COLONIAL AMERICA

for R. A. K. *and* J. R. M.

Colonial AMERICA

A HISTORY, 1565–1776

THIRD EDITION

RICHARD
MIDDLETON

Blackwell
Publishing

© 1992, 1996, 2002 by Richard Middleton

BLACKWELL PUBLISHING
350 Main Street, Malden, MA 02148-5020, USA
9600 Garsington Road, Oxford OX4 2DQ, UK
550 Swanston Street, Carlton, Victoria 3053, Australia

First published 1992
Second edition published 1996
Third edition published 2002

4   2005

Library of Congress Cataloging-in-Publication Data has been applied for.

ISBN-13: 978-0-631-22141-8 (paperback)
ISBN-10: 0-631-22141-7 (paperback)

A catalogue record for this title is available from the British Library.

Set in 11 on 13 pt Goudy Old Face
by Graphicraft Ltd, Hong Kong
Printed and bound in the United Kingdom
by TJ International, Padstow, Cornwall

The publisher's policy is to use permanent paper from mills that operate a sustainable forestry policy,
and which has been manufactured from pulp processed using acid-free and elementary chlorine-free
practices. Furthermore, the publisher ensures that the text paper and cover board
used have met acceptable environmental accreditation standards.

For further information on
Blackwell Publishing, visit our website:
www.blackwellpublishing.com

Contents

Illustrations

Maps

Documents

Preface to the Third Edition _____

Although this edition continues to focus on the English-speaking colonies, I have included a new chapter on the colonies of Spain and France that subsequently became part of the United States. Such broader coverage will undoubtedly continue as the demographic balance of the United States changes, for the writing of history is necessarily one of constant reinterpretation: what one generation sees as essential to an understanding of its past, the next commonly downplays. For this reason I have also updated the existing text with numerous corrections, additional points, and materials. The bibliography has also been extensively revised. I hope that this new edition will continue to meet the needs of students and their teachers.

In the preparation of this edition I would like to acknowledge the assistance of Dr David Hayton for help on the background to emigration from Ireland in the seventeenth and eighteenth centuries. I should also like to acknowledge the helpful comments of various students over the years regarding the content and layout of this book. Finally, I should like to thank the ever helpful staff of Blackwell Publishers, especially Ken Provencher, and the copy-editor, Sue Ashton.

Richard Middleton
The Queen's University, Belfast

Acknowledgments ———————————————

The author and publisher would like to thank the following for permission to reproduce illustrative material:

Ancient Art and Architecture Collection for plate 2; American Antiquarian Society for plates 36 and 38; American Museum of Natural History for plate 3; the curator of Berkeley Castle for plate 20; Bodleian Library, Oxford for plates 7–9; the trustees of the British Museum for plates 10, 11; Cahokia Mounds State Historic Site for plate 6; the Controller of Her Majesty's Stationery Office for plate 40; Stephen Davison for plate 48; Elizabeth Donnan for plate 35; Essex Institute, Salem, Massachusetts for plates 27, 29, and 43; Gibbes Museum of Art for plate 37; Gregory Scott Godwin for plate 34; Historical Society of Pennsylvania for plates 25 and 26; Houghton Mifflin, Boston for plate 17; Indianapolis Museum of Art for plate 51; Jesse D. Jennings for plates 4 and 5; Glyn Lewis for plate 18; Library Company of Philadelphia for plate 44; The Mansell Collection, London for plates 1, 13–15, 49, 50, 52–4; Massachusetts Historical Society, Boston for plates 16, 32, and 33; Museum of Fine Arts, Boston for plates 28 and 55; National Archives of Canada for plate 39; National Portrait Gallery, London for plate 22; New Mexico Economic Department and Tourism Department for plate 47; New York Historical Society, New York City for plates 19 and 41; New York Public Library for plate 45; Pennsylvania Academy of the Fine Arts for plate 21; Pierre Pomet for plate 24; Princeton University Library for plate 30; Helen Rountree for plate 12; St. Augustine Historical Society for plate 46; Sterling Memorial Library, Yale University for plate 31; US Library of Congress, Washington D.C. for plates 23, 56, and 58; University of Georgia Libraries for plate 42; Washington/Curtis/Lee Collection, Washington and Lee University, Lexington, Virginia for plate 57.

Part I

Europeans Encounter Another World

1

The Age of European Exploration

1420	The Portuguese discover and settle Madeira.
1440	The Portuguese settle the Azores.
1471	Portuguese mariners reach the Gold Coast.
1487	Bartholomew Diaz rounds the Cape of Good Hope.
1492	Columbus reaches the Americas.
1494	The Treaty of Tordesillas divides the new territories between Spain and Portugal.
1497	John Cabot initiates English exploration by searching for a northwest passage around America.
1498	Vasco da Gama reaches India.
ca. 1500	The first African slaves are brought to Hispaniola.
1519	Hernando Cortés marches against the Aztec empire.
1531–3	Francisco de Pizarro overthrows the Inca empire.
1539–42	Hernando de Soto explores North America from the Gulf of Mexico to the Ozarks.
1558	Elizabeth I becomes queen of England.
1565	St. Augustine is founded by Spain in Florida.
1576	Martin Frobisher resumes the English search for a northwest passage.
1585	The first English colony is founded at Roanoke Island.
1588	The Spanish Armada is defeated by England.
1605	Sir George Weymouth explores the New England coast.
1606	The London and Plymouth companies are chartered.

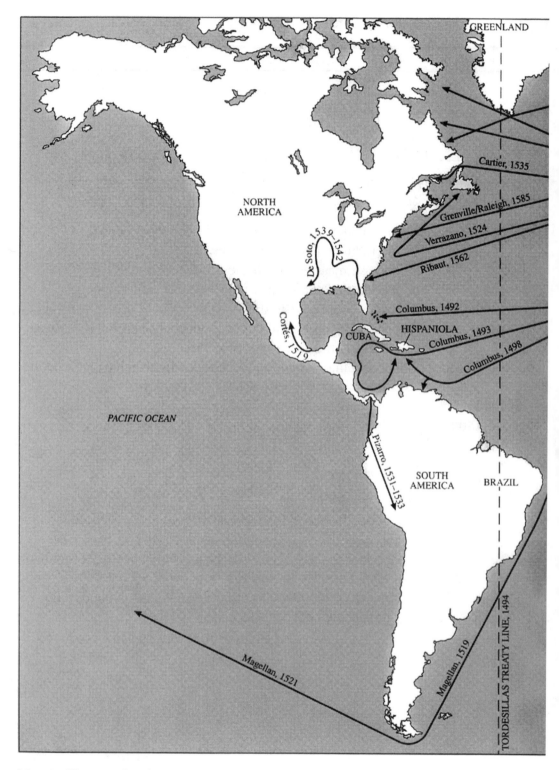

Map 1 The age of exploration.

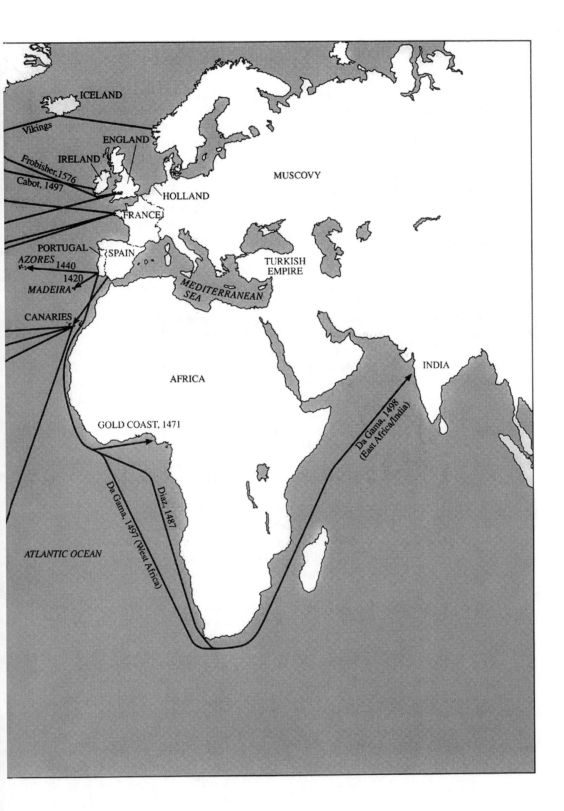

1 SPAIN AND PORTUGAL

THE EUROPEAN INVASION of North America, which ultimately led to the creation of the United States, properly begins with Christopher Columbus. Although Leif Erickson, Thorfinn Karlsefni, and other Vikings explored the northern coasts of North America and even established a temporary colony on the tip of Newfoundland at L'Anse aux Meadows around A.D. 1000, it was Columbus's voyage of 1492 which opened the way for the European conquest of the continent, even though he initially failed to reach the mainland. Ironically Columbus was looking for an alternative route to Asia to bypass the Turkish-controlled eastern Mediterranean when he stumbled on his discovery. Europeans had long suspected that the world was round, not flat, and that by sailing westward a mariner would eventually reach the east. But until Columbus made his famous voyage, such views were merely speculative.

Initially the new territories were a disappointment, since they seemed to present a new barrier to the east while offering little in return. Traces of gold were found in the possession of the native inhabitants, but little else of interest was. Hence Columbus, like many other pioneers, did not gain from his discoveries. His career ended in disappointment, and it remained for others to reap the rewards. The first settlement of any promise was on Hispaniola, where some gold was found, while after 1500 tobacco, ranching, and sugar – which the Spanish already had experience of growing on the Mediterranean coast and Canary Islands – proved profitable.

The pace of Spanish penetration increased with the subjugation of the islands of Puerto Rico, Jamaica, and Cuba from 1509 to 1511. Trading posts were established soon after in Venezuela and Colombia at Santa Marta and Cartagena. However, the sense of having found a new world came only in 1519 with the expedition of Hernando Cortés to Mexico to conquer the Aztec empire of Montezuma. Cortés discovered significant Indian cultures with advanced agriculture, sophisticated building techniques, and knowledge of gold and other precious metals. These expectations of wealth were further realized twelve years later when Francisco de Pizarro overthrew the Inca empire in Peru and thus transformed Spain into a world power, the envy of other European monarchs.

Spain's first problem following the conquest was to find sufficient labor to exploit the new territories. The indigenous inhabitants soon began to die from diseases brought by the Europeans, their numbers being reduced in some areas by almost 90 percent, though an alternative supply of labor was found after 1500 when the Portuguese organized the first shipment of African slaves to Hispaniola.

Other states were inevitably motivated to emulate Spain's success. Within five years of Columbus's first voyage, John Cabot, a Venetian seaman with a patent from Henry VII of England, sailed from Bristol to find a route to China via the northwest, which the Spanish conquest had disappointingly failed to do. The French made similar efforts. But only the Portuguese had much success. Like the Spanish, they were geographically well placed for exploring the Atlantic; indeed Portugal had been engaged in voyages of discovery even longer than Spain. From 1420 the energetic Prince Henry the Navigator had sponsored a series of expeditions down the coast of Africa. Portuguese explorers had also navigated the eastern Atlantic, settling Madeira in the 1420s and the Azores in the 1440s. Here they established sugar plantations, the first outside the Mediterranean, worked by African slaves. By 1471 the Portuguese had reached the Gold Coast, the site of modern Ghana,

DOCUMENT 1

Letters patent to John Cabot, March 5, 1497, reprinted in W. Keith Kavenagh, *Foundations of Colonial America: A Documentary History* (New York, 1974), I, 18–19.

[This document shows the desire of England's King Henry VII to emulate Spain's example by sending an expedition to conquer non-Christian territories. The fact that no moral qualms were felt about such activities represents the typically Eurocentric view of the time. Ironically, like the Spanish, Henry VII had to employ an Italian mariner to undertake the exploration for him.]

Be it known that we have given and granted . . . to our well beloved John Cabot, citizen of Venice [and his sons] full and free authority, leave and power to sail to all parts, countries, and seas of the East, of the West, and of the North under our banners and ensigns . . . to seek out, discover and find whatsoever isles, countries, regions or provinces of the heathen and infidels whatsover they be, and in what part of the world soever they be which before this time have been unknown to all Christians. We have granted to them . . . license to set up our banner and ensigns in every village, town, castle, isle or mainland newly found by them which they can subdue, occupy, and possess as our vassals and lieutenants, getting unto us the rule, title and jurisdiction of the same villages, towns, castles and firm land so found.

---

though it was not until 1487 that Bartholomew Diaz rounded the Cape of Good Hope. Exploration of this route was completed in 1498 when Vasco da Gama reached India, thus pioneering a new passage to the East which avoided the Turks.

Initially it seemed that the Portuguese and Spanish would dispute control over their discoveries. However, under the auspices of Pope Alexander VI in 1494, the two crowns signed the Treaty of Tordesillas, which drew an imaginary line 370 leagues (about 1,000 miles) from the Cape Verde Islands. Spain was to have exclusive rights to all new territories to the west, while Portugal was to enjoy similar advantages to the east. Neither had any qualms about annexing such lands, since Christian doctrine had granted the right to the persons and property of heathens and infidels since the time of the Crusades. Even Cabot had been given full authority to "subdue, occupy and possess" native habitations.

The mainland of North America played little part in this territorial scramble. In 1513 Juan Ponce de Leon of Spain explored the coast of Florida, and in 1521 he tried to establish a settlement there but failed in the face of the hostility of the native inhabitants. In 1526 Lucas de Ayllon made another attempt father north near the Pedee River, but this effort foundered too, owing to the difficulties of the terrain and climate. The process of exploration continued, however, inspired by the twin objectives of finding a passage to China and discovering another El Dorado, or city of gold. In 1524 Giovanni de Verrazzano, acting for the French king, found the Hudson River and sailed as far north as present-day Nova Scotia. Then in 1535 Jacques Cartier, also in the employment of France, penetrated the St. Lawrence to the future site of Montreal. Four years later Spain's Hernando de Soto traveled across the lower Mississippi to the Ozarks, meeting numerous American Indian nations on the way.

Other Spaniards explored the west coast, yet despite many rumors and hopeful promises, the interior of the northern continent was seemingly barren of all but a scattered native population still living in the Stone Age.

Nevertheless, some interest remained, not least among the French, who in 1562 sent an expedition to northern Florida under Jean Ribaut. Sponsored by Gaspard Coligny, the Protestant Admiral of France, its aim was to establish a retreat for his coreligionists in the event of their persecution at home. The initial attempt by Ribaut to establish a post at Charlesfort in modern South Carolina failed, so two years later he led a second expedition, this time to build a fort and settlement on the St. Johns River in Florida. Unfortunately for the French, this second, more substantial expedition merely induced the Spanish to make a new effort to establish themselves in that area. In the summer of 1565, a force of fifteen hundred men under Pedro Menéndez de Avilés first founded the town of St. Augustine and then tracked down and destroyed Ribaut's settlement. The Spanish then placed various missions along the coast to convert the local inhabitants and to prevent any further intrusion by the subjects of a foreign power.

At this point, interest in the northern continent subsided. The Spanish were too busy elsewhere to bother with their less promising northern territories, while the Portuguese had more than enough to do exploiting Brazil, their preserve east of the Tordesillas line. Other European nations, meanwhile, seemed unable to make any impression. England and France were politically weak; Holland was a province of Spain; Germany was divided into small states; and Sweden and the other Scandinavian countries were remote and impoverished. In addition the trauma of the Reformation now swept most of northern Europe, channeling the region's energies away from exploring the New World.

2   ENGLAND: THE ELIZABETHAN PRELUDE

The Reformation in Europe began in 1517 when Martin Luther protested against what he considered to be the corrupt practices of the Roman Catholic church under the pope. Luther and others believed that faith alone, not good works, could secure salvation. They also felt that the church contained too much ceremony, pomp, and superstition to be compatible with the Christian message contained in the Bible. Ultimately most of northern Europe, including England, denounced the pope and separated from Catholicism.

The process of reforming the English church proved tortuous, however, and it was not until 1559 that Elizabeth I effected even a partial settlement. Interest in the New World resumed only in 1576 when Martin Frobisher set off on a series of journeys to seek a northwest passage. Two years later Sir Humphrey Gilbert obtained a patent from Queen Elizabeth for the discovery and colonization of the northern continent. Unfortunately, Frobisher was frustrated by the arctic ice, while Gilbert drowned off the Newfoundland coast in September 1583 before he could accomplish anything. Gilbert's patent was then taken up by his half-brother, Sir Walter Raleigh, who managed to interest a number of influential courtiers and seafaring men like Sir Francis Drake and Richard Grenville. As a result an expedition comprising two small vessels was dispatched in April 1584 under Philip Amadas and Arthur Barlowe to explore the coast of North America. They duly made their way via the West Indies and early in July reach the outer banks of North Carolina, where they made contact with the inhabitants of Roanoke Island and the surrounding area. Before leaving they persuaded (or forced) two inhabitants, Manteo and Wanchese, to accompany them back to England, to provide more information, not least knowledge of their language.

Amadas and Barlowe were sufficiently encouraging about trading prospects and the defensive advantages of Roanoke to persuade Raleigh and his friends to dispatch a major expedition the following year, this time to establish a permanent base. The flotilla comprised five large and two small vessels under the command of Grenville. Raleigh put much thought into the expedition. Not only were Manteo and Wanchese to return as interpreters but Thomas Harriot, a young Oxford graduate and scientist, and John White, an artist, were hired to assess the resources and draw the flora and fauna of the region, now called Virginia, in honor of the celibate queen.

Grenville's force left England in early April 1585 and arrived off the outer banks early in July. Here the expedition suffered its first setback when Grenville discovered that only the smallest vessels could get over the sandbar to the sound beyond, making Roanoke unsuitable as a permanent military base. Next, as the force explored the interior, a silver cup went missing. Grenville's decision to avenge this incident by burning an Indian village was hardly calculated to maintain good relations, though the act was to prove typical of the English in their dealings with the native population.

Grenville then departed for the Caribbean toward the end of August, leaving Captain Ralph Lane with approximately one hundred men to complete a fort and other dwellings. This number was smaller than originally contemplated, which posed a problem because more men were now needed to find another, more suitable site. Fortunately relations with the Roanoke Indians and their chief, Wingina, remained friendly. Lane was accordingly able to reconnoitre the surrounding area, even dispatching a party under White to winter among the Chesapeake Indians. However, when supplies began to run low toward the spring, Lane responded by demanding corn from Wingina, who offered Lane and his men some empty fields and seed corn. Despite this generosity Lane believed that the Indians were plotting an attack and carried out a preemptive strike, murdering Wingina and a number of his people. The triumph proved short-lived, since it soon made the other Indian communities fearful of further dealings with the white men, thus intensifying the food shortage. The Europeans now realized how tenuous their hold was. Not surprisingly, when Drake called unexpectedly in June 1586 after a buccaneering expedition in the West Indies, Lane and his men insisted on returning home.

The timing was unfortunate, for Grenville arrived a few weeks later with fresh supplies and men. After some deliberation he decided to leave fifteen men to hold the fort until a further group of colonists could arrive the following year.

Meanwhile, in England Raleigh's enthusiasm for colonization was beginning to wane. White and a number of others, however, remained optimistic and suggested a new plan to settle the Chesapeake area, which he believed would provide better harbor facilities and a more friendly population. Under White's prompting the scheme this time was less martial and more agricultural, being primarily aimed at establishing a colony of predominantly families and freeholders as opposed to soldiers and servants. It was to be called the City of Raleigh.

Accordingly in April 1587 some eighty-five men, seventeen women, and eleven children set sail, this time for the Chesapeake. Unfortunately the two vessels were late in departing, and the captain insisted on leaving the settlers at the old site on Roanoke. White may have agreed to this, since Manteo was still with him and could be expected to enlist some local support. There was also a chance that the men Grenville had left behind would be present to welcome them. Unfortunately, they turned out to be no longer there, having presumably been driven off by a now enraged native population. This meant that no crops

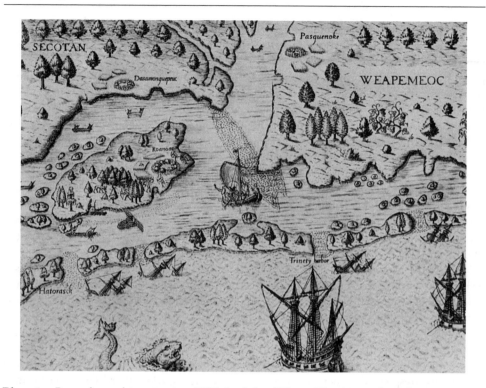

Plate 1   Roanoke and its vicinity 1585, by John White. The Mansell Collection, London.

had been sown, nor habitable accommodation maintained. In this critical situation it was decided that White should return to England for additional help.

Before he could return with fresh supplies, however, war broke out between England and Spain. Philip II had been increasingly angered by Elizabeth I and her policies. Having previously been married to Elizabeth's half-sister and predecessor, Queen Mary, he still had pretensions to the English throne. A devout Catholic, having received from the pope the title of "most Catholic monarch," his religious belief also caused him to oppose Protestant England. In addition, Philip II resented England's support for the Dutch revolt against his rule; and he was also displeased at the activities of Drake and Grenville. By 1588 the solution was clear. With the support of Pope Sixtus V, he resolved to invade England, claim its throne for himself, and rid the world of a dangerous heretic.

The effect of the war was to sever all communication with Roanoke until after the Spanish Armada had been defeated. Not until August 1590 did a relief vessel get through, by which time all trace of the settlers had vanished. White had left instructions that the colonists were to move to a neighboring location in the event of trouble, leaving a message as to their whereabouts. The only message was the word "Croatan" carved on a doorpost, an apparent reference to a neighboring island on which Manteo's people lived. But no clue to the settlers' fate could be found, though diminishing supplies and poor weather prevented a visit to Croatan itself.

The Roanoke episode subsequently gave rise to legends that the settlers had inter-married with the local people and migrated into the interior of the continent. Another thesis is that they went north to join the Chesapeake Indians. More prosaically, their fate can be reduced to one of three possibilities: either they died of starvation; or they were killed by hostile American Indians; or they drowned at sea while trying to make their escape. The last fate now seems the most likely, given the lack of any archeological remains.[1]

There are several reasons for the English failure to sustain a permanent presence on the continent at this time. The first was poor timing. Had the Armada not sailed, the Roanoke settlers would probably have been rescued by White's relief expedition. The second factor against them was the poor nature of the site, which was swampy, not readily accessible, and disease-ridden. But even more important was the project's poor organization, which stemmed mainly from Raleigh's limited funds. Mounting an expedition so far from home in such hostile conditions required huge resources, not to mention luck. It was an enterprise equivalent to exploring the moon today, in which no single individual, however rich, could hope to succeed.

Other factors, too, worked against the would-be colonists. One was the type of settler. Most were soldiers of fortune, not colonizers. They lacked the motivation and practical skills to get a settlement started. They and their patrons were interested mainly in seizing existing wealth, either from newly discovered empires or from Spanish treasure fleets, and the lure of such conquests remained strong until the next century, despite the diminishing returns that even successful buccaneers like Drake and Grenville experienced. As late as 1617, Raleigh was still proposing another expedition to discover a new El Dorado, reputed to be a fabulously rich Indian empire in the interior of Guiana.

Although the last decade of the sixteenth century witnessed no fresh attempt at settlement by the English, a number of changes occurred which ultimately enabled them to colonize North America. The first was the growing realization that precious metals and jewelry were not the only commodities to bring wealth. Increasingly sugar, cotton, cacao, coffee, tobacco, and even fish were seen as having equal value. Indeed, as the Dutch were beginning to demonstrate, shipping these goods alone could be a highly profitable undertaking.

This realization in turn led to the appreciation that a different kind of operation was required to profit fully from the New World. Buccaneering might result in the interception of a treasure fleet; it could hardly enable a crop to be harvested. Clearly a more sober type of colonist was needed. Richard Hakluyt, Jr., advocated this and other ideas in his book *The Principal Navigations, Voyages, Traffiques and Discoveries of the English Nation*, which appeared in 1589. In various chapters Hakluyt listed the advantages which would result from plantations, as he called them. The new settlements could provide naval stores like pitch, tar, and hemp. Ships would be required to supply them, thus increasing the pool of seamen and naval resources of the nation. Other valuable commodities, like olives, vines, and citrus fruit, could be grown, thus ending both dependence on foreign producers and the drain on bullion. In short, the American settlements could "yield unto us all the commodities of Europe, Africa and Asia . . . and supply the wants of all our decayed trades."[2] The poor need no longer burden the rest of the community, while the power of the state would greatly increase, as would the profit of the individual.

---

[1] For the argument that the colonists joined the Chesapeake Indians see Karen Ordahl Kupperman, *Roanoke: The Abandoned Colony* (Totowa, 1984); and David B. Quinn, *Set Fair for Roanoke: Voyages and Colonies, 1584–1606* (Chapel Hill, 1985).

[2] Extracts of Hakluyt's writings are to be found in David B. Quinn, *The New American World: A Documentary History of North America to 1612*, 5 vols (London, 1979), III, 71–123.

English colonization of the New World was given another important boost at this time by the rise of the joint stock company, a new institution which promised to overcome the limitations of exploration by individuals such as Raleigh. By selling shares in an enterprise, such companies could harness the resources of many individuals, making possible a larger and more sustained effort. The first such ventures were the Russia and Eastland companies, formed in 1553 and 1572 respectively to trade with Muscovy, followed in 1592 by the Levant Company, set up to trade in the eastern Mediterranean. The most famous was the East India Company, established in 1600 to trade with India and the Far East. The development of these companies reflected not only the growing concentration of monied wealth, especially in London, but also the increasing opportunities for commerce. Indeed, historians have regarded European expansion in the sixteenth century as proof that the continent was emerging from its feudal, theocratic, and communal past into a more aggressive, individualistic, and capitalistic era.

These opportunities for English colonization and trade were greatly increased in 1604 by the formal signing of peace with Spain. Although Spain did not recognize the right of the English to contravene the Treaty of Tordesillas, the agreement did promise a new era in which their colonial ventures stood a better chance of success. The Spanish implicitly accepted that they had enough difficulty controlling their existing possessions without attempting to police the activities of other nations farther to the north.

Another stimulus to English overseas settlement at this time was the growth in population and rise in unemployment. The latter problem was greatly exacerbated by the enclosure of fields to consolidate holdings; as a result of this policy many tenant farmers lost their lands. Some of these were prepared to try their fortunes elsewhere. So, too, were skilled workers in the woolen industry who were experiencing hard times. As Sir George Popham, one of the first architects of English settlement in Virginia argued, a colony in America could employ not only the ex-soldiers and "poor artisans" but also "the idle vagrants" and many others who could not find work at home.

A further inducement for people to leave England was religious conflict. Although Elizabeth I had tried to devise a religious settlement which permitted theological diversity, many groups were still dissatisfied. The Puritans in particular yearned for greater cleansing of the national church. They believed that there were still too many corrupt Roman Catholic elements in the Episcopalian settlement, and their discontent increasingly brought them into conflict with the authorities. As a result, some Puritan dissenters began to think of leaving England to establish a commonwealth elsewhere which was free from such corruption.

Yet another reason for emigration may have been the Crown's attempts to modernize the English state. Since the middle of the sixteenth century successive monarchs had interfered with local institutions like the borough corporations, the militia, and the governing of the poor. Now new laws like the Statute of Artificers regulating the employment of labor were suddenly imposed on communities which had barely changed in centuries, while additional agencies of government, like justices of the peace, were also created. All of these changes helped produce an atmosphere of uncertainty, encouraging some people to look overseas for a more stable environment.

A final contributing factor may have been the English colonization of Ireland. Since the beginning of her reign Elizabeth I had made determined efforts to anglicize Ireland by imposing English law, customs, and officials to bind the country more securely to the Crown. In the process a number of settlers had also been sent. Of course colonizing Ireland was very different from settling North America. Ireland had a large population with a highly developed agriculture. It was also a Christian country with a long cultural tradition, many of whose people spoke English. Moreover, Ireland was nearby, and the English and the Irish had been visiting each other since the time of the Norman invasion of Ireland in the twelfth century.[3]

North America, on the other hand, was three thousand miles distant. The main challenge there was to tame a totally different environment, and to civilize inhabitants who in English eyes were nothing more than heathen savages. The English colonization of Ireland was nevertheless an important precedent, if only for the experience it provided. Many of those involved in Ireland were also active across the Atlantic, notably Raleigh, Grenville, Gilbert, and Lane. Significantly, their attitude to the Irish was similar to that shown subsequently to the indigenous peoples in North America.

By the turn of the seventeenth century, then, the pace of English interest in the New World was beginning to quicken. Peace with Spain was in the offing, and new possibilities for trade were in prospect. Even the most northern parts of America now appeared attractive, since it was now appreciated that the seas there abounded with fish, while the land contained many fur-bearing animals. These prospects led to renewed voyages of exploration, notably by Sir George Weymouth, who visited the coast of Nantucket and Maine in 1605. He returned with five Abenaki Indians and a highly optimistic account of the possibilities for trade and settlement. One final spur, if any were needed, was the knowledge that from 1603 the French were sending out various expeditions under Samuel Champlain to explore the area of the St. Lawrence.

Toward the end of 1605, therefore, a group of merchants and their friends, including the younger Hakluyt, petitioned the Crown for a charter incorporating two companies, one from the City of London, called the London Company, the other from the ports of Bristol, Exeter, and Plymouth, called the Plymouth Company, to establish two colonies in that part of America "commonly called Virginia." This area was defined as lying between latitudes 34 and 45 degrees north, which James I, Elizabeth's successor, affirmed was outside the dominion of either Spain or France, since neither nation had established any effective settlement there.

The plea was accordingly successful and a charter duly issued on April 10, 1606. The London Company, or South Virginia group, was granted the area between 34 and 41 degrees north: the Plymouth Company, or North Virginia group, could settle anywhere between 38 and 43 degrees north, though neither company was to come within one hundred miles of the other. No difficulties were anticipated in this respect, since the South Virginia group intended to concentrate on the Chesapeake area, which White and others had explored in the winter of 1585. The North Virginia group, in contrast, intended to devote itself to the area to the north reconnoitred by Weymouth.

In America, each venture was to set up a council of thirteen, which was to elect a president and control all local matters. However, the overall direction of the two enterprises was to be in the hands of a royal council of fourteen chosen by the king. The normal joint stock model was not adhered to in this case because the two companies were not simple trading organizations. The fact that they were rather aiming to develop commerce by peopling new lands with subjects of the Crown led James I to believe that his Privy Council should oversee all important aspects of the new venture. Both groups were in any

---

[3] The argument that Ireland provided a model for the English colonization of America is put forward by Nicholas P. Canny. See especially his article, "The Ideology of English Colonization: From Ireland to America," *William and Mary Quarterly*, XXX, 1973, 575–98.

case represented on the new royal council, the northern company by Sir Fernando Gorges and the southern company by Sir Thomas Smith.[4]

Initially few objections were voiced, for the prospects still looked promising. The charter granted the companies "all the Lands, Woods, Soil, Grounds, Havens, Ports, Rivers, Mines, Minerals, Marshes, Waters, Fishings, Commodities, and Hereditaments" within their jurisdiction. In addition they could mine for gold and other precious metals, though one-fifth of any such discoveries would belong to the Crown. They could also mint money, a rare privilege, but could not trade with foreign nations, meaning Europeans. Finally, the companies had the right to expel any interlopers, which effectively gave each an absolute monopoly in its respective area.

The charter also had to address the status of those now going across the sea. It was clearly not intended that they should cease to be subjects of the king. On the other hand, neither should their position be disadvantaged as a result of leaving their homeland. Consequently it was agreed that the colonists and their children should be guaranteed all the "liberties, franchises, and immunities" which Englishmen then enjoyed. These were not defined, although recognized as among the most important was the right to own and inherit property. Nevertheless, all lands in America were to be held as part of the king's demesne in free and common socage, not fee simple.[5] Except in New England, seventeenth-century property rights were never to be as absolute as they later became in the United States.[6]

The charter said little about the treatment of the native inhabitants except that the settlements might "tend to the Glory of his Divine Majesty" by spreading "the christian Religion to such People, as yet live in Darkness and miserable Ignorance." The hope was that such missionary work would "in time bring the Infidels and Savages, living in those parts, to human Civility, and to a settled and quiet Government." No liberties or immunities were mentioned for them. Indeed, the Spanish precedent suggested that Christianity could succeed only when civility had been accomplished and that this could be achieved only by compulsion. Even then, the indigenous peoples could expect no more than a subordinate role as hewers of wood and drawers of water, if the examples set by Raleigh, Gilbert, and others in Ireland were any guide.

In the initial stages of colonization, the Plymouth Company proved the more speedy. By August 1606 it had a ship ready to reconnoitre its designated area. Unfortunately, the vessel was blown off course and then seized by the Spanish. A second attempt at reconnoitring the New England coast was more successful, but by the time the crew returned, the London Company had already dispatched three ships – the *Sarah Constant*, *Godspeed*, and *Discovery* – with the first colonists on board.

---

[4] A complete copy of the charter can be found in W. Keith Kavenagh, *Foundations of Colonial America: A Documentary History* (New York, 1974), III, 1698–1704.

[5] The term *socage* meant that the possessor had to pay a small annual fee, known as quitrent, to the king, as opposed to enjoying an absolute *fee simple*, which would have been equivalent to owning the land outright. Modern English property law uses the term *leasehold* for socage and *freehold* for fee simple. It is these latter terms which are generally used hereafter to describe such property arrangements.

[6] This was true of all "rights" at this time, which basically fell into three categories: privileges granted by the Crown, privileges established by custom, and rights laid down by statute. Crown privileges varied according to the residence and circumstance of the individual. The same was true of custom. Only rights established by statute, notably trial by jury, were common to all. Even these were not absolute in the sense of the later state and federal constitutions of America, since what one parliament had granted another could take away.

2

The Peoples of Eastern North America

30,000–11,000 B.C.	Indian peoples migrate to North America from Asia via the Bering Strait.
11,000 B.C.	The land bridge finally disappears.
5000 B.C.	Agriculture begins to develop in Tehuacan Valley, Mexico.
1500 B.C.	The Eastern Woodland culture begins to emerge.
1200 B.C.	The first Mesoamerican civilization, the Olmecs, emerges.
500 B.C.	Mayan civilization develops.
500 B.C.	The Adena mound builders of the Ohio emerge.
300 B.C.	First maize is grown in eastern North America.
100 B.C.–A.D. 400	The Hopewell mound builders flourish.
A.D. 600	The Mississippi mound builders emerge.
A.D. 700	Use of the bow and arrow becomes widespread among Eastern Woodland peoples.
A.D. 1200	The city of Cahokia's population numbers around 30,000.
A.D. 1500	The Mississippi mound builders disappear.

Comparative Ancient History Chronology
Major material and cultural advances to 1 B.C. (approximate dates)

YEAR (B.C.)	AMERICA (Mexico/Peru)	AFRICA (Central/East)	WEST ASIA	EUROPE (N. Western)	E. MEDITERRANEAN (Egypt/Greece/Rome)	CHINA
1 Million		Homo erectus	Homo erectus	Homo erectus	Homo erectus	Homo erectus
100,000		Homo sapiens Stone Age hunters	Homo sapiens Stone Age hunters	Homo sapiens Stone Age hunters	Homo sapiens Stone Age hunters	Homo sapiens Stone Age hunters
30,000	Homo sapiens Stone Age hunters			Cave paintings		
9000	Ice Age ends	Magosian stone culture		Ice Age ends		
6500			Agriculture – wheat/barley pigs/cattle Pottery			
5000	(Mexico) Agriculture – maize/ squashes/beans			Agriculture – wheat/barley cattle/sheep	(Egypt) Agriculture – wheat/barley Pottery/textiles	Agriculture – rice/millet Pottery
4000	Cotton		Plough	Pottery		
3500	Copper-beaten tools (Great Lakes)		Potter's wheel Pictographic writing	Copper	River sailing craft	Potter's wheel
3000–			Bronze Age Sumer cities Arched tombs Cuneiform hieroglyphs	Bronze Age Stonehenge I	Bronze Age Cities Hieroglyphs	

2500	Pottery		Indus cities Cotton		Pyramids Potter's wheel	Irrigation
2000		Agriculture – wheat/sorghum cattle herding	Babylon city		Minoan culture (Crete)	
1700					(Greece) Mycenae walled city	Shang Dynasty Cities Bronze Age
1500	(Peru) Chavin Culture–irrigation Stone sculptures		Spoked wheel Iron Age	Celts	(Phoenician alphabet) Linear B script	Writing (Ideographic)
1200	(Mexico) Olmecs Stone temples Jade carving			Iron Age	Iron Age	Early writing
750					Greek alphabet (Rome founded)	
500	Hieroglyphic writing (Olmec)	Iron Age Cotton	Buddha		Pythagoras (Mathematician)	Iron Age Confucius
200	Early Maya Pyramids Corbel vaulting				(Rome) Stone bridges Aqueducts	First Empire Canal building
100	Teotihuacán city Irrigation			Potter's wheel		Road network Great Wall
50					Julian calendar	Paper

1   THE PRECONTACT BACKGROUND

THE NORTH AMERICAN continent, which the Virginia Company and Plymouth Company were planning to settle in 1607, was still almost a mystery to Europeans. Not least in the settlers' ignorance was the lack of information about the inhabitants. Since the late fifteenth century, fishermen had been intermittently visiting the northern coasts to catch cod and trade onshore in furs. Elsewhere, contacts had been made during the expeditions of Hernando de Soto, Pedro Menéndez de Avilés, Ralph Lane, and Sir George Weymouth. But the numbers, location, and culture of the peoples of what was ultimately to become the eastern United States were largely unknown.

Since the Indians left no written records and only limited artifacts, information about them is still restricted today, though knowledge is growing as archeologists, anthropologists, and historians continue their researches.[1]

It is generally agreed that the first Indian peoples came to America from Siberia by way of the Bering Strait between 30000 and 11000 B.C. when the Ice Age lowered sea levels, creating a huge land bridge between Asia and America. Bands of nomadic hunters followed game from eastern Siberia to Alaska, eventually penetrating both North and South America.

These first Paleo-Indian peoples were essentially hunter gatherers, their largest quarry being mammoths, large-horned bison, musk ox, large antelope, caribou and, ironically, horses. The rest of their diet consisted of berries, nuts, fruits, fish, birds, and wildfowl. Their material culture was simple but effective. Animals provided skins for clothing; crude shelters were found in caves, rock overhangs, or made from the branches and bark of trees; while simple canoes or even logs provided the means for crossing rivers. Flint knives and scrapers enabled food and other materials to be prepared, while fire was used for keeping warm and cooking.

Around 9000 B.C. the peoples of North and Central America entered what archeologists call the Archaic Age. The inhabitants were still hunter gatherers but now looked to other types of game because of the extinction of the larger mammals. First the mammoth disappeared, then the large-horned bison, followed by the horse. Archeologists are divided as to why these mammals vanished; possible causes include overhunting, climatic change, or some natural catastrophe like that which eliminated the dinosaurs seventy million years before. As the Ice Age ended, the inhabitants became less migratory, confining their activities to smaller areas. It is probable that the main language groups now became established, though each group had many individual tongues. At the time of the European arrival there were still more than two thousand languages being spoken in the Americas.[2]

---

[1]   Until 1945 the study of precontact Indian peoples was left to archeologists. Postcontact eras were the province of anthropologists and ethnologists. American history proper was considered to begin only with the arrival of Europeans, the Indians constituting thereafter passive and disappearing bystanders. During the past twenty years attempts have been made to combine all three approaches in the new discipline of ethnohistory. For an account of these developments see Bruce Trigger, *Natives and Newcomers: Canada's "Heroic Age" Reconsidered* (Montreal, 1985), 1–49, 164–72; and James Axtell, "The Ethnohistory of Early America: A Review Essay," *William and Mary Quarterly*, XXXV, 1978, 110–44.

[2]   The main North American language groups were Wakashan, Salishan, Penutian, Siouan, Iroquoian, Algonquian, Muskogean, Caddoan, Hokaltecan, Azteco-Tanoan, Athapascan, and Eskimo Aleut.

The most momentous phase in the development of North America was the beginning of horticulture, which occurred around 5000 B.C. in the Tehuacan Valley of central Mexico. The reason it began in Mesoamerica so much earlier than in the rest of North America is unknown. Possible factors include an early decline in the availability of game; optimum conditions for cultivation; the need to feed a growing population; the presence of teosinte, a wild ancestor of maize; and the desire for a more secure food supply.

The planting and improvement of crops proceeded in a halting fashion. In some places it began with the growing of beans, elsewhere of squash or gourds; but invariably maize or corn was added at some point. Initially all these crops were cultivated from wild plants, but in time selection of the best seeds or hybridization through cross-pollination produced better strains, giving higher yields. In contrast to Africa, Europe, and Asia, however, no animals except dogs and turkeys (and llamas in South America) could be domesticated. In many ways the lack of livestock did not matter, since the cultivation of beans and maize ensured a high-protein diet, especially when supplemented by meat from hunting.

The development of horticulture was to have profound consequences. Cultures were radically altered as communities became more settled to allow the planting, harvesting, and protection of their crops. Horticulture also allowed the support of larger populations, which in turn permitted greater diversification and specialization. It is no coincidence that the beginnings of agriculture corresponded with the appearance of ceramics and the first advances in metallurgy; previously implements were made from either stone or bone. Nor did the transformation of Indian societies stop here. Specialized skills encouraged trade and the growth of towns. These in turn required more complex administrative systems, which led to the emergence of temporal and religious elites. The eventual results in Central America and the Andean highlands were the great civilizations of the Olmecs, Mayas, Toltecs, Aztecs, and Incas.

The first major Mesoamerican civilization was that of the Olmecs, who were active between 1200 and 500 B.C. Among their achievements was the building of large temple mounds faced with stone. They also devised irrigation systems and carved huge heads from blocks of basalt, suggesting not only craftsmanship but sophisticated beliefs and organizational ability.

The most sophisticated civilization to emerge in Mesoamerica was that of the Mayas. From 500 B.C. to A.D. 700 they domesticated dogs, wove elaborate cotton textiles, used gold and silver to fashion intricate jewelry, and constructed large stone buildings incorporating the corbeled vault. Equally impressive was their development of hieroglyphic writing carved in stone or painted on paper, invention of an elaborate calendar based on detailed observation of the solar system, and knowledge of mathematics.

The last great Mesoamerican civilization before the European invasion was that of the Aztecs. The Aztecs were recent arrivals from northern Mexico, who in the fifteenth century overthrew the other, more advanced city-states of Texcoco and Tlacopán. They brought sufficient organization and energy to create an empire of six million people, centered on the capital city of Tenochtitlan, which at its height had over one hundred thousand people. Built on an artificial island in the middle of a lake and joined to the mainland by stone causeways, Tenochtitlan contained numerous squares, paved streets, stone temples, and other buildings that astounded the Spanish on their arrival in 1519.

North of the Rio Grande the pace of development was slower, possibly as a result of climatic conditions in the aftermath of the Ice Age. Another reason may have been the area's remoteness from Mesoamerica. It is significant that North American horticulture

Plate 2   Chichén Itzá. Mayan building with faces of gods. Ancient Art and
Architecture Collection.

began in the Southwest, among the Hohokam and Anasazi pueblo peoples around 2000
B.C., spreading to the lower Mississippi Valley and adjacent areas after 1500 B.C.[3]

The subsequent emergence in eastern North America of other similar cultures partly
based on farming is usually called the Woodland era. Lasting approximately from 500 B.C.
to A.D. 1500 it is customarily subdivided into the Early, Middle, and Late Woodland
periods, which roughly correspond to the three cultures of Adena, Hopewell, and Mississippi.
These cultures possessed a number of common features: all built mounds for burial and other
religious purposes; all developed urban settlements; all practiced some form of horticulture;
all possessed pottery; and all were familiar with copper for making ornaments and tools.

The earliest of these cultures, the Adena people, emerged around 500 B.C. in the Ohio
Valley. They were still largely hunter gatherers but practiced some horticulture, notably
cultivation of gourds and other squashes. Their mounds were primarily burial places, though
one or two animal-shaped structures, for example, the Great Serpent Mound near Hillsboro,
Ohio, clearly had wider religious connotations. The burial mounds were filled with numerous

---

[3] Archeologists are divided as to how technology, institutions, and culture are transmitted. It used to be thought
that a single area of special inventiveness diffused its creativity to neighboring peoples. Hence, European civilizations were all ultimately indebted to Pharaonic Egypt, whereas the great cities of Mesoamerica provided the
catalyst in the Americas. However, radiocarbon dating and other techniques have shown such views to be
mistaken, since many key developments, like the use of iron in southeastern Europe, took place before its discovery
by the supposed center. For a discussion of diffusion theory see Jesse D. Jennings, ed., *Ancient North Americans* (San
Francisco, 1978), 11–12.

Plate 3 The Great Temple of Tenochtitlan, reconstructed by Ignacio Marquina from existing Aztec monuments in Mexico and descriptions by contemporary Spanish conquerors. Courtesy of the Department of Library Services, American Museum of Natural History.

practical and ornamental objects, both to show respect for the dead and to support the deceased in the afterlife. Ancestor worship was widely practiced, since it was believed that the deceased could intervene with the spirit world to aid living relatives. It is likely that servants and even wives were executed for the comfort of an important departed chief. Among the artifacts buried were clay pipes, the first evidence of tobacco smoking.

The Adena were followed from about 100 B.C. to A.D. 400 by the Hopewell people, whose culture flourished not only in the Ohio Valley but in adjacent areas along the Illinois and Miami rivers. The Hopewell sites were of greater size and complexity than those of the Adena. Instead of simple squares, the burial mounds often comprised concentric circles and other geometric patterns. Many were grouped together inside an enclosure to elevate houses or other secular structures, suggesting large-scale habitation. Another difference is that the burial artifacts were more diverse. Some were made of materials originating from great distances, such as obsidian from the Rockies, copper from Lake Michigan, and conch shells from Florida, indicating widespread trade and commerce. Elaborate carvings, especially of animals and humans, were made in wood and stone. Clay was also popular for making decorative figures.

The third and final phase of the mound-building cultures began around A.D. 600, with the emergence of the Mississippian peoples. Their mounds, which were even larger than those of the Hopewell, comprised large platform edifices grouped around a central plaza, suggesting a link with Mesoamerica. The size and complexity of these sites indicate towns of thousands of inhabitants, which in turn suggests that the Mississippian cultures were dependent primarily on agriculture, especially maize and beans, for their subsistence.[4] Significantly, all were concentrated on the rich alluvial soils of the Mississippi Valley and rivers of the Southeast, where flooding regularly regenerated the soil. The greatest of these cities, Cahokia, near present-day St. Louis, had an enclosed area of several square miles, containing over one hundred earthworks. The largest of these had four levels and was more than one hundred feet high. Thirty thousand people may have lived there.

At its zenith, around A.D. 1200, Cahokia almost emulated the great cities of Mesoamerica, though its craftsmen had yet to build in stone or to develop the range of metallurgical skills of those civilizations. Mounds were still simple earthen structures, topped by buildings constructed of wattle and daub under a thatched roof. Metalworking was confined to copper, which was available in such purity on certain rock outcrops that it could be worked into artifacts without the need for smelting. Among the items produced were chisels, awls and punches (for piercing leather), needles, harpoons, spear points, and knives – as well as brooches, bracelets, gorgets, and clasps for decorative purposes. Such items were almost certainly made only for the elite, enabling rulers to preserve their status and claims to supernatural power. Peasant farmers, in contrast, still used arrow heads, scrapers, knives, hoes, and axes made of bone, shell, or stone.

Little is known about the beliefs and social structures of the mound builders. Scholars can only examine the remaining artifacts and make rough guesses. The most puzzling aspect of these cultures, especially the Mississippian, is their disappearance. By the time the first Europeans visited Cahokia in the seventeenth century, the town was occupied by a small

---

[4]   Not all archeologists accept the argument that the development of agriculture was the main explanation for the rise of these societies. Some have argued that better distributive systems allowed the growth of towns and cities that still depended primarily on hunting and gathering.

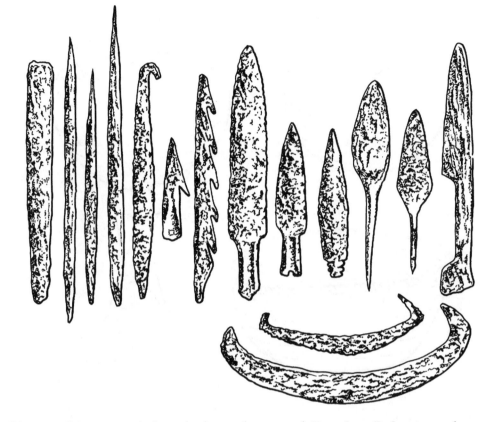

Plate 4 Copper utensils from the late archaic period. From Jesse D. Jennings, ed., *Ancient North Americans* (San Francisco, 1978).

community of Illinois Indians who knew nothing of its history or significance. The only mound builders Europeans described in any detail were the Natchez Indians in the lower Mississippi, and their building was only on a limited scale. When the French visited the Natchez Great Sun chief in 1700, the main village had just one mound and nine dwellings.

Historians can only speculate on the reasons for the disappearance of the mound builders. It is possible that they were unable to sustain such large communities through a lack of organizational ability. Their crops may have failed because of temporary climatic changes like the onset of a minor ice age around 1450 A.D. They may have been attacked by more nomadic peoples, who did to Cahokia what the Huns and Visigoths did to fifth-century Rome. Another possibility is that the introduction of new technology, notably the bow and arrow around A.D. 700, enabled one nation to obliterate another. Alternatively, the mound-building cultures may have collapsed from internal tensions when the mass of their population rose up against their rulers. A final possibility is that many Mississippian peoples were destroyed by disease, since they disappeared about the time the Europeans first arrived. The newcomers' microbes could have attacked the mound builders before the invaders themselves arrived to witness the events. But until more evidence is found, the Mississippians' disappearance remains a mystery.

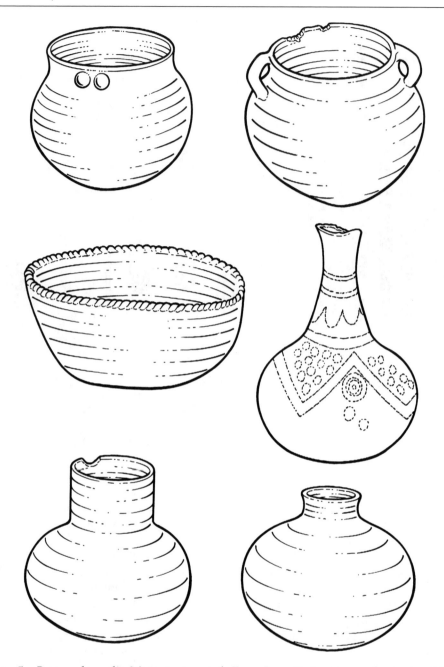

Plate 5   Pottery from the Mississippi period. From Jesse D. Jennings, ed., *Ancient North Americans* (San Francisco, 1978).

Plate 6 Cahokia mounds, ca. A.D. 1150, painting by William R. Iseminger. Cahokia Mounds State Historic Site.

2 THE COLUMBIAN IMPACT

Historians now recognize that the Indian populations of America went into catastrophic decline following the arrival of the Europeans. The true extent of the disaster remains a matter of debate, because it has proved difficult to establish exactly what the population was before the Europeans arrived. It used to be thought that the population was around one million people north of the Rio Grande and about ten million throughout the rest of the Americas. But as historians, archeologists, and ethnologists have continued their research, the numbers have been revised upward. The best current estimate is between two and three million living north of the Rio Grande in 1492, though some authors believe that the figure may have been at least ten million, with another sixty-five million in Central and South America, thus equaling the contemporary population of Europe.[5]

---

[5] The older view is well represented by the work of James Mooney, "Population," in *Handbook of American Indians North of Mexico* (Washington, 1910); and A. L. Kroeber, *Cultural and Natural Areas of Native North America* (Berkeley, 1939). It suited nineteenth- and many twentieth-century historians to believe that the American Indians were few in number to justify their displacement. The impact of European diseases was almost entirely ignored. The first widespread attempt to reassess the population of the indigenous inhabitants occurred only in the 1960s, when there was greater readiness to acknowledge America's ethnic diversity. For more information on the subject see Alfred W. Crosby, *The Columbian Exchange: Biological and Cultural Consequences of 1492* (Westport, 1972); and *Ecological Imperialism: The Biological Expansion of Europe, 900–1900* (New York, 1986); William M. Denevan, ed., *The Native Population of the Americas in 1492* (Madison, 1976, rev. ed., 1992); Henry F. Dobyns,

These revisions make the subsequent reductions all the more dramatic. It is now estimated that the population of Mexico was reduced from perhaps ten million in 1500 to about two million a century later, while the population of Hispaniola shrank from one million to one hundred thousand within a generation.

There are several explanations for such a precipitous population decline. In areas under European occupation, maltreatment of the native peoples, particularly the wide-spread use of slavery to exploit the mineral and vegetable riches of the New World, was an important factor. Another reason could be that the habitat changed through the introduction of different flora and fauna. The Europeans brought horses, cattle, sheep, pigs, chickens, honey bees, sugar cane, wheat, rice, and numerous grasses and weeds – as well as vermin such as rats and parasites such as the cockroach. A third cause was the destruction of the Indians' political, religious, and social systems, which necessarily affected their fertility. But most devastating of all were the diseases the newcomers brought to the Americas.

The reasons for this biological catastrophe are now well known. Since earliest times the peoples of Africa, Asia, and Europe had exchanged pathogens – sometimes with devastating results, such as the outbreak of bubonic plague in fourteenth-century England. However, the long-term effect was constant reimmunization of the inhabitants against a huge array of diseases. No matter how devastating an epidemic, the population always recovered.

The American Indian peoples unfortunately did not participate in this microbiological exchange, having been cut off from the rest of the world since 11,000 B.C.[6] Not that they were free of disease. Syphilis, hepatitis, encephalitis, polio, and dental caries all existed in precontact America. But smallpox, whooping cough, chicken pox, diphtheria, influenza, scarlet fever, typhus, dysentery, cholera, measles, and yellow fever were all unknown; and they had a devastating effect on populations with no immunity to them. Immunity takes several generations to develop. The problem for the Indian peoples was that as soon as one epidemic passed, the survivors were often afflicted by another. Even a single pathogen could devastate a community, leaving crops unattended, the game not hunted, and the sick left to fend for themselves. The result was that the survivors often found their culture all but destroyed. Religious and political institutions were undermined, while a community often no longer had the skills and resources to remain economically viable, let alone defend itself from external attack.

Unfortunately, calculating the effects of these diseases on the peoples living north of the Rio Grande in 1492 is especially difficult given the paucity of the evidence. When early explorers like de Soto traveled through the Southeast, they found deserted towns. Some had been devastated by what the inhabitants called a "pest," but others may have been abandoned through fear of the approaching intruders. What is certain is that complex societies like the Mississippian cultures had disappeared. Most communities were now little more than a few families under a single chief. As one of de Soto's men observed of one such

---

Their Number Become Thinned: Native American Population Dynamics in Eastern North America (Knoxville, 1983); and Ann Ramenovsky, *Vectors of Death: The Archeology of European Contact* (Albuquerque, 1987). For an account of the historical debate, see John D. Daniels, "The Indian Population of North America in 1492," *William and Mary Quarterly*, XLIX, 1992, 298–320.

[6]   Some scholars believe that the Americas were not totally isolated after the submerging of the land bridge. For a discussion of possible transoceanic contacts before 1492 with Australasia, China, Japan, India, Africa, and the ancient Mediterranean world, see Jesse D. Jennings, ed., *Ancient North Americans* (San Francisco, 1978), 557–613.

DOCUMENT 2

A first meeting with the Europeans, printed in Colin G. Calloway, ed., *The World Turned Upside Down: Indian Voices from Early America* (Boston 1994), 35–8.

[The first meeting with Europeans could be extremely disconcerting for native peoples, uncertain who the newcomers were, what they wanted, and how they (the Indians) should react. This account of Henry Hudson's arrival in 1609 was written down in the mid-eighteenth century by John Heckewelder after talking to some Delaware Indians whose ancestors had inhabited the area of Manhattan.]

A long time ago, when there was no such thing known to the Indians as people with a white skin [their expression], some Indians who had been out fishing, and where the sea widens, espied at a great distance something remarkably large swimming, or floating on the water, and such as they had never seen before. They immediately returning to the shore, appraised their countrymen of what they had seen, and pressed them to go out with them and discover what it might be. These together hurried out, and saw to their great surprise the phenomenon, but could not agree what it might be; some concluding it either to be an uncommon large fish, or other animal, while others were of the opinion it must be some very large house. It was at length agreed among those who were spectators, that as this phenomenon moved towards the land, whether or not it was an animal, or anything that had life in it, it would be well to inform all the Indians on the inhabited islands of what they had seen, and put them on their guard. Accordingly, they sent runners and watermen off to carry the news to their scattered chiefs, that these might send off in every direction for the warriors to come in. These arriving in numbers, and themselves viewing the strange appearance, and that it was actually moving towards them (the entrance of the river or bay), concluded it to be a large canoe or house, in which the great Mannitto (great or Supreme Being) himself was, and that he probably was coming to visit them. By this time the chiefs of the different tribes were assembled on York island, and were counselling (or deliberating) on the manner they should receive their Mannitto on his arrival. Every step had been taken to be well provided with plenty of meat for a sacrifice; the women were required to prepare the best victuals; idols or images were examined and put in order; and a grand dance was supposed not only to be an agreeable entertainment for the Mannitto, but it might, with the addition of a sacrifice, contribute towards appeasing him, in case he was angry with them. The conjurers were also set to work, to determine what the meaning of this phenomenon was, and what the result would be. Both to these, and to the chiefs and wise men of the nation, men, women and children were looking up for advice and protection. Between hope and fear, and in confusion, a dance commenced. While in this situation fresh runners arrive declaring it a house of various colours, crowded with living creatures. It now appears to be certain that it is the great Mannitto bringing them some kind of game such as they had not before; but other runners soon after arriving, declare it a large house of various colours, full of people yet of quite a different colour

> than they [the Indians] are of; that they also dressed in a different manner from them, and one in particular appeared altogether red, which must be the Mannitto himself. . . . Many are for running off into the woods, but are pressed to stay, in order not to give offense to their visitors.

habitation, "The town was of seven or eight houses, built of timber, and covered with palm leaves"; another consisted of "forty small and low houses." This was a far cry from the large and numerous habitations of the Mississippian peoples.

Nevertheless, ossuary or burial evidence suggests that some Indian peoples may have been spared the worst ravages of disease, enjoying a similar life expectancy before and after the coming of the Europeans. At a Late Woodland site at Clarksville in southern Virginia, 16 percent of those buried died before age three; another 24 percent died by age eighteen; 26 percent died between the ages of twenty-one and thirty-five; and 15 percent died between the ages of thirty-six and fifty-five, giving an average life expectancy of around twenty-seven. These numbers correspond closely to the figures for an early contact site at Shannon in Montgomery County, Virginia. There 19 percent of those interred died before age three, 15 percent between four and seventeen, 21 percent between the ages of twenty-one and thirty-five, another 13 percent by age forty-five, and 14 percent by age fifty-five; average life expectancy was thus about thirty. Such figures are not suggestive of a sudden biological holocaust.[7] On the other hand William Bradford, while visiting an Indian village near Plymouth colony in 1621, commented, "Their skulls and bones were found in many places lying still above the ground, where their houses and dwellings had been." The failure to bury them reflected "the late great mortality which fell in all these parts about three years before the coming of the English." Similar comments were made by other Europeans at this time, indicating that the native peoples suffered widespread population loss during the contact era. Thus, the North American continent was not an unpopulated wilderness, as often asserted in the past but a recently depopulated countryside, a crucial difference.

Whatever the ravages of disease, recent estimates suggest that some 500,000 people lived east of the Allegheny Mountains in 1600 and that 30,000 of these resided in the vicinity of the lower Chesapeake, to which the London Company was directing its efforts; perhaps another 150,000 lived in New England, where the Plymouth Company was about to attempt a settlement.

3   EASTERN NORTH AMERICA, CIRCA 1600

Four main linguistic groups inhabited eastern North America at this time. Algonquian peoples occupied the coastal regions from Newfoundland to northern Carolina, though a number also resided around the Great Lakes. Siouan peoples inhabited the coastal areas of the Carolinas; while Muskogeans lived in Georgia and the Floridas. The Iroquoian peoples in contrast lived almost entirely inland, inhabiting the St. Lawrence valley and the area

---

[7]   See Douglas H. Ubelaker, "Human Biology of Virginia Indians," in Helen C. Rountree, ed., *Powhatan Foreign Relations, 1500–1722* (Charlottesville, 1993). Average life expectancy in England at the end of the sixteenth century was thirty-nine.

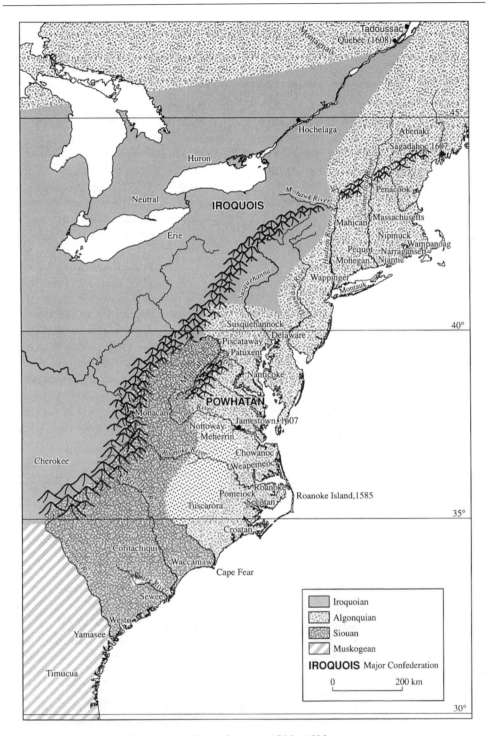

Map 2 Eastern Woodland coastal peoples, ca. 1530–1608.

southward to the piedmont of Virginia and the Carolinas. Common linguistic roots did not mean close political or cultural ties, and in this respect the Indian peoples were no different from their European counterparts. Though the French and Spanish spoke languages derived from Latin, they enjoyed their own cultures and often pursued conflicting paths. The English were similarly different from the Germans.

One consequence of the European arrival is that more is known about the peoples of eastern North America before acculturation changed their way of living.[8] The testimony of these early observers confirms that the material culture of the east coast Indians was roughly similar to that of the earlier Adena peoples. Implements were of wood, shell, or stone, copper being used for ornamentation only.

Horticulture was the principal means of subsistence. Wooden hoes tipped with flint or shell were used to cultivate tobacco, maize, beans, and squash, which were sown together in the same plot. This method allowed the beans and squash to use the maize for support and also helped fertilize the soil, since the beans replaced the nitrogen taken by the maize. John White noted at Roanoke that a first sowing of corn was made in April, with further sowings in May and June, so that successive crops could be harvested from midsummer until the fall.

Evidence about the extent of Indian horticulture varies. When Jacques Cartier visited the Iroquoian settlement of Hochelaga in October 1535, near present-day Montreal, he found it to be a "fine land with large fields covered with the corn of the country." The productivity of Eastern Woodland agriculture was confirmed by Thomas Harriot at Roanoke in 1585. He commented that an acre of corn yielded "at least two hundred London Bushelles," whereas in England forty bushels of wheat per acre was considered a good yield. On the other hand, William Strachey and Henry Spelman described the fields at Jamestown as small, while White's drawing of the town of Secotan near Roanoke in 1585 shows trees close to the settlement and only small cultivated plots in between. These observations suggest that a village of twenty or thirty dwellings would not have more than two hundred to three hundred acres under cultivation.

A major problem for Indian cultivators, shortly also to face Europeans, was clearing the land. Trees could be killed by girdling the bark from the trunk and burning the undergrowth, but this slash-and-burn method did not remove the stumps. Hence planting initially could be done only by digging holes between the stumps and then heaping soil around the plants as they grew. Eventually the stumps were removed by scorching the roots, though by then the soil had lost much of its fertility. As a result, every ten to twenty years the

---

[8] Among the most important sources are the drawings of John White and writings of Thomas Harriot, who were both at Roanoke; the writings of John Smith and William Strachey, who were present in early Jamestown; the comments of Jacques Cartier on his journey up the St. Lawrence in 1535; and the drawings of Jacques Lemoyne, who accompanied Ribaut's expedition to northern Florida in the early 1560s.

The observations of these artists and writers necessarily have to be treated with caution. John White's figures tend to have European rather than Indian faces. John Smith exaggerated his own achievements by distorting everything else. But these sources do provide valuable eyewitness evidence about the numbers and culture of the eastern Indian peoples on the eve of colonization. White's drawings have been published in Paul Hulton, *America 1585: The Complete Drawings of John White* (Chapel Hill, 1984). For John Smith's writings, see Philip L. Barbour, ed., *The Complete Works of Captain John Smith, 1580–1631*, 3 vols (Chapel Hill, 1986). William Strachey's *The Historie of Travell into Virginia Britania* has been edited by Louis B. Wright and Virginia Freund (Cambridge, England, The Hakluyt Society, Second Series, Vol. 103, 1953). Cartier's observations can be found in Ramsay Cook, ed., *The Voyages of Jacques Cartier* (Toronto, 1993).

inhabitants moved to another site, though a lack of wood for fuel and building was another reason. This restricted ability to practice intensive horticulture meant that only a limited population could be supported. Hence to Europeans, accustomed to relatively densely populated countrysides, eastern North America still seemed largely uninhabited.

Horticulture provided between 30 and 70 percent of food requirements, depending on the time of the year and location. Tribes like the Timucua in Florida enjoyed a long growing season and probably secured two-thirds of their subsistence from horticulture. The Abenaki, on the other hand, who lived just south of the St. Lawrence, probably secured less than 50 percent of their food by such means. In any case all Indian peoples made up the shortfall from game, fish, and wildfowl, depending on what was available and whether a settlement was near the coast, by a river, or on higher ground inland.[9]

The principal hunting seasons were fall and early winter when animals were at their prime weight, though more localized hunting also took place in the spring and early summer. Deer constituted the most available source of meat; bear, fox, raccoon, and beaver were also caught. Most animals were either snared or hunted with bows and arrows. However, deer were often caught with the help of fire, being driven by the flames into an ambush. The large trees were not normally affected by such conflagrations, which typically destroyed only the saplings and other undergrowth. Such fires thus not only cleared the woodlands but encouraged the growth of grasses that attracted the deer to return. Fire also helped rid an area of insects and made travel to and from the hunting grounds easier. In addition, clearing the brushwood made it more difficult for an enemy to approach unseen. The undergrowth was often fired twice a year, which accounted for the "parklike" appearance of many woods to the early Europeans.

One source of meat closer to hand was wildfowl, abundant during spring and fall when migratory birds such as passenger pigeons, Canada geese, and other species passed by. John Smith, one of the leaders at Jamestown, noted in 1608 as winter approached, that "rivers became so covered with swans, geese, ducks, and cranes, that we daily feasted."[10] Another prolific wildfowl was turkey, which providentially did not migrate and was available in large numbers.

Fish, too, played an important part in the diet of Eastern Woodland peoples. Along the coast fishing was necessarily confined to shallow waters, since the Indians had only dugout tree logs or wood-framed birch bark canoes. On the rivers they could fish either in boats or from the bank, using nets made from vegetable fibers or weirs constructed with poles or rocks, which channeled the fish into a confined area where they were either speared or caught by hand. They also used lines tipped with bone hooks. Everywhere nature offered a wonderful bounty. The Chesapeake and Delaware bays abounded in shad, bass, sturgeon, and eels; the rivers of New England were equally stocked in spring with spawning runs of alewives, salmon, and eels; and the coastal waters proliferated with clams and other shellfish.

In general the Indian peoples of eastern North America enjoyed a relatively balanced and healthy diet at the time of contact; Europeans were continually struck by their well-proportioned limbs and physical agility. So prolific were their food sources that the

---

[9] For the variations in Indian subsistence patterns within a region, see Kathleen J. Bragdon, *Native Peoples of Southern New England, 1500–1650* (Norman, 1996).

[10] Smith may have been exaggerating here so far as he and his companions were concerned, since it was one thing to describe the game, but another to catch it, see chapter 3, section 1.

Plate 7   Indian hunter, front and back view, by John White, engraved by Theodore de Bry. The Bodleian Library, Oxford.

production or accumulation of surpluses for resale was rarely considered. Only corn was stored year-round, though dried fish and meat were kept for a time. In general the Indians knew that they could survive each season until the next part of the food cycle arrived. This philosophy led many Europeans to condemn them for their want of foresight and lack of work ethic. The Indians seemingly ignored the biblical command to have "dominion" over the earth and every living creature in it. Only thus could Europeans explain what seemed to them the paradox of Indian poverty in a land of plenty.

Woodland Indians made their clothing either from animal skins or fabrics woven from hemp or other vegetable fibers. In the Albemarle region at the time of White's visit, adults mostly wore deerskin aprons tied around their waists during the summer and deer or bear mantles draped over their shoulders in winter. They added leather thongs around the edges of deerskin garments for ornamentation. Woodland Indians generally went barefoot in summer and wore leather moccasins in winter. They wore remarkably light clothing by European standards. Cartier was amazed in 1535 when they approached his ships over the ice almost naked, seemingly unaffected by the cold. One reason for their endurance was the practice of rubbing themselves with bear grease, which also gave protection from insects in summer.

East of the Allegheny Mountains copper was relatively scarce and was used only for ornamentation in the form of gorgets, bracelets, and brooches for both men and women. Other decorative items were made from bone and shell, notably strings of beads. Hairstyles varied according to gender. Women grew their hair full length. Men, on the other hand, customarily shaved one side of the head or created a central crown. Face paint was worn only for religious ceremonies or war rituals.

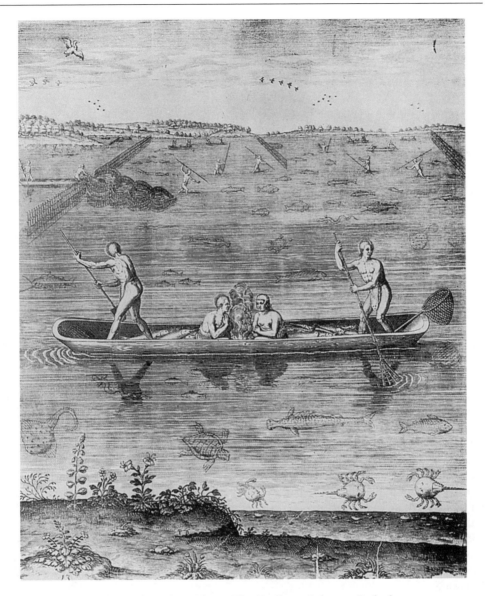

Plate 8 Indians fishing, by John White. The Bodleian Library, Oxford.

Scholars disagree about the role of trade. Until the arrival of Europeans, the Indians were basically self-sufficient. No single item or particular raw material was critical to their way of life. Shell scrapers were nearly as effective as obsidian ones; bone-tipped spears were almost as lethal as those tipped with flint. But burial sites reveal an extensive exchange of artifacts, at least of luxury goods for the elites, notably copper, puccoon (red paint), pearls, and decorative shells. Indian peoples, especially chiefs, wanted to demonstrate their wealth and superiority through their dress and personal appearance, just as Europeans did.

Plate 9 Indian man and woman preparing a meal, by John White. The Bodleian Library, Oxford.

The exchange of goods, however, was part of a gift culture rather than the operation of a commercial market. Among Indians status was measured by the ability to give rather than to possess. Hence many items found in burial sites were originally gifts exchanged to cement alliances and treaties.[11] Nevertheless, some tribes undoubtedly traded because they had a monopoly of a scarce raw material, while others realized that commerce could enhance their power and status. According to the Franciscan monk Pierre Sagard, who visited the Great Lakes in the 1630s, the Huron sowed enough corn for two or three years, "either for fear that some bad season may visit them or else in order to trade it to other nations for furs and other things." Powhatan, the paramount chief of the Pamunkey, Chickahominy and Mattaponi tribes, who was attempting to expand his influence in the Chesapeake at this time, may also have been seeking control of four key items: copper from the Allegheny Mountains; red paint from the Carolinas; shell beads from the coast; and pearls from the Delaware.

Tobacco played an important role in intertribal relations. It was always produced to welcome visitors and smoked during peace conferences. Those making long journeys similarly carried a pipe to signify their desire for peace and friendship. Many Indians believed its smoke could carry their thoughts to the gods.

---

[11] The argument that trade was an essential aspect of American Indian life before European contact is made by Helen C. Rountree, ed., *Powhatan Foreign Relations, 1500–1722* (Charlottesville, 1993). The view that it was less important is argued by Daniel K. Richter in *Ordeal of the Longhouse: The Peoples of the Iroquois League in the Era of European Colonization* (Chapel Hill, 1992), 28; and Bruce G. Trigger, *Natives and Newcomers: Canada's Heroic Age Reconsidered* (Montreal, 1985), 104 and 183.

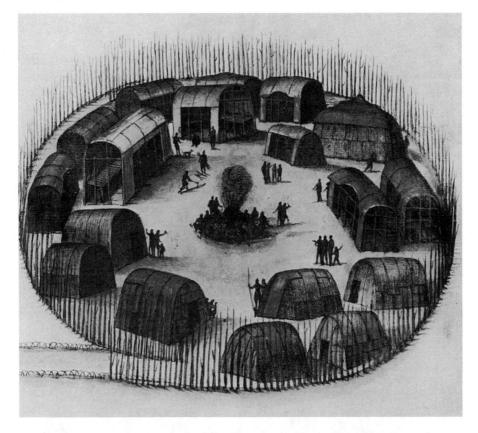

Plate 10 The town of Pomeiock, with protective stockade, by John White.
© Copyright the British Museum.

At the time of European contact the American Indians of eastern North America lived mainly in stockaded villages, unless they felt secure. Stockades were made from wooden poles set close together in the ground. According to Captain John Smith in 1608, the Chesapeake Indians' "buildings and habitations are for the most part by the rivers or not far from a fresh spring. Their houses are built like our Arbors [summerhouses] of small young saplings bowed and tied, and so close covered with mats or the barks of trees" that "not withstanding either wind, raine or weather, they are as warm as stoves." A similar picture was painted by Cartier at Hochelaga, where fifty houses were sited in the middle of fields close to a hill, providing both fine views and early warning of anyone's approach.

House styles varied. In the Southeast, circular structures covered with wattle and daub under a thatch of palmetto leaves were common. In the Northeast, houses were usually rectangular and increasingly elongated, especially among the Iroquoian peoples. At Hochelaga Cartier noted that the houses were some "fifty paces or more in length, and twelve to fifteen in width, built completely of wood and covered in and bordered up with large pieces of the bark and rind of trees, broad as a table, which are well and cunningly lashed after their manner." Houses this size accommodated several families, who were related by blood or fictive kin and were members of the same clan.

Plate 11 The Indian town of Secotan, drawing by John White. © Copyright the British Museum.

Since the Eastern Woodland people were still hunter gatherers as well as agricultural-ists, not all the year was spent in the village, the location of which might be changed for seasonal convenience. The women and children went out to gather fruit, nuts, and berries, while the men fished and hunted nearby. The males departed in the fall to hunt game farther afield, returning with their catches in December or January. Some women accom-panied them to process the catches and to carry the meat and skins back to the village.

Gender roles were well defined. According to Smith and other observers, the men mainly spent their time in fishing, hunting, or making war. The women and children did all the rest of the work, making "mats, baskets, pots, morters." Females also pounded the corn, and did all the other things necessary in the village itself, such as "make their bread, prepare their victuals, plant their corne, gather their corn."[12] A principal reason for this division of labor, observed also by Samuel Champlain in 1608 at Quebec and by William Wood in New Eng-land in the 1630s, was that all the tasks allotted to women were compatible with simultaneous child rearing. Consequently, most eastern societies were matrilineal, since it was the women who owned the crops and remained in the village to educate the young. Children accord-ingly took their mother's name and looked to her relatives for protection and support.[13]

Many have concluded from the comments of Smith and others that American Indian men were lazy. One reason is that hunting and fishing in Europe were largely aristocratic sports. But this view overlooks the fact that hunting for food rather than for sport could be arduous, especially in winter; warfare was inherently dangerous, if intermittent; building cabins and pallisades was hard work. Moreover, when not engaged in these tasks, the men made tools and weapons.

Indeed, whatever the impression of early white visitors, many ethnohistorians believe that greater equality existed between the sexes among the Indian peoples than in Europe, where patriarchy was widespread. One indication of this was the easy availability of divorce, which merely required agreement by the two parties; also, casual liaisons for unmarried members of both sexes were common. Since most tribes were matrilineal and often matri-local, it was the man who left the household once a marriage ended. The absence of patriarchy is also evidenced by the Indians' lenient attitude toward children, who were rarely punished and often indulged as a way of getting them to accept society's norms. On the other hand, women were not allowed to practice polygamy, were sometimes provided as sleeping partners for visiting dignitaries, were usually excluded from formal positions of authority, and seldom received expensive or ostentatious burial gifts. They were also banned from the community during menstruation, for fear of contaminating the village.

An important aspect of Indian society, though it was not recognized during the early contact period, was kinship. As one recent historian commented, "Kin taught children the ways of the world, from the secrets of making pots or arrows to the enemies of their people,

---

[12] John Smith, *A Map of Virginia. With a Description of the Country, the Commodities, People, Government and Religion* (Oxford, 1612), 19–36, quoted in Warren M. Billings, *The Old Dominion in the Seventeenth Century, 1606–1689* (Chapel Hill, 1975). See also Karen Ordahl Kupperman, ed., *Captain John Smith: A Select Edition of his Writings* (Chapel Hill 1988); and Philip L. Barbour, ed., *The Complete Works of Captain John Smith, 1580–1631,* 3 vols (Chapel Hill, 1986).

[13] This caused considerable confusion for Europeans who were accustomed to children taking the name of their father and receiving their inheritance from him. To Europeans, a matrilineal society implied a society without male control or proper order.

DOCUMENT 3

The upbringing of children, Father Gabriel Sagard, 1632, reprinted in James Axtell, ed., *The Indian Peoples of Eastern America: A Documentary History of the Sexes* (New York, 1995).

[Sagard, a Franciscan monk, was horrified, like all Europeans, at the upbringing of Indian children, believing that they were neither educated nor properly disciplined. He failed to appreciate that there were other ways of achieving maturity – notably by example, encouragement, public shaming and social ostracism – and that self-discipline generally worked better than rules imposed by others.]

Nevertheless they love their children dearly, inspite of . . . the fact that they are very naughty children, paying them little respect, and hardly more obedience; for unhappily in these lands the young have no respect for the old, nor are children obedient to their parents, and moreoever there is no [corporal] punishment for any fault. For this reason everybody lives in complete freedom and does what he thinks fit; and parents, for failure to punish their children, are often compelled to suffer wrongdoing at their hands, sometimes being beaten and flouted to their face. This is conduct too shocking and smacks of nothing less than the brute beast. Bad example, and bad bringing up, without punishment or correction, are the causes of all this lack of decency.

from proper behavior toward one's fellow villagers to the mysterious forces controlling the universe . . . Kin met to celebrate a young hunter's first kill or decide on the propriety of a marriage offer. Kin avenged one when one was harmed, took care of one in sickness, and mourned one after death."[14]

Kinship was of two kinds, biological and fictive. The latter was effected through a clan system, to which each family was attached. These were normally called after the name of an animal such as bear, turtle, beaver, or wolf. Clans originated as a means of minimizing conflict and increasing the political and economic effectiveness of families. In due course they facilitated a number of complementary objectives. Hospitality could be sought from someone of the same clan, no matter how distant, which was especially useful in a society where men spent so much time away from home hunting or making war. It also facilitated trade.

One difference in Indian society that early European observers were quick to notice was the relative importance of the community over the individual, especially in material goods. The only items over which an individual could claim possession were those into which personal labor had been invested – notably crops, the produce of a hunt or fishing expedition, a house and its furnishings, tools, and items of personal clothing and ornamentation. Everything else, especially land, was owned in common. However, in times of hardship, even personal resources were pooled, since the needs of the community prevailed over the

---

[14] James H. Merrell, *The Indians' New World: Catawbas and their Neighbors from European Contact Through the Era of Removal* (Chapel Hill, 1989), 20.

claims of the individual. Everyone had an obligation to share, none more so than the chiefs. Indeed the ability to give was the measure of their importance and respect.

Burial practices were restrained compared to those of the earlier Mississippian era. The emphasis now was on a simple honoring of the dead. In the Chesapeake area charnel houses were common. Here the corpses, minus the soft tissue, were laid out so that families could honor their kin before final burial in a communal grave. The belief was that the soul could not go to heaven until the flesh had been removed and the bones cleaned. However, Iroquoian people simply buried their dead after a few days' mourning, during which the deceased were laid out in their best dress. Most burials were accompanied by feasts in honor of the departed, and mourning for close relatives usually continued for about a year. In some cultures bereaved men abstained from sexual relationships during this time and widows did not remarry.

Like all peoples of the Americas, the Eastern Woodland Indians believed in many deities. Most of these were associated with the seasons or heavenly bodies, reflecting the importance of the yearly cycle. A long winter could mean starvation; a late spring might result in a poor harvest; lack of rain could ruin crops; excessive cold affected the game. The most popular ceremonies were those for midwinter, the coming of spring, the start of summer, the eating of the first corn, and the final harvest. Ceremonies often involved dancing to a rhythm provided by gourd and turtle rattles. White noted that the Algonquian peoples of the Chesapeake performed their dances around carved posts representing the heads of the deities. He also noted that during the green corn dance three young women – representing maize, beans, and squash – embraced in the center of the dancers. Feasting was also customary on these occasions, as were orations thanking the deities for their providence.

Indian peoples had various theories about how the world was created, not entirely dissimilar to the Judeo-Christian one contained in the Bible. Thomas Harriot was surprised to learn at Roanoke that the Algonquians of North Carolina believed in one supreme god who had made the lesser gods, who in turn produced water out of which were created all the animals and other creatures, including the first woman. The Iroquois, in contrast, believed that the world began when the pregnant skywoman descended from heaven to the watery darkness below, bringing light and life. Her daughter subsequently gave birth to twins, Good and Evil, who ever after were in conflict with each other. A constant theme among Indian nations was the idea of a supreme being, the great Manitou, who was the ultimate creator of the earth. On the other hand, they had no notion of a hell of brimstone and fire where punishment was meted out to those who had fallen from grace, nor did they have any concept of original sin.

However, religion was not restricted to the worship of these formal gods, since Indians believed that all things had spirits that had to be honored; otherwise, sickness or death might result. Animals in particular had to have their spirits propitiated by certain rituals if the hunter was to continue to hunt. Hence the bones of a beaver were never thrown to the dogs, but returned to where the animal had been killed as a mark of respect for the food it had provided and the warmth its fur would give in winter.[15] This respect for the

---

[15] Such rituals have led one historian to believe that the precontact Indian peoples were the world's first conservationists, living in harmony with nature until the balance was destroyed by the arrival of the Europeans. See Calvin Martin, *Keepers of the Game: Indian Animal Relationships and the Fur Trade* (Berkeley, 1978). The thesis has not been accepted by other historians. See Shepherd Krech III, *Indians, Animals and the Fur Trade: A critique of Keepers of the Game* (Athens, 1981). Other critics include Bruce Trigger, *Natives and Newcomers*, 242–43; and Helen C. Rountree, *The Powhatan Indians of Virginia: Their Traditional Culture* (Norman, 1989), 40.

environment was to prove one of the greatest differences between the Indian and European peoples, since the latter looked on the land and its resources as commodities to be exploited for private profit.

One method of dealing with such phenomena was the seeking of a benign spirit or *okki*, as the Iroquois called them, to act as protector. Adolescents customarily went through various initiation ceremonies to secure one for life. Otherwise, these matters were the particular concern of shamans, who had to act both as priests and physicians, since sickness might have natural causes as well as being the result of vengeful spirits, witchcraft, or the unfulfilled desires of the soul. Natural causes could be treated by herbal medicines, of which the shamans had a wide selection, ranging from ground juniper for colds, milkweed as an antiseptic, spider's web to stop bleeding, senega root for snake bites, birch bark for burns, dogwood for fevers, and sweat baths for ridding the body of its poisons. In contrast, witch-craft or vengeful spirits were combated by charms and incantations. Finally, the desires of the soul could be found in a person's dreams, which the shaman had to interpret so that they could be executed and the soul left in peace.

At the time of European contact, the Eastern Woodland peoples everywhere lived in villages of from one hundred to perhaps a thousand people. These in turn were joined in loose confederacies with neighboring communities of the same language and culture. Each village was governed by a chief, who usually inherited the position, though ability was also essential. Succession among the Algonquian peoples was largely through the female line, passing from a woman's eldest son through the younger brothers to the sisters and then the heirs of the eldest sister. The leaders of the several villages periodically deliberated together in a tribal council. However, the individual chiefs were fairly independent, not least because their own authority was limited. A chief might expect a proportion of the hunt and help in the cultivation of his field, but otherwise he was expected to fend for himself, even to the extent of making his own clothes. Indian society was very democratic in some respects.

There are signs that, by the end of the sixteenth century, individual leaders or groups of tribes were attempting to re-create the kind of centralized authority that had existed during the Mississippian era. It may have been the result of competition for scarce hunting grounds or limited acreage along the fertile river valleys. The most prominent empire builder along the eastern seaboard was Powhatan, who by 1607 had extended his authority over thirty-one tribes in the Chesapeake region. A similar consolidation was taking place among the Piscataway and Patuxent peoples higher up the bay. Farther north consolidation had taken the form of confederation, notably among the Five Nations of the Iroquois. However, the authority of these leaders or confederations was still limited. They could merely expect a tribute of beads, copper, or skins, plus occasional assistance in war from dependent tribes. The Indian peoples of North America had not developed the idea of a state or the means of organizing one.

Warfare played an important role in Indian life, though historians have not always agreed as to its purpose. Smith stressed revenge and the desire for captives as the main factors. The truth is somewhat more complex. Most Indians believed that the spirits of kin slain in battle could not rest until they had been revenged. This meant either killing an enemy or seizing a captive for adoption by way of replacement, a custom known as the mourning war culture. But war was also a means of controlling territory to ensure game and food supplies. Indians did not need to control territory in the European manner; simply depopulating an area was sufficient to assert their claim, a policy that the Iroquois were

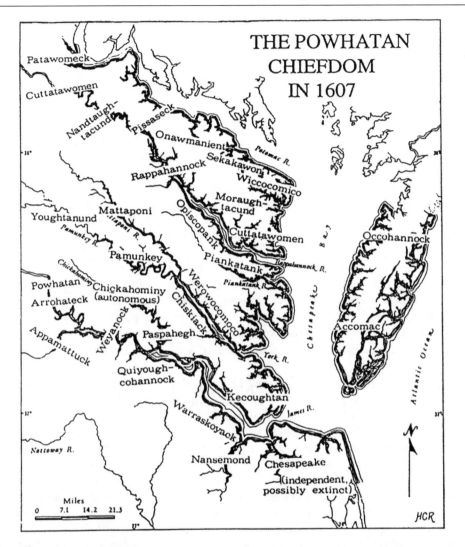

THE POWHATAN
CHIEFDOM
IN 1607

Patawomeck

Cuttatawomen

Nandtaugh-
tacund

Pissaseck

Onawmanient

Potomac R.

Sekakawon

Wiccocomico

Rappahannock

Moraugh-
tacund

Youghtanund

Mattaponi

Opiscopank

Cuttatawomen

Occohannock

Mattaponi R.

Pamunkey R.

Pamunkey

Piankatank

Rappahannock R.

Piankatank R.

Chickahominy

Powhatan

Chickahominy
(autonomous)

Arrohateck

Werowocomoco

Chiskiack

Accomac

Appamattuck

Weyanock

Paspahegh

York R.

Quiyough-
cohannock

Kecoughtan

Warraskoyack

James R.

Nottoway R.

Nansemond

Chesapeake

(independent,
possibly extinct)

Chesapeake Bay

Atlantic Ocean

Miles
0   7.1   14.2   21.3

HCR

Plate 12 Map showing the Powhatan Confederacy in 1607. From Helen Rountree, *Powhatan Foreign Relations* (Charlottesville, 1993).

shortly to pursue in order to gain control of the St. Lawrence Valley and the area of the Great Lakes. Paradoxically, war may also have become a means of replacing lost tribal numbers by the seizure of captives.

Warfare may in consequence have been on the increase by 1600. One indication was the growth in the number of pallisaded towns. Success in arms was certainly esteemed by most Indian peoples, partly because it indicated the physical prowess and stratagem necessary for successful hunting. Hence young males everywhere, especially potential leaders, were initiated into membership of their community by a ceremony, called *huskanaw* among the Algonquian peoples of North Carolina, which involved various tests of endurance, most notably being sent into the woods where they were fed potions designed to obliterate their

DOCUMENT 4

The Indian method of warfare, Thomas Harriot, 1588, reprinted in Karen Ordahl Kupperman, ed., *Major Problems in American Colonial History: Documents and Essays* (Lexington, Mass., 1993), 13.

[Apart from describing traditional methods of fighting, this document emphasizes the dramatic effect the Europeans had on Indian military practices.]

Their manner of wars amongst themselves is either by sudden surprising one another, most commonly about the dawning of the day, or moonlight, or else by ambushes or some subtle devices. Set battles are very rare, except it fall where there are many trees, where either part may have some hope of defence, after the delivery of every arrow, in leaping behind some or other.

If there fall out any wars between us and them, what their fight is likely to be, we having advantages against them so many manner of ways, as by our discipline, our strange weapons and devices else, especially by ordinance great and small, it may easily be imagined; by the experience we have had in some places, the turning up of their heels against us in running away was their best defence.

---

childhood memories. It must be stressed, however, that Indian warfare was often more symbolic than real. War parties were usually small, while arrows and tomahawks tipped with flint or horn were only moderately lethal, especially against the Iroquois, who fought in armor made from wooden slats.[16] There was also no shame in running away. A warrior who survived would be able to fight another time. Unfortunately the rules of warfare were to change significantly with the arrival of the Europeans.

The peoples of the east coast were not without knowledge of the strangers now approaching. Their vessels had been sighted for more than a century and contact had been made, usually to trade. This was especially true in the lower St. Lawrence area, where the Montagnais village of Tadoussac had become a thriving center for furs. But the American Indians were also well aware that the newcomers were potentially dangerous. Misunderstandings during the exchange of goods had produced conflict, while the visitors had shown an alarming readiness to kidnap Indian people. Farther south, the Spanish had made various forays, looking for gold and taking slaves. In 1570 a Spanish Jesuit mission was established at Ajacán in the Chesapeake. When the priests were killed following their failure to help during a drought, the Spanish mounted a punitive expedition in which eight Indians were executed. Fourteen years later, other strangers appeared in Albemarle Sound just down the coast in North Carolina. Once more, Indian hospitality was abused. Powhatan certainly knew of the Roanoke venture and may have contributed to its fate.

---

[16] For a discussion of Indian warfare, see James Axtell, *The European and the Indian: Essays in the Ethnohistory of Colonial North America* (New York, 1981); and Bruce G. Trigger, *Natives and Newcomers: Canada's "Heroic Age" Reconsidered* (Montreal, 1985).

Nevertheless, the newcomers had never succeeded in remaining permanently; and they did have wonderful goods to trade. Glass beads and copper objects made glittering jewelry. Iron hoes and hatches would make the cultivation of crops and the building of houses easier. Their weapons, too, would consolidate the position of a chief like Powhatan as master of all the werowances in the region. There was much to be gained from welcoming the newcomers, at least in the short term.

Part II

The Seventeenth-century Settlements

3

The English Arrive:
Virginia, 1607–60

1607	Jamestown and Sagadahoc are established.
1609–10	Jamestown endures "the starving time."
1611–16	Gates and Dale are governors.
1614	Peace is concluded with the Powhatan Confederacy. John Rolfe marries Pocahontas. The first shipment of tobacco is exported to England.
1618	The Virginia Charter of Liberties is granted.
1619	The first meeting of the Virginia House of Burgesses takes place. The first Africans arrive in Virginia.
1622	The Powhatan Confederacy attacks the Jamestown settlements.
1624	The Virginia Company lapses.
1625	Charles I accedes to the throne.
1635	A county administrative structure is created.
1639	The Crown formally recognizes the Virginia assembly.
1644–6	A second war breaks out against the Powhatan Confederacy.
1651	Virginia acknowledges the authority of Parliament.

1 THE VIRGINIA COMPANY: EARLY SETTLEMENT

THE EXPEDITION WHICH the London Company organized to begin the colonization of Virginia set sail on December 20, 1606, with 105 colonists on board. They were a mixed lot, including some 35 gentlemen, an Anglican minister, a doctor, 40 soldiers, and a variety of artisans and laborers. The journey took them via the Azores to the West Indies – the means of determining longitude were still unknown – and they arrived off the Chesapeake only in late April 1607. The instructions given to Captain Newport, the senior commander, were to find a site which was secure from Spanish attack but had access to the sea. Here he was to build a fort, erect a town, and explore the surrounding countryside.

It was in pursuit of this instruction that Newport sailed up the James River for about fifty miles. After declaring that the territory belonged to James I, he disembarked on a piece of land joined to the shore by a thin natural causeway, which made it more defensible against an enemy. The site had the additional advantage of being close to the deep-water channel, which allowed the ships to anchor nearby. The new settlement was to be called Jamestown.

Initially, everything went well. A sealed box was opened to discover the names of the councillors. Then the colonists began clearing some land to build a fortified palisade with a number of simple dwellings inside. These were one- and two-room timber-frame cottages with thatched roofs and walls of brushwood plastered with clay. The remaining land which had been cleared could now be devoted to crops. Equally promising was the demeanor of the local inhabitants. Initially they had seemed hostile, but within a few days Powhatan, the principal chief in the lower Chesapeake, was offering food and hospitality, a welcome addition to the colonists' supplies. Such fair conditions encouraged the council to divert many colonists to explore the neighborhood, still enticed by the lure of finding some El Dorado which would make them instantly rich.

Even so, there were early danger signs. During the summer and autumn an alarming number of the colonists began to sicken and die, owing to the unhealthy location of Jamestown, on the edge of a swamp. Unknowingly the colonists had brought with them typhoid and dysentery or the "bloody flux," which they now spread through ignorance of hygienic practices. Furthermore, the water on this stretch of the river became contaminated in summer by sea water, so that those who drank it suffered salt poisoning.[1]

With the onset of autumn the colonists found that they did not have enough food to sustain them through the winter. Not enough land had been cleared, nor sufficient crops planted and harvested, because too many men had gone off searching for gold. The newcomers still had not grasped the essential requirements for making a settlement in a strange country like the Chesapeake. For, as one councillor commented: "Though there be fish in the sea, fowls in the air, and beasts in the woods, their bounds are so large, they so wild,

---

[1] The argument about salt poisoning is advanced by Carville V. Earle, "Environment, Disease and Mortality in Early Virginia," in Thad W. Tate and David L. Ammerman, eds, *The Chesapeake in the Seventeenth Century: Essays on Anglo-American Society* (Chapel Hill, 1979), 96–122. Historians have pointed to malaria as another contributor to the mortality, though there is some dispute whether it was already in America or, like typhus and dysentery, brought by the colonists. See Darrett B. Rutman and Anita H. Rutman, "Of Agues and Fevers: Malaria in the Early Chesapeake," *William and Mary Quarterly*, XXXIII, 1976, 31–60.

Plate 13 The colonists land in Virginia, after John White. The Mansell Collection, London.

and we so weak and ignorant, [that] we cannot much trouble them." Fortunately, Powhatan remained friendly and ready to supply food. He hoped to absorb the newcomers by giving them hospitality in the traditional Indian manner, since commerce for profit was alien to Indian culture.

Disease and lack of food were not the only problems to afflict the colonists, however. From the first moment of landing, the settlers had been racked by dissension, since most of the gentleman soldiers refused to undertake the more menial tasks of colonization. The bitterest arguments took place between the councillors and their nominal president, an ineffectual aristocrat, Edward Wingfield. One member of the council was actually executed for mutiny.

The situation was saved only by the energetic leadership of Captain John Smith, a soldier of fortune, who in the next twelve months compelled his fellow colonists to live up to their obligations by planting corn, strengthening their defenses, and building dwellings for the colonists and their goods. Smith also embarked on a series of exploratory voyages to trade with the local inhabitants for food. When negotiations failed, he took what he wanted by force. He believed that the best way to treat the inhabitants was as the Spanish had done, by compelling "the treacherous and rebellious Infidels to do all manner of drudgery, work and slavery" for the colonists, so that they could live "like Soldiers upon the fruits of their labour." Smith was one of those who had served in Ireland.

Smith also tried to fulfill the company's hopes of producing glass, pitch, and potash, but without success. Nevertheless, he did arrange for the shipment of some timber and had another thirty acres of land cleared. Although only thirty-five colonists survived the first winter, further recruits arrived in spring 1608 and in the following October to swell the ranks, among them a few women. The orders remained, as before, to search for gold and to look for a northwest passage. The one additional instruction was for Powhatan to be crowned king to secure his allegiance to the colony.[2]

With such orders it is perhaps unsurprising that 1608 proved another disappointing year. Even the coronation of Powhatan was a failure, since the wily old chief refused to kneel for his crown or make any acknowledgment of his fealty, merely offering Captain Newport his old moccasins and fur cloak in return. Although Powhatan was still prepared to trade for food, his terms were increasingly high: he now wanted an English-style house and a supply of muskets. Another setback was the discovery that rats from the ships had spoilt much of the remaining grain. Since the colony was still unable to feed itself, Smith had to order some of the residents to lodge with the Indians, putting further stress on relations.

By now Smith's dictatorial stance had made him unpopular. His authority was constantly challenged, and he finally left the colony in October 1609. The London Company's concern over the settlement's difficulties was not diminished by news of similar misfortunes to its sister company. Following a preliminary reconnoitre, the Plymouth Company had sent two ships in May 1607 with 120 men on board. A settlement had been established at Sagadahoc on the coast of Maine at or near the Kennebec River. Here, as in Virginia, the settlers built a fort, a church, a storehouse, and fifteen dwellings. And just as in Virginia, disputes soon broke out among the council. As supplies of food ran low, the remaining settlers experienced the full severity of a Maine winter. Although a relief ship arrived there, too, in spring 1608, the survivors refused to stay and with their departure sank the hopes of any settlement.

Despite the evidence, the Virginia Company believed that the failings of both companies were the result of the 1606 charter, which gave the Crown the power to make decisions but left the adventurers with the responsibility and the expense of implementing them. Consequently, in February 1609 an application was made to turn the company into a proper joint stock corporation. The Crown, now less sanguine of an immediate profit, was happy to see its role diminished. A new charter was thus granted in May 1609, including an enlarged territory extending two hundred miles north and south of Point Comfort and stretching from the Atlantic to the Pacific. The royal council was to be abolished and replaced by one elected annually by the stockholders. In future the company could make its own laws and regulations, the only proviso being that they were to be as closely as possible "agreeable to the laws, statutes, government, and policy of this our realm."[3]

Armed with the new charter, the company took immediate steps to put itself on a sounder footing. Stock was sold in lots of £12.10s, £25, and £50, with the promise of a dividend from whatever gold or other valuable commodities, including land, were accumulated after seven years. To avoid further disputes in Virginia itself, the company decided to

---

[2]   Historians have been dependent for information on this period on Smith himself, who often exaggerated his exploits. For an analysis of his claims, see Philip L. Barbour, ed., *The Complete Works of Captain John Smith, 1580–1631*, 3 vols (Chapel Hill, 1986).

[3]   For a copy of the 1609 charter, see W. Keith Kavenagh, *Foundations of Colonial America: A Documentary History*, 3 vols (New York, 1973), III, 1704–14.

Plate 14 Captain John Smith captures the king of the Pamunkeys. From John Smith's *Discovery of Virginia*, 1609. The Mansell Collection, London.

concentrate authority in the hands of a governor with full powers, including that of exercising "martial law in cases of rebellion or mutiny."

This reorganization happened just in time, for events in Virginia were becoming critical. Even before the departure of Smith in the fall of 1609, relations with the local inhabitants had been deteriorating, following accusations of theft and dishonesty on both

Plate 15   An artist's impression of Jamestown ca. 1608. The Mansell Collection, London.

sides. The Powhatans had become disillusioned by the English failure to repay their hospitality and refusal to marry their women, which suggested hostility. Powhatan, who had several times asked Smith when the English intended to leave, now realized that the newcomers had not come to trade but "to invade my people and possess my country." His confederacy accordingly began attacking the settlers, killing their livestock, and burning their crops. The position of the colonists was particularly precarious because they were still not self-sufficient. Consequently, when a large relief fleet of nine ships was scattered by a violent storm in October 1609, the outcome was little short of catastrophic. During this bitter winter, known as "the starving time," most of the settlers perished either from malnutrition inside the fort or in attacks from outside. Many were reduced to eating the flesh of their dead companions or local inhabitants, disguising the taste with herbs and roots. One man even murdered his wife. The situation was so bad that in June 1610 the sixty survivors were on the point of quitting, as at Sagadahoc, when Lord De La Warr, the new governor, arrived with news of the company's new charter and future plans.

De La Warr moved quickly to get the settlement reestablished, ordering buildings to be repaired and fields brought back into cultivation. He divided the settlers into groups of fifteen, so that they could work safely and ward off the hostile native inhabitants. At the same time a policy of search and destroy was launched in a series of raids against the Indians, which resulted in atrocities on both sides. During one such operation the children of the Queen of the Paspaheghs were thrown into the water and shot before she herself was led into the woods to be burnt.

Although De La Warr himself succumbed to sickness and had to leave to save his health, the company remained determined to persevere with its investment and sent out a fresh batch of ships in 1611. An advance guard sailed under Deputy Governor Sir Thomas Dale, who had seen extensive military service in the Netherlands. Dale used the more direct route to Virginia via Bermuda which had been pioneered five years earlier by Captain Argall. By the time Sir Thomas Gates, the new governor, arrived, Dale had forced Powhatan into a truce and established a new settlement, Henrico, at a more healthful spot fifty miles upriver. This change was good news, for Gates had brought with him two hundred more settlers, most of them artisans, who were more suitable for the work in hand. The day of the gentleman adventurer and soldier of fortune was almost over.

For the next two years the colony was governed first by Gates (1611–1613) and then by Dale (1614–1616). Both men made full use of the powers granted them in the charter of 1609. To help manage the colony, Gates drafted a code of laws "Divine, Morall and Martiall," which became a byword for harshness. These laws required daily attendance at divine service and imposed stiff penalties for blasphemy and other crimes against the church. The code stipulated that work hours be from six o'clock till ten o'clock in the morning and again from two till four in the afternoon, the rest of the day being devoted to the personal repair of cottages and the cultivation of garden plots. Harsh penalties were instituted for crimes like sodomy and adultery, suggesting that the colony was suffering from an imbalance between its male and female population. The code also took steps to protect the company's tools, the monopoly of its storehouse, and trade with the local inhabitants. Among the offenses carrying the death penalty were desertion, mutiny, and disrespect to the company or its officials.[4]

Possibly the poor caliber of most colonists necessitated a system of martial law; for it was only now that the settlement finally became self-sufficient, helped by the discovery that a commercial crop could be grown. Although the various staples first favored by the company had not materialized, one crop, tobacco, had been tried. The local plant, *nicotiana rustica*, was extremely bitter; but in 1612 John Rolfe, who had arrived in 1609, introduced the West Indian variety, *nicotiana tabaccum*, which was sweet like the Spanish product. This new crop offered the prospect of a profitable export trade to England; for although James I equated smoking with the fires of hell, his kingdom was a growing market for tobacco. Rolfe's first consignment of four hogsheads – about 2,600 pounds – was shipped in 1614. Three years later 20,000 pounds were dispatched.

The colony also began to prosper because peace with the American Indians was finally achieved. Here, too, Rolfe was instrumental in advancing the colony's fortunes. During a raid in 1613, Samuel Argall, a member of the council, captured Pocahontas, Powhatan's favorite daughter. In due course Rolfe fell in love with the captive and requested Governor Dale's permission to marry her. Much romanticizing has surrounded this event, not least for its implication that the two races might have lived in harmony. The record shows that this was the only formal marriage between the races at this time, though a number of informal liaisons occurred. The overriding reason for this union, however, was simply the scarcity of women during the settlement's first years, though Rolfe may also have calculated some advantage from the fact that Pocahontas was the daughter of a chief. Nevertheless, the marriage did improve relations enough for the colony finally to present an appearance of peace and stability.

---

[4] A copy of the laws can be found in Kavenagh, *Documentary History*, III, 1869–75.

Meanwhile, the company itself had gone through a further metamorphosis. After the first hopes of a quick financial return disappeared, investors became wary of sinking more money into the venture. Accordingly, in 1612 yet another charter was sought, this time allowing the company to run a lottery, a popular form of speculation in the seventeenth century, from which profits could be used to finance other operations. The company also asked to have its domain extended to include Bermuda. Some of those shipwrecked in the storm of October 1609 had reported that the island was suitable both for the production of cash crops and as a protective base against the Spanish. Finally, the new charter provided for more meetings of the general court to facilitate the better government of the company. Complaints had been made that the treasurer, Sir Thomas Smith, and the council were not sufficiently responsive to the interests of the ordinary investors, or adventurers, as they were called. Now at least one meeting had to be held for them every three months in winter, spring, summer, and fall.

2 THE CHARTER OF LIBERTIES

With this second reconstruction it was hoped that the company could now build on what had been established in Virginia, though only the arrival of additional colonists could produce the kind of diversification envisaged in London. Alas, the population remained obstinately static; in 1616 there were a mere 324 men, women and, children at the company's six settlements, as against 450 in 1611. Clearly, few were tempted to endure the harsh rule of Dale and Gates when the rewards were so small. Another difficulty was that by 1614 the surviving servants of the original settlement were due to be released from their obligation to serve the company. Unless they were given some inducement to stay, the company's lands would fast be emptied.

Accordingly, in 1614 Dale allotted to all those who had settled in the colony prior to 1612 three acres of land to farm for their own use, exempt from all payments except one month's service to the colony and twelve bushels of corn in rent. This step did nothing, however, to resolve the even greater difficulty that was looming in 1616 when, according to the terms negotiated in 1609, all stockholders were to receive a dividend of one hundred acres of cleared land. The company had no means of honoring these terms; it could offer the adventurers no more than fifty acres of land, and that only if they subscribed another £12.10s in stock. The problem of profitability had not been solved, nor had that of the settlers' morale.

These failures led to yet more changes in the company, which are normally attributed to Sir Edwin Sandys, although some of the alterations must have been under consideration while Smith was still the treasurer. Sandys himself, believing that the various staple and manufacturing enterprises had failed through want of manpower, embarked on a policy of sending more colonists to ensure a self-sustaining population. Since the company's resources were insufficient, Sandys adopted the expedient of granting subpatents to groups of subscribers or wealthy individuals in return for special administrative and judicial privileges. The most important innovation was that their lands were to be held in free and common socage, subject to only a nominal quitrent. Administratively they were to be equivalent to an English hundred, which was part of a county.

The first grant was made to John Martin in 1617, but Sandys now extended the practice. Although many of the subsequent forty-four patents were not taken up, including that to

DOCUMENT 5

John Rolfe's request for permission from Governor Sir Thomas Dale to marry Pocahontas, 1614, reprinted in Warren M. Billings, *The Old Dominion in the Seventeenth Century: A Documentary History of Virginia, 1606–1689* (Chapel Hill, 1975), 216–19.

[Since the colonists' lives were still strictly controlled by the Virginia Company, Rolfe needed permission to marry Pocahontas. He was clearly aware of the objections to such a union and worried too that he was merely giving way to carnal lust in a society where there were few women. He skillfully played on the desirability of converting Pocahontas to Christianity to win over Dale, one of the authors of the Laws Divine, Morall and Martiall.*]*

Let therefore this [constitute] my well advised protestation . . . if my chiefest intent and purpose be not to strive with all my power of body and mind, in the undertaking of so mighty a matter, no way led (so far forth as man's weakness may permit) with the unbridled desire of carnal affection: but for the good of this plantation, for the honour of our country, for the glory of God, for my own salvation, and for the converting to the true knowledge of God and Jesus Christ, an unbelieving creature, namely Pokahuntas, to whom my hearty and best thoughts are, and have a long time been so intangled. . . .

I have not only examined but thoroughly tried and pared my thoughts . . . I forgot not to set before my own eyes the frailty of mankind. . . . Nor was I ignorant of the heavy displeasure which Almighty God conceived against the sons of Levie [sic] and Israel for marrying strange wives, nor of the inconveniences which may thereby arise . . . which made me look about warily and with good circumspection, into the grounds and principal agitations, which thus should provoke me to be in love with one whose education hath been so rude, her manners barbarous, her generation accursed, and so discrepant in all from my self, that often times with fear and trembling, I have ended my private controversy with this: surely these are wicked instigations. . . .

Now if the vulgar sort, who square all men's actions by the base rule of their own filthiness, shall tax or taunt me in this my godly labor: let them know, it is not any hungry appetite, to gorge my self with incontinency. . . . Nor am I so desperate in estate, that I regard not what becometh of me; nor am I out of hope but one day to see my Country, nor so devoid of friends, nor mean in birth, but there to obtain a match to my great content; nor have I ignorantly passed over my hopes there, or regardlessly seek to lose the love of my friends, by taking this course.

the Pilgrim fathers, enough were established to accelerate the shift from company to private property.

Not that the company had given up all intention of developing Virginia itself, for Sandys continued to send as many servants and tenants as possible to cultivate company lands. His plan was to offer all servants a tenancy after seven years, whereupon they would surrender half their produce to the company so that it could pay a dividend back home.

Sandys also shipped one hundred respectable maids to improve the balance of the population. In addition he endeavored to persuade the City of London and other towns to finance the departure of some of their surplus poor and orphaned children. More artisans were also sent, some in groups under a master, to establish the long-hoped-for silk, glass, brick, iron, salt, naval stores, and shipbuilding enterprises. During the next four years nearly four thousand persons were dispatched to the colony.

While making arrangements to increase the future profitability of the colony, Sandys was aware that his long-suffering shareholders required some immediate reward. He therefore announced that all adventurers would be given one hundred acres of land as their lawful dividend. Furthermore, all those who had arrived at their own expense since 1616 would receive fifty acres, plus a similar amount for every dependent who accompanied them. This provision came to be known as the Virginia headright. Lastly, lands were set aside to support the ministry; to build a school for the native peoples; and, more distantly, to establish a university for the settlers.

To facilitate these arrangements, the company divided up the existing settled areas into four boroughs: Charles City, Jamestown, Henrico, and Kiccowtan. The company was to retain three thousand acres in each of these boroughs for its own servants and tenants.

Sandys was aware, however, that the settlement needed a different form of government if it was to become truly popular. Dale's code of laws had already been abandoned, but further changes were necessary, if only to accommodate the new patentees like John Martin. Perhaps mindful of the adventurers' earlier demand for consultation in 1609, Sandys hit on the device of convening an assembly in America. The scheme may also have been devised partly to accommodate those adventurers who had gone to claim their land and were in consequence unable to attend the quarterly meetings in London.

The new body was to be composed of the governor, his council, and two burgesses from every hundred or parish elected by the inhabitants. It was to meet once a year and have full power to enact measures on all matters for the colony's good government.[5] Naturally all acts would have to conform where practical to English law and would also be subject to the veto of both the governor and the company in London.

The new measure was introduced strictly as a privilege. It was not intended to confer any rights on the settlers as Englishmen, among whom voting was the prerogative of the few. The only right was that of the adventurers to attend company meetings. However, to widen the appeal of the measure, Sandys wisely opened the vote to all male inhabitants. It was a remarkably generous gesture, and one which has rightly been seen as a crucial episode in the development of representative institutions in British North America. It set the pattern for government which within two centuries led to genuine democracy.

The news of these momentous changes was brought by a new governor, George Yeardley, who convened the first assembly late in July 1619 at Jamestown in the church. Sitting in the choir stalls were representatives from the four boroughs and eight plantations. A number of laws were passed, many based on previous company ordinances. The first stated that no injury was to be done to the American Indians "whereby the present peace might be disturbed and ancient quarrels revived." Then followed a series of decrees against drunkenness,

---

[5]   Quoted in Warren M. Billings, *The Old Dominion in the Seventeenth Century: A Documentary History of Virginia, 1606–1689* (Chapel Hill, 1975), 37–8. See Document 6.

DOCUMENT 6

Formal constitution for a council and assembly in Virginia, July 24, 1621, reprinted in W. Keith Kavenagh, *Foundations of Colonial America: A Documentary History* (New York, 1974), III, 1889–90.

[Although Governor Yeardley called the first meeting of the colonists' representatives in July 1619, the company defined the new body only two years later. One interesting feature was that the company intended to make ratification of its own decrees subject to reciprocal approval by the assembly.]

Know that we, the said Treasurer, Council and Company, taking into our careful consideration the present state of the said colony in Virginia and intending, by divine assistance, to settle such a form of government there as may be to the greatest benefit and comfort of the people, whereby all injustice, grievance, and oppression may be prevented . . .

We therefore . . . do hereby order and declare that from hence forward there be two supreme councils in Virginia for the better government of the said colony aforesaid. The one of which councils, to be called the Council of State, whose office shall be chiefly assisting with their care and advice and circumspection to the said Governor, shall be chosen, nominated, placed, and displaced from time to time by us, the said Treasurer, Council and Company. . . .

The other Council, more general, to be called by the Governor, and yearly . . . and no oftener but for very extraordinary and important occasions, shall consist for the present of the said Council of State and two Burgesses out of every town, hundred and other particular plantation to be respectfully chosen by the inhabitants. Which Council shall be called the General Assembly, wherein, as also in the said Council of State, all matters shall be decided, determined and ordered by the greater part of the voices then present, reserving always to the Governor a negative voice. And this general assembly shall have full power to . . . make, ordain, and enact such general laws and orders for the behalf of the said colony and good government thereof as shall from time to time appear necessary or requisite. Wherein, as in all things, we require the general Assembly, as also the Council of State, to imitate and follow the policy of the form of government, laws, custom, manners and administration of justice used in the realm of England, as near as may be . . . provided that no laws or ordinance made in the General Assembly shall be in force and valid unless the same shall be solemnly ratified and confirmed . . . here in England. . . .

idleness, gaming, and the wearing of ostentatious clothing; these were not dissimilar to Dale's laws, except for the severity of the punishment to be incurred. Trade with the American Indians was permitted, though only with the consent of the governor, but constant care was to be taken since the native inhabitants were in general "a most treacherous people." Accordingly, no guns were to be sold, and all settlers were to attend church on Sunday bringing their weapons with them.

Other laws confirmed recent reforms to the storehouse to prevent "certain abuses now complained of in the Magazine." The company's future profit was to be limited annually to 25 percent, while private landowners were excused having to sell their produce to the company storehouse. The assembly also addressed the curing of tobacco, demonstrating the crop's importance to the colony, along with the need for the proper regulation of relations between master and servant. Finally, every household was to have one spare barrel of corn, plant six mulberry bushes, and cultivate vines. The lessons of "the starving time" had finally been learnt.[6]

3   THE MASSACRE OF 1622 AND FALL OF THE COMPANY

It seemed that the colony was now set for a period of growth. One visitor, John Pory, noted in 1619 that, although sickness was still prevalent, the colonists also enjoyed the prospect of growing wheat and excellent grapes; he commented that "a few years may bring this colony to perfection," if the English plow was introduced to improve the preparation of the soil. The only cause for concern was the obsession with tobacco, where one or two planters had made a profit of £1,000. Not surprisingly, John Rolfe reported unqualified contentment the following year. The planters, freed from the company's restrictions, "strive and are prepared to build houses and to clear their ground."[7]

Nevertheless the growth expected by Sandys did not take place. One reason was that barely one-quarter of the four thousand settlers shipped out between 1618 and 1622 survived. Another was that the company, still harboring the delusion that it could develop manufactures in the colony, sent over hundreds of craftsmen who were quite unsuited to the wilderness conditions. Other colonists were simply physically weak, for no medical examination was ever given, so that even if they survived the voyage, they succumbed during the seasoning period which all newcomers had to undergo. Pory advised that people should be dispatched only in the fall, when the weather was reasonably benign. They could then acclimatize during the winter before planting their first crops. His advice, however, was all too often ignored, and Yeardley's resources were severely strained caring for the sick and destitute.

Then in March 1621 James I revoked the company's right to hold a lottery, probably because of the unscrupulous way in which the tickets were being sold. This reversal was a serious blow, since it ended what had been the company's best source of revenue. The likelihood that investors would put more money into the venture after such wretched returns over the past fifteen years was minimal.

As money was still required to meet the operating costs and pay the adventurers' dividends, the company's thoughts turned to the exploitation of tobacco. Initially the company had not welcomed Rolfe's experiments, feeling that they detracted from other activities which would be more profitable in the long term. Several attempts had been made

---

[6]   The full list of acts passed by the burgesses can be found in Kavenagh, *Documentary History*, III, 1884–8.
[7]   The correspondence from Rolfe and Pory can be found in Susan M. Kingsbury, *Records of the Virginia Company of London*, 4 vols (Washington, 1906–1935), III, 152–303.

to reduce the crop, though to little avail, especially after 1616 when most colonists could do what they wanted with their land. Production soared, reaching nearly fifty thousand pounds in 1618. An additional inducement was the decision of the Crown in December 1619 to ban tobacco planting in England. The net result was another leap in production to almost two hundred thousand pounds by 1622.

In these circumstances the company reluctantly recognized that it had no alternative but to exploit this unexpectedly profitable commodity. Unfortunately, under the 1609 charter company products were liable to a customs levy. The Crown now proposed a duty of one shilling a pound, twice the anticipated rate. Even worse, the duties were to be collected by tax farmers, who would thus control the crop's distribution. Sandys was not happy at this loss of patronage and proposed that the company itself should import and distribute the tobacco, allowing the Crown in return one-third of the crop. To this James I consented. Many shareholders, however, were appalled at the extravagent fees proposed for those administering the scheme when so few dividends had been paid. Pamphlets were written attacking Sandys, while his opponents, led by the Earl of Warwick and Sir Thomas Smith, appealed to the king to intervene. In response the Privy Council ordered the tobacco contract to be suspended while it investigated the company's affairs.

In the middle of this rumpus another crisis suddenly devastated the colony itself. One result of Sandys's liberal land policy was that the settlements had become dispersed along the James River for almost a hundred miles, leaving the colonists vulnerable to attack, especially since the total population was still barely fifteen hundred. By this time the Powhatan Confederacy sensed what the continued presence of the English would mean: more plantations, the felling of the forests, the extinction of the game, and the destruction of their way of life. Tobacco, not trade, was now the main interest of the settlers. The American Indians were no longer valued even for their friendship, for as one officer of the company noted, "There is scarce any man amongst us that doth so much as afford them a good thought in his heart."

The deaths of Powhatan and Pocahontas further hastened hostilities. The attempts of George Thorpe, the college tutor, to convert American Indian children to Christianity under the guise of educating them also did not help. Finally, when one of the werowances was murdered early in 1622, no redress from the company was forthcoming. Accordingly, the confederacy, led by Chief Opechancanough, resolved to end the settlers' presence through a series of coordinated assaults. Since the attack on Friday, March 22, 1622, was not preceded by any overt hostility, the American Indians were able to gain access to the settlement on seemingly innocuous business before revealing their true intent. Some even breakfasted with their victims. Jamestown was saved only by a last-minute warning from a native convert to Christianity. In the subsequent bloodbath some 350 colonists – men, women, and children – were struck down before the rest of the population could respond.

At a stroke many of the colonists' gains since 1616 were swept away. Several major plantations were destroyed, notably Martin's hundred and Charles City, along with the precious iron works and college lands. As a result the delicate balance between self-sufficiency and starvation was upset, while the image of the colony as a death trap was once more raised in the minds of potential settlers back home.

The American Indians, too, soon paid a terrible price for their attempt. In the following days and months bloody reprisals were carried out which severely weakened the Powhatan Confederacy.

The attack was also the final nail in the coffin of the Virginia Company. In April 1623 the Privy Council appointed a seven-man commission under Sir William Jones to inquire into the state of the colony, while at the same time it ordered the company to send help. Being bankrupt, it declined to do so, and thus stood in breach of its obligations under the charter of 1612. The council initially proposed a return to the situation of 1606, when the Crown had overall control, but the company refused to accept this proposal. The Privy Council therefore ordered the attorney general to begin legal proceedings, by writ of *quo warranto*, for the annulment of the charter. By May 1624 the Virginia Company was no more.

It used to be considered that the demise of the company, and by implication, that of the assembly, was part of the Stuart kings' design to impose a more absolutist form of government. This interpretation of events linked Sandys with the opposition in Parliament; but while it is true that Sandys did elicit support there during the final crisis, so, too, did his opponents. Moreover, Sandys was responsible for the tobacco contract, which would have given him and his friends a lucrative monopoly. Such arrangements were particularly unpopular in Parliament at this time.[8]

The reality is that the disputes over the company had only tenuous links with those between the king and Parliament. Certainly the court believed that the company's democratic method of proceeding, or "populariness," had exacerbated the situation. Of a plot, however, there is no trace. The annulment of the charter was forced on the Crown by the company's failings, as evidenced by the fact that neither James I nor the Privy Council had any immediate plans for dealing with the ailing enterprise.

Thus the real reason for the demise of the company was its failure to make a profit, which exasperated the shareholders, enough for them first to take their cause to the general court and then to raise it in Parliament, the Privy Council, and anywhere else where they could get a hearing.

The company's affairs were initially put into the hands of a caretaker commission under Lord Mandeville, who decided to send two of its members to Virginia to investigate before taking any action. Then in March 1625 James I died, and his successor, Charles I, wanted time before giving his decision in May 1625. He then merely affirmed by proclamation through the Privy Council the original intent that the colony had been established "for the propagation of Christian Religion, the increase of trade, and the enlarging of his Royal empire." The main change was that Virginia would now be administered by a governor and royal council answerable to the king.

---

[8]   This interpretation was popular with nineteenth-century Whig nationalist historians, who were keen to affirm that the destiny of America was an inevitable progression to liberty and democracy. Independence was still too recent to be questioned in a time of militant nationalism, typified by the mood of manifest destiny. The most famous work in this mold is George Bancroft, *History of the United States*, 10 vols (Boston, 1834–74). The interpretation was first seriously challenged by Wesley Frank Craven in *Dissolution of the Virginia Company* (New York, 1932); and by Charles M. Andrews in *The Colonial Period of American History*, 4 vols (New Haven, 1934–8). Both were members of the imperial school who were keen to emphasize the benefits of the English connection, partly as a result of the greater impartiality that time brings, and partly because they felt that the Anglo-Saxon nations ought to stand together. Both were products of the Ivy League. Andrews got his B. A. at Trinity College, Hartford, his Ph.D at Johns Hopkins, and was later appointed the Farnam Professor of American History at Yale. Craven completed his Ph.D at Cornell and subsequently became the Edwards and then George Henry Davis Professor of American History at Princeton.

One matter undecided in Charles's proclamation was the distribution of the tobacco crop, which for the moment was left to the king's servants. The good news, however, was that the exclusion of all foreign and domestic produce would be enforced, thus ensuring Virginia's producers a monopoly of the home market. Finally, the proclamation assured the colonists that the annulment of the charter was "not intended to take away or impeach the particular interest of any private planter or adventurer." Their just concerns would be protected.

The declaration made no mention of the assembly; most likely the Privy Council simply overlooked its existence. The assembly hardly had the potential to compare with Parliament, that ancient institution which had made and unmade kings. It was rather a mere device to assist in the administration of a colony. No ban was placed on its meeting, indicating that there was no preconceived notion of destroying it. The king's main concern was to end the bitter altercations within the company and perhaps in time to produce some revenue. Beyond that aim he had no plans.

4   GROWTH AND CONSOLIDATION, 1625–60

The imposition of royal government in 1625 was hardly a cause for celebration, since the colonists were uncertain what it would mean. It might merely lead to the reestablishment of the company, for during the next few years Sandys made several attempts to regain the charter. Whatever frame of government was imposed would be at best the lesser of two evils.

The colonists themselves had two main concerns: one was to avoid the imposition of a contract for the marketing of their tobacco; the other was to prevent the reimposition of martial law. They believed that the latter goal could best be achieved if the assembly was allowed to meet. To this end they issued a "Brief Declaration" when the two commissioners, John Pory and John Harvey, arrived to investigate. They also tried to buttress their position by passing an ordinance declaring that "the governor shall not lay any taxes or impositions upon the colony, their lands or commodities other than by the authority of the general assembly." In addition they published a review of the Virginia Company under Sir Thomas Smith, making its maladministration clear.

Regarding the tobacco contract, Charles I eventually settled for a customs duty of one shilling, leaving the colonists to market it themselves. But on the matter of an assembly, the Crown remained obstinately quiet, despite further appeals and the dispatch of Yeardley with a petition in 1625.

Nevertheless, both Sir Francis Wyatt, the first royal governor, and his successor found it convenient to summon meetings to sound out colonists' opinions on matters of special importance. Although the governors had plenipotentiary powers, once in Virgina they found themselves very constrained. They had no soldiers or bureaucracy on which to fall back and found ultimately that they could govern only with the consent of the colonists. Given that state of affairs, some kind of dialogue was required. To this end the assembly was a useful entity. Even the Crown acknowledged the wisdom of occasionally convening such a body, as in 1627 to discuss the issuing of licenses to import tobacco, and again in 1628 for the provision of a palisade between the James and York rivers. Charles I did not grant the assembly formal recognition, however, until 1639, when he authorized Governor Wyatt to summon the burgesses "as formerly once a year or oftener, if urgent occasion shall require." Only then did the king concede the crucial point that the assembly "together with the governor and council shall have power to make acts and laws for the government of that plantation, correspondent as near as may be to the laws of England."[9] It had been a long struggle.

Meanwhile, the physical condition of the colony had slowly improved following the massacre of 1622. After recovering from their surprise, the settlers hit back hard, taking advantage of the opportunity to destroy all the American Indian settlements in the vicinity of Jamestown and the lower peninsula. As Edward Waterhouse, secretary to the Virginia Company in London, enthused, "Our hands which before were tied with gentleness and faire usage, are now set at liberty by the treacherous violence of the Savages. . . . [We] may now by right of War, and law of nations, invade the country and destroy them who sought to destroy us."[10] For the next decade expeditions were sent out three times a year to kill the enemy, seize their crops, and prevent their return. No tactics were too cruel. One detachment talked with the Potomac Indians in 1623 as a ruse to poison two hundred of them, including their chief. Peace was achieved only in the early 1630s, when the two sides agreed to maintain a strict separation by a line across the Jamestown Peninsula, with only limited contacts for trade. The local inhabitants were still formidable but weakening as the English settlements grew.

For the English, the events of 1622 and the subsequent fighting had revealed that the two cultures were incompatible. Even conversion was no longer an option. One culture would have to give way.[11]

It was thus at best an uneasy truce, and another major conflict was almost unavoidable. The 1644–6 war was fought for the same reasons as before. This time the colonists were too strong for the American Indians, even though Opechancanough began hostilities with another surprise attack, in which five hundred settlers were killed. The Algonquian peoples paid dearly for their bid to regain their lands. The settlers no longer needed them, except for a handful of fur traders. What they wanted was the Algonquins' land; and the war provided a convenient excuse for ridding the area of its native inhabitants. After two years of fighting, Opechancanough was captured and brought to Jamestown, where he was murdered by his guards. The result was the final destruction of the Powhatan Confederacy. Under the terms of the peace treaty of 1646 the American Indians were banned from the Jamestown Peninsula under pain of death, and had to acknowledge the king of England as their sovereign. Even their remaining lands on the north side of the York River were not exempt from colonization.

A gruesome pattern had been established in colonist–American Indian relations which was to be repeated elsewhere over the next two and a half centuries. Initially trade

---

[9]   No copy of Wyatt's commission survives. That of his successor, Sir William Berkeley, can be found in Warren M. Billings, ed., *The Old Dominion in the Seventeenth Century: A Documentary History of Virginia, 1606–1689* (Chapel Hill, 1975), 51–8.

[10]   Quoted in Billings, *Old Dominion*, 220–4.

[11]   This is the conclusion of Alden T. Vaughan, "'Expulsion of the Salvages': English Policy and the Virginia Massacre of 1622," *William and Mary Quarterly*, XXXV, 1978, 57–84; and Bernard Sheehan, *Savagism and Civility: Indians and Englishmen in Colonial Virginia* (Cambridge, England, 1980). Other writers have pointed out that peaceful contacts continued after 1622, especially in the fur trade. See Frederick J. Fausz, "Merging and Emerging Worlds: Anglo-Indian Interest Groups and the Development of the Seventeenth Century Chesapeake," in Lois Green Carr, Philip D. Morgan, and Jean B. Russo, eds, *Colonial Chesapeake Society* (Chapel Hill, 1989).

beneficial to both sides occurred, but as the settlers' numbers increased, and they became more confident, their eyes turned to the natives' land and harmony gave way to intermittent warfare, followed by massacre, after which the remnants of the indigenous inhabitants were either enslaved or confined to reservations, where they could be controlled for the convenience of the colonists. Even then the American Indian peoples were not safe, for although sporadic attempts were made to protect them from the excesses of their white neighbors, these were rarely effective.

In consequence the way was now open for the colonists to exploit the land more rapidly, especially for the cultivation of tobacco. Admittedly the Crown, like the Virginia Company before it, continued to cherish delusions of a more diversified economy. On his arrival in 1641, Governor Sir William Berkeley was ordered "to cause the people there to apply themselves to the raising of more Staple Comodities as Hemp and Flax, Rape Seed, Pitch and Tarr, for the Tanning of Hydes and leather." He was also to get every plantation to grow some vines, together with mulberry trees, for the cultivation of silk-worms. To no avail. Although the price of tobacco plunged more than 90 percent, from three shillings to threepence a pound, in the 1630s, the crop still produced a good profit for most planters. Equally fruitless were Berkeley's attempts to induce the inhabitants to live in towns so as to make the settlements more defensible. All planters wanted a riverside jetty where they could load their produce. Towns simply did not suit a plantation system. Instead the assembly created eight English-style counties in 1635, with justices, a recorder, a sheriff, constables, and a coroner.

Now that the basic requirements of settlement had been learnt, the population at last began to grow. A steady stream of persons, mainly male, continued to come to Virginia, encouraged by the demand for tobacco, so that by 1640 the population had reached eight thousand. Many brought enough capital to set up on their own, while those who could not afford to do so arrived as indentured servants.

The origins of the system of indenture have been disputed, since there was nothing precisely similar in England. It seems clear, however, that it was a modification of two English customs: apprenticeship and the practice of short-term husbandry. Some such system was necessary to finance the crossing of the Atlantic. By agreeing to a contract of service, usually from four to seven years, the servant had his passage paid, while the master was guaranteed a supply of labor, plus an additional fifty acres under the headright provision for every person thus brought in. Tobacco was a labor-intensive crop, and planters who wanted to expand their production had to find extra hands. Slaves from overseas were too expensive, while the indigenous inhabitants made poor workers, since they tended either to escape or to die in captivity. There were in any case too few to meet the growing demand of the planters. Indentured servitude proved the answer since there were thousands of young English men and women ready to try their fortune in the New World. It was the prime reason for the steady growth in both the population and the economy, with the production of tobacco reaching one million pounds by 1640.

Indeed, after a few years of royal government, the removal of the company was seen to have been a blessing. One immediate bonus was the ending of the company magazine, with its monopoly on the sale and importation of all goods. Second, the removal of the company further opened the settlement of the land to private individuals. Although the Crown retained some interest, it was only too happy to encourage such settlement in return for a small quitrent.

One other event of note at this time was the arrival of the first Africans on board a passing Dutch warship in 1619. Where they came from is not definitely known, though a great deal of attention has been devoted to their status in the hope of establishing that African slavery was not preordained. Most likely they had been seized from a Portuguese vessel supplying slaves from Angola to the Spanish port of Vera Cruz in Mexico.[12] John Rolfe merely recorded that they were traded for victuals by Governor Yeardley and the director of the company magazine. The likelihood is that they were slaves, because the institution of slavery was well established elsewhere in the Americas. Since the first voyages of the Portuguese, Africans had been transported from their homeland for one reason only: to be used as forced labor. Except for a few interpreters, none had left voluntarily.

Another reason for supposing that these new arrivals were slaves is that from their earliest contacts, Europeans had been disposed to see Africans as inferiors. In the first place, they were not Christian and therefore considered to be outside the normal conventions governing Christian peoples. Second, Europeans believed that Africans were related to the ape, because of their skin color and customary lack of clothing. In European eyes nakedness was akin to bestiality. Third, it was convenient to assume that Africans must be descended from the biblical Ham, whose offspring had been condemned to permanent servitude.

All these presumptions did not necessarily mean that the slave status of the African in North America was predetermined. Indentured servants were also sold and yet attained their freedom. In fact the indications are that before 1660 both African and European servants were treated similarly. Many lived together, they not infrequently absconded together, and a few even inter-married. A number of Africans were provided for in wills. In cases of sexual misconduct, Africans were not necessarily punished more severely than European offenders, another indication that racial attitudes had not yet hardened.[13]

Indeed, there is evidence that in these early decades Africans enjoyed a measure of freedom and prosperity, owning property and suing in the courts. The most famous case was

---

[12]   For the origin of these Africans, see Engel Sluiter, "New Light on the '20 and Odd Negroes' Arriving in Virginia, August 1619", *William and Mary Quarterly*, LIV, 1997, 396–8.

[13]   Among those writers who stress the fluidity of the situation in the early period are Oscar and Mary Handlin, "Origins of the Southern Labor System," *William and Mary Quarterly*, VII, 1950, 199–222; Edmund S. Morgan, *American Slavery, American Freedom: The Ordeal of Colonial Virginia* (New York, 1975); and T. H. Breen and Stephen Innes, *Myne Owne Ground: Race and Freedom on Virginia's Eastern Shore, 1640–1676* (New York, 1980). All emphasize the economic and legal rather than racial grounds for slavery at this time. The contrary view is argued by Carl N. Degler, *Out of our Past: The Forces that Shaped Modern America* (New York, 1959); Alden T. Vaughan, "Blacks in Virginia: A Note on the First Decade," *William and Mary Quarterly*, XXIX, 1972, 469–76; and Winthrop D. Jordan, *White over Black: American Attitudes Toward the Negro, 1550–1812* (Chapel Hill, 1968). Jordan looked at the English background of the colonists and found strong racial antipathy during the Elizabethan period, suggesting that prejudice not only preceded slavery but was essential for its development. More recently, historians have argued that race is a matter of social construction rather than biology; that racial attitudes are the product of unequal relationships and misguided ideology. Such writers have been influenced by modern genetics, which indicate that there are no significant biological differences between the different races. They are also influenced by the desire to show that a multicultural society like the United States can exist. However, opinions remain divided, especially whether racism preceded or followed the introduction of slavery. For a recent view favoring Degler, Vaughan, and Jordan, see J. Douglas Deal, *Race and Class in Colonial Virginia: Indians, Englishmen and Africans on the Eastern Shore during the Seventeenth Century* (New York, 1993). For an interpretation arguing that race was a matter of social construction, see Ira Berlin, *Many Thousands Gone: The First Two Centuries of Slavery in North America* (Cambridge, Mass., 1998). The two approaches are discussed in Michael McGiffert, ed., "Constructing Race: Differentiating Peoples in the Early Modern World," *William and Mary Quarterly*, 1997, LIV, 1–252.

that of Anthony Johnson, who arrived in Virginia around 1621. Johnson may have been an "Atlantic Creole" who had already experienced slavery in the Caribbean and West Africa, and knew how to work the system. Whatever his origins, he first secured his own freedom, then that of his family, and in due course owned several slaves himself, together with a substantial farm. On at least one occasion he successfully sued a white neighbor for the recovery of a slave, receiving damages in the process. His route to freedom, as for a number of others, was the agreement he made with his master that in return for a period of diligent service he would be freed like an indentured servant. The advantage to his master was that he acquired a willing worker with an overriding interest in honoring the agreement.

Only a small number of Africans, however, actually secured their freedom in this way. Anthony Johnson himself lived in Northampton County on the eastern shore, which was relatively poor and contained few large plantations. There was not the same remorseless pressure for the exploitation of human resources as existed along the James River. Even he moved to Maryland in later life, possibly because of harassment. Indeed, the evidence suggests that he was ultimately stripped of his property in Virginia by the Accomack county court because he "was a Negroe and by consequence an alien." His lands in consequence were to revert to the Crown and not pass to his heirs.

Elsewhere during this period most Africans remained firmly at the bottom of the social and economic order. If they were indentured, their period of service might last up to twenty-eight years, and unlike white servants they were rarely given formal contracts. In wills, Africans were usually placed after other servants, next to the livestock, and were recorded only by their first names.

One reason for the confusion about the status of these early African-Americans was the lack of a legal definition for them. Slavery had disappeared as an institution in England before the Norman Conquest. A further complication was that Virginia was a new society, where little was yet written down. It naturally took some years before the status of Africans was codified, especially as their numbers remained small in the early years. In 1634 there were perhaps 200, at a time when the settlers numbered 7,500 so that Virginia was still a "society with slaves" rather than a fully developed "slave society."[14] Hence there was plenty of scope for anomalies like the agreement with Johnson, especially in a frontier society where most people were too busy establishing themselves to notice what others were doing.

Nevertheless, for persons of European descent the path to success was now clear. Extra labor would result in more crops, which could then finance the purchase of more land and servants in a growing spiral of production and wealth. Though most holdings along the James River were still farms rather than plantations, the possibilities had been demonstrated in the late 1620s by Yeardley himself, George Sandys, and Abraham Piercy, all of whom had a mixed labor force of nearly forty servants cultivating several hundred acres.

Because planters preferred male servants for such wilderness conditions, the result was a society that was overwhelmingly masculine. This meant a lack of traditional family life. It also meant that Virginia could only sustain its population if it attracted a constant supply

---

[14] Historians currently make this distinction, based on the ratio between free and enslaved persons, on the grounds that "societies with slaves," where the majority of the population was free, were more likely to be humane and less racist than a "slave society," where the dominant slave population seemingly posed a threat to the white inhabitants.

of immigrants. With the demand for tobacco remaining strong, this did not seem a problem. Most planters, accordingly, had to console themselves with the thought that, once they had made their fortune, they could go home for a wife in England. Virginia was only a temporary residence for most.[15]

It was during the 1630s, 1640s, and 1650s that those who founded some of the more famous Virginian families first arrived. They were minor gentry or substantial yeoman families like the Washingtons, who brought some capital and were keen to profit from the tobacco boom. Often they were younger sons, or members of families who first came to Virginia as traders and stayed to become planters. They had the advantage of being able to learn from the mistakes of the first generation. It was no coincidence that the history of Virginia was to be dominated by the progeny of this second generation, whose names included Washington, Carter, Harrison, Lee, Beverley, and Byrd.

Although civil war broke out in England in 1642, it caused almost no interruption to this pattern of growth and consolidation. The colony affected to support Charles I but offered only token resistance when a commission arrived in 1651 to make Virginia acknowledge Parliament's authority.[16] Berkeley himself retired to his estate at Green Spring, for like Yeardley and Wyatt before him he had elected to become a planter in his adopted country. Even the Anglican church suffered little disturbance. Its ministers were permitted to retain their benefices, though dissenting churches had to be tolerated. As religion had never been a strong factor in Virginia, few people were affected by this policy. The main preoccupation continued to be the planting of tobacco. Although Parliament passed a navigation law in 1651 to exclude the Dutch from the carrying trade, Virginia's economy was not seriously inconvenienced, since the measure was rarely enforced.

---

[15]   For the subsequent impact of skewed sex ratios on society in the Chesapeake, see chapter 5, section 1.

[16]   Popular tradition holds that Virginia provided a refuge for many of the king's more aristocratic supporters. In reality only three members of the gentry came to Virginia during this period, the nobility preferring exile in the relative comfort of Europe to life on the frontier.

4

The Conquest Continues:
New England, 1620–60

1607	The Sagadahoc settlement fails.
1620	The Plymouth colony is founded by the Pilgrim Fathers.
1624–6	The Dorchester Company is established.
1626	The settlement of Naumkeag (later Salem) is founded.
1628	The Dorchester group is revived as the New England Company.
1629	The Massachusetts Bay Company is formed from the Dorchester group.
1630	The Puritans found Boston and ten other settlements.
1632	Watertown's inhabitants protest over arbitrary taxation.
1634	Council members demand to see the Massachusetts charter.
1634–6	The first English settlements in the Connecticut River valley are founded.
1636	Roger Williams founds Providence in Rhode Island after being expelled from Massachusetts (1635).
1637	The Pequots are eliminated in the Pequot War. New Haven is founded. Anne Hutchinson is banished from Massachusetts.
1642	The English civil war begins.
1643	The United Colonies of New England are formed.
1644	Rhode Island is granted a charter by Parliament.
1646	Dr Robert Child protests about church membership.
1648	Book of General Laws: the Cambridge Platform is published.
1649	Charles I is executed. John Winthrop dies.
1656	The first Quakers arrive.
1660	Mary Dyer is executed.

1 THE PILGRIM FATHERS

WHILE VIRGINIA WAS struggling to establish itself, important developments were taking place to the north.

After the failure at Sagadahoc in 1607, the Plymouth Company itself did little beyond licensing voyages of exploration. Among these was one undertaken by Captain John Smith in 1614 to investigate the area's fishing and trading potential. On his return he suggested to Sir Fernando Gorges, one of the few remaining shareholders in the Plymouth Company, that a permanent settlement be established for drying and curing cod.

Gorges was a West Country baronet, who like many of the earlier Elizabethans hoped to make his fortune in the New World. He was accordingly receptive to the ideas of Smith and others. But Gorges realized that he first needed a new charter to prevent a repetition of the quarrels that had ruined not only Sagadahoc but also Jamestown in its early years. Gorges therefore proposed to limit his new enterprise to forty eminent persons, who would be coopted rather than elected to positions of authority. The new body was to be called the Council for New England.

Gorges seems to have been influenced in one respect by the Virginia Company. He was aware that from 1618 onwards Sir Edwin Sandys encouraged groups to apply for patents as subordinate companies, favoring a system whereby the parent company incurred no expense and the hard work and actual risks of colonization were undertaken by others. Such a system also appealed to someone like Gorges with only limited resources. Accordingly he decided that the Council for New England would simply patent an area and lay down its administrative and judicial structures. Profit would accrue either from quitrents, tenancies, or the exploitation of the area's natural resources to which the council held the title deeds.

Among the applications soon received was one by the Pilgrim Fathers, a dissenting sect who wanted to separate from the Church of England. Unlike most Dissenters they believed that the established church was beyond reform and that the faithful must cut themselves off from it completely. Their separatist views had inevitably brought them into conflict with the authorities, for whom uniformity was essential for the maintenance of national harmony. In 1609 the Pilgrims had left their home in Scrooby, Yorkshire, and fled to Leyden in Holland; but many of them were unhappy there, and when they heard that the Virginia Company was offering special privileges to incorporated groups, they applied for a patent.

Unfortunately Virginia was an Anglican settlement. Consequently, when a group of London merchants headed by Thomas Weston offered them financial help to seek a patent from the Council for New England, they decided to adopt this course instead.

In July 1620 a voluntary joint stock company was set up between the merchants and the Pilgrims. The agreement was that the Pilgrims would farm, build houses, and fish for seven years, after which the profits of the operation would be shared between the two parties. The Pilgrims were to be treated as partners with a £10.10s share each, so that they would have an interest in the success of the venture.

At this point the Pilgrims still had a patent only from the Virginia Company, since Gorges's reorganization of the Council for New England had yet to be completed. Nevertheless, despite the legal uncertainties, they determined to set out, leaving their merchant associates to complete any formalities. The Pilgrims were supposed to sail on two vessels, the *Mayflower* and the *Speedwell*, but the latter twice developed a leak and had to be abandoned. Hence it was a reduced complement of 101 persons plus crew which departed

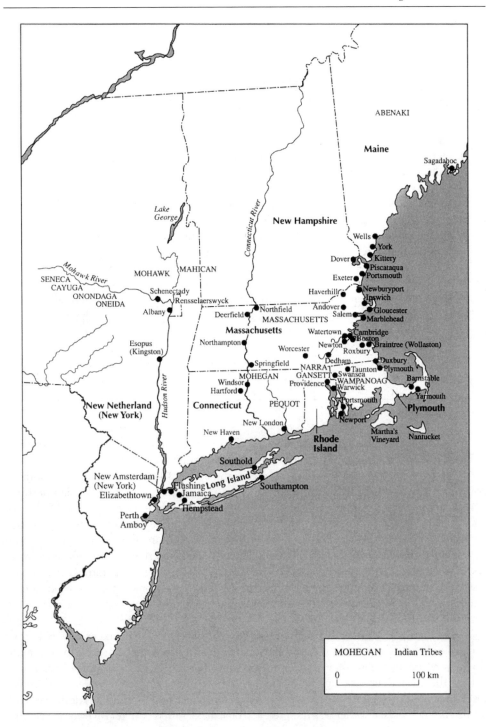

Map 3 Seventeenth-century New England and New York

DOCUMENT 7

The Mayflower Compact, November 1620, reprinted in W. Keith Kavenagh, *Foundations of Colonial America: A Documentary History* (New York, 1974), I, 246.

[The compact was only a declaration of intent and said nothing about the actual institutions of government or the exercise of power. No women were among the forty-one signatories. Another significant point is that eleven of the signatories merited the title of "Mr," indicating class differences among the Pilgrims.]

In the name of God, Amen. We whose names are underwritten, the loyal subjects of our dread sovereign lord King James, by the Grace of God, of Great Britain . . . and Ireland, King, Defender of the Faith, having undertaken, for the glory of God, and advancement of the Christian faith, and the honour of our King and country, a voyage to plant the first colony in the northern parts of Virginia, do, by these presents, covenant and combine ourselves together into a civil body politic for our better ordering and preservation and furtherance of the ends aforesaid; and by virtue hereof do enact, constitute, and frame such just and equal laws, ordinances, acts, constitutions, and officers, from time to time, as shall be thought most meet and convenient for the general good of the colony, to which we promise all due submission and obedience. In witness thereof, we have hereunto subscribed our names at Cape Cod, the eleventh of November 1620.

on the *Mayflower* on September 16, 1620. In contrast to the early shipments to Virginia, a number of women and children were on board in family groups.

The journey took over two months, giving the Pilgrims time to consider what form of government they should establish, for in their haste to depart, they had decided nothing. The matter was pressing, for their leaders – William Bradford, John Carver, Edward Winslow, and William Brewster – knew that not all the passengers on the *Mayflower* were separatists, especially among the servants. Accordingly, forty-one of the male passengers drew up an agreement for the framing of "such just and equal laws, . . . as shall be thought most meet and convenient for the general good of the colony." This agreement formed the famous Mayflower Compact. Traditional accounts have glorified the compact as the beginning of American democracy, but its true intent was the exact opposite: to preserve power and authority in the hands of the few.

Although the Pilgrims first sighted land near Cape Cod on November 11, 1620, they decided to head for the Hudson River. Bad weather and a dangerous shoreline then induced them to return to where they had just come from, but the lack of a suitable harbor prevented them from deciding on the site which they were to call New Plymouth until mid-December. One attraction was the site's combined access to the sea and proximity to a hill for defense purposes; another was the presence of some deserted cornfields. Two years earlier an epidemic had killed most of the local inhabitants, and the remainder were not disposed to dispute the newcomers' arrival, even after they had appropriated a cache of local corn.

On December 25, 1620, the Pilgrims began to erect their first dwellings around a crude palisade – simple frames covered by rough planks. After erecting a common store, each family labored on its own shelter; it was thought that this method would encourage greater endeavor and avoid the kind of disputes that had afflicted Jamestown and Sagadahoc.

Disputes were not likely among the Pilgrims, however, for they were united in their desire to build a godly community. Few wanted to dispute the authority of the church elders who had drafted the Mayflower Compact. The new Jerusalem was not built without cost, despite a relatively mild winter. In the first few months nearly half the settlers died, weakened by the long voyage and the difficulties of adapting to a new environment. Fortunately the Pilgrims had brought enough food to sustain them through the winter; and in the spring they were able to sow their first crop of indian corn.

While engaged in this task they first made contact with the indigenous inhabitants, when an Indian named Samoset walked into the settlement, uttering a few words of English. Shortly afterward he returned with another, more fluent speaker, Squanto, who had been kidnapped some years earlier and taken to England as a slave. He showed the settlers how to plant squashes between the rows of corn and how to fertilize the land with fish offal. He also opened negotiations with the chief of the local Wampanoag nation, Massasoit. Before coming to America the Pilgrims had believed Smith that the American Indians were "cruel, barbarous and most treacherous." Now they were presented with a chieftain anxious to cultivate their friendship. Massasoit's reasons for making a treaty in March 1621 were of course not dissimilar to Powhatan's motives in Virginia. He was attracted by the possibilities of trade and wanted help against the neighboring Narragansett and Massachusetts peoples. Indeed, within two years he had tricked the Pilgrims into making an unprovoked assault on the Massachusetts tribe in which several were murdered after being invited to a feast.

Another unforeseen result of the new relationship was the frequency with which the Wampanoags visited their neighbors in the expectation of receiving hospitality. The Pilgrims felt most uneasy about such intrusions and within a short time informed them that only Massasoit was welcome. Even he had to make an appointment. Nevertheless, the result of the treaty was that the Pilgrims were able to harvest their first crops in safety. In recognition of this divine providence, they killed some wild turkeys and held the first thanksgiving on American soil.[1]

Despite this success the settlement faced serious problems, one being the lack of a minister. The pastor, John Robinson, had stayed in Leyden with the rest of the congregation. For a time John Lyford, an Anglican minister of reforming tendencies, officiated, even though he had not formally separated from the established church. Lyford, however, began intriguing with the merchants in England and had to be expelled. During this impasse the settlers asked one of the church elders, William Brewster, to officiate, although he had no degree or competence in theological matters, nor the right to administer the communion or baptism. It was nine years before a fully trained minister arrived.

Another embarrassment was the arrival of Thomas Weston in 1622 with a fresh batch of settlers, few of whom were separatists. Fortunately, the newcomers were persuaded to

---

[1] Thanksgiving was not observed on a regular basis in Plymouth until 1630 after which the practice slowly spread to the other New England colonies. It only became a national holiday in 1864, following a proclamation by President Lincoln.

move up the coast to their own settlement at Wessagusset, which survived for only a year. The problems really began in 1625 when a second group, led by Thomas Morton, a lawyer of dubious reputation, developed a new settlement at Mount Wollaston, later Braintree, into what has been called "America's first Woodstock." Morton's primary aim was the establishment of a trading post, but to increase his turnover, drink flowed, and the local inhabitants were entertained with a maypole. Morton even took to writing lascivious poetry. To the godly Pilgrims this was too much, especially when Morton compounded his offenses by selling arms to the American Indians. In 1628 they dispatched their militia under Miles Standish to end Morton's venture by sending him and his companions back to England.

The most serious problem faced by the Pilgrims during the first decade of settlement was financial. The initial expectation was that fishing and fur trading would be sufficiently profitable to fulfill their agreement with the merchants. Some attempts were made to build fishing vessels, but most Pilgrims devoted themselves to farming, since this was what they were accustomed to do. Unfortunately, farming in the area offered subsistence at best, even when carried out communally. A further problem was that most settlers wanted to farm their own land. For the first few years only personal gardens of up to one acre had been allowed. By this time, however, most of the adventurers in England were disillusioned with the project, and in November 1626 they agreed to sell their shares for nine annual installments of £200.

This agreement made it possible to distribute the settlement's collective wealth. Each of the surviving fifty-three original shareholders was allotted twenty acres and a proportion of the sheep, goats, cattle, and poultry. But to find the money for these nine installments, Bradford and the other leaders had to form a trading monopoly of all the colony's commercial enterprises. The most promising commodities remained fish and furs, since the latter could be traded for corn with the Abenaki peoples to the north. Sadly, the London end of the business was not well managed, and the debt was extinguished only in 1648 after much vexation and expense.

Fortunately, the general economic situation brightened in the 1630s with the arrival of the much larger and wealthier Massachusetts Bay Company. Suddenly Plymouth's livestock and grain were in great demand. Slowly the population began to rise, aided by the arrival of one or more ships each year bringing fresh settlers. According to William Bradford, now the governor and historian of the colony, by 1624 the number of inhabitants stood at 124. In 1630 it had risen to 300, and the town had more than one street and was surrounded by a stockade with gates at the exits. At the top of the hill was a meeting house which supported six cannon on its upper floor. The continued expansion of the population, which had reached 550 by 1637, led to several new settlements at Yarmouth, Taunton, Marshfield, Duxbury, Scituate, and Sandwich, though several of these simply housed overspill population from Massachusetts.

Until 1630 Plymouth had no proper charter or frame of government other than that granted to Weston and his group. In that year the Pilgrims approached the Council for New England for a new patent confirming their right to frame laws and settle the area. Not until 1636 was a formal constitution adopted, providing for a governor and court of seven assistants to be elected by the freemen, or shareholders, of the colony, who also had to be church members. In 1638, as additional settlements sprang up, each town became entitled to send two deputies to join the court in the making of "all such laws and ordinances." This action was taken to relieve the freemen from the "many inconveniences and great expenses," of constantly attending the court, scattered as they now were.

Plymouth was doomed by its separatist origins to remain a small, uninfluential colony, isolated from mainstream Puritanism and thus denied recruitment from a wider population. Financially, too, it lacked the resources to expand in the manner of Virginia, nor did it have a decent harbor or staple. Most of its inhabitants were simple folk who had few ambitions other than to survive and worship in their own fashion. The result was that Plymouth was soon to be totally overshadowed by Massachusetts to the north.

2 MASSACHUSETTS: A CITY ON THE HILL

In the years immediately after the Pilgrim Fathers' departure, several other patents were issued by the Council of New England for settling the area. One was granted to a group of Dorchester merchants who wished to exploit the fishing grounds. Their project at Cape Ann did not prosper, however, the climate being too harsh and the fishermen too refractory. The settlement was accordingly abandoned in 1626, though some of the inhabitants moved to Naumkeag, or Salem, as it was soon to be called.

Among the Dorchester group was a Puritan minister, the Reverend John White, who refused to be discouraged. Although the fishermen were clearly unsuitable material, White began to envisage a settlement similar to the one at Plymouth, consisting of persons whose goals were religious rather than material.

White soon found that other groups in London and East Anglia were thinking similarly. Consequently the decision was made in 1628 to revive the Dorchester Company by means of a further patent from the Council for New England. That body, however, was almost moribund, as Gorges was away on military service and only the Earl of Warwick attended to its proceedings. It was therefore decided to approach the Crown for a more authoritative grant. The new group had many influential friends, not least Warwick himself, who had Puritan leanings.

A patent was accordingly secured on March 4, 1629, similar to that of other joint stock companies. The new entity, to be known as "The Company of Massachusetts Bay," would have title to all the lands between the Merrimack River and the tip of Massachusetts Bay, as well as the right to any minerals, subject to the usual percentage for the Crown. The lands were to be held from the king in free and common socage.

The company was to be managed by a governor and council of eighteen assistants, elected annually by the ordinary freemen. The general court itself was to have full power "to make, ordain, and establish all manner of wholesome and reasonable Orders, Lawes, Statutes, and Ordinances," providing these were consistent with the laws of England. However, routine business was to be in the hands of the governor or deputy governor and six assistants. As in Virginia, those emigrating were to "enjoy all Liberties and Immunities of free and natural Subjects . . . as if born within the Realm of England."[2]

Significantly, little mention was made of converting the American Indians. Although the charter asserted that this was "The Principal end of this plantation," it was only mentioned near the end of the document. Moreover, the newcomers were not expected to

---

[2] The full text of the charter can be found in W. Keith Kavenagh, *Foundations of Colonial America: A Documentary History*, 3 vols (New York, 1973) I, 45–58.

proselytize the Indians. It would suffice if their "good Life and orderly Conversation" set an example that brought in due course "the Natives of the Country, to the Knowledge and Obedience of the only true God and Saviour of Mankind." This reticence may have indicated a lack of interest among the Puritans, but more likely it reflected the general feeling following the 1622 massacre in Virginia that converting the indigenous inhabitants was of doubtful benefit.

It might be wondered why the Crown would issue another such charter in view of the recent history of the Virginia Company. In reality, however, the turmoils of that enterprise could be seen as exceptional. The format for joint stock companies was well established, and Charles I did not want to become directly involved in another venture, since royal control of Virginia had yet to prove the best model for colonization. Finally, the list of subscribers to the Massachusetts Bay Company contained some eminently respectable names, among them Mathew Cradock, Sir John Younge, Sir Richard Saltonstall, and Sir Henry Rosewell. There was no reason to expect trouble from such loyal subjects.

What Charles I did not know was that divergencies were emerging between those who wanted the company to be a normal trading venture and those who, like White, had a more spiritual end in view. Among the latter was a Suffolk squire from the village of Groton, John Winthrop. A justice of the peace and graduate of Trinity College, Cambridge, Winthrop was typical of many Puritan gentry who were alarmed at the direction of events. Charles I had dissolved Parliament in 1629, apparently determined to rule as an absolute monarch. He seemed equally determined to maintain an unreformed church by promoting high Anglicans like William Laud. Another cause for Puritan concern was the number of severe defeats that the forces of Protestantism had suffered in Europe during the opening phases of the Thirty Years' War. It has been suggested that Winthrop was motivated by financial inducements to emigrate at this point, since not long before buying into the company he had been deprived of an attorneyship in the Court of Wards and Liveries. He was also in debt and had a large family to support.[3]

All the lessons of the past thirty years, however, had shown colonization to be a risky business. Raleigh had reputedly spent upwards of £40,000 on his various enterprises, and it is unlikely that Winthrop would have undertaken such a risky venture when he still had so much to lose at Groton. Religious zeal was clearly the main reason for his departure from England. Winthrop and the others believed that Armageddon was not far away and that all true believers must remove themselves before God visited his wrath upon the land. From a twenty-first century perspective it is hard to appreciate the intensity of religious feeling among the population at large in this period, coupled with the prevailing sense that God was all-powerful and man merely a weak mortal. Religion helped to explain a harsh world over which individuals had little control and of which they had even less understanding.

---

[3] The view that Winthrop and other Puritan leaders went to America for economic reasons was popular in the first decades of the twentieth century with Progressive historians like James Truslow Adams, *The Founding of New England* (Boston, 1921). The Progressives were anxious to show that American democracy had always been threatened by wealthy business elites. More sympathetic is Edmund S. Morgan, *The Puritan Dilemma: The Story of John Winthrop* (Boston, 1958). This account was written during the cold war when it was fashionable to reaffirm traditional views about America, especially the contribution of Puritan New England. The importance of religious motivation has most recently been restated by Virginia DeJohn Anderson in *New England's Generation: The Great Migration and the Formation of Society and Culture in the Seventeenth Century* (Cambridge, England, 1991).

Plate 16   Portrait of John Winthrop. Courtesy of the Massachusetts Historical
Society, Boston.

But although the Puritans were not leaving for material reasons, they had no wish to
be poor. What they desired was "competency," or a comfortable independence, so that they
could avoid the dilemma of too much wealth, which would lead them into sin, and too
little sustenance, which would inhibit the leading of a godly life.

It was in this climate that the zealots formed a plan to take over the company and
emigrate to New England with the charter. For while the company's headquarters were in
England anyone could buy into the enterprise. Removal was also necessary to avoid the
prying eyes of the king's officials, notably the bishops. It was hoped that the company could
slip away unnoticed, given the distance of America from England and the distractions of
the Crown back home; it was not intended to disavow the English church or state but to
make interference impossible.

In pursuit of this dubious idea, Winthrop and his group were aided by a remarkable
oversight in the charter, which failed to specify that the company had to retain its headquarters in England. An agreement to buy out the non-Puritan elements was accordingly
concluded at Cambridge, England, on August 26, 1629. Three days later the plan was
accepted at a hastily convened meeting of the general court in London attended by just 27
freemen out of 125. Not long afterward Winthrop himself was elected governor.

Amidst all these maneuvers the process of getting the scheme launched had already commenced. On the first formation of the company in 1628, a ship had been sent out under John Endecott, an associate of White, to take possession of the remnants of the Dorchester settlement at Salem. Here Endecott found perhaps eighty people eking out a tenuous existence. The following April, the company had sent a further five ships carrying two hundred additional settlers. Thus when the main group of the Puritans left in March 1630 in a fleet of eleven ships, they already had a substantial base on which to build. Unlike the Pilgrims, the Puritans had considerable financial resources; and, unlike the Virginia Company, they had realistic expectations.

The *Arabella*, with Winthrop on board, sighted the coast of Maine early in June before going on to Salem, where Endecott had built a formidable settlement. This location did not please the group's leaders, however, and the main fleet went on to another site near the Charles River. It was here that they noticed a thin neck of land protruding into the bay and decided to make this site the focus of their new enterprise, not least because of its central position and defensive capabilities. They called it Boston after the town in Lincolnshire from which some of the emigrants had come.

Not everyone stayed with Winthrop and the council, as there was not enough land or water to sustain so many people. Other settlements sprang up round the bay, organized in congregations. A group of people pooled their resources and applied to the council for a grant of land. This was given in freehold or fee simple without the payment of a quitrent as specified in the royal charter. They then repaired to their site, made a covenant to create a godly community, and began to build a church and clear enough land to support themselves. In this they were widely successful.

As at Plymouth, the local inhabitants had been decimated by disease and were in no condition to resist the newcomers. Winthrop himself believed that the Massachusetts tribe had been smitten by God to make the land available for his chosen people. Nevertheless, from the start the Puritans insisted on formal purchase, since they wanted no legal complications in the settling of their commonwealth. The American Indians of course had little idea what they were signing. Their assumption was that they were sealing friendships rather than selling their lands in perpetuity.

Another favorable factor for the new colonists was the climate, which, though harsh, was healthy, resulting in fewer diseases than in Virginia. A number of settlers did die during the first winter, but the Puritans brought a great sense of mission to the enterprise which enabled them to overcome most obstacles. Lastly, settlements had been established in the area since the turn of the century, and with their experience to build on, the Puritans had come well equipped with livestock and every kind of tool. They could also rely on the support of Plymouth. By the end of 1630 eleven towns had been established with a total of over one thousand inhabitants.

The Puritans did everything communally at first to overcome the initial problems of settlement. However, once enough land had been cleared, they distributed plots of one to four acres and in 1635 began the permanent division of much larger areas, according to the amount invested by each family. Although the religious impulse was always strong, the Puritans were practical businessmen too. Settling new towns in the wilderness was expensive, since lands had to be surveyed and titles purchased from the Indians. The role of the proprietary families who subscribed the initial capital was crucial, and their reward was a share of the land proportional to their investment. Hence major contributors like Winthrop were given two hundred acres, the lesser settlers from thirty to one hundred acres.[4] In general the settlers replicated the type of agriculture with which they were familiar in East Anglia, Yorkshire, and elsewhere. They could do this because the average temperatures and growing season were similar to those in England.

As already mentioned, the Puritans were not separatists. They had come to America to await either the reform of the Church of England or the second coming of Christ. The Puritans' denial of separatism was important, since it enabled them to claim descent, and hence legitimacy, from the first church of Christ, that is, the early Christian church. What they objected to in the Anglican church was government by bishops, for whom they could find no biblical justification. In their view authority lay with the congregation as it had, they believed, after the death of Christ. They also quarreled with much of the liturgy in the Book of Common Prayer, believing the Bible to be the only source of Christian authority. In addition, they detested what they regarded as the many traces of popery, for example, in the vestments and altar cloths still lavishly used in Anglican churches. The same reasoning led them to abandon feast days, including Christmas, as pagan or popish relics, preferring instead simple acts of thanksgiving in accordance with the Scriptures.

The Puritans were theologically the disciples of John Calvin, the Genevan reformer, and herein lay their greatest criticism of the Church of England. Calvin stated that, because of original sin, the world was irrevocably corrupt. Only a few, whom God had chosen through his divine grace, could be saved. Although clause 17 of the Articles of Religion of the Church of England acknowledged this doctrine, the thrust of Anglicanism lay elsewhere. Luther had preached that all men could be saved if they repented of their sins. Most Anglicans went one step further, accepting the arguments of the Dutch theologian Arminius that good works were themselves a necessary demonstration of that faith. To the followers of Calvin this view was anathema, since it threatened to lead to all the old abuses of people trying to buy their way to heaven with good works and minimal faith, which they associated with the Catholic church. Such behavior in their eyes spelt total depravity, for God was not to be bargained with.

The Puritans did modify Calvin's doctrine of predestination slightly, arguing that if they kept their faith and lived a godly life, salvation would be theirs. For as Winthrop stated in an address on board the *Arabella*, "Thus stands the cause between God and us: we are entered into Covenant." The new settlements were to "be as a city upon a hill," an example to all the world. The idea of the covenant was to be a persistent theme in Puritanism.

One problem now facing the Puritans was to establish just who were God's elect, or saints, as they came to be called. In England, everyone could take communion after confirmation by a bishop. One or two churches, notably Southwark, had experimented with a congregational form of government, but most had only a hazy notion of what it required. The Puritans now developed a special process of public examination before the congregation to solve this problem. This relational experience consisted of four main stages. First, the intending saint had to acknowledge humanity's innate depravity – God alone could save. Next the individual had to show true repentance and desire to be saved. Then followed the hardest part of the examination, justification, whereby the examinee had to

---

[4] For the financial aspects of Puritan town building, see John Frederick Martin, *Profits in the Wilderness: Entrepreneurship and the Founding of New England Towns in the Seventeenth Century* (Chapel Hill, 1991).

convince the interrogators that the Holy Spirit had entered the soul and that the individual was open to God's covenant of grace. If the answers were satisfactory the fourth stage, sanctification, followed, indicating that the person was of the elect. Even then no relaxation was possible, for sin could quickly lead to a loss of grace. Godliness had to be worked at constantly until the saint was called to a higher place.

Since the Puritans intended to create a purer commonwealth, it was important that corrupt elements be kept in check. Many of those who had crossed the Atlantic were servants who had not come by choice; others had come primarily for economic reasons. Consequently, in 1631 the general court ruled that none but the saints could participate in public affairs or vote. The godly must not be put at risk.

At the same time, Winthrop and the assistants began issuing various edicts for the better government of the colony. Naturally these had a strong moral tone. All gaming, blasphemy, sexual misconduct, excessive drinking, and lascivious entertainment like the theater were to be severely punished, while church attendance was compulsory. Restrictions were also placed on commerce to ensure that prices were just and that profiteering and hoarding were avoided. Although many of the same restrictions had been imposed in Virginia, the difference in Massachusetts was that the majority of the population wanted to abide by them so that they might join the elect.

Massachusetts has often been accused of being a theocracy in its early years as proudly affirmed by one of its leading ministers, John Cotton; but most writers today dispute this charge, since the clergy in the settlement were not granted temporal authority, and were indeed specifically forbidden from wielding such power. Nevertheless, in these early years the dividing line between minister and magistrate was thin. The minister was essentially the most learned member of the congregation; his sacerdotal authority was limited. Second, many magistrates, not least Winthrop himself, had pretensions to theological expertise; if there was no actual priestly caste, the saints were close to being one. Third, punishment for breaches of the moral code were imposed according to biblical, not common law. Lastly, the settlement's whole ethos was religious, its purpose to establish a godly community. Church and state were thus inextricably intertwined. The church existed to enunciate the moral law, the state to enforce it. Those who deviated from the accepted path could expect to be punished.

3 THE STRUGGLE FOR ORTHODOXY

Despite its strong sense of mission, the settlement of Massachusetts was not to remain free of controversy, although the first disputes were of a political rather than religious nature.

Since the last general meeting of the company in England had taken place in March 1630, another meeting of the general court was called in October of that year, at which a couple of important changes were engineered by Winthrop and his colleagues. The first was that the freemen should elect the assistants, as provided under the charter, but that the assistants alone should elect the governor and deputy governor. The second was that the governor and the assistants would henceforth "have the power of making laws and choosing officers to execute the same," a change which represented a huge increase in their power. During the next eighteen months, Winthrop and the magistrates directed the settlement without any further resort to the general court, confident that the meeting of October 1630 had given them a complete mandate. As Winthrop later told a delegation of town deputies,

"It is yourselves who have called us to this office, and being called by you, we have our authority from God."

This view was not to remain unchallenged. To raise the money required to execute their mandate, the governor and his colleagues levied contributions from the towns. This arbitrary measure met with protest, notable from Watertown, which as an outlying community had less influence in the choice of assistants. In 1632 its inhabitants argued that under the charter the magistrates had no power to levy taxes. The justice of their case could hardly be denied, and after some prevarication Winthrop and his colleagues grudgingly agreed that every town should send two representatives to the general court each year to discuss such matters. Another concession was the restoration of the freemen's right to elect the governor and deputy governor.

While this concession constituted a substantial victory, it left the magistrates with the right to promulgate laws, resulting in further calls for more frequent meetings of the general court and greater participation by the freemen in the government of the colony. The matter finally came to a head at the annual meeting of the general court in May 1634, when some members of the council, notably Thomas Dudley, Israel Stoughton, and Roger Ludlow, supported the demand to see the charter, which was then in the possession of Winthrop. The charter confirmed the sole right of the general court to raise money, make laws, and dispose lands. The dissatisfaction which resulted was so widespread that Winthrop was subsequently defeated for the governorship, first in 1635 by John Haynes and again in 1636 by Sir Henry Vane. He maintained his seat on the council, however, and bided his time.

Because the settlements were now too dispersed for most freemen to attend the general court, it was agreed that in future each town would be represented by two deputies on all matters, not just taxation. The result was that Massachusetts, like Virginia, now had a representative system of government, which owed much to its company origins but was in no sense democratic. The franchise was still limited to freemen who were full church members. In a town like Dedham 70 percent of the adults may have been communicants; in Boston the figure was about 50 percent. Up to half the adult males – and all females – thus remained disenfranchised. Nevertheless, Massachusetts had a constitution which was capable of being liberalized in time. The first breach had been made in the theocratic and autocratic system of government.

Within twelve months the new system was put to the test when its authority was challenged by Roger Williams. Williams had come to Massachusetts in 1631, having trained for the ministry in England. Like many people of his time, he was passionately concerned about Christian purity, arguing that outward conformity did not mean salvation. His belief led him into separatism and a two-year stay at Plymouth, where Bradford described him as "godly and zealous . . . but very unsettled in judgement." It also took him to Salem, where a number of the original Dorchester Company settlers had similar leanings. Between 1633 and 1635 Williams began calling for the complete separation of his church from the other New England congregations, which had not disavowed the Church of England. He also publicly tore the English flag because it contained the cross of St. George, a popish symbol. The general court responded by expelling Salem's deputies until they saw the error of their ways.

At this point Williams revealed his radical tendencies, for he promptly denied that the general court had any authority in spiritual matters, arguing that church and state should be totally separate. He also gratuitously denied the court's power to sequestrate American Indian lands merely because of a charter from the king. In effect he was denying both the religious and political authority of the Puritan establishment. Clearly such schismatic behavior could not be tolerated; in October 1635 Williams was banished, while pressure was brought on his congregation to conform. The episode underlined a major difficulty for the Puritan church. How could orthodoxy be preserved without compromising the rights of the congregation? One solution was the formation of a ministerial synod similar to that of the Presbyterian church, but the congregationally minded Puritans loathed the idea of undermining the authority of the laity in favor of the ministry. The matter was a perplexing one.

While the threat posed by Williams was being successfully contained, another, more insidious danger was emerging in Boston itself. It concerned Mrs Anne Hutchinson, who had arrived in 1634 with her family and had joined the church where John Cotton was minister and Governor Vane a member of the congregation. Her formidable intellect and love of argument soon made her influential, not least with Cotton and Vane, whom she met at private gatherings.

Hutchinson's views veered toward an antinomian form of predestination, which affirmed that God had decided from the beginning of time who would be saved; nothing that the individual did could change this, not even the strictest observance of the moral law. Hutchinson, like many Puritans, believed that the church still contained many unregenerate persons even among the clergy, who disguised their lack of belief by a veneer of good works and outward conformity to the moral law. She therefore denounced some ministers for preaching a covenant of deeds rather than one of grace.

Hutchinson's antinomian views posed a number of challenges. The first was the attempt to undermine the ministry implicit in her argument that the elect had no need of spiritual guidance, God having revealed directly that they were saved. No established church could allow such bypassing of its authority, as the Pharisees had demonstrated when confronted by Christ. The second challenge was to the authority of the Scriptures as the revealed word of God on which the whole religious polity of the Puritans was based. Lastly, Hutchinson's beliefs implied that if salvation were predetermined, then logically no one need bother even to demonstrate the possession of faith. This view completely contradicted the Puritan emphasis on sanctification. Although it was not Hutchinson's intention to do so, her arguments could equally justify the life of a libertine, posing a threat to society itself.

Unlike Williams, Hutchinson had powerful supporters; indeed, her struggle in its later stages can be seen as an extension of the political battle between Winthrop, Vane, and Dudley. For a time the eventual outcome was uncertain. Not until Winthrop had the general court convened at Newtown, outside Boston, in May 1637 was his victory assured. First, Winthrop was elected governor. Next the general court was purged of two of its errant deputies from Boston. Then a meeting of the church elders and magistrates was held to reaffirm the view that grace was a state that had to be constantly sought. Following these proceedings, action could be taken against the antinomians. First, Anne Hutchinson's brother-in-law, the Reverend John Wheelwright, was banished, along with one of the errant deputies. Then Cotton was persuaded to retract. Finally, in November 1637 Hutchinson herself was called to face her accusers before the general court. When she claimed that her views had been revealed by God, she was duly condemned and banished.

Some writers have suggested that Hutchinson received this treatment because she was a woman, who encouraged other women to discuss religion independently of their husbands. While in Boston she had presided over a weekly gathering of some sixty of her sex. Although the Puritans went further than most churches in admitting women to full

DOCUMENT 8

The examination of Mrs Hutchinson, November 1637, reprinted in Thomas Hutchinson, *The History of the Colony and Province of Massachusetts Bay*, edited by Lawrence Shaw Mayo (Cambridge, Mass., 1936), II, 366–91.

[Mrs Hutchinson gave a spirited and able defence until her confession that she had been directly instructed by God. Apart from the menace of antinomianism, the magistrates were clearly troubled that their authority was being challenged by a woman.]

GOVERNOR WINTHROP: "Mrs Hutchinson, you are called here as one of those that have troubled the peace of the commonwealth and the churches here; you are known to be a woman that hath had a great share in the promoting and divulging of those [antinomian] opinions that are the causes of this trouble, and to be nearly joined not only in affinity and affection with some of those the court had taken notice of and passed censure upon, but you have spoken divers things as we have been informed very prejudicial to the honour of the churches and ministers thereof, and you have maintained a meeting and assembly in your house that hath been condemned by the general assembly as a thing not tolerable nor comely in the sight of God nor fitting for your sex, and notwithstanding that was cried down you have continued the same, therefore we have thought good to send for you to understand how things are, that if you be in an erroneous way we may reduce you so you may become a profitable member here among us, otherwise if you be obstinate in your course that then the court may take such course that you may trouble us no further. . . ."

MRS HUTCHINSON: "I am called here to answer before you but I hear no things laid to my charge."

WINTHROP: "I have told you some already and more I can tell you."

MRS HUTCHINSON: "Name one Sir . . . What have I done?"

WINTHROP: Why for your doings, this you did harbour and countenance those that are parties in this faction [the antinomians]."

MRS HUTCHINSON: "That's a matter of conscience, Sir. . . ."

WINTHROP: "Your conscience you must keep or it must be kept for you."

MRS HUTCHINSON: "Must not I then entertain the saints [church members] because I must keep my conscience?"

[Thomas Dudley] DEPUTY GOVERNOR: "I would go a little higher with Mrs Hutchinson . . . it appears by this woman's meeting that Mrs Hutchinson hath so forestalled the minds of many . . . that she now hath a potent party in the country. Now if all these things have endangered us . . . and if she in particular hath disparaged all our ministers in the land that they have preached a covenant of works and only Mr Cotton a covenant of grace, why this is not to be suffered. . . ."

MRS HUTCHINSON: "I pray Sir prove it that I said they preached nothing but a covenant of works."

DEPUTY GOVERNOR: "Nothing but a covenant of works, why a Jesuit may preach truth sometimes."

MRS HUTCHINSON: "Did I ever say they preached a covenant of works then?"

DEPUTY GOVERNOR: "If they did not preach a covenant of grace clearly, then they preach a covenant of works."

MRS HUTCHINSON: "No Sir, one may preach a covenant of grace more clearly than another, so I said . . . if you please to give me leave I shall give you the ground of what I know to be true. Being much troubled to see the falseness of the constitution of the church of England, I had like to have turned separatist; whereupon I kept a day of solemn humiliation and pondering of the thing . . . the Lord was pleased to bring this scripture out of the Hebrews. 'He that denies the testament denies the testator,' and in this did open unto me and give me to see that those which did not teach the new covenant had the spirit of antichrist, and upon this he did discover the ministry unto me and ever since, I bless the Lord, he hath let me see which was the clear ministry and which the wrong. . . ."

MR NOWEL [a magistrate]: "How do you know that?"

MRS HUTCHINSON: "How did Abraham know that it was God that bid him offer his son, being a breach of the sixth commandment?"

DEPUTY GOVERNOR: "By an immediate voice."

MRS HUTCHINSON: "So to me by an immediate revelation."

membership, women were still barred from the ministry; a woman could not become a freeman, vote, or be elected a deputy or magistrate. The female role was strictly subordinate, and even in religious matters a woman was supposed to derive her "ideas of God from the contemplation of her husband's excellencies." This superior male attitude was expressed most bluntly by Winthrop himself when he told Anne Hutchinson, "We do not mean to discourse with your sex." She had offended against not only God's laws but those of men, preferring, as one minister commented, to be "a husband than a wife, a preacher than a hearer, and a magistrate than a subject." Her fate was sealed.[5]

---

[5] See Lyle Koehler, "The Case of the American Jezebels: Anne Hutchinson and Female Agitation During the Years of Antinomian Turmoil, 1636–1640," *William and Mary Quarterly*, XXXI, 1974. 55–78; and *A Search for Power: The "Weaker Sex" in Seventeenth Century New England* (Urbana, 1980). Koehler's work was the result of the greater interest in women's studies that began to emerge in the 1970s, reflecting feminist anger at the traditional position of women in American society. For the view that women enjoyed more genuine equality in seventeenth-century New England, see especially Cornelia Hughes Dayton, *Women Before the Bar: Gender, Law, and Society in Connecticut, 1639–1789* (Chapel Hill, 1995), who argues that Puritan women enjoyed greater access to the courts because procedures were less legalistic. In addition, Puritan magistrates, concerned with morality rather than legality, were more disposed to listen to women of good repute. For more information on the subject see chapter 12.

The Williams and Hutchinson affairs came at a critical time for Massachusetts when the colony was also under attack from opponents in England.

The first threat came from Gorges and the Council for New England. Gorges had been busy preventing a French invasion of England in 1629, and it was some time before he realized that the king had issued a patent to another group in an area claimed by the council. He was not opposed to the Puritan emigration; he merely required that the Puritans should acknowledge the council's authority and accept its plan of government. Gorges was supported by Thomas Morton, who had been expelled from Mount Wollaston once more in 1629, this time by Endecott. Several others, however, joined the clamor to have the affairs of Massachusetts investigated.

Accordingly, in 1634 a special committee of the Privy Council was set up under Archbishop Laud to look into the affairs of the Massachusetts Bay Company. On discovering that the charter was no longer in England, the committee began legal proceedings to have the company terminated. These were slow, and it was not until the summer of 1637 that a verdict was given in favor of the king. Charles I then announced that he would govern Massachusetts, as he did Virginia, through a governor and council, with Gorges as his first representative.

Fortunately for Massachusetts, the king's gesture proved hollow, as his attempts to govern without Parliament while his Scottish subjects were in rebellion had proved a dismal failure. Gorges was left without support and had to be satisfied with an empty title to Maine.

Another cause of unease during these years was the first outbreak of hostilities between the settlers and the American Indians. The Massachusetts tribe had initially been too weak to pose any threat, but the continuing tide of settlement brought the Puritans into conflict with the Pequot nation along the Thames River. The Pequots may also have been newcomers to the area, as their presence was certainly resented by most of the neighboring tribes, notably the Narragansetts. Another cause of contention was the desire of all the contestants to control the region's trade, especially the production of wampum.[6]

As often happened, hostilities were precipitated by murder, on this occasion the killing of two white traders, Captain Stone in 1634 and John Oldham in 1636. In neither case was it clear who the perpetrators were, but everyone found it convenient to blame the Pequots. The Pequots themselves offered to negotiate, but their overtures were rejected since they refused to surrender Stone's alleged killers, which the Puritan clergy demanded as evidence that the Pequots were not in league with the devil. Had they acceded to this demand they would have effectively been acknowledging the jurisdiction of Massachusetts and lost their independence. However, perhaps more importantly, a number of settlements had recently been established on the Connecticut River, and war offered Massachusetts the best means of both securing these and opening up fresh lands for settlement. Endecott was therefore dispatched with a punitive expedition, first to Block Island and then to Pequot Harbor. Block Island was Narragansett territory, and Endecott's action could have brought the Narragansetts into league with the Pequots. Ironically, Massachusetts received assistance not only from neighboring Plymouth and Connecticut but also from Rhode Island, where Roger Williams persuaded the Narragansetts not to join the Pequots.

Following these maneuvers the outcome of the conflict could not be in doubt. The Pequots had just sixteen guns and little powder. The English colonists had not only guns

---

[6] See chapter 5, section 2, for information on wampum.

Plate 17 "Underhill's Diagram of the Pequot Fight." From John Fiske, *The Beginnings of New England or the Puritan Theocracy in its Relations to Civil and Religious Liberty* (Boston: Houghton Mifflin & Co., 1898).

but swords, armor, and overwhelming numbers in their favor, as well as the support of the surrounding indigenous peoples. The Pequots did surprise the town of Wethersfield in April 1637, killing nine settlers. The attackers, however, were quickly trapped in their fort on the Mystic River and burnt alive by a Connecticut force under Captain John Mason. Five hundred perished in the flames despite protest by the Narragansetts, who realized that they were witnessing a new and terrible kind of conflict. When an even larger group of Pequots was trapped in a swamp, the Puritans did not hesitate to kill the fighting men and sell the rest into slavery, believing that the American Indians, like the Philistines in the Old Testament, had rightly been put to the sword.

The destruction of the Pequots was not without its effect on the other tribes. The following year the Narragansetts and Mohegans had to agree not to go to war without the permission of the English. And in 1643, when rumors were afoot that the Narragansetts were about to attack, their Chief Miantonomo was summoned to Boston and his nation forced to pay tribute. This episode precipitated the formal signing of an alliance between Massachusetts, Plymouth, and Connecticut, styled the Confederation of the United Colonies of New England.

Meanwhile the collapse of Charles I's personal rule in England and his summoning of Parliament in 1640 promised a new chapter in English politics, for a principal aim of the majority was the reform of the Church of England. Some New Englanders therefore advocated going back to England to help. Among those who returned were several ministers, along with others who were simply homesick, having been unable to adapt to a strange environment. The vast majority stayed put, however, being too firmly attached to their new country.

Unfortunately, Parliament in England was dominated by Presbyterians, with whom the Puritans had a number of disagreements, not least concerning the relationship of a congregation to its minister, and it was a Presbyterian, Dr Robert Child, who mounted the next challenge to the commonwealth. Having first visited Massachusetts in 1641, Child returned in 1645 following Parliament's triumph in the civil war. Child was well educated and quickly recognized the disabilities under which he labored in Massachusetts. In November 1646, together with several associates he wrote *A Remonstrance and Humble Petition* in which he made a number of charges: that his rights as an Englishman were being infringed; that the charter was being used beyond its intended purpose, being merely equivalent to an English corporation; that the laws of Massachusetts did not conform to those of England; and that the church lacked proper regulation, since it excluded most inhabitants from the sacrament and their children from baptism. Only a Presbyterian system, Child argued, would correct these faults.[7]

The attack by Child was seen as dangerous because it might be supported from England. Nevertheless, the Puritan leadership was not disposed to admit any of his charges. Child was charged with writing "divers false and scandalous passages . . . against the Churches of Christ and the civil government here established." The general court asserted that a proper body of laws had been enacted and that their only obligation under the charter was to ensure that these laws were not contrary to those of England. As to the charge that Massachusetts constituted no more than an English corporation, the court asserted that the position of a foreign plantation was necessarily different. The debate uncannily foreshadowed that between Thomas Hutchinson and Samuel Adams in 1773.

Initially, the court determined to impose a stiff fine, but when Child and his coauthors implied that they would appeal to Parliament, they were imprisoned while the court dispatched its own courier to London. Fortunately the army, dominated by the Independents, as the congregational Puritans were known in England, shortly took control as it gained the upper hand in England's civil war. Child's complaint, therefore, was not well received when he finally reached London. From 1648 Massachusetts was seemingly safe for the first time in the affections of an English government.

Nevertheless, the Child episode was not without consequences. The general court was aware that Massachusetts still had no proper legal code. Many settlers had from the beginning been worried by the arbitrary nature of the justice dispensed by the court of assistants, with its unsystematic use of the Bible, common law, and individual whim. In 1636 John Cotton had drawn up a code which Winthrop called "a model of Moses" because of its biblical references. This code had been modified in 1639 by the Reverend Nathaniel Ward,

---

[7] A copy of Child's trial and the response of the Massachusetts general court can be found in Kavenagh, *Documentary History*, I, 306–13.

DOCUMENT 9

A call for Indian unity by Chief Miantonomo, 1642, reprinted in Karen Ordahl Kupperman, ed., *Major Problems in American Colonial History: Documents and Essays* (Lexington, Mass., 1993), 135.

[The disastrous impact of the Europeans on the culture and ecology of the Indian peoples is well expressed in this document. Miantonomo, like Opechancanough in Virginia, having tried coexistence with the colonists, could see no alternative to all-out war with them if the native peoples were not to be exterminated. This required the burying of old feuds among the Indians so that unity could be achieved.]

A while after this came Miantenomie from Block Island to Mantacut with a troop of men . . . instead of receiving presents, which they used to do in their progress, he gave them gifts, calling them brethren and friends, for so are we all Indians as they English are, and say brother to one another; so must we be one as they are, otherwise we shall be all gone shortly, for you know our fathers had plenty of deer and skins, our plains were full of deer, as also our woods, and of turkies, and our coves full of fish and fowl. But these English having gotten our land, they with scythes cut down the grass, and with axes fell the trees; their cows and horses eat the grass, and their hogs spoil our clam banks, and we shall all be starved; therefore it is best for you to do as we, for we are all the Sachems from east to west, both Moquakues and Mohauks joining with us, and we are all resolved to fall upon them all, at one appointed day; and therefore I am come to you privately first, because you can persuade the Indians and Sachem to what you will . . . and when you see the three fires that will be made forty days hence, in a clear night, then do as we, and the next day fall on and kill men, women, and children, but no cows, for they will serve to eat til our deer be increased again.

though the intent was still "to compose a model of the judicial laws of Moses." It was this draft which had finally been issued in 1641 as the Body of Liberties. Many deputies, however, felt that it still left too much to the arbitrary judgment of the magistrates and quirks of the mosaic law. Accordingly, in 1648 a further revision was undertaken, during which a number of legal volumes were imported from England. The result, published as *The Book of General Lawes and Libertyes*, defined more precisely the powers and functions of the magistracy, the "liberties" of the individual, and the due process of the law. Another important step had been taken in the evolution of Massachusetts from a semitheocratic state to a constitutional polity.[8]

---

[8] *Book of the General Lawes and Libertyes Governing the Inhabitants of the Massachusetts* (Boston, 1648), reprinted in Kavenagh, *Documentary History*, I, 295–306.

4 THE COMMONWEALTH SECURED

We have seen that Massachusetts had lived precariously during its first twenty years, threatened first by internal dissension and then by external forces. However, the triumph of the Independents in England at last promised a more settled existence. Parliament might still interfere in matters of trade, but the Puritans knew that their religious settlement at least would be respected.

It was about this time that the Puritans completed the final details of their church government. In 1641 the general court passed a bill confirming the right of each congregation to elect its own officers, control its membership, and worship according to conscience. But with the Williams and Hutchinson cases in mind, the court decreed that "it shall be lawful for the ministers and leaders of the churches" to discuss and resolve "any such doubts and cases of conscience concerning matters of doctrine, or worship, or government of the church." A fine line still existed between a Presbyterian and congregational system. In reality the ministers had been meeting since the beginning in what they called consociations.

One result of the Child affair was the need to address the charge that nonmembers of the church were being discriminated against. In addition, there was a wider need for a definitive statement of the congregational church's theology and procedures. Accordingly, the Cambridge Platform of August 1648 attempted to do for the church what the *Book of General Lawes and Libertyes* had done for the state. On relations between the two it asserted, "As it is unlawful for church officers to meddle with the sword of the magistrate, so it is unlawful for the Magistrate to meddle with the work proper to church officers." The days when Winthrop could dominate both were over. The dividing lines were now clear. The church pronounced on matters of doctrine, the magistrates enforced them. As to doctrine, the ministers decided to adopt the 1648 Westminster Confession, bringing them into line with their colleagues in England. The Platform, however, made no concession on church membership, arguing that the issue of "saints by calling" was a matter for the congregations to decide. There must be no lowering of standards, whatever the civil disabilities for the rest of the community.[9]

In general the church's position was secure, though further challenges were made to its authority. In the early 1640s, the followers of Samuel Gorton, a self-styled preacher, disturbed the peace in a display of disrespect for Puritan orthodoxy. At about the same time the first Baptists, or Anabaptists, appeared and insisted on adult immersion because the Bible did not authorize infant baptism. Most troublesome were the Quakers, who first arrived in 1656. They wished to dispense with almost all traditional Christian practice, including use of the Bible, since they believed that everyone could experience God's grace through prayer and the "inner light."[10] All these groups were small in number, however, and could initially be fined, whipped, placed in irons, banished, or (in the case of four Quakers) executed.[11] Such harsh punishments, however, often proved counterproductive, since they merely encouraged others to proclaim their faith by defying the magistrates. Accordingly, one concession to the Dissenters was that they might hold private meetings, providing "it be without just offense." But formal congregations could be established only with the

---

[9] For the full text, see Max Farrand, ed., *The Laws and Liberties of Massachusetts* (Boston, 1929).
[10] For further information on the Quakers, see chapter 7, section 3.
[11] Among those executed was Mary Dyer, a former associate of Anne Hutchinson.

consent of the local magistrates and elders by such persons as "be orthodox in judgement." There were to be no rival establishments in the Puritan commonwealth.[12]

The number of church members in general was gratifyingly high, though by 1650 Boston had only 625 saints out of a total populace of 3,000. Among the smaller towns the proportion of saints remained as high as 60 percent. More problematic was the fact that many male members did not apply for freemanship, thus imposing a heavy civil burden on their fellow saints. Accordingly, the 1648 code laid down that church members who failed to qualify might still serve as constables, jurors, selectmen, and highway surveyors. An additional law permitted nonfreemen to vote for selectmen and serve as jurors.

One early problem, the provision of a trained ministry, had been tackled in 1636 by the founding of Harvard College, which henceforth lessened the colony's dependence on England for qualified clergy. The first candidates were ordained in 1641, by which time over twenty scholars were in residence.

In 1647 action was also taken to ensure that the population at large received some instruction. Since knowledge of the Scriptures was essential for salvation, all towns with fifty households were to appoint someone to teach their children to read and write. Larger towns were also to establish a grammar school for teaching Latin so that their youths might "be fitted for the university," where Latin was the language of instruction.

Serious attempts were also begun to convert the American Indians. The only noteworthy missionary activity up to this time had been undertaken by Thomas Mayhew at Martha's Vineyard. The decision to proselytize now was in part a response to criticism by Williams and others of the Puritans' failure in this matter. But the time was also propitious because many southern New England Indians were ready to embrace Christianity, following the breakdown of their own societies under the impact of war and disease. Accordingly, in 1646 the Reverend John Eliot, the minister at Roxbury, established a mission for the surviving Pequot and Massachusetts peoples. They were herded into four settlements known euphemistically as the "praying towns," the chief one being at Natick. The problem of the lack of any written liturgy was partly rectified in 1654, when Eliot published a version of the catechism, followed in 1660 by a translation of the New Testament. Plans were also made for the training of an Indian ministry at Harvard. About the same time, the Natick congregation was admitted to the Roxbury Church, though only after much reluctance on the part of the white community, who believed that the new converts had not yet attained sufficient religious understanding. Racial prejudice was probably a factor too.

The Puritans have traditionally been portrayed as humorless killjoys who believed that all leisure was sinful, as evidenced by the law of 1633 banning idle amusements such as the theater, cards, and dice. The fear was that such activities not only led to sinful actions, but also represented an unprofitable use of time. In reality, however, except for the European aristocracy and merchant class, few seventeenth-century people anywhere had time for such diversions or leisure in a modern sense. Life was certainly too demanding in a frontier society, although some diversions were permitted so long as they did not become an end in themselves. Hence hunting and fishing were approved because they produced a valuable

---

[12]   The Baptists managed to establish a meeting house in 1679 in Boston, but for a long time it was the sole one. The Anglicans only established their first formal place of worship in Boston in 1689, a wooden structure known as King's Chapel. This was superseded in 1723 by a handsome brick building, known as the old North Church or Christ Church; see chapter 13, section 1.

supplement to the family diet. Reading and music were also seen as lawful recreations, provided they were done "with thankfulness to God." As a result, some poetry was produced, notably Anne Bradstreet's *The Tenth Muse*, published in London in 1650, and Michael Wrigglesworth's *The Day of Doom*, which appeared in Boston in 1662. The latter, however, was intended to make Puritan theology memorable by versification, and even Bradstreet's poems had religious themes.

One activity that the Puritans might have been expected to condemn was the consumption of alcohol. But although drunkenness itself was one of the seven deadly sins, the Puritans by no means favoured total abstinence, which might have been difficult to enforce since most of the settlers were from England where alcohol was widely consumed. As with most things, the Puritan leadership proved eminently practical. Cider, beer, and wine were seen as legitimate refreshment, providing they were consumed in moderation. Indeed, alcohol was often served at public functions to emphasize the symbolic nature of the occasion, though the custom of toasting acquaintances and business deals was frowned on as likely to lead to excess. Another consideration was the need for places of refreshment for travellers. Hence a number of taverns were licensed in Boston and the neighboring towns. In due course some establishments grew sufficiently large to host meetings of the justices and other events in lieu of more suitable accommodation. But to prevent lascivious amusements like dancing, the general court ordered town officials regularly to patrol all such establishments.

Since the Puritans came mainly in family groups, the ratio of men to women was always relatively equal and family life was therefore far more pronounced than in the Chesapeake. In addition, New England was blessed with a healthy, if bracing climate, being isolated from most of the epidemics that continually swept Europe. Most couples therefore raised large families, with between five and seven children commonly surviving to adulthood. This fertility led to New England's remarkable expansion throughout the seventeenth century and made up for the lack of immigration after 1640. Twenty thousand people came to New England in the 1630s; thereafter the flow slowed to a trickle. The natural population increase, however, caused the number of towns in Massachusetts to grow from twenty-one in 1641 to thirty-three by 1647.

This expansion necessitated some additional administrative structures, notably the creation of a county system in 1643. Initially four were established: Suffolk, Middlesex, Essex, and Norfolk. Here was another reminder of how closely the Puritans followed their English ways. Each county had a bench of justices commissioned by the general court for determining petty criminal and civil matters. Major cases were still referred to the court of assistants, the colony's superior court of judicature.

Most communities in Massachusetts were close to the sea, though some, like Dedham, were beginning to be sited inland. Farming was necessarily the main occupation. The Puritans had always realized that souls could not be saved if mouths were not fed. Most farming was initially of a subsistence nature, the main produce being hogs and corn, though those with servants were soon able to diversify into cattle and wheat. Settlers along the coast could also fish, though few had the skills or capital to do so on a commercial basis. Nevertheless, this activity encouraged a nascent boat and later shipbuilding industry.[13] In

---

[13] For the early development of the fishing industry in Massachusetts, see Daniel Vickers, *Farmers and Fishermen: Two Centuries of Work in Essex County, Massachusetts, 1630–1850* (Chapel Hill, 1994).

general the colony was remarkably prosperous during its first ten years, largely because a continuous stream of immigrants arrived bringing cash to buy livestock and other supplies with which to establish themselves.

The decline of immigration after 1640 therefore appeared initially to be something of a calamity. On the other hand, new markets were beginning to appear in the West Indies, where planters were happy to exchange sugar for other provisions, primarily fish, beef, pork, and corn. Lumber and fish from Maine were also important products which found a ready market in England, where the civil war allowed New Englanders to supplant English merchants in the supply of fish to Spain and Portugal. Some trade with the local inhabitants was also possible, though the furs in New England were not of the best quality. Lastly, attempts were made to improve the colony's self-sufficiency by establishing an ironworks near Lynn on the Saugus River. Unfortunately, the plans for the production of finished goods proved too ambitious, in part because of a lack of skilled labor, and the project folded after a few years, though small-scale smelting and the fashioning of items like nails and simple tools did continue at a number of sites.

But whatever the obstacles, there was never any doubt that the Puritans would succeed in both their religious and economic endeavors. Indeed, many writers have seen a link between the two. Ministers and magistrates frequently mentioned the "parable of the talents" in which Christ extolled those servants who worked hard for their master, while condemning those who did not. It is argued that this emphasis on the work ethic helped the accumulation of capital, the development of skills, and the encouragement of enterprise, three key factors that explain New England's successful economy. Not that Massachusetts was a fully developed market-led capitalist system. The general court still regulated prices in the interests of the community, while attempts were also made to prevent conspicuous consumption through the passage of sumptuary laws. The general court also granted monopolies to favoured individuals. Nevertheless, important advances towards a free-market economy had been made.[14]

As to their material culture, the immigrants in Massachusetts initially constructed simple cottages, as in Virginia, but in contrast they soon began improving their residences, thus giving their settlements a greater sense of permanence. The first houses were mainly one-room affairs with a stone hearth for cooking and a loft to sleep in. The more affluent soon added a second room and loft. Next came a second type of dwelling with a cellar and raised ground floor plus a kitchen at the back, a style known as the salt box. The exterior walls of these were covered with clapboard, the roofs with shingles or thatch, and the walls inside with plaster. The furniture consisted of simple wooden tables, benches, stools, beds, and coffers, with rush mats on the floor. Seventeenth-century New England housing, though plain, was always effective.

---

[14]   The link between Protestantism, the work ethic, and capitalism was first made by the German sociologist, Max Weber, *The Protestant Ethic and the Spirit of Capitalism* (1904–5). A similar but more critical analysis was provided by the British historian R. H. Tawney, *Religion and the Rise of Capitalism* (London, 1926), who pointed to the undesirable consequences of the Protestant ethic, namely the destruction of social obligation, the worship of wealth, and the denigration of the poor. The thesis about the Protestant work ethic and economic growth has recently been restated by Stephen Innes, *Creating the Commonwealth: The Economic Culture of Puritan New England* (New York, 1995). Innes, however, emphasizes the restraining influence of Puritanism on the rampant individualism that Tawney condemned.

5 RHODE ISLAND, CONNECTICUT, AND NEW HAMPSHIRE

Plymouth and Massachusetts did not constitute the only colonizing efforts at this time. Massachusetts itself spawned several further settlements, though not always in a manner approved by Winthrop and his colleagues.

The first was that of Roger Williams after his expulsion in 1635. During that winter he retired to southern New England, taking with him some of his Salem supporters. Williams knew the area of Rhode Island, which was not then claimed by any white group, from his earlier stay at Plymouth; and he was acquainted with the indigenous inhabitants, from whom he purchased some land. His group then chose a site fifty miles up the Blackstone River, where each person was given a plot of land with a river frontage. Williams called his straggling community Providence.

Initially, government was by heads of households, who met once every two weeks. Later a system was devised for the election of five disposers, who were to govern by arbitration. This compact was to relate only to civil matters; Williams had had enough of magistrates interfering in church affairs. The godly and the damned alike must be free to tend their own consciences as they saw fit. Here was perhaps the first example of frontier democracy and religious toleration.

Three years later another town, Portsmouth, was established on the island of Aquidneck in Narragansett Bay. Its principal founders were Anne Hutchinson and William Coddington, a friend of Williams, who had been implicated but not charged in the antinomian controversy. Here, too, freedom of conscience was permitted, on the grounds that nothing could be done for the damned. But Coddington was less generous in his ideas concerning government, and he was soon ousted from the town. He subsequently formed another settlement at Newport on the other side of the island. By March 1641, however, the two had joined together again in what they described as "a democracy or popular government," based on the right of the freemen to make "just laws."[15] The two groups had discovered that only by tolerating each other could they hope to survive. Their democracy certainly emanated more from necessity than principle, though in both England and America voices were now asserting that civil authority could be derived only from the people, and not from God, as most magistrates and kings liked to claim. The early settlement of Rhode Island was completed in 1643 when Samuel Gorton arrived with his followers to establish the town of Warwick.

For the first few years relations between the settlements were restricted. Nevertheless, the need for unity was emphasized in 1643, when Rhode Island was pointedly not asked to join the New England confederation. Both Massachusetts and Plymouth claimed parts of its territory and did not look kindly on this collection of outcasts. Williams accordingly journeyed to England to secure a patent, despite his earlier condemnation of such contrivances. He was aided by the publication of his pamphlet, *The Bloody Tenet of Persecution*, which won him many friends, notably the Earl of Warwick, who was now in charge of Parliament's colonial affairs. A patent was therefore issued on March 24, 1644, granting the petitioners

---

[15] For a copy of the agreement see Kavenagh, *Documentary History*, I, 343–5.

"a free and absolute Charter of Incorporation ... with full Power and Authority to rule themselves." The only qualification was the customary one that all laws should "be conformable to the Laws of England." Effectively Rhode Island was given corporate status with the right of local self-government.[16]

Despite this success, internal dissension prevented any further progress until 1647, when the several towns finally came together to frame their government. Not surprisingly, their union was federal in character. The spirit was remarkably democratic. Each town could initiate legislation, and all had to be consulted before any law was passed. The government was to be "held by the free and voluntary consent of all, or the greater part of, the free inhabitants," assembled together in a general court. Between meetings, political authority would be exercised by a committee, to which each town would send six representatives. After 1650, this effectively became the legislative body, though a majority of the freemen could still have any law disallowed.

Rhode Island during the seventeenth century never represented more than a refuge for a few outcasts, who practiced unconventional ideas on religion and politics. That it survived was in no small measure due to the skill of Williams and his friendship with Warwick. With only four settlements before 1660, Rhode Island remained on the periphery of events, and its contribution to colonial development was small.

More important in this period was the settling of the Connecticut River valley, first explored in 1632 by Edward Winslow of Plymouth. His proposal for a joint venture with Massachusetts to exploit the fur trade there was not adopted, but interest soon quickened following reports of lush meadows along the river, and by 1635 several groups had emigrated there from both Plymouth and Massachusetts. In addition, the Dutch had established a settlement at Fort Hope. The most important migration, however, was that from Newtown, where Thomas Hooker was minister, in May 1636.

Although the main reason Hooker and his congregation removed was economic – the land around Newtown was rocky – it seems that the inhabitants were also unhappy about the dissension then affecting Massachusetts. While Hooker and his congregation had no sympathy with either Hutchinson or Williams, they appear to have disliked the arbitrary actions of the general court. Another cause for concern was the restrictive nature of church membership and the problem of determining who was saved. Hooker's answer was to widen the membership by offering communion to all who professed the faith. He also advocated a broader base for political authority. In a famous sermon in May 1638 he propounded the view that political authority must stem from the people. For Hooker, of course, "the people" meant the godly, but it was an important step to claim that authority was vested in them rather than in a higher being, as Winthrop had suggested.

Since there were several claimants to the lands in Connecticut, Massachusetts arbitrated among the different groups. Eight persons were nominated to be magistrates, with John Winthrop, Jr. acting as governor until a more permanent arrangement could be devised.

In the summer of 1638, the representatives from the three principal towns of Hartford, Windsor, and Wethersfield duly met to draft a frame of government. Agreement was finally reached in January 1639 on what came to be known as the Fundamental Orders. These were "to maintain and preserve the liberty and purity of the gospel of our lord Jesus as ... is

---

[16] See Kavenagh, *Documentary History*, I, 109–10.

now practised." To this end there was to be a general court consisting of a governor, six assistants, and four deputies from each town. The governor and magistrates were to be elected by the freemen, for whom church membership was implicitly required. The deputies, however, were to be elected "by all that are admitted inhabitants in the several towns." Another innovation was the recognition that the deputies had different functions from the magistrates and should meet separately, a practice which Massachusetts adopted only in 1644. The deputies could also convene the general court, should the governor and assistants fail to do so, for an all-powerful magistracy such as had existed in Massachusetts was not to be allowed. Later in 1650 a code similar to the 1648 *Book of General Lawes and Libertyes* was enacted.[17]

Settlements were also springing up elsewhere. In June 1637 the Reverend John Davenport established New Haven, after purchasing a tract of land from the local inhabitants. Davenport was invited to stay in Massachusetts but declined because some of his congregation were merchants and wanted to settle on the coast. The Davenport group adopted a frame of government similar to that of Massachusetts, restricting the franchise to church members and instituting a legal code based on the 1641 Body of Liberties. The similarity was not surprising, since Davenport was a friend of Cotton.

About the same time, the Reverend John Wheelwright was establishing Exeter in present-day New Hampshire. Wheelwright, one of the antinomian refugees, formed his simple community with a compact similar to that of the Pilgrims. During the early 1640s additional settlements were established at Dover and Portsmouth and at York and Kittery in Maine. Many of these settlers were fishermen or woodsmen, unlike the inhabitants of Massachusetts. All settled on land subject to claims by Gorges and the heirs of Captain John Mason, another patentee, though none could make good their title because of the civil war in England. In this administrative vacuum, Massachusetts was not slow to act. By 1643 the New Hampshire settlements had acknowledged its authority. Then in 1651 Maine was annexed on the grounds that it was part of Massachusetts's own grant. The Maine settlements protested, but to no avail. Kittery was organized as a town with the right to send a deputy to the general court. Since it had no covenanted church, all the male inhabitants were made freemen and allowed to vote. Such a step, however, was the exception not the rule.

---

[17] For a full copy of the Fundamental Orders see Kavenagh, *Documentary History*, I, 352–5.

5

Maryland and New York, 1624–60

1609	Henry Hudson explores the Hudson River.
1624	The Dutch West India Company establishes New Netherland.
1624–8	The Mohawks triumph over the Mahicans.
1626	Manhattan is purchased for sixty guilders.
1627	Lord Baltimore abandons his settlement of Avalon in Newfoundland.
1629	Kiliaen Van Rensselaer establishes the first patroonship in New Netherland.
1632	A charter is issued to the first Lord Baltimore for the colony of Maryland.
1634	The colony of Maryland is established by the second Lord Baltimore.
1635	The first assembly of freemen in Maryland takes place.
1638	The first Swedish settlement is founded on the Delaware.
1641	The first representatives meet in New Netherland.
1643–5	War breaks out between the Dutch and the American Indians.
1644–6	Maryland endures "the plundering time."
1646	Peter Stuyvesant is appointed director general of New Netherland.
1648	Maryland grants headrights to servants.
1649	Maryland passes an act for religious toleration.
1655	The Dutch take control of New Sweden. The Peach War is fought between the Dutch and American Indians of the lower Hudson. The Battle of the Severn River is fought in Maryland.
1657	Jews are permitted to become burghers of New Amsterdam.

1 MARYLAND: A CATHOLIC PROPRIETARY

W HILE THE PURITANS were establishing their commonwealth, members of the Roman Catholic church in England were also planning a refuge, for they too were being persecuted on account of their religion.

The Catholics had of course opposed the break with Rome and the changes to the liturgy in the Book of Common Prayer. They also insisted that the pope, not the monarch, should be head of the church. Their position worsened following the excommunication of Elizabeth I in 1570, which seemingly condoned the subsequent attempt by Guy Fawkes to kill James I on the opening of Parliament in November 1605 in what came to be known as the gunpowder plot. In addition English paranoia against Catholicism had increased with the war against Spain, in which the most Catholic state in Europe had seemingly committed its vast wealth to a crusade against the Protestant nations.

A series of progressively harsher penal laws against Catholics was therefore introduced from 1571. Graduated fines were imposed for anyone attending mass and severe punishment was inflicted on priests who were caught officiating, while generous rewards were offered to informers.

Despite these difficulties many Catholics persisted in their faith, including some members of the aristocracy who sought to balance their attachment to Rome with loyalty to the Crown. Although they refused to take the oath of supremacy recognizing the monarch as head of the church, they denounced regicide. Fortunately, the accession of Charles I in 1625 promised a more relaxed regime, since his queen, Henrietta Maria, was a Catholic herself.

It was inevitable in an age of colonization that the idea of Catholic emigration would surface. The Catholics, like the Puritans, felt an obligation to protect their religion and believed that ultimately the true faith would be restored. In their view Protestantism was merely an aberration in the Catholic church's sixteen-hundred-year history. America, in the meantime, might provide a refuge.

Among those interested in such a scheme was George Calvert, the first Lord Baltimore. For most of his life Baltimore had not been a Catholic. Indeed, for two decades he was a prominent courtier, holding the position of secretary of state. His conversion in 1625 was, however, not unexpected, for both his parents were of that religion, while his son had recently married into a recusant (i.e., Roman Catholic) family.

Calvert's interest in the New World was first stimulated by one of his Protestant relatives, the Earl of Warwick, who persuaded him to invest in the Virginia Company. Later Calvert joined Warwick on the reconstituted Council for New England and started a small settlement of his own in Newfoundland to exploit the fishery. Unfortunately, when he visited the site at Avalon in 1627 he found the winters too harsh and the soil too barren for any hope of success.

During these early ventures, Calvert was motivated mainly by profit; and even after his conversion his actions were not entirely altruistic. Like his colleagues on the Council for New England, he hoped to increase his fortune by settling a plantation in America. As befitted a member of the nobility, his ambition was also to increase his estates, for more land would bring not only more income but more power and honor. So while the merchants saw Virginia in terms of expanding their trade, Baltimore and the nobility saw the New World primarily as a way of enlarging their estates.

After his experiences in Newfoundland, Baltimore went in search of somewhere warmer, setting sail in the summer of 1629 to explore Virginia. Once the Virginians knew he was a Catholic, however, they refused him entry and sought to prevent him obtaining a patent at all. Baltimore persevered, and only his death prevented him from seeing a charter issued on June 20, 1632, for a grant of territory in the upper Chesapeake, to be called Maryland in honour of the queen.

Baltimore's patent was necessarily different from those issued to Virginia and Massachusetts; his primary aim was the advancement of his family rather than of a group of shareholders, whom he believed had ruined the Virginia Company. Earlier he had discovered an old patent issued in the fourteenth century to the Bishop of Durham, giving that prelate extensive powers on the frontier between England and Scotland in the form of a palatinate. Baltimore had used this palatine model for his Avalon project. Now he persuaded Charles I to issue a similar grant of princely authority once again. The document, customarily called a proprietary charter, was strongly feudal in tone. Baltimore and his heirs were to be "absolute Lords and Proprietors," with the right to all minerals, except for the usual 20 percent of any precious metals reserved for the Crown. He could create his own titles and grant lands with manorial rights. In addition he could incorporate towns, create ports, license all trade, raise customs, and levy other revenues. He could also license "Churches, Chapels, and Places of Worship . . . according to the Ecclesiastical Laws" of the kingdom. Most remarkably, Baltimore was to be excused all duties to the Crown, delivering only a symbolic two arrows every year in acknowledgment of his fealty.

Regarding legislation, the proprietor had "full, and absolute Power . . . to ordain, Make, and Enact Laws" subject to "the Advice, Assent, and Approbation of the Free Men of the same Province . . . or of their Delegates or Deputies." The reason Baltimore included this article is uncertain. It may have reflected his support for Parliament at this time; more likely he recognized that some such concession was necessary if he was to compete with Virginia for settlers. In any case an exemption clause was included which allowed the proprietor to promulgate ordinances unilaterally in an emergency, including martial law. The only restriction was that both kinds of law were to be "agreeable to the Laws, Statutes, Customs and Rights" of England. Those emigrating were otherwise entitled to the same "Privileges, Franchises and Liberties" as at home.[1]

This grant was indeed remarkable. In the fourteenth century the bishop had been given sweeping powers because of Durham's exposed position on the Scottish border. Similar reasoning may have influenced the issue of this grant, for Virginia's experience had proved the need for strong, decentralized government. Nevertheless, such authoritarian powers were already anomalous in England and were likely to prove so in America once the initial period of settlement was over.

The feudal nature of the document may have appealed to Baltimore for another reason, too. His colony clearly needed investors. If gentlemen of quality could be induced to purchase land, the need for shareholders would be eliminated. Accordingly the manorial rights were offered as a special inducement to the aristocracy and gentry.

The new patent mentioned the native inhabitants only as savages who might have to be repelled. The days of pretending that the conversion of the American Indian was part of God's noble work were clearly over.

---

[1] The full text can be found in W. Keith Kavenagh, *Foundations of Colonial America: A Documentary History*, 3 vols (New York, 1973), II, 756–63.

It took Baltimore's heir, the second Lord Cecilius, almost eighteen months to organize an expedition of about two hundred people. One reason for the delay was the disappointing response of wealthy investors, despite the charter's offer of special privileges. Protestant gentry were not attracted by the prospect of having a Catholic proprietor, while most Catholics had given up the idea of emigrating now that persecution had subsided. Nevertheless, some twenty-five gentlemen, mostly Catholics, did depart and contribute to the cost. The rest of the passengers were servants, artisans, or yeoman farmers, some of whom were Protestant.

From the start Baltimore emphasized that all Christian denominations would be welcome, for he realized that there were unlikely to be enough Catholics to make the scheme a success. In addition, Cecilius seems genuinely to have believed that coexistence was the best policy to ensure that his coreligionists would not remain an isolated and distrusted minority.

Cecilius's two ships finally left Portsmouth in November 1633, reaching the upper Chesapeake by way of the West Indies in March 1634. The first mass was celebrated on the Potomac near Blakiston. They then moved back down to begin the settlement of St. Mary's on the northern bank, having first bought the land from the local inhabitants in exchange for some axes and other implements. A fort was built with several cannon mounted on top, followed by a storehouse and chapel. Since the American Indians had already cleared some land, a crop of corn was possible. Fortunately, both the local Yoacomacos and the nearby Piscataways were friendly, seeing the newcomers as potential allies against their common foe, the Susquehannocks.

Baltimore himself was not one of the passengers, preferring to send his younger brother instead. During the next few years it was Leonard Calvert who began the task of organizing the colony according to the charter. The Catholic gentry with their servants proved invaluable in providing the nuclei for the first manors, the details of which were spelt out in an edict in 1636. The original gentlemen adventurers were to qualify for a grant of two thousand acres for every five servants they brought with them. Those who arrived thereafter would receive a grant of one thousand acres for the same number of retainers, while anyone bringing over a male servant would receive one hundred acres, or fifty acres for a maid. In return there was to be a sliding scale of rents, though all grants of over one thousand acres would qualify for manorial status, each with its own court in which the owner dispensed justice for petty misdemeanors, collected fees, and enjoyed certain other administrative privileges. Initially some twenty-five manors were patented and a total of sixty were to be established, ranging in size from one thousand to six thousand acres.

Although the Privy Council had overruled belated attempts by the Virginians to prevent this settlement, Baltimore was to experience further friction from that quarter. In May 1631 one of their number, William Claiborne, had obtained a commission from the Crown to develop Kent Island as an independent trading station. Apart from wishing to preserve control himself, Claiborne did not want to be the tenant of a Catholic landlord. The main conflict concerned Claiborne's right to trade, which according to Baltimore's charter had to be licensed from him. Shots were fired several times between vessels representing the rival elements. Fortunately for Baltimore, Claiborne was then disowned by his merchant associates in England; and the dispute ended in 1635 with Baltimore's men taking possession of the island by force.

The episode may have been one reason for the calling of the first representative assembly in Maryland. Leonard Calvert had apparently called all the freemen together earlier that

Plate 18 First Maryland State House, 1634–94 (reconstructed). St. Mary's City. Photographed by Glyn Lewis.

year. Baltimore, however, nullified their acts, insisting that only he had the right of proposing laws. The capture of Kent Island necessitated the calling of a more formal and representative body, since the inhabitants of the new territory could not travel so readily to St. Mary's. Accordingly a summons was issued for an assembly on January 25, 1638. Some freemen still attended in person, others sent a deputy. Altogether nineteen people were present, claiming to represent sixty-five freemen.

Among the acts passed was one prescribing an oath of loyalty to Charles I promising to defend him "against all conspiracies," a gesture necessary to reassure the authorities that Maryland was not going to be a haven for regicides like Guy Fawkes. Another defined the future nature of the legislature, which was to comprise the governor, council, lords of the manor, and one or two freemen elected from every hundred. A third, equally remarkable act laid down that an assembly was to be summoned at least once every three years, with "the like power, privileges, authority, and jurisdiction . . . as in the House of Commons." Clearly the assembly was seeking to acquire the characteristics of a parliament. An act was also passed attempting to secure all the rights of freemen in England "saving in such cases as . . . may be altered or changed by the laws and ordinances of this province."[2] The representatives were apprehensive because these rights had not been defined in the charter itself.

Because the assembly had no legal right to initiate this legislation, Baltimore nullified these acts too. The following year, however, he permitted Leonard to be more flexible. As

---

2 Kavenagh, *Documentary History*, II, 1009–12.

a result most of the laws were passed, though still not in the language demanded by the proprietor, being full of expressions about the rights of Parliament and the individual reminiscent of Magna Carta and other such precedents.

Ironically, these disagreements involved the people Baltimore most wanted to help. Among the Catholics was a group who wanted to expand the role of the Jesuits, led by Thomas Cornwallis, a wealthy investor. Baltimore, on the other hand, feared that the Jesuits would ruin his hopes of peaceful coexistence between Catholic and Protestant. Hence the early meetings of the assembly were dominated by two factions bidding for Protestant support.

Despite these disputes Maryland now contained perhaps five hundred inhabitants in three main clusters: St. Mary's, St. Clements, and St. George's, all organized as hundreds on the English model. They in turn contained sixteen manors, occupying over 80 percent of the patented land. Even at this stage, however, Baltimore's hopes for a European-style aristocracy were not high; only a handful of the original gentry remained, though several others had arrived to take their place.

Economically, though, the colony had established itself quickly, mainly because the requirements of settlement in the Chesapeake were now well known. Hence all the settlers immediately concentrated on making themselves self-sufficient in food by raising corn, cattle, hogs, and other livestock which flourished in the region. As in Virginia and New England, the Indian slash-and-burn method was used to clear the land. Corn was fenced rather than the livestock, in contrast to European practice. Cattle and hogs were left to fend for themselves because it was more profitable to use cleared land for crops. Only cows in milk were temporarily fenced. There were risks to this method of husbandry from wolves and other hazards, but the savings in labor more than offset the dangers.

During the early years most farmers also planted an orchard for cider, since growing barley for beer, or any other European grains, required the use of a plow, which was not feasible while the ground was full of stumps. Draft animals were in any case costly to maintain, and plows were therefore not common during the first fifty years of English settlement.

Once these initial tasks were completed, attention was devoted to tobacco growing, especially after the fur trade failed to develop. Although tobacco prices were only a fraction of what they had been ten years earlier, the market now was much wider. Consequently the settlers could sell all that they grew.

Even so, the following years were not tranquil. The ascendancy of Parliament, with its anti-Catholic majority, after 1640 was fraught with danger for the new settlement. Furthermore, the outbreak of hostilities in England meant that Baltimore was cut off from his province, a situation which worsened in 1642 when Leonard came to England to consult with his brother, leaving a political vacuum in America. Soon Claiborne reappeared to seize Kent Island, while Richard Ingle, a London tobacco trader masquerading as the protector of Protestantism, succeeded in capturing St. Mary's. Thus when Leonard returned to Maryland in the autumn of 1644 he was compelled to flee to Virginia. For two years Maryland, without any government, endured "the plundering time," which continued until Leonard returned with aid from Governor Berkeley of Virginia. Ingle then returned to England to accuse Baltimore and Leonard of harboring treasonous recusants. In the event he did not prove his case and Baltimore, by dexterous maneuvering, not least the appeasement of the London merchants, managed to keep his charter. Parliament still had many aristocrats anxious to show that proprietary rights were not incompatible with the parliamentary cause.

The effects on Maryland were nevertheless deplorable. Neighbor was set against neighbor in a climate of suspicion and fear. To calm the situation Baltimore appointed a Protestant, William Stone, as governor, but even more was required. In 1649 he presented the assembly with a bill for religious toleration, introduced for a number of reasons. One was the continuing need to pacify the authorities in England. Another was perhaps the hope that such a bill would induce a predominantly Protestant assembly to acknowledge the proprietary authority. A third reason was that the Catholics themselves now needed protection. The Protestant population had greatly increased with the arrival in 1643 of Richard Bennett and some four hundred Puritans from Virginia, following the expulsion of their ministers by Governor Berkeley and the Anglican church. Indeed, the Act Concerning Religion can be seen as the first attempt to protect a minority group, an unusual phenomenon in the seventeenth century, when the reverse was usually the motivation behind religious legislation.

Baltimore was undoubtedly sincere in wanting to calm the religious passions in Maryland. He may have been inspired by the new climate in England itself, where the belief was growing that Christian unity was unobtainable and that toleration was the only course. Certainly Cecilius's own measure was influenced by such reasoning. The act did not positively affirm toleration, but it made intolerance a crime, at least among Christians. Non-Christians, of course, were not included.[3]

Unfortunately, the measure served to exacerbate the tension, since the Puritan newcomers were interested in toleration only for themselves. They were soon aided by events in England, where in 1650 Parliament decided to dispatch a commission to seize Bermuda, Antigua, Barbados, and Virginia. Maryland was included by implication, for Baltimore's old enemy, Claiborne, was on the commission, as was Bennett. These men quickly seized the chance in 1651 to install themselves in power.

Nevertheless, the continuing instability in England encouraged Baltimore to try to reassert his authority. Maryland was divided between the lower counties of St. Mary's and St. George's, which were loyal to the proprietor and the Act for Religious Toleration, and Anne Arundel and Kent counties, which wanted a commonwealth like Massachusetts from which Catholics and even Anglicans were barred. When Governor Stone's advance toward the Severn River in March 1655 resulted in a complete victory for the Puritans, four of the invading proprietary party were executed, while many of the rest had to pay heavy fines or flee for their lives.

This battle was not the end of the conflict, which could ultimately be decided only in London. Here Baltimore's contacts and diplomatic skills gave him an advantage. Oliver Cromwell now ruled England as lord protector, and he had little sympathy for the extreme demands of the Maryland Puritans. In consequence the two parties had to compromise. At the end of 1657 Baltimore was reinstated as proprietor, in return for which he pardoned his opponents, who then accepted the Act Concerning Religion. It was essentially this situation which prevailed when the monarchy was restored under Charles II in 1660, though Baltimore experienced more trouble when his first governor, Josiah Fendall, aligned himself with the Puritan opposition.

During the mid-1640s Maryland's population had fallen to under four hundred. Thereafter it grew, aided by immigration from Virginia. Maryland's popularity may have increased

---

[3] For the full text see Kavenagh, *Documentary History*, II, 1322–4.

DOCUMENT 10

An Act Concerning Religion, reprinted in W. Keith Kavenagh, *Foundations of Colonial America: A Documentary History* (New York, 1973), II, 1322–4.

[This unique act anticipated George Mason's Virginia Bill of Rights by 130 years in its provisions for religious toleration. Unlike Mason and the later federal Bill of Rights, Baltimore's act extended only to Christians, excluding American Indian and African religious beliefs. Remarkably, the second article introduces the concept of "politically correct" language as a way of calming tensions in a multicultural society.]

Be it therefore ordered and enacted that . . .

[2.] whatsoever person or persons shall, from henceforth upon any occasion of offense or otherwise, in reproachful manner or way declare, call or denominate any person or persons whatsoever inhabiting, residing, trading, or commercing within this province an Heretic, Schismatic, Idolator, Puritan, Independent, Presbyterian, Popish Priest, Jesuit, Jesuited Papist, Lutheran, Calvinist, Anabaptist, Brownist, Antinomian, Barrowist, Roundhead, Separatist, or any other name or term in a reproachful manner relating to matters of religion, shall, for every such offense forfeit and lose the sum of ten shillings sterling [half to the victim, the other half to the Proprietor].

[4] And whereas the enforcing of conscience in matters of religion has frequently [proved] of dangerous consequence in those commonwealths where it has been practised; and for the more quiet and peaceable government of this province and the better to preserve mutual love and amity amongst the inhabitants thereof. Be it therefore also by the Lord Proprietary, with the advice and consent of this Assembly, ordained and enacted . . . that no person or persons whatsoever within this province . . . professing to believe in Jesus Christ, shall, from henceforth, be any ways troubled, molested, or discountenanced for or in respect of his or her religion, nor in the free exercise thereof within this province or the islands thereunto belonging, nor any way compelled to the belief or exercise of any other religion against his or her consent. . . . [Offenders to pay treble damages to the wronged party or suffer a severe whipping and imprisonment at the discretion of the Proprietor.]

owing to Baltimore's liberal land policy. In 1640 the legislature provided that on completion of their service, all male servants were to receive three barrels of corn, a new outfit of clothes, some tools, and fifty acres of land. This headright was later confirmed by Baltimore in 1648.

Even so Maryland was no paradise for servants. Both males and females were expected to work long hours in the field, on the farm, or in the household, being constantly at the call of their masters and mistresses, whose main aim was the extraction of productive labour. Those who ran away could expect to do extra time, as could women servants who became pregnant. Despite various laws, beatings were common, diet was rarely sufficient, clothing and housing were frequently inadequate, and medical attention was negligible. A wasting sickness like malaria was often mistaken for laziness; and because sickness meant that someone else had to do that person's job, bullying by fellow servants, overseers, and masters was common. Not surprisingly, 40 percent did not survive their period of indenture. Those who did, who wished to become planters, still had to pay the surveyor's fees and register their land, as well as buy essential items to get their farms established. Such an outlay being initially beyond the means of most servants, the usual options were to continue as laborers or to lease some land, possibly on a sharecropping basis. Fortunately, wages were high, as the price of tobacco rose during the 1650s, so many servants, perhaps as many as half of those attaining their freedom, did acquire their own farms in time, though some took as long as twelve years to become freeholders. In one respect the 1650s was a golden period for servants, there being no elite other than the proprietor and a few gentry. Never again were social classes to be so fluid.[4]

Like Virginia, Maryland had an overwhelmingly male social structure, the ratio in some areas being perhaps six males to every female. Male servants were preferred, since they were generally physically more capable of performing the exhausting tasks of clearing the land, working the soil, and erecting houses and barns. Domestic maids in such wilderness conditions were an unnecessary luxury. Maryland's population too, therefore, could grow only by means of constant immigration.

The social consequences of this imbalance between the sexes were enormous. For men it meant a late marriage and little family life, causing many ex-servants to band together to form their first households. For women, paradoxically, the imbalance meant the opposite. Not only could they expect an earlier marriage, but they generally had a choice of suitors, usually someone with property. Remarriage was also much easier if a partner died. Some women, blessed with exceptional health, married three or four times. The scarcity of women also meant that many female servants did not have to complete their indenture, if an acceptable suitor was prepared to buy out their remaining period of service.

Another factor inhibiting family life was the high mortality rate among both men and women. Only one-third of marriages lasted more than ten years. As a consequence, 20 percent of all children were orphaned by age twelve, and most experienced the death of one parent before their majority. This led to the establishment of special orphan courts, something quite unknown in England. Thus stable family life was virtually impossible, and few enjoyed the kinship patterns which prevailed in New England. One compensation was that children came into their inheritances early and could marry without parental constraint. Women, too, benefited, as their scarcity allowed them to insist on better marriages.[5] Of

---

[4] The traditional view has been to see America as a land of opportunity for all emigrants. This view was especially popular in the nineteenth century when the examples of Andrew Carnegie and others were regularly cited. More recently the tendency has been to emphasize that only the lucky few made such progress, even in the earliest years when the social and economic structures were fluid. See Lois Green Carr and Russell R. Menard, "Immigration and Opportunity: The Freedman in Early Colonial Maryland," in Thad W. Tate and David L. Ammerman, eds, *The Chesapeake in the Seventeenth Century: Essays on Anglo-American Society* (Chapel Hill, 1979), 206–42.

[5] Until twenty years ago the structure of the population in the Chesapeake was totally overlooked because historians limited their investigations to evidence from the small, literate part of the population. Since the late 1960s, the availability of computers and new statistical methods have allowed early colonial society to be reconstituted using hitherto ignored parish registers, tax lists, wills, conveyances, and account books. See Russell R. Menard, "Immigrants and their Increase: The Process of Population Growth in Early Colonial Maryland," in Aubrey C. Land, Lois Green Carr, and Edward C. Papenfuse, eds, *Law, Society, and Politics in Early Maryland*

course families of a kind did exist. Surviving parents usually remarried, creating a new type of family, comprising half-brothers and half-sisters, stepfathers and stepchildren. Although such unions created problems of inheritance and emotional adjustment, they often fostered a sense of community, love, and affection.

Meanwhile the relative availability of land had proved to be the death knell of the manorial system, since it became difficult to keep people on the manor. One manor, St. Clements, owned by Thomas Gerard, was still functioning in 1660, with sixteen tenants and nine freeholders. Nevertheless, the returns were poor, and within a few years Gerard began to buy slaves as a more profitable way of developing his land. The hundreds became parishes, and they in turn were grouped into counties on the English model. Although one or two manors continued to function, justice and administration were increasingly dispensed by the county courts.

Indeed Maryland was increasingly adopting the appearance of its neighbor to the south in many other respects, having the same pyramidal social structure of gentry planters, yeoman farmers, dependent tenants, and indentured servants. As in Virginia, there was a complete absence of towns, because the planters here too insisted on having a waterfront from which to export their crops. Their housing, comprising mostly timber-frame cottages, was also similar. And from Virginia to Maryland came the first Africans, though their numbers were small – around one hundred – and their status was equally unclear until after 1660. Thus whatever the initial differences, the two Chesapeake societies were rapidly converging in their economic and social, if not their political, structures.

2 NEW YORK AND DELAWARE: THE DUTCH AND SWEDISH BEGINNINGS

England, of course, was not the only European nation colonizing North America after 1600. The Spanish had a presence in Florida, while the French were establishing themselves along the St. Lawrence at Quebec. Of more immediate concern to the English, however, were the activities of the Dutch on the Hudson River.

Ironically, the first real exploration of this area was carried out by an Englishman, Henry Hudson, operating on behalf of the Dutch East India Company. Hudson's mission in 1609 was to find the elusive northwest passage, in pursuit of which he proceeded as far as present-day Albany. Since the Dutch interest was trade rather than settlement, Hudson's employers merely established an outpost called Fort Nassau in 1613 to barter with the local inhabitants for furs. It lasted only a couple of years.

When it appeared in 1620 that war was about to break out again between Spain and Holland, Dutch interest in the area revived, because a base might be required for operations across the Atlantic. Since the Dutch East India Company was preoccupied elsewhere, a new corporation was formed to establish a base and exploit the area's commercial opportunities.

(Baltimore, 1977); Lorena S. Walsh, "Till Death Us Do Part: Marriage and Family in Seventeenth Century Maryland," in Thad W. Tate and David L. Ammerman, eds, *The Chesapeake in the Seventeenth Century: Essays on Anglo-American Society* (Chapel Hill (1979); Gloria L. Main, *Tobacco Colony: Life in Early Maryland, 1650–1720* (Princeton, 1982); and Russell R. Menard, *Economy and Society in Early Maryland* (New York, 1985). Similar problems were experienced in Virginia: see chapter 7, section 1.

Initially, the Dutch West India Company devoted its attention to Bahia in the Caribbean. In 1624, however, a group of settlers was dispatched to the mainland of North America under Cornelius May. Since the threat of war had by this time receded, most of the party went to the site of the earlier post, now called Fort Orange, to resume the fur trade. A smaller group settled on Governor's Island at the mouth of the Hudson, while a further detachment went to the Delaware Valley, establishing Fort Nassau near the future city of Philadelphia.

The following year, as more settlers arrived, a post was set up on Manhattan Island called New Amsterdam. Here a fort was built, together with a church and residence for the governor, or director general. Clustered round it were several farms. It was this settlement which Willem Verhulst and his successor, Peter Minuit, made good when they purchased the island from the Manhattan Indians for sixty guilders in 1626.

In many respects the Dutch company resembled that of Virginia in its early stages. Governmental authority lay primarily with the director general and his officials, though they were supposed to seek the occasional advice of a council drawn from the inhabitants. Most settlers arrived as servants of the company, usually for a period of six years. After this they could take up tenancies, as in Virginia. The Dutch colonists, however, were required only to grow food. To get themselves established they were given land, tools, livestock, and grain. Those who came as freemen could farm on their own, but everyone had to buy and sell through the company storehouse.

Although the settlement was slow to grow, it never experienced the tribulations of Virginia. Since the land on Manhattan and the surrounding area proved suitable for growing wheat, rye, barley, and oats, the settlement was self-sufficient from the outset. Shipbuilding, too, was possible, given the plentiful supply of timber, while the growing of barley and oats meant that beer could be brewed.

Despite these attractions, the colony remained unappealing to most Dutchmen, for by 1630 it contained only three hundred inhabitants, many of them Walloons from southern Flanders. The reluctance to emigrate was mainly on account of prosperity at home and more enticing prospects in the East and West Indies. In addition, New Netherland had proved disappointing financially. In 1626 one vessel had returned with 7,246 beaver skins and by 1635 exports had risen to 16,304 pelts. But much of this production remained outside the company's control. Agriculturally the settlement was also unrewarding, for it produced no really valuable staple. Hence by 1628 the company determined not to invest any more in the project.

Since the desirability of having a privateering and trading base remained, the directors decided to adopt one of the Virginia Company's earlier expedients, that of offering special privileges to private investors. Anyone bringing over fifty able-bodied persons would be offered a large tract of land with manorial rights, called a patroonship. Each patroon was to receive a four-mile stretch of the Hudson River extending back east or west as far as the land went. The only restriction was that the proprietor must first secure title by purchasing the land from the local inhabitants. The patroon had the right to the minerals and game on his land, and he could also trade along the coast, subject to a 5-percent duty payable at New Amsterdam. He was not to engage in manufacturing, however, and in due course he had to support a minister and schoolmaster. A doctor also would be desirable.[6]

---

[6] See Kavenagh, *Documentary History*, II, 984–8, for the full text.

Although several patents were issued, only Kiliaen Van Rensselaer, a wealthy merchant and investor in the Dutch West India Company, made any real attempt to establish a patroonship. He secured a large tract of land in the vicinity of Fort Orange. During the next fifteen years he sent out over two hundred tenants to cultivate his patrimony.

The grant to Van Rensselaer was one sign that the company's monopoly on the economic life of New Netherland was being eroded. During the ensuing years a number of smaller grants were made to those who paid their passage and had money to invest, though land was granted only on condition that one-tenth of all produce was payable as quitrent. Still, it was enough to attract a larger trickle of settlers, especially after 1638, when the company relaxed its monopoly on the fur trade and commerce with Holland and introduced a headright scheme, granting a freehold of two hundred acres to each colonist who brought over a family of five. Thereafter some Germans from Westphalia, a few Jews, some French Protestants, and Puritans from New England arrived, the latter by way of Long Island. Some Africans were also imported to work as domestic servants and laborers. A French Jesuit who visited New Amsterdam in 1643 commented on the town's "confusion of tongues."

Like all Europeans, the Dutch in New Netherland were not free from troubles with the American Indians. There were two main causes of conflict, the first being control of the fur trade north of Albany, the second the use of land around New Amsterdam. The fur trade was conducted principally from Fort Orange. For the first few years the company tried to steer a middle course between the Mahicans, an Algonquian-speaking tribe, and the Mohawks, one of the Five Nations of the Iroquois, as the two battled for control of the area. After the triumph of the Mohawks in 1628, however, the company had to change its policy, formally aligning itself with the Mohawks after Arent van Curler, a relative of Van Rensselaer, visited their country in 1642.

Meanwhile the principal activity on Manhattan and the lower Hudson was farming, which inevitably brought the colonists into conflict with the indigenous inhabitants, notably the Manhattan and Wappinger peoples. Initially, the company tried to avoid such conflict by insisting on proper treaties for the purchase of all land. However, American Indian understanding of the concept of purchase extended for a limited period only; it did not in their eyes mean permanent and irrevocable surrender. The Dutch were in any case Calvinists like the New Englanders, and they saw no reason to treat the American Indians according to the conventions which governed behavior between Europeans. As the colony grew, so the need to accommodate them lessened. Relations were not improved when Director General Kieft began levying a tribute on wampum in 1639 to solve the company's financial problems. The native inhabitants of the lower Hudson had large quantities of wampum, which they made from the abundant supply of oyster shells along the Long Island coast. The belts had two colors: white represented peace and health; purple implied war and death. They had become highly valued by the northeastern tribes because of their fine workmanship and symbolic significance. Wampum had in consequence become an important medium of exchange.[7]

Nevertheless, serious trouble was delayed until 1643, when Kieft resolved on retaliation for a number of murders. The recent treaty with the Mohawks may have contributed

---

[7] The commerce in wampum was relatively new, since the iron tools necessary for its mass production had only been available since the arrival of the Dutch.

to subsequent events, since there is evidence that the Dutch invited their new allies to assist them in the assault. The hostilities began on February 25, 1643 with a bloody massacre, reminiscent of the destruction of the Pequots, when a contingent of Dutch soldiers surrounded the village of Pavonia and set it on fire. All those trying to escape, including women and children, were brutally cut down. The attack was especially reprehensible because most of the victims were refugees who had fled the Mohawks to seek asylum with the Dutch. This assault in turn provoked reprisals. Among the victims was Anne Hutchinson, who had settled with her family on eastern Long Island. Peace was reestablished only in 1645, by which time much of the province had been devastated and a thousand American Indians killed.

Another reason for the slow growth of New Netherland was the autocratic nature of its government, which reflected an ownership concentrated in the hands of a few wealthy persons. There was no general assembly of stockholders as in Virginia and Massachusetts through which power could be diffused to the settlers. New Netherland was ruled for most of its history by the director general and a few officials who implemented company policy, dispensed justice, and levied the company's dues. When trouble with the native inhabitants was brewing in 1641, Kieft did order the heads of households to choose twelve men to represent them. When they demanded a more responsive administration, however, they were promptly dismissed. Two years later Kieft arranged another meeting, this time summoning eight representatives, who immediately repeated their predecessors' protests against the company's arbitrary taxation. Even more boldly, they wrote home demanding a new director general.

This action led to a partial reorganization of the colony in 1645. Authority in future was to be concentrated in the hands of three officials: a director general, his deputy, and a fiscal. Together they were to make up a council, though they were to continue the concession of allowing "one or two persons to inform the director and council, at least every twelve months, of the state and condition" of their settlements, foreshadowing a possible future assembly.

To help the economic development of the colony, permission was given to private individuals to import Africans, which pleased the larger merchants and landowners since it eased the labor shortage, while another concession granted the right to trade overseas on payment of a customs duty. Here, effectively, was New Netherland's equivalent to Virginia's Charter of Liberties.

These changes were inaugurated by Peter Stuyvesant, who was appointed director general in July 1646, having previously been in charge at Curaçao. Stuyvesant was a military man, and his background may explain much of his subsequent directorship. He duly allowed the election of nine inhabitants to consult about the levying of taxes but soon terminated the experiment. Indeed, within two years the inhabitants were writing to the States-General in Holland complaining about the autocratic manner of the director general, who browbeat everyone "in foul language better fitting the fishmarket than the council board." They charged Stuyvesant with openly breaking the contraband laws by selling arms to the American Indians, even though others were hanged for doing so. They also asserted that he had arbitrarily confiscated property for the nonpayment of taxes, ignoring the fact that many people were late in paying because they had suffered heavily in the recent war. New Netherland's bad reputation was affecting trade, the petitioners urged. Compared with Virginia and New England, the Dutch colony presented a miserable spectacle, the only remedy for which was the disbanding of the company, for it was apparently indifferent to the settlers' fate.

These complaints have a perennial ring to them, reflecting as they do the conflicting interests of the center and the periphery. Perhaps for this reason they were largely ignored, the only concession being to turn New Amsterdam into a municipality in 1652. The sheriff and Burghermaster, however, were still appointed by the director general. The following year Stuyvesant did summon representatives from the various settlements, mainly because war threatened with England; but when no offers of money were forthcoming he unilaterally imposed additional taxes on land, livestock, and rents. Additional revenue was also the motivation for creating two new classes of burgher in 1657; the purpose was to raise enough money to complete the city's defenses by selling full or half memberships. The privileges were in any case commercial not political.

During the 1640s a number of New Englanders began settling on Long Island, and by the 1650s both Dutch and English villages were demanding local government. In due course this was granted, but it was hardly what the New Englanders wanted, since the officials were chosen by the director general. The one concession was that the appointees were residents, but this was as far as local participation could go.

The only other freedom enjoyed by the inhabitants of New Netherland was that of religious toleration. Jews were permitted to settle there, and from 1657 became burghers, as in Holland. Though only a handful did so, their status was testimony to the tolerant nature of the Dutch back home, in contrast to other European nations.[8] The arrival of the Quakers, however, prompted the director general to issue an edict in 1656 banning all Christian services which were not held according to the Calvinist Synod of Dort. Given the heterogeneous nature of the population, the edict proved unworkable, and it was relaxed in 1663.

The relatively benign nature of Dutch society was also reflected in the company's treatment of its African slaves. Manumission was possible and many worked for wages. A few even bought small farms on securing their freedom so that by 1650 one in five Africans was free. The records of the Dutch Reformed church also show that the enslaved had their marriages blessed and infants baptized. On occasion they were even successful in the courts. However, many of those of manumitted were elderly and of little further use. Significantly, their children were not freed and, as in Virginia, the opportunities for both free and enslaved blacks diminished as their numbers increased and the colony became more settled. By 1660 two out of every five households in New York City had a black slave.

In general the province offered a mean prospect during its first forty years. New Amsterdam itself had over three hundred dwellings by 1660, with thirteen hundred inhabitants. Nevertheless, its housing was poor and there were few buildings of any distinction. The fort was dilapidated. The streets were an open sewer, for many residents had their privies close to the highway, and the offal was constantly scattered by hogs roaming the neighborhood. The director general and council issued several ordinances in an effort to clean up the town, imposing fines against those who did not control their animals by putting a ring through the nose. Other penalties were imposed for siting a privy near a public highway.

---

[8] For the rise of the Jewish community in the Americas, see Jacob R. Marcus, *The Colonial American Jew, 1492–1776*, 3 vols (Detroit, 1970). The number of Jews throughout the colonial period was small.

Another problem during these years was rowdy behavior on the Sabbath. In 1647 an edict prohibited the sale of all alcohol during divine service. The following year another ordinance urged everyone to attend church and stop trading for a couple of hours. Perhaps not surprisingly, New Netherland remained an unpopular destination for the potential settlers back home. This state of affairs was unfortunate for, as the remonstrants in 1648 had said, more settlers would lead to increased trade. But people would not come to a place without good government, and in this respect New Netherland's reputation remained low.

On the other hand, the province was by no means destitute. The fur trade brought in a steady income, and the colony was more than self-sufficient. In the late 1650s, however, a scarcity of beaver depressed the value of wampum, so that Stuyvesant had to issue a proclamation to stabilize prices and prevent profiteering. Also, further trouble with the Algonquian Indians resulted in what came to be called the Peach War. This time the trouble began when a squaw was killed as she took fruit from an orchard; before hostilities ended a considerable number of Dutch and Algonquian settlements had been ravaged. One consequence was the need for an office in New Amsterdam to look after orphaned children.

Dutch settlement was not confined to the Hudson Valley, for the company also had claims to the Delaware or South River. These claims were disputed by Sweden, which first became involved when King Augustus Adolphus chartered a general company to trade with Africa, Asia, and America. It achieved little until 1636, when a new charter was secured specifically for the Delaware region. Ironically the first group of Swedes was taken there late in 1637 by the former director general of New Netherland, Peter Minuit, who established Fort Christiana near present-day Wilmington.

New Sweden was always a struggling entity, dependent for its existence on Dutch capital and expertise. Sweden was remote, and its energies were devoted mainly to the Protestant cause in Europe. More important, the venture on the Delaware was inveterately opposed by the Dutch West India Company. On first hearing the news of Minuit's settlement, Kieft had warned that New Netherland would preserve its sovereignty. For a time Johan Printz maintained the Swedish presence by building several stockades. However, the enterprise was starved of investment, and Swedish control finally ended in 1655 with the capture of Fort Casimir by the Dutch.

Under the terms negotiated between Stuyvesant and the Swedish director, all the inhabitants were allowed to depart with their possessions. Those who stayed were to swear loyalty to the Dutch States General. Stuyvesant then appointed a deputy director general to govern the area as a province of New Netherland. To consolidate Dutch control, the Burghermasters of Amsterdam offered prospective emigrants various inducements to leave Holland, for example, exempting settlers from all rents or taxes for ten years and providing a schoolmaster and minister. About 160 recruits took up the offer.

Swedish encroachments were not the only problem facing the Dutch. More threatening was the spread of the English settlements on Long Island and along the coast. During the 1643 hostilities with the American Indians the Dutch and English had cooperated, but once that danger receded the tension between them returned. The Dutch still occupied Fort Hope on the Connecticut River but were becoming increasingly isolated by the presence of English colonists in that area.

The Dutch recognized that they could not treat the English as they would later treat the tiny colony of New Sweden in 1655. Consequently, Stuyvesant decided to negotiate, and in September 1650 he met with representatives of the New England confederacy and agreed to a boundary line dividing Long Island in the vicinity of Oyster Bay. Two sources of potential conflict remained, however: the Dutch were to keep their post at Hartford, and the English settlements of Flushing and Hempstead remained on the Dutch side of the border.

Although this treaty was not recognized by Cromwell, Massachusetts insisted on honoring it when war broke out between England and Holland in 1654, being reluctant to fight a Protestant neighbor merely for the sake of England's commerce. Connecticut, however, took a different view and unilaterally seized Fort Hope. With the remaining English settlements in New Netherland still expressing discontent, it was clear that another conflict was only a matter of time.

6

The Restoration Era

1658	Oliver Cromwell dies.
1660	The English monarchy is restored under Charles II. The first Navigation Act enumerates exports from the colonies.
1662	Charters are confirmed for Rhode Island and Connecticut.
1663	The second Navigation Act regulates exports to the colonies. A proprietary grant is issued to the Carolinas.
1664	A royal commission investigates New England. New Netherland is captured by the English in the Second Dutch War.
1665	The Duke's Laws are issued for New York.
1666	Much of London is destroyed in the Great Fire.
1669	The Fundamental Constitutions are drawn up for the Carolinas.
1670	Old Charles Town is founded.
1672–4	Third Dutch War
1673	The third Navigation Act regulates intercolonial trade.
1677	Culpepper's rising takes place in North Carolina. Governor Andros negotiates the Covenant Chain with the Iroquois.
1680	The Westo Indians in South Carolina are destroyed. Charleston is moved to the junction of the Cooper and Ashley rivers.
1683	New York holds its first assembly and issues the Charter of Liberties.

1   THE RETURN OF CHARLES II

OLIVER CROMWELL DIED in September 1658. His son Richard succeeded him but soon proved unequal to the task, especially that of controlling the army. Within eighteen months it was clear that only the recall of the Stuart dynasty could save the country from anarchy.

Charles II has traditionally been portrayed as the "merry monarch" of the Stuart dynasty. In contrast to his inflexible and haughty father, Charles I, he had a great sense of fun and love of life, not to mention his mistresses, of whom Nell Gwyn was the best known. Easygoing and relaxed, the new king wanted above all to enjoy a quiet life politically after his eleven years as a refugee.

The restoration of Charles II in the spring of 1660 produced a mixed response from England's North American colonies. Virginia and Maryland were generally favorable. Virginia had been strongly loyal to the Stuarts until the dispatch of the Claiborne–Bennett commission. The Maryland settlers were more divided, but the colony's affiliations were determined by its proprietor, who was firmly for the Crown.

In the northern colonies the Restoration received a much cooler reception. Only Rhode Island, which was in need of friends, acted expeditiously, proclaiming Charles II king in October 1660. Elsewhere the various settlements delayed, weighing the dubious advantages of recognition against the likelihood of punishment should they fail to do so. The possible ramifications were enormous, as all acts passed by the English Commonwealth were likely to be overturned. It was not yet certain, however, that the monarchy's restoration would be permanent, and the penalties for a premature declaration might be severe. Thus Connecticut did not proclaim for the new monarch until March 1661; New Haven followed in June 1661. In August 1661, Massachusetts became the last settlement to recognize Charles II, though a loyal address had been sent privately the previous November.

When Charles II ascended the throne, the affairs of the North American colonies, whose population was after all still less than eighty thousand, were not paramount. The king was much more concerned with regaining his authority, summoning a new Parliament, and determining the religious settlement of England.

Initially it was hoped that the overall settlement would be reasonably favorable to Dissenters. Once Parliament met, however, the Tory majority quickly restored the Church of England to its former position, complete with bishops and other symbols inimical to the Puritans. Even worse, it was soon clear that those who dissented would be penalized. First, the Corporation Act of 1661 prohibited all Dissenters from holding office. Next, the Act of Uniformity required all services to be conducted according to the Book of Common Prayer. Later, the Conventicle Act fined Dissenters for holding meetings, while the Five Mile Act effectively prohibited their ministers from entering any town.

Amidst all this legislation there was one small comfort. These harsh laws were imposed by Parliament, not the Crown, and seemingly applied only in England. Charles II himself had little stomach for them, preferring a more tolerant stance. His main concern was the maintenance of royal authority, not the extension of Parliament's power. Hence the only immediate effect of the Restoration in the colonies was the royal instruction of September 1661 to cease the prosecution of Quakers. In future Quaker offenders were to be sent to England for trial.

Most New England colonies, including Massachusetts, now sent emissaries to express their loyalty. Rhode Island and Connecticut in addition took the opportunity to have their charters confirmed. It proved an expedient move, for in his formal response on colonial matters in April 1662 Charles II made only four relatively lenient demands. The first was that while regicides were to be prosecuted, all other infractions of the laws were to be pardoned. Second, everyone was required to take an oath of allegiance and all laws derogatory to the royal authority were to be annulled. Third, anyone conforming to the Book of Common Prayer was to receive the sacrament. Lastly, "all freemen, of competent estates, not vicious in conversation, and orthodox in religion" were to have the vote.

Rhode Island, Connecticut, and Plymouth quickly accepted these conditions. They harbored no participants involved in the execution of Charles I and were glad to take the oath of allegiance, since it merely reinforced the temporal authority of the king. Admission to the communion concerned only Anglicans, of whom there were very few, and there was nothing else in the royal instructions which undermined their existing religious arrangements.

Connecticut and Rhode Island were duly rewarded. Rhode Island had its grant of 1644 confirmed under the great seal; Connecticut was similarly granted a charter which conformed closely to its existing Fundamental Orders. Especially pleasing to its emissary, John Winthrop, Jr., was the incorporation of New Haven as part of its grant. New Haven itself bitterly protested this measure, justly accusing Winthrop of sharp practice, since he had agreed to represent its interests. New Haven may have been punished because it had concealed two of the regicide judges, William Goffe and Edward Whalley, and was slow to recognize Charles II.

The king made a similar offer to confirm Massachusetts's charter, but to no avail, the general court holding the view that its existing grant endowed sufficient authority. Allegiance to the king merely meant not conspiring against him, nor aiding any foreign prince, nor harboring any fugitives from justice. Nothing more was required.

The slow response of Massachusetts and some other New England settlements led Charles II to renew his four demands in April 1664. This time he dispatched four commissioners to back them up. Compliance was urgent, since war with Holland was threatening. Indeed, the commissioners were to travel as part of a force for the capture of New Netherland. The tone of their instructions was conciliatory, since Charles II wanted New England's help against the Dutch. The commissioners, therefore, were to reassure the colonists that their various churches would be respected and indeed, were told privately not to listen to self-appointed friends of the Church of England, who might stir up animosity. In addition the commissioners were to create no apprehension about taxes, as any necessary revenues would be raised through the existing assemblies. Their main objective was to secure the "obedience and loyalty" of the New England colonies, which could best be done if the Crown had a say in the nomination of their governors and militia officers.

The commissioners, led by Colonel Richard Nicholls, duly visited the several settlements. All except Massachusetts were anxious to show that they had conformed to the king's four points of April 1662. When the commissioners arrived at Plymouth, its leaders raised the question of a new charter, explaining that the colony had been too poor to send a special mission to London. They then produced their old grant from the Council of New England. The commissioners agreed to forward this and then suggested that Plymouth name three men from whom the king might select a governor. This offer was politely declined, though with great protestations of loyalty.

The commissioners' hope that the conduct of the other New England colonies would make Massachusetts more amenable was dashed in October 1664, when the general court actually petitioned the king to recall the commission. The Puritan leaders reiterated that the existing charter had given them permission to go into the wilderness at their own expense to govern themselves and practice their religion. If this freedom of worship was not respected, they might have to remove to another jurisdiction, by which they meant that of Holland. The Massachusetts Puritans' only concession was to enact a new franchise law in August 1664. In future, property with a rental value of ten shillings would qualify an individual for freemanship and thus the right to vote, provided a certificate from their minister confirmed that the person was "orthodox in religion." While the royal intention was to allow Anglicans to participate in affairs, this new law was clearly designed to do the exact opposite by keeping the saints in control.

In the event Massachusetts remained obdurate on all the points specified by Charles II. The commissioners had been authorized to hear appeals from the local courts, but the magistrates refused to acknowledge their authority, affirming that "the general court was the supremest judicatory." Another cause for disquiet was the Massachusetts *Book of General Lawes and Libertyes* which contained not a single reference to the king. The commissioners recommended that the king's name be substituted for "commonwealth" and similar titles. The commissioners also recognized that the new freemanship law was a sham, since only three persons in a hundred had ratable property of ten shillings; church membership was still the real criterion for participation in the colony's affairs.

Earlier the general court had ordered the New Hampshire settlements not to cooperate with the commissioners during their visit there. The commissioners were further angered by the knowledge that Whalley and Goffe had passed through Boston with much feasting, even though they had been declared traitors. Clearly, they felt, unless a firm stand was taken the province would continue to produce schismatics and rebels.

The commissioners noted that the general court set much store by the possibility that the Dutch war might produce political unpheaval in England, and that the court was quite likely to adopt the tactic of writing letters and doing nothing.[1]

In the event the commissioners were proved right. First, they themselves were captured on the voyage home by a Dutch warship, so that they were unable to make their report until December 1665. When Charles II then offered the colony one last chance to explain itself, Massachusetts simply prevaricated. Such defiance might have seemed foolhardy, but although the Dutch war had not produced the hoped-for political deliverance, Charles II had too many other concerns to enforce his demands. London was devastated first by the plague and a year later by the Great Fire, while in Europe the ambitions of Louis XIV were of increasing concern. For the moment Massachusetts was able to do as it pleased, even annexing Maine, though the commissioners had arranged for that area's settlements to be administered independently.

In reality the Crown still lacked the machinery of government to enforce its decisions. At the start of his reign Charles II had created a council of trade, but its members invariably had other responsibilities, and the body received little money for bureaucratic support.

---

[1] The full text of the commissioners' report can be found in W. Keith Kavenagh, *Foundations of Colonial America: A Documentary History*, 3 vols (New York, 1973), I, 133–42.

Provided the New England colonists acknowledged Charles II, recognized the laws of trade, and did not harbor regicides, they could still expect to remain self-governing.

2 MERCANTILISM: THE NAVIGATION LAWS

Although the Crown had only limited political objectives regarding the colonies, it had taken decisive action to regulate their economic relationship with England through the introduction of what later came to be known as the mercantilist system.[2]

The material benefits of owning colonies had been a prime reason for chartering the first trading companies. Attention had initially been fixed on the discovery of precious metals, a phase usually associated with bullionism. But once the colonies began producing valuable commodities like tobacco, this perspective changed. Now the key to wealth and national power was a favorable balance of trade. This could best be achieved by monopoly in the production and export of such commodities. Mercantilists believed that there was a fixed amount of wealth in the world and that the greater the share secured by one nation, the less remained for others. Accordingly, in 1621 James I announced that all tobacco must first be carried to England to pay customs; he later ordered that no foreign ships were to enter Virginia's waters.

In the turbulent era of the English civil war these edicts had not been observed. As a result the Dutch had steadily appropriated much of the trade from the colonies. Dutch shipping rates were cheaper and their masters more adept at finding markets for their cargoes. The Dutch also carried a wider range of goods to exchange, so that by 1648 England had lost much of its colonial trade, while it seemed that the Dutch would not be content until they had an absolute monopoly.

Accordingly, in 1651 Parliament passed the first Navigation Act, which laid down two basic principles. The first was that all goods imported into England from any plantation in America, Africa, or Asia must be shipped in vessels owned and manned by Englishmen or English colonists. The second was that all European goods destined for the colonies had to be carried in English vessels or vessels belonging to their country of origin. The act's aims were twofold, first to exclude the Dutch from the carrying trade and, second, to increase the customs revenues, without which it seemed pointless from a governmental viewpoint to carry on a trade at all.

The success of the act has been disputed. The Dutch, however, considered it sufficiently damaging to fight the first of its three wars against England in the period 1652–1674.

The 1651 act lapsed following the Restoration, because the Crown refused to recognize any measure of the interregnum. However, the exclusion of the Dutch from the carrying trade had now become a cardinal aim of the merchant community, and some alternative measure was essential if Charles II was to retain their support in Parliament. Many believed

---

[2]   The term mercantilism was first used by Adam Smith in his book, *The Wealth of Nations*, published, ironically, in 1776. Before this, contemporaries referred either to the navigation laws, plantation duties, or acts of trade. Historians, following Smith, have traditionally seen mercantilism as a monolithic system with a coherent philosophy. However, as Joyce Olham Appleby shows in *Economic Thought and Ideology in Seventeenth Century England* (Princeton, 1978), English economic thought was anything but coherent during the seventeenth century. Regulation was largely the result of uncoordinated pressure, often from competing interest groups.

that the 1651 act had not gone far enough because it did not prevent the shipment of colonial goods to Holland or elsewhere in foreign vessels. As a result, a considerable proportion of the colonies' trade was not directly benefiting the mother country, particularly with respect to customs revenue. In October 1660, therefore, Parliament passed a new act which excluded foreign traders altogether by permitting only vessels owned and three-quarters manned by Englishmen to enter English colonial ports. Second, this act enumerated a list of colonial goods which had to be exported to England before being shipped elsewhere: tobacco, sugar, cotton, indigo, and other dyes. All those trading in such goods had to give bonds of up to £2,000 to the governors to ensure that they brought their cargoes to England.

The act of 1660 by no means completed the economic regulation of the colonies, for it was recognized that the provinces were not simply producers of raw commodities but also an increasing market for English goods. Consequently, in 1663 a further measure was passed, this time requiring all foreign goods going to the plantations to be shipped via England, where they could be taxed and thus denied any competitive advantage.

Finally, in 1673 an act was passed requiring the colonists to pay the same enumerated duties as their compatriots at home. In future all enumerated goods shipped from one colony to another were to be treated as though they were destined for England. To ensure that these "plantation duties" were properly collected, the Crown arranged for customs commissioners to be appointed in every colony.

These measures promised to secure the commerce of England for the sole benefit of England. Parliament was of course only copying the example of Spain, Portugal, and France, for as the 1663 act averred, "It was the usage of other nations to keep their plantation trade to themselves." As already noted, however, it was not simply the commodities but the method of commerce itself which was now important. The carrying trade helped sustain a large mercantile marine, giving employment to thousands of seamen. That in turn provided the sinews of naval power, which was increasing in importance as the century progressed. If the king's navy was to match its rivals, it must have a ready reserve of seamen, which the mercantilist legislation promised to supply.

3 NEW YORK BECOMES AN ENGLISH COLONY

The challenge to England's naval strength was not long in appearing and came once again from the Dutch. As before, the main cause of hostilities was economic. Rivalry between the two powers had spilled over into Africa after Charles II chartered the Royal Africa Company in 1663 to monopolize the supply of slaves to the English West Indies, thus threatening a long-established Dutch trade.

An additional cause of conflict was the position of New Netherland, sandwiched between two fast-growing areas of English settlement, the Chesapeake and New England. In English eyes the Dutch colony was a serious impediment. Much coastal trade was calling there to evade the newly passed navigation laws. If they were to be effective, this loophole would have to be closed. A further pretext was the plight of the English settlers on western Long Island, who were still complaining about their arbitrary treatment at the hands of the Dutch.

The final catalyst in England's decision to conquer New Netherland was the ambition of James, Duke of York, Charles II's younger brother. James was anxious to extend his patrimony: where better than in the New World at the expense of the Dutch? Charles II readily consented, for his brother's wishes coincided with his own interests. Accordingly a charter was issued on March 12, 1664, to the area between the Connecticut and Delaware rivers, granting powers similar to those in the Durham palatinate. The duke was given all the lands in free and common socage, with the right to make laws and appoint such officers as he wished, providing the former were "as conveniently may be, agreeable to the laws, statutes and government of this our realm of England. . . ." Like Baltimore, James owed a nominal tribute, forty beaver skins a year, to the king, though Charles II retained the right to hear appeals.[3] Another difference was that there was no mention of an assembly in the duke's charter.

An expedition was quickly organized under the command of Richard Nicholls, one of the commissioners who were to investigate the condition of New England. Accompanying him were 400 troops, several frigates, and a bomb vessel. This force was more than enough for the intended target, for help was also expected from New England. Nicholls arrived off New Amsterdam on August 18, 1664, where he linked up with a force from Connecticut under John Winthrop, Jr. Stuyvesant, with the fortifications at New York still incomplete, found himself hopelessly outnumbered. He had only 150 troops, and even the Dutch population, at least the commercial class, was lukewarm about resisting. He accordingly surrendered on August 27 after Winthrop had acted as intermediary. Generous terms were granted: the property of the Dutch inhabitants, including that of free blacks, was to be protected; those who wished to leave were given a year to do so, while new settlers from Holland would be admitted; liberty of conscience was guaranteed; and Dutch inheritance laws were to be respected.

Nicholls decided to call his conquest New York in honor of the duke. He then dispatched Sir Robert Carr, another of the commissioners, to seize the settlements on the Delaware. It was anticipated that victory would be easy here too, with the Swedish population welcoming deliverance from the Dutch. In the event, force was required to take the main post, Fort Casimir, which resulted in some looting by Carr and his men, much to the anger of Nicholls.

The territory now had to be reorganized to ensure the loyalty of the population. Nicholls himself was an able person, both as a commander and as an administrator. Though a strict disciplinarian, he recognized the need for conciliation and was rightly annoyed at Carr's looting activities. Fortunately, the Dutch and English had been accustomed to living together as refugees and coreligionists for the past hundred years. In addition James lightened Nicholls's immediate task by selling the lands between the Hudson and Delaware to two friends, John Lord Berkeley and Sir George Carteret, who had helped plan the expedition. The disadvantages of giving away so much of New York's natural hinterland were not immediately apparent.

Meanwhile Nicholls began adapting the institutions of government to reflect those of England more closely. At the beginning of March 1665 he issued what came to be known as the Duke's Laws. These laws attempted to integrate English practice with those Dutch customs protected under the recent treaty and were heavily influenced by the laws of New

---

[3]   A copy of the full text can be found in Kavenagh, *Documentary History*, I, 793–6.

England. One reason behind Nicholls's action was the need to appease the towns of eastern Long Island, which were now to become part of the duke's province. In the aftermath of the campaign, Winthrop had ceded Connecticut's claims to the island in exchange for a more favorable boundary on the mainland.

Twelve crimes were to merit the death penalty, among them the denial of God, murder for gain, sodomy, conspiracy to overthrow the government, treason, and resistance to the king's lawful authority. Rules were also laid down for the conduct of the magistrates, sheriffs, and constables. Justice itself was to be administered through courts of session, with assizes meeting once a year in September.

Local government similarly reflected New England practice. Responsibility in each town was to be in the hands of overseers, who were to be elected by all freeholders. The overseers were to have the same functions as selectmen and the same powers as petty magistrates. Their meetings, however, were to be presided over by a justice chosen by the governor. Later a county structure was added, consisting of a panel of justices who were also to be appointed by the duke or his representative.

New Amsterdam, now renamed New York, was also remodeled politically. The Dutch municipal officials were replaced by a "mayor, aldermen and sheriff, according to the custom of England." However, these officials were to be appointed by the duke, rather than nominated from among themselves. The Dutch burghers protested at what they considered a breach of the surrender terms, but to no avail.

Although the peace treaty guaranteed liberty of conscience to the Dutch, it was not intended to open the floodgates to other religious denominations. Ministers of religion had to show that they had been properly ordained. Nevertheless, no congregations were to "be disturbed in their private meetings" nor anyone "molested, fined, or imprisoned for differing in judgement in matters of religion who profess Christianity." Although tithes were to be levied, it was left to the overseers in each town to decide which church to support. This liberality was similar in many respects to Baltimore's Act Concerning Religion. Perhaps it was no coincidence that James, like Baltimore, was a Catholic.[4]

Compared with English common law, the Duke's Laws were a model of clarity and restraint. They had just one weakness, the absence of any mechanism to amend them or deal with complaints. Disputes or grievances could be referred to the assizes and then to the duke, but this recourse was hardly adequate. The principal omission, of course, was the absence of any assembly to make laws and levy taxes, partly because such a body would have had a Dutch majority. Nevertheless, by 1665 all of England's other American colonies had an assembly, and the lack of one in New York was to be a source of much grievance, especially among the towns in eastern Long Island which had formerly been represented in the Connecticut general assembly. It was these towns which led the protest against Nicholls's plan in 1665 to register all land titles as the prelude to collecting a quitrent. The same towns led the refusals in 1669 and 1670 to pay their rates, on the grounds that they were "inslaved under an Arbitrary Power" and denied the "Liberty of Englishmen." In 1672 several of them requested to be returned to Connecticut's jurisdiction.

Nicholls and his successor, Governor Lovelace, also had little success in appeasing the Dutch. Nicholls initially refused to have any of them on his council. However, in 1668

---

[4]   Kavenagh, *Documentary History*, II, 1037–45.

DOCUMENT 11

The Duke's Laws, April 2, 1664, reprinted in W. Keith Kavenagh, *Foundations of Colonial America: A Documentary History* (New York, 1973), II, 1037–45.

[The influence of New England can be seen in the laws concerning children and sexual misconduct. Homosexual relationships were considered especially heinous.]

1. If any person within this government shall, by direct expressed impious or presumptuous ways, deny the true God and his attributes, he shall be put to death.

2. If any person shall commit any willful and premeditated murder, he shall be put to death.

3. If any person slays another with sword or dagger who has no weapon to defend himself, he shall be put to death.

4. If any man shall slay or cause another to be slain by lying in wait privately for him or by poisoning or any such wicked conspiracy, he shall be put to death.

5. If any man or woman shall lie with any beast or brute creature by carnal copulation, they shall be put to death and the beast shall be burned.

6. If any man lies with mankind as he lies with woman, they shall be put to death, unless the one part were forced or be under fourteen years of age; in which case he shall be punished at the discretion of the Court of Assizes.

7. If any person forcibly steals or carries away any mankind, he shall be put to death.

8. If any person shall bear false witness maliciously and on purpose to take away a man's life, he shall be put to death.

9. If any man shall traitorously deny his Majesty's right and titles to his crown and dominions or shall raise arms to resist his authority, he shall be put to death.

10. If any man shall treacherously conspire or publicly attempt to invade or surprise any town or towns, fort or forts, within this government, he shall be put to death.

11. If any child or children above sixteen years of age and of sufficient understanding shall smite their natural father or mother, unless thereunto provoked and forced for their self-preservation from death or maiming, at the complaint of the said father and mother, and not otherwise . . . shall be put to death.

12. Every married person or persons who shall be found or proved . . . to have committed adultery with a married man or woman, shall be put to death.

13. Every single person or persons who shall be found or proved . . . to have committed carnal copulation with a married man or woman, they both shall be grievously fined and punished as the Governor and Council or the Court of Assizes shall think meet, not extending to life or limb.

Lovelace did promote two Dutchmen, appointing a third to be mayor of New York City. He also delayed implementing the Duke's Laws in some areas, but trouble arose between his soldiers and the Dutch inhabitants of New York, Esopus, and Albany. Dutch merchants also feared that they were about to lose their commerce to English rivals, following a ban in 1668 on any further trade with Holland.

Then in 1672 news arrived that England and Holland were at war again. This third conflict was mainly the result of the 1670 secret Treaty of Dover in which Charles II had promised to assist Louis XIV in any conflict with the Dutch. The war was extremely unpopular in England, since it merely served the ambitions of Europe's most powerful Catholic monarch against a fellow Protestant ruler, William of Orange. This time it was the Dutch who took advantage of the hostilities to change the status of New York. After assembling a force in the West Indies, they first visited the Chesapeake, destroyed the English tobacco fleet, and then arrived off New York. Here they met little opposition, since the English towns refused to resist the forces of a Protestant prince who had close ties with the English royal family. The Dutch expedition enjoyed similar success in retaking the settlements on the Delaware.

This respite from the duke's rule was to be short-lived, however, for by the 1674 Treaty of Westminster New York was returned to English control. The duke accordingly reissued his code of laws, though he now allowed the governor and council to amend them if necessary. He also appointed a new governor, Major Edmund Andros, who had served in the West Indies and had also fought in the Dutch service. It was the confident and authoritative Andros's first civil appointment.

The problems previously faced by Nicholls and Lovelace were not long in resurfacing, the most pressing being lack of money. Attempts to raise revenue soon provoked the English towns to renew their clamor for an assembly, a demand which Andros rightly accused Connecticut of helping to incite. The episode convinced the governor that James must take over either all of New England or at least western Connecticut and New Jersey if New York was to be a viable settlement. Andros subsequently undertook an exploratory visit to Connecticut but was warned off by the local militia. He also tried to give instructions to the authorities in New Jersey but had limited success. The only other way of raising money, he suggested, might be the summoning of an assembly.

James quickly responded that such notions must be discouraged. As he told Andros in January 1676, an assembly "would be of dangerous consequence, nothing being more known than the aptness of such bodies to assume to themselves many privileges which prove destructive to . . . the peace of the government." The colonists had been guaranteed their rights and property under the laws. If they had a grievance they could appeal to him through the assizes. However, he confided to Andros that he would be "ready to consider of any proposals you shall send to that purpose," thereby suggesting that he was less inflexible on the matter than is commonly supposed.[5]

Andros also had problems when the burghers of New York refused to take an oath of allegiance. Perhaps his earlier service in Holland made him believe that firmness was the best policy, for he eventually imprisoned seven of the resistance leaders, including Nicholas Bayard, forcing them to forfeit one-third of their estates. In this situation there could be no question of having any Dutch in positions of authority. But from 1677 Andros gradually relaxed his stance, admitting several leading merchants to the council, most notable among them Frederick Philipse and Stephanus Van Cortlandt. The first signs of integration among the elite were beginning to take place.

---

[5]   The correspondence is published in Michael G. Hall, Lawrence H. Leder, and Michael G. Kammen, eds, *The Glorious Revolution in America: Documents on the Colonial Crisis of 1689* (Chapel Hill, 1964).

Plate 19   The Stadt Huys of New York, corner of Pearl Street and Coentje Slip. Lithograph by G. Hayward. Collection of the New York Historical Society, New York City.

But although Andros began the process of rapprochement, New York's financial problems remained intractable, given the truncated condition of the settlement. Despite all Andros's endeavors, the colony was not producing an adequate revenue. Its main burden was the cost of defense. Andros had succeeded in negotiating a Covenant Chain of friendship with the Mohawks at Albany in 1677. In addition to continuing the trade in arms and furs, the two sides agreed a mutual assistance pact. The Iroquois would protect English settlements from French raids in return for English recognition of their suzerainty over other neighboring Indian peoples.

Nevertheless, the Iroquois remained uncertain allies, since their aim was an expansion of their political and economic control. Since the beginning of the seventeenth century they had been engaged in a series of wars for control of the fur trade, known as the Beaver Wars. As they told the Ursuline nun, Marie de l'Incarnation, they wanted "to be alone in all these lands, in order to live without fear, and to have all the game to live off, and to give pelts to the Dutch." Accordingly, they had already destroyed the Huron in the 1640s, defeated the Erie, Petun, and Neutral nations in the 1650s, savaged the Ottawas in the early 1660s, and more recently dispersed the Susquehannock and Mahican peoples. Having now secured the necessary weapons and supplies through the Covenant Chain, they proceeded to invade the Illinois country in an attempt to extend their hegemony. No one could predict where this conflict would end.[6]

For a time Andros endeavored to increase the revenue using the traditional Stuart devices of arbitrary taxation and the sale of monopolies. In particular, the decision in 1678 that all overseas trade must pass through New York City effectively gave its merchants a stranglehold on the colony's trade, for which they paid handsomely. The agreement also helped facilitate the collection of customs by eliminating Southampton and Southold on Long Island as ports of entry. Andros's alliance with the city merchants was further consolidated two years later when he gave them a monopoly over the milling of flour for export.

These monopolies and trading privileges were immensely unpopular in the colony as a whole. The Long Island towns were especially bitter at the loss of their customs privileges, which threatened their trade with New England. Equally hurt were the merchants of Albany, who had previously enjoyed a significant share of the flour trade. Although they retained their monopoly of the fur trade, they were clearly disadvantaged by the need to channel everything through their rivals. The discontent quickly boiled over in 1680 when Andros neglected to renew the customs duties while on a visit to England. Many merchants not only refused to pay the the levies but also took William Dyer, the collector, to court. During the subsequent assize, the grand jury demanded that James place the province "upon equal ground with our fellow Bretheren and subjects of the realm of England," by which it meant the granting of an assembly.

These disturbances finally led James to the conclusion that the colonists were themselves perhaps best qualified to extract money. He therefore resolved to make a fresh start. First he appointed a new governor, Thomas Dongan, to replace the unpopular Andros. Then he decreed an assembly and gave its deputies full "liberty to consult and debate among themselves all matters" for the drafting of "laws for the good government of the said colony." Public revenues were to be levied in the duke's name, however, and Dongan was privately told to raise sufficient revenue to make further meetings of the assembly unnecessary. In addition he was to reorganize the militia and consider the special position of New York City.

The first assembly in the history of New York met in October 1683. A majority of the deputies were from the Dutch towns, but the English deputies from Long Island took the lead, being more familiar with such institutions. They began by drafting a charter of liberties or frame of government similar to that of Connecticut. The supreme legislative authority under the proprietor was to lie with the governor, council, and "the people in general assembly," who were to meet at least once every three years "according to the usage, custom and practice of the realm of England." All freeholders or freemen were to have the vote. New York City was to return four deputies, the other counties two each, except Schenectady, which was to have one. Members were to have all the privileges of a parliament: freedom from arrest, free speech, and the right to adjourn. Together with the governor and council, the deputies were to impose all taxes.

What followed effectively constituted a bill of rights for New York's inhabitants, based mainly, though not entirely, on English precedents. Trial was to be by jury, due process of the law was to be observed, and punishment was to fit the crime. In accordance with an

---

[6] For further details about the role of warfare in Iroquois culture, see chapter 15, section 2.

act of 1679, no soldiers were to be quartered on any settlers against their will except in wartime, and martial law was to be restricted to the military. Lands were to be an "estate of inheritance, not chattel or personal" which could be seized on some technical fault, and they were to be free of feudal dues as in England. The charter also addressed the question of religion. All peaceably behaved Christians were guaranteed freedom of conscience, though they still had to support a minister chosen by a majority of the local inhabitants. Lastly, widows were to be protected and women with property were to have the right to affirm in open court that it was their wish to sell.[7]

This was a remarkable document. Other fundamental orders in America had been designed to protect the position of a dominant group. Since New York had no such group, the assembly had had to devise a bill establishing the rights of all its settlers. The document has a modern ring to it, being comparable to the 1776 Virginia Bill of Rights, which was similarly designed for a society which was no longer homogeneous.

The action of the assembly was more than Dongan or James had anticipated, but it was not specifically against the ducal instructions. Dongan had in any case secured a substantial revenue as the *sine qua non* for convening the assembly. Consequently, he accepted its measures pending approval from England. Meanwhile New York, like Virginia in 1619, seemed set on a happier course, though many problems remained, notably high taxes, large land grants to favored individuals, and the continued monopoly of New York City over the trade of the colony.

Another reason for optimism was the slow but steady growth of the population and resources of the colony. By 1685 the number of colonists had risen to fifteen thousand. Of these, three thousand were in New York City, fifteen hundred in Albany, and six thousand on Long Island, where Southampton was the largest settlement with seven hundred people. Integration of the two main ethnic groups had unfortunately made little progress. Albany and Esopus remained almost exclusively Dutch, while Long Island was divided between five Dutch and twelve English settlements. Only in New York City did the two nations come close together, and even there assimilation was limited.

4 THE CAROLINAS: EARLY SETTLEMENT

Although trade was the main reason for the conquest of New York, it was not the only cause of continued interest in the New World. Land, too, was increasingly important, now that colonization on a substantial scale had proved possible. Although Baltimore had not increased his fortunes dramatically, his experiment still seemed to have much to offer. As has been mentioned, the noble families of England were anxious to enlarge their holdings. The Durham palatinate might be archaic in England, but it offered a compact and disciplined model for colonization that was seemingly well suited to the frontier conditions of America.

The Crown itself had few objections. Charles II had no definite policy regarding the internal administration of the colonies, as his grant to Connecticut and Rhode Island showed. Some profit might accrue if the venture was successful, and such grants were also

---

[7] For the full text, see Kavenagh, *Documentary History*, II, 1051–5. For women's property rights during the colonial period, see Marylynn Salmon, *Women and the Law of Property in Early America* (Chapel Hill, 1986).

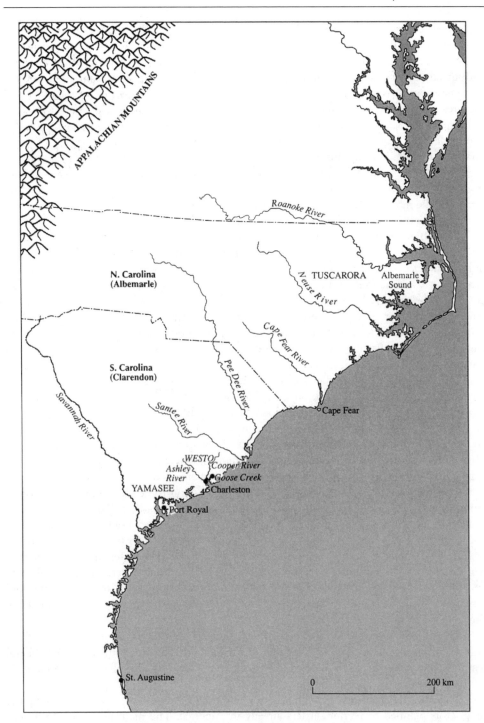

Map 4 The early Carolinas.

useful because they allowed the king to pay off financial obligations which he had incurred in exile.

Interest in the area south of Virginia had been growing for some time. Indeed, settlers had already begun moving from Virginia into the area around Albemarle Sound, though settlement farther south had so far been inhibited by the threat of Spanish retaliation and the presence of numerous American Indian nations. England's capture of Jamaica in 1655 indicated that Spanish power was on the decline; the American Indians, however, were another matter. The nations in this area were among the most advanced north of the Rio Grande and included the Muskogean-speaking Yamasee and Creek nations, the Iroquoian-speaking Cherokee, and the Siouan-speaking Catawba. All were relatively numerous and lived in well-defined territories, supporting their population by a mixture of hunting and farming. Like most American Indians, however, they were eager to trade, so that any initial settlement had a good chance of being accepted.

The chief promoter of English colonization at this time was a Barbadian planter, Sir John Colleton. Barbados, like other West Indian islands, was experiencing a crisis, all of its land being either exhausted or claimed. Sugar was an expensive crop to grow, and its production was becoming concentrated in the hands of a wealthy few, which left an increasingly discontented mass of poor planters or younger sons no longer able to compete. An opportunity to settle elsewhere was thus likely to be well received. Colleton was on good terms with Sir William Berkeley of Virginia, his brother John Lord Berkeley, and an ambitious young politician, Anthony Ashley Cooper, who had once owned a plantation in Barbados.

Even the four men together had insufficient resources to mount such a project. Consequently, they decided to seek support from four of the most powerful figures in the kingdom: Edward Hyde, Earl of Clarendon, the king's chief minister; George Monck, Duke of Albemarle, whose march from Coldstream had made possible Charles II's restoration; and the Earl of Craven and Sir George Carteret, two prominent friends of the Duke of York. Having the necessary requirements for establishing a colony, the eight men agreed to approach the king for a palatinate grant on the Durham model.

The grant was duly issued on March 24, 1663, giving the eight proprietors all those lands from Luck Island on the thirty-sixth parallel to the St. Matthias River on the borders of Florida. They were to be "absolute Proprietors of the Country," holding the land in free and common socage for the nominal rent of twenty marks, or £13 6s 8d. They could sell or lease land, create titles and manors, make war in defense of their territories, and declare martial law for the suppression of any rebellion. They were empowered to make all laws and raise taxes subject to "the advice, assent and approbation of the freemen of the said province." As in Maryland, however, they could issue emergency decrees which would have the same force as acts of the assembly.

The inhabitants were to remain the king's subjects, enjoying the same "liberties, franchises and privileges of this our Kingdom of England." In keeping with the king's liberal leanings, they were also to be allowed liberty of conscience, provided all settlers periodically affirmed their loyalty to the throne.[8]

To avoid the problems of acclimatization and the expenses of an Atlantic crossing, the proprietors planned to recruit settlers already in America. The main fields of recruitment

---

[8] Kavenagh, *Documentary History*, III, 1738–47.

were to be Barbados and New England. The proprietors believed that the lack of available land in Barbados and the coldness of the New England climate would be sufficient inducement to get the enterprise started. They expected settlers in both areas to be lured by the rich alluvial lands along the many rivers, which would, they hoped, support the cultivation of silk, vines, ginger, waxes, almonds, and olives.

In the event a party of New Englanders did go to the Cape Fear region, but they found it singularly uninviting and returned home. It was therefore left to Colleton and the governor of Barbados, Sir John Yeamans, to continue the enterprise. Between 1663 and 1665 they organized a number of exploratory voyages under Captain William Hilton, which proved sufficiently encouraging for a substantial group of Barbadians to offer themselves as colonists. But despite relatively generous land provisions, including fifty acres for every slave imported, the enterprise did not last long. The newcomers disliked the demand for quitrents and found the Cape Fear region relatively infertile, so that within two years the settlement had broken up. Some colonists went on to Virginia; the rest returned to Barbados.

Nevertheless, the proprietors, notably Cooper, now Earl of Shaftesbury, determined to persist, not least because the Privy Council had announced that in future such grants would lapse unless settlement was effected within a reasonable period. Another incentive to continue was that a peace treaty had been concluded in 1667 with Spain, reducing the fears of a Spanish attack.[9] But this time settlers were to be sent from England in the hope that they would be more amenable to the ideas of the proprietors.

First a system of government was put in place, called the Fundamental Constitutions of Carolina, of which the chief architects were Shaftesbury and his secretary, John Locke. The stated purpose of the constitutions was the "better settlement of the government," which was to be effected by defining the powers of the proprietors to make them compatible with monarchy, while avoiding "an arrogant aristocracy" or the creation of "a numerous democracy." The province was to be administered by a palatinate court, which could call the provincial "parliament," prepare legislation, appoint officers, and dispose of public money. The parliament itself was to consist of the proprietors and other nobility, together with deputies representing the freeholders of every precinct. Each representative had to possess five hundred acres and each voter fifty. The parliament was to sit every other November, and its first action would be to reaffirm the Fundamental Constitutions.

Although the Church of England was to be supported from public funds, other Christian sects would be tolerated. The American Indians, too, would be shown forbearance as their "idolatory, ignorance, or mistake gives us no right to expel or use them ill." The hope was that Jews, heathens, and other dissenters would convert, after "having an opportunity of acquainting themselves with the truth and reasonableness" of the Anglican church.

The most remarkable feature of the Fundamental Constitutions was that its landholding structure was pyramidal. Carolina was to be divided into two provinces, Albemarle and Clarendon, each comprising a number of counties. Each proprietor would own twelve thousand acres in every county. Next in rank would be a landgrave, who would possess four baronies of twelve thousand acres each, followed by two caciques, holding two baronies apiece. The landgraves and caciques would constitute the nobility. After them would come the lords of the manor, each with three thousand to twelve thousand acres, followed by the rest of the freeholders, who collectively would own three-fifths of the land.

---

[9] For further information on Anglo-Spanish relations at this time, see chapter 18, section 1.

Shaftesbury and Locke were seemingly influenced here by the writings of James Harrington, who argued that the English civil war had occurred because of an imbalance between the landed classes, though Harrington favored the gentry and yeomanry over the aristocracy or monarchy as bulwarks of stability. Shaftesbury and Locke believed that their pyramidal structure would achieve the same effect.[10]

The authors realized that the Fundamental Constitutions could not be implemented immediately in an infant colony. Accordingly they issued a set of temporary laws, restricting the initial size of the baronies until enough settlers had arrived to make the scheme workable. The expectation was that each barony would contain between fifteen and thirty persons within seven years.

The first batch of settlers departed in August 1669 in three ships, financed by a contribution of £500 from each proprietor. They arrived off the Ashley River in April 1670, after journeying by way of Barbados where additional settlers were recruited. An immediate start was made clearing a site on the south bank for the building of a stockade around the principal settlement of Charles Town. Two years later the settlement had 271 men and 69 women, but this number was not nearly enough to implement the Fundamental Constitutions, since there were as yet no caciques or lords of the manor and only one landgrave – Sir John Yeamans, the governor. A further postponement was necessary.

Nevertheless, Yeamans had already summoned the first parliament in July 1671 and had begun implementing a survey. Squares of twelve thousand acres were marked along the Ashley River: six for the people, two for the proprietors, and two for the nobility. The proprietors amended their scheme, however, by reserving two squares for the American Indians where one of their towns already existed.

Alas, from the start the plan was unworkable. Many of the initial settlers were more interested in furs than farming. The area was rich in game, especially deer, and the local Westo Indians were anxious to trade. Thus the hopes of growing silk, vines, ginger, and olives quickly disappeared. The surveyor also had neither the skill nor the resources to carry out his task. Although all proprietors had agreed to contribute £100 annually for seven years, this sum was never enough to finance the exercise. A number of landgraves and caciques were created, but most grantees, like the proprietors, waited for other people to turn their dreams into reality.

In 1682 another attempt was made to organize a survey. New counties were created, and all free inhabitants were promised a headright of fifty acres, including servants on the expiry of their service. The only charge would be a quitrent of one penny an acre. Most settlers resented paying even this, given that the proprietors were absentee landlords, and responded by refusing to take the oath acknowledging the Fundamental Constitutions. This attitude stymied the whole scheme, since the proprietors had accepted that their system of government could be considered lawful only after it had been ratified by the people as part of an original compact.[11]

Another bone of contention was the fur trade. The proprietors argued that an unlicensed trade would alienate the Westos, whose friendship was essential to the colony.

---

[10] For the full text of the Fundamental Constitutions, see Kavenagh, *Documentary History*, III, 1761–74. Harrington's book *Oceana* was first published in 1656.

[11] This provision foreshadowed Locke's *Second Treatise of Government* (1690) in which he argued that government must be based on a contract reflecting the consent of the people.

There was some justification for this concern, since the colonists began kidnapping the local inhabitants to work as slaves on their farms. In 1677 the proprietors accordingly issued an edict banning all settlers from engaging in the trade for seven years. This action caused much bitterness in the parliament, where it was rightly seen as an attempt by the proprietors to engross the one profitable activity in Clarendon province. The policy was in any case doomed to failure, for those excluded simply began trading with other nations hostile to the Westos. This behavior led to the Westos' destruction in 1680, much to the anger of the proprietors.

Most of the opposition to proprietary rule came from the Barbadians. They had returned to the Carolinas with Yeamans in 1670 to settle the area of Goose Creek, a tributary of the Cooper River. Yeamans himself was typical of their kind – aggressive, resourceful, and determined to make his fortune. Like many Barbadians he arrived with several slaves and other servants, and his group quickly dominated both the council and the assembly. It was to counter their influence that the proprietors began recruiting French Huguenots and English Dissenters, thereby creating another source of contention, for the Barbadians were Anglican.

In 1680 the main settlement – hereafter referred to as Charleston – was moved to the junction of the Ashley and Cooper rivers, a much healthier site open to the Atlantic breezes. Disease had not been a major problem, for the Barbadians were well seasoned, though they had added to the misery of other settlers by bringing malaria and yellow fever with them.

The population of Charleston at this time was about three hundred. It remained a small struggling outpost. An act of 1685 stated that the inhabitants were to clear the roads of bush and weeds in front of their houses to make the town worthy of being the province's chief port. In 1692 another act was passed to deal with stray swine which, as in New York earlier, roamed the streets to the great annoyance of all. In future any colonists except slaves could lawfully kill any such animals and receive five shillings for their trouble.

Economically the colony had no obvious staple apart from furs, but it quickly became self-sufficient in food. Hogs and cattle did particularly well, since they did not have to be killed in winter. Indeed, surplus provisions provided Clarendon County with a useful export, the main market for which was the West Indies, where the Barbadians exchanged their provisions for sugar.

If the province of Clarendon was proving unprofitable to the proprietors, Albemarle to the north was even more so. It was hoped that this area could be controlled by Governor Berkeley of Virginia, since its first settlers came from that colony.

Accordingly, from 1664 Berkeley issued a number of permits, guaranteeing the holders their lands on the same terms as in Virginia. Others, however, simply bought titles from the local inhabitants without regard to the proprietors' rights. To prevent further chaos, in 1667 the proprietors nominated Samuel Stephen as governor with more complete instructions. He was to appoint a surveyor to sell lands, reserving to the proprietors a quitrent of one halfpenny an acre and 50 percent of all precious metals. Freedom of conscience was guaranteed and an assembly was to be called, composed of the governor, council, and twelve representatives elected by the freemen. This assembly had the sole right to raise taxes and was empowered to make laws, provided they were consistent with the laws of England and did not contravene the interests of the proprietors.

When the Fundamental Constitutions were drawn up in 1669, the proprietors expected Albemarle to conform to them. Indeed, one or two manors were actually created, but the proprietors realized from an early stage that Albemarle was too remote to offer much profit, hence they preferred to devote their limited resources to Clarendon instead.

Since most of Albemarle's settlers were from Virginia, it quickly took on the appearance of that colony. The settlement's main activity was subsistence farming, supplemented by the production of a little surplus tobacco and corn, which were sold to passing New England traders. Albemarle itself had little institutional cohesion, since it contained no towns and few churches. The governor on Roanoke Island had to shift for himself with the aid of a motley council. The one institution which did thrive was the assembly, because the inhabitants were familiar with Virginia's House of Burgesses.

The settlers in general quite failed to comprehend the proprietary system, except to recognize that it was incompatible with their existing land titles. They also resented the demand for quitrents and were further irritated by the passage of the 1673 Navigation Act, which threatened to stifle the province's small trade. The result was a climate of instability.

The governor at this time was John Jenkins, one of the early settlers from Virginia. He and other leading planters, notably John Culpepper and George Durant, were especially unhappy about the new trade laws. This group was opposed by another faction, led by Thomas Miller and Thomas Eastchurch, which succeeded in persuading the proprietors to transfer authority to them by appointing Eastchurch governor and Miller collector of customs. Miller then began confiscating his opponents' property as punishment for contravening the 1673 act, provoking an uprising by Culpepper and his associates in December 1677. Miller was seized, while Culpepper, with the support of the assembly, established his own government before going to England to defend his actions.

Since Culpepper and his followers had not overtly challenged the authority of the king or the proprietors, they were exonerated, and calm returned to the province. But the incident underlined the weakness of proprietary government. It was the proprietors' poor judgment in appointing Jenkins and Miller which had sparked off the trouble in the first place. Then they had passively watched as the struggle unfolded. Mercifully, bloodshed had been avoided, a remarkable achievement in light of the fact that Virginia to the north had just emerged from a bloody civil war.

7

The Later Years of Charles II

1660	Sir William Berkeley is restored as governor of Virginia.
1662	The Congregational church agrees to the Half-Way Covenant.
1673	Virginia land rights are awarded to Lords Culpepper and Arlington. The Lawne's Creek protest takes place.
1675	King Philip's (Metacomet's) War breaks out in New England; Northfield is abandoned. The Privy Council sets up a committee for supervising the colonies. Fighting breaks out with Doeg and Susquehannock Indians.
1676	Bacon's Rebellion is quashed. Metacomet is finally defeated. William Penn and other Quakers purchase West New Jersey.
1679–81	In the Exclusion crisis in England the Whigs attempt to bar James, Duke of York from the succession.
1680	New Hampshire becomes a royal colony.
1681	Penn is granted a charter to establish Pennsylvania. Edward Randolph is appointed customs collector for New England.
1682	Philadelphia is founded. Plant cutter riots break out in Gloucester County, Virginia.
1686	The first German Pietists arrive in Pennsylvania.
1689	The Keithian Schism divides Quakers in Pennsylvania.

1 VIRGINIA: BACON'S REBELLION AND ITS AFTERMATH

W HILE PROPRIETARY GOVERNMENT in seventeenth-century America has been widely criticized, it is salutary to remember that royal government, too, did not escape difficulties. What is perhaps surprising is that when disturbances occurred they took place in England's oldest, most valuable, and loyal colony, Virginia.

In 1660 Sir William Berkeley had returned there as governor without bloodshed to almost universal acclaim. His previous period in office had been widely approved because of his handling of the American Indian war of 1644–6 and his readiness to work with the assembly. Slowly this esteem eroded, partly because of his failure to call fresh elections for the House of Burgesses. Berkeley found the 1662 house so amenable that he determined to retain it. Coincidentally, the colony was growing rapidly, with many new counties being added and fortunes being made. By 1670 the population was close to thirty thousand.

The sense of exclusivity was reinforced by the Franchise Act of that year. In future only freeholders and housekeepers were to have the vote, to prevent propertyless and disorderly elements from disrupting elections. Parish councils were similarly ceasing to be elective, their membership being instead coopted. Thus at both a provincial and a local level, government was becoming the preserve of a small clique of colonists who owed their position to Berkeley. Among the most prominent were Philip and Thomas Ludwell, Henry Chicheley, Francis Moryson, and Robert Beverley.

The navigation laws were another cause for concern. The legislation of 1660 and 1663 had been, in Berkeley's words, "mighty and destructive" of Virginia's economy, having reduced the market for tobacco while excluding the cheaper goods and services of the Dutch. Virginia was seemingly being sacrificed for the benefit of a few English merchants. The economy was already depressed because of a slump in tobacco prices caused by over-production; annual output was now running at between seven million and nine million pounds for the Chesapeake as a whole. The situation was so bad that in 1666 Virginia, Maryland, and North Carolina agreed not to plant any crop that year, but their action did little to increase demand. In response Berkeley vainly repeated the need to develop other commodities.

Unfortunately, the catalogue of woes continued. In 1667 eighteen tobacco vessels were seized at the end of the second war with the Dutch. Next the crops themselves were affected by bad weather, and in 1671 a plague struck the cattle. Two years later the province had to contend not only with another Navigation Act but also with a third Dutch war, during which eleven tobacco vessels were captured by the fleet heading for New York. This was despite the construction of several forts near the entrance to Chesapeake Bay. Coming as it did on top of reduced markets and poor prices, this misfortune was a body blow. Many planters, especially bitter that so much money had been spent on the defense of the Chesapeake to so little effect, protested at Lawne's Creek in Surry County in an attempt not to pay any taxes.

Even these setbacks were not the end of Virginia's troubles, for that same year news arrived that Charles II had consigned his land rights in Virginia to Lord Arlington and Lord Culpepper for thirty-one years. They could create new counties, appoint sheriffs, and dispose of all unsettled lands. Moreover, they were empowered to collect quitrents throughout

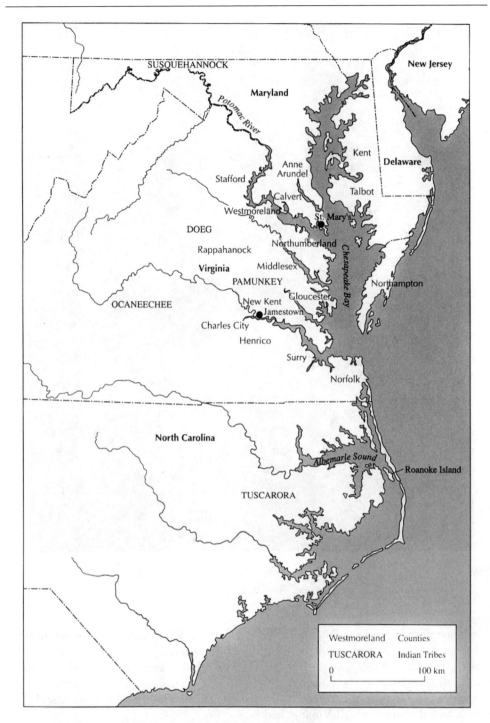

Map 5 Mid-seventeenth-century Maryland and Virginia.

Plate 20 Portrait of Sir William Berkeley, by Sir Peter Lely. Reproduced by the kind permission of the curator, Berkeley Castle.

Virginia and to control the Anglican church. Charles II had acted to pay off yet another debt, but his measure was singularly ill-considered, threatening as it did the existing institutions. Berkeley himself was quick to express "the people's grief" at an act which undermined all confidence in the future. A delegation was immediately sent to England to try to overturn the grant, while to prevent the recurrence of such an action, it was decided to seek a formal charter, which Virginia had lacked since 1624.

The grant to Culpepper and Arlington was eventually reduced, but by then the damage was done. The history of English North America shows that nothing so disturbed its inhabitants as the questioning of their land titles and the diminishing of their assemblies. Such measures inevitably caused trouble, and this case was to prove no exception.

Virginian society at this time was extremely volatile. As in Maryland, the population contained a high proportion of male indentured servants or ex-servants. The composition of the servant population has been the cause of some dispute. One contemporary asserted, "Some are husbands who have abandoned their wives: others wives who have abandoned their husbands: some are children and apprentices who have run away from their parents and masters." Whatever their social origins and reasons for coming to America, these servants were hardly the most stable elements on which to build a society, especially given the unbalanced sex ratios. On average four to six times more young men than women entered Virginia, ensuring a lack of family life and, consequently, of social stability.[1]

The condition of the servants was also harsh in other respects. Virginia at this time was obsessed by the search for wealth, and its society was ruthlessly exploitative. Servants were worked to the limit, their existence made doubly hard by the lack of prospects once that service was completed. Although land itself was relatively cheap, they still had to pay the surveyor's fees and then find enough capital to buy livestock and other essential equipment, for which the dues from the master were totally inadequate. Another problem was that by this time all the best land had been claimed. Thus 25 percent of all servants failed to become landowners, and only 6 percent actually became successful planters owning their own labor force. Many of the rest remained tenant farmers, foremen, or laborers. Such men were hardly pillars of society, especially when their prospects were further eroded by the actions of Berkeley's assembly, which paid itself generously for the privilege of taxing others. The governor himself was aware of the potentially explosive situation when he commented, "Six parts of seven at least are Poore, Indebted, Discontented and Armed."

Finally, trouble with the local inhabitants broke out again. Since 1646 there had been a general peace, mainly because Berkeley had removed all the indigenous inhabitants from the Jamestown Peninsula, leaving that territory free for white settlement behind a defensive perimeter of forts. Since then the colony had grown rapidly and new counties had been created, bringing the settlers back into contact with the American Indians. It was this contact which sparked off the traumatic events of 1676.

---

[1] The quote is from Abbot Emerson Smith, *Colonists in Bondage: White Servitude and Convict Labor in America, 1607–1776* (Chapel Hill, 1947), 82–3. Smith in general categorizes most servants as "Rogues, Whores and Vagabonds." This view was challenged by Mildred Campbell in "Social Origins of Some Early Americans" in James Morton Smith, ed., *Seventeenth Century America: Essays in Colonial History* (Chapel Hill, 1959). Campbell found that most immigrants were respectable maids and skilled artisans. Her view has in turn been qualified by David W. Galenson in " 'Middling People' or 'Common Sort'?: The Social Origins of Some Early Americans Re-examined," to which there is a rebuttal by Campbell, *William and Mary Quarterly*, XXXV, 1978, 499–524. Most recently, Russell R. Menard has concluded that the truth lies somewhere in between. See "British Migration to the Chesapeake Colonies in the Seventeenth Century," in Lois Green Carr, Philip D. Morgan, and Jean B. Russo, eds, *Colonial Chesapeake Society* (Chapel Hill, 1988), 99–132. The distorted sex ratio of Virginian society was first noted by Wesley Frank Craven in *White, Red and Black: The Seventeenth Century Virginian* (Charlottesville, 1971). Craven arrived at his conclusions by looking at the hitherto unused headright patents. The subject is explored in greater detail by Edmund S. Morgan, *American Slavery, American Freedom: The Ordeal of Colonial Virginia* (New York, 1975); and by Darrett B. Rutman and Anita H. Rutman, *A Place in Time: Middlesex County, Virginia, 1650–1750* (New York, 1984). Similar conclusions have been reached for Maryland; see chapter 5, section 1.

Throughout the 1660s there had been periodic disputes in which the settlers accused the local inhabitants of stealing hogs and cattle and were in turn charged with letting these animals invade the natives' corn fields and disturb the game. In the spring of 1675 Doeg Indians killed an overseer in a dispute over some missing hogs. The Doegs were pursued by a detachment of the Stafford County militia, commanded by Colonel George Mason and Captain John Brent. Coming upon two cabins, they began shooting the inmates; only after killing fourteen of them did Mason discover that he had shot friendly Susquehannocks by mistake. The Susquehannocks had recently moved to the area after being driven from their homeland by the Mohawks following a battle for control of the trade between the Chesapeake, Ohio, and Great Lakes.

The result was an escalation of the fighting, necessitating another expedition; this time Colonel John Washington commanded the militia of all the Rappahannock counties. Washington's orders were to inflict "such Execution upon the said Indians as shall be found necessary." In due course the force joined a party of Marylanders and surrounded a Susquehannock fort. Indicating a desire to treat, five chiefs came out to parley, denying any knowledge of the recent murders and blaming a Seneca war party from the north. Their answer did not satisfy the Virginians, since several Susquehannocks had been found near the scene of recent incidents with the clothing of murdered whites. The chiefs were accordingly executed, though on whose orders it is not clear, since the Virginians subsequently tried to exculpate themselves by blaming the Marylanders.

The Susquehannocks quickly went on the warpath with further attacks on the Virginian backcountry as far south as Surry County. Berkeley's first response was to propose a new expedition under Colonel Chicheley, but fearing an escalation of the troubles and recognizing that the American Indians were not entirely to blame, he ordered the expedition to return. Berkeley was perhaps influenced by news that a ferocious war had broken out with the American Indians in New England and may have acted to avoid uniting those involved in a similar struggle to the south. The Virginians were accordingly ordered to remain inside their perimeter forts. Unfortunately, the extension of white settlement had made such forts inadequate; soon Berkeley was accused of pursuing this policy simply to protect his fur trade interests. An act of 1661 stated that anyone engaged in this trade must first get a license from the governor and be of "known integrity," which of course meant friendly with Berkeley.

Feeling was especially bitter on the frontier in Charles and Henrico counties, which were isolated and seemingly ignored by the governor and his clique at Jamestown. When a meeting of angry farmers was held to discuss the situation, it was attended by a young man who had recently come from England to establish a plantation. Nathaniel Bacon was well connected. He had an uncle on the council and had himself been invited to join because, as Berkeley commented, "Gentlemen of your quality come very rarely into this country." As he was also a good speaker, it was natural for the Henrico farmers to make him their leader; and since his own overseer had just been murdered, he accepted willingly.

Agreement was quickly reached to launch an expedition against the Susquehannocks in defiance of Berkeley. Bacon and his men were joined on the way by the Ocaneechee Indians, who tracked down a party of the Susquehannocks, butchering most of them in a surprise attack. In the aftermath Bacon and his native allies fell out, possibly over the division of spoils, which the Ocaneechee rightly felt belonged to them. Bacon did subsequently attempt to justify what followed by asserting that the Ocaneechees had refused him food for his return home. Whatever the reason, three or four of his men were killed, while nearly all the Ocaneechee men, women, and children were burned to death or shot as they attempted to flee. Bacon proudly boasted, "In the heat of the Fight we . . . destroyed them all," and he gloated that his forces had "left all nations of Indians . . . ingaged in a civil war amongst themselves [to] their utter ruin and destruction." Later he justified his action to Berkeley by declaring that the American Indians were "all our enemies."[2]

The news of these events naturally infuriated Berkeley, especially as it was a member of the council who had defied his orders and thus jeopardized his own attempts to calm the situation. He therefore declared Bacon a traitor. Berkeley, however, was aware of his own unpopularity, and not simply with the frontiersmen. The tidewater counties, too, were alienated from the Green Spring clique which controlled the assembly, local government, and the granting of land. Accordingly, in May 1676 Berkeley ordered fresh elections for the first time in fourteen years, inviting all those with grievances to state them openly. At the same time he issued a declaration defending his long association with the province, though privately he wrote to England requesting to be relieved by a younger "more vigorous Governor." The assembly was to meet on June 5 at Jamestown.

Initially, this ploy seemed to work. Bacon himself was elected for Henrico County and requested the governor's pardon for his late escapade. Berkeley agreed, though by now both men distrusted each other, as Bacon demonstrated by keeping a considerable guard about him. Meanwhile the assembly got down to business. First, an act was passed to pacify the frontier counties by granting Bacon a commission to march against the American Indians. Another measure prohibited all trade except with "friendly Indians," while any deserted land was to revert to the colony. The assembly then turned to the question of the better government of Virginia. An act was passed preventing sheriffs from holding their posts in consecutive years and also placing restraints on their collection of taxes and on the fees paid to them. Another act gave freeholders the right to elect the vestries in an attempt to reopen public office holding. A similar measure was adopted for the county courts. Next the annulment of the Franchise Act of 1670 restored the vote to all freemen rather than just freeholders.[3]

The actions of the assembly were rudely disturbed on June 23, 1676, by the arrival of Bacon with four hundred armed men. The plan to levy a force from the whole population apparently did not please him or his associates – Giles Bland, William Drummond, and William Lawrence – who wanted to recruit men from Henrico and New Kent, believing that they would be more effective and doubtless more amenable. Bacon also desired his commission immediately, not in three months' time when the necessary taxes had been raised. A confrontation ensued on the steps of the general assembly, with the timorous representatives beseeching Berkeley to give in and Bacon threatening fire and the sword if his demand was refused. Although Berkeley finally gave way, Bacon and his comrades would not depart until they had compelled the assembly to pass an act of indemnity in compensation for their proceedings.

This humiliation was too much for the governor. As soon as Bacon had marched off to attack the American Indians, Berkeley declared him a traitor again and summoned the

---

[2]   Quoted in Warren M. Billings, ed., *The Old Dominion in the Seventeenth Century: A Documentary History of Virginia, 1606–1689* (Chapel Hill, 1975), 267–9. The original document is in the Public Record Office, London (Colonial Office 1/36, 77).
[3]   The complete list of acts passed by Bacon's assembly is printed in Billings, *Old Dominion,* 274–5. The full text can be found in William W. Hening, ed., *The Statutes at Large: Being a Collection of All the Laws of Virginia from the First Session of the Legislature, in the Year 1619* (Richmond, 1809–23), II, 341–65.

DOCUMENT 12

Declaration of Nathaniel Bacon in the name of the people of Virginia, July 30, 1676, reprinted in W. Keith Kavenagh, *Foundations of Colonial America: A Documentary History* (New York, 1973), III, 1783–4.

[Bacon's declaration was calculated to appeal both *to the tidewater areas about high taxes and the monopolization of office by the clique that surrounded Berkeley, and the backcountry, which wanted better protection from the American Indians.]*

Charges against Sir William Berkeley
1. For having, upon specious pretenses of public works, raised great unjust taxes upon the commonalty for the advancement of private favorites and other sinister ends . . .
2. For having abused and rendered contemptible the magistrates of justice by advancing to places of judicature scandalous and ignorant favorites.
3. For having wronged his Majesty's prerogative and interest by assuming monopoly of the beaver trade and having for unjust gain, betrayed and sold his Majesty's country and the lives of his loyal subjects to the barbarous heathen.
4. For having protected, favored, and emboldened the Indians against his Majesty's loyal subjects, never contriving, requiring, or appointing any due or proper means of satisfaction for their many invasions, robberies, and murders committed upon us.
5. For having . . . when we might with ease have destroyed them . . . sent back our army by passing his word for the peaceable demeanor of the said Indians, who immediately prosecuted their evil intentions . . .
6. And lately, when upon the loud outcries of blood, the assembly had, with all care raised and framed an army for the preventing of further mischief . . . for having, with only the privacy of some few favorites without acquainting the people . . . forged a commission, by we know not what hand, not only without but even against the consent of the people, for the raising and effecting civil war and destruction.
   Of this and the aforesaid articles we accuse Sir William Berkeley as guilty of each and every one the same.

[While Bacon claimed unanimous support, other tidewater residents were complaining of his arbitrary actions and looking to Berkeley for protection.]

To the Right Honorable Sir William Berkeley, Governor and Captain General of Virginia. The humble Petition of the county of Gloucester, 1676, reprinted in Kavenagh, *Colonial America*, III, 1780–1.
That whereas your petitioners have always been ready to give all due and just obedience to all laws, especially the late laws for securing our neighbors the frontiers of this county from the incursions of the barbarous Indians, and for the total destruction of them by our speedy raising men, horses, arms, and provisions according as the laws required, since which time Mr Nathaniel Bacon Jr. having sent several warrants to this county for the impressing more men, horses, and arms, grounded, as he pretends, upon a commission from your Honor to be general of all the forces in Virginia against

the Indians; which commission, although we have never seen or heard published, we have not failed to comply with . . .

Nevertheless, Mr Bacon . . . lately came down into the county with a consider-able number of armed men and horses, who went into all parts of our county and took what horses and arms they pleased . . . and not only so but did in many places behave themselves very rudely both in words and actions to the great disturbance of the peace of the county [so that] we have just reasons to fear for the county in general . . .

militia to his aid. Now Berkeley experienced the full effects of his alienation from the tidewater counties. Though adherents like Henry Chicheley tried to muster the Gloucester and Middlesex levies, the militia simply melted away when Bacon reappeared in July 1676. This time Berkeley had to flee to the eastern shore, while Bacon issued a manifesto "in the Name of the People of Virginia," accusing Berkeley of graft and corruption, of levying huge taxes for personal profit, and of condoning murder by the native inhabitants to preserve his illegal trading monopoly. Bacon's intention was "to represent our sad and heavy grievances to his most sacred majesty." But in the meantime, being "general by Consent of the people," he issued a list of Berkeley's "wicked and pernicious councillors" who were to surrender immediately, among them Chicheley, Philip Ludwell, Robert Beverley, Richard Lee, and William Sherwood. Any colonists giving them aid would have their property confiscated.[4]

Having secured his position, Bacon marched inland once more. His target this time was the friendly Pamunkey people, who had to flee into a swamp for safety. Berkeley meanwhile returned to Jamestown, only to be attacked by Bacon once more. During the assault on September 18 the town was burned, and Berkeley for a second time had to take refuge on the eastern shore. In the aftermath armed servants and slaves took advantage of the general lawlessness to exact revenge on those who had used them ill. Among the sacked plantations was Berkeley's at Green Spring.

It is difficult to predict quite how long these events might have lasted had not Bacon fallen ill and died in October. Deprived of his charismatic influence, the movement soon disintegrated. Bacon's confederates were steadily rounded up and brought before the embittered Berkeley. Twenty-three were summarily hanged, despite a royal proclamation pardoning everyone except Bacon. The executions continued until April 1677, when Berkeley finally surrendered the governorship to Colonel Herbert Jeffreys, who arrived in February with a thousand troops to quell the disorders. Accompanying him were two other commissioners charged with conducting an inquiry.

It was a sad end to Berkeley's career. He had been in the province thirty-four years and had rendered many public services. In most respects he was a Virginian himself. Therein lay his weakness. He was too personally involved and too old to handle affairs dispassionately.

The commissioners took depositions from various colonists. The inhabitants of Gloucester County emphasized the hardship caused by the various taxes, the fear that the Arlington–Culpepper patent would lead "to the enslaving" of the inhabitants, and the terror created by the American Indians which gave Bacon the opportunity to exploit the

---

[4] For a copy of the declaration, see Billings, *Old Dominion*, 277–9.

situation. The commissioners themselves blamed Bacon's ability to exploit the "giddy headed multitude," most of whom "had but lately crept out of the condition of servants." However, they conceded that high taxes had been a factor.

In the nineteenth century this episode was frequently portrayed as a bid for independence, with Bacon playing the role of a George Washington, but this interpretation no longer holds credence. Bacon had been in Virginia less than two years. Apart from his demand for an American Indian commission, he had no program or philosophy. He was certainly not fighting against the English government. If he intended to resist the redcoats, as one bystander subsequently claimed, it was only until he could inform the king of the situation. In many respects Bacon's cause seems to have been little more than a vendetta against Berkeley dressed up in seventeenth-century opposition rhetoric.[5]

Why, then, was Bacon able to make so much mischief? For one thing, Virginia was still a frontier society which lacked institutional cohesion and was therefore vulnerable to rumors and demands for wild action against supposed enemies. For another, the colony had developed two distinct societies: the frontier counties of Henrico, New Kent, and Stafford; and the more settled counties of James City, Gloucester, and Middlesex. Berkeley's misfortune was to fall foul of both. Later governors usually made sure to preserve the goodwill of the tidewater counties in case they needed their support against the piedmont.

The consequences of Bacon's Rebellion were less severe than might have been expected. Some of the reforms passed by Bacon's assembly were lost, notably that relating to the franchise, while several others were amended. The request for a royal charter also met with a setback. Although one was ultimately granted, it ominously failed to give the assembly any overt recognition. Indeed the next royal governor, Lord Culpepper, had specific instructions not to allow the burgesses the right to initiate legislation. In addition he was to seek a permanent revenue to strengthen royal control. The planters were sufficiently cowed to grant him a two-shilling duty on each hogshead of tobacco exported.

Interestingly it was Berkeley's faction, led by Ludwell and Beverley, which resisted the royal plan. Beverley's punishment was to lose his position as clerk to the assembly, while Ludwell was dismissed from the council. The Crown soon discovered, however, that it could govern only with the help of the elite, and within a year both men had been restored to their positions.

The crushing of the rebellion did not mark the end of Virginia's troubles, for in 1682 serious riots in Gloucester County were provoked by the low price of tobacco. Nevertheless, Bacon's Rebellion did constitute a watershed, heralding significant changes in Virginian society. One such was the substitution of African servitude for white indentured labour. The reasons for this switch are in dispute. Some historians argue that the planters began using African slaves after Bacon's Rebellion in the belief that they would be easier to control. Others maintain that a population decline in England, combined with competition from Pennsylvania, simply made fewer servants available, prompting the wealthier planters to turn to African sources instead.

---

[5]   The view that Bacon was an early George Washington can be found in Thomas J. Wertenbaker, *Torch-bearer of the Rebellion: The Story of Bacon's Rebellion and its Leader* (Princeton, 1940). For a contrary view, see Wilcomb E. Washburn, *The Governor and the Rebel: A History of Bacon's Rebellion in Virginia* (Chapel Hill, 1957). A more recent version of the old interpretation is Stephen Saunders Webb, *1676: The End of American Independence* (New York, 1984).

There were in any case a number of other contributing factors. The ending of the Royal African Company's monopoly in 1698 encouraged more traders to enter the slave business. At the same time a decline in the demand for slaves in the Caribbean, where the production of sugar had peaked, forced many slave traders to look for other markets, dropping their prices at the same time.

The main reason for the increased trade in Africans, however, was the changing attitude of the planters. Until the 1680s most planters aimed to make their fortune quickly so that they could retire to England. It did not make sense to pay the extra cost of a slave whose labor the owner might not live to enjoy. Short-term white indentures were far more cost-effective even if it meant replacing the workforce every four or five years and knowing that some ex-servants would buy plantations and become competitors.

Now profound demographic changes in the colony were encouraging more planters to think in the long term. Until 1680 Virginia had been overwhelmingly a land of immigrants with short life spans. Now a growing percentage of the population were native born, with greater immunity to disease than their parents and, consequently, a longer life expectancy. The new Creole generation were also able to marry earlier and raise larger families.[6]

In consequence a white native population evolved which could see not only the advantages of a permanent slave labor force, especially one that reproduced itself, but also the attractions of their environment. Virginia was their home, not a temporary refuge, and as a result they now built for the future. At last, after nearly a hundred years, the crude wattle and daub structures began to give way to more grandiose houses, often of brick, or at least with brick chimneys and foundations. The wealthier inhabitants at least began to enjoy English standards of comfort.[7] Political and social horizons also changed. Even the most successful no longer thought of returning to England, preferring instead to serve on the council or assembly and develop institutions like the College of William and Mary, which received its charter in 1692. Local pride was also behind the writing of Robert Beverley, Jr.'s *History of Virginia*, in which he described the province as the "best poor man's country." Unknowingly the colony had changed from a crude frontier society to the more sophisticated type of province which was to be so conspicuous a feature during the eighteenth century. Tidewater Virginia was also now a "slave society" not a "society with slaves."

There was one other important, though unanticipated development which resulted from these demographic and economic changes, namely, the different relationship between the elite and the rest of the white population. No longer was it one of exploiter and exploited; that position had been taken over by the African-Americans. Herein lay the reason for the new amity among whites. The small planters constituted the bulk of the

---

[6] The view that Africans were substituted for servants because they were more reliable is put forward by Morgan in *American Slavery, American Freedom*, though he believes that the decision was more subconscious than rational. The argument that the switch occurred primarily because of a decline in the supply of servants is presented in Russell R. Menard, "From Servants to Slaves: The Transformation of the Chesapeake Labor System," *Southern Studies*, XVI, 1977, 355–90. The effects of greater life expectancy and the creation of a white native class are discussed by Allan Kulikoff in *Tobacco and Slaves: The Development of Southern Cultures in the Chesapeake, 1689–1800* (Chapel Hill, 1986). For a useful summary, see Warren M. Billings, John E. Selby, and Thad W. Tate, *Colonial Virginia: A History* (New York, 1986).

[7] See James Horn's *Adapting to a New World: English Society in Seventeenth Century Chesapeake* (Chapel Hill, 1994), in which the author argues that most people suffered a drop in their standard of housing before 1700 compared with what they would have enjoyed in England.

militia and would be responsible for suppressing any uprising by the slaves. Almost sub-consciously the grandees began to cooperate more with their less affluent neighbors, helping them market their crops, giving them credit, and assisting them in numerous other ways. They were encouraged to do so because this attitude complemented the new image they had of themselves as leaders of a civilized provincial society.

2 MASSACHUSETTS: THE STRUGGLE TO REMAIN SELF-GOVERNING

Virginia was not the only colony to experience trouble in the second decade of the Restoration; an equally bitter conflict was taking place in New England.

These had not been happy times, especially for the people of Massachusetts. In 1672 the Crown had announced plans for a new commission to investigate the condition of the colony. Although the third Dutch war intervened, few could doubt that further efforts would be made.

Another reason for doubt and uncertainty was an apparent decline in religious zeal. The second generation appeared forgetful of why the first had come to Massachusetts and displayed a distinct preference for material goods. As one leading minister commented, "Land hath been the idol of New England . . . they that profess themselves Christians, have foresaken Churches, and Ordinances, and all for land." A young woman visitor from Plymouth was equally critical after a visit to Boston in 1676. She observed, "Through all my life I have never seen such an array of fashion and splendour . . . silken hoods, scarlett petticoats with silver lace, white sarsenet plaited gowns, bone lace and silken scarfs." Even the men sported "fancy ruffles and ribbons."

Typical of this new materialism was the example of Winthrop's own son, John. From an early stage he was involved in the settling of the Connecticut Valley, driven by specu-lative rather than spiritual considerations. Then in 1644 he tried to establish a blast furnace and iron foundry on the Saugus River and also tried to exploit other metals like lead, tin, and copper. His later involvement in the capture of New York was similarly rooted in commercial motives, as was his participation in the activities of the Atherton Company, which sought to secure the Narragansett country from its native owners. Winthrop also helped found several Massachusetts towns, notably Ipswich, even though he resided there for only a few months. New settlements were always anxious to attract the support of wealthy sponsors, offering them in return a share of the land.

The Pynchon family of Springfield presents a similar example. John Pynchon followed his father, William, in establishing a virtual monopoly of wealth in this frontier community. Thirty percent of the population were Pynchon's tenants, and few escaped that status, unless they were foreclosed. Pynchon helped too in the establishment of several new towns. Such activities made Winthrop and Pynchon, in effect, professional town promoters.

But it was not only the wealthy who were acting in an entrepreneurial fashion. The proprietors of Dedham, anticipating the day when land might no longer be available for their descendants, obtained a grant from the general court for the establishment of Deerfield in western Massachusetts. Few actually left Dedham, and only those with capital to invest stood to benefit. Similar ventures were undertaken by other long-established towns.

Some historians believe that what was taking place was a fundamental transition from a community-based society, dedicated to the observance of God's covenant, to one which was aggressively capitalistic and individualistic. The concept of the just price had given way to the more competitive values of the marketplace. Usury, or lending money for interest, was no longer considered extortion. In consequence, capital was triumphing over labor. The Puritan was being replaced by the Yankee.[8]

Of course such materialism was not incompatible with religious zeal. The early Puritans had never ignored the economic benefits of their new commonwealth, and most historians have rejected the view that religious zeal was in decline, though the imbalance in the number of church members relative to the total population presented a serious problem. Especially perplexing was the dilemma surrounding the children of the unregenerate, who could not be baptized and therefore could not become saints, thus further decreasing the church's eligible membership. Although many parents accepted their own exclusion from full membership, they were aggrieved that their children must always be denied the chance of salvation.

Accordingly, in 1662 the ministers agreed to the Half-Way Covenant, permitting the baptism of children even though the parents were not of the elect in the hope that the offspring might succeed where the parents had failed. Since the Puritans were congregational, however, it was left to the individual churches to implement the new covenant. Ironically many refused, on the grounds that the Half-Way Covenant undermined the fundamental standards of Puritanism. This stance has led many historians to believe that declension was not as serious as has often been suggested.[9]

A lack of commitment to God manifested itself in other ways too. Even the elect increasingly settled their disputes in court rather than as members of a covenanted

---

[8] For the changing values of seventeenth-century New England, see Richard S. Dunn, *Puritan and Yankee: The Winthrop Dynasty of New England, 1630–1717* (Princeton, 1962); Darrett B. Rutman, *Winthrop's Boston: Portrait of a Puritan Town, 1630–1649* (Chapel Hill, 1965); Frederick Martin, *Profits in the Wilderness: Entrepreneurship and the Founding of New England Towns in the Seventeenth Century* (Chapel Hill, 1991); Stephen Innes, *Creating the Commonwealth: Economic Culture of Puritan New England* (New York, 1995); Mark Valeri, "Religious Discipline and the Market: Puritans and the Issue of Usury", *William and Mary Quarterly*, LIV, 1997, 746–68; and Margaret Ellen Newell, *From Dependency to Independence: Economic Revolution in Colonial New England* (Ithaca, 1998). The continued predominance of the community over the individual is argued by Helena M. Wall, *Fierce Communion: Family and Community in Early America* (Cambridge, Mass., 1990). For the entrepreneurial Pynchon family, see Stephen Innes, *Labor in a New Land: Economy and Society in Seventeenth Century Springfield* (Princeton, 1983). Historians are unable to agree on when the market became predominant. Gary B. Nash finds traces of the old communal values as late as the 1730s, notably in Boston when there was a dispute over the building of a new market house. See *The Urban Crucible: Social Change, Political Consciousness; and the Origins of the American Revolution* (Cambridge, Mass., 1979). In contrast, James Henretta, *The Origins of American Capitalism: Collected Essays* (Boston, 1991); and Alan Kulikoff, *The Agrarian Origins of American Capitalism* (Charlottesville, 1992) believe that the era of the American Revolution and federal Constitution was the time when capitalism, wage labor, and free markets first triumphed. Other writers, in response to the collapse of socialism in Eastern Europe, are now pushing the origins of the market further into the past. See chapter 10, section 2.

[9] The view that Puritanism was in decline was popular with Progressive historians during the two World Wars. See James Truslow Adams, *The Founding of New England* (Boston, 1927); and William W. Sweet, *Religion in Colonial America* (New York, 1942). It was to counter such views that Perry Miller wrote *Orthodoxy in Massachusetts, 1630–1650: A Genetic Study* (Cambridge, Mass., 1933) and *The New England Mind*, 2 vols (New York, 1939). However, even Miller admitted that Puritanism was in decline by the end of the seventeenth century. This interpretation has been challenged subsequently by, among others, Robert G. Pope, *The Half Way Covenant: Church Membership in Puritan New England* (Princeton, 1969); and by Gerald F. Moran and Maris A Vinovskis, "The Puritan Family and Religion: A Critical Reappraisal," *William and Mary Quarterly*, XXXIX, 1982, 29–63. The debate has more recently shifted to declension in the eighteenth century; see chapter 13, section 1.

community. Many ministers remained unpaid; others were not given permanent positions. Their frustration increasingly resulted in jeremiads, or sermons forecasting damnation and hell for their flock unless they returned to the way of the Lord.

For many, God's anger was shortly to be displayed when in 1675 the New England colonies became engaged in a bitter struggle with the American Indians which became known as King Philip's War. The conflict was the natural result of population pressure on the native peoples immediately to the west and north, notably the Wampanoags, Narragansetts, Mohegans, Poducks, and Nipmucks. For some time relations had been deteriorating. The sachems resented the activities of missionaries like John Eliot, which undermined the authority of the chiefs and shamans, while the Narragansetts were alarmed at the machinations of the Atherton Company, which spuriously claimed part of their lands because of some unpaid debts. In 1659 the commissioners of the United Colonies, who included John Winthrop, Jr., had fined the Narragansetts for some alleged property offenses. Winthrop and the Atherton Company had then paid the fine for the Indians, claiming Narragansett Bay as security, a typical piece of white sharp practice. All the native peoples were hurt by the white settlers' hogs and cattle, which strayed into their fields. Worse, their economies were destroyed as the game was driven away and the fur trade ceased. Even wampum declined in value, being superseded by the pine tree shilling as the medium of exchange.

Following the death of Massasoit in 1662 there had been several warning signs. Massasoit's successor, Philip, or Metacomet as he is often called,[10] had twice been summoned, first to Plymouth and then to Boston, to be fined and ordered to surrender his weapons. This was despite the breach of an understanding by Plymouth that it would not proceed with plans for a new town of Swansea. Metacomet was a proud warrior. Like Opechancanough in Virginia, he now recognized that he must fight or lose his country altogether.

The actual hostilities began in June 1675 when a native informer was murdered, supposedly at the instigation of Metacomet himself. Initially only the Wampanoags took up arms, beginning their campaign with an assault on the offending settlement at Swansea. At this point a general uprising by the native peoples does not seem to have been planned, but once Massachusetts went to the aid of Plymouth, a wider conflict was almost inevitable. After Metacomet persuaded the Nipmucks to enter the war, fighting spread to the upper Connecticut Valley and the town of Northfield had to be abandoned in September 1675. Up to this point the Narragansetts had remained neutral, but the colonists were suspicious of their good intentions. When information was received in November that they were harboring some of Metacomet's women and children in an area of Rhode Island known as the Great Swamp, the New Englanders sent a combined force under Josiah Winslow against them which killed three hundred men, women, and children. As at the Pequot fort in 1637, most of the victims were burnt to death, since the first thing Winslow did was to surround the Narragansett fort with a ring of fire. This savage assault promptly increased support for Metacomet, since most American Indians now realized that they were fighting for their lives. Plymouth and Providence came under fire, as did Weymouth and Sudbury, only twenty miles from Boston. Most notable was the routing of a force under Captain Lathrop

---

[10]   There is no agreement among scholars about the correct spelling. Some shorten Metacomet to Metacom. However, Jill Lepore, *In the Name of War: King Philip's War and the Origins of American Identity* (New York, 1998), xix–xxi, argues for keeping the traditional name of Philip.

in the Connecticut Valley, in which sixty of Lathrop's men were killed. Metacomet achieved another success near Providence when sixty men under Captain Pierce died.

At this point the war seemed to favor Metacomet and his allies, whose daring raids had proved too much for the slow-footed colonists. Metacomet received additional support from the Abenaki people to the north, but when he sought the assistance of the Mahican nation, he was attacked by the Mohawks and forced to withdraw with heavy losses. The setback proved especially calamitous because the winter fighting had robbed Metacomet's people of their reserves of food, ammunition, and shelter.

In truth, though, Metacomet and his allies had no real chance against the combined resources of the United Colonies with their population of seventy thousand and reserves of food and ammunition. American Indian society, with its delicate balance between humans and nature, was far too easily disrupted. Women and children were especially vulnerable once their crops and habitations had been destroyed prior to the onset of winter. In addition, Metacomet had to contend with the Indian allies of the colonists, notably the Mohegans under chief Uncas, though ironically such help was not initially appreciated. This failure by Massachusetts in particular proved significant, for it was not until Indian allies were enlisted that the war finally changed in the colonists' favour, as John Eliot readily confessed: "In our first war with the Indians, God pleased to show us the vanity of our military skill, in managing our arms after the European mode. Now we are glad to learn the skulking way of war."

As a result the various tribal groups were steadily tracked down, killed, or sold into slavery in the West Indies, as indeed were Metacomet's own family, after he had been cornered and shot in a swamp. Although some sporadic trouble continued in Maine, by the summer of 1676 it was all over. The American Indians of southern New England had effectively been reduced to a few remnants cooped up in special villages, their way of life and environment destroyed forever. Among the casualties were Eliot's praying towns, most of whose inhabitants, though friendly, had been interned on Deer Island near Boston in conditions of great hardship. Indeed, in the confusion some were shipped to the West Indies, despite the protests of Eliot and Samuel Gookin that this contravened the Puritan obligation to convert the native peoples. Afterwards only four towns remained, while Eliot's seminary at Harvard produced only one Indian minister before it closed in 1692.[11] The prospects for racial harmony even among the converted had been hopelessly compromised.

As in Virginia, the net result was the clearing of the coastal areas for exclusive white settlement. But the war had been fought at a terrible price. Twelve towns had been destroyed, almost half the rest had suffered some damage, one out of every fifteen men of military age had been killed, and all of the United Colonies had incurred large debts. Moreover, damage of another kind had been inflicted, that to the New Englanders' sense of identity and purpose. During the war they had committed as many atrocities as the enemy, disembowelling their dead and placing their heads on poles as trophies. The conundrum of living in a wilderness while attempting to remain a civilized and Godly people was profoundly unsettling.[12] The scars of the war were to remain for a long time.

---

[11] The four surviving towns were Natick, Punkapaug, Hassanamesit, and Wamesit.

[12] The publication in 1682 of Mary Rowlandson's account of her capture by the Nipmuck Indians at Lancaster also highlighted the dilemma. Not only was Rowlandson's life spared, but she was treated with something akin to respect in contrast to the New Englanders' treatment of their captives.

It was to address such doubts that the general court of Massachusetts agreed to a new congregational synod in 1679. At the top of the agenda was the perceived declension in New England's religiosity. The ministers, however, were unable to suggest anything other than the old shibboleths of a more rigorous observance of the sabbath, stricter parental control of unruly children, a closer regulation of taverns, and a turning away from material goods. The last, they believed, could be achieved by new sumptuary laws.

Meanwhile the threat of further English intervention remained omnipresent. The 1673 Navigation Act had empowered the governor to appoint a naval officer in each colony to monitor its implementation. This Massachusetts had not done. Then in 1675 the king appointed a special subcommittee of the Privy Council, called the Lords of Trade, to supervise the colonies, which issued a stern warning requiring all the acts of trade to be observed. Shortly afterwards it sent a special envoy, Edward Randolph, to check on New England's compliance. His presence was deeply offensive to the general court, determined as it was to remain self-governing. The members believed that since Massachusetts was not represented in Parliament, Parliament's laws were not valid in the colonies. As Governor John Leverett bluntly told Randolph on his first visit in 1676, "The Laws made by your Majesty and your parliament obligeth them in nothing but what consists with the interest" of the colony, for "the legislative power abides in them solely" by virtue of the charter. The most that the commonwealth would do was to pass duplicate legislation as a gesture of goodwill.[13]

Another act of defiance was the continued minting of the 1652 pine tree shilling, an abuse of one of the Crown's most cherished privileges. The province had also unilaterally reasserted control over New Hampshire and Maine, despite the recommendations of the commissioners in 1665. New Hampshire was finally declared a royal province in 1680, but Massachusetts kept its grasp on Maine, angering the Crown further by buying out the heirs of Sir Fernando Gorges in an attempt to make good its claim. This move prompted the Privy Council once more to order Massachusetts to send envoys to England to answer Randolph's charges.

Massachusetts still hoped that the government of Charles II would either lack the means to implement its plans or be overthrown by a coup d'état. During 1680 England was convulsed by a Whig opposition attempt in Parliament to curb the Crown. God had saved Massachusetts from the ravages of King Metacomet; a similar miracle might also save it from Charles II.

The general court thus continued to drag its feet. It was slow to appoint envoys and gave them little power. It also obstructed Randolph when he returned in 1681 with a permanent commission as collector of the customs by appointing its own naval officer. Of the thirty-four vessels prosecuted by Randolph, the courts released every one and made Randolph pay the costs. The collector was not completely friendless, however. A number of wealthy merchants engaged in the transatlantic trade, such as Joseph Dudley, were anxious to cooperate for the sake of their commerce. Also, Randolph catalogued so many colonial misdemeanors that even the lackadaisical Charles II could not but take action eventually. Apart from their infractions of the trade laws, Randolph noted that the Puritans

---

[13]   A copy of Randolph's report can be found in Michael G. Hall, Lawrence H. Leder, and Michael G. Kammen, eds, *The Glorious Revolution in America: Documents on the Colonial Crisis of 1689* (Chapel Hill, 1964).

continued to persecute Quakers, failed to take the oath of allegiance, and omitted the king's name in their official proceedings. The day of reckoning could not be far off.

3 NEW JERSEY AND PENNSYLVANIA: THE BEGINNINGS

Randolph's concern for the Quakers was judicial rather than religious, for like most people he did not believe in toleration. Persecution was rife in England too, as the Test and Corporation acts demonstrated. The Test acts of 1673 and 1678 had been passed to fill loopholes in the penal laws by specifically excluding Catholics from holding office and sitting in Parliament. In the colonies, however, few suffered so severely as the Society of Friends, or Quakers, as they were commonly called because they allegedly trembled or quaked at the name of the Lord.

The Quakers were followers of George Fox, an itinerant preacher who wanted to restore Christianity to its original simplicity. Essentially Fox and his followers were extreme Protestants, though of a different kind from the Puritans. They believed that everyone could be saved, since all were the children of God and could experience his inner light. They therefore had no need of a formal priesthood or liturgy like the Bible and Book of Common Prayer. Even the holy trinity was of little importance. They relied solely on the innate goodness of the individual and the power of communal prayer to produce an environment in which they could live in "holy conversation."

These views were naturally abhorrent to the other churches, which considered them a denial of everything they believed necessary for salvation. Unfortunately the Quakers exacerbated their persecution by further deviations from accepted community standards. One problem was their refusal to swear oaths on the Bible, an act which, they argued, would imply that they were not telling the truth on other occasions. Another was their view that the taking of life could never be justified. This belief led them to refuse to perform militia service or to pay taxes even for self-defense. Finally they made a fetish of wearing plain black garments which visibly set them apart from the rest of the population. They suffered cruelly both in England and America.

The Quakers, however, did not lack support. Many of them did well in commerce, because of their truthfulness and penchant for hard work. They also made an exceptional convert in William Penn. Penn's father, who had been a senior naval commander during the first and second Dutch wars, subsequently introduced his son to both Charles II and James, Duke of York. This personal connection was to be of immense value, for it enabled Penn, like Baltimore, to use his influence to secure a refuge for his coreligionists. Penn's motives were not totally altruistic; like all New World proprietors he was anxious to build up his own patrimony by acquiring land and participating in the fur trade.

Penn first attempted to establish a settlement in America in 1676, when he and several other Quakers became trustees for the estate of Edward Byllinge in West New Jersey. The Jerseys had been part of New Netherland until the Duke of York granted them to Sir George Carteret and John Lord Berkeley in 1664. At this point the population did not exceed two hundred (mainly Dutch) settlers living in Bergen County, though the number grew following the sale by Nicolls of 400,000 acres to some Long Island Puritans, who created the townships of Elizabeth and Newark. The two proprietors, who were also involved in the Carolinas, did little to advance their new possessions and subsequently divided the territory between them, but in 1674 Berkeley sold his holdings in West New Jersey to Byllinge and another Quaker, John Fenwick.

It was when these two men quarreled over their purchase that Penn became involved. The area's current legal status was, however, unsatisfactory from his point of view, as the Jersey grant gave title to the land but did not officially grant governmental authority to pass laws protecting the Quaker religion. York did finally confirm the right of government in August 1680, and two years later Penn and eleven other prominent Quakers jointly purchased East New Jersey from the Carteret family. In that very transaction lay another problem: with so many proprietors, confusion was inevitable.

Penn therefore decided to seek a more substantial grant elsewhere. Knowing from his current investment that the lands behind the Delaware were still unclaimed, he decided to seek a formal charter for them. Charles II, who had borrowed heavily from his father, the admiral, owed Penn a considerable sum. Once again the king found it convenient to pay off his debts by a grant of land in America.

Under the charter of February 1681, the new province was to extend from twelve miles north of Newcastle along the Delaware River until the forty-third parallel. The land was to be held in free and common socage for the payment of a small annual quitrent. Penn could grant lands on such terms as he chose, including the creation of manors, and could make all laws and raise taxes, subject to "the advice, assent, and approbation of the Freemen of the said Country." In an emergency he could promulgate ordinances without the assembly, provided all such edicts were consonant with the laws of England "as conveniently may be."

No mention was made of religion beyond the right of twenty inhabitants to petition the Bishop of London for a minister. Penn's own intention was that there should be no established church but that toleration would be the norm, resulting in a society where all Christians lived in harmony bound by mutual respect. Penn called this his "holy experiment."

Despite Penn's considerable powers, the charter contained several deviations from the earlier Durham palatinate grants. The Privy Council was to be the last court of appeal, while to prevent any "misconstruction" of the proprietary power, all laws were to be forwarded within five years for inspection, with those found inconsistent to be disallowed. Another check on Penn's power was the requirement that he must have an agent in London answerable for any infractions of his patent. Furthermore, all commerce was to be "according to the lawes made or to be made within our Kingdom of England" and Penn was obliged to admit any officers sent for their enforcement. In return the king promised to levy no taxes except with "the consent of the Proprietary, or chief governor, or assembly, or by act of Parliament in England."[14]

The reason for these restrictions was that colonial administration was beginning to change. A new type of bureaucrat was emerging who believed that authority should be concentrated in the Crown, not some feudal palatine. Another notable feature was the mention of Parliament for the first time, reflecting its new role in the administration of the colonies following the passage of the Navigation acts. Ironically, at this very moment Charles II was trying to reduce Parliament's influence at home.

---

[14] For the full text of Penn's charter, see Kavenagh, *Documentary History*, II, 849–56.

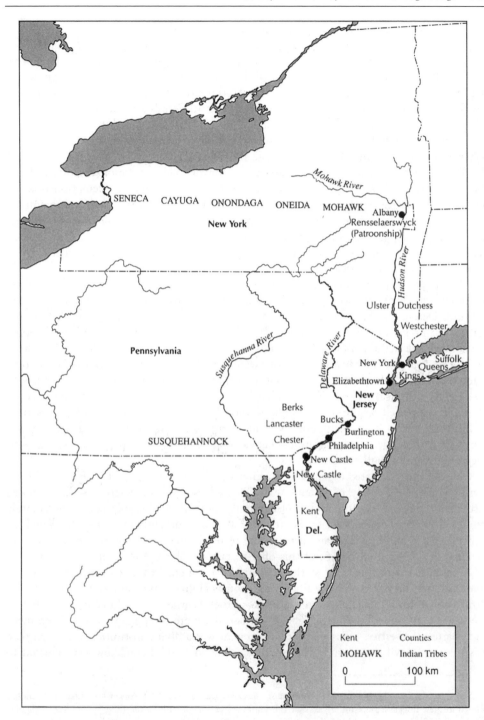

Map 6   The middle colonies in the later seventeenth century.

These restrictions did not worry Penn unduly, since the kind of holy experiment he sought was very different from the one envisaged earlier by John Winthrop, a point which has often been overlooked by historians.[15] Penn, like all Quakers, believed that people were intrinsically good and needed only marginal direction. This view was the exact opposite of the Puritan concept of human depravity. Hence the kind of harsh, repressive government which Winthrop regarded as necessary had no place in Penn's scheme of things. To him persecution, not dissent, was the real crime.

Although Penn was sole proprietor, he did not have the financial resources to fund the settlement project on his own. He therefore turned to a group of wealthy Quakers, called the Free Society of Traders, who arranged for the purchase of various holdings of ten thousand acres each and also negotiated special privileges, including exemption from all quitrents and choice of the best waterfront sites in the new city which Penn was planning. They also reserved seats for themselves on the governing council. These concessions were shortly to cause some bitterness, but it was the Free Society which organized the dispatch of over fifty ships between 1682 and 1683 and made possible the rapid settlement of Pennsylvania in its early years.

Penn's first step on obtaining his charter was to dispatch his cousin, William Markham, to America in April 1681 to appoint a council and ensure that the several hundred English, Swedish, Dutch, and Finnish settlers already there, as well as the American Indians, recognized the proprietary authority. At this stage Penn referred to himself as governor, hoping to take up his duties in person. Shortly afterwards he issued a document called "Concessions to the Province of Pennsylvania." Its terms were remarkably generous: fifty acres were to be granted to every male servant on completion of his service, and all lands were to be in free and common socage, subject only to a small quitrent of one shilling per hundred acres. No limit was placed on the size of holdings, though a certain proportion had to be settled within three years. Strict instructions were also issued concerning disputes with the American Indians which were to be arbitrated between six whites and six American Indians, with everyone treated equally before the law.[16]

Next Penn circulated a pamphlet in England, Wales, and parts of Holland and Germany, where the Society of Friends was also well established, describing the proposed settlement. Several English and Welsh groups, not all of them Quaker, immediately expressed interest, encouraged by Penn's offer that anyone participating in the purchase of the first five hundred thousand acres would receive a free lot in the new city. Some six hundred people took advantage of this offer to become "First Purchasers."

An initial detachment of settlers departed for America in October 1681 with four commissioners on board. Among them was Thomas Holme, who was to survey the site for Penn's new town, Philadelphia, on the banks of the Delaware and Schuylkill rivers. Before the next group landed in August 1682, Penn issued a more complete frame of government and charter of liberties, asserting that government was a divine institution whose purpose was to "terrify evil doers" and "cherish those that do well." Penn, however, affected to

---

[15]   See especially Daniel J. Boorstin, *The Americans: The Colonial Experience* (New York, 1959). Like most scholars trained in New England, Boorstin argues that the Puritans were pragmatists, while the Quakers were inflexible doctrinaires. (Boorstin received his B.A. from Harvard and his Ph.D. from Yale.)

[16]   The full text is printed in Kavenagh, *Documentary History*, II, 1131–4. The right of servants to a headright of fifty acres was abandoned after a few years.

believe that the form of government was less important than the spirit. His philosophy, "Let men be good and the government cannot be bad," was to demonstrate that people of varying religious persuasions could live in peace and harmony.

Nevertheless, Penn agreed that some institutional framework was necessary and decreed that power was to be vested in him as governor, together with the freemen of the province, meeting as a provincial council and general assembly, "by whom all laws shall be made, officers chosen and public affairs transacted." Freemanship was accorded to any male who owned fifty acres of partially cultivated land or who paid the local taxes. Some Quakers wanted to deny the vote to non-Quakers to maintain their control. Penn, however, believed that so benign a regime would not be challenged, even by outsiders.

Superficially Penn's document was remarkably liberal, in keeping with the egalitarian nature of the Quaker religion. In practice, however, Penn believed that government ought to be left to "men of wisdom and virtue," though he was quick to deny that by this he meant wealth. The council was to comprise seventy-two persons "of most note for their wisdom, virtue and ability," who were to serve on a rotating basis for three years, helping the governor to prepare all legislation. The assembly's role, in contrast, was to be restricted to accepting or rejecting bills, though its members could propose amendments. The frame of government itself could be amended only with the consent of the proprietor and six-sevenths of the freemen.

Penn's frame of government also included a list of privileges and liberties. Trial was to be by jury, fees were to be moderate, and punishment was to fit the crime. Servants were to be protected, while everyone who acknowledged "the one almighty and eternal God . . . [would] in no ways be molested or prejudiced in their religious persuasion." This protection included exemption from tithes, as there was to be no established church.[17]

The first settlers had now arrived on the Delaware, where a pleasing prospect awaited them. Penn had fortuitously obtained the best real estate on the east coast of America. The land along the river was extremely fertile, and a favorable site was quickly found for the principal town and port of Philadephia, so called after the Greek word for brotherly love. The town was soon laid out in neat rectangular blocks as Penn desired, anticipating the later American gridiron style of urban planning. Houses were to be a certain distance apart to contain fires and to prevent the spread of disease.

Several factors aided the establishment of Pennsylvania. One was Penn's insistence on negotiating proper treaties with the indigenous peoples, who were paid £1,200 for these first lands along the Delaware. Another was the fact that Pennsylvania faced no immediate external threats, being protected by New York to the north, Maryland to the south, and the mountains to the west. Lastly, even the humbler Quakers were fired with a sense of mission to make the most of God's bounty. Like the Puritans, they were firm believers in the Protestant ethic.

The settlement around Philadephia thus experienced rapid growth. Within a year crops were being harvested and the surplus shipped for export. When Penn himself arrived late in 1682 to take up the governorship, he was well pleased to see that the settlement already had some four thousand inhabitants and contained eighty dwellings in Philadelphia alone. Among the early arrivals were several groups of Welsh and Irish Quakers, together

---

17   Kavenagh, *Documentary History*, II, 1134–44.

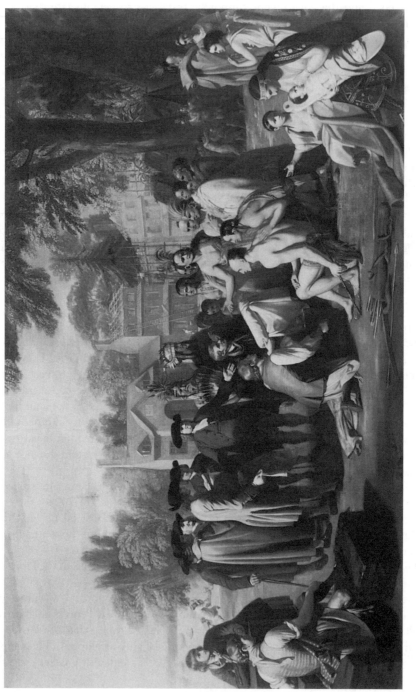

Plate 21 *Penn's Treaty with the Indians*, by Benjamin West, 1771. The Pennsylvania Academy of the Fine Arts, gift of the Joseph and Sarah Harrison Collection.

with some African slaves whom Penn bought to work on his farm. Soon Penn announced that the Duke of York had sold him the three counties of Delaware: Newcastle, Kent, and Sussex, which were then annexed to Pennsylvania subject to the new colony's laws and privileges.

Problems concerning the frame of government of May 1682, liberal as it was, were not slow to appear. One was the unwieldy size of the council and house of assembly, which were both far too big for the number of inhabitants. Accordingly, in April 1683 Penn reduced their membership to eighteen and thirty-six persons respectively. Fortunately, the legislature had already passed a series of laws imbued with the Quaker spirit. Anyone settling a dispute by violence was to be sentenced to three months in the house of correction; ten days was the punishment for riotous behavior or cruel sports. Provision was also made for the destitute. There was, too, a heavy emphasis on honesty between the inhabitants, and meticulous attention was given to weights and measures. Finally, in December 1682 a bill was passed confirming religious tolerance. All freemen who declared "Jesus Christ to be the son of God" and "saviour of the world" could hold office and participate in the affairs of the province. As a legal code it was a model of reasonableness and humanity.

The harmony was short-lived. The three lower counties of Delaware constituted one discordant factor, since they resented their inclusion in the new colony. Most of the inhabitants were Swedish or Dutch, while even those of English descent were Presbyterians or Anglicans. Also, the initial grant of special privileges to the Free Society of Traders now became an issue. Their claims to the choicest lands along the Delaware and best plots in Philadelphia rankled with the poorer Quakers, most of whom owned small farms. The result was a split in their ranks. The wealthy Friends led by Thomas Lloyd dominated the council, while the poorer inhabitants looked to the assembly for protection.

The main issue now became the role of the lower house itself, especially its inability to initiate legislation. An assembly without this power was no assembly at all, and the lack of it caused much trouble, especially after Penn returned to England in 1684 to fight the territorial claims of Maryland.

In 1688 Penn appointed Captain John Blackwell, another relative, to be governor. Blackwell's past service in Cromwell's army immediately affronted the Quakers' pacific sensibilities, and his position only worsened with the outbreak of war in 1689. When Blackwell demanded money to defend the province, the Quakers in both houses refused supplies, even for those willing to fight.

The appointment of Blackwell was another example of Penn's own failings as an administrator. Though genuinely concerned for his coreligionists, he was too full of his own importance to appreciate their point of view, believing instead that he deserved their gratitude and deference. Like many others, he failed to see that the pursuit of his own material advantage conflicted with his professed altruism. Before he died he was to be sadly disillusioned.

Communal divisions were unfortunately soon compounded by religious schism too, following the arrival in 1689 of George Keith from New Jersey. Keith basically believed that the Friends were losing their purity, but his proposed remedy was not a return to the simple ways of the movement in its early years but rather a purification of the Quaker religion through stricter discipline, thus threatening its spontaneity and freedom of conscience. In the resulting split in the Quaker ranks, perhaps a quarter of the Society took Keith's position. His followers were drawn mainly from the poorer Quakers, many of them Scots like himself, and the dispute began to have political ramifications when Keith took issue with Lloyd and his wealthy supporters in Philadelphia's main meeting house.

The new colony nevertheless continued to take shape, aided by the influx of capital and willing hands. Philadelphia was well established and three counties – Bucks, Philadelphia, and Chester – had been founded. Already the population had reached ten thousand, with more settlers on their way. In 1686 some pietists from Frankfurt and Quakers from Kreveld, led by Francis Pastorius, purchased a tract of twenty-five thousand acres and established a settlement which in 1691 became Germantown. Even this development was not free from controversy, however, for the Welsh settlers then argued that they should have been similarly privileged with a county of their own. Pennsylvania was already set to become a society of many ethnic groups and religions, just like the later United States.

8

James II and the Glorious Revolution

1681   The City of London loses its charter.

1683   *Quo warranto* proceedings are instituted against Massachusetts.

1685   James, Duke of York becomes King James II.
Articles of Misdemeanour are drawn up against Rhode Island and Connecticut.
The Dominion of New England is created.

1686   Sir Edmund Andros is named governor-general of the new dominion.
New York's assembly and Charter of Liberties are revoked by James II.

1687   The New England towns protest against arbitrary taxes.

1688   New York is included in the Dominion of New England.
William III invades England and initiates the Glorious Revolution.

1689   (April) The Dominion of New England is overthrown in Boston.
(June) Jacob Leisler takes control in New York.
(July) The proprietary government in Maryland is overthrown. War breaks out with France.

1690   Schenectady is devastated by the French and American Indians.

1691   Jacob Leisler is executed in New York.
A new charter is issued for Massachusetts.

1695   An act of Parliament overturns the verdicts against Leisler and Milborne.

1702   Nicholas Bayard is tried for treason.

1 THE DOMINION OF NEW ENGLAND

CHARLES II DIED in February 1685. For most of his reign his administration had been neither wise nor consistent. Except for the Navigation acts, which were the work of Parliament, his policy had lacked direction, at least until 1680. Charles II's main concern was to avoid the mistakes which had led to his father's execution. Expediency was therefore his guiding principle, laziness his natural bent. He preferred to put off today what could be done tomorrow.

His successor, his brother James, Duke of York, was a very different character, being a man of strong convictions. No fear of exile or upsurge of militant republicanism had ever made him consider giving up his Catholic religion or moderating his policies for strengthening the English Crown. It is important to note here that James was greatly influenced in this respect by Louis XIV, under whom France had replaced Spain as the most powerful state in Europe. Louis XIV's power stemmed not least from the bureaucratic abilities of his chief minister, Jean Colbert, who had centralized many branches of French government. Discordant groups, notably the aristocracy and Huguenots, as the French Protestants were known, had been brought to heel, while the army and navy had been placed on a professional footing. France was now the envy of Europe.

It was this model that James II sought to emulate, for the new king was himself a keen administrator. Indeed as lord high admiral he had carried out a number of reforms to the navy. In this period of bureaucratic expansion, James II brought a centralizing direction to the management of his government.

In 1685 England's status was still minor compared to the grandeur of France under Louis XIV. There seemed to be two roads which the English state could now take. Either it could remain dominated by special interest groups concerned only with their own rights and privileges. Or it could become a modern, centralized monarchy which was powerful at home and abroad. The possibility of a third option, constitutional monarchy, which was just as efficient and more conducive to prosperity than the other two systems, was inconceivable to James II and most of his contemporaries, the dominant political theory at this time being the divine right of kings. Sir Robert Filmer and other royal apologists held that the English monarchs were descended from Adam and were divinely appointed. Hence all rights were merely privileges which the monarch could summarily take away. The idea that government must rest on the consent of the people, originating from some kind of contract, was quite inadmissible to proponents of this view. Monarchs received their powers from God and were answerable only to him.[1]

By the time James II became king, these centralizing and absolutist tendencies were already evident, for Charles II had been provoked into action in the last years of his reign. In 1680 Shaftesbury and the Whig opposition in Parliament attempted to have James excluded from the succession because he was a Catholic. The king and his brother finally realized that radical action was necessary if the English Crown was to survive. Parliament must be tamed. Accordingly, Charles dissolved Parliament and began to remodel the borough charters by writ of *quo warranto*. This step was necessary because these charters determined the method by which each town chose its member of Parliament. By changing

---

[1] Sir Robert Filmer, *Patriarcha: Or the Natural Power of Kings* (London, 1680).

Plate 22 Portrait of James II, by Sir Godfrey Kneller, 1684–5. The National Portrait Gallery, London.

the rules governing the election of members, James II hoped to ensure the return of a more friendly House of Commons. The first borough to suffer such proceedings was the City of London in 1681.

Since many colonial institutions were based on similar charters, it was always likely that these centralizing processes would be applied to them also. The American colonies at this time were a mosaic of small units, vulnerable to attack and difficult to administer. For twenty years Massachusetts had defiantly claimed that its charter placed it outside royal control while collector Randolph reported numerous breaches in the trade laws and loss of revenue to the king.

Accordingly, late in 1682 Massachusetts was ordered to send envoys to London to discuss the revision of its charter. Among the powers sought by the Crown were the appointment of governors and the hearing of appeals. The general court rejected both as undermining the political and religious purposes of the colony. The magistrates still believed that it was better to defy the king than to sin against God. They also noted that those English corporations which had already surrendered their charters had gained nothing by doing so. The magistrates were encouraged to resist by the Reverend Increase Mather, who argued that God would deliver them, as he had in 1637 and 1664, if they remained true to the covenant. Thus although envoys were finally sent, they were given no instructions to negotiate.

The Crown's law officers accordingly commenced *quo warranto* proceedings against Massachusetts in June 1683. The list of infractions presented by Randolph was extremely damaging. Although Massachusetts sent its attorney general, he unfortunately did not contest the suit to indicate the province's disavowal of the action. The tortuous methods of the English legal system were extremely slow not least because the actual charter was still in America. Indeed, the Crown was reduced to seeking an alternative procedure, a warrant known as *scire facias*, to complete its case. Nevertheless, the inevitable verdict of the Court of King's Bench in October 1684 was that the charter was invalid.

This precedent opened the door for a more radical reorganization of James II's other North American possessions. The Crown already controlled New Hampshire, while Plymouth had no charter other than that issued by the defunct Council of New England. It was therefore decided to combine these with Massachusetts and Maine into one colony called the Dominion of New England. Not yet satisfied, the bureaucrats quickly turned their attention to Connecticut and Rhode Island, against which Articles of Misdemeanour were submitted by Randolph in July 1685. Among his charges were the misuse of the judicial power, the failure to administer the required oaths, and the persecution of Anglicans. Proceedings were also to be undertaken against the Jerseys and New York, on the grounds that these struggling entities were prejudicial to the king's authority and the collection of his revenue.

If the members of the Massachusetts general court thought they could still maintain their independence, they were mistaken. For once England had a royal government capable of making its views prevail. James II had met his first Parliament in the spring of 1685 and secured a large revenue, a sign that the remodeling of the charters was working. His enemies were either in hiding or in sanctuary abroad and, unlike his predecessor, he had a professional army of twenty thousand men and an efficient navy. Although the house of deputies in Massachusetts still talked of resistance, the magistrates knew that the end had come. To some extent the old leadership had lost confidence in the wake of the disasters of the past few years. In May 1686 the final meeting of the general court concluded with a short prayer amid tears.

Initially, James II appointed Joseph Dudley president of the council and Randolph secretary until a governor-general could be appointed for the whole dominion. The council was effectively the old court of assistants and contained several notable names: Simon Bradstreet, Nathaniel Saltonstall, William Stoughton, John Pynchon, Wait Winthrop, and Fitz-John Winthrop, though the first two refused to serve. But no formal charter was issued to replace the old; the king's commission was considered sufficient authority. Power was to be vested in the governor and council, who could try cases, convene the militia, appoint all officers, and make other arrangements for the defense of the dominion. Liberty of conscience was to be allowed, especially to such people "as shall be conformable to the rites of the Church of England." No mention was made of the house of deputies or the passing of laws. For the time being the council would levy the existing taxes.

The readiness of so many distinguished Massachusetts inhabitants to serve on the council has been ascribed to the appearance of a moderate party among the merchants, who recognized the need to compromise in a world of commercial and imperial expansion, being more forward-looking in their outlook than the old Puritan leadership, with its community and precapitalist values. Self-interest was clearly a factor. The Winthrop brothers' main concern was to secure the claims of the Atherton Company to the Narragansett country. Stoughton and Pynchon had similar interests, both having ventures in the Connecticut Valley. Nor were they disappointed, since Dudley obliged them with generous land grants. It was not long before Randolph was criticizing the new order for its lack of commitment to the Anglican church and failure to observe the navigation laws.

These complaints ensured the temporary nature of Dudley's presidency. In June 1686 James II nominated Sir Edmund Andros as governor in chief. His appointment has been seen as part of a plan to create a garrison or military style of government throughout the American colonies. In reality Andros was selected for the much more mundane reason that he had already served James II in New York ten years earlier and was therefore familiar with America. In addition, as a faithful servant, Andros had a claim on James II's patronage, while as a military man he was qualified to build the defenses which James II believed were vital. In any case he had no orders to impose martial law.[2]

Andros's commission specifically gave him and the council power to make all laws and raise taxes. To ensure that the former were conformable to English practice, they were to be sent for approval by the government in Whitehall within three months. The Privy Council was also to be the final court of appeal.

The imposition of the dominion was a bitter blow to all the colonies, and to none more so than Massachusetts. Practically all that the commonwealth had fought for was abolished. The general court was replaced by a nonelective council nominated by a royal governor. Equally upsetting was the ending of the special position of the Congregational church and the likelihood that Anglicanism would become the established church, since Andros was an Anglican. These fears were hardly dispelled when Andros took over the Old

---

[2] The view that the Crown had a persistent design to establish military government is argued by Stephen Saunders Webb in *The Governors General: The English Army and the Definition of Empire, 1569–1681* (Chapel Hill, 1979). For a critical assessment of this idiosyncratic view, see Richard R. Johnson, "The Imperial Webb: The Thesis of Garrison Government in Early America Reconsidered," *William and Mary Quarterly*, XLIII, 1986, 408–30; and Ian Steele, "Governors or Generals?: A Note on Martial Law and the Revolution of 1689," *William and Mary Quarterly*, XLVI, 1989, 304–14.

South Meeting House and kept the regular congregation waiting while the Anglican minister celebrated morning service.

Taxes were another grievous matter. Although Andros adopted the assembly's 1680 book of rates, there was nothing to prevent him from raising these later when it suited him. In 1687 several towns, notably Ipswich in Essex County, protested that the taxes were illegal, not having received the consent of the inhabitants according to the fundamental right of Englishmen. Andros quickly arrested the leading protesters and crushed the opposition. Indeed, one of the remarkable aspects of the period was the speed with which the commonwealth collapsed. Equally remarkable was the reliance the Puritans now placed on their rights as Englishmen. The third generation clearly did not have the same confidence as the first in the claim to be a covenanted people.

Other shocks lay in store. The courts of justice were streamlined; juries were to be appointed by the sheriffs rather than the local justices. All lands purchased from the native inhabitants henceforth had to be validated by new deeds and were subject to quitrents. Such purchases had been widespread and, although most titles were confirmed, the expense and uncertainty involved left the population deeply anxious, especially as certain holdings were challenged. This step suggested that all freehold titles would be terminated in due course as the prelude to the levying of a quitrent. The merchants, too, were shocked when the number of ports available for customs clearance was reduced to five. Equally disturbing was the decision that all infractions of the trade laws were to be determined in an admiralty court with no jury, only a presiding judge.

In March 1688 curbs were imposed on the towns to prevent a repetition of the events at Ipswich. In future meetings were to be held only once a year for the election of officials and no selectman could serve more than two consecutive terms, making it difficult for local leaders to establish themselves.

Lastly, Andros's troops created a disturbing presence. Although he had arrived with only one company of redcoats and a frigate, the sight of these raised apprehensions about arbitrary rule, not least because Andros was given full power to declare martial law should an insurrection occur. Such fears were greatly increased by the general belief that James II's grand design was to impose popery on the people of America. Although no Catholics had yet arrived in New England, New York had an Irish Catholic governor, Thomas Dongan, and other Catholic officials. It was feared that James II might ally with the French and American Indians to achieve his purpose.

The outbreak of trouble on the frontiers of Maine thus did nothing to allay the New Englanders' apprehensions, even when Andros marched northward with three hundred militia to attack the Abenaki. Inadvertently, he repeated Berkeley's offense fifteen years earlier of appearing too lenient by attempting to negotiate rather than fight with the native peoples. Moreover, the campaign was undertaken in winter conditions which left his men fractious and ready to desert.

As a result, Andros had few friends even among the councillors appointed by Dudley. Their dissatisfaction stemmed partly from the fact that Andros had his own coterie of advisers from New York and partly from Andros's refusal to confirm the land grants made by Dudley, even though Randolph and other friends had received similar favors.

Nevertheless, the inhabitants of New England were seemingly powerless to prevent events from taking their course. In December 1686 *quo warranto* proceedings were completed against Rhode Island. A year later it was the turn of Connecticut to join the dominion, after its inhabitants had indicated a preference for union with Massachusetts rather than New York. Their compliance meant that the legal surrender of the charter was never completed. In spring 1688 New York was included, though it retained a deputy governor and council.

Although the situation seemed hopeless, early in 1688 the opposition in Massachusetts determined to send Increase Mather to London to plead their cause. The previous April, James II had issued his Declaration of Indulgence, suspending the Test and Corporation acts against Catholics and Dissenters in England. The Puritans correctly interpreted this as an attack on the Anglican supremacy. More naively they speculated that James II was ready to look more favorably on his American dissenting subjects. It was clutching at a straw. Nevertheless, God moved in mysterious ways; perhaps a direct appeal might have some effect. Andros's council thought so too, for its members tried to prevent Mather from sailing, but without success.

2 MASSACHUSETTS RECLAIMS CONTROL

Unknown to the troubled New Englanders, deliverance was indeed at hand. James II's plans to create an absolute monarchy were rapidly alienating the English too. Nevertheless, he would probably have succeeded but for his simultaneous attempt to return England to Catholicism. It was one revolution too many.

Although James never published his plans, it is clear that he hoped to reverse the Reformation in the manner in which it had begun, by royal example and decree. The first steps in this scheme had been to suspend the Test and Corporation acts in 1687 and thus permit Catholics to serve in the army and hold public office. At the same time pressure was put on members of the nobility to convert to Rome. In so hierarchical a society the nobles were likely to be followed by their retainers, thus beginning the great work of returning England to Catholicism.

It was a monumental miscalculation on the king's part. There were enough Tories to help James II curb Parliament, but they were deeply upset by his open encouragement of Catholicism and lack of support for the established church. It was by no means simply a question of religion; the Reformation had seen a change in the ownership of land following the dissolution of the monasteries and reorganization of the church. These titles were implicitly threatened should the religious settlement be undone.

Until 1688 the nation was sustained by the knowledge that James II was old and apparently infertile, and that his daughter Mary, the heir, was a Protestant. In spring 1688, however, James's second wife, Mary of Modena, gave birth to a son, raising the prospect of a Catholic succession and the continuation of James II's policies in both church and state. This was too much. The Whigs were already alienated by the persecution of their leaders following the Exclusion crisis. Now even prominent Tories began to look for an alternative. One beckoned: William of Orange, Stadholder of Holland and husband of James's daughter, Mary. Accordingly, in June 1688, seven prominent Whigs and Tories wrote to William to come and rescue the people of England.

William was more than happy to oblige. Holland was again threatened by Louis XIV, and the possibility of enlisting England in the struggle against France was reason enough. In addition, William did have claims to the English throne, both through his own family and that of his wife, should the allegations that James II's son was illegitimate prove true. In the fall of 1688 William swiftly assembled an army and fleet, landing in the West Country at Torbay. Everywhere he was greeted as a savior, while James II's army melted away or joined the invader. By the middle of November the king found it expedient to flee to France, first throwing the great seal into the Thames.

Rumors of William's landing began to reach America in early spring 1689. They had been preceded by a warning from James II himself about the imminent danger of a Dutch invasion. Hence some discussion had already taken place in Massachusetts among the former elite about whether they ought to take control should the news prove true. It was not until April 1689 that William's success was confirmed and the colonists realized that the English had secured what they still sought: the right to an assembly, the supremacy of the laws, protection from Catholicism, and protection against external foes.

During these critical weeks Andros was handicapped by lack of orders from London, for which Mather was to blame. The minister had persuaded William that Andros ought not be entrusted with his command, even though non-Catholic officials were being confirmed in their posts. In this vacuum rumors abounded, including one that Andros was about to join the French and American Indians in an attack on the English! In this situation it needed only a trivial incident to bring Massachusetts and the other New England provinces to arms. The occasion was provided when some militia seized the captain of the *Rose* man-of-war near Boston harbor on the morning of April 18. The whole population spontaneously came out onto the streets and went to the town house, where Randolph was seized and put in jail. Andros himself took refuge in Fort Hill, where he was surrounded and eventually persuaded to surrender without bloodshed. Most of his troops were in New Hampshire, and the rest were mutinous for want of pay.

In this crisis the old Puritan leadership came forward, led by Increase Mather's son, Cotton, and Simon Bradstreet, the last of the old governors. One point already agreed at the earlier secret discussions was the need to form a "Council for the Safety and Conservation of the Peace," similar to the former court of assistants. Bradstreet was quickly chosen president. Many wanted to resume the old charter immediately by holding elections for the house of deputies. Others were aware that the old frame of government was invalid and that such action would be illegal. In the end it was agreed to convene an interim general court pending further directions from England. There was to be no bid for independence, for the fate of Massachusetts would clearly be settled in London. The council therefore issued a public declaration supporting the new King William III and Queen Mary II and sent a denunciation of Andros, along with a plea that the old charter be restored. This request was to be handled by Mather in London.

Elsewhere in New England events were similarly bloodless. In Rhode Island Dudley was seized while acting as a circuit court judge and sent to Boston. An impromptu assembly then acknowledged the new regime in England and reactivated the charter until more specific instructions arrived. Connecticut, too, sent early congratulations to William and Mary and a plea that its charter be reconfirmed, as it had technically never been surrendered. Later that May an unofficial meeting of the general court voted to "reestablish the government as it was before . . . until there shall be a legal establishment."

The action of the New Englanders, especially in Massachusetts, was a calculated risk. There was no guarantee that William III would remain on the throne or that he would be sympathetic to the pleas now being put forward. He certainly had not come to dismantle the powers of the Crown; indeed he was surrounded by many of the men who had assisted James II to build them up. The liberties that William had been invited to protect were somewhat different from those to which the colonists aspired; their rebellions were unwelcome and even dangerous.

Mather nevertheless had some advantages as he walked the corridors of power in London. Massachusetts had promptly proclaimed William and Mary king and queen, and the coup had been bloodless. Since the dominion itself was no more, it would have to be replaced by something. Moreover, William was immersed in other, more urgent matters. By 1690 James had invaded Ireland, and William's presence was also required in Flanders to oppose the French. It would obviously be advantageous if the American colonies could be pacified quickly. Here Mather showed considerable skill as he lobbied both the Whig and Tory factions. The Whigs were the more natural allies, given their sympathy for Dissenters, but Mather wisely courted the Tories too, despite their Anglican and authoritarian leanings.

A compromise was arranged in October 1691 with the issue of a new charter, for there could be no going back to the 1629 version. In future there would be a royal governor, appointed by the Crown. Liberty of conscience was to be granted, except for Catholics, and the Privy Council was to be the ultimate court of appeal. The governor also had the right to veto all legislation, which was also to be submitted to England for approval. Several important concessions were included, however. The council was to be elected by the lower house, provided that the candidates were acceptable to the governor. The rights of the towns were also to be restored. Land titles, too, were confirmed in freehold and no quitrents levied.

Massachusetts thus had much to be thankful for. Though the Congregational church was no longer technically established, liberty of conscience in practice amounted to indulging the governor and his entourage. Outside Boston the towns could do as they pleased in the levying of tithes and maintenance of their churches. The only thing they could not do was prevent other Protestants from holding services. Another bonus was that Massachusetts was not only to keep Maine but also to incorporate Plymouth. The latter had never had a royal charter, and there was little incentive to restore its independence, since it had barely ten thousand inhabitants. Although some protest occurred, it quickly died down.

The concessions to Rhode Island and Connecticut were even greater. Since neither province had Massachusetts's reputation for defying the English government, their charters were accordingly restored intact. Lastly, New Hampshire again became a royal colony with a governor, nominated council, and elected assembly. New England was not so different from what it had been before.

3 NEW YORK: LEISLER'S REBELLION

If the settlement of New England was to prove relatively harmonious, events in New York were to take a rather different course. One reason was that the province did not have a tradition of self-government. Though the towns on Long Island had seemingly won their case for an assembly in 1683, James II had never confirmed the Charter of Liberties or subsequent legislation. The Privy Council in due course advised that the acts of the New York assembly conceded too many rights and set too many dangerous precedents respecting the legislative power. The disappointment over this was still keen when James II finally disavowed both assembly and charter in May 1686.

New York was unstable for other reasons, too. In the first place it lacked homogeneity: English, Scots, Dutch, Germans, and Huguenots were all present in substantial numbers. The integration of the Dutch in particular had not extended beyond a few wealthy families, and this inherent ethnicity was exacerbated by religious differences. The New Englanders were Congregational; the Scots, Presbyterian; most of the English, Anglican; while the Dutch, Germans, and Huguenots followed their own brand of Calvinism. These disparate groups were united only in their hatred of Catholicism. In addition, there were geographic divisions. Long Island was separate from Manhattan and the Hudson Valley. Most important, however, was the rivalry between New York and Albany, especially over the control of the flour and fur trades.

Finally, defense presented a problem because New York was particularly exposed to American Indian attacks and invasion from the north via Lake Champlain and the Mohawk River. For the previous forty years New York had been protected by the Iroquois. By the end of the 1680s it was clear that the balance of power was changing in favor of the French and their allies. In 1684 the Iroquois had humiliated a French invasion force under Governor Barre, after it had been devastated by sickness. The French had responded by reinforcing their colony under Governor Denonville. At the same time many of the Iroquois' bitterest enemies had been linked into a military alliance, resulting in a devastating attack on the Seneca villages in 1687. The inhabitants of New York believed that the French would use the Jesuits to stir up the native inhabitants even more, giving rise to the prospect of a quasi-religious war in which the divided New Yorkers would be pitted against a united foe using the Hudson River as an invasion route.

James II was not oblivious to these problems. After revoking the Charter of Liberties, he ordered Dongan to raise additional revenue to shore up New York's defenses. Dongan's means, however, soon stirred up discontent, for by confirming New York as the sole port of entry in 1687, he inevitably aroused further protests from the Suffolk ports. Next, Dongan tried to levy quitrents on all land grants issued since the time of Andros, forcing most communities to seek new patents and therefore causing much unease, for those who failed to do so were prosecuted in a new court of exchequer. Lastly, he affirmed that he would continue the taxes voted by the ill-fated assembly, even though these had been part of the bargain for its right to meet. Further protest predictably ensued, this time from Staten Island and the town of Jamaica. A final blow, for the Dutch community at least, was the announcement in 1688 that New York was to be annexed to the Dominion of New England. A lieutenant governor and subcouncil would run New York separately, but this provision offered little consolation, since the officials would be answerable to Andros in Boston.

The man chosen to bring the situation under control was Colonel Francis Nicholson, a newcomer to America just thirty-three years old. Nicholson had the advantage of not being a Catholic, unlike Dongan, but the fact that several persons on his council were of that persuasion, including the customs collector, Matthew Ploughman, made Nicholson suspect. Like Andros, he initially tried to conceal the news of events in England until they could be confirmed. Like Andros too, he faced a cruel dilemma. To announce William's invasion too soon would be tantamount to treason, while to do nothing would only increase tension among the population. All kinds of rumors were circulating, the most insidious being that Andros was plotting to help the French destroy the Five Nations. To calm popular fears, Nicholson agreed at the end of April 1689 to garrison the main fort with units of the militia.

Once news of the rising in Boston became widespread, however, an explosion was almost unavoidable. The trouble began, not surprisingly, among the inhabitants of Suffolk County on eastern Long Island who followed Boston's example early in May by ousting their royal officials. The predominantly Dutch population of Queen's and Westchester counties then followed suit. They were especially eager for a declaration supporting William, since his arrival in England might presage a return to Dutch rule. In the middle of May many of them marched to Jamaica, not far from New York City. About the same time some of the merchants refused to pay the customs because of the collector's religion. In response Nicholson declared that all such levies would be devoted solely to the defense of the city.

Even this assurance did not suffice, especially as it was rumored that war was about to be declared between England and France. The final provocation came on May 30 when Nicholson, in an altercation concerning the placing of a sentry in Fort James, told a militia officer that he would rather burn New York than put up with any more insubordination. The next day the city militia repudiated the authority of its commander, Nicholas Bayard, and took over the fort, though without bloodshed.

Prominent among those participating in these events was Jacob Leisler, one of the militia captains, who had originally come to New York in 1660 as a soldier of the Dutch West India Company. He had subsequently prospered as a merchant and married a rich widow, ranking among the colony's seven richest men by 1676. Leisler, however, had made himself unpopular with the leading Dutch families. In 1674 he had denounced Nicholas Van Rensselaer's attempt to become a minister in the Dutch Reformed church because Van Rensselaer had originally been ordained in England as an Anglican. Leisler was a deacon of his local congregation and was determined that no crypto-Catholic enter the church at a time when Protestantism was under threat from the ambitions of Louis XIV and the designs of James, Duke of York.

Although no real violence had yet occurred, the council deemed it prudent for Nicholson to leave immediately for England to seek assistance. Leisler and the other militia captains quickly filled the vacuum by forming a committee of safety similar to that in Massachusetts, on which there were two representatives each from Westchester, Kings, Queen's, Staten Island, and Manhattan counties, and one from Esopus in Ulster County. The committee proclaimed William and Mary king and queen on June 3, 1689.

As in Massachusetts, events had so far gone relatively smoothly, with no bloodshed or apparent support for the ousted council. Here the similarities ended. Nicholson had powerful connections to plead his cause in England. Leisler subsequently sent envoys to London, but they had no standing or experience, though initially Leisler and his associates seemed to have affairs under control. Ploughman, the customs collector, was dismissed and the revenues collected on the grounds that they had been authorized by the last assembly under the Charter of Liberties. This action caused some murmuring from those calling themselves "English freemen."

In December 1689 a letter from William III arrived addressed to Nicholson or "such as for the time being do take care for the preservation of their Majesties' Peace." Leisler interpreted this message as giving him the authority to do as he pleased, even though it had been written before Nicholson got to England. He accordingly replaced the aldermen of the city and imprisoned his most implacable opponents, Nicholas Bayard and William Nichols. The committee of safety was then superseded by a council with Leisler as lieutenant governor. The council was heavily Dutch in composition – even English members such as

Jacob Milborne and Samuel Edsall had Dutch wives. Only Thomas Williams and William Lawrence, from Westchester and Orange counties, were of a different persuasion.

Leisler's lack of support among the non-Dutch groups was amply demonstrated in August 1689 when he tried to summon a representative meeting of the counties. No deputies arrived from Suffolk or Ulster counties. Even Albany, which did have a heavy concentration of Dutch people, sent none, its inhabitants being still fearful that the New Yorkers had designs on the fur trade.

Another element in the struggle now taking place was that the wealthy Anglo-Dutch families simply resented the intrusion of mere traders like Leisler and Milborne into the affairs of the colony. As a memorial of Nicholas Bayard later emphasized, the leaders of the uprising were "all men of mean birth, sordid Education, and desperate Fortunes," who sought to consolidate their power "by inflaming the people." In contrast, they were opposed by "all the men of best repute for Religion, Estates and Integrity of the Dutch nation." Leisler's support was thus confined to the lesser tradesmen and farmers in the vicinity of New York, a limitation which proved a crucial handicap.[3]

Not that Leisler did not try to widen his support, especially in Ulster and Albany counties. His first step was the dispatch of a force to protect the exposed northern frontier. Unfortunately, this expedition arrived too late to save Schenectady, where some sixty inhabitants were killed on the night of February 9, 1690, by a combined French and American Indian force. Leisler was blamed because he had not secured the cooperation of Albany's principal residents, Philip Schuyler and Robert Livingston. Livingston was a Scot who had lived in Amsterdam before coming to work as a clerk in Albany. Like Leisler he had made a good marriage into the Van Rensselaer family; but he had managed to stay on terms with his Dutch relatives and had prospered accordingly, first in the fur trade and then as a landowner.

In spring 1690 Leisler decided that the best means of protecting the frontier was to join Massachusetts and Connecticut in an invasion of Canada. The New Englanders were to attack by sea while the New Yorkers advanced overland via Lake Champlain. Reluctantly the burghers of Albany opened their gates after Livingston had retired to Connecticut. In the event both attacks proved abortive, whereupon Leisler tried to imprison the commander of the land force, Fitz-John Winthrop, a member of the Connecticut Provincial Council, thus embroiling him in that province's affairs. Moreover, both campaigns still had to be paid for, and Leisler's unpopularity increased when a threepenny tax was imposed on both real and personal property.

Leisler made a second effort to widen his support by calling an assembly in April 1690, partly to diffuse an earlier clash with the English inhabitants of Queen's County under Major Thomas Willett, who had protested against the high taxes and oppression of the Leislerians. Also on the agenda was a bill to abrogate New York City's flour milling

[3] Historians have inevitably differed in their reasons for the rebellion. Thomas Archdeacon, *New York City, 1664–1710: Conquest and Change* (Ithaca, 1976), stresses the threat posed to the Dutch community by the imposition of English culture. Robert C. Ritchie, *The Duke's Province: A Study of New York Politics and Society, 1664–1691* (Chapel Hill, 1977), emphasizes the frustration of the population in general and fears of a Catholic plot in particular. He asserts that the leadership was mainly middle class. The view that the rebellion was a class struggle between rich and poor is argued most strongly by Jerome R. Reich in *Leisler's Rebellion: A Study of Democracy in New York, 1664–1720* (Chicago, 1953).

monopoly, which had so angered Albany. Not surprisingly, this proposal in turn further alienated the powerful New York merchant families, who were already upset over Leisler's arbitrary proceedings.

Meanwhile England's response continued to be slow, for New York was no more a priority for William III than Massachusetts. Not until December 1689 was Colonel Henry Sloughter appointed governor of the province, Nicholson being sent to Virginia instead. Sloughter had other military duties and did not leave until the end of 1690, accompanied by Major Richard Ingoldsby and several hundred troops. There was nothing hostile in Sloughter's commission respecting Leisler, however. New York was to be on the same footing as Virginia, with a governor and council appointed by the Crown and an assembly chosen by the freeholders "according to the usage of our other plantations in America." The only reference to the existing troubles was an injunction to all civil and military personnel to be "obedient, aiding and assisting" unto Sloughter. This language was very different from that of the commission given to Colonel Jeffreys in 1676, when Bacon had been declared a traitor.

Unfortunately Sloughter's vessel was separated in a storm, so that Ingoldsby and the troops arrived before him in February 1691. Leisler offered them accommodation but refused Ingoldsby's demand to be quartered in the fort, believing he ought to remain in command until Sloughter arrived. Three times Ingoldsby issued his demand and three times Leisler refused. The confrontation proved fatal, resulting in some sporadic firing and several deaths which allowed Leisler to be branded as a traitor. Even when Sloughter finally appeared six weeks later, Leisler still delayed handing over the fort, attempting to conduct negotiations through emissaries. This behavior outraged Sloughter and convinced him that Leisler was a rebel who should stand trial for his crimes.

Leisler, Milborne, and six of their lieutenants were then accused of treason. To the end Leisler affirmed that the king's letter of December 1689 had been sufficient authority for his actions. It did him no good, since on Nicholson's departure authority ought to have been exercised by the council. He was found guilty, much to the delight of the oligarchy. Indeed, Bayard wanted to hang all eight defendants, but Sloughter determined to execute just Leisler and Milborne.

The rebellion had been a messy affair, reflecting the province's diverse political and religious composition. It bore some similarity to Bacon's Rebellion, in that the colony was beset by American Indian troubles and heavy taxation. Like Bacon, Leisler was supported mainly by the poorer sections of the population opposed to an aristocratic elite, and he showed similar poor judgment in assessing how far he could go. However, the bloodshed during Leisler's rebellion was minimal and could have been overlooked; had Leisler acted with greater circumspection, the handover of power could have been trouble free. Leisler seems to have put too much faith in his Protestantism and the letter from William III, assuming that a Dutch king would be generous to his own compatriots. In addition, ranged against him were the great Anglo-Dutch families of New York, who were able to plead their cause more effectively in England. They particularly emphasized Leisler's lack of gentlemanly accomplishments, especially his inability to speak or write proper English, which reinforced the impression that he and his followers were a dangerous rabble.

The consequences of the rebellion were not as catastrophic as might have been expected. The overthrow of James II at least ended the Dominion of New England and meant that New York could no longer be denied an assembly. From 1691 the colony's government conformed to the standard pattern of royal governor, appointed council, and elected assembly. The first royal governor was Benjamin Fletcher.

The legacy of the past was not quickly forgotten, however. The Long Islanders renewed their efforts in 1692 for a bill declaring their rights as Englishmen, only to have it disallowed once more by the Privy Council. The Leislerians simultaneously sought to have the verdicts against their dead leaders overturned. Their cause was aided by sympathetic Whigs in England, who succeeded in having a special act of Parliament passed to that end in 1695.

Despite this the Leislerians continued to be proscribed from political life by Fletcher, who was a Tory. Their chance for revenge came in 1698 when Richard Coote, Earl of Bellomont, was appointed governor. Bellomont was a Whig who wanted to distance himself from his predecessor, not least because of Fletcher's corrupt land grants to the Anglo-Dutch grandees. He accordingly invited the Leislerians to join the council. This action led to the trial and conviction of Nicholas Bayard for treason in 1702. Bayard was reprieved only after he had begged forgiveness for his alleged crimes.

Not until the arrival of Robert Hunter in 1710 did the old divisions subside. Hunter judiciously invited both factions to serve on his council. By then many of Leisler's more irreconcilable followers had gone to New Jersey, while the bodies of Leisler and Milborne had received a proper burial. Anglicization was also beginning to work, though many schools continued to use Dutch until the 1750s, and churches conducted services in that language as late as 1770. If New York remained a divided polity, at least its disputes were now being carried on within a constitutional framework.

4 MARYLAND

One other colony which experienced serious trouble during the Glorious Revolution was Maryland. As in Massachusetts and New York, the seeds of the disturbance were to be found in the previous decades.

The years following the Restoration were a time of depressed tobacco prices, as already noted in regard to Virginia. Despite this the proprietor, Cecilius Calvert, the second Lord Baltimore, still expected his duty on every hogshead of tobacco exported to England. Nor did he make any concessions after the 1673 Navigation Act imposed additional burdens on the colony's trade.

Religion was another cause of discontent. Protestants now comprised four-fifths of the population but had few places on the council, a state of affairs which was especially disturbing since the governor and council made all land awards and inevitably favored Catholics. The Protestants also felt that the Act Concerning Religion discriminated against them. Although no church was officially established, a number of generous grants were made to Catholic chapels and their priests, while the Protestant ministers, in contrast, had difficulty supporting themselves.

A further point of conflict was the distribution of patronage. Since most offices went to Catholics, and in particular to relatives of the proprietor, ambitious outsiders had no chance of advancing themselves. The one institution in which rising planters could express themselves was the assembly.

The first serious confrontation between the proprietor and the lower house occurred in 1669, after a Protestant minister had urged the deputies to model themselves on the

House of Commons. His suggestion led to charges of mutiny and sedition, especially when the assembly drew up a document listing its "Grievances." Among the practices complained of were the proprietor's disallowing of the acts of the assembly, the levying of taxes without consent, the arbitrary actions of the proprietary officials, and the demand for exhorbitant fees.

The response of the proprietor was to restrict the franchise to freeholders rather than freemen. Too many discontented persons seemed to be using the elections to disturb the peace, for Maryland, like Virginia, contained a large number of discontented servants and tenant farmers. Voters now had to have landed property worth £50 or a personal estate worth £40. Baltimore also reduced the number of representatives from each county, perhaps in an attempt to conform to English parliamentary practice but more likely to copy the Virginia House of Burgesses.

The colony also experienced trouble with the American Indians and when Bacon's Rebellion broke out in 1676, sixty armed men gathered that August in Calvert County under the leadership of William Davies and John Pate. Their principal grievance was the high poll tax of three hundred pounds of tobacco. Fortunately for Charles Calvert, now the third Lord Baltimore, few others from the population of fifteen thousand joined them; the rebels were easily hunted down and the two ringleaders were executed.

The next disturbance arose in 1680, when news was received that Shaftesbury and the Whigs were attempting to exclude James, Duke of York from the succession. This effort had special significance for Maryland, since it was rumored that the Catholic proprietary government too would fall. Baltimore responded by having two of his leading opponents, Josiah Fendall, the former governor, and John Coode, a militia officer, arrested on charges of mutiny and sedition. In the event Coode was acquitted, though Fendall was fined and banished, having offended once too often. The incident prompted the Lords of Trade to recommend that Baltimore appoint more Protestant, officials, but to no avail.

These events coincided with another slump in tobacco prices, causing plant-cutting riots in Virginia. Baltimore rightly feared these would spread to Maryland but refused to make any concessions when the assembly met in 1682. The representatives began by insisting on their rights as Englishmen, including the right to conduct their affairs as the House of Commons did. Baltimore replied by reaffirming his position as absolute proprietor. He argued that the rights of Englishmen had no relevance to Maryland, the colonists having surrendered these when they emigrated. Indeed, they could enjoy only what he was graciously pleased to give them, for their status was that of inhabitants in a conquered territory. To demonstrate his authority, the following year he unilaterally abolished the headright system on the ground that it had been abused. While this charge may have been true, Baltimore's action closed an important avenue whereby planters could increase their holdings.

Dissident colonists were not Baltimore's only problem, however. By 1684 he had to deal with a border dispute with Pennsylvania and was then accused of defrauding the royal customs. The situation was made worse when Baltimore's nephew, the acting governor, George Talbot, killed the chief revenue collector, Christopher Rousby. The incident gave James II, who was now king, every justification to begin *quo warranto* proceedings.

Despite these setbacks, Baltimore continued to act as though his authority was unquestioned, as reflected in his last choice of governor, William Joseph. Joseph was an Irish Catholic who began by addressing the assembly on the doctrine of divine right: "The Power by which we are assembled here is undoubtedly derived from God to the King and from the

King to his Excellency the Lord Proprietary." A new oath of fidelity incorporating this doctrine was required. Worse, Joseph brought an order from the Crown that in future only high-quality cask tobacco was to be exported, to exclude the inferior bulk product. This measure threatened the smaller producers with ruin, especially when Joseph also served notice that in future the proprietor expected all dues to be paid in specie, not tobacco, since the depressed market price was diminishing his income.

Although the deputies finally agreed to take the new oath of fidelity, they transacted little other business. Instead the members concentrated on a further statement of their grievances, notably the excessive taking of fees, the arbitrary dispensing of the laws, the insistence of the proprietor on money rather than tobacco in the payment of rents, the imprisonment of persons without indictment, and the interference of proprietary officials in the colonists' trade.

It was at this point that news arrived of James II's warning about an invasion. The council responded by ordering all public arms to be brought in for inspection by the local gunsmiths, ostensibly to be put in order, but in reality to be distributed among the proprietor's own supporters. To the majority this was simply a device to disarm them as the prelude to a combined American Indian and Catholic attack. During March 1689 wild rumors circulated of an impending assault by the Senecas, causing a panic among the militia of Calvert county, though the officers, chief among them a prominent Protestant, Henry Jowles, were able to quieten their men.

Because conditions in Maryland were so volatile, the proprietary government decided in April 1689 not to call an assembly. By now news had arrived that Virginia and the provinces to the north had declared for William and Mary. The response of Coode and others was to organize "an Association in arms for the defense of the Protestant Religion." Still the proprietary government did nothing, mainly because Baltimore was waiting for Parliament formally to declare William and Mary king and queen; then the messenger carrying Baltimore's instructions died. When no action had been taken by mid-July, Coode and his association marched on St. Mary's.

Little resistance was offered and no blood shed. Some attempt was made to rally the proprietary forces at Baltimore's mansion on the Patuxent River, but to little effect. An assembly was summoned and a declaration issued which affirmed Maryland's commitment to William and Mary, as well as expressing the belief that the colonists' cause was the same as England's: to stop "Slavery and Popery." Once the assembly met, Coode wisely surrendered the "supreme power" which he had momentarily exercised. A committee was appointed to investigate the American Indian–Catholic conspiracy, after which the assembly was dissolved pending approval from England, leaving an interim council under Coode to protect what had been won.

Later in 1690 a further meeting was held to draw up charges against Baltimore, which Coode and another deputy then took to London. The charges were a compilation of all the previous grievances: the monopoly that Catholics enjoyed in the council, the support enjoyed by their religious establishments, the disallowance of the assembly's acts, the excessive fees demanded by the proprietary officials, the conspiracy with the French and American Indians, and the failure to declare for William III and Mary II.

Coode's reception in London was generally favorable, since the charges against Baltimore confirmed the current prejudice against proprietary government. The decision was accordingly made in August 1691 to strip Baltimore of his governmental rights, leaving him only his property interests. In future there was to be a royal governor with similar powers and instructions as in New York. Thus the principal objectives of the Maryland majority had been obtained: proprietary government had been overthrown, the Protestant religion saved, and the place of the assembly assured.

5 AFTERMATH

Elsewhere in America the changes of 1689 were relatively peaceful. Pennsylvania and the Carolinas were too recently settled and remote for there to be much reaction.[4] More surprising was the lack of violence in Virginia. One explanation may be that the colony remained cowed in the aftermath of Bacon's Rebellion. The governor, Lord Effingham, a strong supporter of James II, was in England when William invaded and the acting governor, Nicholas Spencer, sensibly proclaimed the new order toward the end of April 1689. Some unrest occurred in the northern counties of Stafford and Rappahannock, but it was due mainly to fears of an attack by American Indians rather than a rejection of the authorities in Jamestown.

The disturbances in New England, New York, and Maryland have certain similarities. All were inspired by a fear of Catholicism and the dread of a native attack; all occurred in frontier societies which felt vulnerable to such attack; and everywhere was heard the demand for the rights of Englishmen, even in Massachusetts, where the charter was equated with that end.[5]

What the colonists did not realize was that their version of these rights was not quite the same as that of the English themselves. Even more important, the English did not necessarily believe that the colonists should enjoy exactly the same rights as they did. The colonial relationship was seen as one of mother and children. Dependents therefore did not change their governments; they waited for the mother country to do it for them. Although James II's policies in England were disavowed, much of what he had been trying to do in America was approved. Indeed, attempts were subsequently made to retain some of his measures.

The colonists also missed one other change. They rejoiced in the overthrow of the Catholic James II and his replacement by the Protestant William III. They talked much about their rights as Englishmen, citing the English Bill of Rights in their support. But they failed to appreciate that this was less a declaration of individual rights than an expression of parliamentary authority. One form of absolute sovereignty, divine kingship, had been replaced by a new one, that of the king in Parliament, which institution was eventually to display as exalted an opinion of its authority as any Stuart monarch.

All these developments lay in the future. For the moment, the overthrow of James II and the granting of new charters or governments was sufficient to satisfy colonial aspirations. Even Cotton Mather declared, "It is no little Blessing of God that we are part of the English nation."

---

[4] The governor of North Carolina had to flee, but for reasons unconnected with events elsewhere. See chapter 9, section 4.

[5] Traditional accounts of 1689 have stressed the participants' American aims. The fact that the colonists were seeking the rights of Englishmen is the theme of David S. Lovejoy, *The Glorious Revolution in America* (New York, 1972).

DOCUMENT 13

The Bill of Rights, 1689, *The Statutes at Large*, 1 William and Mary, Session 2, Chapter 2.

[Unlike the 1683 New York Charter of Liberties or later American Bill of Rights, the English version was concerned mainly with the rights of Parliament rather than those of the individual. Only articles 5, 7, 10, 11, and 12 are aimed at protecting the ordinary person.]

1. That the pretended power of suspending of laws or the execution of laws by regal authority without consent of Parliament is illegal.
2. That the pretended power of dispensing with laws or the execution of laws by regal authority, as it has been assumed and exercised of late, is illegal.
3. That the commission for erecting the late Court for Ecclesiastical Causes, and all other commissions and courts of like nature [i.e. prerogative courts], are illegal and pernicious.
4. That levying money for or to the use of the Crown by pretence of prerogative without grant of Parliament, for longer time or in other manner than the same is or shall be granted, is illegal.
5. That it is the right of the subjects to petition the King, and all commitments and prosecutions for such petitioning are illegal.
6. That the raising or keeping a standing army within the kingdom in time of peace, unless it be with consent of Parliament, is against the law.
7. That the subjects which are Protestants may have arms for their defense suitable to their conditions and as allowed by law.
8. That the election of members of Parliament ought to be free [from interference by the Crown].
9. That the freedom of speech and debates or proceedings in Parliament ought not to be impeached or questioned in any court or place out of Parliament.
10. That excessive bail ought not to be required, nor excessive fines imposed, nor cruel and unusual punishments inflicted.
11. That jurors ought to be duly empanelled and returned, and jurors which pass upon men in trials for high treason ought to be freeholders.
12. That all grants and promises of fines and forfeitures of particular persons before conviction are illegal and void.
13. And that for redress of all grievances and for the amending, strengthening, and preserving of the laws, Parliaments ought to be held frequently.

The Revolution of 1689 was a crucial turning point in the political and constitutional life of the colonies. Prior to 1689 they were subject to the whim of Stuart monarchs who believed themselves above the ordinary law, unlike their subjects, who must meekly submit. The arbitrary and inconsistent nature of their rule was reinforced by the poor caliber of the officials who carried out their orders; most of these men were motivated by personal gain. There was always an extortionist element in the practice of Stuart government.

After 1689 this situation changed significantly. Just as William and Mary had to abide by the laws of England, so their agents in America increasingly had to observe a similar code of conduct. In 1700 Parliament passed an act permitting the prosecution of governors who "oppressed their provinces." In 1703 the Privy Council ordered that to prevent corruption, officials must not accept presents from their assemblies. More extensive instructions were formulated for them to follow; for example, all expenditure was to be monitored and the details sent to the Treasury.

Of course the scions of noble families still came to America to recoup their fortunes, but they could do so only in well-regulated ways. Those who stepped beyond the line were punished, as Lord Cornbury shortly discovered while governor of New York (see chapter 16, section 3). Above all, the Glorious Revolution guaranteed the sanctity of property. In this respect the colonists benefited as much as their English compatriots. A new era of constitutionalism had arrived, in which the provincial assemblies were given a key role. Whatever the ultimate disagreements about colonial rights, the events of 1689 and the regranting of the charters gave the colonists lawful protection against the worst abuses of arbitrary government. That was a great step forward.

9

The Era of William and Anne

1689	The League of Augsburg is formed; war begins in Europe.
1690	Sir William Phips attempts to invade Canada.
1692	Witchcraft trials take place in Salem.
1696	The Board of Trade is established.
1697	The Peace of Ryswick is signed.
1700	The Iroquois conclude a treaty of neutrality with the French. Captain Kidd is arrested in Boston.
1701	William Penn issues his last frame of government. Delaware is granted a separate charter.
1702	East and West New Jersey become a royal province. War in Europe is renewed. South Carolina attacks St. Augustine.
1704	The French and American Indians attack Deerfield.
1707	Colonel Benjamin Church's assault on Port Royal fails.
1710	Francis Nicholson captures Port Royal.
1711	The British fail to take Quebec.
1711–12	Fighting with the Tuscaroras takes place in North Carolina.
1713	The Treaty of Utrecht is signed.
1715	Fighting with the Yamasee takes place in South Carolina.
1718	William Teach (Blackbeard) is killed by Virginian naval forces.
1719	South Carolina ousts its proprietary officials.
1729	Proprietary rights to North and South Carolina are formally surrendered.

1   WILLIAM III'S COLONIAL POLICY

TWO MAIN PRINCIPLES guided English policy after 1689: the first was that the colonists must pay their way; the second, that colonial trade must be arranged for the benefit of the mother country.

The accession of William and Mary is often described by historians as a counter-revolution; for in both England and America the centralizing and innovative policies of James II were overturned. However, as Massachusetts had already discovered, the clock could not be turned back completely; the colonies were too important. As Sir Robert Southwell, a leading bureaucrat, emphasized to one of the king's principal ministers in March 1689, North America's 250,000 inhabitants furnished "a full third part of the whole Trade and Navigation of England . . . a great nursery of Our Sea Men and the King's Customs depend mightily thereon." Closer supervision was essential.

The result was a continued strengthening of the bureaucracy, and in this sense the Glorious Revolution was by no means a total defeat for Randolph and his colleagues. Many, like Andros and Nicholson, went on to new posts, while Randolph was promoted surveyor general of the customs for all of North America.

Since their founding the colonies had been haphazardly supervised by various committees of the Privy Council. Clearly some more permanent body was required for the sake of cohesion. At the same time the Commons were denouncing the Crown's failure to enforce the navigation laws. The merchants' feelings on this subject ran so strong that in 1696 the House of Commons proposed setting up a parliamentary agency to do the job. To preempt such an outcome, William III created a new department, the Board of Trade, consisting of a president and seven other salaried members, plus clerks. Apart from enforcing the navigation laws, these "knowing and fit persons" were to sift through the colonial laws and governors' reports before forwarding them to the Privy Council for action. A huge backlog of business awaited them, including the vetting of over a hundred provincial laws.

That same year Parliament extended to the colonies an act regulating the customs, which gave revenue officers greater powers of search by means of writs of assistance. These writs allowed entry to any premises where smuggling was suspected. In addition the Privy Council ordered the governors of Massachusetts, New York, Pennsylvania, Maryland, and Virginia to establish vice-admiralty courts, which had no jury, only a presiding judge, to facilitate convictions for breaches of the trade laws.

Thus, although the Dominion of New England had been overthrown, the central bureaucracy which oversaw the governance of the colonies was not without success. Maryland and New York had become royal colonies. With war now sweeping Europe, the opportunities for further rationalization remained considerable, not least in Pennsylvania, where the proprietor, William Penn, was in trouble.

2   THE SALEM WITCHCRAFT TRIALS

Before looking at the proprietary difficulties in Pennsylvania, mention must be made of the traumatic occurrences in Massachusetts during 1692, known collectively as the Salem witchcraft trials.

Prosecutions for witchcraft were not a new phenomenon. They had been a feature of Christianity since its foundation, though their incidence had increased with the Reformation. The Protestant churches, in their search for purity, were less tolerant of any deviation which could be linked to Satan, including many popular superstitions. Nevertheless many occult practices associated with alchemy, astrology, and chiromancy continued to be widely observed on both sides of the Atlantic as part of popular culture.

In Massachusetts charges of witchcraft had been relatively infrequent. Between 1630 and 1690 there were only twenty-four indictments, seven convictions, and five executions. The first capital offenses occurred in 1647 and 1648 when two women were executed; further executions took place in 1651 and 1656. Cases were relatively more prevalent in the Connecticut Valley, where serious outbreaks occurred at Wethersfield and Springfield in the late 1640s and in Hartford in the early 1660s.

Most of those accused in New England were charged with malefic magic, of doing someone harm, rather than with heresy. Cases often arose out of indictments for slander, in which the defendant tried to prove the truth of a defamatory statement by bringing a charge of witchcraft. Another cause for indictment after 1656 was association with the Quakers, because of their strange clothing and manner.

Charges of witchcraft thereafter steadily declined in both Massachusetts and Connecticut. A small upsurge occurred in the 1680s, but nothing presaged the deluge of accusations, indictments, and convictions that was to sweep Salem and the neighboring communities of Massachusetts in 1692.

The first signs that something was amiss occurred in February 1692, when Betty Parris and Abigail Williams, the nine-year-old daughter and eleven-year-old niece of Samuel Parris, the local minister of Salem village, a suburb of Salem town, began experiencing fits which the local physicians diagnosed as bewitchment after failing to find any physical cause. Proof was supposedly obtained when it was discovered that both girls had been dabbling in occult practices to foretell who their future husbands might be. This had involved putting the white of an egg in a glass of water to see if it produced an image. An image duly appeared in the shape of a coffin and it was shortly after this that the fits began. Next Parris discovered that his Caribbean Indian slave, Tituba, had used an old English folklore remedy, or species of white magic, to find out the cause of the girls' distress. A cake made of rye meal and the girls' urine had been fed to a dog in the belief that this would reveal the names of their tormentors. To Parris this was tantamount to witchcraft itself, and after further questioning Abigail and Betty named two women, Sarah Good and Sarah Osborne, as the cause of their affliction, adding Tituba for good measure. They were supported in their accusations by two other girls, Ann Putnam, the twelve-year-old daughter of a prominent local farmer, Thomas Putnam, and Elizabeth Hubbard, a seventeen-year-old servant girl.

All three accused were then interrogated by the local magistrates at the end of February 1692. Though Good and Osborne stoutly maintained their innocence, the magistrates were quickly convinced of their guilt because of Tituba's confession that she was familiar with Caribbean occult practices and had been helped by the other two women. If further proof was needed, it was supplied by the children themselves, who began writhing in agony, claiming they were being tortured by the spectres of Good and Osborne. The magistrates accordingly ordered the three to be sent to Boston jail pending a formal trial before an assize court.[1]

Despite the drama surrounding the girls, the proceedings so far had not been particularly different from other witchcraft episodes in New England. What changed now was that

---

[1] For Tituba's role in the early stages of the event, see Elaine G. Breslaw, *Tituba, Reluctant Witch of Salem: Devilish Indians and Puritan Fantasies* (New York, 1996).

several more young women and a few older ones too began experiencing fits, blaming not only Tituba, Osborne and Good, but three relatively prominent members of the community, Martha Corey, Rebecca Nurse, and Elizabeth Proctor as well. Nor did the charges stop there for by May more than two dozen people had been accused, including several men who had sought to defend their wives and a former minister of Salem, George Burroughs.

In this situation, the governor, Sir William Phips, decided to appoint a special court to try the cases. During its proceedings the accusers frequently fainted or screamed when confronting the defendants, accusing them of having appeared as specters weeks or even years before. The accused in turn were subjected to minute inspection to check whether they had any marks of the devil on their body, the most important of which was a teat for suckling Satan's young. They were also required to recite the Lord's Prayer fluently, which it was believed no one possessed by the devil could do. The problem for the accused was that such evidence was hard to disprove; specters could be summoned up at any time of the day or night, while the absence of marks could be attributed to the cunning of the devil. Even recitation of the Lord's Prayer was difficult in the tension of a crowded court-room. Lastly, the accused were denied any form of council to ensure that their defence was conducted properly.

In these circumstances the normal judicial processes were completely over-turned, as was demonstrated in the case of Rebecca Nurse. Although she was initially acquitted, her accusers set up such a clamor that the magistrates ordered the jury to reconsider their verdict, which they dutifully did. Given the prevailing mood, many of those accused preferred to confess, since a confession normally entitled a person to leniency. Unfortunately, those like Tituba who took this course had to name their accomplices in order to be convincing, so that even children denounced their parents in the general hue and cry.

Until May 1692 the charges were confined to the vicinity of Salem village and town. In June, however, accusations began to be made at Andover, Haverhill, Topsfield, and Gloucester. By October over one hundred and forty people had been indicted, of whom fifty had confessed, twenty-six had been convicted, and twenty executed, nineteen of them by hanging. The exception among those executed was Giles Corey, whose wife had already been condemned because she had protested her innocence, the presumption being that she would not give up the devil. Corey refused to implicate himself or his wife any further by pleading before the court, since even a confession would probably have led to the forfeiture of all his lands. His ploy did him no good; he was ordered to be crushed under a pile of stones. Many prominent persons now went into hiding or fled to neighboring provinces.

By this time ministers like Increase and Cotton Mather were becoming uneasy at the court's excessive reliance on spectral evidence. They were also alarmed at the contradiction of sparing confessing witches while executing those who asserted their innocence. Equally disturbing was the correlation that the more people confessed the greater the number of accused. Indeed, the net was being cast so wide that even members of the civil and clerical establishment were being mentioned. Among those incriminated were the wives of Governor Phips, the Reverend John Hale, Parson Samuel Willard, and Dudley Bradstreet, a leading magistrate in Andover, all of whom had voiced their opposition to further prosecutions. Although the courts refused to take these latter charges seriously, their refusal to do so further undermined the legitimacy of their proceeding against others. At this point the credibility of the accusers themselves finally came into question, especially when early in October Increase Mather delivered a sermon suggesting that it was better that ten suspects went free rather than one innocent person was hanged. Even Parris, who had been most

Plate 23 Salem witch trial, artist's reconstruction. The Library of Congress, Washington, D.C.

DOCUMENT 14

Recantation of the women of Andover, 1692, reprinted in Thomas Hutchinson, *The History of the Colony and Province of Massachusetts-Bay*, edited by Lawrence Shaw Mayo (Cambridge, Mass., 1936, II, 31–2).

[This document shows how innocent people, suddenly accused of a crime and deprived of their liberty, can be induced to make a false confession.]

When . . . at Mr Parris's house, several young persons, being seemingly afflicted, did accuse several persons for afflicting them . . . we [were] informed that if a person was sick, the afflicted person could tell what or who was the cause of that sickness. Joseph Ballard of Andover, his wife being sick at the same time, he, either from himself or by the advice of others, fetched two of the persons, called the afflicted persons, from Salem Village to Andover, which was the beginning of that dreadful calamity that befell us in Andover. . . . After [the Reverend] Mr Barnard had been at prayer, we were blindfolded, and our hands were laid upon the afflicted persons, they being in their fits and falling into their fits at our coming into their presence, as they said; and some led us and laid our hands upon them, and then they said they were well, and that we were guilty of afflicting them. Whereupon, we were all seized, as prisoners, by a warrant from the Justice of the Peace and forthwith carried to Salem. And, by reason of that sudden surprizal, we knowing ourselves altogether innocent of that crime, we were all exceedingly astonished and amazed, and consternated and affrighted even out of our reason; and our nearest and dearest relations, seeing us in that dreadful condition and knowing our great danger, apprehended there was no other way to save our lives, as the case was then circumstanced, but by our confessing. . . . Indeed that confession, that it is said we made, was no other than what was suggested to us by some gentlemen, they telling us that we were witches, and they knew it, and we knew it, which made us thinking that it was so; and our understanding, our reason, our faculties, almost gone, we were not capable of judging of our condition; as also the hard measures they used with us rendered us incapable of making our defence, but said anything and everything which they desired, and most of what we said was but, in effect, a consenting to what they said. Some time after, when we were better composed, they telling us what we had confessed, we did profess that we were innocent and ignorant of such things; and we hearing that Samuel Wardwell had renounced his confession, and quickly after condemned and executed, some of us were told we were going after Wardwell.

Confession of Sarah Carrier, age seven, August 11, 1692, reprinted in Thomas Hutchinson, *The History of the Colony and Province of Massachusetts-Bay*, edited by Lawrence Shaw Mayo (Cambridge, Mass., 1936, II, 34).

[The ludicrous and tragic excesses of the witch hunt can be gathered from this examination of Sarah Carrier, whose mother had already been condemned to death.]

It was asked Sarah Carrier by the Magistrates or Justices: How long hast thou been a witch. Answer: Ever since I was six years old. Question: How old are you now? Answer: Near eight years old, brother Richard says, I shall be eight years old in November next. Question: Who made you a witch? Answer: My mother, she made me set my hand to a book [of the devil]. Question: How did you set your hand to it? Answer: I touched it with my fingers and the book was red, the paper of it was white. . . . Being asked who was there beside, she answered her Aunt and her cousin. Being asked when it was, she said, when she was baptized. Question: What did they promise to give you? Answer: A black dog. Question: Did the dog ever come to you? Answer: No. Question: But you said you saw a cat once. What did it say to you? Answer: It said it would tear me in pieces if I would not set my hand to the book. She said her mother baptized her, and the devil or black man was not there, as she saw, and mother said when she baptized her, thou art mine for ever and ever and amen. Question: How did you afflict folks? Answer: I pinched them. . . . Being asked whether she went in her body or her spirit, she said in her spirit. And she said her mother carried her thither to afflict. Question: How did your mother carry you when she was in prison? Answer: She came like a black cat. Question: How did you know that it was your mother? Answer: The cat told me so that she was my mother.

zealous in pursuit of those who had afflicted his children, began to recoil. A week later the governor, Sir William Phips, ordered the special court of oyer and terminer to be dissolved. By early 1693 the Superior Court of Judicature, which had replaced the previous tribunal, refused to hear further charges, based solely on spectral evidence, in an implicit acknowledgment that wrong had been done. Several of the accused, however, remained in jail, unable to pay their gaolers' fees. The first public apology only came in 1697 from Samuel Sewall, one of the judges, but not until 1711 was compensation paid to the surviving victims whose lives and those of their families had been ruined. Even then most people preferred to believe that the devil was to blame, even if innocent blood had been shed. For this reason no action was taken against either the accusers or the prosecuting justices. Most of the accusers drifted into obscurity, but the magistrates like William Stoughton, the Lieutenant Governor and presiding judge, remained in high office.

Many interpretations have been offered to explain this extraordinary episode. One is that the afflicted children, brought up in a repressive manner, used the trials to attract attention and turn the tables on their parents. Another suggestion is that the initial accusations came from young girls who were approaching puberty, a time when the psychological and physical stresses caused by hormonal imbalance are most acute. This made them prone to irrational behaviour, especially after they had been discovered dabbling in the occult. It was easy for them to become hysterical, making wild accusations to disarm their parents' anger and avoid blame. Nevertheless, this means that the accusations were essentially fraudulent.[2]

---

[2]   The charge of fraud was first hinted at by Thomas Brattle, a Boston merchant, in an open letter on 8 October 1692. It was later taken up by Thomas Hutchinson in his *History of the Colony and Province of Massachusetts-Bay*, vol. 2 (Boston, 1768). For a similar more recent interpretation, see Bernard Rosenthal, *Salem Story: Reading the*

Others prefer to place the blame on blind panic among the population at large. Once the accusations had been made, they gathered a momentum all their own. Everyone accepted the presence of evil spirits and, as Cotton Mather argued, "Where will the Devil show the most malice but where he is hated . . . most?" When the accused themselves confessed, this seemed the final proof.

Religion may also have contributed to the furore in other ways too. Parris was a stern opponent of the Half-Way Covenant and used this to exclude members of his congregation from taking communion. George Burroughs was distrusted because he appeared to have Baptist leanings. Finally, the Proctor and Nurse families had relatives who belonged to the Quakers, still an object of suspicion in the minds of many country people.

Another widespread view is that the episode was simply an extreme case of the persecution of the most vulnerable members of society. Most of the accused were women who became suspect because of their age, misfortune, or refusal to conform to social norms. For example, Good had a reputation for being a quarrelsome beggar, while Bridget Bishop, the first to be executed, had been accused of witchcraft a decade earlier. But such an interpretation does not explain the inclusion of persons like Elizabeth Carey, the wife of a wealthy Charlestown merchant, and Martha Corey, however, who were neither old, poor, widowed nor social outcasts, though one common factor seems to have been that most of the women were beyond their childbearing years. Women beyond the menopause were thought to resent those who could still have children, which made them vulnerable to satanic influences. But that does not explain the inclusion of Elizabeth Proctor, who was pregnant at the time of her indictment.

A related interpretation is that the trials were largely a case of gender exploitation and repression. Although the outbreak began with hysterical claims of possession by young females, much of the supporting testimony came from male relatives or friends, especially by those aged thirty to forty-five. These were men in their prime of life, who expected to have their way both politically and economically. All too often they found their ambitions stymied by older female neighbors or relatives, who were reluctant to step aside or sell their property. Charges of witchcraft provided a convenient way of removing such women, especially if they were widows with no direct heirs, since they had no husbands or sons to protect them. Ironically, the accusers were often aided by the accused themselves. Like everyone else, they subscribed to the view that women were the weaker sex, since it was Eve who had succumbed to the temptations of the serpent and caused the Fall. Perhaps they too were in some way to blame for their plight.[3]

Witch Trials of 1692 (Cambridge, England, 1993). Apart from hysteria, there are two other medical interpretations. One is that the accusers had contracted ergot poisoning after eating contaminated rye bread, which caused them to hallucinate. Another is that the accusers were suffering from encephalitis, or inflammation of the brain, caused by a virus. However, the ergot interpretation fails to explain why the afflicted were the only sufferers, not the population at large. For this interpretation, see Linda Caporeal, "Ergotism: Satan Loosed in Salem," *Science*, 192, 1976, 21–6. It was promptly rebutted by Nicholas P. Spanos and Jack Gottlieb, "Ergotism and the Salem Village Witch Trials", *Science*, 194, 1976, 1390–4. The possibility of encephalitis is advanced by Laurie Winn Carlson, *A Fever in Salem* (Chicago, 2000).

[3] For an interpretation of the trials based on gender, see Carol F. Karlsen, *The Devil in the Shape of a Woman: Witchcraft in Colonial New England* (New York, 1987). The seventeenth-century belief that women were morally weaker is discussed by Elizabeth Reis, *Dammed Women: Sinners and Witches in Puritan New England* (Ithaca, 1997).

A different line of inquiry has suggested that the trials originated in the tensions between Salem town and Salem village. The town was modern, commercial, and prosperous. The village, on the other hand, especially its western half was largely agrarian, steeped in more medieval and communitarian values. Most of its inhabitants were subsistence farmers, at the bottom of the tax list, who felt threatened by their more prosperous neighbours. Interestingly, twelve of the fourteen initially accused came from the eastern part of the village closest to the town, where the greatest wealth lay, whereas almost all of the accusers were from the western side. This may explain why John Proctor was among the accused. Besides being a successful farmer, he ran a thriving tavern for travelers on the main road running north from Boston to the east of the village. Such commercialism hardly squared with the older puritanical values of the rural interior. The same entrepreneurial activity was also true of Israel Porter and his family, who lived on the eastern side of the village. They too had considerable wealth, not only in land but milling enterprises and were friendly with the Proctors. Among the accused was Porter's brother-in-law Daniel Andrew.[4]

Certainly Salem had a long history of contention. Roger Williams had been one of its first pastors, and other notable disputes had included a quarrel with George Burroughs over his salary as minister of Salem village which led to his departure in 1683. Parris, the next minister, had been involved in a similar dispute. Among his supporters were the Putnam family, who favored a tax to fund the minister's stipend. Opposed to this faction were the Porters, Proctors, and others who were subsequently victimized. One of the factors behind the salary dispute was that many living on the eastern side of the village disputed the need for a separate church at all, since it was convenient for them to worship in Salem town. They were also angry that the village parsonage had been surreptitiously given to Parris, rather than leased, as required under the original bequest granting the land. They accordingly used their influence in Salem to block the demands for the tax to fund Parris's salary. In response, the Putnam group decided to seek town status for the village so that they could have a fully covenanted church and run their affairs without interference from Salem. However, in October 1691 they were thwarted once more when the Porter group gained control of the village committee. Within six months the first charges of witchcraft were being made, fanned by Parris's sermons about the dangers facing the community and the need to destroy the ungodly.

These facts suggest that the trials may have been partly the result of personal grudges. In the past, charges of witchcraft had sometimes been brought by those who had a grievance against an individual. The Putnam family apparently had designs on some woods owned by the Nurse family, while several of those accused in neighboring Topsfield had pursued litigation against the Putnams over land. Vengeance might also explain the spread of witchcraft charges to other towns, as former neighbors caught up with their longtime adversaries. This interpretation would also further explain the prosecution of Rebecca Nurse, who, although a good church member, had earlier been involved in a heated dispute over some stray pigs. The fact that the owner of these had subsequently died in strange circumstances seemed to support a charge of malefic magic. Lastly, vengeance might account for the charges made by servants against their master. John Proctor and George Jacobs both

---

[4] For the thesis concerning the location of the accusers and accused, see P. Boyer and S. Nissenbaum, *Salem Possessed: The Social Origins of Witchcraft* (Cambridge, Mass., 1974).

became suspect when Mary Warren and Sarah Churchill accused them of witchcraft, following unsympathetic treatment at their hands. George Burroughs was another person to fall foul of a former servant, Mercy Lewis.

One factor which certainly cannot be ignored is the propensity of human beings to copy one another. Once news of Salem's outbreak spread, it was almost inevitable that neighboring communities would find similar evils in their midst. The recent publication of several books on the subject may have acted as an added stimulus. Most notable among these was Judge Matthew Hale's account of some trials in Suffolk, England. Hale himself, an eminent judge, clearly believed in the presence of witches. His opinions were supported by Cotton Mather, who wrote an essay on the subject in 1689. From the beginning the Puritans had been obsessed about preserving the purity of their commonwealth. For twenty years the ministry had been threatening the people that they would suffer for their errant ways. The surprise is that there had not been more charges of witchcraft. Certainly many ministers were disposed to see the Salem trials as justification for their jeremiads. In such a climate the subsequent excesses become understandable.

Finally, historians have emphasized what might be called the stresses of the times. Massachusetts had undergone two decades of crisis beginning with King Philip's War, continuing with the loss of the charter, and culminating in the turmoil surrounding the events of 1689. War then had broken out with France. This catalogue of misfortunes seems to have considerably undermined the confidence and, hence, the government of the third-generation Puritans. The clergy stood aside, while the magistrates simply lost control. They allowed those with spectral visions to behave as they liked, permitted the Putnam family to intervene in support of witnesses, and made statements about the defendants in blatant disregard of all due process. Such undisciplined proceedings would never have been allowed in the time of Winthrop.[5]

Ultimately the explanation of the Salem witchcraft trials depends on a fusion of all these factors. The obsession with sin, the belief in the devil, the social and political turmoil, personal vendettas, all created a climate in which the excesses of the trials were understandable. The episode in some respects constituted the death throes of a passing era, as old orthodoxies succumbed to more secular forces, though belief in the supernatural remained widespread. The church and magistracy, however, found it safer to distance themselves from Satan and his agents, leaving God to decide on the punishment of deviants. After 1700 no further charges of witchcraft were entertained by the courts in Massachusetts or elsewhere.

3 PROPRIETARY PROBLEMS IN PENNSYLVANIA AND NEW JERSEY

We have seen that even before the tumultuous events of 1689 Penn had found the management of his settlement difficult. Now he came under attack for his vigorous support of James II's policy of religious toleration and his reluctance to welcome William and Mary. In the immediate aftermath of the Glorious Revolution, rumors and plots abounded. Penn

---

[5] For the failure of the judiciary, see Peter Charles Hoffer, *The Salem Witchcraft Trials: A Legal History* (Lawrence, 1997).

was more obviously antagonistic to the new regime than most and in July 1690 he was accused of high treason. His control of the province was thus put in jeopardy, for although Penn made his peace with William III, other misdemeanors could not be so easily overlooked. One involved alleged infractions of the laws of trade; another concerned his inability to defend Pennsylvania.

Penn's proprietary rights were suspended in October 1692 when William III appointed Benjamin Fletcher to be joint governor of Pennsylvania and New York. Officially Fletcher's appointment was justified "by reason of the great neglects and miscarriages" which had occurred in Pennsylvania during Penn's absence. Another, unstated reason was the desire to create a more effective system of defense now that the Dominion of New England had been disbanded. Fletcher was therefore also given command of the New Jersey militia.

If Fletcher imagined that he would have more authority as the king's representative than Penn had enjoyed, he was soon disabused of this notion. Fletcher did have the advantage of nominating his own council, but the effect of this provision was merely to concentrate opposition in the lower house, where the demand for the right to initiate legislation soon resurfaced. The assembly also insisted on auditing all public monies, out of concern that funds might be siphoned off for military purposes. On that matter the Quakers were adamant; war was unlawful no matter how perilous the situation might be.

Fletcher's difficulties led to Penn's being restored to his proprietorship in August 1694, despite the opposition of the bureaucracy. William III could hardly claim to be the savior of English rights if he abolished one of its most distinctive species, proprietary government. In any case a Quaker proprietor might be more effective in securing the supplies the government so desperately wanted.

Penn had to guarantee a number of conditions to get his title back, the most important of which was his return in person to secure Pennsylvania's defense. This news was announced at a council meeting in Philadelphia in March 1695 by William Markham, who was to be lieutenant governor until Penn arrived.

The restoration of proprietary government was by no means welcome to the lower house, since it brought with it the return to an elective council with a rival claim to represent the people. Consequently the assembly immediately demanded a fresh charter. At length, in November 1696 Markham issued a new frame of government in return for a supply bill. The one major change was the right of the lower house to initiate legislation.

Markham's frame nevertheless allowed the governor and council considerable powers, including the same right to initiate legislation as the assembly. Claiming the sole right to initiation, the assembly could not accept this measure. Furthermore, the deputies now demanded the authority to audit the public accounts, which was presently reserved to the council. The majority in the lower house now had a new leader, David Lloyd, a cousin of the former councillor. Trained as a lawyer in England, he was well versed in constitutional procedures. Under his leadership the acrimony between the assembly and the council continued unabated.

Historians have rightly criticized the Quakers for being unable to conduct their affairs amicably and for constantly taking quarrels beyond sensible bounds. The fact that the wealthy merchants of Philadelphia dominated the council hardly justified such fractiousness, since both houses were elected by the freemen. In such a hierarchical age, wealth was bound to predominate; indeed, in that respect the upper house was little different from the Senate today.

In 1699 Penn finally left England, still believing that Quaker principles founded on reason could produce calm. After two years, however, he recognized that further concessions were necessary, not least because his proprietorship was under attack once more in England. Accordingly, in 1701 Penn issued a further frame of government. It was remarkably short, making no mention of the council and declaring that all laws were to be made "By the Governor with the consent and approbation of the freemen in general assembly met." Pennsylvania was to have a unicameral legislature, a unique phenomenon in England's American colonies. The only check on the assembly was that all bills were still subject to the veto of the proprietor and, ultimately, of the Privy Council.[6]

The assembly quickly accepted Penn's concessions, though the pattern of Pennsylvania politics did not change. The proprietary family still controlled the executive branch and the granting of all land, which were the issues behind the next dispute with the assembly.

In a separate proviso Penn indicated that the three Delaware counties could separate from Pennsylvania. They would keep the same governor and privileges, the only difference being that their representatives would meet at Newcastle to frame their own laws. Delaware's inhabitants quickly seized this option, since most of them disliked the Quakers. Nor was their departure in November 1702 opposed, since they had been overrepresented in the assembly. One element of contention was thus removed, though Delaware itself remained in an anomalous position, since its separation was never formally recognized by the Crown.

The new frame of government effectively ended Penn's "holy experiment." Instead of proposing what was good for Pennsylvania, he now limited himself to accepting or rejecting the resolve of others. After twenty years' endeavor his ideal of a benign, deferential society was dead. Equally disappointing for Penn was the lack of profit on his investment, neither his land sales nor trade with the American Indians having rescued him from debt. He was so disillusioned that within a few years he tried to sell his proprietorship back to the Crown.

Historians have rarely given Penn and his fellow Quakers a good press. Their factional in-fighting and inflexibility on issues like defense laid them open to criticism, especially when compared with the Puritans. In addition, their refusal to marry outside their sect, to maintain tribal purity, has been seen as incompatible with American values. It should be noted, however, that the Quakers also displayed traits which were to become regarded as quintessentially American. First, they alone believed in religious toleration at this time and as a result they welcomed other groups, making Pennsylvania the first province to offer refuge to the oppressed – had the Statue of Liberty been commissioned in the eighteenth century it would have had to be sited on the approaches to Philadelphia. The Quakers also believed in simplicity of manners, another American trait, and in human equality, holding that God created all human beings in His image. Thus only the Quakers attempted to treat the American Indians as equals, while this same egalitarianism was leading them to denounce slavery as well. It also led them to be more generous in their treatment of women. Moreover, only in Pennsylvania was charity distributed without the recipient being expected to acknowledge shame. Finally pragmatism made the Quakers exponents of technology, on which American economic greatness was subsequently built.[7]

---

[6] For the full text see W. Keith Kavenagh, *Foundations of Colonial America: A Documentary History* (New York, 1973), II, 1160–4.

[7] The hostility of Daniel J. Boorstin to the Quakers in *The Americans: The Colonial Experience* (New York, 1958) has already been noted in chapter 7, section 3. For a more sympathetic account, see Frederick B. Tolles, *Quakers and the Atlantic Culture* (New York, 1960). For a more recent, generally neutral analysis, see Richard S. Dunn and Mary Maples Dunn, eds, *The World of William Penn* (Philadelphia, 1986).

While Penn was making his final dispositions for Pennsylvania, another province in which he had once had an interest was also undergoing change. The situation in East and West New Jersey was becoming increasingly confused as one group of proprietors sold its interest to another. These changes necessarily had an unsettling effect on the population. Some of the settlers had originally been invited to settle by Colonel Nicholls and many had subsequently purchased land from the native inhabitants, whose titles had then been challenged by successive proprietors. Since neither the East nor the West New Jersey proprietors had done anything to protect the provinces, in 1700 some two hundred inhabitants of East New Jersey appealed to the Crown to release them from their predicament.

The charges they presented were sufficiently damaging for the Board of Trade to take note, not least because the old suspicion resurfaced that the acts of trade were being ignored. Accordingly, William Blathwayt, a leading bureaucrat, wrote a memorandum based on a long list of misdemeanors prepared by Randolph, which recommended that all the proprietary colonies be taken over by the Crown. To this end a bill was introduced into the House of Lords.

Although the measure was stopped short by the death of William III in March 1702, Blathwayt and his colleagues were not to be denied in the case of the Jersey provinces. The proprietors rejected the charges regarding the lack of defense and evasion of the navigation laws, but they were ready to negotiate. In return for keeping their land rights, they agreed to surrender their governmental powers to both East and West New Jersey.

To help unify the province, Queen Anne, William III's successor, ordered that the council should comprise six men from the east and six from the west, with the assembly alternating between Perth Amboy and Burlington. Freeholders who held one hundred acres of land would qualify for the vote. Although New Jersey was to have the same governor as New York until 1738, it was now a full-fledged royal colony.

4 THE END OF PROPRIETARY GOVERNMENT IN THE CAROLINAS

Pennsylvania and New Jersey were not the only proprietary governments in North America under attack. Although the Carolina palatine court was quick to acknowledge William and Mary, both the Clarendon and Albemarle provinces – South and North Carolina, as they were beginning to be called – were under scrutiny by the bureaucracy in England.

We have already seen that the proprietors were armchair developers who expected others to realize their dreams. The net result was that most aspects of the Fundamental Constitutions had not been achieved. Few landgraves or caciques had been established, and the only element of the scheme which showed vitality, the provincial assembly, remained hostile to the proprietors.

Nevertheless, the proprietors still hoped that the Fundamental Constitutions would eventually be implemented, at least in South Carolina. By 1693 they were sufficiently optimistic to think that the time had arrived. The assembly disagreed, causing a deadlock, as article seventy-four stated that all parties had to subscribe to the Fundamental Constitutions before they could come into force. After various rebuffs, the proprietors declared the document invalid, only to make a further attempt to have it confirmed in 1698.

An equally contentious issue was the claim of the assembly to be allowed to initiate legislation. Under the Fundamental Constitutions this right was reserved to the grand council, but the lower house gradually got its way. The deputies were aided paradoxically by one of the proprietors, Seth Southel, who had bought the interests of Lord Clarendon and had then come to America, the first proprietor to do so. Initially Southel went to North Carolina to be governor, where his administration turned into a catalogue of misdemeanors arising from the view that his purchase gave him a license to do whatever he pleased.

In 1689 the inhabitants of North Carolina, perhaps also stirred by events elsewhere, ousted Southel, who then claimed the governorship in Charleston. For the next eighteen months he arbitrarily imprisoned and fined both the inhabitants and the proprietary officials until he was recalled by the palatine court. It was Southel, however, who first allowed the assembly to initiate legislation, albeit as a means of gaining support for himself. His successor, Philip Ludwell, was ordered to overturn this practice, but to no effect; the grand council had become effectively redundant.

Another cause of dissension in South Carolina was the establishment of the Anglican church, which little was done to implement in the first twenty years, partly because of the presence of so many Baptists, Puritans, Huguenots, and Quakers, and partly because of the need to attract further immigrants. However, the end of the century marked a time of resurgence among the Anglicans, not least in Goose Creek. The outbreak of war with France gave them a pretext to expel the Huguenots from the assembly as a danger to the province's security. Then in May 1704 they passed a bill requiring all members of the assembly to be members of the Church of England, clearing the way for a second act in November 1704 which divided Clarendon province into six parishes, each with its own church. Any shortfall in construction costs was to be made good by the public treasury, while the clergy were to receive a public stipend. The vestrymen, too, had to be Anglican. Both these acts were accepted by the palatine court, where Lord Granville, a strong supporter of the Church of England, was now the principal influence.

The Anglicans, however, constituted a bare majority of the population, and their opponents promptly petitioned the authorities in England to have the two acts disallowed. They were successful mainly because the Board of Trade believed that the second act gave the vestries too much power over the clergy, but the dissenters' victory lasted only until a similar bill to establish the Anglican church was passed in 1706, which gave the vestries less clerical authority. This time it was not challenged.

Nevertheless, the days of proprietary government in the Carolinas were numbered, for another major issue, defense, was about to demonstrate even more clearly the inadequacy of the palatine court. Throughout its existence South Carolina had been exposed to attack from the Spanish in Florida, the French on the Mississippi, and the Creek, Cherokee, Chickasaw, and Yamasee nations. The situation was generally uncertain because these Indian nations were often in conflict with one other, the tensions among them fostered by each of the European powers struggling for supremacy in the fur trade.

The outbreak of war in Europe in 1702 marked a critical point, especially as it followed the unification of France and Spain under the house of Bourbon. The Spanish in Florida, long jealous of the settlements around Charleston, could now call on the French in Mobile for help.

Governor James Moore decided to anticipate the enemy by equipping a small expedition to attack St. Augustine. Eight ships embarked with fifty Carolinians and thirteen hundred Yamasee. Alas, the expedition found the stone walls of the Castillo de San Marcos at St. Augustine impenetrable, though the coastal missions provided an easy target, and the operation achieved little beyond saddling the colony with a large debt. The proprietors, to whom the colonists appealed for assistance, had neither the means nor the will to take any action; most of them were either too young or too busy to exercise their responsibilities, so that the running of the palatine court devolved on one or two individuals. The foray therefore simply fueled calls for an end to proprietary government. Fortunately for the settlers, the Spanish ability to retaliate was limited, and when the enemy did muster a force to attack Charleston, it was even less successful than Moore's expedition. The French, however, worked hard to stir up the American Indians, among whom the balance of power was changing.[8]

Up to this time the most important nation in South Carolina was the Yamasee, who inhabited the coastal plain to the south of Charleston. During the first forty years of the settlement, they had been generally friendly, especially after they had supplanted the Westos as the principal channel for the fur trade. They not only provided the bulk of the forces for Governor Moore in his expedition to St. Augustine in 1702 but also gave him help when he decided to attack the Spanish missions in western Florida at the end of 1703. In due course, however, the initial harmony declined, reflecting the increasing scarcity of game in the area through overhunting and the growth of the white population, which by the turn of the century had reached ten thousand. These deteriorating relations in turn led many traders to begin dealing with the Cherokee and other nations to the west, bypassing the Yamasee altogether. An additional grievance was the fraudulent practices of the traders, which kept the native peoples in perpetual debt.

The situation developed into a classic case of aggrieved native peoples against indifferent white settlers with no further use for their former allies. War finally broke out in 1715, after the Yamasee had enlisted the support of the Creeks. The conflict was as serious for South Carolina as King Philip's assault had been for New England. The Yamasee carried hostilities to the very gates of Charleston, killing over four hundred settlers. Once more the colonists appealed to the proprietors for aid, again to no effect. Virginia offered help, but only if the Carolinians sent a large number of slaves in compensation, and the few volunteers who did arrive were described as useless. So desperate was the situation that even slaves had to be armed, while the outcome seemed to depend on which side the Cherokee supported. Only the inability of the American Indians to form a common front saved the colonists. With Cherokee help the Yamasee were tracked down and the majority of them killed or sold into slavery.[9]

The proprietors' failure to send aid led to further pleas for South Carolina to be placed under royal protection, especially as the colony was by now on the verge of bankruptcy. Any residual support for the proprietors was further undermined when they disallowed several pieces of legislation, including a new electoral law. The inhabitants also resented proprietary attempts to restructure the council and quadruple the price of land. Another war with Spain threatened, and in November 1719 the assembly took control by electing its own governor, James Moore. The colonists, however, were careful to send a full explanation of their actions to the king, accompanied by yet another denunciation of the proprietors. The ploy was successful since the officials in Whitehall remained hostile to the

---

[8] See chapter 18, section 1, for the Spanish perspective on these events.

[9] This was the last time that Indians were enslaved in any significant number.

concept of proprietary government, especially its ability to enforce the laws of trade. Accordingly, in August 1720 the veteran Francis Nicholson was appointed royal governor with power to appoint a council, summon an assembly, and take all measures for the admin‑ istration of the colony.

The Board of Trade then began the long process of buying out the proprietors, which was only completed in 1729 by an act of Parliament. Most of the proprietors yielded readily enough, not least because of their poor financial return. They finally agreed, with one exception, to relinquish the government and land rights to the Carolinas in return for £2,500 each.[10]

The demise of proprietary government, the expulsion of the Yamasee, and the ending of the war in Europe all helped foster some important economic and social changes. For its first forty‑five years the colony had survived largely on the fur trade. Now the expulsion of the native inhabitants opened the colony to wider settlement and a more diversified economy. Rice was introduced in 1693, its cultivation aided by the importation of African slaves. It was the Africans' familiarity with the crop as well as their labour which made successful cultivation possible. Soon a plantation system developed along the main rivers and their tributaries, while at the same time Charleston became a center of commerce and admin‑ istration to which the planters gravitated during the fall and winter months when the assembly was sitting. South Carolina was finally changing from a frontier to a provincial society. It had also become a "slave society" rather than a "society with slaves."

The agreement between the Crown and the proprietors in 1729 also covered North Carolina, whose development was both similar to and different from that of its southern sister. One difference was that the proprietary interest there was almost nil. Since Culpepper's rising the proprietors had endeavored to govern the province as part of South Carolina, an experiment which had not proved a success.

As in South Carolina, the Anglican church was a cause of contention. In 1701, and again in 1704, the assembly attempted to pass a vestry bill, excluding Dissenters from parish affairs while compelling them to contribute to the church's upkeep. This policy caused much antagonism, especially among the Quakers, who were the second most numerous group. The dispute was intensified by the Anglicans' refusal to let Quakers affirm rather than swear on the Bible when taking oaths, as they were allowed to do in England under the Toleration Act of 1689.

Fortunately for the Quakers, the Anglican majority was divided into two factions, led by Thomas Cary and William Glover respectively. Although Cary had readily harried the Quakers when in office, he quickly began to affect great concern for them when Glover replaced him in 1700 as the proprietors' acting governor. The disputes became so bitter that in 1711 the Privy Council ordered the proprietors to appoint a permanent governor to calm the situation. The man selected was Edward Hyde, a descendant of the Earl of Clarendon, one of the original proprietors.

Initially it seemed that the aristocratic Hyde might bring the conflict to an end, especially after the assembly passed a number of conciliatory declarations asserting that in future all laws would be based on those of England. Hyde, however, soon committed himself to the Anglican party, whereupon Cary attempted to overthrow the government. Hyde

---

[10]   The exception was Lord Carteret who gave up his governmental but not his property rights.

then called for assistance from Virginia and had Cary seized and sent to London for trial; but the proprietors were already disillusioned with their governor and the case was dismissed.

The release of Cary did not prevent the Anglican majority from introducing another vestry bill in 1715. Each parish was to be administered by a self-coopting vestry whose members were to take an oath of loyalty to the king, with a promise not to "impugne the liturgy of the Church of England." These bodies were to have extensive powers, including the right to build churches and to fund them by a five-shilling poll tax or other tithe. Furthermore, only marriages celebrated by the Church of England were to be recognized. The Anglicans' only conciliatory gesture was a toleration bill allowing the Quakers to affirm rather than take an oath on the Bible.

As in South Carolina, the proprietary government had difficulty defending the province. Though North Carolina was not vulnerable to attack by France and Spain, it did experience problems with the American Indians. Here, too, the province had previously been blessed by the initial protection of a friendly nation, the Tuscaroras, who then became disillusioned after being abused by local traders and subjected to an advancing line of white settlement. Despairing of any satisfaction, in September 1711 the Tuscaroras fell upon the settlements of Bath County in a surprise attack. Although about two hundred settlers were killed, the North Carolinians were able to obtain help from both Virginia and South Carolina, the latter reinforced, ironically, by the Yamasee. The Tuscaroras were eventually defeated, but as usual the settlers received no assistance from the proprietors; and this failure did not go unnoticed in London.

Another cause of royal displeasure was the suspicion that North Carolina was providing a haven for pirates. The ending of the war in Europe led many licensed privateers to become pirates, perhaps the most notable of whom was Captain Teach, or Blackbeard, who found the waters of Albemarle Sound a most convenient haven. Tobias Knight, the provincial secretary, and possibly Charles Eden, Hyde's successor, were suspected of complicity in providing Teach with harbor facilities and help in the sale of his booty. An expedition from Virginia, organized by Nicholson, was required to bring the scourge to an end. Teach was finally cornered and killed on the Albemarle outer banks near Ocracoke Inlet.

Once more the corruption and incompetence of the proprietary government had been exposed. From 1718 North Carolina was effectively a royal province, since the Crown insisted on vetting the next nominee for governor, but formal surrender was achieved only through the same act of Parliament which ended the proprietors' title to South Carolina.

Traditional accounts have tended to view proprietary experiments like those in the Carolinas as doomed to failure, the Durham palatine model being simply incompatible with the seeds of liberty already planted in American soil.[11] Proprietary colonies, however, were established successfully by the French in Canada, the Spanish in central America, and to some extent by the Dutch in New York. One reason for the system's failure in the Carolinas was that the proprietors did not put enough into their scheme; another was that the Durham model was an anachronism in England itself. Where a manorial system was still the norm, as in France, it proved quite possible to transplant it to the New World, albeit in modified form.

---

[11]   See, for example, Louis Hartz, *The Liberal Tradition in America* (New York, 1955).

The paradox is that a pyramidal society was eventually established in the Carolinas, though not in the way envisaged by Locke and Shaftesbury. By the middle of the eighteenth century a local aristocracy had emerged, though it owed nothing to the proprietors and placed little reliance on a yeomanry, preferring to depend on African servitude for its labor requirements. Thus were the projects of the Old World turned upside down in the New.

5   WAR AND THE AMERICAN COLONIES, 1689–1713

The southern proprietary colonies were not alone in being engaged in conflict at this time. Almost all the colonies were affected to some extent by the wars between England, France, and Spain in the period 1689–1713. Prior to 1689 colonial wars had been localized. Now they became part of much wider struggles.

The most serious fighting outside the lower south occurred on the frontiers of New England and New York. These northern colonies, which were closest to the center of French power in the St. Lawrence, were also the most vociferously Protestant and antagonistic to their Catholic neighbors. In addition, they had long experienced American Indian attacks in Maine. To New Englanders, French and American Indian were synonymous. Accordingly, once war broke out, in May 1690, Massachusetts determined to organize an expedition under William Phips to attack Port Royal in Nova Scotia and thus secure its eastern frontier.

It was at this point that Jacob Leisler suggested a joint offensive against Canada. But instead of abandoning the Port Royal operation, Massachusetts insisted on carrying it out before commencing the combined assault on Canada. As a result, Phips did not reach Quebec until October 15, far too late to begin a siege. In any case Phips found his force of 2,300 militia insufficiently equipped and had to retreat. Fitz-John Winthrop, commanding the forces marching by way of Lake George, made even less progress. His forces were too small, lacked supplies, and were then beset by smallpox. After reaching Wood Creek he determined to withdraw, although he dispatched a raiding party toward Montreal.

These operations revealed the limited capacity of the colonists to change the strategic balance in North America. Hereafter they wisely limited themselves to frontier forays, though Phips was rewarded with the governorship of Massachusetts and control of the militias of Rhode Island, Connecticut, and New Hampshire. The plan in London was to improve the colonial effort by a backdoor revival of the Dominion of New England, but the action had the opposite effect, especially when Connecticut's militia was transferred in May 1693 to the authority of Governor Fletcher of New York. The Connecticut assembly claimed that this step contravened its charter rights and thereafter offered minimal cooperation.

As a result the initiative passed to the French and their allies. Retaliation was meted out first on York and Wells in Maine during the spring and summer of 1692; on Durham, New Hampshire, in June 1694; and on Haverhill, Massachusetts, in March 1697. Nor was it only the white settlers who suffered, for the French also attacked the Iroquois. The Seneca had already had their settlements razed by Governor Denonville in 1687. First the Mohawks lost three hundred of their people in 1693. Then in 1696 it was the turn of the Onondagas and Oneidas to have their villages razed, in retaliation for an Iroquois raid in 1689 in which the French settlement at Lachine had been mercilessly devastated.

Slowly the fighting died out. The provincials on both sides did not have the resources for sustained warfare, while their respective mother countries were much too engrossed in Europe to send assistance. Hostilities formally ended with the signing of the Peace of Ryswick in September 1697, and the prewar status quo was restored.

Many recognized that the respite was only temporary. Consequently, the government in England made another attempt at consolidation in 1698, when the Board of Trade appointed Richard Lord Bellomont not only governor of New York, Massachusetts, and New Hampshire but also commander of the Connecticut, Rhode Island, and New Jersey militias. In 1700 Bellomont invited the governors of Virginia, Maryland, Pennsylvania, and New Jersey to New York for a conference with the Iroquois, the first time that so many officials had gathered together. Although Bellomont was personally able, however, the task of coordinating all these governments was too great. In addition, colonial distrust of any-thing that smacked of the Dominion of New England remained strong. When Bellomont died three years later, the experiment was not repeated.

The French meanwhile increased their presence along the upper Mississippi and began the construction of a series of forts, among them Detroit, to exclude the English from the western fur trade. At the same time French Jesuits used their influence among the Indians of the St. Lawrence Valley and Great Lakes to secure support for the French cause.[12]

Neither side needed much excuse for renewing hostilities when war broke out once more in Europe in 1702. Initially the French proved more aggressive, reflecting the fact that the governor-general of Canada commanded all that colony's resources, whereas the English settlements were fragmented and often in dispute with each other. Indeed, in this respect the English colonies were worse off than ever, as even the United Colonies of New England had ceased to exist. One reason for the lack of cooperation among the New England colonies was the appointment in 1702 of Joseph Dudley as governor of Massachusetts. Dudley was extremely efficient but widely distrusted. The inhabitants of Connecticut and elsewhere had not forgotten the role he had played as chief justice in the Dominion of New England. Consequently, Dudley found himself locked in several battles even with his own house of representatives, first over the choice of the council, then over the appointment of a speaker for the lower house, and again on the question of a permanent salary for himself and the judges. In 1706 he was accused of trading with the French under the ruse of exchanging prisoners.

New York presented another problem. In 1701 the Iroquois had signed a treaty of neutrality with the French, as their continuous warring since 1680, together with several outbreaks of smallpox, had so drastically reduced their numbers – from 2,550 to 1,230 braves – that peace was essential. Any desire to continue fighting was extinguished by the feeling that they had been repeatedly let down by the English. Moreover, many Dutch traders at Albany were keen to follow the Iroquois example to preserve their commerce. This left the defense of New York's frontier extremely precarious.

Hostilities commenced in earnest in August 1703 when the Abenaki, in retaliation for various attacks on their own people, first devastated the Maine settlements and then in February 1704 attacked Deerfield in Massachusetts. Being in the depths of winter,

---

[12] For further information on the Jesuits' success with the native people, see chapter 15, section 2, and chapter 18, section 4.

the attack came as a surprise. Forty-seven colonists were killed and over one hundred captured, among them the local minister, the Reverend John Williams. All attempts to convert him to Catholicism failed, but his daughter, Eunice, became a squaw.[13] Massachusetts quickly countered with another attack on Port Royal. Benjamin Church destroyed the villages of Minas and Beaubassin but failed in his main objective. Fortunately the frontier of New York remained quiet following the peace between the Iroquois and the French. Neither side saw much profit in local skirmishing.

In 1707 Massachusetts made another attempt on Port Royal. This attack too failed, as did a return visit, even though Church commanded twelve hundred men against a mere three hundred defenders. The fiasco finally led to the realization that help was needed from England. The political climate there was now more favorable, for the public was becoming tired of the endless war in Europe, where each success of the Duke of Marlborough merely led to the need for another campaign.

Consequently, when Samuel Vetch, a Scots merchant and former soldier, argued how advantageous it would be if the French were removed from Canada, his ideas fell on sympathetic ears. Accordingly, in 1709 plans were made for the dispatch of a force from across the Atlantic to sail up the St. Lawrence. They were to be supported by twelve hundred Massachusetts men, while another fifteen hundred recruits from New York, Connecticut, New Jersey, and Pennsylvania advanced overland under Nicholson, accompanied by some Mohawks. One of their chiefs, Theyanoguin, had converted to Anglicanism and was anxious to demonstrate his attachment to the English, despite the recent agreement with the French. The colonial preparations were extensive and considerable sums were expended, indicating what could be achieved when backing was provided from the mother country. Sadly it, too, proved abortive. At the last minute the troops in England were diverted to Portugal, rendering the colonial forces redundant, for they were insufficient to mount such an ambitious operation on their own.

Despite this disappointment, Massachusetts sent Nicholson to England early in 1710 to argue the case for a further renewal of the assault on Port Royal. He duly returned the following June with several frigates and four hundred marines. This time Nicholson was able to put his military training to good effect. Port Royal fell in October 1710.

His achievement duly impressed the government in London, as did the dispatch of four Indian "Kings," led by Theyanoguin, who was introduced as "Emperor" of the Iroquois.[14]

---

[13] For an account of the attack on Deerfield, see Richard I. Melvoin, *New England Outpost: War and Society in Colonial Deerfield* (New York, 1989) and John Demos, *The Unredeemed Captive: A Family Story from Early America* (New York, 1994) which also describes the attempts of the Williams family to reclaim Eunice over a period of almost seventy years. The readiness of whites, both captive and other, to accept the American Indian way of life is dealt with by James Axtell in "The White Indians of Colonial America," *William and Mary Quarterly*, XXXII, 1975, 55–88. The astonishment of contemporary white society is equaled only by the neglect of later historians. Both found it difficult to understand how anyone could abandon civilization in favor of savagery. More recent writers with less ethnocentric values have emphasized the simplicity of the American Indian way of life and its attractions, not least for runaway servants and army deserters, though the numbers who did so were probably small, a point made by Alden T. Vaughan, *The Roots of American Racism: Essays on the Colonial Experience* (New York, 1995), 213–52.

[14] In reality, only one of the Indians was a sachem, let alone a king or emperor in the European sense. See Eric Hinderaker, "The 'Four Indian Kings' and the Imaginative Construction of the First British Empire," *William and Mary Quarterly*, LIII, 1996, 487–526.

The Tories were now in power and anxious to match the earlier Whig successes in Europe with some measures of their own. Consequently the administration agreed to another expedition up the St. Lawrence in conjunction with a colonial advance by way of Lake George. The amphibious force was to comprise fifteen warships and seven regular regiments under the command of Admiral Walker. The colonists were to be led by Nicholson advancing north from Albany. Once more, Massachusetts voted £40,000 for the project, while all the other northern colonies contributed either men or money, including £2,000 from Quaker Pennsylvania "for the Queen's use."

Alas, this operation was even less successful than that of Winthrop and Phips in 1690. Admiral Walker's fleet with seven thousand troops on board arrived in Boston in June 1711, but their reception was not entirely cordial, the colonists being offended by the visiting army's airs of superiority. The military responded by describing the inhabitants as republicans, bigots, and smugglers. Nevertheless, the required supplies and shipping were assembled, and the expedition proceeded for the St. Lawrence in good time. Unfortunately the navy had no charts of the river, and on the night of August 23, Walker lost eight ships and seven hundred men. This misfortune unnerved him and he sailed back across the Atlantic. Nicholson was left waiting to advance at Lake George until news of Walker's departure finally reached him in October, by which time it was too late to do anything except throw his hat on the ground in frustration, shouting "rascals, damned rascals."

Soon peace was again in prospect, and the European conflict finally ended with the signing of the Treaty of Utrecht in April 1713, whereby the French made important concessions in North America. These concessions were to benefit the New England colonists in particular. The ceding of Newfoundland consolidated their dominance of the fisheries, while the acquisition of Nova Scotia promised to give the frontiers of Maine greater security.

The signing of the peace coincided with the beginning of a new era for the American colonists. Up to this time they had been struggling frontier settlements. Now in most areas the American Indians had been subdued and the coastal areas cleared, so that the frontier was often a hundred miles away. With this protective screen and increased space, the population, culture, and economy of the colonies were set for rapid development.

Part III

The Eighteenth-century Provinces

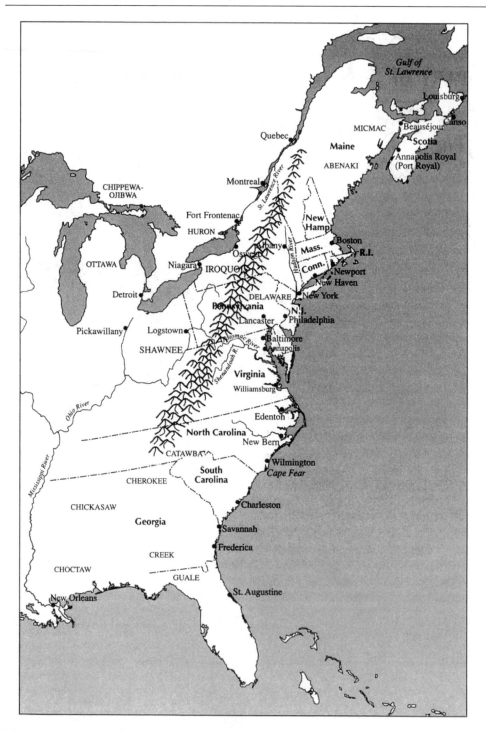

Map 7   Eastern North America, 1715–60.

10

The Provincial Economy and Labor System

1690	Paper money is first issued in the colonies by Massachusetts.
1693	Rice culture is introduced into South Carolina.
1699	Parliament bans the export of colonial woolens.
1704	Parliament grants bounties for the production of naval stores.
1707	Parliament regulates the silver content of colonial coinage.
1718	Parliament passes the Transportation of Convicts Act.
1720	The South Sea Bubble causes financial panic in Britain.
1723	The Pennsylvania loan office issues its first notes.
1725	Pennsylvania passes the Flour Inspection Act.
1730	Virginia passes the Tobacco Inspection Act.
1732	Parliament passes the Hat Act.
1733	Parliament passes the Molasses Act.
1735	The first poorhouse is established in Boston.
1740	The Land and Silver banks are established in Massachusetts. Commercial wheat cultivation begins in the Chesapeake.
1741	Indigo cultivation is introduced into South Carolina.
1748	Maryland passes the Tobacco Inspection Act.
1750	The Iron Act prohibits rolling and slitting mills.
1751	The New England Currency Act is passed.
1755	Paper money is first issued in Virginia.

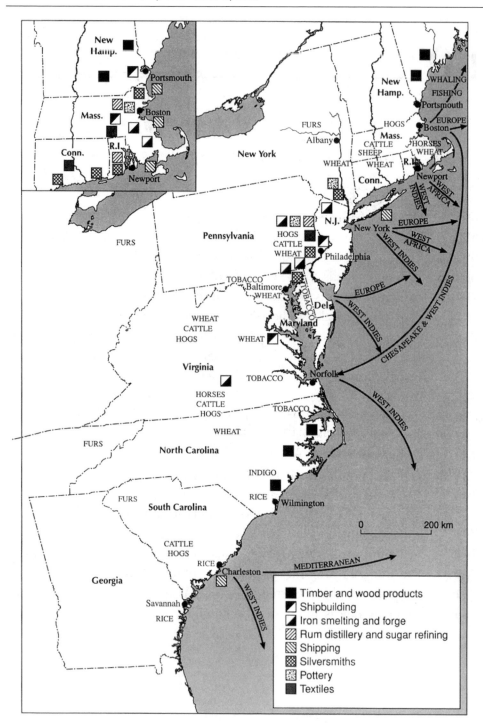

Map 8   The provincial economy, 1700–60.

1 THE SOUTHERN PLANTATION SYSTEM

ONEY MAKES THE world go round, it is popularly said. This aphorism was certainly true of the colonial world, which was dominated by the need to make a living. The possession or creation of wealth determined people's goals, tastes, and living standards. For this reason the provincial economy is considered before the family, religion, and culture.

With some exceptions, the colonial economy had matured by 1713. As Benjamin Franklin later commented, "The first drudgery of settling new colonies, which confines the attention of people to mere necessaries, is now pretty well over." Most colonists were increasingly becoming part of a wider market economy, producing primarily to sell to others. This was the difference between the tidewater and piedmont regions: one was essentially commercial, the other subsistence.

Historians are divided as to whether the dynamics of growth in the colonial period were the result of a Malthusian increase in population, that is, of supply, or of an export-driven demand for staples. A related question is whether the domestic market was more important than the export market in the southern economy.[1]

To some extent such distinctions are artificial, since supply and demand are two sides of the same coin. Exports were certainly important to the South, because the region was geared to the production of cash crops. On the other hand, the majority of its population were owners of small farms who produced primarily for their own needs. Since the export of staples is usually considered the most dynamic element in the southern economy, it will be considered first.

The most important staple in British[2] mainland North America was tobacco. Even by 1700 production had reached twenty-eight million pounds and it continued to climb, reaching eighty million pounds by 1760. By this time tobacco comprised almost 45 percent of mainland colonial exports. The total value of the exported crop was some £700,000. Seventy percent of it was grown in Virginia.

This increase had been achieved as a result of both supply and demand factors. Among the more important supply elements was the growth in the labor force. In 1660 the population of Virginia had been 25,000, Maryland had 10,000 settlers, while North Carolina had only a few hundred. By 1760 Virginia had almost 350,000 inhabitants, Maryland 160,000, and North Carolina 120,000.

---

[1] The view that population is the most important factor in growth was first made by Thomas Malthus. However, he believed that eventually growth in population would always exceed the increase in production and result in famine. Malthus concentrated his attention on Europe, where land was relatively limited. America, in contrast, had a plentiful supply, a fact noted by Adam Smith in *An Inquiry into Nature and Causes of the Wealth of Nations* (Glasgow, 1776). Among those writers who believe that exports were the main dynamic in the colonial economy are Gary M. Walton and James F. Shepherd, *The Economic Rise of Early America* (New York, 1979). The debate is surveyed in John J. McCusker and Russell R. Menard, *The Economy of British North America, 1607–1789* (Chapel Hill, 1985). See also David W. Galenson and Russell R. Menard, "Approaches to the Analysis of Economic Growth in Colonial British America," *Historical Methods*, XIII, 1980, 3–18.

[2] The noun *Britain* or adjective *British* is hereafter used in place of *England* or *English* to take into account the 1707 Act of Union between England and Scotland, which created the United Kingdom of Great Britain. Too many writers use England when they mean Britain, to the annoyance of most Scots and Welsh.

Another supply factor was improved efficiency. By the eighteenth century, the average tobacco worker was able to attend between two and three acres or up to ten thousand plants, producing between seven hundred to one thousand pounds of tobacco. The seventeenth-century average attendance was only three thousand plants.

Also on the supply side was the availability of land. Without this, extra hands would have been to no avail. Land and people were two advantages enjoyed by the Chesapeake colonies in particular.

But demand factors were also important. During the eighteenth century exports of tobacco grew steadily, especially to France. Exports were further stimulated after the 1707 Act of Union between England and Scotland by the advent of an aggressive Scottish merchant community to market the crop. This was especially beneficial to smaller producers who until then had to rely on the intermediary services of the larger growers. Even the decline in price was advantageous, as it widened the market. By the middle of the eighteenth century, tobacco was no longer a luxury for most of Europe's population.

Two kinds of tobacco were cultivated during the eighteenth century, one the sweet-scented variety originally introduced by John Rolfe, the other the Orinoco from South America. The type planted was partly a matter of climate. The Orinoco was a hardier plant and better able to thrive in the shorter summers of the upper Chesapeake and less fertile soils of the piedmont. Much of this was exported to continental Europe. However, most tidewater planters continued to grow the more traditional sweet-scented variety, since this was most popular in Britain.

Despite the growth in production, the cultivation of tobacco was not without its problems. Late frosts posed a serious hazard in the early stages, while too much rain was similarly disastrous before harvesting. In between, pests like the tobacco fly and hornworm could ruin a crop. The owner then had the difficult decision of when to cut his tobacco, since a mistake here would leave him with an inferior product. Curing and packing were also delicate operations that required great care if the tobacco was to get to market in good condition.

To protect its industry, Virginia developed a system of inspection. For almost a century various attempts to control the quality of the tobacco had met with fierce opposition from the small-scale planters, who feared that their inferior bulk product would be excluded. An act passed in 1712 was subsequently disallowed by the Privy Council, but an amended version, passed in 1730, required all tobacco to be brought to a public warehouse for inspection to ensure that it was properly cured. One unanticipated benefit was that the receipts provided a useful circulating medium. The system of inspection was sufficiently successful to be copied by Maryland in 1748.

A common criticism of the tobacco industry in the eighteenth century was its extravagant use of land. Tobacco made heavy demands on the soil, wearing it out in three or four years, after which the planter had to move on to fresh acreage. While land was so abundant, however, this practice made economic sense, for as Jefferson later noted, it was cheaper for Americans to buy a new acre than to manure an old one. Such reasoning was not generally appreciated by European visitors, who forgot they were looking at agriculture from a different perspective when making derogatory remarks. In Europe labor was plentiful and land scarce; moreover, the countryside had been under intensive cultivation for many centuries. Hence behavior in America that seemed slovenly and wasteful was often the result of attempts to avoid the high cost of labor. Best practice on the two continents necessarily differed at times.

Like all industries, tobacco suffered cyclical movements in its prosperity. Prices were highest – around two and a half pence a pound – in the periods 1700–1704, 1714–1720,

1735–1743, and 1747–1753, which generally coincided with peace in Europe. In between, prices often fell below one penny a pound.

This uncertainty concerning prices and the difficulties of production led many Chesapeake planters to turn to wheat after the outbreak of war in the 1740s. Wheat could be grown in fields left fallow after tobacco, often as a winter crop. Over a twenty-year period twelve crops of wheat might be grown to three of tobacco, though the value of tobacco was approximately six times greater. George Washington was one of those who switched to wheat after the French and Indian War ended in 1763. Wheat permitted the use of ox-drawn plows, making it less labor-intensive and therefore allowing more time for building and other improvements. Production climbed steadily throughout the later colonial period, though its export value, around £150,000 by 1760, was still less than one-fifth that of tobacco. Most wheat was shipped to southern Europe or to the West Indies.

By comparison, South Carolina's economy was still in transition in 1713. The fur trade had been its lifeline during the seventeenth century, and although the number of deerskins exported reached 150,000 by 1750, worth perhaps £50,000, overall it was facing decline as the supply of game decreased.[3] Rice, however, had been introduced in the 1690s and a profitable market was beginning to develop in both the Mediterranean and northern Europe. Production, which rose from ten thousand to one hundred thousand barrels between 1720 and 1760, was boosted by the expansion of cultivation to the adjacent areas of North Carolina and Georgia. Other factors also helped production. One was the partial removal of rice from the enumeration list in 1730, which allowed its direct export to Spain, Portugal, and the Mediterranean. Production was also aided toward the end of the colonial period by the use of wind-powered fans for winnowing the rice and of draft animals for pounding it, which made processing easier and more efficient. By 1760 rice accounted for about 20 percent of colonial commodity exports, bringing in about £300,000. This made it the second most valuable export after tobacco. However, like tobacco, it was susceptible to market fluctuations. This was especially true during the War of Jenkins' Ear, when the price plummeted from nine to two shillings a hundredweight.

Rice, unlike tobacco, was a relatively hardy plant to grow. The main requirement (and difficulty) was the need to immerse the crop in water at various stages during the growing season. This meant the construction of special fields protected by embankments, with ditches, sluice gates, and reservoirs to control the water supply. A dry spring or early summer could mean disaster if the reservoirs ran dry, while too much rain might lead to flooding at the wrong time. For this reason some planters began experimenting with river tidal flows to get a more dependable supply of water, but the technology and capital to do this were not widely available during the colonial period.

Another crop developed in South Carolina after 1740 was indigo. Its production at this time was the result of attempts by the planters to diversify in response to the problems caused by the war in Europe. When boiled in special vats, the leaves of this plant yielded a brilliant violet dye, which was especially prized before the invention of chemical substitutes. The advantage of indigo was that it could be grown on land where rice cultivation was not possible. The disadvantage was that it was not easy to produce, since the periods of fermentation, distillation, and drying were difficult to assess, making quality control a

---

[3] For the economics of the southern fur trade, see Kathryn E. Holland Braund, *Deerskins and Duffels: Creek Indian Trade with Anglo-America, 1685–1815* (Lincoln, 1993).

Plate 24   West Indian slaves processing indigo. From Pierre Pomet, *A Compleat History of Drugs*, 1725. Eliza Lucas Pinckney was the first to make indigo a profitable crop in South Carolina by perfecting a new production process and making use of slave labor.

nightmare. Nevertheless, production rose steadily, helped after 1748 by a bounty of sixpence a pound from Parliament. Indigo provided an export value of approximately £100,000.

Cotton, the crop usually associated with the Deep South, was still almost unknown. The short staple variety was impracticable to harvest on any scale until Eli Whitney invented his famous gin, though some slaves and poor whites spun a little yarn for their own use. Otherwise, all the colonies at this time imported sea island cotton from the West Indies if they wanted fabric from this material.

The first southern colonizers had envisioned a mixed economy of commerce, manufacturing, and farming, but their hopes had been sadly disappointed. Timber was plentiful, but shipbuilding was restricted by a lack of skilled labor. In the eighteenth century, however, a lumber industry developed using water-powered saw mills. Its principal product was staves for making barrels to export the South's cash crops. Shingles for roofing and clapboard were also produced, and found a ready market in the West Indies, where all wood products were scarce. Sales of these products brought in perhaps £50,000.

Timber also supported the naval stores industry. As the century progressed, the Royal Navy required ever larger quantities of pitch and tar for making vessels watertight, as well as turpentine for varnishing woodwork. Until the eighteenth century these items were obtained mainly from the Baltic, but political uncertainty in that area eventually induced the navy to seek alternative supplies from the colonies. To encourage this Parliament passed an act in 1704 providing for bounties on the production of masts, hemp, pitch, and tar. The pitch and tar industry was especially important for the Carolinas, since both had a vast supply of suitable pine trees. The resinous timber was heated slowly to make the tar run out without catching fire. Initially the industry flourished in South Carolina, but as rice cultivation became more widespread there, production shifted to North Carolina. The export value of this product was about £60,000 annually.

The continued expansion of cash crops in the South was made possible by the growth of the labor force, primarily through the purchase of slaves. As was pointed out in Part I, before 1700 Virginia and Maryland had relied on indentured servants, although South Carolinians had always preferred slaves. The eighteenth century witnessed a rapid increase in the size of the African labor force in both the upper and lower South, as planters sought to extend their holdings and increase their profits. In 1680 Virginia had 3,000 slaves and 15,000 indentured servants. By 1715 the ratio of free to nonfree labor was almost exactly the reverse, with 23,000 slaves in the province, and another 1,000 being imported annually. Even these figures were dwarfed by the dramatic increase between 1743 and 1756. The total number during this period rose from 42,000 to 120,000 as a result of both importation and the fertility of the existing population.

Maryland and the Carolinas experienced similar increases. In 1690 there had been 1,500 slaves in South Carolina; by 1720 the figure had risen to 12,000, reaching 57,000 in 1760. By then Virginia and South Carolina were each importing over 2,500 slaves annually; and even North Carolina was buying several hundred. During the 1750s imports often exceeded 7,000 slaves a year.

The reasons for the growth of slavery have already been dealt with (see chapter 7, section 1). Most indentured servants left their masters at the end of their service and thereafter became too expensive. According to the Reverend Peter Fontaine of Virginia, in 1750 a free white servant would expect to be paid almost £20 a year, while for another £7 or £8 a planter could "have a slave for life." The cost of slaves relative to indentured servants had significantly decreased since the seventeenth century.

The buying of slaves also suited the planters in other ways too. Their demand for skilled labor was limited. A cooper, smith, and tanner might be required, but most plantation tasks were of a dull, routine nature for which most male and female slaves were admirably suited. They were inexpensive to keep, requiring only a meager diet and simple shelter. In addition, by the eighteenth century they reproduced themselves.

It has been traditionally assumed that slave ownership was limited to the wealthy few. Recent scholarship has shown that it was more widespread, especially in the tidewater, where 40 percent of households in many counties had three or more slaves. Even in the piedmont 20–30 percent of households owned one or two slaves. Of course ownership was distributed unevenly, many households having only one, while others had half a dozen or more. Large plantations of more than twenty slaves were relatively scarce and were found most frequently in South Carolina, where rice and indigo cultivation and the production of naval stores were expensive businesses which could be undertaken only by large producers.[4]

---

[4] The claim that slave owning was relatively widespread in the Chesapeake is advanced by Allan Kulikoff, in *Tobacco and Slaves: The Development of Southern Cultures in the Chesapeake, 1680–1800* (Chapel Hill, 1986). His argument that large concentrations of Africans were rare is challenged by Philip D. Morgan and Michael L. Nicholls in "Slaves in Piedmont Virginia, 1720–1790," *William and Mary Quarterly*, XLVI, 211–51, who found that in many piedmont counties 30 percent of Africans lived on plantations of twenty-one slaves or more.

Despite the widespread ownership of slaves, their use did not go unquestioned. Many South Carolinians feared that slaves would become too numerous and eventually overpower them. Accordingly, attempts were made in the early 1730s to restrict slave imports by imposing a tax, linked to a promise of fifty acres of land without quitrents for ten years for every white person settling new townships in the backcountry. The Crown saw the tax on slaves as a restriction on trade and disallowed the measure.

Similar efforts were made in Virginia, though concern there was not as great as in South Carolina, since Africans were not a majority of the population. Nevertheless, some thoughtful Virginians already recognized that they were trapped in a vicious cycle. The expense of free labor drove most people to employ slaves and become planters; as a result there were no merchants, traders, or artificers. Recent evidence suggests that considerable numbers of white coopers, smiths, joiners, wheelwrights, leather workers, weavers, and bricklayers were indeed working in the countryside. The absence of many skills was real, however, though the full consequences of this lack were not felt until the onset of the Industrial Revolution in the nineteenth century. Then the South was to find itself increasingly disadvantaged by its lack of skilled labor and commercial acumen.

One possible alternative to slave labor was the use of convicts. In 1718 Parliament passed a law providing for their transportation to America. While occasional convicts had been sent over since the time of the Restoration, the numbers now greatly increased, reaching a total of 30,000 by 1760. Some two-thirds went to the Chesapeake, where they worked in gangs like the slaves, serving sentences between seven and fourteen years. The advantage for employers was that convicts were cheaper than any other hired labor. No purchase or transportation charges were incurred, nor were freedom dues payable when their sentences were completed. Not all were hardened criminals; many were first offenders convicted of minor crimes for whom transportation was a chance to make good. However, the practice did not become popular with most colonials, and the convicts were invariably blamed for increases in crime. Franklin suggested America should send her rattlesnakes to England in "return for the Human Serpents sent us by the Mother Country." Various attempts were made to restrict the traffic, but all fell foul of the Privy Council acting on behalf of the merchant interest.

Although slavery was now the predominant form of labor, its prevalence did not cause the disappearance of white servitude. Many indentured servants continued to be imported into the Chesapeake, especially from Ireland. Most masters still preferred a mixed labor force to give them some control over their African slaves. Others had to invest in servants because they required a smaller initial outlay. In all, 18,000 came to Maryland between 1718 and 1760.

The employment of slaves, convicts, and indentured servants was confined largely to the production of staples for export. Fifty percent of the white population were subsistence farmers with no labor other than their own. Although this chapter has focused on colonial exports, at least 80 percent of all economic activity was purely domestic, a fact which has led some historians to suggest that the role of exports in shaping the colonial economy has been grossly exaggerated.[5]

Small-scale tenant and freehold farmers were especially numerous in the backcountry of Virginia, Maryland, and North Carolina, where they grew a little tobacco in exchange

---

[5]   Edwin J. Perkins, *The Economy of Colonial America* (New York, 1988).

for other essentials. In the lower South the common surpluses were wheat, horses, cattle, and hogs. Since there were few towns to buy their produce, their opportunities were necessarily limited. Toward the end of the colonial era, however, corn and wheat began to be exported to the Mediterranean and West Indies. Even the meanest farmer wanted to market some produce so that he could improve his lot. By 1760 farmers in the Shenandoah Valley and south side of Virginia were trading up to one-quarter of their produce in the market.[6]

Almost no manufacturing took place in the South, except for the production of pig and bar iron. Most foundries were concentrated in Maryland close to the Delaware, though there were some furnaces scattered throughout Virginia and North Carolina. Another obvious aspect in which the southern colonies differed from their northern neighbors was lack of towns, which for many southerners explained the failure of their economy to diversify. Of course, South Carolina had a commercial center at Charleston and Maryland the beginnings of a port at Baltimore by 1760. Virginia, however, remained stubbornly rural despite numerous attempts by the House of Burgesses to establish towns.

The lack of diversification in the southern economy has induced much speculation. It is usually attributed to the institution of slavery, which absorbed the region's available capital while burdening it with an unskilled labor force. In reality southerners preferred to invest in the area which they knew best and in which they had the greatest competitive edge: growing cash crops.

Certainly diversification was not a major worry in the eighteenth century. The South paid its way vis-à-vis Britain, something that the North found more difficult. Nor did it feel itself to be a beleaguered or inferior region. The planter class bought the best goods from Europe and displayed far more obvious wealth than did the northern elites. Indeed, the per capita income of the region's white inhabitants was twice that of either New England or the middle colonies.[7]

---

[6] For the development of the Virginian piedmont, see Robert D. Mitchell, *Commercialism and Frontier: Perspectives on the Early Shenandoah Valley* (Charlottesville, 1977); and Richard R. Beeman, *The Evolution of the Southern Backcountry: A Case Study of Lunenburg County, Virginia, 1746–1832* (Philadelphia, 1984). The commercialization of backcountry farming is also discussed by Allan Kulikoff in "The Transition to Capitalism in Rural America," *William and Mary Quarterly*, XLVI, 1989, 120–44; *The Agrarian Origins of American Capitalism* (Charlottesville, 1992); and "Households and Markets: Towards a New Synthesis of American Agrarian History," *William and Mary Quarterly*, L, 1993, 342–55. In addition, see Winifred Rothenberg, "The Market and Massachusetts Farmers, 1750–1855," *Journal of Economic History*, XLI, 1981, 283–5; and Richard L. Bushman, "Markets and Composite Farms in Early America," *William and Mary Quarterly*, LV, 1998, 351–74. The contrary view that social values dominated colonial economic activity is advanced by James A. Henretta, "Families and Farms: *Mentalité* in Preindustrial America," *William and Mary Quarterly*, XXXV, 1978, 3–32; and *The Origins of American Capitalism: Collected Essays* (Boston, 1992). See also James A. Henretta and Gregory H. Nobles, *Evolution and Revolution: American Society, 1600–1820* (Lexington, 1987).

[7] For the distribution of income, see Alice Hansen Jones, *Wealth of a Nation to be: The American Colonies on the Eve of the Revolution* (New York, 1980); and section 5 of this chapter. Historians have traditionally seen the southern economy, with its concentration on a few staples, as an anomaly, compared to the diversification of the North. However, since the 1970s scholars have suggested that is was New England and the Middle Colonies that were anomalous in the wider context of the Americas, where cash-crop economies were the norm. See Jack P. Greene and J. R. Pole, *British Colonial America: Essays in the New History of the Early Modern Era* (Baltimore, 1984), and John J. McCusker and Russell R. Menard, *The Economy of British North America, 1607–1789* (Chapel Hill, 1985).

DOCUMENT 15

An Act for the Better Governing and Regulating White Servants, 1717, Statutes of South Carolina, reprinted in W. Keith Kavenagh, *Foundations of Colonial America: A Documentary History* (New York, 1973), III. 2095–102.

[Because of the need for an adequate supply of labor, all the colonies regulated the employment of servants. But while ostensibly giving servants protection, such laws in practice favored the masters.]

Be it enacted . . . that all servants shall serve according to his contract or indentures and where there is no contract or indenture, servants under the age of sixteen years on their arrival in this province shall serve until they are of the age of one and twenty years and if they be above the age of sixteen years, they shall serve for five years and at the expiration of the time aforesaid, shall receive from their master, mistress, or employer a certificate of their freedom on demand, and whoever shall refuse, without good cause, to give such certificate to any servant whose time is expired shall forfeit forty shillings for every refusal . . .

3. [All indentures to be registered before a justice of the peace within six months of the servant's arrival.]

7. And be it further enacted . . . that if any servant or hired laborer shall lay violent hands or beat or strike his or her master, mistress, or overseer and be convicted thereof . . . the said justices of the peace are hereby required and authorized to order such servant or laborer to serve his or her master or mistress or their assigns any time, not exceeding six months, without any wages after his or her time by indenture or otherwise is expired, or such corporal punishment to be inflicted by the hands of the constable or some other white person not exceeding twenty-one stripes as they shall in their discretion think fitting. . . .

8. And be it further enacted . . . that any servant or servants unlawfully absenting him, her, or themselves from his, her, or their said master, mistress, or overseer shall, for every such day's absence, serve one week and so in proportion for a longer or shorter time, the whole punishment not to exceed two years over and above the time he or she was to serve by indenture . . . and shall satisfy or pay to his, her, or their master or mistress all such costs and charges as shall be laid out and expended for their taking up.

12. And be it further enacted . . . that in case any servant shall run away in the company of any slaves, that every such servant . . . shall, upon conviction thereof at the general sessions of the peace and gaol delivery of this province, be deemed a felon and the punishment of a felon be inflicted on him accordingly. . . .

13. And to prevent the barbarous usage of servants by cruel masters, be it enacted, that every master or mistress shall provide for his servants competent diet, clothing, and lodging, and that he shall not exceed the bounds of moderation in correcting

them beyond the merit of their offenses, and that it shall be lawful for any servant, upon any master or mistress . . . denying and not providing sufficient meat, drink, lodging, and clothing, or shall unreasonably burden them beyond their strength with labor or debar them of their necessary rest and sleep or excessively beat or abuse them, to repair to the next justice of the peace to make his or her complaint. . . .

20. And in case one servant shall beget another with child, then the man-servant shall, after the expiration of his term, serve the master or mistress of the woman-servant during the time she had to serve from the time of her delivery. And if any man shall marry without his master or mistress's consent, he shall serve one year for such offense or forfeit the sum of twenty pounds. But if any freeman shall marry a servant, he shall be liable to pay the full value of the said servant to her master or mistress and she shall be free.

22. And as it is customary in other of his Majesty's colonies in America to make allowances of clothing to servants at the expiration of their servitude, be it enacted . . . that every manservant shall, at such time of expiration of their servitude, as aforesaid, have allowed and given to him one new hat, a good coat and breeches, either of kersey or broadcloth, one new shirt of white linen, one new pair of shoes and stockings; and all women servants, at the expiration of their servitude as aforesaid, shall have allowed and given them, a waistcoat and petticoat . . . a new shift of white linen, a new pair of shoes and stockings, a blue apron, and two caps of white linen.

2 NORTHERN FARMING AND COMMERCE

While the South was dominated by the production of cash crops, the northern colonies from an early stage had a more varied economy. This diversity increased during the eighteenth century, though somewhat paradoxically the actual percentage of persons engaged in agriculture remained around 85 percent. The region nevertheless had a growing commercial sector and even the beginnings of manufacturing, though mainly of a craft or cottage kind.

Northern farm sizes ranged from between fifty and one hundred acres to three hundred acres. Not all the land could be cultivated at one time. Like his southern counterpart, the northern farmer exhausted his soil and then moved on to freshly cleared land. In general a man could harvest only between five and ten acres. So even with two or three sons and a couple of servants, a farmer could not cultivate more than fifty acres, though a much larger pasturage could be handled.

The most common products on the northern farm were hogs and corn. Indian corn was an extraordinarily productive crop and easy to grow. It provided bread for the family and fodder for the animals, especially hogs, which were said to fatten best on this crop. The usual method of cultivation was to sow the plants six feet apart in small hillocks, which were created by scraping the surface of the soil with a hoe, an unavoidable procedure in ground not yet clear of roots and stumps. But even in well-cultivated land, this method was often used, since it avoided the necessity of plowing – no mean consideration for small-scale farmers who had neither plow nor draft animals. Approximately twelve hundred to fifteen hundred could be planted to the acre. On the larger farms, especially in Pennsylvania, wheat became an increasingly popular and valued crop, since it produced a finer flour than Indian corn and hence better bread. Barley and rye were also grown in some areas. These crops all required the ground to be plowed.

The other pillar of American agriculture, the hog, was also easy to raise. Hogs foraged for themselves and provided meat for much of the year. By the latter part of the colonial period, however, cattle were also becoming popular, especially in New England, as better pasture became available following the importation of European grasses. Unfortunately, the readiness of farmers to let their cattle forage made breeding improvements difficult and also meant the loss of much valuable manure, something that European visitors were quick to criticize.

All farmers tried to produce whatever their families needed. Poultry provided extra protein, while most farms had a good orchard. Beer was brewed with barley malt, and in the spring the maple trees could be tapped for syrup. Many farmers also kept some sheep; their wool, although coarse, made excellent working garments. Unfortunately, the lack of pasture resulted not only in inferior fleeces but also in the loss of much wool in the scrubby terrain. For this reason some farmers cultivated flax for making linen yarn.

Although northern farmers had no southern-style cash crops to sell, they were still keen to market their produce. The opportunities were twofold. One was the growth of towns, especially the seaports along the coast, which by mid-century had a total population of 120,000. The other was the development of export markets to the West Indies and southern Europe.

Prosperous commercial farming was confined largely to the coast or major river valleys like the Hudson, Connecticut, and Delaware, which offered not only the best land but also water transport. The majority of northern farmers were not blessed with such resources, especially in New England, where the rivers were not generally navigable, the soil was often rocky, and the climate harsh. As a result most of the population in these areas engaged mainly in subsistence farming.

Since the time of Jefferson the individual who worked a small farm has been glorified as someone who provided for himself and his family in the best American tradition. This idealization should be qualified on at least two counts. In the first place subsistence did not equal self-sufficiency, something that no farmer could ever attain completely. He always needed tools or other equipment and of necessity bartered surpluses to secure them. Second, a farmer's existence was by no means enviable. Farming was a hard business, dependent on the climate, and precarious too should the breadwinner be injured or fall sick. Hence the farmer always aimed to increase production beyond mere subsistence level, initially by relying on the labor of his family. If he was fortunate he might secure additional land and employ servants. Only then could he provide for his wife and children in a more dignified, less squalid manner. Subsistence farming was never seen as anything other than a prelude to entering the market.[8]

The principal provisions exported by the east-coast producers were pickled beef and pork from New England; wheat from New York; and wheat, flour, and bread from Pennsylvania and New Jersey.

---

[8]   On the Jeffersonian image of farming, see Joyce Oldham Appleby, "Commercial Farming and the 'Agrarian Myth' in the Early Republic," *Journal of American History*, LXVIII, 1982, 833–49. On the impracticability of being self-sufficient, see Bettye Hobbs Pruitt, "Self-sufficiency and the Agricultural Economy of Eighteenth Century Massachusetts," *William and Mary Quarterly*, XLI, 1984, 333–64, and Bushman, "Markets and Composite Farms." The continued glorification of farming has been greatly reinforced by the perceived decline in the quality of urban life.

Meat exports from New England reached a value of approximately £80,000 by mid-century, the most important area of production being the Connecticut River valley. However, most farmers kept a few head of cattle on their limited pasture, driving them to Boston and other seaports for slaughter and pickling.

The middle colonies also produced some meat, though from the early days they concentrated on the cultivation of grain, especially wheat. Pennsylvania in particular produced some of the finest flour, instituting a rigorous inspection system in 1725 to maintain its high quality. Pennsylvania and New Jersey in addition exported some corn and peas, and the total annual value of their combined exports amounted to about £300,000 by 1760.

As in the South, the principal export markets were southern Europe and the West Indies. By 1750 the value of shipments of flour and pickled meat to southern Europe amounted to some £150,000 a year. Equally important, those trading there brought little back with them, thus ensuring a net gain to the balance of payments. Most cargoes comprised wine from Madeira and the Canary Islands.

The annual value of victuals exported to the West Indies was about £200,000 during the same period. This market existed because these islands were no longer self-sufficient, being devoted to the production of sugar. Most captains brought back with them a cargo of sugar and molasses, the thick syrup that was drained off from the sugar. Molasses was an important commodity because it could be fermented and distilled into rum, a useful stimulant after a long day's work and a valuable anesthetic in the event of injury. Rum was also a key item in the trade with American Indians. Its manufacture consequently supported over a hundred refineries and distilleries in the northern colonies, with the heaviest concentration around Boston and Newport. Other goods imported from the Caribbean included cocoa, coffee, cotton, and mahogany.

A variant on direct trade between America and the West Indies was the triangular voyage via Africa to purchase slaves. However, ships clearing for Africa made up little more than 1 percent of the whole export trade, and their importance is now discounted. The most active slave traders were the merchants of Newport, while a few also operated from New York.[9]

At the start of the eighteenth century the dominant force in the export of victuals was Boston, whose merchants had pioneered the trade in provisions with the West Indies and elsewhere. When supplies from its own hinterland proved scarce, the Boston merchants had scoured the other colonies for alternative sources, effectively replacing the Dutch as general carriers. By the third decade of the eighteenth century, however, both Philadelphia and New York were developing their own commerce at Boston's expense, resulting in a stagnation in its growth after 1720.

New Englanders were involved in two other forms of commerce: fishing and whaling. Fish was a common ingredient in many colonial diets and was similarly important in southern Europe, where the Catholic church proscribed the eating of meat on Fridays. Like rice, fish could be shipped directly, not being an enumerated product, and consequently numerous vessels were employed for this purpose. What made the industry so important in New England was the region's proximity to the great fishing banks of Maine and Newfoundland.

---

[9] For a critique of the traditional view of the slave trade, see Gilman M. Ostrander, "The Making of the Triangular Trade Myth," *William and Mary Quarterly*, XXX, 1973, 635–44. For its relative importance to Rhode Island, see Jay Coughtry, *The Notorious Triangle: Rhode Island and the African Slave Trade, 1700–1807* (Philadelphia, 1981). By 1740, 6 percent of its shipping was clearing for Africa.

Each catch was usually dried or pickled with salt and put into barrels. The highest-quality fish were dispatched to Europe, while the inferior refuse fish were sent to the West Indies to feed the slaves. Fishing was New England's most valuable industry, its exports amounting annually to some £150,000.

Whaling constituted a similarly valuable commerce both for the domestic market and for export to England. Whale meat was an important addition to the colonial diet, while the fat could be made into candles or used as oil for lamps and for tanning leather. Whale bone was also used for decorative combs and for stays in women's corsets. Lastly, the intestines of the whale produced the odoriferous ambergris, which was used as an ingredient of perfume. The whaling industry has traditionally been associated with Nantucket, but whalers operated from most New England and eastern Long Island ports, mainly patrolling the areas around Newfoundland and Greenland; the searching of the Seven Seas occurred only in the nineteenth century. Annual export values of whale products were in the region of £50,000 by 1760.

Although the fur trade had declined in relative importance since the seventeenth century, it remained significant for the merchants of Albany and other centers near the frontier. Indeed a fierce rivalry continued between New York and Pennsylvania for access to the Great Lakes and Ohio country. The principal pelts were deer and beaver. Deer hides were used for making leather goods like saddles, bags, belts, and shoes. Beaver pelts were prized for making hats. It is difficult to put a total value on the trade, but it probably averaged around £30,000 a year for the northern colonies.

Another important commodity industry in the north was lumber. In the early settlement period each man cut his own crude requirements. However, as areas became well established, settlers increasingly demanded finished products for their timber-frame and clapboard houses. Such quality necessitated water-powered saw mills. By the middle of the eighteenth century all the colonies had such mills near the fall line. New Hampshire was particularly blessed in this respect, having both timber and water power near the coast. For this reason New England exported more timber than any other region, mainly to the West Indies, where many of the sugar islands lacked even firewood. Consequently, on voyages there vessels usually carried items like hoops for making casks, boards, and posts for building houses, and shingles for covering roofs. Though the annual export value of such commodities was about £60,000, this was one industry whose products were intended mainly for the domestic market.

Maine and New Hampshire, like the southern colonies, also benefited from the 1704 Naval Stores Act. Their forests produced the timber for the very large masts required for the battleships of the Royal Navy. Here, too, bounties were paid to encourage production, and the result was an important trade, centered on Portsmouth, worth perhaps £20,000 in an average year.

Commerce provided employment for hundreds of ships and thousands of seamen. In addition the export of provisions required a sizable processing industry for their preparation and packing. Warehouses were needed to store the goods, middlemen to distribute them once they had arrived, and clerks to settle accounts between customers who lived thousands of miles apart. Increasingly complicated logistics led to the emergence of counting houses. Insurance was also increasingly used, as was credit. Although no banks were actually set up during the colonial period, attempts were made to establish one in Boston. Here was the economic sophistication and diversification which eluded the Chesapeake economy.

Another way in which commerce benefited the north was by stimulating manufacturing. So much tonnage required a considerable shipbuilding industry to sustain it. Ships needed replacing on average every ten to fifteen years and had to be repaired in between. The northern colonies were extremely well placed to develop shipbuilding; they had almost inexhaustible supplies of timber and could supply practically all the materials required for the construction of the largest ocean vessels, in addition to having a skilled labor force.

Much of what the colonists built they exported to Britain. Indeed, it was frequently the practice to sell both the ship and the cargo on arrival there. The reputation of colonial builders was such that by 1760 their yards were producing twenty-five thousand tons a year, one-third of all British requirements. This trade was an important element in enabling the northern colonies to pay their way, contributing perhaps £140,000 annually to their balance of payments.

As the century progressed, other types of manufacturing also began to develop, although unlike shipbuilding, they were devoted mainly to supplying the domestic market. Most of these enterprises were concentrated either around the Delaware, where Quaker pragmatism was conducive to manufacturing skills, or in southern New England, where a similar environment and concentration of skills existed.

Among the more important manufacturing processes were the smelting of iron and production of metal wares. John Winthrop, Jr., had made the first attempt to produce iron in Massachusetts in the 1640s. But the industry did not become established until the second decade of the eighteenth century. Most of the furnaces for producing pig iron, slitting mills for fashioning it into bars and forges for making finished goods were concentrated in the two key regions of the Delaware and southern New England. By 1750 colonial iron output was sufficiently important for Parliament to pass an act controlling the industry, by which time America was producing one-eighth of the world's pig iron.

Also concentrated in these two areas was the silver industry, with numerous workshops in Connecticut and the towns of Philadelphia, New York, and Baltimore. Here also were located other key metalworkers, notably gunsmiths and clock makers. Another significant craft industry was cabinetmaking. As colonial standards of living improved, so did the demand for furniture designed in the latest European fashion.

Other manufacturing industries which had developed by 1760 were pottery and glass. Both had existed as cottage industries from the early days, but the production of finer pieces had to await technical improvements and a more skilled work force. By 1760 a number of factories had been established in the two main areas of manufacturing. The paper industry, too, established mills in these two areas.

One other incipient manufacturing activity was woolen and linen goods. Most colonists produced their own homespun, but increasing urbanization stimulated production on a commercial basis. Yarn was still spun at home, but specialist weavers produced cloth for sale in shops. The native wool was coarse and unable to compete with English cloths, but British producers were sufficiently apprehensive to have an act passed in 1699 prohibiting the export of colonial woolens. They need not have worried, since the colonists never had enough yarn to meet even their own domestic needs.

All this activity meant that the northern economy required additional labor to sustain its multifarious activities, especially skilled personnel like coopers, smiths, tanners, weavers, shipwrights, printers, and clerks. In New England this demand could be met from the resources of the local population. Not all fathers had sufficient land for their sons after

1700, as the population grew, and many younger sons had to be apprenticed to ensure themselves of a livelihood. Others did casual labor when not required on the family farm. One consequence was the emergence of a flexible multi-skilled workforce.

The middle colonies, in contrast, continued to use the system of indentured servants as the mainstay of their labor force. Almost 100,000 were imported from the British Isles in the period 1700–75, while another 35,000 came from Germany. About half of all servants went to Pennsylvania, which became the great entrepôt for servants. One result of indenture was an absence of the English apprenticeship system with its restrictive guilds. Employers either recruited already trained servants from Europe or chose suitable persons from the many eager young men anxious to learn a trade. The opportunities for developing skills were always greater in America than in Europe.

One resource which was not employed to solve the labor shortage to any extent was African slavery. Northern cereals and husbandry were less labor-intensive than southern cash crops. And since the growing season was shorter and the winters were longer, there was less year-round work. In these circumstances the family was usually sufficient to work most farms. Additional hands or casual labor could be found from the local white community if required. The same was true of manufacturing. Employers generally preferred to employ indentured servants, living and working as they did in close proximity to one another. Prejudice may also have led them to believe that Africans were incapable of mastering the necessary skills.

Some historians believe that the growth of commerce helped produce a distinctive working class, since the market economy, with its differentiation between owners and operatives, reduced labor from having a dignified status to that of a mere commodity. The argument is not entirely convincing. One reason is that labor in a preindustrial era was anything but dignified to start with. Furthermore, a true working class in the Marxist sense could not emerge until industrialization produced both capitalist and propertyless classes which were mutually antagonistic. This stratification had yet to occur except on southern plantations.[10]

One reason for the lack of a rigid class structure is that most servants lived with their masters in considerable intimacy; only a small class labored for wages. Many servants later became masters and property owners, further blurring class distinctions. Of course, differences in rank, skill, and wealth were commonplace; but the segregation of the workplace from the home by the payment of a flat wage had yet to be adopted, though some signs of it were appearing in Philadelphia and the other large towns by 1760.

One other question that has concerned historians is the extent to which the northern (and southern) economies were true capitalist systems operating through a market economy. Many key ingredients were certainly there. Property could be sold without restrictions like primogeniture and entail (other than in some southern colonies), which facilitated the accumulation of capital. An incipient system of wage labor was developing (except for slavery) which allowed the workforce to be deployed in a flexible and efficient manner,

---

[10] The emergence of a proletariat is implicit in Gary B. Nash, *The Urban Crucible: Social Change, Political Consciousness, and the Origins of the American Revolution* (Cambridge, Mass., 1979). For a recent interpretation, see Ronald Schultz, *The Republic of Labor: Philadelphia Artisans and the Politics of Class, 1720–1830* (New York, 1993). The concept of class in America has generally been unpopular. See chapter 11, section 3.

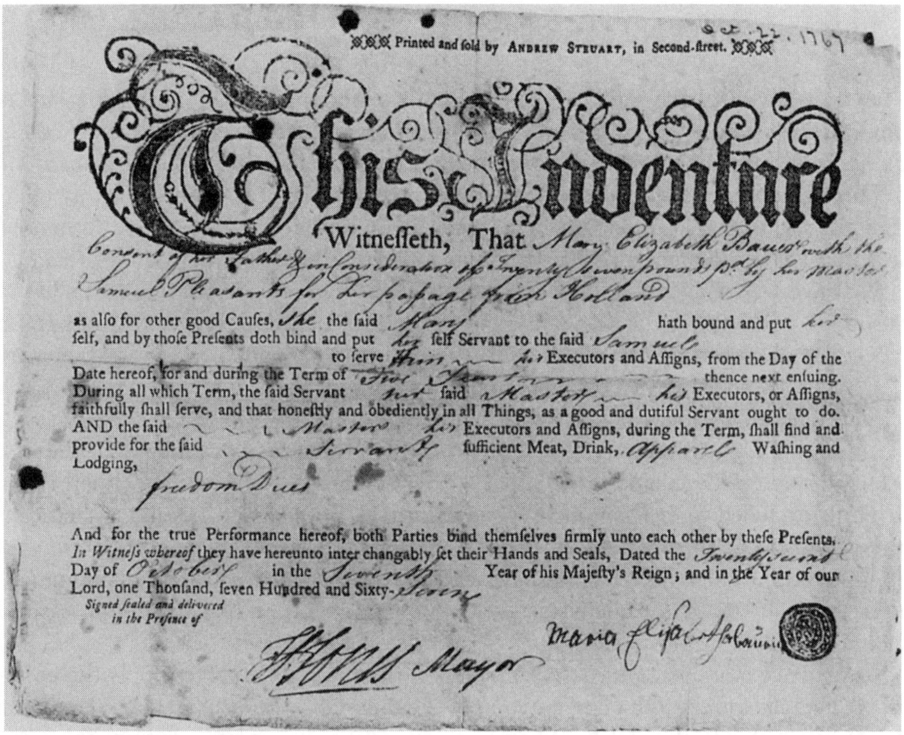
Oct. 22. 1767

Printed and sold by ANDREW STEUART, in Second-street.

This Indenture

Witnesseth, That Mary Elizabeth Bauer with the Consent of her Father & in Consideration of Twenty Seven pounds pd. by her Master Samuel Pleasants for her passage from Holland

as also for other good Causes, she the said Mary hath bound and put her self, and by those Presents doth bind and put her self Servant to the said Samuel to serve him his Executors and Assigns, from the Day of the Date hereof, for and during the Term of Five Years thence next ensuing. During all which Term, the said Servant her said Master his Executors, or Assigns, faithfully shall serve, and that honestly and obediently in all Things, as a good and dutiful Servant ought to do. AND the said Master his Executors and Assigns, during the Term, shall find and provide for the said Servant sufficient Meat, Drink, Apparel Washing and Lodging,

freedom Dues

And for the true Performance hereof, both Parties bind themselves firmly unto each other by these Presents. *In Witness whereof* they have hereunto interchangably set their Hands and Seals, Dated the Twenty second Day of October in the Seventh Year of his Majesty's Reign; and in the Year of our Lord, one Thousand, seven Hundred and Sixty-Seven

Signed sealed and delivered in the Presence of

Mayor

Maria Elisabetha Bauerin

Plate 25 Copy of servant's indenture. The Historical Society of Pennsylvania, Society Miscellaneous Collection Box 9c, "Apprentices and Indentures."

unencumbered by the restrictive practices of guilds and other craft associations. Sumptuary laws had been dispensed with, leaving individuals free to spend their money. They could also use their capital for investment without fear of prosecution for usury. Compared to the seventeenth century, the economy was now predominantly a cash-based one rather than one determined by barter and exchange.

On the other hand, many restrictions still operated, including restraints on wages, prices, and working conditions, and there was as yet no modern banking system. Moreover, in a society where most inhabitants still lived on small family farms, prices were never determined solely by impersonal economic forces. Equally important were social factors like the good of the community and the personal needs of the household. Most farmers, for instance, assisted their neighbors at certain times of the season, receiving help in return, which made cooperation rather than competition the underlying principle of economic activity.[11]

---

[11] Unsurprisingly, historians have not been able to agree when a true market economy emerged. See chapter 7, section 2, n. 8 for the historiography concerning this topic.

3 THE MERCANTILIST SYSTEM

We have already seen that the colonial economy had to function within the parameters of the mercantilist system, or navigation laws, as they were called, to ensure that the colonies' trade and domestic economy were controlled for the benefit of the mother country.

There has been considerable debate about this system's utility. Some historians have asserted that it strangled development, others that it was an irrelevance, still others have claimed that it was beneficial.[12] The truth undoubtedly lies somewhere in between.

We have seen that the system was not entirely benign at its inception, particularly for the southern colonies. By the turn of the eighteenth century, however, its teething troubles had been largely overcome. Britain had displaced Holland as the financial and commercial leader of Europe and was also experiencing the beginnings of the phenomenon known as the Industrial Revolution.

Industrialization in the mother country brought a number of advantages to the colonists. First, it increased demand for colonial goods, which enjoyed a protected market, since high tariffs excluded foreign producers from selling in Britain. Second, it supplied capital to the colonists. As members of the landed classes still sent younger sons or relatives to build up estates, so merchants similarly sought trade outlets and partners, extending credit to their colonial contacts. Equally important was the export of human capital, especially skilled labor.

As the pace of industrialization quickened, Britain was also able to supply the best and cheapest manufactured goods. These included machinery like saws, cogs, axles, crankshafts, and gears; nails, hooks, files, chisels, hammers, shovels, knives, plows, and anchors; implements of war, notably cannon, firearms, shot, and gunpowder; and navigational instruments like compasses and sextants. The wealthy imported British fabrics made from wool, linen, cotton, lace, silk, and felt. Many other household goods, such as lanterns, taps, mirrors, curtain rings, pewter, cutlery, kettles, sieves, measuring cans, and brass items like candlesticks could also be obtained from the mother country at ever keener prices. So, too, could books and fine-quality paper.

Being part of the British mercantilist system brought the colonists other advantages too, one of which was the benefit of insurance from Lloyds, which helped the flow of trade and furthered colonial economic development. Another was lower transportation costs,

---

[12] One of the earliest critics of the navigation system was George W. Bancroft, *History of the United States*, 10 vols (Boston, 1834–74). Bancroft was a member of the Whig nationalist school and was anxious to justify America's separation from Britain in 1776. Like most nineteenth-century writers, he was overly influenced by Adam Smith and the doctrines of free trade. In the early twentieth century, Progressive historians also criticized mercantilism, believing that its restrictions left the colonies in debt. See especially Charles A. Beard and Mary R. Beard, *The Rise of American Civilization*, 2 vols (New York, 1930); and Lawrence A. Harper, *The English Navigation Acts: A Seventeenth Century Experiment in Social Engineering* (New York, 1939). This view was challenged by members of the imperial school. They, too, were products of the Progressive era but had more obvious Anglo-Saxon leanings which led them to emphasize the benefits of the British connection. See especially Charles McClean Andrews, *The Colonial Period of American History*, 4 vols (New Haven, 1934–8); and Oliver M. Dickerson, *The Navigation Acts and the American Revolution* (Philadelphia, 1951). Most recent writers have been favorable to the navigation laws as a system of economic management, notably John J. McCusker and Russell R. Menard, *The Economy of British America, 1607–1789* (Chapel Hill, 1985); and Gary M. Walton and James F. Shepherd, *The Economic Rise of Early America* (New York, 1979). The latter emphasize the advantages of competitive shipping rates, capital investment, and access to technology.

which were halved during the later colonial period. A third advantage was the protection afforded by the British navy. In wartime British trade suffered less disruption than that of any other European state. This continuity was crucial in a period of so much strife, with major wars from 1689 to 1713, 1739 to 1748, and 1755 to 1762. Moreover, after 1700 an increasing number of warships were employed in commerce protection, so that by 1720 the day of pirates like Teach and Kidd was over. In addition, mercantilism offered the collective advantages of British financial policies, which allowed many goods shipped for re-export incentives in the form of customs repayments. After 1704, Britain also gave various bounties to colonial industries which would otherwise not have been viable, notably naval stores.

Lastly, the colonial economy was greatly helped by one other aspect of British policy, free immigration. Most other European powers controlled the flow of people to their colonies so as to exclude subversive elements. These restrictions starved their settlements of population, which proved especially critical for French Canada and Spanish Florida. For instance, fewer than 10,000 people were allowed to emigrate to New France in the period 1608–1775. Britain, on the other hand, placed few obstacles in the way of troublesome elements like the Quakers and was even ready to open the door to the refugees of other nations, such as the Huguenots, many of whom were skilled craftsmen or persons with capital. Britain's liberal policy continued into the eighteenth century, even though it led to a considerable influx of non-English-speaking immigrants; and it is estimated that almost 500,000 people entered the thirteen continental colonies in the period 1607–1775. It was this open-door policy that facilitated the extraordinary speed with which British North America was settled.

Unfortunately no economic system can satisfy all its constituent elements. The British liked to assert that mercantilism was complementary: Britain sold its manufactures to the colonies, while they sent their produce in return. The disadvantage of enumeration was theoretically offset by the advantage of a protected market. In practice the system did not work so well. In the Chesapeake a planter might receive £5 on a thousand-pound hogshead of tobacco. After the shippers had added their charges and the Crown had collected duties of nearly £17, the same hogshead sold for £25. The amounts suggest a less than adequate return, as is also indicated by the fact that the Virginia and Maryland planters were constantly in debt to their British factors.

The question of Virginian indebtedness is a complex one, however. Contemporaries in Britain argued that such debts were the result of extravagance; the planters were simply too much given to importing expensive luxuries. Later historians believe that the planters should have been more efficient and made greater efforts to control the tobacco trade itself. Others have seen the planters' indebtedness as evidence of their creditworthiness and their debts as basically an investment in the system.[13] What is not in doubt is that some planters resented their dependency on British merchants and that this may have been one reason why the Virginian elite later supported the Revolution so ardently.[14]

To some extent the Virginian tobacco industry was the victim of its own success. The planters overproduced, causing the depressions of 1704–13, 1720–34, and 1756–65, with

---

[13] For a discussion of Virginian indebtedness, see Warren M. Billings, John E. Selby, and Thad W. Tate, *Colonial Virginia: A History* (New York, 1986).

[14] See especially T. H. Breen, *Tobacco Culture: The Mentality of the Great Tidewater Planters on the Eve of the Revolution* (Princeton, 1985). Similar resentments existed among the rice growers of South Carolina, according to Kenneth Morgan, "The Organization of the Colonial Rice Trade," *William and Mary Quarterly*, LII, 1995, 443–6.

their consequent loss of income. The eighteenth-century Chesapeake also demonstrated the classic weakness of a single-crop economy: reliance on tobacco left the planters especially vulnerable to market forces because they had little else to supplement their income. The same difficulties afflict many Third World countries today.

Another, more obvious flaw in the argument that mercantilism was complementary is that New England and the middle colonies actually produced few raw materials for the mother country. This problem was partially solved by their supply of foodstuffs to the West Indies, which restored the principle of complementarity. Unfortunately, the middle colonies expanded so fast that by 1720 Britain was unable to use all that they produced. As a result surplus foodstuffs were sold to the French and Spanish colonies. Although this practice did not contravene the navigation laws in peacetime, the colonists began buying so much cheap French and Spanish sugar for their return voyages that the British islands then found themselves being undercut on their own market. The result was the Molasses Act of 1733, whereby all foreign sugar products imported into the colonies had to pay a duty of sixpence a gallon.

Had this act been enforced, it would have dealt a serious blow to the northern economy. However, customs machinery in the period 1714–60 was still rudimentary. The coast was divided into a number of districts, but they were poorly staffed. Many of the officers were corrupt and levied only a nominal duty of one penny a gallon, though the low yield suggests that some illicit trade must also have occurred.

This situation has led to the assertion that the mercantilist system was in fact maintained by smuggling. Unfortunately, the extent of such activity is difficult to assess; as with social security fraud today, the perpetrators did not keep records. People certainly talked as though smuggling was common, though the evidence suggests that outside the West Indies most merchants obeyed the rules, especially when trading with Europe, since American vessels were very conspicuous and could be easily policed by their British counterparts. Even in the West Indies there was a tendency to abide by the law. A Newport ship-owner instructed the master of one vessel on a voyage to St. Eustatius in 1750 as follows: "You may perhaps meet with some Frenchman . . . who may propose to make a French bottom of your vessel; but desire that you will not take up with any such proposal, as I would not have you go on any illicit trade."[15]

Religion was one reason for such a law-abiding attitude, since conscience clearly dictated that it was improper to deny the king his due. Quakers were especially insistent on the ethical conduct of business and had a vested interest in ensuring that others kept within the law. If there were infractions, these are likely to have occurred as a result of the 1733 Molasses Act, which seemed to have been passed to allow British sugar planters to live in idleness and luxury.

The increasing development of manufacturing in the northern colonies indicates a third discrepancy in the theory of complementarity. Shipbuilding especially ought to have been the preserve of the mother country, but the demands of British merchants for cheap ships overrode the cries of protest from British shipbuilders, who did not have the advantage of cheap timber. Protectionism prevailed, however, in other areas where colonial producers were seen as a threat. Wool, for example, was one of the oldest industries in England, accounting in the past for 80 percent of her exports. By the end of the seventeenth

---

[15] William Johnston to David Lindsay, March 13, 1752, printed in David C. Douglas, ed., *English Historical Documents*, vol. IX; Merrill Jensen, ed., *American Colonial Documents to 1776* (London, 1964), 495–6.

century the industry was under attack not only from America but from Ireland too. Accordingly a Woollen Act was passed in 1699 stating that no wool or finished items were to be exported from Ireland or the colonies, even to a neighboring province. All domestic produce must be sold where it was made. The hat industry, too, was regulated in this way. When this long-established British trade found itself in danger of losing its traditional markets to colonial producers, a ban was placed on the export of colonial hats in 1732. Regulations were also laid down concerning the number of apprentices who must be employed in the trade, ostensibly to maintain quality but in reality to restrict production. No slaves could be employed, and all apprentices had to serve for seven years.

The third major activity to be regulated in the interests of Britain was the iron industry, where the conflict was similar to that in the shipbuilding industry. British smelters wanted all American activity banned, while the makers of finished goods wanted cheap pig and bar iron from the colonies. The latter group eventually won. In 1750 Parliament enacted legislation banning the colonists from building or operating any "mill or other engine for slitting or rolling of iron, or any plating forge . . . or any furnace for making steel," but in accordance with the principle of complementarity, no duties were to be levied on the import of any pig or bar iron. America was to produce the raw materials, Britain the finished products, the latter of course being the more profitable activity.

The same reasoning led Britain to annul various colonial laws encouraging local manufactures. In 1705 the Privy Council disallowed a Pennsylvania law encouraging shoe making. The following year it was New York's turn to have a sail-making venture condemned. In 1756 a Massachusetts law to facilitate the production of linen suffered a similar fate.

It is difficult to say how effective these prohibitions were, since governors and other officials had neither the information nor an inspectorate to stop them. In any case, British concern was generally premature. The quality of American wool, for instance, was too poor to be exported. The number of slitting mills and forges for iron was relatively small, and the infant industry was not seriously inconvenienced. The ability to ship as much pig and bar iron as could be produced seems to have satisfied the American iron industry. There was no outcry before 1760.

Nevertheless, these prohibitions on colonial manufacturing suggest that by 1750 there had been a qualitative change in the operation of the mercantilist system caused by British recognition that its economy now depended as much on the export of manufactured goods as on the import of cheap raw materials. In the seventeenth century the colonists had been encouraged to produce as many goods as possible: now they were being restricted in what they could do. It has been argued that this indicates that the system was being increasingly managed for the benefit of special interests, notably the merchants of London, in contrast to the seventeenth century when the aim had been to strengthen the kingdom as a whole. The evidence on this point is not conclusive, since the original navigation laws had been largely prompted by English merchant interests. Nevertheless the continued commitment of Britain to a system designed to benefit the imperial center certainly contained the potential for discord in the future.[16]

---

[16] The shift to the protection of Britain's manufacturing was first noted by George Louis Beer, *British Colonial Policy, 1754–1765* (New York, 1907). For the thesis about special interests, see John J. McCusker, "British Mercantilist Policies," in Stanley L. Engerman and Robert E. Gallman, eds, *The Cambridge Economic History of the United States*, Vol. 1: *The Colonial Era* (Cambridge, 1996), 337–62. For a discussion of special interests before 1700, see Joyce Oldham Appleby, *Economic Thought and Ideology in Seventeenth Century England* (Princeton, 1978).

4 MONEY AND TAXATION

One problem faced by all the colonies in the period 1689–1760 was a lack of specie. The condition used to be attributed to a chronic imbalance of payments with Britain, but modern scholars have largely discounted this interpretation. Although exports to the mother country often equaled only half the value of imports, the imbalance was generally corrected by colonial surpluses on trade with the West Indies and southern Europe.[17]

Even so the domestic economy was invariably short of specie. Minting fresh coinage was not permissible, since this was a Crown prerogative. The colonies in any case had little gold or silver to mint. Barter solved the problem on the frontier, but it was a hindrance elsewhere as the colonial economy became more sophisticated.

One alternative was the use of commodity money, the most common forms of which were tobacco and wampum, though the latter was largely a seventeenth-century device. Most colonies passed acts regulating such items in terms of their sterling value. North Carolina, for instance, rated sixteen commodities in 1715, including tobacco, corn, wheat, tallow, leather, beaver, butter, cheese, pitch, whale oil, pork, and beef.

The difficulty was fixing the value of a commodity satisfactorily. In times of a glut, the commodity was devalued and the creditor was hurt; in times of scarcity, the debtor was at a disadvantage. In addition, commodities used in payments could often be spoilt or become unmarketable. Complaints were made in New Haven that worthless wampum was being put into the church collection plate, to the distress of the minister and his family. Although the provincial assemblies constantly tried to regulate commodity prices, it was an almost impossible task.

A third option was the use of bills of exchange, whereby those wishing to settle an account or buy some goods would go to a local merchant and buy a bill that was negotiable with a third party with whom the purchaser wanted to do business. This procedure was really only feasible for merchants or persons dealing in large sums, usually overseas or in another colony.

Most colonists had to make do with whatever specie was available: Spanish pesos or pieces of eight, Flemish ducatoons, Portuguese crusadoes, Dutch guilders or florins, German and Danish talers or dollars, and French ecus. Apart from their bewildering variety, such specie often had variations in their silver or gold content. Many coins were also clipped. Nevertheless, some specie was better than none, and many colonial legislatures passed laws placing higher values on certain coins to attract them to their province. The ploy was rarely successful, since it merely stimulated other colonies to do the same. This practice so alarmed British merchants, who were apprehensive of being paid in artificially inflated coin, that in 1704 the Privy Council issued a proclamation regulating the value of foreign coins according to their silver content. In future such specie was not to exceed the sterling equivalent by more than one-third. Three years later Parliament enacted legislation to this end, though with only limited effect.

---

[17] For the old view about the imbalance of payments see Curtis P. Nettels, *The Roots of American Civilization* (New York, 1938). For more recent analyses see Gary M. Walton and James F. Shepherd, *The Economic Rise of Early America* (New York, 1979); and John J. McCusker and Russell R. Menard, *The Economy of British North America, 1607–1789* (Chapel Hill, 1985).

By this time the colonies had discovered a new solution to their lack of money, namely the printing of paper. Essentially two types of paper currency were issued during the colonial period: tax anticipation bills and asset-backed currency. Tax anticipation notes were first issued by Massachusetts in 1690 to finance the expedition of Sir William Phips against Quebec. The bills had to be repaid within a short time at the insistence of the British merchants, who feared that otherwise they would be paid in depreciated paper. The Board of Trade in consequence was under constant pressure either to prevent their issue or to ensure that such notes were not legal tender and obligatory in the settlement of debts. Nevertheless, the device was too useful to ignore, especially in wartime, and other colonies followed Massachusetts's example: South Carolina in 1703, New York and New Jersey in 1709, and North Carolina in 1712.

Most of the notes were in denominations of between five shillings and twenty pounds and were more like bills of credit than modern currency. The individual had to purchase them from the provincial treasurer and pay interest for the privilege of doing so. The advantage was that they could be circulated more widely than bills of exchange, which were restricted to the name of the eventual payee.

So useful did these emissions prove that a number of colonies continued their use long after the official redemption date, sometimes to pay their government expenses, sometimes to redeem other bills, and sometimes as a means of stimulating the economy. However, their unpopularity in London led some colonies to experiment with the second type of paper money: asset-backed currency based on land. The most notable scheme was that of Pennsylvania in 1723 whereby individuals could obtain notes ranging from £10. 10s to £100 from the local loan office. The borrower had to pay 5 percent interest and provide as security land twice the value of the total loan, for what was effectively a mortgage. That same year New Jersey adopted a similar scheme, using the interest on the notes to meet the expenses of government.

The benefit of paper currency was not lost on some royal officials. As Governor William Burnet of neighboring New York explained in November 1724, such schemes had widespread advantages: "The officers of the government might otherwise be kept out of their money for a very long time and have difficulty to subsist." Essential expenditures like repairs to the fort and diplomatic contacts with the American Indians would also suffer. Indeed, Burnet asserted, "Under good regulation, these acts are both of service to the trade of the plantations and of Great Britain." Burnet also pointed out that the colonists were merely imitating Parliament, anticipating revenues by means of paper.[18]

In the aftermath of the 1720 South Sea Bubble in Britain, in which thousands of investors were ruined by fraudulent share schemes, Burnet's arguments were not appreciated. Hence in 1725 the Privy Council ordered South Carolina to redeem its £55,000 of outstanding bills. Nevertheless, the need for a circulating medium led to the acceptance of two New Jersey acts in 1730 and 1733 for an emission of £60,000 and one in Maryland. The following year Connecticut managed to secure an issue of £35,000 "to promote trade." Even the South Carolina assembly managed to pass another bill in 1736 for an emission of £210,000, arguing that its trade was in great distress for want of a circulating medium.

---

[18] Governor William Burnet to the Board of Trade, November 21, 1724, printed in Douglas, ed., *English Historical Documents*, vol. IX; Jensen, ed., *American Colonial Documents to 1776*, 429–33.

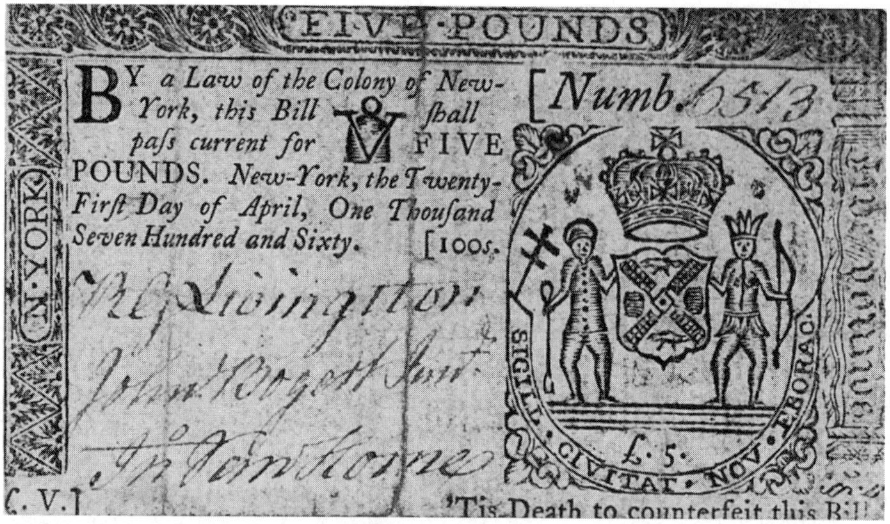

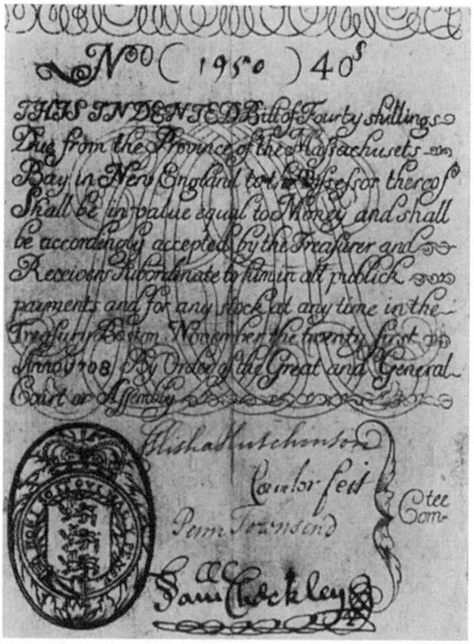

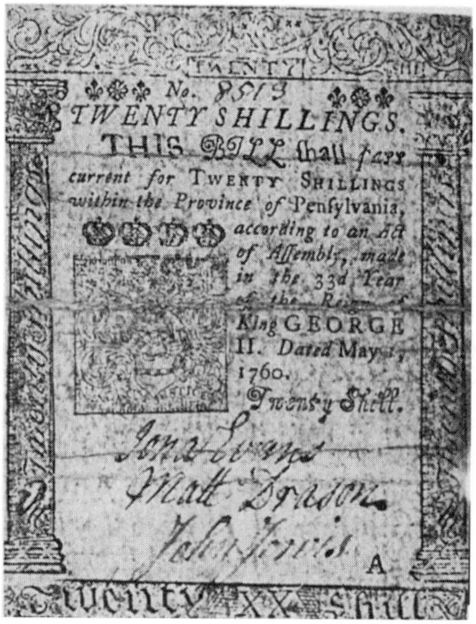

Plate 26   Colonial money. The Historical Society of Pennsylvania.

The problem of sustaining the value of such currency became acute only in the late 1730s when there was a renewed threat of war. By then the Massachusetts pound was trading at £5.5s to £1 sterling; and the South Carolina currency at £7.19s to £1. Fearing new issues of depreciated paper, the Privy Council sent a circular letter in August 1740 telling the governors to allow no more emissions. If any such acts did have to be passed, they must contain a suspending clause until they had been approved in Britain. The following year the Board of Trade ordered the Massachusetts assembly to retire all its paper money, except for £30,000 to finance its government.

In response, a group of merchants decided to set up a Land Bank to print notes, using their landholdings as security. The idea had been mooted during the previous decade, but it was the recall of the provincial bills which now led to its execution. A more conservative group then proposed a rival Silver Bank, with notes redeemable in silver. Both groups proposed to operate without a charter from the provincial legislature. At this point the British vetoed both measures by declaring that they fell within the scope of the 1720 Bubble Act, which had been passed to prevent just such enterprises. The closing of the Land Bank hurt a number of people, including the father of Samuel Adams.

None the less, the Privy Council's attempts to restrict the issue of paper proved difficult in the 1740s, for military expenditures would not wait. A number of issues were accordingly made, much to the dismay of British officials. The New England colonies were particular offenders, though they were provoked by the need to meet the cost of capturing Louisburg in 1745. Worse, their emissions were not well managed, lacking any redemption date or security in the form of tax revenue. By the end of the war the exchange rate had slumped to £12 of Massachusetts currency for £1 sterling. Fortunately Massachusetts was owed a large sum in reimbursement for its war effort, and Thomas Hutchinson persuaded the assembly to use this to redeem its near worthless currency.

Despite this farsighted initiative, Parliament passed an act in 1750 requiring the redemption of all existing bills in New England. In future, only sufficient paper for the government salaries and other necessary expenditures could be issued, and this amount had to be redeemed in two years, though in an emergency the period could be extended to five years. Such notes were not to be legal tender, thus restricting their use as a circulating medium.

Nevertheless, further emissions continued to be made, especially of asset-backed paper, which suffered little depreciation due to the rising value of the land offered as collateral. Hence New Jersey was allowed another £60,000 worth of bills in 1754 in recognition of its earlier judicious handling of paper. As the Board of Trade commented, the previous issues were "found to be the least burthensome method of levying taxes for the support of government" and had "also been of great service in enabling the inhabitants to extend and improve their trade." The bills were not to be legal tender.

Even that restriction had to be lifted to stimulate the colonial war effort during the final conflict with the French and American Indians. The British merchants then renewed their clamors, even though Virginia stipulated in its first issue of 1755 that any discount would be made good in the settlement of sterling debts. The issue of paper was to be one element in the subsequent conflict between Britain and the colonies after 1760 (see chapter 20, section 2).

The supply of money generally seems to have sufficed. Even Britain in the eighteenth century had to manage with a mixture of barter, commodity money, paper, and coin. The colonial economy was no exception.

One aspect of the colonial economy which was favorable throughout the period was tax rates. Though the colonies had to pay the navigation duties, which could be heavy, the burden fell on the consumer rather than on the population at large. In contrast, internal taxation was light, since the government expenses were low except in wartime. The bureaucracy was tiny, and there was no standing army or fleet. Poor relief was the responsibility of the local authorities. Spending on roads or other facilities was minimal.

One reason for the popularity of paper money was that it could finance extraordinary expenditures in wartime, though ultimately such issues had to be redeemed and other obligations met. To this end taxes were most commonly levied on land or personal property. Poll taxes on adult males over sixteen were another option; in the Chesapeake an export duty on tobacco was imposed, and excise duties on liquor were also adopted. But with the exception of quitrents, none was so onerous as to cause significant protest before 1760.[19]

5 THE STANDARD OF LIVING: POVERTY AND PROSPERITY

Whatever the restraints of the mercantilist system, the colonies developed at a remarkable pace throughout the later colonial period. Growth was by no means even, there being periods of stagnation. Nevertheless, the evidence suggests that the system cannot have been too restrictive. Colonial trade with Britain grew by 700 percent in the period 1689–1760, while the population increased from 250,000 to around 1.5 million. At the same time per capita income rose by at least 0.5 percent a year in real terms, so that the standard of living for most of the population improved by between 50 and 100 percent. The American colonies were one of the first societies to escape the Malthusian cycle in which increased resources merely stimulated population growth and ultimate decline in per capita income. America never experienced the kind of famines which afflicted most European societies until the nineteenth century.

One indication of colonial well-being was the reaction of visitors. In the seventeenth century it was the wild appearance of the continent which drew comment, whereas by the 1750s visitors were impressed by the general prosperity of the inhabitants. Most people had land, and there seemed to be little poverty or unemployment. As a British officer commented, "Everybody has property and everybody knows it." The general progress was well symbolized by the rise of Philadelphia, a town which did not exist in 1682, but which by 1760 was on a par with Dublin, Edinburgh, or Bristol.

The attractions of living in America were constantly emphasized by Franklin. He pointed out how much better off the inhabitants of America were compared with their counterparts in the British Isles. After a trip through Scotland he commented, "I should never advise a nation of savages to submit to civilization." He believed that even the American Indian lived the life of a gentleman compared with an Irish peasant.

The same points were made more prosaically by Thomas Hutchinson in his *History of Massachusetts*. He wrote, "Property is more equally distributed in the colonies . . . especially those to the northward of Maryland than in any nation in Europe. In some towns you see scarce a man destitute of a competence to make him easy." The reason, of course, was the availability of land, which led "most men as soon as their sons grow up endeavour to procure tracts in some new township where all except the eldest go out one after another

---

[19]   For the accepted view that taxation was light, even during the final French and Indian War, see Lawrence Henry Gipson, *Connecticut Taxation, 1750–1775* (New Haven, 1933). The fact that Parliament by no means reimbursed all the costs of that struggle and that considerable taxation was necessary is argued by Harold E. Selesky in *War and Society in Colonial Connecticut* (New Haven, 1989).

with a wife, a yoke of oxen, a horse, a cow or two and maybe a few goats and husbandry tools. . . . A small hut is built and the man and his family fare."[20]

A few such statements could be misleading, and more recently historians have also been paying attention to other types of evidence. Wills, for example, tend to support the view that living standards were improving. Whereas in the seventeenth century most decedents left a few tools, some rough furniture, and livestock, eighteenth-century inventories reveal a much richer standard of living, including china rather than coarse pottery, silverware, furniture, clocks, warming pans, and other household items designed for decoration or comfort rather than mere survival. Additional evidence can be obtained from the records of colonial imports. After 1700 these increasingly included what earlier would have been considered inessential luxury items: tea, coffee, French wines, Indian silks and calicos, glass, porcelain, and even furniture. Previously colonials had made their own, found substitutes, or done without. The first sixty years of the eighteenth century witnessed a consumer boom which seems to suggest a standard of living 20 percent higher than in Britain, for the middle classes at least.[21]

Of course, this wealth was not evenly spread even within a single class. The evidence from wills for the year 1774 reveals that the Charleston area of South Carolina, with its large rice plantations, had by far the highest concentration of wealth, with the estates of decedents there averaging £2,337. The next most wealthy area was Ann Arundal in Maryland, with an average inventoried estate of £660. Philadelphia, in contrast, for all its commerce, could manage a figure no higher than £396, while Suffolk County, Massachusetts, was just £312. New York City was even lower with a mere £278, though this was still indicative of a comfortable existence.[22]

How was this prosperity achieved? One answer was greater efficiency. Although historians have generally condemned the American colonial farmer for his wasteful land usage, improvements did occur through greater knowledge of the climate and terrain. Some modest technological improvements occurred in manufacturing and commerce, though less so in farming. Most colonials were still using tools similar to those of their seventeenth-century ancestors, though implements like plows were now used more widely. In addition, the colonial period was generally one of price stability. The price of manufactured goods actually fell as production methods improved and transport became cheaper, giving settlers greater purchasing power. Throughout the period the colonists continued to enjoy that almost unique combination of abundant land, cheap food, and unlimited fuel.

Lastly, the growth in living standards was ironically fueled by the consumer boom itself. Until the end of the sixteenth century only gentlefolk were expected to live sump-

[20]   Thomas Hutchinson, *The History of the Colony and Province of Massachusetts-Bay* (Boston, 1764. Reprinted, Lawrence Shaw Mayo, ed., Cambridge, Mass., 1936).

[21]   Considerable work is now being done on the eighteenth-century consumer revolution. See Carole Shammas, *The Pre-industrial Consumer in England and America* (New York, 1990); and Ronald Hoffman, Cary Carson, and Peter J. Albert, *Of Consuming Interests: The Style of Life in the Eighteenth Century* (Charlottesville, 1993). Some historians have attempted to link the growth in consumption to the separation from Britain, positing that the taxing of America frightened colonial consumers into rebellion. See T. H. Breen, "Narrative of Commercial Life: Consumption, Ideology, and Community on the Eve of the American Revolution," *William and Mary Quarterly*, L, 1993, 471–501.

[22]   For further information, see Alice Hanson Jones, *Wealth of a Nation to be: The American Colonies on the Eve of the Revolution* (New York, 1980).

tuously as a sign of their rank and a means whereby the social order could be maintained. Ordinary people, it was assumed, would merely be corrupted by such consumption into idleness and vice. By the end of the seventeenth century such attitudes had changed in favor of personal improvement. Now it was argued that many of these same luxuries were items of refinement which could be defended on moral grounds as leading to gentility. This change in attitudes had two consequences. One was a surge in demand. The other was an increase in production, as people sought to improve their standard of living. The Protestant work ethic was now geared to the god of consumption.

The contemporary statements of Franklin, Hutchinson, and others have encouraged the belief that America was the first society to banish poverty. Interestingly, Hutchinson did not say that no towns experienced any deprivation, and more recent historians have shown that poverty was a constant problem in cities like Boston, New York, and Philadelphia. In the case of Boston the first serious poverty occurred after the 1690–1713 war. That conflict had precipitated a boom in shipbuilding and privateering; when it ended many seamen and carpenters were left in straitened circumstances. War widows were also badly hit. Indeed, the advent of peace ushered in a period during which the population of Boston actually fell. By 1740, 25 percent of the town's inhabitants were living below the poverty line. This situation necessitated the provision of workhouses and an ambitious scheme to

DOCUMENT 16

Benjamin Franklin on the Protestant ethic: the advice of Poor Richard, reprinted in Kenneth Silverman, *Benjamin Franklin: The Autobiography and Other Writings* (New York, 1986), 216–17.

[The following maxims, published by Franklin in his Poor Richard's Almanac, typify the Protestant ethic which Americans traditionally believe has led to their success as a nation.]

The Taxes are indeed very heavy; and if those laid on by the Government were the only ones we had to pay, we might more easily discharge them; but we have many others, and much more grievous to some of us. We are taxed twice as much by our *Idleness*, three times as much by our *Pride*, and four times as much by our *Folly*. . . . However let us hearken to good Advice, and something may be done for us; *God helps them that help themselves, as Poor Richard says,* in his Almanack of 1733. . . .

How much more than is necessary do we spend in Sleep! forgetting that *The sleeping Fox catches no Poultry,* and that *there will be sleeping enough in the Grave, as Poor Richard* says. If Time be of all things the most precious, *wasting Time* must be, as Poor Richard says, *the Greatest Prodigality,* since, as he elsewhere tells us, *Lost Time is never found again;* and what we call *Time-enough always proves little enough:* Let us then be up and be doing, and doing to some Purpose; so by Diligence shall we do more with less Perplexity. *Sloth makes all things difficult, but Industry all easy,* as Poor Richard says; and *He that riseth late, must trot all Day, and shall scarce overtake his Business at Night.* While *Laziness travels so slowly, that Poverty soon overtakes him,* as we read in Poor Richard, who adds . . . *Early to Bed, and early to rise, makes a Man healthy, wealthy and wise.*

build a linen factory where the unemployed might work and repay the cost of their upkeep. Unfortunately, this attempt to use private capital to solve unemployment in Boston was not a success: the factory was unable to compete with low-priced imports and had to close after a few years. Other towns were similarly affected by the scourge of poverty, and by 1760 even Providence had a workhouse.

However, Philadelphia perhaps best demonstrates the reality of urban deprivation, since many artisans and laborers there were rarely above the poverty line. This was especially the case in winter, when perhaps a quarter of the workforce required relief. Many tried to avoid this humiliation, since recipients had to wear a large letter P (for pauper) on their garments. Even when the economy was robust, many seamen, shoemakers, and journeymen tailors earned barely enough to feed, clothe and house their families. As a result they were never able to amass enough capital to break out of their cycle of poverty, no matter how hard they worked or observed the aphorisms of Franklin's *Poor Richard*.[23]

But poverty was not limited to the towns. New England farming communities increasingly warned away strangers for fear they would become a charge on the inhabitants. In Virginia the House of Burgesses passed a law in 1723 against vagabonds who were becoming a burden on the parish and county authorities. According to the most recent calculations, 30 percent of the population in that colony were poor even by the standards of the time. A similar picture pertained for Maryland, while in South Carolina the governor calculated that 6,000 of its 26,000 white population lived in dire poverty, with another 10,000 possessing only the bare necessities of life.

Historians are also now aware how large was the proportion of tenant farmers – perhaps 30 percent of all those engaged in agriculture. Since 20 percent of the population were laborers, this figure actually indicates that close to 50 percent of white males owned no land. Of course, tenancy could be the first step on the ladder to ownership; and many young men with no land were simply waiting to inherit from their parents or relatives. A study of conditions in Connecticut suggests that most males owned no land on reaching adulthood. However, by the time they were married they possessed an average of around forty acres, which had typically increased to one hundred acres by age forty. Only 5 percent remained permanently poor.[24]

While the evidence is conflicting, it can still be asserted that most white persons in colonial America had a better chance of a comfortable existence at some point in their lives than did their counterparts in the mother country which was why most of them, or their ancestors, had come in the first place.

---

[23] The issue of urban poverty is dealt with by Gary P. Nash, *The Urban Crucible: Social Change, Political Consciousness, and the Origins of the American Revolution* (Cambridge, Mass., 1979); and Billy G. Smith, *The "Lower Sort": Philadelphia's Laboring People, 1750–1800* (Ithaca, 1990).

[24] For the view that tenant farming was widespread and led to poverty, see Gregory A. Stiverson, *Poverty in a Land of Plenty: Tenancy in Eighteenth Century Maryland* (Baltimore, 1977); Gloria L. Main, *Tobacco Colony: Life in Early Maryland, 1650–1720* (Princeton, 1983); and Sharon V. Salinger, *"To serve well and faithfully": Labor and Indentured Servants in Pennsylvania, 1682–1800* (New York, 1987). Salinger points out how difficult it was for servants to make the transition to owning property in Pennsylvania. For a more optimistic account of tenancy, see James T. Lemon, *The Best Poor Man's Country: A Geographical Study of Early Southeastern Pennsylvania* (Baltimore, 1972); Sung Bok Kim, *Landlord and Tenant in Colonial New York: Manorial Society, 1664–1775* (Chapel Hill, 1978); and Lucy Simler, "Tenancy in Colonial Pennsylvania: The Case of Chester County," *William and Mary Quarterly*, XLIII, 1986, 542–69. The details on Connecticut can be found in Jackson Turner Main, *Society and Economy in Colonial Connecticut* (Princeton, 1985).

11

European-American Family and Society

1648 Massachusetts passes a law condemning rebellious children over sixteen to death for striking their parents.

1690 The first birth control devices become available in London.

1693 John Locke publishes his *Thoughts Concerning Education*.

1700 The European-American population reaches three hundred thousand. Sex ratios in the Chesapeake become more balanced.

1 THE FAMILY STRUCTURE

T HE FAMILY WAS the foundation of colonial society. It protected individuals at birth, provided a reason for their working lives, and shielded them in old age. It was everyone's means of traveling through life. The family was also the basis around which other institutions were built. Government, the church, and the community all worked through this key unit.

It used to be thought that the modern nuclear family, comprising only parents and their offspring, originated in America. Previously the extended family was the norm. Parents, children, brothers, sisters, aunts, uncles, nephews, nieces, and grandparents all stayed in the same village, if not under the same roof. Lack of mobility was partially responsible for this state of affairs. Until the Industrial Revolution people in Europe rarely traveled, having neither leisure, nor means, nor need to do so. The vast majority were tied to the land – living, working, and dying near their place of birth.

According to the traditional view, the lack of economic opportunity and mobility had the further effect of increasing dependence on parents, especially fathers, who owned what little property there was. Society was hence intensely patriarchal, with fathers dictating where their families lived and how they made their living. As a result, individuals married late, men usually being closer to thirty than twenty and women generally in their twenties before marriage. The further result was to retard the fertility of the population and produce generally stagnant population growth.

It was this cycle of extended family, patriarchal control, late marriage, and low fertility which the colonists were thought to have broken. Only young adults traveled to America, thus cutting traditional patriarchal ties. Crossing the Atlantic by definition induced a new mood of mobility, accentuated by the frontier, which beckoned the new arrivals with the hope of a better life. The natural wealth of America allowed parents and their children to support themselves without the extended family, who were in any case far away, at least in the first generation. The net result, according to this view, was a whole new lifestyle based on the nuclear family.[1]

One consequence was earlier marriage for most couples and, consequently, increased fertility. Men normally married around the age of twenty-one and women around the age of eighteen, the most fertile period for both sexes. The combination of early first birth and a greater number of subsequent offspring explains the rapid growth from 300,000 whites in 1700 to 2.5 million by 1776.

Most of these views on the structure of the colonial family were first expressed by Benjamin Franklin, who was an incurable optimist about all things American, though similar opinions were also expressed by the Swedish traveler Peter Kalm in the early 1750s. Some of these observations were accurate, notably those concerning the fertility of the colonial population, which was doubling itself every twenty-five years. Since the 1960s, however, their belief that American society was exceptional has been shown to be inaccurate. More recent demographic studies have shown that the picture traditionally presented of European society was distorted. In reality, 30 percent of the population moved considerable

---

[1] This view is well summarized in Bernard Bailyn, *Education in the Forming of American Society: Needs and Opportunities for Study* (Chapel Hill, 1960).

distances in search of work, and families were far less extended than had been thought. The nuclear family in Europe actually predated the Industrial Revolution by several centuries.[2]

These findings have prompted American scholars in the past thirty years to examine once more the structure of the colonial family, with remarkable, though varied, results; significant differences emerged between north and south, and between the seventeenth and eighteenth centuries.[3]

Demographers have found a marked similarity between the family in New England and its counterpart in the mother country. The average marrying age by the eighteenth century was twenty-six for New England men and about twenty-two for women. On average couples married two years earlier than in England, a significant though not decisive difference. Even at the height of the migration in the 1630s, the average marrying age of New Englanders was about twenty-one for women and twenty-five for men.

The figures for births show a similar correlation. During the seventeenth century the average number of children born to each couple in the town of Andover was 8.2. What was remarkable was that 7 of these survived to age twenty-one. Across the Atlantic the average survival rate tended to be only between 4 and 5 out of approximately 7 births. In the eighteenth century, the number of children born to each New England colonial family had decreased slightly, to around 7.5; but the average of those surviving had dropped to 5.3, which was much closer to the English norm.

The reasons for the discrepancies in fertility are easily explained. In the seventeenth century New England was relatively isolated from the epidemics which regularly swept Europe, but by the middle of the eighteenth century this was no longer the case. The number of children surviving to adulthood therefore dropped significantly.

The traditional view of New England as an exceptionally fertile society is thus subject to qualification. White fertility remained higher in America than in Europe throughout both the seventeenth and eighteenth centuries, but much of the difference can be explained simply by lower infant mortality and greater life expectancy due to a healthier climate and better diet. The natural abundance of the American landscape meant that no one starved; the famines which were so common in Europe simply did not occur. Most people had enough land, and no one was dependent on a single crop.

We have already seen that the structure of the family in the southern colonies before 1700 was quite different. Here the terms "extended" or "nuclear" were irrelevant; the family

---

[2]   The new demographic history began appearing in the late 1960s. See especially Peter Laslett, *The World We Have Lost: England Before the Industrial Age* (New York, 1973); and Peter Laslett, ed., *Household and Family in Past Time: Comparative Studies in the Size and Structure of the Domestic Group* (Cambridge, England, 1972). The new studies in demography came about because social changes in Europe, not least the democratization of political structures, generated interest in the history of the common man. An early survey of the new methodology and its implications for American history can be found in Philip J. Greven, "Historical Demography and Colonial America," *William and Mary Quarterly*, XXIV, 1967, 438–54.

[3]   The first major demographic works on America were Philip J. Greven, Jr., *Four Generations: Population, Land, and Family in Colonial Andover, Massachusetts* (Ithaca, 1970); and John Demos, *A Little Commonwealth: Family Life in Plymouth Colony* (New York, 1970). Other, later studies include Vivian C. Fox and Martin H. Quitt, eds, *Loving, Parenting, and Dying: The Family Cycle in England and America, Past and Present* (New York, 1980); John Demos, *Past, Present and Personal: The Family and the Life Course in American History* (New York, 1986); and Barry Levy, *Quakers and the American Family: British Settlement in the Delaware Valley* (New York, 1988).

DOCUMENT 17

The fertility of the American population, from Peter Kalm, *Travels into North America, Containing Its Natural History and a Circumstantial Account of Its Plantations and Agriculture . . .* , translated by John Reinold Forster, 3 vols (Warrington, 1770), II, 3–5.

[Although historians now discount Kalm's views and those of others like him, his opinions about the fertility of the American population during the colonial period were typical.]

It does not seem difficult to find out the reasons why the people multiply more here than in Europe. As soon as a person is old enough, he may marry in these provinces without any fear of poverty; for there is such a tract of good ground yet uncultivated that a new married man can, without difficulty, get a spot of ground where he may sufficiently subsist with his wife and children. The taxes are very low and he need not be under any concern on their account. The liberties he enjoys are so great, that he considers himself as a prince in his possessions. I shall here demonstrate by some plain examples. . . .

In the year 1739, May 30, the children, grandchildren and great grandchildren of Mr Richard Buttington in the parish of Chester in Pennsylvania were assembled in his house; and they made together one hundred and fifteen persons. The parent of these children, Richard Buttington, who was born in England, was then entering his eighty-fifth year; and was at that time quite fresh, active and sensible. His eldest son, then sixty years old, was the first Englishman born in Pennsylvania. . . .

In the year 1739, on 28 January, died at South Kingston, in New England, Mrs Mary Hazard, a widow in the hundredth year of her age. She was born in Rhode Island . . . [and] could count altogether five hundred children, grandchildren, great grandchildren and great-great-grandchildren. When she died 205 persons of them were alive. A granddaughter of hers had already been a grandmother near fifteen years.

itself was the exception rather than the rule, mainly because most immigrants were male and unable to procreate. After 1640 the South was the opposite of New England, where immigration had ceased and the family was the norm.

By the eighteenth century, however, social structures in the South were beginning to assume more traditional patterns. An increasing percentage of the population were native born, so that sex ratios were more balanced and family life became possible for most of the white population. Moreover, a greater percentage of imported servants were now female, further increasing the potential fertility of the population. From 1700 onwards, white births in the Chesapeake outnumbered white deaths.

As a result, most southern children now grew up in a nuclear family instead of as orphans. After 1700, the average marriage in Virginia lasted twenty-five years rather than fifteen as previously. Children were also far more likely to grow up with grandparents. Another result may have been to increase patriarchal influence, since fathers now survived to supervise their adult offspring. Perhaps it was no coincidence that by 1750 the average

age on marriage in the Chesapeake was twenty-seven for men and twenty-two for women, close to the norm for New England, where patriarchal influence had never been broken.

These findings, however, are drawn mainly from the gentry, for whom the best documentary material exists. Other evidence suggests that in less affluent areas the average marrying age for men was under twenty-three and for women not much more than twenty. With little property to bequeath, parents had both less control and less incentive to keep their families together, so that their sons and daughters likely found fewer obstacles in the way of marriage. In addition, poorer families may have found it more difficult to remain together because of the need to look for work.[4]

Little has been said so far about the middle colonies. Here generalizations are more difficult. The assertion has often been made that the decision to marry depended on the availability of land. If true, New York's development was retarded by the manorial system, which made freeholds difficult to secure. Certainly the growth of population there was slow compared with the other English-speaking colonies.

Pennsylvania and New Jersey, by contrast, were closer to New England in their family structure. Men generally married around the age of twenty-six, women at the age of twenty-two, except among Quakers, where the average marrying age for women was about twenty-five. Other factors which favored fertility were a relatively benign climate and the ready availability of land. Some historians have suggested that the Quaker practice of marrying among themselves inhibited their numbers. But such "tribalism" had been equally true of the Puritans. The real issue for the Quakers in Pennsylvania was the weight of other groups coming into the colony, for immigration was crucial to the rapid growth of the population. With perhaps two hundred thousand people arriving in the province before the Revolution in 1776, Pennsylvania was truly a land of immigrants. Another factor assisting growth was that many arrived in family groups, while the distribution of males to females among servants was also more even. Hence Pennsylvania and New Jersey did not suffer the same kind of demographic imbalance as the Chesapeake had earlier.

One myth about the colonial family which has generally proved grounded in reality is that nearly everyone married. In most colonies single people comprised a mere 3 percent of the population, compared with a European norm of 10 percent. The reasons for this difference were partly social and partly economic. Unmarried men were rarely admitted to church membership, since it was assumed that their physical passions had yet to be controlled. Materially speaking, two people could nearly always live better than one. Only the Quakers in Pennsylvania had a higher proportion of single people than prevailed in Europe, ranging from 12 to 15 percent of all males and females. This percentage may be attributable to the pressure to marry within the sect, which reduced the pool of available partners, though Quaker respect for women and their right to choose for themselves may also have been a factor.

If many traditional assumptions about the structure of the colonial family have proved wrong, similar corrections also need to be made concerning its mobility. Recent

---

[4] The structure of gentry families is examined in Daniel Blake Smith, *Inside the Great House: Planter Family Life in Eighteenth Century Chesapeake Society* (Ithaca, 1980). For the situation of less affluent families see James M. Gallman, "Determinants of Age at Marriage in Colonial Perquimans County, North Carolina," *William and Mary Quarterly*, XXXIX, 1982, 176–91.

demographic studies have revealed that during the seventeenth century the population of New England was remarkably static. Once a group had established a community like Andover or Dedham, its members were unlikely to move. Their reluctance was natural; despite the popular view, few relished moving to the frontier, which was wild and inhospitable.[5]

Another constraint on mobility was economic. A life's work was usually required to establish a farm. Hence what one generation had built, the succeeding one wanted to enjoy. Often there was sufficient land for all the sons and their offspring too, at least in New England, where the general court during the seventeenth century granted the towns extensive lands. Subdivision was therefore possible. Patriarchal influences further reinforced this tendency to stay. Crossing the Atlantic had not changed most attitudes. A father might provide a house on the marriage of a son, but the couple were expected to remain and work for him. Such an arrangement guaranteed that the father and mother would not die in penury. In this respect colonial society reflected European practice. Only Quaker parents deviated significantly from this norm, most of them giving sons outright ownership of land within a year of the marriage.

The incentive to leave did not arise until the third generation in New England, when younger sons found for the first time that there was insufficient land to keep a wife and family. Even then the migrants usually went to a better-endowed neighboring town, and they still went home for a spouse. Most moved with the blessing of their family, for fathers usually tried to buy some acreage for all their sons. The European tradition of primogeniture, that is, of leaving everything to the eldest son by means of an entail on the family estate, was never adopted in America, outside the Chesapeake, to any extent, though the first son sometimes received a double share.[6]

People in the South equally preferred not to move unless the exhaustion of their land or lack of other opportunities forced them to. By the turn of the eighteenth century this was beginning to be the case in some tidewater counties of the Chesapeake. In due course many families or their offspring joined the exodus through Virginia into the Carolinian backcountry. Perhaps the most mobile were the people of the middle colonies, where the lack of homogeneity undermined any sense of community and induced a greater readiness to move.

One other aspect of the colonial family structure which deserves attention is that of patriarchy, though scholars are by no means agreed on its role and importance. One view is that patriarchy was on the increase, since the father had taken over responsibilities which had previously been shared by all male kin. This trend was reinforced by the Anglicization of the law, which brought colonial practice into line with that of England where patriarchy had long been entrenched. A contrary view is that patriarchy was beginning to crumble

---

[5] On mobility, see Greven, *Andover*, 122–6; and Linda Auwers Bissell, "From One Generation to Another: Mobility in Seventeenth Century Windsor, Connecticut," *William and Mary Quarterly*, 1974, XXXI, 79–110.

[6] It used to be thought that primogeniture and entail were rare even in the South. South Carolina had abandoned entail in its legal code of 1712, while Virginia was believed to have largely given up the practice, a view based on C. Ray Keim, "Primogeniture and Entail in Colonial Virginia," *William and Mary Quarterly*, XXV, 1968, 545–86. However, recent work by Holly Brewer suggests otherwise. See "Entailing Aristocracy in Colonial Virginia: 'Ancient Feudal Restraints' and Revolutionary Reform," *William and Mary Quarterly*, LIV, 1997, 307–46, in which she argues that up to three–quarters of all estates were entailed at the time of the Revolution when Jefferson brought in his bill abolishing the practice.

under the forces which led to the Revolution, as Americans began to question all forms of authority.[7]

Patriarchical views were widespread, as a letter to the *Spectator* magazine suggested in 1712. The writer commented: "Nothing is more gratifying to the mind of man than power or dominion: and this I think myself amply possessed of, as I am the father of a family. I am perpetually taken up giving out orders, in prescribing duties, in hearing parties [disputes], in administering justice, and in distributing rewards and punishments. . . . In short, Sir, I look upon my family as a patriarchical sovereign, in which I am myself both king and priest."[8] Such views were reminiscent of Sir Thomas Filmer and his model of the patriarchal family which he used to justify absolute monarchy in the seventeenth century. However, after 1700 a softer version of patriarchy was becoming fashionable, reflecting the ideas of John Locke. He denied that any authority was absolute or divinely appointed, since it had to be contractual, giving protection to all the family. But Locke still believed in the natural superiority of men.[9]

One indication that patriarchy may have been in decline was the greater readiness of fathers after 1700 to let younger sons leave home. Certainly sons were becoming more independent in their choice of work and selection of a marriage partner. The same may also have been true to a more limited extent of daughters since another indication was the considerable increase in bridal pregnancy. During the seventeenth century, when fathers kept strict control of their daughters, such incidents never rose above 10 percent in New England. By the mid-eighteenth century, the rate had increased to around 30 percent, suggesting a more relaxed paternal authority, though a decline in religious feeling may also have been a factor.

Whatever the cause, the greater freedom enjoyed by young people was sufficient for Harvard undergraduates to debate the issue of "bundling" or sharing a bed without undressing. The proposition asked "Whether it be Fornication to lye with one's sweetheart (after contract) before Marriage?" Bundling was now a widespread practice, whatever patriarchs liked to pretend.

The picture of the colonial family in the eighteenth century is usually one of fecundity, long life, and contentment. In reality this was often far from the case, especially in a society like South Carolina which suffered fifty-nine epidemics in the years 1670–1775, among them smallpox, cholera, and yellow fever. In Christ Church parish, eighty-six out of every

---

[7] The argument that conformity to English law was strengthening patriarchy is made by Cornelia Dayton Hughes, *Women Before the Bar: Gender, Law, and Society in Connecticut, 1639–1789* (Chapel Hill, 1995). Among other contributors to the debate are Allan Kulikoff, *Tobacco and Slaves: The Development of Southern Cultures in the Chesapeake, 1680–1800* (Chapel Hill, 1986); he argues that patriarchy was increasing in the eighteenth century; Daniel Blake Smith, *Inside the Great House: Planter Family Life in Eighteenth Century Chesapeake Society* (Ithaca, 1980), believes it was in decline. The argument that the decline of patriarchy was linked to the American Revolution is made by Melvin Yazawa in *From Colonies to Commonwealth: Ideology and the Beginnings of the American Republic* (Baltimore, 1985); and by Jay Fliegelman in *Prodigals and Pilgrims: The American Revolution Against Patriarchal Authority, 1750–1800* (New York, 1982). Kenneth A. Lockridge, *On the Sources of Patriarchal Rage: The Commonplace Books of William Byrd and Thomas Jefferson and the Gendering of Power in the Eighteenth Century* (New York, 1992) offers a different reason for the decline, arguing that misogyny accounted for the patriarchal impulses of many men and that such attitudes were becoming less acceptable as a result of the Enlightenment.

[8] Quoted in Julia Cherry Spruill, *Women's Life and Work in the Southern Colonies* (Chapel Hill, 1938), 43–4.

[9] For a discussion of the Filmer and Locke models of the family, see Mary Beth Norton, *Founding Mothers and Fathers: Gendered Power and the Forming of American Society* (New York, 1996).

hundred children failed to see their twentieth birthday. Moreover, an ailment like malaria could be crippling, chronic, and depressive, since there was no known cure, given the state of medical knowledge. Although some discoveries had been made during the seventeenth century regarding inoculation and the circulation of the blood, most branches of medicine were still the same as in Roman times. Indeed, the most popular theory about the body was that of Galen, who had practiced in the second century A.D. According to him, health resulted from a natural balance between the four dominant bodily fluids: blood, phlegm, black and yellow bile. Each of these produced a particular effect. Hence if a patient was feverish a physician might prescribe blood letting to lower the temperature. Those suffering from colds would be wrapped in blankets to keep them warm while their symptoms dried out. A patient producing dark-coloured faeces would be considered to have an excess of black bile and given emetics to clear the bowels. Similar logic was used in the treatment of yellow bile, the cause of jaundice. There was no understanding that disease was the result of bacteria or viruses. This would only be discovered in the late nineteenth century.

Physicians accordingly were extremely limited in what they could do. They could talk to patients about their symptoms, observe their bodily fluids and examine their bodies, but what they prescribed was necessarily a matter of faith. The problem was compounded by the lack of hospitals and proven medicines. Surgery was rarely an option except as a last resort for the removal of infected limbs and even then death was likely because of trauma due to a lack of anaesthetics. Apart from the scalpel, medical equipment was limited to a few items like the catheter for draining the bladder. In general physicians could only advise people to follow nostrums similar to those of George Cheyne in *An Essay on Health and Long Life*, published in London in 1724. This recommended temperate living as the best protection from illness, the most important precautions being a proper diet, correct clothing, regular exercise, hygiene, the movement of the bowels, and plenty of sleep.

For most of the population, therefore, pain was a constant possibility and calling the doctor an act of desperation. Sufferers could only seek herbal remedies or take comfort in their religious beliefs, ascribing their maladies to the will of God, though attitudes were beginning to change. The Enlightenment was making scientists look more rationally at the world, producing a better understanding of sickness, though practical treatments were still far distant. Nevertheless, pain was no longer necessarily seen as the reward for sin, but something to be studied, analyzed, and possibly treated. In the meantime people must endure their ailments as best they could, since public displays of suffering were frowned upon.

2 CHILDREN

Writers on the subject of children often quote the Massachusetts law of 1648 which stated that any youngster over sixteen who struck or cursed a parent was to be put to death. There is no evidence that the penalty was ever implemented, but the law does give an indication of the prevailing social attitude that children existed primarily to do their parents' bidding.

Like their contemporaries in Europe, the colonists did not see childhood as an age of innocence; play was not an acceptable concept. The seventeenth-century view that children were the product of original sin remained the received opinion for most of the colonial period. Children were inherently naughty and had to be taken in hand by stern but loving parents. As one minister asserted, "There is in all children . . . a natural pride, which must in the first place be broken and beaten down." This approach was essential to instill a sense of obedience, responsibility, and self-control, without which no one could survive either the tempting of the devil or the inclemency of the environment for in such a wilderness children would otherwise degenerate into savages like the Indians. Corporal punishment consequently was used frequently, except by Quaker parents, who not only disliked violence but believed that children, like the rest of humanity, were innately good. According to Quakers, all that was required to achieve good behavior was a proper example, supported occasionally by verbal admonition.

Childhood therefore had one main purpose: to prepare a person for adult life with all its problems and responsibilities. Children were constantly told of the need to earn their living by the sweat of their brow. They were also repeatedly warned of the possible imminence of death. As one seventeenth-century schoolmaster commented to his class, "Remember death, think much . . . how it will be on the death-bed." This was no abstract danger, as the family of Paul Revere, the Boston silversmith and future Son of Liberty, well knew. Seven of his eleven brothers and sisters died before attaining their majority, while ten of his sixteen children expired in infancy or adolescence.

Why did people have children in colonial times? Sexual appetite and lack of birth control methods were necessarily important factors. The only widely known method of control, apart from abstinence, was withdrawal, which was considered a sin, Onan having been condemned in the Bible for spilling his seed on the ground. Sheaths made of sheep's gut could be purchased in London from the 1690s, but they were unavailable to most colonists. Some women resorted to herbal abortifacients or tried riding on horseback to induce miscarriage; attempts at surgical abortion, however, were rare. The dangers were too great, as was demonstrated by one case in Connecticut in 1742 in which a young woman died after her boyfriend persuaded her to submit to the attentions of a physician. The medical skills to carry out such an operation were still unknown.

One other solution to an unwanted child was infanticide, which was of course murder; the slaying of infants could not have been extensive in so religious a society. Of the sixteen women executed for this offense in seventeenth-century New England, most were servant girls or single women who could not marry or had been jilted. Concealment for them was difficult, though the tendency to wear loose-fitting garments made pregnancy less obvious than it is today. The infant was usually first smothered before being buried.

For married couples the situation was easier, if they could find a sympathetic midwife. By denying the newborn child nourishment or warmth the parents could claim that it had been stillborn. Since many families found additional children burdensome, this practice may have been more widespread than realized, though any attempt to quantify it remains necessarily speculative.

Notwithstanding the situations just described, most births were welcome. A large family was the best insurance that sons and daughters would be available to provide security for a couple who could no longer fend for themselves. A large family was also the surest means of developing a farm or business. The more affluent wanted to have children to whom they could bequeath their possessions. Finally, the Christian religion taught that God would provide bountiful blessings through a loving union between husband and wife. It was the duty of a married couple to have children, and those who did not could expect unflattering comment.

For the first few months of infancy children were dressed in swaddling clothes. These consisted of pieces of linen bound tightly round the body from the ankles to the neck.

Parents feared that otherwise their offspring might not grow straight. Infants therefore wore the same clothing at night to prevent them from sleeping in the fetal position.

The obsession with straightness stemmed from the premise that children were essentially uncivilized and had to be molded physically as well as morally before taking their place in society. Humans, it was often noted, were the only occupants of the earth to walk in an upright position. Consequently when the swaddling clothes were dispensed with after a few months, the next task was to prevent children from crawling and developing beastlike qualities. Various devices were used to effect this, the most popular being standing stools, gocarts, and leading strings. All were designed to speed the transition to walking.

Toilet training in contrast caused parents less concern. Living conditions were necessarily odoriferous even for the upper classes, not least because most adults were lax about their own toilet habits. The dangers of disease from poor sanitation and lack of hygiene were not understood, and most people relieved themselves close to the house. Children simply copied their elders once they could walk.

The period of infancy lasted for about six years, during which time boys and girls were dressed in identical long garments, these being the easiest to wash and pass on from one child to the next. Few children could expect new clothes.

During these early years young children were left mainly to their own devices, although under the watchful eye of an older child or servant. Parents were too busy running the farm or managing the household to spend much time with their offspring. Orthodox opinion held that too much affection was undesirable, since it made adults self-indulgent and children selfish. Hence even the cries of infants were largely ignored, since it was assumed they were either exercising their lungs or expressing their frustration at not being gratified in some excessive want. It was inconceivable that beings so young could know what was good for them.

Infants usually slept in a cot with their parents. As they grew they were given beds in any convenient space. Houses were too small and space too precious to allow separate bedrooms, even in the homes of the affluent, until the end of the colonial period. Most children slept on a mattress which could be rolled up during the day. Everyone shared a bed. Even single adults slept with someone of the same sex for warmth and company. The modern obsession with privacy would have struck provincials as strange.

Few children had toys; most had to make do playing imaginatively with whatever was lying around the house, though lucky youngsters might have a wooden doll or other carved figure. Those who could walk would play hide and seek, blind man's buff, leap frog, hopscotch, skipping, marbles, and shuttle-cock, using improvised wooden implements. In spring and summer they would explore their outside surroundings, and in winter skating and tobogganing were popular with older children when conditions allowed. Infants were necessarily confined to the house.

Around the age of six decisive changes occurred. Boys were given breeches, while girls remained in skirts. This development was the prelude to another important step on the road to adulthood. Both sexes began to be given small tasks, the girls helping in the kitchen or dairy, the boys doing light farm work. In New England and the middle colonies most children would also receive some schooling for a few hours each morning.

As colonial society developed and land became scarcer, many boys around the age of ten began an apprenticeship, normally lasting about nine years, during which the apprentice lodged with the master. Though this might seem a harsh and unloving step on the part of the boy's parents, in most households the relationship between master and servant was similar to that between parent and child – stern but affectionate.

Not that abuses didn't occur, especially among the offspring of the poor. Children as young as five were sometimes "put out," either because of poverty or the death of a parent. The receiving master was supposed to provide a certain level of care and education in return for the child's labor. Inevitably exploitation occurred in some cases.[10]

A small proportion of boys from the richer families progressed to a grammar school and even college in preparation for a career as a minister, lawyer, or merchant. The majority, however, stayed with their parents to help on the farm or in the workshop. Even the offspring of the wealthy would finish their education by their early teens unless they were destined for college. The boys then helped their fathers run their farms and plantations, or worked as clerks in their businesses. Middle-class girls remained with their parents, learning how to manage the household; girls from poorer families were sent to be maids. Life was necessarily a serious business.

Colonial society knew no such phenomenon as adolescence. Teenage boys and girls were expected to face up to the burdens of life, though it was recognized that they were not yet ready for life's main concerns: running a farm, having a family, and participating in public affairs. The young were seen as being still susceptible to temptation and irresponsibility because they had not yet shed the last traces of their childhood. Hence the emphasis was on achieving maturity as soon as possible, as this represented the key to making one's way in the world, both morally and materially.

Maturity was commonly assumed to have been reached by age 21, at least for males, when they could take control of any inherited property (providing it was free of legal constraints), participate in politics (if they met the necessary property qualifications), and marry without parental consent. However, young women gained no such privileges. They rarely inherited property outright, nor were they eligible to vote. Even their right to marry was constrained by their economic dependency on their families.[11]

Regarding the upbringing of children, Cotton Mather, as in so many matters, was full of advice. He believed that parents should "consider how to enrich their minds with valuable knowledge; how to instill into their minds generous, gracious, and heavenly principles; how to restrain and rescue them from the paths of the destroyed, and fortify them against their peculiar temptations." Certainly the task could not be left to the young persons themselves for "'tis folly for them to pretend unto any Wit and Will of their own." In pursuit of his own advice, Mather questioned his six children every night, asking them what they had done during the day, whether they had "sought the Face of God and read His Word." At mealtimes Mather sought to make the conversation "facetious as well as instructive." Not a moment should be lost for improvement.[12]

Such accounts have led most writers to believe that the colonial family was less affectionate in its relationship than its modern counterpart, on the assumption that high infant mortality made emotional investment relatively pointless and that the main purpose

---

[10]   Edmund S. Morgan, *The Puritan Family: Religion and Domestic Relations in Seventeenth Century New England* (New York, 1966), 77, argues that New England families adopted this practice to protect themselves from being excessively indulgent. The economic reasons behind such family disruption are emphasized in Helena M. Wall, *Fierce Communion: Family and Community in Early America* (Cambridge, Mass., 1990), 97–125.

[11]   For more information on the constraints on women, see chapter 12.

[12]   Quoted in Fox and Quitt, *Loving, Parenting, and Dying*, 313.

of having children was, as always, economic. The actual evidence is conflicting. In the case of Mather, only six of his fifteen children survived to adulthood. He was nevertheless a relatively indulgent parent, much more so than his father had been. As the eighteenth century progressed, attitudes among the wealthier classes seem to have begun to change. Influential in this respect were the writings of John Locke, who argued in his *Essay Concerning Human Understanding* (1690) and *Some Thoughts Concerning Education* (1693) that example and environment, rather than precept or innate character, determined behavior. Locke still emphasized firm discipline but believed that it should be moderated by a little indulgence to secure gratitude and affection. The child would then respond more readily to the challenge of adulthood. A sense of shame was generally most effective, for this would naturally induce a desire for self-improvement. Corporal punishment should be administered only as a last resort, since it could make a child resentful and less open to reason and moral persuasion. The new attitude was reflected in depictions of the biblical prodigal son. Earlier versions stressed the folly and ruin that would result for children who defied their parents. By 1760 the emphasis was on the need for parental affection and forgiveness to prevent children leaving in the first place.

Another factor behind the changing attitude to children was the rising standard of living. The more affluent no longer had to think constantly of survival. They could spend more time with their family in leisurely pursuits, without worrying where the next meal was to come from. Increasing longevity also meant that more people became grandparents with time to devote to the young. In addition, as families created substantial estates, the importance of handing on their wealth became a greater consideration. Greater wealth and longevity enabled people to plan not only for their children but for their grandchildren too and provided an additional incentive to develop a close and loving relationship.[13]

Whatever the reason, wealthier parents became steadily more indulgent, seeing childhood in a benign light. By 1760 innocence was emphasized more than malignity. Swaddling clothes were given up for more comfortable wear, while crawling was no longer seen as evidence of bestiality. Play became increasingly acceptable, and a greater range of toys and presents was available. Parents took more delight in their children's company, indulging them in their childish amusements. The uniqueness of each child was also given greater weight, an indication, perhaps, that the seeds of individualism were already being planted in the American colonial character.

These changes have led some writers to believe that by 1760 social structures were almost modern. The nuclear family, not community, was supreme; and the focus of attention was the home, where love and affection took precedence over disipline and obedience. Although the father was head of the household, obedience was voluntary, since it was recognized that other members of the family had rights in equity if not in law. Among the more important of these were privacy, the choice of a marriage partner, and the seeking of personal fulfillment. These developments have led some historians to suggest that perceptions of the self and the place of the individual in society had undergone a radical change by the late colonial period.[14]

---

[13]   This view is argued by Daniel Blake Smith in *Inside the Great House*. See also his review article, "The Study of the Family in Early America: Trends, Problems, and Prospects," *William and Mary Quarterly*, XXXIX, 1982, 3–28.
[14]   See J. E. Crowley, *This Sheba, Self: The Conceptualization of Economic Life in Eighteenth Century America* (Baltimore, 1974); Philip J. Greven, *The Protestant Temperament: Patterns of Child Rearing, Religious Experience, and the Self in Early America* (New York, 1977); Jay Fliegelman, *Declaring Independence: Jefferson, Natural Language, and*

3 SOCIAL STRUCTURE: RANK AND CLASS

Americans have long prided themselves on being a classless society. Three reasons are usually given in support of this contention: one, that the frontier was a great leveler; two, that in crossing the Atlantic, Americans left class distinctions behind; three, that America was a land of opportunity. In the words of Benjamin Franklin, the question was not what a person was, but what a person could do. Ability, not birth, determined status and rewards in life.[15]

Along with the nuclear family, this view is one more example of American exceptionalism that recent writers have questioned. Of course the colonists did leave behind them the strict hierarchical structures of Europe. No feudal aristocracy or peerage existed as in Britain. But the result was not that they arrived in America as equals. The Virginia Company had dispatched a number of gentlemen to help build the colony; the Puritans were led by gentry families like the Winthrops, Saltonstalls, and Vanes; Lord Baltimore sent over his brother and a number of gentry to Maryland; while the Carolinian proprietors planned a leading role for their aristocracy. Only Penn had a consciously egalitarian view, and even he relied on a monied class to get his settlement established.

It is true that most of this first aristocracy went home and that for a time colonial society was relatively fluid. By the end of the seventeenth century, however, local elites were emerging everywhere, usually from among the families of lesser rank who had come from England and decided to stay. A smaller number were also ex-servants who had made their way to the top. Massachusetts had its merchant families like the Dudleys, Hutchinsons, Pynchons, and Sewalls. New York was dominated by the Anglo-Dutch dynasties of Van Rensselaer, Livingston, Stuyvesant, Bayard, and Philipse; Virginia was controlled by the planter families of Beverley, Randolph, Carter, Harrison, Lee, and Byrd; while South Carolina had its Pinckneys, Rutledges, Draytons, and Manigaults. And in every province the gentry or merchants dominated social and political life, especially at the level of the provincial council. In New York during one decade twenty-five of the twenty-eight councillors were from the landed families of the Hudson Valley. Similarly, in Virginia, nine families

---

the *Culture of Performance* (Stanford, 1993); and Ronald Hoffman, Mechal Sobel, and Fredrika J. Teute, *Through a Glass Darkly: Reflections on Identity in Early America* (Chapel Hill, 1997). The recent concern of historians with identity in the United States has several causes, notably the ending of a dominant Anglo-Saxon culture, the massive immigration of the 1980s and 1990s, and the development of a multicultural society in which the different ethnic groups feel the need to define who they are. A similar process is happening in Europe as a result of the European Union and the erosion of the nation-state.

[15] It was a foreign visitor, J. Hector St. John Crèvecoeur, who first propounded the notion that America was exceptional in its social structure. In an oft-quoted passage from his *Letters from an American Farmer* (1782), he asked: "What then is the American, this new man?" The answer was clear: "He is an American, who leaving behind him all his ancient prejudices and manners, receives new ones from the new mode of life he has embraced, the new government he obeys, and the new rank he holds. . . . Here individuals of all nations are melted into a new race of men, whose labors and posterity will one day cause great changes in the world." "From involuntary idleness, servile dependence, penury and useless labor" in Europe the newcomer "has passed to toils of a very different nature, rewarded by ample subsistence." The belief in the egalitarian nature of American life was then passed down in American mythology, along with the story that George Washington never told a lie and that Abraham Lincoln was a lifelong friend of the slaves. Among the more notable expositions on this theme in the twentieth century was that by Louis Hartz, *The Liberal Tradition in America* (New York, 1955). For a recent discussion, see Jack P. Greene, *The Intellectual Construction of America: Exceptionalism and Identity from 1492 to 1800* (Chapel Hill, 1993).

made up one-third of the council in the period 1700–60, while in Connecticut twenty-five names accounted for two-thirds of that body. Whatever equality there might have been during the mid-seventeenth century had vanished after 1700.

This domination by the elites was accepted almost without question, since the colonists' attitudes had been formed in Europe. Their acquiescence was reinforced by religious sanction. As John Winthrop asserted on board the *Arabella* in 1630, "God Almighty, in his most holy and wise providence, has so disposed of the condition of Mankind" that "some must be rich, some poor, some high and eminent in power and dignity, others mean and in subjection." Inequality was so evident that few either questioned it or were ashamed to acknowledge it. It was part of the natural order. Members of the provincial council were addressed as "honorable," justices merited the term "esquire," town officials and persons of property expected to be called "mister."

Nevertheless, until thirty years ago many scholars suggested that colonial America was an equal society because it offered unrivaled economic opportunity. Robert E. Brown in particular argued that the presence of the frontier made land both plentiful and cheap, while the high level of wages opened its purchase to all whites. Since property was the only qualification men required to vote or hold office, entry into the political and social life of a colony was unrestricted. Brown called this situation economic democracy, a society in which the majority of the population was middle class.[16]

Unfortunately, the Brown thesis contained several flaws, which most historians now recognize. Though land may have been cheap in many areas, it was not necessarily accessible, while its development was potentially a most expensive and backbreaking enterprise. Moreover, the frontier itself was far from having a leveling effect, as another earlier historian, Frederick Jackson Turner, suggested. Settlers simply did not arrive there in an equal condition, for of course the scions of the rich were able to secure the best tracts from their relatives on the council and gain a head start before coming west with slaves or servants. Such "pioneers" included William Byrd of Virginia, who purchased one hundred thousand acres in what became Lunenburg County; and John Pynchon, who developed the frontier settlement of Springfield, high up the Connecticut River in western Massachusetts.[17]

Historians now accept that significant discrepancies in wealth prevailed throughout the colonial period. In Virginia only half the adult male population owned land and 50 percent of these did not have the necessary one hundred acres to make life comfortable. The same was true in Maryland. In Talbot County 150 men owned land and slaves, 220 owned some land, but 420 owned no land at all. In neighboring Prince George County during the 1730s the average tenant was worth just £26; the owner of a small farm was worth £117; but a planter with slaves possessed almost £600. Perhaps most significant is the fact that some 60 percent of households still possessed less than £100.

Admittedly the distribution of wealth was not so unbalanced in the north. In Dedham, Massachusetts, the top 5 percent of the population owned a mere 15 percent of the wealth by 1730, though the gap in Boston was considerably greater. There the top 5 percent owned as much wealth as the rest. Boston, however, was perhaps the exception since in Philadelphia

---

16 Robert E. Brown, *Middle Class Democracy and the Revolution in Massachusetts, 1691–1780* (Ithaca, 1955).

17 The Brown thesis incurred considerable criticism at the time of publication, not least for its flawed statistical methodology. See John Cary, "Statistical Method and the Brown Thesis on Colonial Democracy," *William and Mary Quarterly*, XX, 1963, 251–64. For the thesis on frontier democracy see Frederick Jackson Turner, *The Frontier in American History* (New York, 1920).

the same percentile owned under half the taxable wealth, though the imbalance was growing.[18]

It was these discrepancies which helped to create an upper class in colonial America. However unintentionally, those who were successful began distancing themselves from the rest of society. Their way of life changed. They built larger houses and furnished them with the latest fashions from Europe. They bought carriages, dressed better, and now that they no longer had to engage in manual work, gave greater attention to personal hygiene and appearance. Their pattern of acquaintances changed too; former friends, smelling of toil in the field or workshop, called at the back door if they called at all. These changes helped to alter their own perception of their worth. Wealthy settlers now saw themselves as leaders of society, rightfully chosen to serve as selectmen, justices, members of the assembly, and even councillors. They could advance their interests by obtaining land or business contacts in an ever-widening sphere of wealth and influence, as the case of the Pynchon family shows.

Nor did the process of gentrification and class stratification stop here. The new elite recognized the importance of being able to read, write, keep accounts, and have some knowledge of the law. Hence they were quick to educate their children, sending them to school and later college, where they could develop a network of acquaintances. Such children mixed only with their peer group and soon absorbed the manners and attitudes of a governing class. This status was reinforced through suitable marriages, which helped the elites to consolidate their wealth.

Two factors, however, helped to conceal an overt class structure, especially in the northern colonies. The first was religion. All the dissenting churches emphasized that ostentatious display was to be equated with more than one of the seven deadly sins. Everyone was familiar with Christ's assertion that salvation for the rich would be a feat as difficult as that of a camel passing through the eye of a needle. The second factor was that the largest fortunes in the North were usually made in commerce, the field which offered the greatest opportunities to outsiders. The relative openness of the region's economic and social structure always permitted ambitious apprentices like Franklin to make their way.

The southern elites, by comparison, had different attitudes to wealth and its creation, while the Anglican church there placed few inhibitions on its enjoyment. Moreover, their wealth derived from land, as did that of the aristocracies of Europe. It was thus easier for southern planters to develop exaggerated notions of their class and right to govern and it is no coincidence that they viewed primogeniture as a means of maintaining their family name and status.

Not that the rest of the population was resentful. They had not come to America expecting radically different social structures. Most wanted to emulate their betters, not pull them down. The wider economic opportunities of America meant that every white person could dream of becoming a great planter or merchant. Only a minority did, but that was beside the point, for unlike Europe, America created the possibility.

---

[18] For wealth distribution in Maryland, see Paul G. E. Clemens, *The Atlantic Economy and Colonial Maryland's Eastern Shore: From Tobacco to Grain* (Ithaca, 1980); for Dedham, see Kenneth A. Lockridge, *A New England Town, the First Hundred Years: Dedham, Massachusetts, 1636–1736* (New York, 1970); for Boston and other cities, see Gary B. Nash, *The Urban Crucible: Social Change, Political Consciousness, and the Origins of the American Revolution* (Cambridge, Mass., 1979).

12

European-American Women

1696	Dinah Nuthead is appointed printer to the Maryland assembly.
1700	Witchcraft accusations end.
1712	South Carolina allows *femes couverts* to be sued for trading debts.
1716	Mary Stagg helps found the first theater in America at Williamsburg.
1718	Pennsylvania grants sole trader status to abandoned wives or those with absent husbands.
1723	A Connecticut law allows married women to own property through a settlement or trust.
1739–42	Elizabeth Timothy manages the *South Carolina Gazette*.
1741	Eliza Pinckney introduces indigo to South Carolina.
1744	South Carolina grants sole trader status to married women engaged in business.
1745	Widow Roberts runs a coffee house in Philadelphia.
1749	Elizabeth Murray Smith (Inman) starts her dry goods and millinery business in Boston.
1766	Mrs Catherine Blaikley, "an eminent midwife" from Williamsburg, dies aged 76, having presided over three thousand births.

1 OLD WORLD LEGACIES: NEW WORLD OPPORTUNITIES?

THE STATUS OF European women in colonial America is traditionally thought to have been higher than in their countries of origin.[1] Three reasons are usually given. The first is that until the onset of industrialization, the household had important economic functions which brought status to those employed therein. The second concerns the egalitarian nature of the frontier. Setting up a farm required both sexes to shoulder the work, and women mastered most occupations inside and outside the home, helping to sow crops and feed the livestock. Only the heaviest plowing or timber cutting were beyond their capabilities. Consequently, gender roles were less clearly defined than in more traditional European societies. The third argument is that women enjoyed a higher status because their scarcity enabled them to control their lives in a way which was not possible when sex ratios were balanced.

As with so many themes in American history, traditional views have subsequently been challenged, if not overturned. First, the Industrial Revolution may have undermined many traditional domestic skills, but it did offer lower class women the opportunity of earning a wage and of advancing their economic independence. Secondly, the scarcity argument may have held true to some extent for the seventeenth century, when sex ratios were extremely unbalanced. Southern women especially often managed the family estate when their husbands died, there being generally no male relatives to take on this responsibility. Such experience gave them considerable authority until the eldest son came of age. Women were also able to negotiate better marriages, or remarriages if they were widowed. However, by the eighteenth century greater longevity and the development of kinship enabled husbands to turn over their estates to male executors. More balanced sex ratios also meant that single women could no longer lay down conditions to suitors, while widows had difficulty remarrying at all.

Lastly, the thesis concerning the frontier needs similar qualification. The blurring of gender roles was a transitory phase. Once a family was established and the wilderness cleared, women reverted to their more traditional household occupations. This development was in line with the general tendency toward specialization which occurred in the eighteenth century even before the onset of industrialization.

Another point to note is that because of the primitive conditions on the frontier, most women were not keen to go there. During a tour of the South Carolina backcountry in the 1760s, one observer wrote that many of the inhabitants "have nought but a Gourd to drink out of, not a Plate, Knive or Spoon, a Glass, Cup, or anything." If equality did exist, it was one of misery, not opportunity.

The general view of a more egalitarian culture is further open to challenge on the ground that men by no means changed their attitudes on coming to America. As we have seen in Part I, the settlers brought their traditional laws and customs with them. These explicitly reflected the universal assumption that women were the weaker sex, in need of

---

[1] For African-American and Indian women, see chapters 14 and 15.

protection and, by implication, inferior. The only group to qualify this were the Quakers, who stressed the equality of the sexes in the garden of Eden before the Fall.[2]

The origins of male prejudice are as old as humanity itself, though there is little agreement on the reasons for it. Many feminists view it as the result of an inferiority complex arising from man's limited role in the propagation of the species. To compensate for inner fears, men responded by asserting their own physical superiority, turning biological differences into sex discrimination to subordinate women. Male dominance, accordingly, was the result of social construction rather than something innate to the species.

The fact that the average man was stronger than his female counterpart was a crucial factor in a society dominated by the requirements of manual labor. The value placed on strength was reinforced on the frontier, where the use of weapons was often necessary. If the species was to be propagated, homesteads had to be built and defended, two key roles for which the male was generally better suited.

The most common contemporary argument in favor of male domination was that women were intellectually inferior and ruled by their passions. Typical of such views was a pamphlet *The Lady's New Year's Gift or, Advice unto a Daughter*, published in London in 1688 and frequently reprinted. The author, a male, began by observing to his reader what seemed a fundamental truth: "There is *Inequality* in the *Sexes*, and that for the better Oeconomy of the World, the Men, who were to be the Law givers, had the better share of *Reason* bestowed upon them; by which means your Sex is the better prepared for the *Compliance* that is necessary for the performance of those *Duties* which seem to be most properly assigned to it." He continued: "We are made of differing *Tempers*, that our Defects may the better be Mutually Supplied: Your sex wanteth our *Reason* for your *Conduct*, and our *Strength* for your *Protection*; Ours wanteth your *Gentleness* to soften and entertain us." By way of compensation, he told his audience, "you have more strength in your *Looks* than we have in our *Laws*, and more power by your *Tears*, than we have by our *Arguments*."[3]

Contemporaries were perhaps understandably misinformed on the subject of temper. Hormonal cycles were unknown to them. They assumed that variations in female temper could be ascribed only to an excess of passion and evidence of irrationality. The eighteenth century prided itself on being the Age of Reason; it was this quality which divided humanity from the beasts. Any deficiency in this respect could mean only that women were inferior.

---

[2] The frontier thesis and view that the colonial period was a golden era were popular in the 1930s. See Elizabeth A. Dexter, *Colonial Women of Affairs: Women in Business and the Professions in America Before 1776* (Boston, 1931); Julia Cherry Spruill, *Women's Life and Work in the Southern Colonies* (Chapel Hill, 1938); and Richard B. Morris, *Studies in the History of American Law, with Special Reference to the Seventeenth and Eighteenth Centuries* (1930, 2nd edn, Philadelphia, 1959). Later works to endorse the thesis are John Demos, *A Little Commonwealth: Family Life in Plymouth Colony* (New York, 1970); and Roger Thompson, *Women in Stuart England and America: A Comparative Study* (Boston, 1974). More recent challenges to the interpretation are Mary Beth Norton, *Liberty's Daughters: The Revolutionary Experience of American Women, 1750–1800* (Boston, 1980); Marylynn Salmon, *Women and the Law of Property in Early America* (Chapel Hill, 1986); Cornelia Hughes Dayton, *Women Before the Bar: Gender, Law, and Society in Connecticut, 1639–1789* (Chapel Hill, 1995); Kathleen Brown, *Good Wives, Nasty Wenches, and Anxious Patriarchs: Gender, Race and Power in Colonial Virginia* (Chapel Hill, 1996); Elaine Forman Crane, *Ebb Tide in New England: Women, Seaports and Social Change, 1630–1800* (Boston, 1998); and Cynthia A Kierner, *Beyond the Household: Women's Place in the Early South, 1700–1835* (Ithaca, 1998).
[3] Quoted in Spruill, *Women's Life and Work*, 216.

Such thinking encouraged other male notions of female inferiority. Women were considered vain, given to gossip, passive, and, therefore, helpless in a crisis. Men invariably had to take the initiative.

Finally, male views were reinforced by the Bible, especially the early chapters on the creation, which presented Eve as having been created from Adam's rib as an afterthought for his comfort. It was Eve who had eaten the apple and brought about the Fall. As punishment she had been told, "Thy desire shall be to thy husband and he shall rule over thee." Since all European settlers in American subscribed to the literal veracity of the Bible, these stories were powerful weapons in support of male domination. The repercussions were profound, here as everywhere else: every aspect of a woman's life was affected by the assumption that she was physically, mentally, and morally inferior and must at every stage be kept dependent.

2 LIFE CYCLES

The accident of her sex determined a female child's destiny for life, since society assumed that she could aspire only to being a wife and mother. From their early years young girls were encouraged to imitate their mothers. As soon as possible they were given small tasks like churning some butter, assisting in the milking, doing simple sewing, and helping with the cooking. The aim was to ensure that by the age of twelve or thirteen they could take their place alongside the adult women in the household.

Girls accordingly received little education in the modern sense. Outside New England a majority probably had no formal schooling whatsoever. In New England the desire for a godly society ensured that many could at least read. The ability to write, however, was thought to be a male prerogative, of use only in the active lives which men would lead. No girls went to grammar school or college before 1760.

Toward the end of the colonial period, upper-class families began to recognize the desirability of giving their daughters a more complete education. The curriculum began to include all three Rs, together with French, music, and dancing, though the aim was still to produce better wives. It should be remembered that education is not always a liberating medium but one which can just as readily be used to condition people. The variety in the new curriculum for females merely reflected the greater sophistication of elite colonial society, which now required an upper-class woman to be a hostess rather than a drudge. To some extent this was a backward step, since it helped stereotype women as frivolous and wasteful.

Marriage thus remained the goal for which all young women prepared themselves. It was their *raison d'être*, the importance of which was reinforced by the absence of alternative careers. This point was emphasized by the seemingly terrible fate of being an old maid, "the most calamitous creature in nature." Constant jokes were made about the ugliness, frigidity, and desperation to secure a mate of those despised, unmarried females; and young women inevitably felt that any husband was better than none. The proof seemed all too obvious since most spinsters, lacking their own means of support, lived with relatives in a demeaning dependency. The alternative of seeking independence through employment was not open to middle-class women, since the opportunities were mainly menial ones like washing, cooking, sewing, and cleaning. A single life in these circumstances was simply degrading.

Among upper-class families the selection of a husband was invariably taken under strict parental guidance, which was considered desirable for several reasons. As the "weaker vessel," a woman was more easily led astray, especially if she was young and impressionable. Another reason was that among middle- and upper-class families, marriage involved a transfer of property. While today a couple expect to obtain employment and thereby security, in the eighteenth century families had the duty of ensuring that their offspring were sufficiently endowed to maintain themselves. This obligation usually required the prospective husband's father to transfer part of the farm or make a commitment to do so when he retired, meanwhile offering the couple a roof and means of subsistence. The bride's family was similarly expected to contribute a dowry in money, livestock, and household items to ensure the economic viability of the marriage.

Because marriage among wealthier families was a union of economic interests, the woman especially was expected to show a proper respect for the wishes of her parents. If she refused a match, as one of William Byrd II's daughters threatened to do, she could expect to be disowned for ignoring "the sacred duty you owe a parent." Indeed, in some colonies the consent of the father to a marriage was statutorily required. As the author of *The Whole Duty of Man*, published in London in 1684, stated, "Children are so much the goods, the possessions of their Parents, that they cannot without a kind of theft, give away themselves." Life was so precarious that economic necessity had to be given due weight. Couples simply could not marry on emotional impulse.

In most cases a daughter welcomed guidance, recognizing that her choice of partner was the most momentous decision of her life. Most women appreciated the desirability of avoiding a bad match from which there could be no escape other than death. They had little experience of their own and were constantly being told by ministers, teachers, and society to respect their parents. Most readily turned to them for advice.

A further incentive to accept parental guidance was that a genteel woman could not initiate courtship. If she made advances she was considered flirtatious, even immoral, and ran the risk of eliciting sexual advances which could irrevocably damage her reputation. Respectable families prized virginity above all else as a sign of godliness, character, and virtue in an unmarried daughter. A forward woman might also be compared to an Amazon and accused of possessing a domineering and tyrannical nature. Contemporary literature was full of such examples. Modesty and discretion were the proper qualities in a young woman looking for a suitor.

Premarital sexual contact among the upper classes was avoided at all costs for fear of pregnancy. As one young New Yorker asserted in the 1750s, although she considered herself a "giddy girle," she "never suffered any [beaux] to approach too nearly" and always "had a very great aversion to familiarity of any sort." Otherwise, she knew, her reputation would suffer and her chances of a good match evaporate. As one Chesapeake plaintiff in a slander suit contended: "no greater misfortune can befall a young Woman, whose well being depends upon her having a good husband, than to be reputed a Whore."[4] Admittedly, toward the end of the colonial period bridal pregnancy was on the increase, but most such instances occurred among lower-class families, where the same proprieties of courtship were not observed because little or no property was involved.

For that small group of women who were jilted and left with a child, their prospects were severely damaged. Until the end of the colonial period they were liable to be

---

[4] Quoted in Larry D. Eldridge, ed., *Women and Freedom in Early America* (New York, 1997), 295.

summoned to court and fined or whipped, depending on their social class, though one advantage was that the court would ensure the payment of maintenance, if the father was named. However, many women were too embarrassed to do this. However, as fornication ceased to be considered a criminal matter, it was left to the woman or her family to seek support by means of a civil suit. But, whatever the outcome, the woman's aspirations for normal married respectability were seriously compromised.

Although it seems that little attention was given to the feelings of an upper-class bride, love and companionship were not entirely ignored. What differed was the manner in which these qualities were regarded. Most parents recognized that intending couples must feel attracted to one another and be likely to be sexually compatible. Though the colonials never equated lust with love, revulsion on the woman's part clearly would lead neither to a happy marriage nor one that God would bless. And the sanctity of the marriage vows, embodying a lifetime commitment, was a factor which few colonials ignored. Provided that mutual respect was present, however, the assumption was that love would grow as the couple made a home together, sharing its pleasures and tribulations.

By 1760 there were signs that love and personal attraction were beginning to predominate over economic and family considerations when it came to marriage. Even in the 1690s Fitz-John Winthrop observed how "it has been the custom of the country for young folks to choose." Forty years earlier Fitz-John Winthrop had had to subordinate "his own will and desires" to those of his parents, though of course he belonged to the elite. Lower-class families may have allowed greater choice throughout the period because parents had fewer means of controlling their children once they reached adulthood. Most indulgent were Quaker parents, who even accepted the wish of their daughters not to marry at all. In any case, personal attraction was not necessarily inimical to patriarchy, if the new genre of romantic novel was to be believed. Almost without exception they emphasized that the virtuous young woman, who followed her parents' advice as well as her heart, would achieve ultimate happiness.

Careful vetting of partners was essential because a woman's status changed completely on her marriage. Legally she became a *feme couvert*, meaning that her civil identity was subsumed into that of her husband. Her personal property now belonged to him, and he also had the right to manage her real estate and to enjoy its profits. The same was true of income from her labor. In addition a married woman could no longer make contracts, take legal action, or draw up a will without her husband's consent.

Because a husband's powers were so absolute, some upper-class families took the precaution of placing legal restrictions on any real estate belonging to their daughters so that it could not be alienated by the husband. Another reason for such action was to protect the daughter and her children in the event of widowhood. The traditional dower right to a third of the estate was often ineffective, since the husband's property could be seized by creditors during his lifetime.

The usual method of protecting a daughter's estate was by means of a trust, although such devices were never popular in New England. The Puritans saw them as the prelude to a separate household, a corrupt device of the English aristocracy to substitute a mistress for a wife. They believed that a harmonious marriage was the only protection a wife needed. Connecticut did not recognize such settlements until 1723.

The one device which the Puritans did permit was a jointure, or marriage settlement, according to which the bride's family contributed a sum of money or personal property as a dowry. In return, the groom or his family set aside an equivalent amount in real estate in the bride's name. The property was still managed by the husband but could not be alienated to pay off creditors. If the couple did subsequently wish to sell, they could do so only with the agreement of the wife. In the southern colonies her consent had to be given to a magistrate independently of the husband to ensure that the wife was not acting under duress. Elsewhere only her signature, which could be appended at home, was required.

None of these formulas was designed to give a woman personal freedom, either as a wife or widow. The main purpose of setting up a trust was to protect the rights of any future children, especially male heirs. Similarly, the dower rights or jointure were a form of damage limitation to ensure that the woman and her offspring did not want in the event of a husband's death. If the woman subsequently remarried she usually forfeited her rights, which either passed to her children or reverted to the husband's family if there were no offspring.

A woman had three principal responsibilities in her marriage: to please her husband, have children, and manage the household.

Pleasing her husband meant not disputing his wishes. As the *Virginia Gazette* advised its female readers in 1737, "Never dispute with your husband whatever be the Occasion. . . . If any Altercations or Jars happen, don't separate the bed," since that would only compound the animosity. If in doubt, "Read often the Matrimonial Service, and overlook not the important word OBEY."[5] Similar advice was tended by Cadwallader Colden, the future lieutenant governor of New York, to his daughter Elizabeth. He wrote "You have been a Dutyfull Child to your Parents. . . . Let your Dress, your Conversation and the whole Business of your life be to please your husband and to make him happy." This was a woman's natural role and route to happiness.

One important way in which a woman could please her husband was by submitting to his sexual advances. Colonial attitudes to sex were somewhat ambivalent. Copulation had been ordained by God for the procreation of children; on the other hand it was the consequence of the Fall. Women could not thus be regarded merely as sexual objects, for men themselves were constantly being reminded that lust was the result of original sin. Nevertheless, within marriage the sexual act was seen as something that should be enjoyed as part of the loving relationship between husband and wife. Certainly most men believed that sexual satisfaction was their proprietary due and refused to abstain even after several infants had died and their wives had been imperiled. The assumption was always that such things were the will of God. On the other hand, men were expected to satisfy their wives, since male impotence was justification for a separation or divorce in New England.

Because women were expected to submit sexually to their husbands, a first child usually appeared within twelve months after marriage and another one thereafter every two to three years. Prolonged lactation could delay the next pregnancy, and some women deliberately delayed weaning their children for this reason. Herbs like savin and snakeroot were also taken in the hope of restoring menstruation, which it was thought would improve a woman's health. Pregnancy was not without its compensations for upper-class women. It usually made their husbands more solicitous, for superstition held that wives who were denied their longings might miscarry. Their condition was looked upon as a mild sickness

---

[5]   Quoted in Spruill, *Women's Life and Work*, 164.

during which it was important to eat a correct diet. Spicy foods were to be avoided for fear of tainting the fetus. Travel was regarded as dangerous, since it might cause a miscarriage; and rest was considered advisable.

Naturally, among poorer groups this last piece of advice especially was not easily followed. The requirements of the existing family meant that there was little respite from the daily grind, and few if any concessions could be made to diet or the need for rest.

Childbirth itself was an event from which all men were excluded, since until the 1760s the midwife reigned supreme. Female friends and relatives attended the birth to give assistance and reassurance, since it was a time of considerable apprehension, especially in the case of a first child. The pain of labor and delivery was well known, since most colonial women had helped their mothers, sisters, and relatives on similar occasions. The possibility of death was also recognized, though the risks may not have been as high as has been supposed. Statistically, the chance of a complicated birth was about one in 30 though of course all births were painful and took several hours to complete. The worst situation was if the baby was trapped inside the womb, for a Cesarian operation then had to be performed, and this was nearly always fatal to the mother. Anne Bradstreet wrote during one of her pregnancies:

> How soon, my Dear, death may my steps attend;
> How soon it may be thy lot to lose thy friend.

Another young wife, Mary Clapp, prayed with her husband each night during her pregnancies that God would continue their lives together. She did so with reason. By the time she was twenty-four she had buried four of her infants before going to the grave herself.

Except for the wealthy, most mothers rested only a few days before resuming their household chores. Among poor families the lying-in period was usually a couple of days, though that was generous compared to the lot of American Indian women, who returned to work immediately. Almost all mothers breastfed their babies, since their milk was a natural and easy method of subsistence and the preparation of baby foods would have been difficult. In the South some women resorted to an African wet nurse, but the practice was rare elsewhere. Weaning normally took place between one year and eighteen months, unless painful feeding necessitated an earlier cessation. By this time the next child had probably been conceived.

One consequence of giving birth so many times was that women mothered extensively rather than intensively. This contrasts with the present day, when most women rear children for just one period of their lives and devote as much time as possible to their upbringing. Naturally, upper-class mothers had more time for their children, since they could employ servants and slaves to do their housework. Poor colonial women, on the other hand, had no option but to continue with their daily chores. Relief from this cycle of pregnancy and child rearing came only with the menopause or death. Roughly 30 percent of married women died before they reached fifty.[6]

---

[6] The view that child rearing was extensive rather than intensive and thus involved less emotional commitment is argued by Laurel Thatcher Ulrich, *Good Wives: Image and Reality in the Lives of Women in Northern New England, 1650–1750* (New York, 1982); and Catherine M. Scholten, *Childbearing in American Society: 1650–1850* (New York, 1985). The emotional commitment of mothers to their children is emphasized by Mary Beth Norton in *Liberty's Daughters: The Revolutionary Experience of American Women, 1750–1800* (Boston, 1980).

Plate 27 Typical eighteenth-century kitchen hearth from the Abraham Browne, Jr. House, Watertown, Massachusetts. Courtesy of the Samuel Chamberlain Collection at the Essex Institute, Salem, Massachusetts.

The third responsibility of married women was the management of the household. This obligation included cooking, baking, washing, cleaning, sewing, preserving food, fermenting beverages, spinning yarn, making clothes, and producing soap. Farm women were also responsible for looking after poultry, milking the cows, and making dairy products. Women in less affluent households also worked in the fields at harvest time.

Then as now, most household work was of a dull, monotonous nature with little seasonal variation. Those not conveniently close to a mill had to grind wheat or corn with a mortar and pestle most days for a couple of hours to provide bread for the family. Meals had to be cooked every day, while washing and cleaning had to be done two or three times a week. Another continual occupation was spinning, much time being required to produce even a little yarn. Fortunately, a task like sewing could be done in the company of neighbors to help relieve its tedium. Food preserving also made a change from more routine tasks.

The minority of women living in towns had a marginally easier time, since they could purchase many items. Townswomen thus did little spinning or dairy making. On the other hand the majority of them had to pay for such products by washing and cleaning in the households of the elite.

Only the wives of well-to-do merchants and plantation owners escaped the drudgery by employing servants or slaves to do it for them. These women's tasks were mainly managerial, though supervising servants and feeding and entertaining guests was not always easy. The wife of Robert Carter of Nomini Hall during one year had to oversee the consumption of 27,000 pounds of pork, 20 head of cattle, 550 bushels of wheat, 4 hogsheads of rum, and 150 gallons of brandy.

Amidst all this activity, women had little time to themselves. Most got up with the sunrise and continued their labors even when the sun had set. As a result, they rarely read or thought for themselves, let alone had the opportunity to be creative in any areas other than those connected with their work. As one poetess observed:

> Ah yes! tis true, upon my life,
> No Muse was ever yet a Wife,
> Muses in poultry yards were never seen
> [who] from Books and Poetry must turn,
> To mark the Labours of the Churn[7]

Perhaps most dispiriting for women was that many derived little satisfaction from their work, which was increasingly separated from that of men as the workplace became more complex and impersonal. Husbands might compliment them on their efforts, but most wives and their helpers regarded their work as of a meaner kind than that performed by men. They constantly referred to their "humble duties," "little domestick affairs" and "necessary duties of life." Their chores were a penalty to be endured, not a task to be enjoyed. Here was yet another consequence of Eve's curse.

Women rarely challenged their daily existence, since there were few alternatives. The best a woman could hope for was that she and her husband might prosper sufficiently to be able to employ servants to do the most laborious work. Otherwise she remained trapped in her daily tedium, unable to prepare herself for another role, since neither education nor careers were available. As we shall see, some women did engage in business, but unless they were single or widowed they required their husband's consent.

Perhaps the worst aspect of a married woman's existence was her inability to escape a bad match. Legally a husband had the right to chastise his wife physically, and many did so, though in cases of grievous bodily harm a woman could appeal to the courts for protection. Mental cruelty was not a ground for complaint. Occasionally a separation order might be granted if the woman or her children were thought to be in mortal peril. She was then allowed to set up her own household with her children and receive support from her erstwhile husband. Such separations were only granted in exceptional cases, however, since the assumption was always that the husband had a proprietary right to the services of his wife. Securing alimony could also be a problem, especially from husbands who had little property or had absconded. Indeed, the lack of financial support was often the real reason for not granting separations, no matter how severe the abuse. No community wanted the burden of supporting a broken family, nor the embarrassing reminder that a marriage had failed. The moral, legal, and financial implications were too great. Decisions concerning separations accordingly were taken in the interests of the community: the happiness of the individual was only a minor consideration.

Absolute divorce with the right of remarriage was available only in New England and was rare even there. The Puritans took the view that marriage was a civil institution and could be dissolved for adultery, impotence, bigamy or desertion. However, this step required

---

[7]   Quoted in Norton, *Liberty's Daughters*, 36.

application to the superior court, and few wives were prepared to face the expense or humiliation of such proceedings. The presumption remained that the bonds of marriage were sacred and were to be severed only in extreme cases. Ironically, some petitions for divorce in New England were filed by men claiming that they had been deserted when in reality their wives had fled because of their physical violence. A plea of cruelty only began to be accepted by the courts in the 1780s.

Elsewhere in the colonies divorce could be obtained only by a special act of the legislature, a procedure beyond the means of nearly all women. Divorce was difficult in the southern colonies for another reason. Southern planters not infrequently had liaisons with their female slaves, and few legislators were prepared to see the misdemeanors of their colleagues exposed in their presence, though they had fewer reservations about dealing with adulterous wives. The same double standard governed separation orders, which were granted only if the adultery was accompanied by physical violence and neglect. Southern women consequently were advised not to be jealous or give way to recrimination if they suspected their husbands of infidelity. Rather, they should carry themselves with dignity, knowing that they at least had kept their marriage vows and were faithful to God.

In reality colonial women everywhere were subject to the double standard of male sexual morality. If a married woman had an affair it was adultery no matter what the status of her lover. According to biblical custom, if a married man erred with a single woman it was merely fornication, the logic being that husbands had a property right in their spouses. As the eighteenth century progressed, attitudes to male sexual misdemeanors became steadily more relaxed. Men still preached the necessity for faithfulness but were increasingly less faithful themselves. Some even bragged about their sexual conquests since prosecutions for fornication and adultery became steadily less frequent after 1700, while rape was often treated as though the woman herself was responsible. By 1750 there were even brothels in Boston. A woman with an illegitimate child, however, was still subject to severe penalties, including whippings and standing on the gallows, if she had no means of support. As an eighteenth-century Virginian poetess bewailed:

> Custom alas doth partial prove,
> Nor gives us equal measure.
> A pain it is for us to love,
> But is to man a pleasure.
>
> They plainly can their thoughts disclose,
> whilst ours must burn within.
> We have got tongues, and eyes, in vain
> and Truth from us is sin.
>
> Men to new joys and conquests fly,
> And yet no hazard run.
> Poor we are left, if we refuse,
> And if we yield, undone.[8]

---

[8] Quoted in Robert E. Brown and Katherine B. Brown, *Virginia, 1705–1786: Aristocracy or Democracy?* (East Lansing, 1964).

A few women did attempt to escape a bad marriage, if only temporarily. Younger women sometimes fled to their parents, though the usual outcome was reconciliation. Few parents were prepared to endure the shame of an open breakdown, but such action did serve to remind a husband not to push his wife too far. A smaller number of women ran away alone or with another man, in which case they forfeited all rights to their children and any property in the marriage. This was another case of the double standard since a man found guilty of desertion or adultery merely had to hand over one-third of his estate, the woman's dower entitlement. Most women, therefore, had no option but to remain with their husbands, hoping that chance or fate would in some way alleviate their situation. Toward the end of the colonial period a few separations were mutually agreed whereby the husband allocated certain property for his wife's maintenance. Since a woman could not technically make such a contract, a trustee had to be nominated to make the agreement legal. In such cases, which were very much the exception, an advertisement in the newspaper informed tradesmen and other creditors of the new situation.

The only condition in which a woman might avoid the constraints of masculine domination was widowhood. Even then her freedom was limited, since most husbands placed restrictions on what wives could do with their estates. Here was yet another example of the double standard: if the wife died, the husband retained the use of her property during his lifetime, the assumption being that the family still existed, but should the woman outlive her husband, she could claim only the dower portion of his estate, since the family was held to have ceased.

Seventeenth-century English law stipulated that if a man died intestate his widow was entitled to one-third of his personal property and a life interest in one-third of his real estate. Most of the colonies initially followed this custom, but by the eighteenth century this provision had been whittled down to the life interest plus clothing. Only Virginia and Maryland continued the former, more generous allocation. In reality, many husbands who made wills provided much less, though a widow could appeal to the courts if she felt she had been treated unfairly. The courts usually adopted as their yardstick a life interest in one-third of the real estate when giving judgment.[9]

Such provision rarely mounted to a fortune, since the average farm was not very substantial. A widow's financial prospects were generally doubly bleak: she was rarely able to work the land herself; and she could not sell the property because she had only a life interest or tenancy. Accordingly, most women had to appoint a manager, thus further diminishing their income.

Even when a widow was left a substantial estate without restrictions, her position was not always enviable. She still had the problem of adjusting to a completely new way of life. If her children were young she had to take over the responsibilities of her late husband, dealing with creditors and debtors who often tried to take advantage of her distress. For most women this was an unnerving experience, since few had been trained to handle the business of a farm, shop, or counting house.

---

[9]   Dutch law in New Netherland had been even more generous than English practice in the seventeenth century, giving a widow the husband's entire estate during her lifetime and a half share if she remarried. However, these entitlements rapidly disappeared after 1700.

DOCUMENT 18

An Act to Enable Feme Couverts to Convey Their Estates, Georgia, 1760, reprinted in W. Keith Kavenagh, *Foundations of Colonial America: A Documentary History* (New York, 1973), III, 2505–6.

[The fear of dower rights on some properties inhibited land sales and the ability of owners to develop their estates. But like all southern colonies, Georgia made strict provision to ensure that the wife was a willing party to such transactions.]

II. Whereas it is necessary to secure the property of future purchasers of lands and tenements as well to prevent husbands disposing without the consent of the wife what of right did or would belong to them . . . where a *feme couvert* has or may have any right in part or the whole of the lands and tenements to be conveyed and the said *feme couvert* does willingly consent to part with her right by becoming a party with her husband and in the sale of such lands and tenements, in such cases as these the said *feme couvert* shall become a party with her husband in the said deed of conveyance and sign and seal the same before the chief justice or assistant judges, or one of his Majesty's justices of the peace for the parish where such contracts shall be made, declaring before the said judge or justice that she has joined with her husband in alienation of the said lands and tenements of her own free will and consent without any compulsion or force used by her husband to oblige her so to do. Which declaration shall be made in the following words: "I, A.B., the wife of C.D. do declare that I have freely and without any compulsion signed, sealed and delivered the above instrument of writing passed between E.F. and C.D.; and I do hereby renounce all title or claim of dower that I might claim or be entitled to after the death of C.D., my said husband."

Most widows therefore opted to divest themselves of such responsibilities, especially if they had a relative to look after them. Many husbands in fact anticipated this situation by stipulating that the eldest son should provide his widowed mother with a room, food, and fuel for the duration of her life. Unfortunately for the woman, such an arrangement exchanged one form of dependency for another. Most sons were undoubtedly dutiful. Nevertheless, inheriting their father's estate was for them a time of liberation, and some resented having to look after their mother. For the woman, the widowhood brought about a complete reversal of relationships. Previously she had controlled her children; now she was dependent on them.

It used to be thought that most widows could choose to remarry to escape such dependency. Recent research has shown this not to be the case after 1700 as sex ratios everywhere became more balanced and women began living longer than men. A young widow with property and few children certainly had good marriage prospects. But middle-aged or elderly widows with estates entailed in favor of their children offered no great attractions to potential suitors. Most were condemned to remain single in a society which all too often viewed them as relics. Only a few had the means and energy to seek a more independent and satisfying existence by establishing their own economic base.

3 HOUSEHOLD ENTERPRISES, BUSINESS, AND THE PROFESSIONS

Although managing the household and rearing children were a married woman's main responsibilities, many women did have an economic dimension which gave them at least some income, if not independence. While most women were of necessity Jills of all household activities, many were also mistress of one which they could market as wares or services to neighbors and nearby townsfolk. They could then purchase other items which they were less adept at making or had no time to produce.

Among these household microbusinesses were spinning, weaving, butter and cheese making, soap manufacturing, and laundering.

All colonists needed clothes, and a large number of colonial women engaged in the basic task of spinning wool or linen yarn. Not all women could afford a spinning wheel, which was a relatively expensive item. When Benjamin Franklin bought his sister one as a wedding gift he assumed that he was doing her a good turn. The evidence from inventories suggests that only 50 percent of colonial households possessed such an item, the most common being the linen wheel. Spinning was a tediously repetitive occupation, but households with plenty of hands could produce useful quantities of yarn.

After spinning, the next stage in the production of cloth was weaving. Only 10 percent of households had a loom, which was another expensive item and one which required room to house. None the less, those who had one could produce woolen and linen cloth which could then be sold back to neighbors for making clothes, tableware, curtains, and bedding. However, the actual weaving was invariably done by men. The one exception was in New England where a more diversified economy and shortage of skilled labor opened this occupation to women by the end of the colonial period.

Another important household industry was dairy produce, for which the main markets were the towns. Unlike rural folk, who could produce their own butter and cheese, townsfolk did not have the space for cattle and had to purchase dairy produce from the surrounding farms. The main instrument in butter making was the churn, which until 1760 was usually a simple plunger unit with a disk on the end of a handle to agitate the cream. Churning in this way was hard work; it took three hours to produce even a few pounds of butter. This time was cut in half by the more efficient barrel churn, which was beginning to appear by 1760, though only the more affluent could afford it.

Cheese making, in contrast, needed little sophisticated equipment. The milk was first cooled with spring water before being put into wooden vats for curdling. The bacterial process was usually controlled by adding a small amount of rennet, a substance obtained from the gut of a sheep or unweaned calf. Once coagulation was complete, the curd would then be pressed to squeeze out the remaining liquid or whey. It was then cut into cakes either for immediate consumption or for ripening to improve the texture and taste.

Soap making also involved equipment no more sophisticated than a large iron container for boiling the potash and separating the potassium carbonate. The resulting alkali was then mixed with animal fat (an acid) to produce soap. Soap manufacture was sometimes done in conjunction with candle making, which involved boiling animal fat to yield tallow. Both processes involved the considerable labor of stoking the fire, stirring the mixture, and extracting the product.

Many women also offered domestic services such as washing, starching, and ironing clothes. Cleaning silks and lace was especially lucrative, since both fabrics required delicate handling. The demand for such laundering services increased as the colonies grew in wealth and sophistication.

The evidence for New England, at least, indicates that by 1755 many women were being paid wages, suggesting employment outside the household and greater financial independence. Such employment included farm work and other occupations traditionally held by males like tailoring and weaving, though rates of pay for women were only half those earned by adult men. The key factor influencing the employment of women of course was the state of the economy. When labor was scarce, the economic opportunities improved. However, New England may have been unique in this respect, given its westward movement of population and lack of immigration. Rates of pay for women in Chester County, Pennsylvania, in contrast were barely one-quarter to one-third those of males.

Although most women found farming too strenuous to handle on their own, a few did manage their estates in cases where no legal restrictions were imposed on them. Female management was particularly feasible on southern plantations, where an existing supply of labor meant that the woman's tasks were supervisory. Margaret Brent, for example, arrived in Maryland in 1638 as an independent heiress and developed several plantations. She showed such skill that Governor Calvert gave her power of attorney to look after his property in his absence and made her the executor of his will. Significantly, Margaret Brent never married, thus maintaining her *feme sole* status.

Another southern woman to show exceptional talent in plantation management was Eliza Lucas Pinckney. She was the daughter of a British army officer, George Lucas, who entrusted her with the management of his plantations in South Carolina while absent on military service. Both father and daughter were interested in developing imported plants, especially from the West Indies, including indigo, ginger, cotton, and cassava. The most successful was indigo, though it was not easy to grow since both the soil and the processing of the leaves required careful preparation. The first crop was harvested in the early 1740s, and in 1744 Eliza Pinckney selflessly produced only seeds so that her neighbors might profit from her endeavors. The industry was sufficiently promising by 1748 for Parliament to offer a bounty of sixpence a pound to encourage production. Eliza Pinckney was fortunate in having a father and husband who both encouraged her enterprise.

Apart from farming, a number of women also ran various businesses, among which one of the more popular was millinery. As the colonies prospered in the eighteenth century, the demand for hats and other fashion items, such as dresswear, greatly increased. Many women often ran their businesses as partnerships with their husbands' haberdashery or dry goods shops, thus acquiring sufficient business skills to continue if their husbands died. This arrangement partly explains why so many businesswomen were widows.

One of the more notable milliners was Elizabeth Murray Smith (Inman) of Boston, who in 1749 established a small dry goods shop before her marriage to a Boston merchant. After his death she returned to the millinery business before deciding to remarry. This time she protected her right to trade by insisting on a prenuptial agreement. When her second husband died, Murray was one of the wealthiest individuals in town. Murray was exceptional in her dedication to a career, and in her constant encouragement of other young women to follow her example by developing skills without regard to their traditional roles as wives and mothers.

Plate 28   Portrait of Mrs James Smith (Elizabeth Murray), by John Singleton Copley, 1769. Gift of Joseph W. R. and Mary C. Rogers, courtesy of the Museum of Fine Arts, Boston.

The keeping of grocery shops was also popular with urban women. The most important items for sale were tea, coffee, spices, salt, sugar, rum, brandy, tobacco, and possibly kitchenware. Other establishments offered delicatessen items or operated as bakeries. Some women also kept drugstores, selling various powders and herbs.

Other women engaged in keeping inns and taverns. Usually they took these over from deceased husbands or fathers from whom they had learnt the trade. The selling of alcohol required a license, but magistrates readily granted one where a woman had already revealed a capacity for management, especially if doing so would ensure that she would not be a burden on the community. Some southern widows turned their plantation homes into inns if they were adjacent to a road. Many such houses had sufficient rooms and facilities to accommodate guests. A sign was easily erected at the gates; and thereafter the business consisted largely of doing what the woman had always done – feeding and accommodating people.

By the middle of the eighteenth century, a few women had begun to capitalize on the English fashion for coffee houses. The first mention of one run by a woman was that of Widow Roberts in Philadelphia in 1745. Ten years later Mary Ballard more ambitiously advertised her establishment in Boston for the "entertainment of gentlemen." She provided all the regular colonial newspapers, together with the best English magazines, which the customers could peruse while drinking their tea, coffee, and chocolate.

A few exceptional women found other commercial niches too. Dinah Nuthead inherited her husband's printing press at St. Mary's and was sufficiently successful to be appointed printer to the Maryland assembly. Similarly, Elizabeth Timothy inherited the *South Carolina Gazette*, Charleston's first newspaper, which her husband had taken over. Although she had six small children and was pregnant with a seventh, she successfully continued the paper until her eldest son was ready to take over.

Nevertheless, running a business was by no means easy, for a woman. Most had no training in bookkeeping and probably could not even do simple arithmetic. They also had little knowledge of the workings of credit or dealing in commodity money, though they soon learned the power of resorting to an attorney. Colonial newspapers often carried advertisements from businesswomen requesting their customers to settle their accounts. Those who did not could expect to be sued.

Most disadvantaged in this respect were married women since they could not sue or make contracts. This impediment did not matter if they had the support of their husbands, but if a husband opposed his wife or had deserted, her predicament was severe, as Susannah Cooper of Virginia discovered. She brought her husband a substantial dowry on her marriage in 1717. Three years later he deserted her, leaving a mass of debts. She nevertheless developed a moderate plantation, owning several slaves, but because she was technically still married, she could neither sell any of her assets nor sue anyone who trespassed on her property or refused to honor an obligation. She was even barred from making a will in favor of her children. On this occasion the Virginia assembly passed a private bill allowing her to act as a *feme sole*.

The only colony to address the role of women in business was South Carolina. In 1712 the assembly passed a law allowing a woman trader to be sued as though she were a *feme sole* to prevent women from pleading couverture when pressed by creditors. However, the reciprocal right of suing debtors was not granted. In 1744 the assembly rectified this injustice by allowing businesswomen the status of sole traders so that they could sue and carry on their businesses effectively. Paradoxically this generosity toward women emanated from the double standard. The South Carolina legislators felt obliged somehow to compensate for the sexual license of the colony's menfolk by giving women greater economic freedom should they become divorced or separated.

The only other province to provide any relief to businesswomen was Pennsylvania, where in 1718 the assembly gave sole trader status to any woman whose husband was away for a long period – a mariner, for example – or had deserted her. The main purpose of the law was not to benefit women but to prevent them from being a burden on the community. Once the husband returned the woman lost her sole trader status.

One occupation which posed no legal problems was teaching, and many women consequently kept a school. Communities often could not afford a qualified instructor but were prepared to pay a woman to teach their children to read and write and, in the case of girls, sew. Many of these "dame" schools were little more than nurseries; others were effectively orphanages. Toward the end of the colonial period a few women also opened boarding schools for the daughters of the well-to-do which offered the wider curriculum now in fashion.

Of the three principal professions – the church, law, and medicine – the first two were closed to women. The Bible revealed that Christ chose only male disciples, and all denominations followed his example when selecting their ministry. The one exception was the Quakers. The Society of Friends of course had no separate priesthood, relying on licensed members to preach the inner light. They took the view that souls knew no gender. Accordingly, a considerable number of women were licensed for such missions, often traveling hundreds of miles in the company of one or two colleagues. The most famous Quaker female missionary in the seventeenth century was Mary Dyer, whose visits to Boston ended in her martyrdom in 1660 after she repeatedly refused to stop preaching to the townsfolk. After 1689 that danger ceased, though until the 1720s speaking in public was often difficult. Another Quaker innovation was the practice of holding separate women's meetings.

The legal profession was similarly out of bounds to women, in part because they were given no education beyond the primary level. Most colleges were after all founded primarily as seminaries for professions from which women were excluded. In addition, there was a strong presumption that the "weaker sex" did not have the intelligence to handle such complex matters as the law or to derive any benefit from higher education.

The one profession which did offer women opportunity before 1760 was medicine, mainly because it was not yet professionally organized. No formal qualifications or vetting bodies had been established which could close the door to female practitioners. Women were particularly active as physicians through their skills as herbalists, offering various remedies for a fee to the population at large. Many women also combined their knowledge of herbs with nursing skills, though few practiced as surgeons.

The area of medicine in which women were most dominant was midwifery. Modesty seemingly required men to be absent from the delivery of babies until the 1760s, when some male doctors began to offer gynecological services. Midwifery had the additional advantage of not requiring any formal training. Only two colonies, Massachusetts and New York, laid down regulations in this area, and they were concerned largely with the legal aspects of a child's birth and parentage. A successful midwife usually began by helping neighbors and building up her reputation from there. In the seventeenth century midwives risked accusations of witchcraft if a child was born deformed or some other evil consequence resulted from the birth. After 1700 that occupational hazard subsided, inaugurating a golden age for midwives, since those with a good reputation could command considerable fees.

Much debate surrounds the question of whether the status of women was improving in the eighteenth century. Some historians argue that it was, especially for upper-class women. The most important evidence of progress was the increasing readiness of fathers to give their daughters a share of land, money, livestock, and, in the South, slaves. Families also more frequently negotiated a marriage settlement to protect the bride's property; and more women made wills and engaged in business.

On the other hand, the formal legal position of women changed little. They remained excluded from all aspects of public life: a woman could not vote, sit in the assembly, be a magistrate, or hold any local office. Moreover, this exclusion was not simply a legal technicality. Women were now physically excluded from public places where official business was transacted. In the seventeenth century justices had often met in private homes where procedures had been informal so that women like Anne Hutchinson could express their opinions. All this changed in the eighteenth century with the Anglicization of the law and the building of special court houses. Now wigs and gowns were worn and the whole process was conducted in such technical language that women, who lacked legal sophistry, were reduced to being mere bystanders of proceedings that only male lawyers and judges could understand. The result was to push them even further into the private world of the family. Even here they still faced the insidious consequences of the double standard.[10]

Perhaps the most reasonable conclusion is that the position of women both improved and deteriorated after 1700. Materially it undoubtedly got better, except on the frontier. Women generally did less manual labor, unless they were servants or slaves. But better living conditions were not paralleled by greater equality. Indeed some of the gains in this area made during the seventeenth century, especially in the South, were lost. As society became more complex, specialization increased, placing women firmly in the household to their detriment elsewhere.

---

[10] The argument that women were being progressively excluded from the legal process is made by Cornelia Dayton Hughes in *Women Before the Bar*.

13

European-American Religion, Education, and Culture, 1689–1760

1689	Parliament passes the Toleration Act.
1693	The College of William and Mary is chartered. John Locke publishes his *Thoughts Concerning Education*.
1701	The Society for the Propagation of the Gospel (SPG) is founded. Yale is founded to train a more orthodox New England ministry.
1704	*The Boston News-Letter* begins publication.
1706	The Anglican church is established in South Carolina. Francis Makemie forms the first presbytery in Philadelphia.
1708	The Connecticut churches adopt the Saybrook Platform.
1722	The first Anglican church in Connecticut is established.
1726	William Tennent's Log College is founded at Neshaminy.
1727	The Junto Club (later the American Philosophical Society) is founded by Benjamin Franklin in Philadelphia.
1729	Jonathan Edwards is appointed minister at Northampton.
1731	The Library Company of Philadelphia is created. The first public music concert is given in Boston.
1739	George Whitefield arrives in America.
1746	The Presbyterian College of New Jersey is established at Elizabethtown (and moved to Princeton in 1754).
1751	Franklin's Academy of Philadelphia is established.
1752–4	Lewis Hallam's theater company tours the colonies.
1754	King's College, New York (later Columbia College) is chartered.

1 RELIGION

EXCEPT FOR WORK, religion remained the most important aspect of colonial life, even in the South. Although the fires of religious conviction perhaps burned less fiercely after 1689, religion was still a crucial element in people's lives, particularly in their limited periods of relaxation.

Religion retained its hold for a number of reasons. It provided the community with a sense of purpose; it was a socially desirable habit; it still provided the best explanation of the world; and it gave people the hope of an afterlife. When existence was so harsh and its duration so uncertain, religion offered at least some comfort to most people. Not that salvation was easy; God was still seen as a vengeful deity who punished the wicked by sending them to hell. Only a minority would go to heaven.

Nevertheless, important developments had taken place. In New England the need to expand the elect had led some ministers to extend the communion. The first tentative steps in this direction had been taken by Thomas Hooker in seventeenth-century Connecticut. Toward the end of his ministry, Hooker had opened communion at Hartford to all adults of good behavior, believing that only God could judge whether someone was of the elect. At the same time he urged everyone to prepare for salvation. Hooker argued that God had not necessarily made up his mind about every individual. Grace might still be achieved if the covenant were observed.

Hooker's ideas were later adopted at Northampton, further up the Connecticut Valley, where Solomon Stoddard was the minister. Opponents like Cotton Mather understandably argued that Hooker and Stoddard were preaching a covenant of works. Nevertheless, Stoddard was not prevented from continuing these practices when the Massachusetts synod of ministers was convened in 1679 to discuss the issue of church declension. Increasingly others followed his lead, notably the Brattle Street Church in Boston. After 1740 most churches began offering communion to all who appeared of a godly disposition, effectively ending the distinction between the elect and the rest of the congregation. All that was now required in most places to take communion was a satisfactory preparatory examination before a minister.[1]

Other philosophical influences were also at work. By the start of the eighteenth century the European intelligentsia was moving toward a more rational, less theological explanation of the world, based on the scientific work of Galileo and Newton and the deductive philosophy of Locke. An intellectual revolution was in progress which even the churches could not escape. Especially important was the view that man was not the product of original sin. A benign deity had given humanity reason so that it could understand the environment and benefit therefrom. Opinion, in other words, was shifting toward those who believed in free will rather than predestination as the answer to salvation. Among

---

[1] On the abandonment of the requirement that all candidates relate their conversion experience, see Baird Tipson, "Samuel Stone's Discourse against Requiring Church Relations," *William and Mary Quarterly*, XLVI, 1989, 786–803. Stone was Hooker's deputy at Hartford. The importance of Stoddard is argued by Perry Miller in *The New England Mind from Colony to Province* (Cambridge, Mass., 1953). This view is challenged by Paul R. Lucas, *Valley of Discord: Church and Society Along the Connecticut River, 1636–1725* (Hanover, 1976). More recently Stoddard's influence has been reasserted by Philip F. Gura in "Going Mr Stoddard's Way: William Williams on Church Privileges, 1693," *William and Mary Quarterly*, XLV, 1988, 489–98.

those affected by these intellectual currents were the two Mathers. Although they continued to believe in an elect chosen through grace, they now sought to reconcile theological explanations of the world with the new insights of the natural sciences. Hence the elder Mather accepted the scientific explanation for the periodic appearance of comets, but also affirmed that they were God's way of indicating his divine purposes. Cotton Mather argued similarly for the workings of providence when he published his views on the natural world in *The Christian Philosopher* in 1721.

This intellectual approach helped narrow the gap between the Congregational and Presbyterian churches, since both subscribed to many of the new ideas. One sign of this rapprochement was the readiness of the two Mathers to attend the consecration of a Presbyterian church in Boston. Clearly the Massachusetts establishment had come a long way since the time of Robert Child. Exclusivity was now less important than standing together against the growing irreligion of the population at large.

The most dramatic closing of the gap between these two churches occurred at the Connecticut synod of 1708, when the Congregational ministry adopted the Saybrook Platform, which effectively instituted a Presbyterian form of discipline. Another sign of the retreat from congregationalism was that the ordination of the clergy was now done entirely by the laying on of ministerial hands rather than those of the laity. The ministers felt that their congregations contained too many unregenerate elements for the old practice to continue, though another reason may have been the disproportionate number of women now comprising most congregations. The result was a further distancing of the ministers from their flock.[2] The drift toward clericalism caused considerable disquiet and may have been one cause of the subsequent Great Awakening.

Officially or unofficially, most colonies continued to have an established church. In most of New England it remained the Congregational church. The Massachusetts charter of 1691 stated that "there shall be a liberty of conscience allowed in the worship of God to all Christians, except papists." This provision was interpreted to mean that each town could levy tithes for the support of a congregational minister. Liberty of conscience did not mean the right to equal treatment. Not until 1727 and 1728 were laws passed exempting Anglicans, Baptists, and Quakers from the payment of tithes for the support of the Congregational ministry. Even then it was a case of applying for an exemption rather than an automatic right.

Connecticut and New Hampshire similarly tried to exclude other religious groups. Connecticut did grant the Baptists the right to worship in 1708, but they still had to pay tithes and obtain permission from the county court to hold their services. In this hostile climate the Anglicans did not manage to form their first church there until 1722. Between 1727 and 1729 the tithe requirement was finally abated for most denominations, including Quakers, though the exemption was still hedged by various restrictions and Connecticut was far from accepting genuine toleration. The presumption remained that minority religious groups undermined the established order and ought to be discouraged.

The only province in New England not to have an established church was Rhode Island. Here the legacy of Roger Williams prevailed: all churches had to be supported by

---

[2] The view that congregationalism as a form of church government was in decline is challenged by James F. Cooper, Jr., *Tenacious of their Liberties: The Congregationalist in Colonial Massachusetts* (New York, 1999).

their congregations without the aid of a tithe. The result, as Cotton Mather sarcastically observed, was that Rhode Island had "Antinomians, Familists, Anabaptists, Antisabbatarians, Arminians, Socinians, Quakers, Ranters – everything in the world but Roman Catholics and real Christians."

Elsewhere, except for Pennsylvania and Delaware, the Anglican church superficially reigned supreme. It had prospered in the aftermath of the Glorious Revolution, securing establishment in the Carolinas, Maryland, and part of New York. One sign of its growing confidence was the founding in 1701 of the Society for the Propagation of the Gospel in Foreign Parts, the SPG, which dispatched numerous missionaries, books, and pamphlets to the colonies. The Anglicans were also helped by the desire of several groups to ingratiate themselves with the British authorities. By 1750 many Dutch in New York City had joined Trinity Church, and Huguenots acted similarly in South Carolina. By the end of the colonial period the Anglicans had built over four hundred churches, including seventy in New England. The Dutch Reformed church in contrast had barely sixty congregations, concentrated in New York and New Jersey.

The newfound confidence of the Anglicans was reflected in the building of Christ Church, otherwise known as the Old North Church in Boston in 1723. Its steeple dominated the Puritan capital, compelling the Congregational community to respond with a similar adornment for the Old South Church in 1729. Other churches were given steeples also in an attempt to dominate the skyline. But perhaps most shocking to Congregationalists was the defection to Anglicanism in 1722 of the rector of Yale, Timothy Cutler, and another leading minister, the Reverend Samuel Johnson.

Despite these successes, the Anglican church suffered from a number of weaknesses. In the South it tended to remain the religion of the planter class, who seemingly adopted it for reasons of social snobbery rather than conviction. Conversation among the congregation was usually about tobacco prices and social matters rather than the content of the sermon. Among the backcountry farmers it was unable to compete with the Baptists and Presbyterians. Although the South structured its local government around the parish vestry, the arrangement did not usually benefit the Anglican church, since many vestries contained persons belonging to other denominations.[3]

One fundamental weakness of Anglicanism was its lack of locally trained clergy. The failure to create an American bishopric contrasted sharply with the position of the other major denominations, who had no such problems in the ordination of their ministers. The decision to place the colonies under the episcopal authority of the Bishop of London in 1691 did not help, since he was too remote to exert effective leadership. Hence the church, like other institutions of the English establishment, was starved of local input and later withered like the proverbial seed in stony ground on the outbreak of the Revolution in 1776.

In addition to Rhode Island, by the eighteenth century Pennsylvania and Delaware were two other provinces not to have an established church. The Quaker conviction that religion was a matter for the individual meant that uniformity was not sought there. Only Catholics were excluded from full toleration, at the insistence of the authorities in the mother country.

---

[3] For the Baptist advance in Virginia, see Rhys Isaac, *The Transformation of Virginia, 1740–1790* (Chapel Hill, 1982).

Three churches – Presbyterian, Lutheran, and German Reformed – enjoyed major growth during the eighteenth century. There had been Presbyterians in America since the time of Robert Child, but they remained an insignificant group. Indeed, the church was not properly organized until 1706 when Francis Makemie, an Edinburgh-trained Scots-Irishman, succeeded in bringing the various English, Welsh, Scots, and Irish congregations together under a presbytery in Philadelphia. The subsequent arrival of more Scots following the Act of Union in 1707 and, more important, of the Scots-Irish from Northern Ireland after 1717, led to such remarkable growth that by the end of the colonial period Presbyterians made up the largest denomination in the middle colonies and had significant support in Virginia and the Carolinas. By then they possessed nearly four hundred congregations.

The Lutheran and German Reformed churches also flourished because of immigration, in this case from Germany. Most of the new immigrants went to Pennsylvania, though some later took the great road down the Shenandoah into the backcountry of North and South Carolina. The Lutherans, like the Church of England, subscribed to salvation through faith and similarly retained much of the former Roman liturgy. The Reformed churches, on the other hand, were strictly Calvinist and believed in purging their worship of all traces of Catholicism. By 1760 the Lutherans had around 200 churches and the German Reformed 150.

Finally, mention should be made of the German Pietist sects, the Mennonites, Amish, Dunkers, and Moravians. The Mennonites and Amish believed in the supremacy of the laity, reliance on the Gospel, and the need for personal religious experience. They were in many respects close to the Quakers. The Dunkers, on the other hand, were the German equivalent of the Baptists, believing in the need for adult immersion. All three were inward-looking, concerned about their own salvation, and were limited to a few scattered communities in eastern Pennsylvania.

The Moravians, in contrast, affected to believe in St. Paul's dictum about going out to preach to the world. Another difference was that they claimed to be part of the Lutheran church, though in reality they were much closer to the Quaker movement. Despite their outward stance, their numbers were small even in Pennsylvania, where they comprised perhaps two thousand believers. Their main proselytizing success proved to be with the native American peoples, where the simplicity of their message about the love of Christ and readiness to interpret Indian dreams made them welcome. Their most important mission was at the Delaware village of Shamokin, near the forks of the Susquehanna River.

Although religion remained the single most important activity outside work, nearly all the churches believed that their flock were sinking into irreligion and godlessness. An inquiry at the end of Queen Anne's War in Connecticut concluded that the spirit of the original covenant had "departed from us" and called for an inquiry into the state of religion.

Historians now believe that no serious declension in religious belief was taking place.[4] Nevertheless, attempts continued to be made to enhance the appeal of the churches by

---

[4] See Patricia U. Bonomi, *Under the Cope of Heaven: Religion, Society and Politics in Colonial America* (New York, 1986); and John Butler, *Awash in a Sea of Faith: Christianizing the American People* (Cambridge, Mass., 1990). Butler argues that, except for New England, America was essentially unchurched in the seventeenth century, a situation that began to change only after 1700 with the imposition of more effective discipline and organization. An increase in religious faith was also found by Christine Leigh Heyrman, *Commerce and Culture: The Maritime Communities of Colonial Massachusetts, 1690–1750* (New York, 1985).

relaxing membership requirements and adopting a more rational approach. Paradoxically these attempts at modernization were to cost the major churches dear. As sermons became ever more theoretical and philosophical in content, they provided opportunities for the Baptists to pick up converts from denominations which had lost their fire. The Baptists, as we have seen, had first arrived in the 1650s, preaching the need for adult baptism and attacking the idea of state-supported churches. Their simple style was beginning to win them many converts, especially in the South, where their ministers courageously journeyed to the farthest habitations. By the late colonial period they had perhaps three hundred congregations.

The most persuasive challenge to the major churches came from the phenomenon known subsequently as the Great Awakening, which began in a number of different places as individual ministers, mainly of a Calvinist variety, sought to revive religious feeling through evangelical methods.[5] Their efforts involved placing greater emphasis on the four gospels with their message of glad tidings and salvation, stressing the need for individual religious experience rather than formal acknowledgment of established doctrine. The Calvinist churches, with their greater concern about heaven, hell, and the millennium, were perhaps more open to such appeals. Accordingly, one of the first to adopt this method was Theodore Frelinghuysen of the Dutch Reformed church in the Raritan Valley in 1726. His success in rousing his congregation was emulated by other ministers, notably the venerable Solomon Stoddard, who was still seeking to re-create the first church of Christ at Northampton, Massachusetts. In New Jersey the evangelical style of preaching was first adopted by the Presbyterian William Tennent and his son Gilbert, a close associate of Frelinghuysen. They in turn inspired Jonathan Edwards, Stoddard's successor at Northampton, to deliver a series of sermons aimed at stopping young people from "night walking, and frequenting the tavern" and other "lewd practices." This was in 1735. Two years later Edwards claimed in his published account, *Faithful Narrative*, that five hundred persons had been saved.

But the movement's most important boost came with the arrival of George Whitefield, one of the founders of Methodism. Methodists were generally Anglicans who, like many denominations, found that their church had lost its vitality in the face of abstract theology and the defense of established privileges. They preached a new evangelical message that all men could be saved if they turned to God. In some respects the Great Awakening was a return to the old belief in salvation through faith and God's saving grace, though without the concept of an exclusive elect. Since the turn of the century most churches had veered implicitly toward a brand of Arminianism which was linked to the concept of free will and the belief that humanity could save itself.

All this the Great Awakening rejected, seeking instead to center religion once more on the heart rather than the head, on faith rather than reason, and on grace rather than good works. Even more important than its theology was the movement's style; its proponents reached out to the mass of the population by preaching in fields in what became the first mass revivals of modern times.

Whitefield himself came to America in 1739 on the first of seven tours. Beginning in Savannah, he proceeded up the coast to Philadelphia before returning via the backcountry to Charleston. In August 1740 he traveled to New England, after drawing crowds of many

---

[5] The term "Great Awakening" was first used in 1841.

thousands all along his route. In Philadelphia he impressed even the cynical Franklin with the power of his delivery, the simpleness of his message, and his ability to be heard.

Whitefield's greatest triumphs, however, came in New England, where his itinerant style of preaching was as yet hardly permitted. When pulpits were denied him, he took to the fields, followed by huge crowds. Everywhere he subjected his listeners to the certainty of hellfire and eternal damnation unless repentance was immediate and complete. Thousands wept for their sins.

Whitefield and his imitators posed a serious challenge to the established churches. The speed of their conversions and indifference to denominational boundaries inevitably caused dispute. Many ministers, recognizing the revivalists' appeal, opened their doors in the belief that their techniques would help rekindle the religious zeal of their own congregations. Others, notably Charles Chauncey of Boston's First Church, rejected this approach, feeling that such enthusiasm was of little value in awakening real spirituality and that only a proper appreciation of Christ could bring an individual real grace. Among the doubters, the need for caution was soon reinforced by the antics of James Davenport, who urged his followers to give away their worldly goods, including much of their clothing, and follow him dancing and singing through the streets of Boston and other New England towns.

The result was an internal split in many churches, notably among the Presbyterians of the middle colonies and the Congregationalists of New England, where both denominations established rival congregations in many towns. Among the Presbyterians divisions were especially bitter after Gilbert Tennent published his pamphlet *The Danger of an Unconverted Ministry*, which attacked the conservatives. The two groups came to be known as the New and Old Lights representing the radical and conservative wings respectively. Some of these rifts healed after a few years; others remained. Many New Lights subsequently found that the Baptist church met their desire for a more informal, less institutionalized religion.

The dilemma posed by the twin challenges of revivalism and orthodoxy is aptly illustrated by the career of Jonathan Edwards himself. As we have seen, Edwards, like many ministers, tried to adapt the new enthusiasm to revitalize the existing Congregational church. The theme of his most famous sermon, delivered in 1741, was "Sinners in the Hands of an Angry God" during which individual members of the congregation cried out "What shall I do to be saved?", "Oh I am going to hell." However, Edwards soon came to distrust the idea of simple conversion, emphasizing instead the old Calvinist view that God could not be bargained with. Repentance had to be deep and sustained. Being of the elect was still the key to salvation. He increasingly felt that the revivals could only create a better environment in which God's purpose might be revealed. Significantly, this attempt to return to the old standards cost Edwards his pulpit in 1750.

Some historians believe that there were social and economic factors behind these divisions, arguing that the supporters of the Great Awakening tended to be drawn from the young, the new commercial classes, or the poorer elements of the population, notably artisans, small farmers, and traders. Opponents, on the other hand, were largely drawn from the governing elite and merchant aristocracy. All three of the former desired to challenge the existing religious order, the exclusiveness of the political establishment, or the restrictive nature of the economy. Thus in Connecticut, the New Lights were strong in the growing commercial center of New London and recently settled towns of the interior. The Old Lights in contrast were dominant in the older towns of Hertford and New Haven.

However, the evidence is by no means conclusive; for while most New Lights wanted to break the existing religious mold, they were by no means in favor of political reform or the development of a market economy and trend to consumerism.[6]

The area least affected by the Great Awakening in its early stages was the South, partly because the Anglican church dominated the tidewater and partly because the backcountry was so isolated. The Anglicans were afraid of the impact that the new style of religion might have on their slaves. During the 1750s, however, Baptists like Shubal Stearns traveled through the piedmont preaching the message of salvation, so that by the end of the decade revivals were still common there long after they had ceased elsewhere. The uneven impact of the Great Awakening has led some scholars to doubt the meaningfulness of the term, suggesting that it was either an invention of later nineteenth-century writers or that it amounted to little more than a self-seeking publicity drive by its supporters.[7]

Finally, some historians have suggested a link between the Great Awakening and the American Revolution, arguing that revivalism destroyed the old deference for established institutions and made it easier for the colonists to break free from Britain politically and intellectually. Furthermore, the Calvinist emphasis on an elect and the popularity of millennial thought reinforced the colonial view that they were a special people, like the children of Israel, who would be released from their bondage. Lastly, it has been argued, the Awakening provided the first opportunity for an intercolonial exchange of ideas, thus helping the development of an American identity and desire for independence.

Certainly, the emphasis on personal salvation strengthened those elements in colonial culture which placed the individual ahead of the group and paved the way for a more democratic culture in the nineteenth century. Equally important was the revivalists' adoption of the open-air mass meeting, where not much was required for religious topics to be supplanted by political and social ones. It was this dangerous implication of revival meetings which made so many Old Lights wary of the new movement. Nevertheless, most scholars downplay the importance of the links. They stress the time lag between the Great Awakening and the Revolution, especially in New England and the middle colonies. Another point is the fragmented nature of the movement and the fact that it had an international dimension: it was not specifically an American phenomenon. Moreover, if Calvinist theology and millenarianism were so strong, they are curiously absent from the rhetoric of the

---

[6]   The suggestion that the Awakening tended to attract the young is made by Peter S. Onuf, "New Lights in New London: A Group Portrait of the Separatists, 1740–1745," *William and Mary Quarterly*, XXXVII, 1980, 627–44. The argument that it created divisions between new and old commerce is suggested by Rosalind Remer, "Old Lights and New Money: A Note on Religion, Economics and Social Order in 1740 Boston," *William and Mary Quarterly*, XLVII, 1990, 566–73. The view that the Awakening stimulated non-elite political consciousness is made by Gary B. Nash, *The Urban Crucible: Social Change, Political Consciousness, and the Origins of the American Revolution* (Cambridge, Mass, 1979); Isaac, *The Transformation of Virginia*; and Mark Valeri, *Law and Providence in Joseph Bellamy's New England: The Origins of the New Divinity in Revolutionary America* (New York, 1994). Valeri points out that class differences affected the ministry itself. Among those writers stressing the movement's wider appeal are Edwin Scott Gaustad, *The Great Awakening in New England* (New York, 1957) and James Walsh, "The Great Awakening in the First Church of Woodbury, Connecticut," *William and Mary Quarterly*, XXVII, 1971, 543–62.

[7]   For the debate over the origins of the term, see Jon Butler, "Enthusiasm Described and Decried: The Great Awakening as Interpretative Fiction," *Journal of American History*, LXIX, 1982, 305–25. The view that the Great Awakening was largely a publicity stunt is argued by Frank Lambert, *Inventing the Great Awakening* (Princeton, 1999).

DOCUMENT 19

Benjamin Franklin on George Whitefield, reprinted in Kenneth Silverman, ed., *Benjamin Franklin: The Autobiography and Other Writings* (London, 1986), 116–19.

[Whitefield was the first of many great evangelical preachers to call the American people to repent. He was influential in breaking down old sectarian barriers, appealing to people from a variety of religious persuasions. His techniques were later used by Charles Grandison Finney and other nineteenth-century revivalists.]

In 1739 arrived among us from England the Reverend Mr Whitefield who had made himself remarkable there as an itinerant preacher. He was at first permitted to preach in some of our churches; but the clergy taking a dislike to him, soon refused him their pulpits, and he was obliged to preach in the fields. The multitudes of all sects and denominations that attended his sermons were enormous, and it was a matter of speculation to me, who was one of the number, to observe the extraordinary influence of his oratory on his hearers and how much they admired and respected him, notwithstanding his common abuse of them, by assuring they were naturally "half beasts and half devils." It was wonderful to see the change soon made in the manners of our inhabitants, from being thoughtless or indifferent about religion, it seemed as if all the world were growing religious, so that one could not walk through the streets in an evening without hearing psalms sung in different families of every street. . . .

I happened soon after to attend one of his sermons, in the course of which I perceived he intended to finish with a collection and silently resolved he should get nothing from me. I had in my pocket a handful of copper money, three or four silver dollars, and five pistoles in gold. As he proceeded, I began to soften and concluded to give the coppers. Another stroke of his oratory made me ashamed of that and determined me to give the silver; and he finished so admirably that I emptied my pocket wholly into the collector's dish, gold and all. . . .

Some of Mr Whitefield's enemies affected to suppose that he would apply these collections to his own private emolument, but I who was intimately acquainted with him (being employed in printing his sermons and journals, etc.) never had the least suspicion of his integrity, but am to this day decidedly of opinion that he was in all his conduct a perfectly honest man.

Revolution, which produced political institutions that were profoundly secular in design. Finally, the idea that the New Lights were the backbone of the Revolution is not borne out by the subsequent careers of many Old Lights, notably Charles Chauncey, who took the lead in the controversy about an American episcopacy and remained a strong supporter of the patriot cause.[8]

---

[8] The thesis that the Great Awakening prepared the way ideologically for the Revolution is advanced most explicitly by Alan Heimert in *Religion and the American Mind from the Great Awakening to the Revolution* (Cambridge, Mass., 1966); William G. McLoughlin, "The Role of Religion in the Revolution," in S. G. Kurtz and

One important, though unintended, consequence of the Great Awakening was the advancement of toleration, for even New Englanders recognized that uniformity was an ideal which could no longer be attained. In other respects the movement's religious effects seem to have been limited. Within a few months of Whitefield's preaching, the population began to lose its enthusiasm. Soon the ministers were warning once more of the failings of their flock. The most insidious threat to the godly kingdom was that of materialism, the constant desire for "improving and advancing." One sign of this trend was the increasingly female composition of congregations as men turned their attentions to other pursuits. The danger seemed most obvious in the larger towns, where churchgoing was in decline.

Whatever the complaints of the ministers, the colonists remained overtly religious in their attitudes and culture. Deism, which was to threaten traditional Christianity after the Revolution, was still in its infancy, as was freemasonry. Most inhabitants attended church on Sunday to listen to sermons of an hour or more. Concern for religion continued to dominate the thoughts of legislators and the governing classes. Most colonies retained laws like Virginia's 1691 act for the "more Effectual Suppressing of Swearing, Cursing, Profaning God's Holy Name, Sabbath Abusing, Drunkeness, Fornication, and Adultery." The desire was still to effect a godly society, even if the laws were breached increasingly in both letter and spirit.

2 EDUCATION

America has a long tradition of providing free schooling for its citizens and was the first nation to do so. The origins of this achievement can be traced back to the colonial period.

We have seen that the first educational establishments, notably those in New England, were motivated by religious considerations. Persons wishing to be saved must be conversant with the word of God and therefore required the ability to read the Bible. Another consideration was the need for a trained ministry.

To these ends schools and colleges were established from an early stage in New England. A Massachusetts law of 1647, the first regulating eduction, stated that if parents neglected to instruct their children, the selectmen could apprentice them so that they could "read and understand the principles of religion and the capital laws of the country." Connecticut passed a similar law in 1650.

In smaller communities most instruction was provided in "dame" schools, where the teacher was a female member of the church. Only the larger towns could afford a qualified master to run a grammar school, and these were restricted to boys. Nevertheless, by 1700

J. H. Hutson, eds, *Essays on the American Revolution* (Chapel Hill, 1973); and J. C. D. Clark, *The Language of Liberty, 1660–1832: Political Discourse and Social Dynamics in the Anglo-American World* (Cambridge, England, 1993). The argument that the Awakening stimulated new forms of communication is advanced by Harry S. Stout, "Religion, Communications and the Ideological Origins of the American Revolution," *William and Mary Quarterly,* XXXIV, 1977, 519–41. Among those questioning the links are Butler, *Awash in a Sea of Faith,* who stresses the Revolution's secular nature; and Bonomi, *Under the Cope of Heaven,* who affirms both the time lag between the two events and the fact that the Great Awakening occurred during a period of political stability. The international connections with Europe are stressed by Perry Miller, *Errand into the Wilderness* (Cambridge, Mass., 1956), and the intercolonial impact by Richard Hofstadter, *America at 1750: A Social Portrait* (New York, 1973).

some 70 percent of men and 45 percent of women could read and write. The figures continued to climb throughout the colonial period as communities became more settled, but literacy remained essentially a religious rather than a secular quest. This is reflected in the principal book used by children after 1686, the *New England Primer*, which, apart from the alphabet and a list of syllables, mostly contained hymns, prayers, biblical stories, and accounts of Protestant martyrs. Not until the 1760s were materials like *Tom Thumb's Song Book* and Daniel Defoe's *Robinson Crusoe* used. The value of education in advancing a person's skills and livelihood was not generally accepted until after the Revolution.[9]

Outside New England, schooling was more haphazard, on account of different attitudes among the other churches. Most left the attainment of salvation to guidance by the minister rather than personal study by the individual. Such elitist views were especially prevalent in the Anglican church. The rector's sermons, services, and parish visits were thought to be sufficient guidance for the congregation, though education was seen as a legitimate part of the missionary process. The least concerned with education were the Baptists and Quakers, who relied on inspiration and spontaneity, for which neither formal training nor literacy was necessary, though this attitude started to change once these sects became more institutionalized.

In the middle and southern colonies schooling was accordingly left to individual parishes and communities. Large towns like New York and Philadelphia had schools by the end of the seventeenth century, though the emphasis remained religious. The first school in New York was established by the Dutch Reformed church, followed in 1710 by Trinity School, an SPG foundation. In Philadelphia the first educational institution was the Friends' School, founded by the Quakers in 1689, in part to maintain their tribal purity which made separate educational facilities seemingly necessary. Elsewhere, especially in the South, the only instruction available was by private tutor, though many parents did their best to pass on their skills. In reality, appreciation of the need for education had not advanced much beyond the time of Sir William Berkeley, who proudly boasted that Virginia had neither printing presses nor free schools, which he believed was a blessing, since they merely encouraged sedition and rebellion.

As the eighteenth century progressed, the need for better schools outside New England was recognized not just by the churches. This increased awareness in part reflected a growing need for clerks and other literate persons in commerce, law, and administration. The growth of education was also a response to the Enlightenment, as the more affluent began to sense that they could improve themselves materially as well as morally if they were educated.

These factors resulted in greater efforts to provide schooling. In Maryland attempts were made in 1723 to set up county schools for the poor, albeit unsuccessfully, while in the Charleston area a number of "free" schools were established where only the better off had to pay. This increase in schools in turn led more people to contemplate a career in teaching, which had now become accepted as a separate vocation from the ministry, though

---

[9]   The traditional view was that America's commitment to mass education laid the foundations for its phenomenal progress in the past two hundred years. See Bernard Bailyn, *Education in the Forming of American Society: Needs and Opportunities for Study* (Chapel Hill, 1960). For the argument that religion remained the basis of education, see Kenneth Lockridge, *Literacy in Colonial New England: An Enquiry into the Social Context of Literacy in the Early Modern West* (New York, 1974).

Plate 29 "A Westerly View of the Colledges . . ." (Harvard College), attributed to Paul Revere. Courtesy of the Essex Institute, Salem, Massachusetts.

many people continued to practice both. Another aid to educational expansion was an increase in the number of legacies left to schools. The consequence was a respectable increase in literacy even in Virginia, where perhaps two-thirds of males could read documents and sign their names by 1760, though an ability to read did not necessarily mean an ability to write. Pennsylvania had roughly the same literacy level.

The figure for women's literacy is less definite, but it was certainly lower, perhaps only half that of males. Since women could not be ministers or participate in public life, the benefits of educating them were less apparent. An ability to read was all that was required except for the daughters of the elite, who required additional social graces. Literacy among them was undoubtedly aided by the new form of literature, the novel. Especially influential was Samuel Richardson's *Clarissa*, which took the form of an exchange of letters between two young women.

We have already seen that New England was also at the forefront of higher education with the founding of Harvard in 1636 to provide a trained ministry. The college was never intended solely as a seminary, for in addition to theological topics, instruction was offered in "good literature, arts and sciences." Nevertheless, until the end of the colonial period any male wishing to graduate in anything other than classics, divinity, and philosophy had to journey across the Atlantic for his education. The most popular subjects were medicine in Edinburgh and law in London.

Life at Harvard was very formal. Freshmen were not allowed to wear gowns or carry canes, and all undergraduates had to doff their caps on passing the president's house. They were similarly required to salute at fifty yards when meeting the president in the street and had to acknowledge professors and tutors at forty and twenty-five yards respectively.

Harvard remained the only institution of higher learning in America for fifty years until the College of William and Mary was established at Williamsburg in 1693 as a belated response by the Anglican community there to the need for a trained ministry. The lack of a higher institution to prepare Anglican clergy had hampered the Episcopalian cause, although with no bishop in America, candidates still had to cross the Atlantic to be ordained. The first president and founding father was a Scottish Episcopalian, James Blair, who always intended William and Mary to be a college as well as a seminary to cater for the needs of the Virginian planters.

Blair's friendship with John Locke was reflected in the college's curriculum, which provided for the study of medicine and law in addition to the more traditional classics and theology. In 1717 the first chair in natural philosophy and mathematics was created. But though generously endowed, the college languished because of internal squabbles. A serious fire also destroyed most of the main building in 1705. As a result some planters continued to send their sons to England for their education, especially in law.

By the turn of the eighteenth century, Harvard had begun to adopt more liberal attitudes in religious matters, reflecting the growth of Arminian views. Not everyone welcomed this trend, and as a result Yale was founded in 1701 to produce ministers of a more orthodox stance. The curriculum at the new college was similar to that of Harvard in the previous century, having a heavy emphasis on classics, divinity, and philosophy. In due course Yale, too, found that it could not divorce itself from the intellectual currents which were sweeping Europe. By 1760 it was little different from its rival.

The middle colonies had to wait longer for an institution of higher learning. New York lacked a single dominant religious group, while Quaker Pennsylvania felt no need of one, having no trained ministry. The Quakers in any case laid more emphasis on the "university of life," as Benjamin Franklin termed it. However, as the Presbyterians grew in strength, they became increasingly eager to have some institution to train their ministers. A few candidates attended Harvard, and in 1726 William Tennent established a "log college" at Neshaminy in Bucks County, Pennsylvania, which trained some twenty ministers before closing its doors through lack of funding. Accordingly, in 1746 a group of New Light Presbyterians, led by Jonathan Dickinson, a Yale-trained New Englander, with the enthusiastic support of the Neshaminy-trained ministers, founded the College of New Jersey. Initially this operated from Dickinson's house in Elizabethtown, before moving on his death to Newark. Finally, in 1754 new premises were established at Princeton, though the college was not known by that name until the 1760s. From the beginning it was interdenominational; indeed, its third president was Jonathan Edwards. And like Harvard, Yale, and William and Mary, Princeton had many students who were not candidates for the ministry.

Meanwhile, under Benjamin Franklin's guidance, in 1751 the Academy of Philadelphia had been founded, with the distinction of being the first secular institution to impose no religious test for admission. Initially it was designed to be only a school, but in 1755 a three-year undergraduate program was added, after which the title was changed to the Academy and College of Philadelphia. From the beginning its aim was to increase knowledge as an end in itself. As Franklin argued in his initial appeal, this was the surest way to advance "the happiness both of private families and of commonwealths." Franklin was heavily influenced by his Quaker surroundings and by the educational philosophy of Locke. The academy therefore placed a heavy emphasis on what was useful. Among the proposed subjects were arithmetic, accounts, geometry, and astronomy. Also included were English

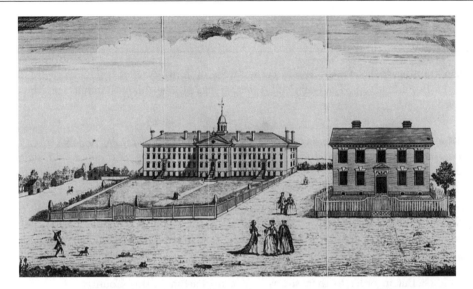

Plate 30   College of New Jersey (later Princeton University), engraving by Henry
Dawkins, 1764. A northwest prospect of Nassau hall with a front view of
the president's house. Department of Rare Books and Special Collections,
Princeton University Library.

and history, to show "the beauty and usefulness of virtue"; natural history and botany, to
contribute to the "improvement of agriculture"; and mechanics, "by which weak men perform such wonders, labour is saved, [and] manufactures expedited." The academy also taught
Greek and Latin, which were useful in the study of divinity, law, medicine, and modern
languages.[10] Franklin's academy has often been seen as the forerunner of the future public
school system of the United States. It was certainly no coincidence that the University of
Pennsylvania was later to be the first institution of higher learning in 1765 to have a
medical school.

Lastly, in 1754 New York obtained its first institution of higher learning with the
establishment of King's College. The Anglicans had tried to charter a college in 1746 but
had been prevented by the Presbyterians in the assembly, where neither group was sufficiently dominant to dictate its wishes. When King's College finally opened, therefore, it
was effectively a nondenominational institution. Its curriculum was centered on "the learned
languages" and "liberal arts and sciences." Entrants had to be able to read and write, have
basic arithmetic, and possess a good knowledge of Greek and Latin. It, too, added a medical
school in 1767.

By 1760, then, six colonies had institutions of higher learning, five of them in the
North. This distribution reflected the concentration of dissenting churches there rather
than a northern commitment to education itself, though urbanization may also have been
a factor. All were exclusively male. An increasing number of students no longer intended

---

[10]   For the full text, see Albert H. Smyth, ed., *The Writings of Benjamin Franklin*, 10 vols (New York, 1905–7),
II, 386–96.

DOCUMENT 20

On training to be a lawyer: the early career of John Adams, 1758, reprinted in L. H. Butterfield, ed., *The Diary and Autobiography of John Adams* (Cambridge, Mass., 1961), I, 54–61.

[The law was just beginning to become more professional when John Adams set out to be a lawyer after graduating from Harvard. Before this anyone who could read, write, and had a smattering of knowledge about the subject could argue a case before the justices of the county and superior courts.]

Went in the morning to Mr Gridleys, and asked the favour of his Advice what Steps to take for an Introduction to the Practice of Law in this Country. He answered "get sworn" [i.e. at the bar] . . .

ADAMS: But in order to that, sir, as I have no Patron in this County.

GRIDLEY: I will recommend you to the Court. Mark the Day the Court adjourns to in order to make up Judgements. Come to Town that Day, and in the mean time I will speak to the Bar for the Bar must be consulted, because the Court always inquire, if it be with the Consent of the Bar.

Then Mr Gridley inquired what Method of Study I had pursued, what Latin Books I read, what Greek, what French. What I had read upon Rhetorick. Then he took his Common Place Book and gave me Lord Hale's Advice to a Student of the Common Law, and when I had read that, he gave me Lord Chief Justice Reeves' Advice to his Nephew, in the Study of the Common Law. Then he gave me a Letter from Dr Dickins, Regius Professor of Law at the University of Cambridge, to him, pointing out a Method of Studying the Civil Law. Then he turned to a Letter he wrote himself to Judge Lightfoot, Judge of the Admiralty in Rhode Island, directing a method of Studying the Admiralty Law. Then Mr Gridley run a comparison be-tween the business and studies of a Lawyer or Gentleman of the Bar, in England, and that of one here. A Lawyer in this Country must study Common Law and Civil Law, and natural Law, and Admiralty Law, and must do the duty of a Counsellor, a Lawyer, an Attorney, a Solicitor, and even of a Scrivener, so that the Difficulties of the Profession are much greater here than in England . . .

I have a few Pieces of Advice to give you Mr Adams. One is to pursue the Study of the Law rather than the Gain of it. Pursue the Gain of it enough to keep out of the Briars, but give your main attention to the study of it.

The next is not to marry early. For an early Marriage will obstruct your Improve-ment, and in the next Place, twill involve you in Expence.

Another thing is not to keep much Company. For this application of a Man who aims to be a lawyer must be incessant. His Attention to his Books must be constant, which is inconsistent with keeping much Company.

to be ministers, however, having more secular ends in view. For a growing segment of society, saving the world was no longer a primary aim. But although all the colleges were broadening their curriculum, they still only partially met the needs of professions like law and medicine. Nor did the situation change dramatically in the 1760s. Of the three new institutions of higher education founded before the Revolution, two – Rutgers (Dutch Reformed) and Brown (Baptist) – were overtly religious; and Dartmouth, though affecting to be interdenominational, provided a traditional curriculum based on Christianity and the classics. Until the Revolution, those who could not afford to study in Europe almost all had to graduate from a colonial college and then practice with someone already qualified in the profession (see Document 20).

3 LIBRARIES, LITERATURE, AND THE PRESS

The earliest libraries in America belonged to private individuals and were relatively small and few in number. The first collection of a public nature was set up in Boston's town house and comprised mainly the books of Robert Keayne, a merchant who died in 1656 and bequeathed his collection to the town. Most of its stock was of a religious nature.

Book collecting, like education, was motivated largely by religion in its early stages. At the turn of the eighteenth century Dr Thomas Bray, one of the founders of the SPG, established several libraries, primarily for the benefit of the Anglican clergy. Among the most notable were those at Annapolis, Maryland, and Charleston, South Carolina.

As the century progressed the demand for more secular collections grew, leading to the founding of the Library Company of Philadelphia in 1731, in which development the indefatigable Franklin played a prominent role. It was funded by a subscription of forty shillings and prominent among its early purchases were various works on science. The scheme proved sufficiently successful for Charleston to establish a similar library in 1748, followed by New York City in 1754. The joining fee for the latter was £5, with an annual subscription thereafter of ten shillings. The New York Society Library, as it was called, inherited a collection of books originally donated by Bray, but it quickly set about expanding its selection to meet the changing tastes. A new form of literature, the novel, proved popular, especially works by Richardson and Smollett. By 1760 some twenty such libraries had been established.

Outside the main towns, people had to buy their own books. As they were relatively expensive, purchasers were limited to the clergy, lawyers, and the small but increasing number of people who affected to believe in the enlightened mind, not least the Virginia plantocracy. Among the more notable collections were those of Robert Carter, who had twelve hundred volumes at his death in 1732, and Cotton Mather, whose collection amounted to some three thousand volumes when he died in 1727.

By mid-century books were beginning to be classified into sections. Hence a good subscription library would contain the poetry of Pope, Dryden, Milton, and Spencer; the plays of Shakespeare, Molière, Congreve, and Addison; the novels of Smollett, Richardson, Fielding, and Sterne; and the political and philosophical works of Montesquieu, Voltaire, Locke, Sidney, Swift, Bolingbroke, and Hume. Also indispensable was a good selection of the classics: Cicero, Tacitus, Livy, Seneca, Aristotle, Terence, Virgil, and Homer; the historical works of Robertson, Hume, and Clarendon; and the scientific works of Buffon and

Newton. Finally, no library was considered complete without some sermons and the legal works of Coke, Bracton, and Fortescue.

Sadly, few of these books were published in the colonies, though an increasing number of printing presses were being established. The first press opened in Boston in 1638, but it was mainly for official business. Most of its other publications were of a religious nature, for example, the Bay Psalm Book in 1640. Not until 1678 was a second printing press authorized, and its literary output too was mainly religious, though it did print the poetry of Anne Bradstreet. One literary genre to attain popularity in New England was the narratives of those captured by the American Indians in the war of 1675, the most notable being that of Mary Rowlandson, which appeared in 1682.

Elsewhere the development of printing was considerably slower. Nevertheless, by the eighteenth century nearly all the colonies had at least one press for producing official documents, while the larger provinces had several. In 1738 the first non-English press appeared in Pennsylvania to cater for the colony's German community.

Relatively few books were written by Americans before 1760, and even fewer were actually published there, though the number was growing. In 1702 Cotton Mather produced his *Magnalia Christi Americana* in Boston. This work consisted of a history of New England, supposedly from the ecclesiastical point of view of explaining divine providence, although it included most of the key events concerning the colony's settlement and expansion. Three years later Robert Beverley Jr. produced his *History and Present State of Virginia*, a more secular account. This work was the first to be written from a consciously American point of view. The newfound pride of the Virginian elite led the Reverend Hugh Jones to produce a similar volume in 1726, entitled the *Present State of Virginia*. Elsewhere the desire to understand the American environment stimulated John Lawson to write his *New Voyage to Carolina* in 1707, Cadwallader Colden to produce his *History of the Five Indian Nations* in 1727, while in 1757 William Smith published his *History of the Province of New York*. By then most provinces had seen some work published about their history or physical environment.

Of course not all that was written found a publisher. Among the items not printed were several notable works from the seventeenth century: William Bradford's *History of Plymouth Plantation*; John Winthrop's *Journal*; and the poetry of Edward Taylor. Others, like William Byrd's *Diary*, were written solely for personal amusement. All had to wait until long after the colonial period for publication.

Apart from works of a religious, historical, or topographical nature, the most regularly printed work was the almanac. This useful compendium of information about the political and physical world was an indispensable tool for the emerging professional and mercantile classes. The most famous was Franklin's *Poor Richard's Almanac*, which first appeared in 1732, though there were a number of competing publications.

The first weekly newspaper in the colonies was the *Boston News-Letter*, founded in 1704. The second was the *Boston Gazette*, established in 1719. That same year marked the appearance of Philadelphia's first newspaper, the *American Mercury*, on which the youthful Franklin was employed. New York followed in 1725 with the *New York Gazette*, while Charlestonians saw the appearance of the *South Carolina Gazette* in 1732. By 1760 Boston had four newspapers and five other printing establishments; Philadelphia, two newspapers and three other presses; New York, three newspapers; and Charleston, two. Other newspapers were published in Williamsburg, Annapolis, Germantown, New Haven, New London,

Newport, and Portsmouth. The distribution, if not the sale, of newspapers was assisted by the establishment of a post office in 1710, which had a network of some sixty-five offices by 1770, serving all thirteen continental colonies.

Most of these newspapers were simple sheets, containing advertisements for the sale of goods and the arrival and departure times of ships. News usually took the form of letters from merchants or correspondents overseas, which the papers shamefully reproduced from one another without acknowledgment. However, when Franklin and his partner David Hall took over Pennsylvania's second newspaper, the *Pennsylvania Gazette*, in 1729, they announced that they would provide more coverage of public events, history, diplomatic affairs, and matters of cultural and scientific interest. Their model was the London *Spectator*, which was popular on both sides of the Atlantic. Even so there was no such thing as editorial comment, let alone investigative journalism. One attempt to do so was that by William Livingston, John Morin Scott, and William Smith in the New York *Independent Reflector* in which they declared their intention "to oppose superstition, priestcraft, tyranny, servitude, public mismanagement and dishonesty in office." Their paper lasted barely one year, from 1752 to 1753, though Livingston produced a number of similar individual items under various titles. If individuals wanted to criticize someone publicly, they resorted to the anonymous pamphlet to avoid legal repercussions.

Otherwise, the only publisher to breach this convention before 1760 was John Peter Zenger, a German printer who had come to New York in 1720 and had served an apprenticeship with William Bradford, the founder of the *New York Gazette*. In 1733 Zenger established his own paper, the *New York Weekly Journal*, which printed letters criticizing Governor Cosby. Zenger was soon arrested and charged with seditious libel. Under English law any derogatory statement, true or false, which undermined the government in the affections of the people was considered seditious. Andrew Hamilton, a prominent Philadelphia lawyer, was unable to defend Zenger on a plea of truth, but he incidentally produced enough material against Cosby to have his client acquitted before a sympathetic jury. Although the case is usually seen as a landmark in press freedom, its real significance was to illustrate the difficulty of obtaining a conviction from a jury for libel where the libel appeared true and the plaintiff was unpopular. This was in part because attitudes were changing in the colonies, for, as Franklin commented, a man who could not express his thoughts was not in a position to improve himself. Wisdom and freedom of expression were inseparable. By the 1750s even officials like Cadwallader Colden were conceding that the free exchange of ideas could assist government in avoiding rash and ill-judged decisions.

4 SCIENCE AND THE ARTS

The eighteenth century was an age of science, and upper-class Americans were keen students. Living in a new world, they were especially eager to understand their environment, not least because they found many of the traditional religious explanations no longer convincing. In this context the Enlightenment in Europe, with its stress on understanding the universe through analysis and observation, proved an important influence.

Philadelphia was perhaps the most important center of science and technology, its position reflecting the Quaker belief in reason and the notion that God had given man his intellect to understand his environment. Equally, it was no coincidence that from 1743

Plate 31 Portrait of Benjamin Franklin at the age of fifty-four, engraving by James McArdell after Benjamin Wilson. Benjamin Franklin Collection, Sterling Memorial Library, Yale University.

Philadelphia was the home of the American Philosophical Society, the first colonial institution dedicated to scientific enquiry. Five of its first nine trustees were Quakers or had been members of the Society of Friends.

The most famous of these, was Benjamin Franklin, though of course he was not a Quaker. He was a New Englander by birth but had left Boston when still a youth. In many respects Franklin personified the embryonic American, being inquisitive, active, ingenious, and optimistic. It was Franklin who was instrumental in getting the society started. He conducted numerous experiments himself, notably those in which he identified electricity's positive and negative qualities. Out of his observations came the lightning conductor, a useful invention which reduced the risk of fire. This was the attraction of science: the production of useful gadgets which would improve the quality of life. Later, Franklin helped devise a stove which required less air, burned more slowly, and gave out greater heat, thus making homes less draughty and easier to keep warm.[11]

Another Philadelphia Quaker interested in science was James Logan, who helped classify the flora and fauna of America. Also resident in the city was John Bartram, who in 1728 established the first botanical garden and later traveled throughout the continent collecting the plants of North America. It was in Philadelphia, too, that David Rittenhouse, a clock maker, subsequently built the first orrery, or model for explaining the planetary system.

Of course scientific enquiry was not restricted to Philadelphia. Paradoxically Boston, the home of Puritanism, was not without its cognoscenti. We have seen that many ministers accepted the new scientific revolution to keep their theology relevant, and some even engaged in scientific enquiry themselves. Increase Mather, in cooperation with Dr Zabdiel Boylston, experimented with inoculation after learning of its use in Africa from his slave Onesimus, persuading some inhabitants of Boston to adopt the practice during a smallpox epidemic in 1721.[12] In general New Englanders excelled in the more theoretical sciences. Thomas Robie identified the nature of a meteor. John Winthrop IV, the Harvard professor of mathematics and natural philosophy, worked on sunspots, the transit of Venus, the lunar eclipse, and Halley's comet.

All these individuals recognized the desirability of a forum in which to exchange their ideas. One such was of course the Royal Society in London, to which no fewer than eighteen Americans belonged during the colonial period. Colonials contributed substantially to the society's published transactions, and the establishment of an American post office in 1710 facilitated the dissemination of its ideas. Traveling across the Atlantic, however, was not feasible on a regular basis.

Accordingly, in 1727 Franklin and several others established the Junto Club in Philadelphia. This group, which helped John Bartram to continue his observations about the botanical nature of the American continent, later expanded to become the American Philosophical Society. Elsewhere, several New Yorkers attempted to establish a similar project in 1748 with their Society for the Promotion of Useful Knowledge. Despite its title it was designed to complement the activities of the Royal Society, though it indicated that later American tendency to view all knowledge as potentially useful. In the event it failed to survive. So too did the American Philosophical Society. Before 1760 colonial science was not yet ready to stand on its own feet. Its practitioners remained essentially field workers for scientists in Europe, on whom they depended for the manufacture of accurate instruments and the publication of learned materials. The American Philosophical Society was only reestablished on a permanent basis in 1768.

The fine arts meanwhile had barely begun to emerge. Indeed, their absence was inevitable in a society which was still establishing itself and had only a tiny leisured class to

---

[11] However, the links between science and technology remained relatively weak. See Brooke Hindle, *The Pursuit of Science in Revolutionary America* (Chapel Hill, 1956).

[12] The experiment caused considerable controversy at the time, since most people believed that it would spread the disease. These fears subsided only when Boylston subsequently demonstrated that about 15 percent of the naturally infected died, compared with 2.4 percent of those inoculated.

support such activities. No distinguished painters appeared until after 1760. Not that portraiture was unpopular before then. Simple pictures were commissioned, but the artists were invariably craftsmen, perhaps engravers or house painters, who practiced portraiture to enhance their incomes. However, several artists emerged in the 1760s who were to win recognition at the highest level, notably John Singleton Copley, Benjamin West, and John Wilson Peale. Significantly all had to travel to Europe to complete their development.

Classical music was also in its infancy. Some concerts were arranged in the principal towns, where there were sufficient violinists, cellists, flautists, and other instrumentalists to perform the works of composers such as Handel, Bach, and Vivaldi. The first formal concert of classical music took place in Boston, in 1731. By the 1750s New York had a regular series of subscription concerts. The performers were almost all amateurs, there being as yet no professional class of musicians.

Equally undeveloped was the theater. Until the 1700s going to a play was considered the equivalent of visiting a brothel and most colonies banned both forms of entertainment. Even in the eighteenth century many considered theater immoral, but the growing secularization and sophistication of the colonial upper classes induced some desire to see the works of great dramatists performed. Previously people could only read these works, though the magistracy occasionally allowed them to be enacted in some form.

The first permanent theater was established in Williamsburg in 1716 when two dancers, Charles and Mary Stagg, obtained permission to erect a stage. Here they produced a number of plays for several years. Slowly other groups emerged, mostly of a private or amateur nature. The most popular productions were George Farquhar's *The Recruiting Officer* and Joseph Addison's *Cato*. By the 1730s all the major cities had hosted some kind of theater. In 1749 a group of actors led by Thomas Kean and Walter Murray toured the towns, performing works by Shakespeare, Congreve, Dryden, Addison, and Farquhar. Another theatrical group from London, led by Lewis Hallam, came to the colonies in 1752 and stayed for several years. By this time Shakespeare had become the most popular playwright. No play, however, had yet been written or performed by a colonial author, though Robert Hunter, while governor of New York, had written one entitled *Androborous: A Biographical Farce*. In reality the time was not ripe for colonial theater, and the climate did not change until after the Revolution.

5 POPULAR CULTURE

Buying books, attending college, joining learned societies, and going to classical concerts were the enjoyments of the few. Most colonists had neither the time nor the money for these activities, for few breaks could be taken in the incessant routine of earning a living. Survival necessarily came first.

For most people the sabbath remained the most important cultural focus, being the one time when some measure of relaxation was possible. The commandment to rest on the seventh day was generally observed, though livestock still had to be cared for and other light tasks done which had been neglected during the week. However, by the end of the colonial period strict observance was breaking down in favor of a more recreational sabbath.

Culture centered largely on the family. In winter people had to make their own entertainment once the sun had gone down. Some families would read the Bible. Others would take to storytelling. Singing was popular and often accompanied by a fiddle, banjo, or some other crude instrument like a flute. When space allowed dancing may also have occurred, but most families would usually devote themselves to needlework or other indoor tasks. The daily grind rarely stopped.

In summer social activity increased, the most important occasions being the markets, fairs, and meetings of the county court. In the South these three events were often combined. The courts gave planters a chance to discuss business and traders to exhibit their goods, while those wishing to see an attorney could do so at the same time. Inevitably such occasions also attracted traveling showmen. Bear baiting and cock fighting were common, drinking at the local tavern more so. Local groups of musicians invariably gathered, and the high-spirited could dance. Some of the gentry might also arrange a horse race on which bystanders could bet.

Northern court meetings tended be more decorous, though entertainments were customary at ceremonies like the installation of a governor or celebration of the king's birthday. Here again fringe activities would be organized so that those attending could combine business with pleasure. The monthly exercising of the militia was a similar chance for socializing as the women and children watched their menfolk go through their drill.

For town dwellers the opportunities for social activities were obviously greater, especially at night. Unlike country folk, who retired to their firesides and beds once the light had gone, the town dweller came alive in the evenings. Artisans and laborers would go to their taverns, gentlemen to their clubs to talk about the world or play cards. Among these clubs were the first Masonic lodges, notably Philadelphia in 1730 and Boston, Charleston, and Savannah shortly afterwards. Tea and coffee houses were also popular in the larger commercial centres.

The most ubiquitous places of recreation, however, were the taverns and inns in every community along the eastern seaboard. As was noted in chapter 4, such places earlier had been limited to the provision of refreshment and accommodation only. Now there was a new emphasis on entertainment as well. Establishments varied according to size and clientele. Those aimed at the upper classes provided newspapers, billiard tables, and rooms for private meetings. Lower-class establishments were more likely to provide pugilistic contests and covert gaming. But all provided alcoholic beverages, which was one of the few pleasures available on a daily basis. Providing consumption was not excessive, most men (if not women) saw no contradiction between going to church in the morning and visiting the tavern at night. Taverns provided men with an opportunity to socialize, talk business, and increasingly discuss political issues after 1760. It has been suggested that the extension of tavern life in the eighteenth century contributed to the democratization of colonial society and politics.[13]

One activity which occupied the wealthier classes was the display of fashionable attire. According to William Smith, by the 1750s New York had an elegant air; the young ladies promenaded on the now well-paved streets or attended concerts, while the men dressed for their coffee houses or clubs. Balls were popular in the South, where the existence of more lavish houses enabled the gentry to accommodate their guests for a prolonged entertainment.

---

[13] For the impact of taverns on colonial society, see especially David W. Conroy, *In Public Houses: Drink and the Revolution of Authority in Colonial Massachusetts* (Chapel Hill, 1995); and Peter Thompson, *Rum, Punch and Revolution: Tavern Going and Public Life in Eighteenth Century Philadelphia* (Philadelphia, 1999).

Two recreations enjoyed by most men were hunting and fishing. Here the common people had an advantage not enjoyed in Britain: the hated game laws did not operate and all could legally engage in such activities, provided that they did not trespass on someone's property. Apart from providing sport, such activities also yielded food, no mean consideration.

By 1750 horse racing had become sufficiently popular for the wealthier gentry to start breeding thoroughbreds so that races could be held over longer distances than the traditional quarter-mile sprint. This led to the marking of dedicated tracks and the forming of jockey clubs to establish proper rules. Fencing was another sport to adopt a formal code, at least among the gentry. In contrast, for pugilistic entertainment, the lower orders preferred wrestling or fist fighting, where there were few or no rules. As always, rank and wealth determined the recreational activities of each person.

Otherwise, sport in the modern sense was almost unknown. Groups of youngsters or adults might engage in improvised contests with a ball or other object, but organized games played according to fixed rules had to await a time when society had more leisure and wealth. As almost everyone depended on constant physical exertion for their livelihood, few wished to exhaust themselves in their few periods of relaxation by doing something which was, by their standards, totally unproductive.

6 ARCHITECTURE: THE ANGLICIZATION OF TASTE

The first six decades of the eighteenth century saw a steady improvement in the quality of housing, reflecting the rising standard of living which the majority of the white population enjoyed. Wood was still the principal element of construction. In the houses of the gentry brick was increasingly used, not only for chimneys and foundations but also for walls. Brick was also favored for most dwellings in the towns, where fire was a significant hazard.

The houses of the elite were now more elaborate. The fashion favored a colonial Georgian style based on British architectural styles, which were in turn based on the columns, friezes, pediments, and other decorative devices popular in ancient Greece and Rome. Generally square or rectangular (twice as long as high), the houses of the gentry consisted of two main floors and an attic. The windows were much larger and the ceilings higher than the structures of the seventeenth century, giving the houses an airy feeling. At the front of the typical house was a large hall, perhaps with a colonnaded entrance, from which doors led to four large rooms. These rooms were reserved primarily for eating and entertaining, though one of them was likely to be a library. The kitchens and other domestic offices were usually located in an adjacent block or adjoining the rear. The bedrooms would be on the second floor and would be reached from the hall by a broad staircase, while the smaller, third-floor rooms accommodated the children and their nurse. Finally, formal gardens now surrounded the house to enhance its appearance, emphasizing through symmetry the triumph of civilization over the wilderness.

Middle-ranking farmers or self-employed craftsmen also lived in rectangular houses, consisting of two main rooms on the first floor and two bedrooms between the eaves, with a lean-to kitchen at the rear. The typical construction was clapboard over a timber frame. In towns like Boston, however, where land prices were on the rise, tenement-style buildings were beginning to be built, usually with a return at the rear to accommodate a kitchen and storehouse. Most had glass windows, though with smaller panes and overall dimensions than in the houses of the gentry.

Plate 32 Thomas Hancock House, Boston, 1736. Courtesy of the Massachusetts Historical Society, Boston.

Only on the frontier did housing still reflect the earlier period. By now the Scandinavian log cabin had become almost universal there, being the sturdiest and easiest building to construct.[14] Such homes merely had shutters for windows and dirt for flooring, and most were quite small, comprising one or two small rooms in an area of between three hundred and six hundred square feet. As they had to shelter several persons, hovel, not house, was perhaps the appropriate description.

Important improvements were also made to the interiors of colonial housing in the period 1700–60. The better dwellings no longer used crude boards for their inner walls; these were now either paneled or plastered and after 1750 had a decorative covering of wallpaper. Except in the homes of poor and backcountry families, furniture, too, was more elegant. The trestle tables and stools of the seventeenth century had been replaced by Queen Anne drop-leaf tables, sideboards, and chairs, all with matching cabriole legs and pad feet. Beds were raised from the floor, those in the better houses usually having four posters to provide curtaining protection from the cold. By the end of the colonial period the elaborately carved designs of Thomas Chippendale, often with a Chinese motif, were becoming popular. Few could afford to import their furniture, but there was no want of local cabinetmakers to turn out finished items which showed a high degree of skill and knowledge of fashion.

Perhaps the most spectacular architectural development was the transformation of public buildings, which were increasingly built of brick, usually in the Palladian style of

---

[14] Numerous claims have been made for the origin of the log cabin. Among the more recent is that by Terry G. Jordan and Matti Kaups, *The American Backwoods Frontier: An Ethnic and Ecological Interpretation* (Baltimore, 1989), in which they argue that the type of cabin built in colonial America originated with settlers from the Karelia region of Finland, who came to settle the colony of New Sweden in the late 1630s.

Plate 33   Faneuil Hall, Boston, 1742. Courtesy of the Massachusetts Historical Society, Boston.

William and Mary. Among the most distinctive were the state house in Philadelphia, erected between 1733 and 1735, Faneuil Hall in Boston, begun in 1740 and completed in 1742, and the governor's palace and College of William and Mary in Williamsburg. Some churches and numerous courthouses also adopted a similar design, especially in the South.

Traditionally, the colonial period has been viewed as a time when the colonies were becoming distinctively American. More recently some historians have suggested that in reality the colonies were becoming anglicized as the century progressed.[15]

It is true that when the colonists first came over during the seventeenth century they were clearly English in their cultural attitudes. It was the strange environment, however, which compelled them to adapt their dress, food, housing, and farming methods. Moreover, a landscape full of unfamiliar animals and potentially hostile native inhabitants caused the colonists to change their language and adopt new words used by the American Indians.

---

[15]   The thesis of anglicization is associated with the work of John M. Murrin, *Anglicizing an American Colony: The Transformation of Provincial Massachusetts* (Unpublished Ph.D. thesis, Yale University, 1966). Other works in this genre are David Grayson Allen, *In English Ways: The Movement of Societies and the Transferral of English Local Law and Custom to Massachusetts Bay in the Seventeenth Century* (Chapel Hill, 1981); and T. H. Breen, "An Empire of Goods: The Anglicization of Colonial America, 1690–1776," *Journal of British Studies*, XXV, 1986, 467–99. See also Richard L. Bushman, "American High-Style and Vernacular Cultures," in Jack P. Greene and J. R. Pole, eds, *Colonial British America: Essays in the New History of the Early Modern Era* (Baltimore, 1984), 345–83. The reason for this trend is not clear but most likely stems from the changing demographic structure of America. In a period of high immigration, the majority community is tempted to reaffirm its cultural roots.

Plate 34 Governor's Palace, Williamsburg, Virginia. Photographed by Gregory Scott Godwin.

Finally, their standard of living seemingly deteriorated as they battled for survival and mastery over this environment. They still felt English, however, and wherever possible they grew the crops and built the houses with which they had been familiar at home.

With the advent of the eighteenth century, colonists in the more settled areas were becoming more affluent and, as a result, eager to acquire the better things in life. They therefore bought English books or copied London furniture styles. This inclination was natural. England was a land of five million people in 1700, whereas America still contained barely three hundred thousand. The mother country had a sophistication which the colonists wanted to imitate. In this respect, incidentally, they were no different from their counterparts at home, for England itself was in the throes of a consumer revolution, in which the emerging middle classes were beginning to ape the fashions, dress, and lifestyles of the aristocracy.

Indeed more affluent Americans were quick to copy another transatlantic fashion, namely observance of the new code of gentility. This began in the royal households of

Europe before spreading to the gentry and commercial classes. Among its requirements was politeness of speech, especially the use of "please" and "thank you." Gentility also required individuals to be clean and their surroundings to be neat. Particular attention was given to improving eating habits through the use of cutlery, plates, chairs, and linen rather than hands, bowls, and stools, which latter methods inevitably led to stained and smelly clothing. The aim everywhere was to elevate and refine in order to make a pleasing impression.[16]

On the other hand, while looking instinctively to England to replenish their cultural roots, many colonists were third- or fourth-generation settlers. They spoke American English and had a distinct accent. Increasingly they sent their offspring to local academies, modeled on English institutions but inevitably distinctive in what they taught. The virtues of a colonial education were first expressed when students at the College of William and Mary asserted, at a May Day address in 1699, that a Virginian education was to be preferred even to one in England. This sentiment might have been an overstatement at the time, but it was a portent of things to come.

---

[16]   The doyen of refinement was Lord Chesterfield, though his *Letters of Philip Dormer Stanhope, Earl of Chesterfield to His Son*, were not published until 1774. See Richard Bushman, *The Refinement of America: Persons, Houses, Cities* (New York, 1992).

14

African-American Society and Culture, 1689–1760

1619	The first Africans arrive in Virginia.
1638	Slavery is first mentioned in the laws of Maryland.
1662	A Virginia law declares that children take the status of their mother.
1691	South Carolina passes an act for the better ordering of slaves.
1699	Free African-Americans are required to leave Virginia.
1704	South Carolina allows the arming of slaves in time of war.
1705	Virginia institutes a slave code.
1712	Nine whites are killed by slaves in New York.
1720	Slaves become the majority in South Carolina.
1723	Virginia passes an act to deal with slave conspiracies.
1730	A majority of Chesapeake African-Americans are now American born.
1732	South Carolina attempts to ban the import of slaves.
1735	Slavery is banned in Georgia.
1739	The Stono Rebellion in South Carolina is put down.
1740	South Carolina revises its slave code.
1741	A slave conspiracy is suspected in New York.
1750	Slavery is permitted in Georgia.
1758	The first African Baptist congregation is established at Lunenburg, Virginia.

1 COMING TO AMERICA: THE MIDDLE PASSAGE

U NLIKE IMMIGRANTS OF European descent, Africans did not come to America by choice. Almost without exception they were forcibly taken or kidnapped by African and Arab traders to be sold as slaves to the Spanish, Portuguese, Dutch, French, and English, whose American possessions required an endless supply of labor.

Most slaves came from the region of West Africa which now comprises the states of Senegal, Gambia, Guinea, Sierra Leone, Liberia, the Ivory Coast, Ghana, Nigeria, Cameroun, Republic of the Congo, Zaire, and Angola. Here were many populous kingdoms or peoples: Dahomey, Mali, Songhay, Asante, Yoruba, Benin, Igbo, Luango, Kongo, and Luba. Most of the actual captives belonged to interior nations which were at war with the coastal states. The latter, eager to trade with the Europeans, found these human cargoes highly lucrative. A small number of slaves came from East Africa and Madagascar, where Arab traders were active.

These African peoples were not the spear-throwing savages traditionally portrayed by Europeans. Most had advanced political structures and considerable material culture, including a knowledge of iron, which they used to produce tools like hoes. Among their other manufactures were cotton textiles, pottery, and jewelry. Their similarly advanced agriculture included the cultivation of rice, millet, sorghum, okra, and cotton; they also kept livestock, notably cattle.

The enslavement of Africans did not begin with the Europeans in the fifteenth century. The institution was developed by the Islamic states of North Africa and Arabia as early as the eighth century A.D. and then copied by the Africans themselves. Until the Europeans appeared, however, Muslim and African slavery were relatively benign. Under Islamic law it was often the prelude to conversion, and many captives were used as soldiers or employed in other positions of trust. Women frequently became their captors' wives, and once a female slave had a child neither she nor her offspring could be sold. Only a minority of slaves were used purely for economic exploitation.

The European brand of slavery was different in two key respects. First, it was based on race. Second, it was adopted for one purpose only: unremitting labor for profit. In contrast to slaves of Muslims and Africans, few of those enslaved by European masters could expect ever to be released or to better their position.

The nightmare for the slaves began with their initial passage to the coast, invariably in groups tied together with ropes round their hands and necks. On arrival, they were sold to European traders, who, after branding their purchases, put them on board a vessel for America. Here they were stripped and shaved to prevent disease, thus completing their degradation and depersonalization. The sexes were then separated for the duration of the voyage.

In their handling of the slaves, the traders were usually assisted by Atlantic Creoles, persons of mixed European and African descent, who used their linguistic skills to facilitate the exchange. Some took ship as interpreters and even stayed in America, though not always voluntarily.[1]

---

[1] For information about this much-neglected group, see Ira Berlin, "From Creole to African: Atlantic Creoles and the Origins of African-American Society in Mainland North America," *William and Mary Quarterly*, LIII, 1996, 251–88; and *Many Thousands Gone: The First Two Centuries of Slavery in North America* (Cambridge, Mass., 1998).

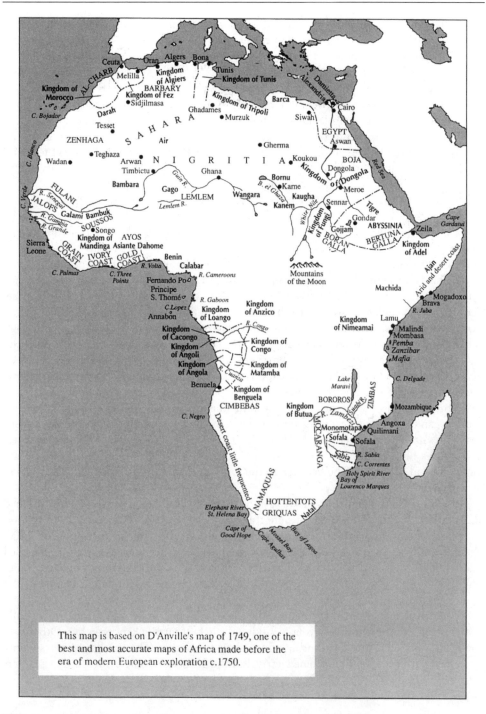

Map 9 Africa as known to Europeans in the mid-eighteenth century.

If the slaves' capture was traumatic, this trauma paled in comparison with their journey across the Atlantic. Most captives had never seen the sea, and its strangeness increased their desperation. Some believed that their European captors were cannibals who had eaten their own people before turning to Africans. Many committed suicide even before the ships sailed, since conditions on board were appalling even by the standards of the age. Most slave ships were between one hundred and three hundred tons and normally carried cargo at the ratio of one and a half slaves to each ton. The slaves were accommodated below deck on platforms, each having a space eighteen inches across and six feet deep to lie on. The most a slave could do was sit, for the height of the deck above was usually about four and a half feet. The accommodation has been compared to that of "books on a library shelf." Toilet facilities were at best an open tub.

In good weather the slaves might be taken on deck for exercise to the beat of a drum or cat-o'-nine-tails. In bad weather, or if the crew were fearful of being overpowered, the slaves were kept chained permanently below deck in conditions whose horror can only be imagined. One doctor commented about his ship, "The floor of their rooms was so covered with the blood and mucus, which had proceeded from them in consequence of the flux, that it resembled a slaughterhouse." The "flux" was usually dysentery, which was quick to take hold. In such circumstances it was surprising that so many slaves survived the voyage. Certainly slave traders expected a substantial proportion of their cargo to perish before arrival. Modern estimates suggest that on average between 12 and 18 percent died, though individual voyages would vary, depending on the weather, length of voyage, and care of the crew. Diseased slaves were often thrown overboard. But whatever the casualty rate, a deep melancholy afflicted every slave ship, each voyage being punctuated by incessant weeping, hysteria, refusal to eat, and attempted suicide.

This ordeal did have one important consequence. Those who survived the first few weeks began to acquire a new identity, stimulated by the recognition that their enslavement was the result of race, not ethnicity. This helped the captives to view their fellow passengers as comrades rather than foes, for whatever the previous differences, they now suffered a common bond as victims. The first step to the forming of an African-American identity had been made.

It used to be thought that most slaves who arrived in British North America reached the mainland via the West Indies, where they were seasoned and introduced to plantation discipline. Modern research shows this not to have been the case, at least not after 1700, when demand increased and direct shipment became more profitable.[2] Direct passage prevailed even in South Carolina, which had close ties with Barbados. Africans from the West Indies might have been seasoned, but they would have been ruined by the brutal regime of the sugar plantations. Strong young Africans were preferred, even if they were unruly for a time.

On arrival at their final destination, the slaves were put up for sale, either individually or as a group. Mothers and very young children were customarily kept together. Otherwise, no regard was paid to the relationship of one slave to another. The purchasers were mainly concerned with the health of the new arrivals, though there is some evidence that planters

---

[2]   Susan Westbury, "Slaves of Colonial Virginia: Where They Came From," *William and Mary Quarterly*, XLII, 1985, 228–37. For the traditional view, see John Hope Franklin, *From Slavery to Freedom: A History of American Negroes* (New York, 1947).

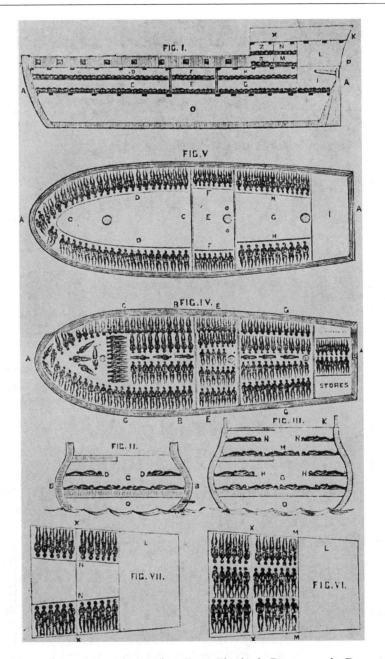

Plate 35 Plan of slave ship *The Brookes*. From Elizabeth Donnan, ed., *Documents Illustrative of the History of the Slave Trade to America*, II (Washington, D.C., 1930–5). The sketch was originally drawn by opponents of the slave trade and may exaggerate the overcrowding on the ship.

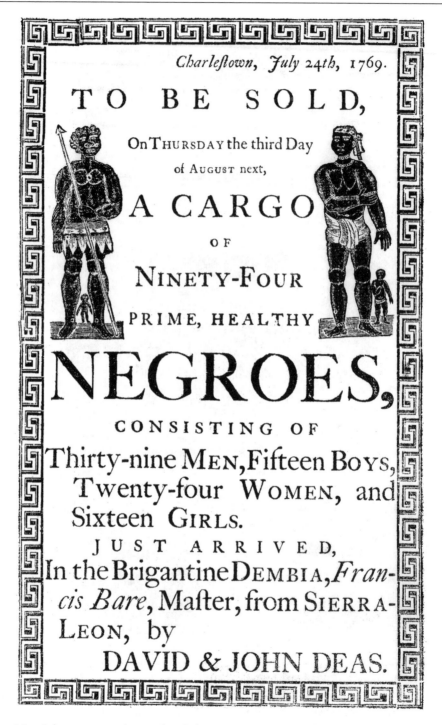

Plate 36   Advertisement for a sale of slaves, 1769. From *William and Mary Quarterly*, LIII, 1996, 141. Courtesy American Antiquarian Society.

DOCUMENT 21

A slave market, circa 1755, reprinted in Karen Ordahl Kupperman, ed., *Major Problems in American Colonial History: Documents and Essays* (Lexington, Mass., 1993), 454.

[The indignity of being sold, as well as the distress of being parted from friends and relations on arrival in America, was an additional torture placed on the Africans after the perils and distress of their passage. That Christians could hand out such treatment was incomprehensible to Africans.]

We were not many days in the merchant's custody, before we were sold after their usual manner, which is this: On a signal given (as the beat of a drum), the buyers rush at once into the yard where the slaves are confined, and make their choice of that parcel they like best. The noise and clamor with which this is attended, and the eagerness visible in the countenances of the buyers, serve not a little to increase the apprehension of terrified Africans, who may well be supposed to consider them as the ministers of that destruction to which they think themselves devoted. In this manner, without scruple, are relations and friends separated, most of them never to see each other again. I remember, in the vessel in which I was brought over, in the men's apartment, there were several brothers, who, in the sale, were sold in different lots; and it was very moving on this occasion, to see and hear their cries at parting. O, ye nominal Christians! might not an African ask you – learned you this from your God, who says unto you, Do unto all men as you would men should do unto you? Is it not enough that we are torn from our country and friends, to toil for your luxury and lust of gain? Must every tender feeling be likewise sacrificed to your avarice?

from South Carolina preferred purchases from Senegal and Sierra Leone because they were familiar with rice cultivation. Akan-speaking peoples from the Gold Coast were also well thought of, but not the Igbo from Biafra because they were thought to be prone to suicide, absconding, and disease. Virginia and Maryland planters, on the other hand, had few prejudices regarding the origin of their slaves. In any case, the planters often had to take what they were offered, which meant purchasing slaves from other areas, notably Angola and the Congo.

Accurate numbers are difficult to establish, but it is thought that around 55,000 Africans were shipped to the Chesapeake area in the period 1700–40, 50,000 of them directly from Africa. South Carolina imported approximately 40,000 slaves during the same period. Thereafter imports into the Chesapeake began to decline, with fewer than a thousand arriving annually. In contrast, South Carolina continued to buy at least two thousand Africans a year until the conflict with Britain made the trade more difficult. Even then the trade continued, if at a reduced level.[3]

---

[3] According to Philip D. Morgan, *Slave Counterpoint: Black Culture in the Eighteenth-century Chesapeake and Lowcountry* (Chapel Hill, 1998), 59, during the eighteenth century, Virginia imported a total of 77,650 African slaves and South Carolina 110,900.

2 THE AFRICAN-AMERICAN FAMILY

Information about the African-American family before 1760 is extremely sparse. The slaves themselves left no written records; even white sources are limited, and most writers have tended to compensate by assuming that late-eighteenth-century material is equally valid for the earlier period.

What is known is that African-American family life took a whole generation to develop, for the same reasons which inhibited the growth of white southern family life in the seventeenth century: disease and an unbalanced sex ratio. Like Europeans, African-Americans had to undergo a seasoning process as they adjusted to their new environment. Almost without exception the slaves were debilitated by the rigors of their passage, which included not just the sea crossing but also the journey along the coast. They then had to face the perils of smallpox and respiratory diseases like pleurisy, so that about 25 percent of those who survived the passage perished in the first year. This high mortality would have cut short many potential relationships.

An even greater inhibition to family life was the imbalance in the sex ratios. At least two out of every three arriving slaves were males, preferred because they were capable of heavier physical work. Also, most slaves imported before 1720 were scattered on isolated plantations and found themselves living either on their own or in predominantly male groups. This situation could change only if more females were imported or if the existing population began to reproduce itself.

The imbalance was most acute in the Chesapeake and northern colonies. In South Carolina the plantations were not only larger but had better sex ratios because the planters obtained female slaves from the American Indian population after most American Indian males were killed in the wars with the Westos and Yamasee. The evidence is circumstantial, but it seems that African men and American Indian women did form relationships. The Chesapeake, in contrast, offered few such opportunities, since the indigenous population had largely disappeared by the time most Africans arrived.[4] Lastly, the imbalance in New England and the middle colonies was exacerbated because the number of African slaves was small and they were widely dispersed.

The capacity of the African-American population to reproduce itself was accordingly negligible in the early decades. Even those women who survived the crossing were generally infertile. One reason may have been the physical and psychological trauma of the passage. Another was poor diet, which unquestionably affected the fertility of many African women. A third reason is that some female slaves must have passed their peak child-rearing period. Still others undoubtedly found no congenial mate, since the restrictions on their movement made the search for a suitable partner difficult.

As the eighteenth century progressed, however, the situation changed dramatically in both the upper and lower south, to the extent that the second generation was surprisingly fertile. Several reasons account for this turnaround. Children born in America automatically had a better chance of survival, since they received some environmental immunity from their mothers. Nature also ensured an equal number of male and female births, so that

---

[4] This point is made by J. Leitch Wright, Jr., in *The Only Land They Knew: The Tragic Story of the American Indians in the Old South* (New York, 1981).

the sex ratio began to correct itself. Also, the second generation had not experienced the trauma of the passage; they had been born into slavery and knew no other life. They were accordingly more ready to accept the situation by reproducing themselves. As the number of slaves increased, so the opportunities for social intercourse improved. Lastly, a society with so many males exerted intense pressure on the females to meet its sexual demands.

As a result, most native-born African women formed relationships from early puberty, ensuring their high fertility through early first birth. This fertility in turn had a dramatic effect on the sex ratio and balance between imported and native-born slaves. In 1725, 60 percent of the slave population in the Chesapeake was still African-born. By 1750 this proportion had dropped to 30 percent, in spite of recent levels of importation. At the same time 40 percent of the slave population in many tidewater areas was now female. In the words of one recent historian, therefore, the second-generation African-Americans had proved a "prolifick people."[5] A similar process was also happening in the lower south.

Reproduction of the labor force of course benefited the owners, though planters were slow to recognize this. For several decades they continued to believe, like their Caribbean counterparts, that the most effective way of increasing their labor force was by importation. They therefore did not interfere in their slaves' sexual behavior. This was a wise policy, since forcing them to have sexual intercourse could have caused much resentment.

But the lot of the African female slave was far from enviable. Sexual harassment and violence were never far away: since there were no laws, provincial or plantation, to protect them from such violations. Even if masters refrained from violence, they were not above exploiting their position for sexual favors. The problem was most acute in South Carolina and Georgia, where there was a culture of tolerance toward interracial sex, stemming from planters' links with the West Indies, the absence of many owners' families in Charleston, and the fact that such liaisons were easier to conceal because the rice plantations were relatively self-contained and remote from the white population. By contrast, in the Chesapeake and northern colonies such liaisons were more difficult to hide and were usually condemned on both moral and social grounds. But for a few slaves, such advances were not completely unwelcome; they were one way of improving their lot. Though freedom was rare, the offspring of such unions might benefit from better working conditions. The disadvantage was that such liaisons made relations with other slaves difficult. The extent of miscegenation is difficult to quantify but may have accounted for 10 percent of the slave population by 1750.

In these circumstances African-American women had to be circumspect. Mothers undoubtedly tried to protect their adolescent offspring for as long as possible, the best course usually being to guide their children toward protective relationships with those male slaves who were most privileged on the plantation and in good standing with the master. Nevertheless, most unions, of course, were decided by the couple themselves on the basis of mutual attraction. However, when they lived on separate plantations, the approbation of both owners was advisable to facilitate visiting. This was not usually a problem in the

---

[5]   Allan Kulikoff, " 'A Prolifick People': Black Population Growth in the Chesapeake Colonies, 1700–1790," *Southern Studies*, XVI, 1977, 391–428. See also Allan Kulikoff, *Tobacco and Slaves: The Development of Southern Cultures in the Chesapeake, 1680–1800* (Chapel Hill, 1986).

later colonial period because masters recognized that such arrangements facilitated a more contented labor force.

Slave marriages were usually simple affairs, held after the working day was over. The man began the proceedings by giving his bride a brass ring or other token of his attachment, after which friends and relatives gathered for a celebration. If the owners approved the match, they might contribute a hog and barrel of rum to facilitate the proceedings.

Despite the greater readiness of masters to accomodate slave unions, immense obstacles still inhibited the development of stable family relationships, the most pernicious of which was the lack of legal recognition. White slave codes did not recognize African-American marriages. This is hardly surprising, as in law slaves were classified not as human beings but as either real or personal estate. Families could thus be torn apart in a variety of circumstances. Owners might have to sell some of their slaves to pay off a debt; they might die and their estates be broken up; they might purchase new lands in the interior and send part of their labor force to work there; or they might give their children plantations of their own. In all these instances the slave family could be split up in an instant with no redress. For some the pain was so great that suicide or infanticide resulted. When Henry Laurens of South Carolina considered breaking up some of his slave families in the 1760s, he predicted "*great distraction* among the whole."

In these conditions the African-American family had to adapt. West African societies were mainly patrilineal, the children taking the name and status of their father. Polygamy was also common there, but was simply impossible in America given the lack of females, though serial monogamy may have been one method of sustaining this custom. African-American families became matrilineal for more basic reasons, however. Small children were invariably kept with the mother if a family was split up. Since female slaves might of necessity have several partners during their lives, the mother was the one who provided the child's identity and place.

Infants were normally looked after by elderly relatives or other slaves who were too old to labor, since their mothers were sent back to work a few days after giving birth. Older children were usually left to play among themselves until the age of nine or ten. They would then be rated as a quarter hand and given small tasks until the age of sixteen or so, when they would be sent into the fields or assigned such other work as they were considered best fitted for. It was these young adults who were most likely to be sent to another plantation or sold. Fortunately, the spreading patterns of kinship meant that they would usually be accompanied by an uncle, brother, half-brother, sister, half-sister, cousin, nephew, or niece. If the white family was increasingly nuclear, its African-American counterpart was of necessity extended; and it was this extended kinship which protected the African-American through a harsh life.

3 WORK AND CULTURE

The life of a slave was dominated by one activity: labor. For this reason Africans were imported, and for this reason they remained in bondage. Whites believed that Africans were an inferior species fit only for menial work. The morality of slavery was rarely questioned.

Since the prime economic activity of the South was the production of cash crops, most adult male and female slaves were employed in field work, organized either by individual tasks or in gangs. The former system was generally preferred in South Carolina, since the clearing of ditches and weeding of rice fields could be readily monitored without the need for constant supervision. Also it provided an incentive for each slave to complete the assignment. The danger from the master's point of view was that the slaves might rush their work in a slipshod fashion. Nevertheless, the task system made for a more contented labor force, as long as the master did not set too high a requirement.

The alternative method, used generally in the Chesapeake, was for the master to work his slaves in gangs where they could be watched. Such supervision was necessary with tobacco since each plant had to be carefully tended throughout the season. This system, too, had its disadvantages. The pace tended to be that of the slowest member, and the slaves had less incentive to work diligently. Whenever the overseer's eye was turned, furtive secession from labor invariably occurred. As one owner commented; the slaves "work hard and seem diligent, while they think anybody is taking notice of them, but when their masters' and mistresses' backs are turned, they are idle and neglect their business."

A lack of commitment was hardly surprising, since the cultivation of cash crops was both tedious and onerous. Tobacco, for instance, required much stooping, especially when the seedlings were being transplanted in the spring, since each plant had to be placed in a small mound of earth at the rate of 350 a day. Not surprisingly, it was at this time that slaves in the Chesapeake were most likely to run away. Next came a period of constant hoeing to control weeds, interspersed with inspections of each plant to destroy hornworms and caterpillars. In addition, the heads and suckers of each plant had to be removed to encourage growth in a few selected leaves only. These labours continued until the fall when it was time to harvest the crop, after which the leaves had to be dried, have their stalks removed before being packed into large barrels, called hogsheads, for export. The whole process, from germinating the seeds in February to the packing of the barrels in November, took about nine months of unremitting labor.

Rice was even more onerous and physically demanding to grow. At new plantations the swampy land first had to be cleared after which ditches and banks were constructed to control the flow of water into and out of the fields. Reservoirs also had to be built to supply water at certain times of the season. Only around April could the sowing of the seed begin, which was done in the African manner by making a small hole with the heel before covering the seed with a flick of the toes. For the next three months the fields had to be constantly hoed, to control the weeds which grew prolifically in such a wet and warm environment. It was at this time that many masters offered their slaves additional food and even rum to keep them at their work. The intensity of labor eased a little in August when the fields were flooded a second time, which helped control the weeds, though some owners used the intermission to divert their workers to the production of indigo. Finally, from mid-September the harvesting and processing of the crop began. The plants first had to be cut and dried after which threshing and winnowing were necessary to separate the grains. Then came the worst part, the removing of the inner film, which, until the 1760s, had to be done by hand with a mortar and pestle. This process began in late November and could take weeks or even months to complete, producing arms that constantly ached and hands that were covered with calluses.

Indigo, the third major cash crop, was another entity that required constant attention by the workforce. Apart from hoeing, it too was subject to the hazard of caterpillars and grasshoppers, which had to be plucked by hand to prevent the crop from being destroyed. The plants were usually cut twice, first in July and again in late August. Production of the dye began immediately after cutting to avoid a loss of quality. First the cuttings were steeped in a fermentation vat for 12–15 hours. Next the contents were removed to a second container where the liquid was constantly stirred to oxidize it before being transferred to a third vessel in which lime was added to precipitate the blue sediment which was the object of the exercise. This was then strained through muslin bags, dried, and cut into cakes for dispatch (see plate 24). For the slaves none of this work was particularly pleasant since the process created a foul stench which attracted flies. Mercifully the production season was considerably shorter than that for tobacco and rice.

For the slaves, these routines changed little from year to year, though some improvements did occur toward the end of the colonial era. In Virginia and Maryland, plows and horse-drawn carts were used more widely, which made the preparation of the ground and harvesting marginally easier. The shift to wheat and cattle also resulted in more varied and less onerous routines for many slaves. In the lower south some rice planters began to invest in threshing machines and pounding mills driven by draft animals, which spared workers the most debilitating part of the production process. Also beneficial to slaves in the lower south was the adoption after 1760 of tidal power to water the crops, which allowed the fields to be flooded more frequently, dramatically reducing the growth of weeds and the need for constant hoeing.

Not all slaves in the South were employed in field work. On larger plantations some male slaves might be trained as carpenters, coopers, smiths, and tanners. Indeed, self-sufficiency became the objective of many eighteenth-century planters. Specialization offered some amelioration from the dull routine of most work, though the number employed as craftsmen was small. A small number of slaves who lived in southern towns also had the chance occasionally to acquire skills, because some urban masters were flexible in how they employed their slaves. This was particularly true of Charleston and Savannah where owners on occasion allowed their slaves to hire themselves out, provided they returned at the specified time with an agreed sum of money. This was a valuable privilege since it allowed slaves to work for themselves once they had met their obligations to the master. Not that southern towns were places of opportunity, since white artisans normally demanded the exclusion of blacks from all skilled occupations. The whites were often supported in their demands by provincial legislatures, as in Georgia, where an act was passed in 1758 curtailing "the employing of Negroes and other Slaves being handicraft Tradesmen." Nevertheless, many owners did see the value of training one or two trusted slaves in certain key occupations.

The provision of such skills served another, if unintended purpose. It created an elite group which had a vested interest in maintaining its position on the plantation and thus made control of newly arrived Africans easier. House servants fulfilled a similar function as they invariably felt superior to the unskilled field workers, not least because many of them were mulattos.[6] Specialization of the labor force thus allowed the owners to divide and rule and gave them no need of an overt force of white retainers to control their slaves. Even the position of overseer was on occasion filled by a trusted slave who had demonstrated an ability to manage the labor force effectively. This was especially true in the lower south for the position of driver or assistant foreman.

In the northern colonies slaves were far less numerous, except in towns like New York. They were most commonly used as house servants and general laborers, though a number

---

[6]   For a discussion of color differentiation among plantation workers, see Michael A. Gomez, *Exchanging our Country Marks: The Transformation of African Identities in the Colonial and Antebellum South* (Chapel Hill, 1998).

were employed in boat building, sail making, and rope spinning. Some were also used on the larger cereal farms of Pennsylvania, New Jersey, and the Hudson and Connecticut river valleys. The decline in the number of indentured servants also led some craftsmen to buy slaves in their place, allowing African-Americans to become skilled coopers, carpenters, blacksmiths, weavers, and silversmiths. Others were used on fishing boats and other vessels. Their navigational skills were often recognized in the South too, since the river ferries were usually worked by slaves. The irony of giving such responsibilities to these supposedly inferior beings escaped most white passengers.

For most African-Americans the working day began at dawn and continued until noon when they had a break for lunch, which usually consisted of hominy or hoe cakes, though many owners added some bacon or ham a couple of times a week. Work was then resumed until either the assignment was completed or sunset approached. Some colonies attempted to regulate the working day. In South Carolina the slave code of 1740 stated that slaves were not to work more than fifteen hours in the spring and summer, and no more than fourteen hours during the rest of the year. However no machinery existed for enforcing these regulations.

When their tasks were done, the slaves were usually free to follow their own pursuits, but these could not be described as leisure. Most plantations expected their slaves to feed themselves, at least partially, by growing corn and vegetables and by raising hogs and chickens. Most slaves therefore had gardens, which seem to have been tilled on a family basis. These plots were one activity which brought great pride to the workforce as each family vied to produce the largest squash and corn. Archeological evidence reveals that slaves supplemented their diet with meat from wild animals, notably opossum, racoon, turtle, deer, squirrel, duck, and rabbit. Additional protein was also obtained from fish in nearby streams and rivers. Most meat and fish were stewed to extract the maximum nutrition from the carcass. Stews were also easier to prepare after a long day in the fields.

In addition to feeding themselves, slaves were also responsible on many plantations for the upkeep of their housing. When not gardening, therefore, they worked on their homes. In the seventeenth century, these were old barns and chicken coops arranged as single-sex barracks; as the eighteenth century progressed, slave quarters appeared like small villages on the larger plantations, comprising a series of one- or two-roomed huts. This reflected the fact that most slaves now lived as families, though some planters still insisted on communal dwellings with one room for each family. Timber was generally plentiful, as were skilled carpenters among the slaves themselves. The result was often housing similar to that of Africa, comprising an earthfast timber frame with wattle and daub sides under a gable roof covered with thatch. Chimneys were usually made of sticks covered in clay (see plate 37).

One distinctive feature of slave housing in the Chesapeake was the provision of a root cellar for storing garden produce and other possessions. They could also be used for concealing items taken illicitly from the owners. In the lower south, lofts, not cellars, seem to have been more common, because of the swampy ground.

The slaves could rarely afford to build permanently, at least in the Chesapeake, since at times the cabins had to be relocated nearer the crops. In both the upper and lower south, dirt floors were normal, as were shutters for windows in lieu of glass. Sanitation was non-existent, excrement or offal simply being thrown into a nearby pit. Straw had to suffice for bedding, though as the century progressed slaves often received redundant items from the plantation house, particularly crockery and other simple utensils which their owners had replaced with china and silver. Iron pots were also increasingly available for the slaves to cook with.

Like white females, African-American women had particular responsibility for domestic chores, notably the cooking of meals and the making of clothes. Garments were usually loose-fitting and made from cloth supplied by the owners. The most common material was Osnaburg, a coarse drab linen, though this could be brightened using vegetable dyes. On some plantations the men received a ready-made outfit of jacket, waistcoat, trousers, and cap. But many slaves, both male and female, wore fashionable European clothing as a way of expressing their individuality, which they obtained despite frequent prohibitions to the contrary through barter or with money earned out of hours. As to footwear, most slaves went barefoot or wore sandals fashioned out of wood or leather.[7]

On the larger plantations in South Carolina and in more populated areas of the Chesapeake, a sense of community had become possible by the eighteenth century. The most popular time for socializing was Sunday, which was generally allowed to be a day of rest. With the benefit of their master's absence either at church or visiting relatives, slaves would often invite the workforce from neighboring plantations. Although slaves were generally forbidden to travel, they came none the less, using back roads or paths to evade white police patrols. Indeed, such routes were well established by the middle of the eighteenth century. Most masters ignored these gatherings in the interests of harmony, unless they became too unruly or disrupted work next day.

The slaves mostly came together to eat, drink, talk, smoke tobacco, dance, and relax. The participants provided food from their own gardens and livestock and usually prepared drink from corn or wild fruit, perhaps assisted with sugar stolen from the main house. They played music on drums, flutes, and banjos, and dancing was generally popular. Gambling with cards and dice was undoubtedly widespread, as was cockfighting.

Historians have looked hard to discover whether the slaves retained any of their African customs during these gatherings. The general consensus is that in their music and dancing, African rhythms and movements were certainly remembered. African influences were also present in the way they made their banjos, drums, mats, baskets, and wood carvings. The African origins of a game like Mancala, in which the participants captured each other's counters from shallow containers, was even clearer. The importation of plants like okra, black-eyed peas, yams, sorghum, and watermelons also allowed the continuation of African cooking, as did the importation of guinea fowl. Recently, archeologists have added to the list of African cultural influences. In particular they have shown that African skills were widely implemented in the making of Colono earthenware, which African women seemingly preferred to the iron pots supplied by their masters.[8]

Finally, African influences persisted in hairstyles and items of personal decoration. Many female slaves continued to braid their hair and everywhere African-style jewellery was worn in the form of colored glass necklaces, beaded armbands, bracelets, and brass earrings. Cowry shells also remained popular as decorative charms to ward off disease and other misfortune.

---

[7] For an evaluation of African-American women during the later colonial period, see Jacqueline Jones, "Race, Sex, and Self-evident Truths: The Status of Slave Women During the Era of the American Revolution," in Ronald Hoffman and Peter J. Albert, eds, *Women in the Age of the American Revolution* (Charlottesville, 1989), 293–337.
[8] See especially Leland Ferguson, *Uncommon Ground: Archeology and Early African America, 1650–1800* (Washington, 1992); and Anne Elizabeth Yentsch, *A Chesapeake Family and their Slaves* (Cambridge, England, 1994).

Plate 37 View of Mulberry Plantation (slave quarters), by Thomas Coram. Gibbes
Museum of Art/CAA Collection, Charleston.

Otherwise, the results of historical research have in some respects been disappointing,
though historians and archeologists are slowly removing the veneer of Anglo-Saxon acculturation to reveal far more than was originally thought to exist. Not least is the realization
that the slaves often injected their own meaning into many artefacts of European origin.[9]
Nevertheless, the reality is that most African culture was lost during the passage and
dispersal in America. In the first place slaves were prevented from bringing material possessions with them other than a few small personal items. Secondly, although most slaves
came from West Africa, they still spoke a variety of languages and had separate customs.
It is calculated that there were some several hundred languages at the beginning of the
diaspora. Even if a whole group was transported together, it still had to survive sale in the
marketplace.

Hence the slaves were generally unable to communicate with one other except in
English, unless they were fortunate enough to be lodged with members of their own nation.
The most famous African-American of the colonial period, Olaudah Equiano, an Igbo
prince, commented on his arrival aged twelve in Virginia in 1757, "I was now exceedingly
miserable, for . . . I had no person I could speak to that I could understand." Since language
is the medium through which most culture is transmitted, the loss of native tongues was
critical. The most that was preserved was the Gullah dialect spoken in the islands off the
coast of South Carolina. This contained some two hundred and fifty words from Angola,

---

[9] See Patricia Samford, "The Archaeology of African-American Slavery and Material Culture," *William and Mary
Quarterly*, LIII, 1996, 87–114. As she points out, historians need to compare eighteenth-century West African
societies with colonial plantation society to get a truer picture of the extent of African influence.

Senegambia, and Sierra Leone. It also retained African speech patterns, grammar, and syntax. But even Gullah was basically a form of pidgin English, however incomprehensible it may have been to whites.[10]

Another area where African culture was partially preserved was in naming patterns, though here too serious erosion took place as children were increasingly given the name of one of their master's family. Some owners like Robert Carter of Virginia deliberately imposed English names on new slaves to undermine their African background and make them more amenable. However, English homonyms often allowed the semblance of an African name to be preserved, as in Joe for Cudjo; and many children continued to be called, albeit in English, after the day, month, season, or festival on which they were born, as was the custom in many parts of Africa. In any case slaves invariably used their own names when not in the presence of their master or overseer.

One aspect of African culture which did survive for a time was religion especially on southern plantations. Before 1750 European Americans made only cursory attempts at converting their slaves to Christianity, fearing, among other things that conversion might lead to a demand for emancipation, even though most colonies had passed laws precluding this possibility. Thus when the South Carolina brothers Hugh and Jonathan Bryan attempted to convert their slaves after a visit by George Whitefield, they were quickly told to desist by neighboring planters. Another reason against conversion was the problem of the slaves' limited command of English. In addition, there was a clear reluctance among planters to share their religion, since their racial prejudice made them unwilling to accept that they might go to the same heaven as their slaves.

For most of the colonial period, therefore, the slaves were left to their own devices in spiritual matters, especially on the large rice plantations of the lower south where contact with the white population was minimal. Some Africans from Senegambia and the Gold Coast were clearly practicing Muslims, judging by the advertisements for runaway slaves with Islamic names. Even more, although the evidence is unclear, continued to observe traditional African religious practices. Most Africans believed in a supreme Creator under whom there were various lesser gods usually associated with natural phenomena like thunder, lightning, rain, earth, fertility, spring, summer, and fall. All had the power to do good or ill, and it was considered important to propitiate them by invoking various forms of Obeah or magic through the use of charms and talismans called *minkisi* supplied by the witch-doctor.[11] Since African religion and medicine were closely intertwined, *minkisi* often

---

[10] There is still some debate on this question. See Margaret Washington Creel, *"A Peculiar People": Slave Religion and Community-culture among the Gullahs* (New York, 1988). The idea that African-Americans retained part of their African roots was first stated by the activist W. E. B. Du Bois, who received considerable support from the anthropologist Melville J. Herskovits's *Myth of the Negro Past* (New York, 1941). However, most of Herskovits's material related to Brazil and the Caribbean, and its relevance to America was fiercely denied by E. Franklin Frazier in *The Negro Family in the United States* (Chicago, 1939). Scholarly opinion in the past twenty years has been moving back toward the position taken by Du Bois and Herskovits, following the work of Sydney Mintz and Richard Price, *An Anthropological Approach to the Afro-American Past: A Caribbean Perspective* (Philadelphia, 1976); and the novel by Alex Haley, *Roots* (New York, 1976). See especially John Thornton, *Africa and Africans in the Making of the Atlantic World, 1400–1680* (New York, 1992); Leland Ferguson, *Uncommon Ground: Archeology and Early African America, 1650–1800* (Washington, 1992); and Gomez, *Exchanging our Country Marks*.

[11] Such ideas were similar to many American Indian beliefs, especially the view that good and evil were not absolute and that the devil was a trickster rather than a corrupter. See chapter 2, section 3.

took the form of amulets or medicine bags into which various herbs and charms were placed, depending on the effect to be achieved, for *minkisi* could be used for good or harmful purposes. Most objects were worn as decoration for personal protection. However, if someone was to be punished, the charm would be placed near that person's house. To the disappointment of many, *minkisi* rarely worked against cruel foremen and owners.

Equally important to African religious practice was ancestor worship. All Africans believed that their ancestors' spirits could protect the living, and for this reason they commonly tossed a small amount of food and drink on one side before starting a meal in memory of departed relatives. Even more important, proper offerings had to be made at funerals to propitiate the departed member of the family, for example, placing broken crockery on the grave to free the deceased person's spirit. It was also customary for Africans to be especially demonstrative when accompanying the body to the grave, celebrating the return of the dead person's soul to their ancestral spirits in Africa. This behavior contrasted vividly with the silence maintained by mourners at white funerals.

Even in the area of religion, however, acculturation began to take place as the native-born increased in number. The Creoles spoke English and were therefore easier to convert, as well as more willing to accept Christianity, especially the house slaves, many of whom were mulattos and better able to identify with the culture of their masters. The similarities between African religion and Christianity may have also become more apparent, notably the idea of one supreme being, the presence of lesser spirits, the concept of reincarnation, the belief in miracles, the importance of water baptism, and the need for blood sacrifice. In addition, Christianity dealt with suffering, exile, the promise of freedom, and the punishment of evil at the Day of Judgment. Of course, the hope remained that baptism might lead to emancipation as a reward for being good and faithful servants. At the very least better treatment might be accorded. Christianity also gave slaves the opportunity to appear superior to those recently arrived from Africa; and in the last resort a Christian slave was less likely to be sold than a heathen one.

Where masters failed to offer religious instruction, as was generally the case in the south, slaves increasingly filled the gap themselves. From 1750 they received considerable help from the Baptists, who had no slave owners among their membership and were far more egalitarian in their doctrines than the Anglicans. The interest was quickly reciprocated. African-Americans especially liked the informality and evangelical style of the Baptists, as well as their emphasis on universal salvation. African religions customarily placed great importance on divine revelation; thus the Baptist appeal to salvation through the mediation of the Holy Spirit had an obvious attraction, as did the possibility of conversion without the need to master a complex theology. A further attraction may have been the practice of adult immersion, which reminded converts of African water cults. Also appealing was the fact that the Baptists demanded no specially trained ministry; a simple license from an existing minister and an ability to preach were all that was required though no African-American became a minister until the 1770s. Lastly, the Baptist use of singing and emphasis on trauma during conversion seem to have complemented earlier African religious practices, notably the "ring shout" when participants formed a circle, drumming their feet and clapping their hands, while they sang and danced.

The Baptists began making inroads among the African-American community in the aftermath of the Great Awakening, when Shubal Stearns and other ministers passed through the southern backcountry. The first predominantly African-American Baptist congregation was established at Lunenburg in 1758 near the estate of William Byrd III. Estimates suggest that up to 40 percent of the African-American population in the Chesapeake had converted to some form of Christianity by 1760, though the figure for the lower south was much less due to the slaves' isolation and the higher level of imports. One owner there confessed even in 1779 that his slaves remained as "great strangers to Christianity, and as much under the influence of Pagan darkness, idolatry and superstition, as they were at their first arrival from Africa."[12]

Although specific cultures were lost, African-Americans retained certain cultural traits as a result of their African heritage. Most notable were their lack of distinction between the natural and supernatural world, their informality, their command of rhythm, and their sense of time as cyclical rather than linear. All these gave them a style that was quite different from Europeans and Africans too, for what was emerging among the second generation was a distinctive African-American culture, based on race rather than ethnicity. This is not to say that the Creole blacks had a common identity, given the lack of contact between the different regions of British North America. The sense of unity was also undermined by the presence of a mulatto population which enjoyed privileged positions on the plantation. Nevertheless, a start had been made.

Finally, some scholars now believe that African-American culture became deeply embedded in that of their masters.[13] Certainly African words and speech patterns were commonly used by southern whites. Perhaps the greatest impact was in the dialect itself, for as one traveler commented toward the end of the eighteenth century, "common country folk talk very much like Negroes."

4   WHITE OVER BLACK: THE SLAVE CODES

Historians are divided on the question of whether the conditions of the enslaved African-American population were improving in the eighteenth century. From the legal viewpoint they clearly were not. For much of the seventeenth century slavery had lacked legal definition, permitting anomalies like the case of Anthony Johnson discussed in chapter 3, section 5. These advantages were progressively lost as harsher laws made the bondage more complete.

The first colonies to codify slavery were Virginia and Maryland. In 1662 Virginia passed an act stating that the child of any Englishman born to a slave mother would take slave status. This measure was a response to a suit brought by Elizabeth Key, the daughter of a white father and a slave mother, who successfully sued for her freedom on the grounds that under English law a child took the status of its father. In 1668 another act was passed declaring that baptism did not change the status of slaves. This act followed a court case involving a slave named Fernando who brought suit for his freedom claiming that he was a Christian. The following year a further act exempted any master from being charged if a slave died after punishment, since no one would deliberately "destroy his own estate." In

---

[12]   Gomez, *Exchanging our Country Marks*, 254.
[13]   See especially Mechal Sobel, *The World They Made Together: Black and White Values in Eighteenth Century Virginia* (Princeton, 1987).

1670 the House of Burgesses prohibited free African-Americans from purchasing "Christian servants," meaning whites, on the assumption that Africans could never be Christian and certainly could not rule over whites. The measure did not prevent them from "buying any of their own nation," but even that concession was withdrawn by progressively tighter legislation, as in 1691 when the House of Burgesses banned interracial marriages. Finally, in 1705 a comprehensive slave code was passed which effectively reduced all African-Americans, unless already free, to perpetual slavery.

Maryland acted even more speedily, formally acknowledging the institution of slavery as early as 1638, when the colony excluded slaves from enjoying the rights of Englishmen. Maryland's first slave legislation, passed in 1664, laid down that all "Negroes or other slaves hereafter imported into the province shall serve" for life, as should their children. Any white woman so forgetful of her status as to marry a slave would have to serve the master of her husband until his death, and her offspring would also be slaves.

Until the 1720s most legislation was concerned with the personal status of slaves and was primarily motivated either by racial prejudice or by financial interest. Subsequently another element came into play in the regulation of African-Americans, namely fear of their growing numbers. As long as African-Americans were few in number relative to the white population, they were not seen as a threat; but the proportion had altered significantly by the eighteenth century. In 1680 Virginia had about 3,000 slaves and 50,000 whites; by 1760 the number of slaves had risen to 120,000 and represented nearly two-thirds of the figure for whites. South Carolina experienced an even more dramatic change in its demographic structure; by 1730 the colony had 10,000 whites but 20,000 African-Americans and appeared to one observer "more like a Negro country than a country settled by white people."[14] Fear now provided a strong inducement to reinforce legal boundaries around an institution that had developed with little forethought as to its consequences.

In 1723 the Virginian authorities introduced a bill for the "More effectual punishing Conspiracies and Insurrections." In future any slave guilty of conspiracy was to suffer death. Those committing perjury were to be nailed by the ear, whipped, and then have that ear cut off. Meetings of slaves were also banned, except when working or attending divine service with their masters. Persistent runaways were to be dismembered, and no African-American was to be freed "except for some meritorious services . . . allowed by the Governor and Council." This clause was inserted solely to reward informers who betrayed serious conspiracies.

A similar tightening of the laws occurred elsewhere. Even in Pennsylvania, with its reputation for humaneness, African slaves were tried not by a full jury but by two justices and six "of the most substantial freeholders." Rape was punishable by death, attempted rape by castration, and if more than four African-Americans met together without permission they were to be whipped.

The same harshness was exhibited in New York, especially after 1712 when a group of slaves killed nine whites as the whites tried to extinguish a fire. The assembly quickly passed a stiffer law, preventing more than three slaves from congregating together without the consent of their owner. The death penalty was also prescribed for a wide variety of crimes against white persons and their property. Nor was there any moderation to these restrictions following another series of fires in 1741, when more than thirty slaves were

---

[14] Morgan, *Slave Counterpoint*, p. 95.

DOCUMENT 22

A suspected African rising prevented, 1680, reprinted in Warren M. Billings, *The Old Dominion in the Seventeenth Century: A Documentary History of Virginia, 1606–1689* (Chapel Hill, 1975), 160.

[Even at this stage white Virginians were becoming sufficiently apprehensive about the dangers of a slave uprising to prohibit Africans from assembling for the burying of their dead. As noted in the text, the purpose and style of African funerals was quite different from those of European-Americans, and such misunderstanding may have stimulated fears of a conspiracy.]

His excellency was pleased this day in Council to acquaint the Council that he had even then received from Mr Secretary Spencer intelligence of the discovery of a Negro plot, formed in the Northern Neck for the destroying and killing his Majesty's Subjects the inhabitants thereof, with a design to carrying it through the whole Colony of Virginia, which being by God's Providence timely discovered before any part of the designs were put in execution, and thereby their whole evil purposes for the present defeated. And Mr Secretary Spencer having by his care secured some of the Principal Actors and contrivers, and the Evil and fatal Consequences that might have happened, being by this Board seriously considered, have found fit to order that the Negro Conspirators now in custody be either safely secured until the next General Court, to the Intent they may then be proceeded against according to Law, or if it be found more necessary for the present safety of the country that they be brought to a Speedy trial, that then his Excellency will be pleased to direct a Commission to Mr Secretary Spencer, Col Richard Lee and Col Isaac Allerton, three of His Majesty's Council Inhabitants in the Northern Neck to sit, hear and try according to law the Negro Conspirators, and to proceed to sentence or condemnation and execution, or to such other punishments as according to law they shall be found Guilty of, by such examples of justice to deter other Negroes from plotting or contriving either the death, wrongs or injuries of any of his Majesty's subjects.

And this Board having considered that the great freedom and liberty that has been by many masters given to their Negro Slaves for walking abroad on Saturdays and Sundays and permitting them to meet in great numbers in making and holding of funerals for Dead Negroes gives them the opportunities under pretension of such public meetings to consult and advise for the carrying on of their evil and wicked purposes and contrivances, for prevention whereof for the future, it is by this Board thought fit that a proclamation do forthwith issue, requiring a strict observance of the several laws of this colony relating to Negroes and to require and command all Masters of families having Negro Slaves not to permit them to hold or make any solemnity or funerals for any deceased Negroes.

hanged or burned at the stake on the unsubstantiated testimony of a white servant girl that they had been plotting to destroy the city.

The legal status of African-Americans was worst in South Carolina. By an act of 1691 any African or American Indian slaves showing violence to a white person for a second time were to have their noses slit and their faces burned. Conversely, though, any whites who killed a slave were to suffer no penalty, except in the case of wanton murder, when the offense carried a sentence of three months' imprisonment. In addition, slaves could be sold as chattels, while their quarters were regularly searched for guns and stolen property.

Such harsh laws did not prevent the outbreak in 1739 of the Stono Rebellion, though it was aided by some exceptional circumstances. War was in the offing with Spain, and the authorities in St. Augustine had offered refuge to all slaves who fled the British settlements. In addition, the large number of Christian Angolans from the Kingdom of Kongo who had recently been imported into South Carolina may have given the uprising exceptional cohesion. The Kongo had converted to Roman Catholicism at the end of the fifteenth century, following contact with the Portuguese. The offer of sanctuary in Catholic Florida, therefore, was doubly appealing.[15] On the morning of Sunday, September 9, a gang of fifteen slaves attacked a store and seized some guns. When they advertised their success by drum beat to encourage others to join, several dozen answered the call; but the action unfortunately also alerted the local militia. In a short exchange fourteen slaves were killed while the rest fled. Another, similar engagement a week later on the road leading south brought the rebellion to a close. By way of revenge and to intimidate the rest of the slave population, the whites inflicted a series of brutal reprisals, in which offenders were burned, dismembered, and made to suffer a slow death by being suspended in chains until the birds and other animals had plucked out their eyes and eaten their flesh.[16]

Paradoxically, the savagery of this repression led to a reaction in favor of the slaves. In 1740 the assembly passed a new law which seemingly attempted to redress the balance so that "the slave may be kept in due subjection and obedience, and the owners and other persons having the care and government of slaves may be restrained from exercising too great rigour and cruelty over them." In future all capital offenses were to be tried before two justices and a minimum of three freeholders, while lesser crimes were to be dealt with by one justice and two freeholders. Owners could no longer "wilfully cut out the tongue, part of the eye, castrate, cruelly scald, burn or deprive any slave of any limb or member" since such cruelty was "highly unbecoming those who profess themselves Christians." In future punishments must be restricted to "whipping or beating with a horsewhip, cow-skin, stick," or alternatively "by putting irons on, or confining or imprisoning," though in an emergency, such as the recent Stono uprising, rebellious slaves could be summarily executed. Slaves were also to be adequately fed and clothed and were not to work on Sundays except in cases of "absolute necessity and the necessary occasions of the family."[17]

---

[15] For the Kongo connection, see John Thornton, "The African Dimension of the Stono Rebellion," *American Historical Review*, XCVI, 1991, 1101–13.

[16] However, it should be remembered that punishments for white offenders were hardly less gruesome. Those guilty of treason were first hung by their necks, then cut down while still conscious so that their bowels could be cut out and burnt in front of them, after which they were beheaded and their bodies cut into four parts.

[17] For a copy of the code, see W. Keith Kavenagh, *The Foundations of Colonial America: A Documentary History*, 3 vols (New York, 1973). III, 2102–21.

Slaves were perhaps most humanely treated in New England, largely because there they constituted only 2 percent of the population, or about 5,500, by 1760. Not being subject to any paranoia about the dangers of an insurrection, whites there could afford to be relaxed. Hence slaves in New England were encouraged to convert to Christianity and were generally better clothed and fed. In addition they could testify in court, could often work for themselves when not required by their owners, could keep their earnings, and could even buy their freedom. They might also gain their liberty by serving in wartime with the provincial forces, when a want of manpower persuaded authorities to ignore normal legal obstacles. In the larger towns they were also permitted greater cultural expression, most notably at the annual governor's day parade in Boston, when they held their own mock leadership elections.

Another indication that slavery was more benign in New England is that unions between slaves were usually called marriages and were often celebrated by a minister. However, they had no legal standing and slave families could still be broken up as elsewhere. The example of Jack and Juliet, two Boston slaves of the 1760s, makes this clear. Jack began courting Juliet, who was owned by a neighbor, and after a time they became betrothed with the tacit approval of both owners. When Juliet became pregnant, however, her mistress immediately considered "how best I shall dispose of it." In due course Juliet gave birth to a daughter, making Jack "the happiest of mortals." Despite this the child was given away to a woman who lived three miles distant. The distress of Juliet and Jack can only be imagined. Five years later, when Juliet gave birth to a mulatto child, the owner determined to sell both her and the child, despite Juliet's desire to remain with Jack. Moreover, slaves in New England continued to endure cruelty of a less deliberate kind. In Massachusetts the sex ratio among slaves was the familiar two males to every female, so that family life was difficult, doubly so given the slave population's small number and scattered habitations. Admittedly manumission for slaves was easier here, but only if the master gave them £50 to prevent their becoming a burden on the community. And, in any alarm or emergency, African slaves were always the first objects of suspicion, as was perhaps inevitable in a culture which equated black with evil.

Two further mitigating points need to be mentioned with regard to the slave codes. First, they were designed mainly to deal with deviations from the norm for which special penalties were required. Second, many of their provisions were not always observed; for example, the obligation on whites to maintain patrols at night. When the white population felt secure, which was most of the time, this duty was not carried out, giving slaves considerable freedom during darkness.

Equally, the assumption that slaves were chattels and could not own property was frequently disregarded, not just in New England but in all the colonies. The most popular entrepreneurial activity among slaves was the raising of livestock, and most families kept a few chickens or hogs. The more enterprising took their surplus to the local market or bartered with the neighboring community. Indeed, many plantation owners found they could not compete with their own labor force for the supply of fowl and bought from them instead. Other slaves used their spare time to set traps and go hunting, subsequently selling their catches to the white population. This entrepreneurial activity was especially widespread in the lower south where the task system allowed slaves more free time. Many came to own tools, cooking utensils, furniture, and occasionally horses. Their *de facto* right to such property was sometimes recognized by the courts.

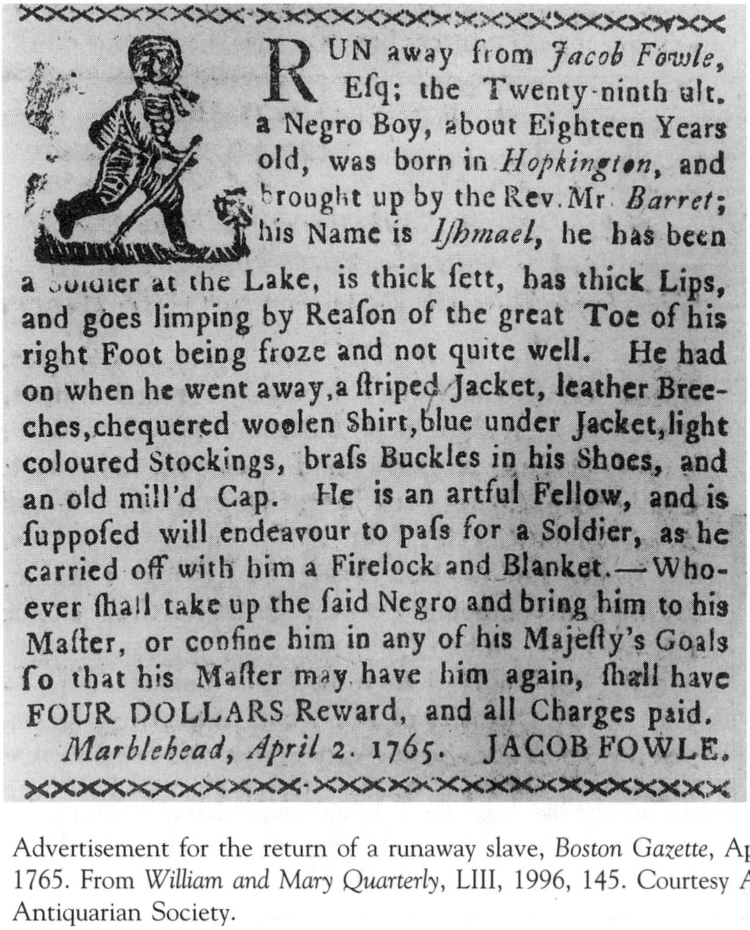

RUN away from *Jacob Fowle*, Efq; the Twenty-ninth ult. a Negro Boy, about Eighteen Years old, was born in *Hopkington*, and brought up by the Rev. Mr. *Barret*; his Name is *Ifhmael*, he has been a Soldier at the Lake, is thick fett, has thick Lips, and goes limping by Reafon of the great Toe of his right Foot being froze and not quite well. He had on when he went away, a ftriped Jacket, leather Breeches, chequered woolen Shirt, blue under Jacket, light coloured Stockings, brafs Buckles in his Shoes, and an old mill'd Cap. He is an artful Fellow, and is fuppofed will endeavour to pafs for a Soldier, as he carried off with him a Firelock and Blanket.—Whoever fhall take up the faid Negro and bring him to his Mafter, or confine him in any of his Majefty's Goals fo that his Mafter may have him again, fhall have FOUR DOLLARS Reward, and all Charges paid. *Marblehead, April* 2. 1765. JACOB FOWLE.

Plate 38 Advertisement for the return of a runaway slave, *Boston Gazette*, April 8, 1765. From *William and Mary Quarterly*, LIII, 1996, 145. Courtesy American Antiquarian Society.

Even the ban on firearms was by no means universally enforced. Some trusted slaves were permitted to go hunting for their masters. Others possessed guns which had been stolen or misplaced. Although slaves were banned from serving in the militia, except as drummers, in emergencies this restriction too could be overlooked. In 1704 the South Carolina assembly passed an act allowing the arming of slaves "in Time of Alarms." Even the unthinkable at times became necessary. Elsewhere slaves were sometimes enlisted in volunteer regiments to make up the numbers.

Historians today tend to suggest that relations between slave and master were tolerable if not harmonious. Most slaves were not overtly defiant, while rebellion was rare. The most serious problems concerned runaways, whose motives varied. Recent African arrivals usually just wanted to return home, however distant and impossible the journey. In South Carolina or Georgia they always had the possibility of reaching St. Augustine. Hence the 1740 law passed in the aftermath of the Stono uprising devoted considerable attention to the problem of runaways. Rewards were to be paid to whites or free American Indians for the return of all fugitives. Most American Indians readily cooperated, though on occasion some runaways were adopted into the captors' nation or kept as slaves for the sachems' own use.

DOCUMENT 23

The problem of runaways, 1729, reprinted in Karen Ordahl Kupperman, ed., *Major Problems in American Colonial History: Documents and Essays* (Lexington, Mass., 1993), 456.

[*Runaways were a constant threat to plantation owners, who feared a similar situation to Jamaica, where African communities had successfully established themselves in the mountainous interior beyond white control. Though the attempt described below was unsuccessful, one such community did develop on the borders of Virginia and North Carolina in the Great Dismal Swamp.*]

Sometime after my Last a number of Negroes, about fifteen, belonging to a new Plantation on the head of the James River formed a Design to withdraw from their Master and to fix themselves in the fastnesses of the neighbouring Mountains. They had found means to get into their possession some Arms & Ammunition, and they took along with them some Provisions, their Cloaths, bedding and working Tools; but the Gentleman to whom they belonged with a Party of Men made such diligent pursuit after them, that he soon found them out in their new Settlement, a very obscure place among the Mountains, where they had already begun to clear the ground, and obliged them after exchanging a shot or two by which one of the Slaves was wounded, to surrender and return back, and so prevented for this time a design which might have proved as dangerous to this Country, as is that of the Negroes in the Mountains of Jamaica to the Inhabitants of that Island. Tho' this attempt has happily been defeated, it ought nevertheless to awaken us into some effectual measures for preventing the like hereafter, it being certain that a very small number of Negroes once settled in those Parts, would very soon be encreas'd by the Accession of other Runaways and prove dangerous Neighbours to our frontier inhabitants.

The reasons which provoked the native-born to run away were often more complex. They might stem from harsh treatment by an unsympathetic master – after all, absconding at least offered temporary relief from the emotional and physical hurt. They might also absent themselves temporarily as a way of negotiating better working conditions, knowing that most masters were dependent on their skills and readiness to work. In South Carolina slaves sometimes absconded during the weeding of rice fields when they had to stand knee deep in mud. But the cause was usually familial. Since slave marriages were not recognized by white laws, families were frequently split up. Even the most loyal slaves might run away in these circumstances, not to freedom, which they knew to be impossible, but simply to see their loved ones. Such defections often occurred on the spur of the moment, and the recalcitrants usually returned of their own accord after a few days. The punishment would normally be a few strokes of the birch or the loss of some privilege, unless the culprit was a constant offender in which case the penalty might include the amputation of a limb or sale to another colony. When native-born slaves did make a conscious bid for freedom, it was usually to go to a town like Williamsburg, where they could pass as free among the free African-American community.

Some historians believe that slaves systematically succeeded in sabotaging the system by passive resistance. Owners certainly bemoaned the incompetence and laziness of their workforce, and theft, too, was widespread. Such complaints, however, are not uncommon in modern industrial societies, where management is incompetent and society fails to reward its workforce adequately. It was the fault of the colonial plantation system that it never gave the slaves any incentive to be efficient or careful. Nevertheless, on the whole the two races learned to accommodate each other. In return for a reasonable day's work, the masters left their slaves alone.[18]

In general, the quality of life for slaves did improve, however modestly, when compared with the harsh exploitative conditions of the seventeenth century. One reason was simply that conditions were also improving for the rest of the population. Better implements for working the land, for example the horse-drawn plow in Virginia and tidal irrigation in South Carolina, made life a little easier. Changing social attitudes also had an effect. Eighteenth-century Chesapeake planters looked upon themselves as patriarchs, not exploiters, viewing their slaves as childlike wards rather than subhuman beasts. William Byrd II liked to refer privately to his slaves as "my family," and spent a considerable time attending to their health and medical problems. Henry Laurens of South Carolina similarly commented on how his slaves "look up to their Master as their Father, their Guardian, and Protector," from whom there was in consequence "a reciprocal obligation," though such attitudes did not prevent a humane planter like Landon Carter from whipping his female slaves if he believed they were feigning pregnancy to escape work. Religious considerations may also have played a part in ameliorating the institution in some respects. After 1700 several denominations began to show an interest in the spiritual if not material well-being of the Africans. The Society for the Propagation of the Gospel attempted to teach some of them to read, as did Cotton Mather, who reminded slave owners: "You deny your *Master in Heaven*, if you do nothing to bring your *Servants* into the Knowledge and Service of that *Glorious Master*." This concern for African-American souls increased with the onset of the Great Awakening when both Wesley and Whitefield condemned the spiritual neglect of the slaves. Among those who responded was Samuel Davies, a New Light Presbyterian, who from 1747 began preaching to the slaves in Hanover County, Virginia, even before the Baptists.

Nevertheless, before 1760 the morality of slavery itself was rarely questioned by whites since even ministers like Cotton Mather and Jonathan Edwards owned slaves and saw nothing wrong in the institution, though Edwards may have had reservations about the

---

[18] The debate over the humaneness of slavery and whether the two races were in irreconcilable conflict is one that has constantly exercised historians. Ulrich B. Philips, *American Negro Slavery* (New York, 1929), put the case for the humaneness of the institution, as did Margaret Mitchell in her novel *Gone with the Wind* (New York, 1936). Both were southerners, writing at a time when there was little sympathy for the plight of the African-American. In *The Peculiar Institution: Slavery in the Ante-Bellum South* (New York, 1956) Kenneth M. Stampp, writing after the first Supreme Court judgments against segregation, argued that the slaves and their masters were in a mutually antagonistic relationship, a view supported by numerous other writers. The problem with past historical writing has been its tendency to view the whole subject in terms of southern oppressors and northern emancipators. More recently the trend has been to suggest that the African-Americans adapted as best they could to the realities of the situation, developing their own culture and lifestyle; see especially Kulikoff, *Tobacco and Slaves*. For a cautionary note on this, see Jean Butenhoff Lee, "The Problem of Slave Community in the Eighteenth Century Chesapeake," *William and Mary Quarterly*, XLIII, 1986, 333–61.

slave trade.[19] The first recorded protest against the institution was made by Francis Pastorius at Germantown in 1688. Samuel Sewall, a Boston merchant and Massachusetts superior court judge, expressed another early critical view in his pamphlet *The Selling of Joseph* in 1700. These were isolated instances, however. Not until John Woolman published *An Epistle of Advice and Caution* in 1754 did the Quakers begin to take a firm stand against slavery. The following year their Philadelphia meeting disowned any member still in the slave trade and advised all others to manumit their slaves as soon as possible.

The rest of the white population found slavery too essential to contemplate its abolition. As the Reverend Peter Fontaine of Westover parish wrote to a correspondent in 1757, the gospels did not ban slavery even though it was widespread at the time of Christ. It was simply impossible to live in Virginia without slaves. Unless a person was "robust enough to cut wood, to go to mill, to work at the hoe" they "must starve, or board in some family." Slavery was an unfortunate necessity whatever the long-term consequences; and no one stopped to speculate what these might be.

5 FREE AFRICAN-AMERICANS

Not all Africans were slaves. A small number of those who arrived in the seventeenth century secured their freedom, and a few also obtained their manumission in the eighteenth century when masters or mistresses rewarded certain slaves who had been faithful over a long period of time. Others were freed because they were infirm, though most provinces had laws against this practice.

Estimating the number of free African-Americans is no easy task. In Virginia there may have been as many as two thousand by 1760, despite a law of 1699 that required all newly freed slaves to leave the colony. Free African-Americans may thus have represented between 2 and 3 percent of the total African-American population in the colony, sufficient for a clause to be included in the 1723 statute banning the manumission of African-American slaves without the permission of the legislature.

In South Carolina the ratio of free to slave was smaller, perhaps 1 percent, or between two hundred and three hundred individuals by 1760. The contrast to Virginia may have been the result of the more rigorous enforcement of the law of 1722 ordering all freed slaves to leave the province, South Carolina, as always, being sensitive about its security.

In the north the proportion of free African-Americans was higher, but because they made up such a small percentage of the general population, the actual number of free African-Americans was small. In Connecticut perhaps 20 percent of the province's two thousand African-Americans enjoyed such status by 1760. The total throughout the North amounted to only a few thousand, or one out of ten blacks living north of Maryland.

The position of free African-Americans everywhere was far from enviable, even when compared with slave status. In Virginia they could not marry whites, vote or hold any office, were excluded from the militia, were forbidden to use firearms, and could only testify in court cases involving other African-Americans. Miraculously, some still managed to get a

---

[19] See Kenneth P. Minkema, "Jonathan Edwards on Slavery and the Slave Trade," *William and Mary Quarterly*, LIV, 1997, 823–34.

small piece of land, usually as tenants. Others used such skills as they had to hire themselves out, mostly as laborers. Some found employment in Williamsburg and other towns where they could use their craft skills. A few owned farms and enjoyed some degree of prosperity, but many apparently slipped back into servitude. Apart from the economic pressures they experienced, they remained continually vulnerable to bullying neighbors, blackmail, or kidnap plots. Use of the courts in these circumstances was not easy.

Conditions were not much better in the North even though these were "societies with slaves" rather than "slave societies."[20] In New York free African-Americans were not allowed to own real estate. Those masters who liberated slaves had to provide sureties of £200, since "it is found by experience that the free Negroes of this colony are an idle slothful people and prove very often a charge." They were always the first suspects in any crime and were also severely fined if they helped slaves to abscond.

The position was little different in Massachusetts, where similar discrimination was the norm. African-Americans were normally excluded from the militia and forced to work on the highways instead. They could not vote or sit on juries, and after 1705 they were forbidden to marry whites. Not the least of their difficulties was dealing with economic discrimination. While slaves found it relatively easy to get work, since their masters arranged it for them, free African-Americans found work opportunities extremely limited and were pushed into the poorest housing and socially ostracized. Although they could use the courts, they were always at a disadvantage before a white jury, and their attempts to purchase property often met with outright refusal. In general the white population considered them a nuisance. Freedom in such circumstances was bittersweet indeed.

There was, however, one place during the colonial period where for a short time free blacks could live with dignity. This was the settlement of Gracia Real de Santa Teresa de Mose in Florida. Mose owed its existence to a 1693 Spanish offer of freedom to any African-American slave who converted to Catholicism. The Spanish had always been more liberal in their attitude to slavery and manumission, though their policy was not entirely disinterested. By encouraging slaves to abscond, they hoped to weaken the economy of South Carolina while strengthening that of Florida.

News of this offer soon spread among South Carolina's African-American population, and during the early decades of the eighteenth century a trickle of refugees attempted to make the difficult and dangerous journey to St. Augustine. The largest influx occurred during the Yamasee war, when a number of slaves joined the Indians in their southward flight. By 1738 there were enough refugees for the establishment of a separate community of about one hundred people two miles north of St. Augustine.

Mose was ostensibly under the command of a Spanish officer, assisted by a priest, since the new settlement was designed as a military outpost for the Spanish capital. But because only the priest lived in the village, the day-to-day life of the settlement was under the control of one of its own freedmen, Francisco Menendez. He had arrived in Florida in 1724 and first organized the male inhabitants into a militia. Otherwise Mose was similar to a Spanish Indian mission. The inhabitants lived in small thatched huts and tilled the land around the fort, fishing in the nearby waters to make ends meet. Some did laboring in St. Augustine.

---

[20] See chapter 3, section 4, for the importance of this distinction.

Unfortunately the settlement was no sooner founded than it was destroyed by James Oglethorpe during his 1740 expedition against St. Augustine and the inhabitants evacuated to the Spanish capital for protection. Menendez and his militia played an important role in Mose's recapture a few weeks later. But the settlement struggled to survive. By 1759 Mose had a population of only fifty-seven; there were twice as many men as women, and one-quarter of its inhabitants were children. The settlement finally came to an end in 1763 when Florida was ceded to the British. The Spanish took Menendez and the refugees to Cuba, where they were reestablished in another frontier post. Conditions there proved even harsher than in Florida, and within a few years the community had disappeared.

15

American Indian Society and Culture, 1689–1760

1677	New York agrees the Covenant Chain with the Iroquois.
1677–88	The Abenaki people seek an accommodation with Massachusetts.
1694	Commissioners are appointed to run the Massachusetts American Indian townships.
1697	The Piscataway people leave Maryland for the Ohio region.
1701	A Massachusetts act prevents the unauthorized sale of American Indian lands. A treaty of neutrality is signed between the Iroquois and the French.
1712	The Tuscarora people in North Carolina are defeated.
1713	By the Treaty of Utrecht the British claim the eastern part of the Micmac homeland.
1715	The Yamasee are defeated and removed from South Carolina.
1722	The Tuscarora join the Iroquois confederation (and are granted full membership in 1750).
1724	The Norridgewock Abenaki are destroyed.
1729	The Natchez people are defeated and dispersed by the French.
1730	The Natick township is taken over by white settlers.
1735	Pennsylvania claims land from the Delawares following the Walking Treaty Purchase.
1742	A peace treaty is signed between the Iroquois and the Cherokee.
1744	The Iroquois offer the Delawares new lands on the upper Susquehanna.
1751	A peace treaty is agreed at Albany between the Catawba and the Iroquois.

1 THE COASTAL RESERVATIONS

I F THE AFRICAN-AMERICANS suffered a bitter heritage after coming to America, this fate was equally true of the continent's indigenous inhabitants. From being the sole occupants of a vast continent, by the turn of the eighteenth century they had all but disappeared from the east coast. As Robert Beverley Jr. commented in his History and Present State of Virginia in 1705, the tidewater nations there, once numbering many thousands, had been reduced to perhaps five hundred people. By 1715 this pattern had been repeated throughout the coastal areas from Massachusetts to South Carolina.

This decline had four principal causes: disease, warfare, deforestation, and the extermination of hunting game. All were the result of the European invasion.

Historians now agree that it was the diseases transmitted by European and African immigrants which had the most lethal impact on the people and culture of the indigenous inhabitants. Smallpox, typhoid, dysentery, yellow fever, and malaria all devastated the indigenous nations just because their previous isolation and lack of exposure had prevented them from developing any immunity and laid them open to attack from several epidemics at the same time. Between one-half and three-quarters of all America's original inhabitants perished from these diseases.

Less insidious, but still destructive, was the development of the fur trade leading as it invariably did to the extermination of the game. Prior to the Europeans' arrival the local inhabitants killed sufficient game to provide meat and clothing for themselves. Such limited culling helped preserve a natural balance between man and nature. Then the Europeans arrived seeking an endless supply of furs in exchange for guns and other useful objects, thus seducing the American Indians into hunting the game to extinction – and with it their own economic system which had endured for thousands of years. In addition, they began to neglect traditional skills like pottery making and weaving in favor of European textiles and ironwares, further compounding their new economic dependence.

Equally deleterious was the destruction of the forests. As early as 1642 the Narragansett chief Miantonomo had noted the devastating ecological effects which had befallen his people as a result of European farming methods.[1] The clearing of the land had gone on remorselessly, resulting in an environmental calamity for all the east coast peoples.

The fourth major effect of white influence was in the area of warfare. Before 1607 American Indian conflicts had been limited, and their prime purpose had been the taking of a few scalps or captives to avenge earlier losses. Now the Europeans introduced them to a style of warfare which was close to genocide as entire confederations were conquered and enslaved. These conflicts were not simply a matter of white against red, in fact most of the killing was done by the American Indians themselves. The indigenous nations now felt compelled to secure a monopoly of the game in their area to assure their access to European technology, which was essential if they were to protect themselves against neighboring enemies. Perhaps one-quarter of the native population perished because the traditional balance of power was upset by these internecine struggles.

Many writers also include a fifth reason for the decline of the American Indians, namely the rum trade. Believing that alchohol put them into contact with their ancestral

---

[1] See chapter 4, section 3, Document 9.

spirits, many American Indians were so keen to obtain rum that a disproportionate amount of furs were traded for this commodity, whose effects were entirely destructive. The effect of alcohol set the braves fighting among themselves, destroyed tribal loyalty, undermined the authority of the chiefs, ruined the health of the males, and reduced fertility.[2]

The effects of disease, extinction of game, deforestation, and war are well illustrated by the experience of the native peoples of southern New England. In 1600 the native inhabitants numbered some twenty-five thousand. Seventy-five years later, at the conclusion of King Philip's War, the Massachusetts, Wampanoag, Narragansett, and Mohegan nations had been reduced to perhaps fifteen hundred people. In eastern Massachusetts they were confined to just four towns: Natick, Punkapoag, Hassamesitt, and Wamesit, which were effectively reservations. Even then their decline continued.

Initially the sachems were left to run these settlements in the manner of other New England towns. However, the Massachusetts authorities repeatedly found that the sachems had only the vaguest notion of what the office of a magistrate or selectman involved. In 1694 commissioners were appointed to run the towns in conformity with the provincial laws, in the hope that in time the American Indians would be assimilated into white society through the twin processes of "civility and Christianity." In the meantime they would be protected both from themselves and their white neighbors, especially from drunkenness and debauchery.

In practice the reservation system continued the downward slide from acculturation to extinction. In the first place, these reservations were not economically viable. Surrounded increasingly by white settlement, the native peoples were unable to sustain game in the old manner, so that they had nothing to trade except land. American Indians in the New England region had always done some farming, but this pursuit was insufficient to sustain their numbers, since they were unwilling to adopt white agricultural methods and forms of ownership which would further erode their community-based society. Many American Indians had to hire themselves out as laborers or trackers to secure their livelihood. Others took to whaling like the Indians of Nantucket in which they proved highly proficient. But, whatever they did, the result of taking such employment was the same, the destruction of their traditional way of life, since it further increased their dependency and acculturation, while at the same time undermining their family structures and, ultimately, their fertility. Indeed, low fertility was now the greatest threat to the survival of the Indians of southern New England. This was the result not only of family separation but the consequence of a poor diet and an unbalanced sex ratio. By 1760 the ratio of female to male was approximately two to one not least because so many men had been killed in the wars with France. Many Indian

---

[2] Among those writers to stress the problem of alcohol are Allen W. Trelease, *Indian Affairs in Colonial New York: The Seventeenth Century* (Ithaca, 1960); James Axtell, *The European and the Indian: Essays in the Ethnohistory of Colonial North America* (New York, 1981); Bernard Sheehan, *Savagism and Civility: Indians and Englishmen in Colonial Virginia* (Cambridge, England, 1980); Kenneth M. Morrison, *The Embattled Northeast: The Elusive Ideal of Alliance in Abenaki-Euramerican Relations* (Berkeley, 1984); Wilcomb E. Washburn, ed., *Handbook of North American Indians*, vol. 4, *History of Indian–White Relations* (Washington, 1988); and, most recently, Peter C. Mancall, *Deadly Medicine: Indians and Alcohol in Early America* (Ithaca, 1995). Mancall shows that the Indian peoples were by no means uniform in their use of and response to drink. Alcoholic addiction, of course, was not confined to the indigenous population. Interestingly, little work has been done on its misuse among whites. A comparative dimension is urgently needed.

women had, in consequence, turned to the black community for a mate, further undermining tribal identity, since many of their offspring were classified as African-Americans.

An equally pernicious threat to native culture was the imposition of white law. The whole concept of an impersonal law enforced by the state was alien to American Indians. In their society, when someone committed an offense, the aggrieved person or clan carried out the appropriate punishment. A murder might require the death of the offender, a lesser crime might be absolved by some form of compensation. In any case, American Indians generally took a more relaxed view of human nature, tolerating many forms of behavior deemed deviant by the Puritans.

The clash of cultural values was most obvious in regard to property. Most possessions, especially land, were considered to be collectively owned, though garden plots might bring a prescriptive right to the produce. Europeans, on the other hand, considered land a commodity which could be bought or sold for the private benefit of the individual. Hence what constituted theft in white eyes was often merely communal use to American Indians. As a result, they were frequently punished for actions which their society viewed as quite legitimate.

The erosion of the native culture did not stop here, however. The native inhabitants were severely disadvantaged when it came to the implementation of the white judicial system. In cases of murder they were granted legal representation, but on most other occasions they had to plead their own cause. Even in the eighteenth century most had only a limited command of English. The technical language of the courtroom was certainly beyond their understanding. Nor did the jury system help, for while American Indians occasionally served in cases involving their own people, they were never called when the defendant in such a case was white. Invariably such juries were quick to condemn American Indian offenders while showing leniency to those of European descent. Appeals to the superior court were usually beyond their means and were generally futile. Whites, on the other hand, were often able to appeal their way out of trouble.

Another disadvantage was that many punishments involved fines which the American Indian found hard to pay. The sachems might sell a piece of land, but the poorer members of the reservation usually had no option but to submit to whipping or servitude in settlement of their offense. Going into servitude of course eroded their cultural identity even more.

Finally, the inability of the American Indians to play the legal game made them vulnerable to exploitation by European Americans, especially when white squatters produced spurious titles to tribal land, thus further reducing the viability of the reservation. An act of 1701 supposedly prevented all such property transactions without the sanction of the general court, but it was rarely effective, especially after 1746 when the general court passed another law allowing the commissioners to lease out what they considered surplus lands. This was an invitation to abuse.

Meanwhile, civility and Christianity made slow progress, for as the efforts of Eliot had shown, Puritan standards were attainable only when the American Indian had become totally acculturated to white society. Most native peoples in southern New England refused to make such a radical change, preferring to keep as many vestiges of their old culture as possible. When acculturation did make advances, notably in the concept of land ownership, it was merely destructive. For example, whites constantly encouraged American Indians to think of garden plots as their own. Since the native people had little understanding of European agriculture and a market economy, all too often such encouragement merely led to the sale of these plots, thus speeding up the destruction of their communal lands.

DOCUMENT 24

An attempt to cheat Indians of their lands, New Jersey, 1716, reprinted in W. Keith Kavenagh, *Foundations of Colonial America: A Documentary History* (New York, 1973), II. 1595–6.

[Using drink to defraud American Indians of their land was a typical device favored by unscrupulous whites. So too was the use of fraudulent deeds, which led Indians to distrust all paper documents, items which were redundant in an oral society. Fortunately, the American Indians were not always bereft of friends, especially in New Jersey and Pennsylvania, where the Quakers were sympathetic. On this occasion the native complaint was upheld.]

John Kay came before me, Jacob Doughty, one of the King's Justices of Peace for the County of Burlington.

Myself [John Kay] with several others sent for John Weitherill and heard the Indian's complaint against him, which was that said John Weitherill had come to said Indian King and treated him with cyder and made him drunk, and that he came again to him the next morning and would have given him more cider and told him he sold him some land the night before, being land which said Indian King and other Indians lived on, and had set his hand to a deed or writing for the sale of said land. The said Indian King declared he remembered nothing of selling any land to said John Weitherill or setting his hand to any paper and further said he had always refused to sell that land and had reserved it for himself and the Indians to live upon and that the Indians had a right in it and would never suffer him to sell it. He had also promised them that he would not sell it and that he loved to live near John Wills and other Englishmen whom he called his bretheren and . . . if John Weitherill had got him to sign any paper it was by defraud and cheating him and that he could neither eat, drink, nor rest with quiet until that writing or paper was destroyed.

We used what endeavours we could with John Weitherill to persuade him to deliver the writing to the Indian King and make him and the rest of the Indians easy, telling him how unjust such an action it was and the dangerous consequences that might thereby happen, but could not prevail with him to give any satisfaction.

[Eventually the governor of New Jersey interceded, and the deed was destroyed].

The native peoples of southern New England were therefore left in limbo, as the fate of the Natick township revealed. After 1675 white settlers steadily encroached on the reservation, and by the 1730s they, not the commissioners, were running its affairs, since the local inhabitants were now a minority. The native position was further weakened when Natick became a parish, as this allowed the white majority to disfranchise the native minority, even though many still had property. After this, those unable to support themselves were unceremoniously told to move elsewhere and seek relief from the provincial government, since they could have no claim on the local community.

A similar process occurred in the other townships, notably the Mahican settlement of Stockbridge in western Massachusetts. The day was not far off when the disappearance of

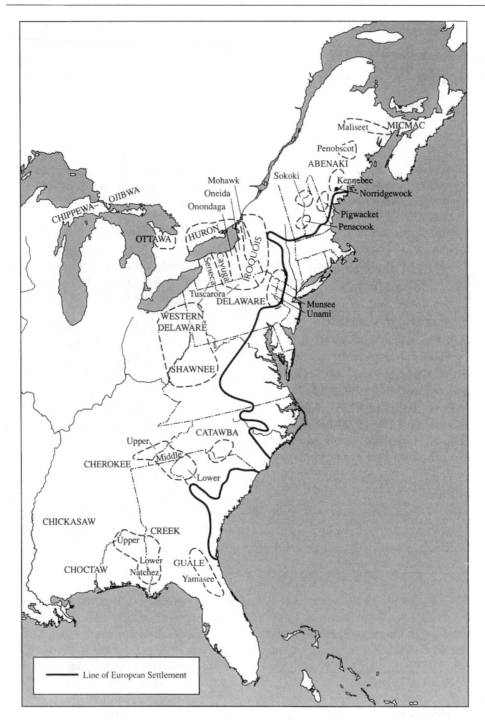

Map 10   The American Indian nations, ca. 1750.

the American Indians as a distinctive group was certain, other than for a few isolated reservations, such as that of the Mashpee people near Cape Cod and the Wampanoags on Martha's Vineyard. The rest now lived in small groups barely distinguishable from their European neighbors, except for their poverty. The situation of Indian women was perhaps the worst. Most of them, without fields to cultivate, had to make baskets, brooms, and pottery to subsist. Many became itinerants and vagrants as they searched for customers. The usual response from European Americans, as at Natick, was an order to leave. Their desperate situation is suggested by the plea of some Massachusetts Indian women in 1756 who, through the absence or death of their men on provincial military service, had been left utterly destitute.[3]

A similar decline was also in process in the other coastal areas. In the lower regions of New York and New Jersey most of the indigenous Algonquian peoples, such as the Wappinger and Manhattan, had either been killed during the seventeenth century or had removed themselves to the interior. Some individual families survived on Long Island, where they were active in the whaling industry. Even in Pennsylvania, the number of American Indians within the white areas was small, though this partly reflected the colony's recent creation and lack of white settlement. The main nation, the Lenni Lenape, or Delaware, still lived beyond the line of settlement, at least until the 1730s. Eastern Pennsylvania was home to some small groups like the Conestogas, a remnant of the Susquehannocks, who had converted to Christianity and eked out a tenuous existence until 1760 protected by their Quaker neighbors. Sadly, they were massacred by backwoodsmen during Pontiac's war.

In Virginia few native settlements remained after Bacon's Rebellion, which had inflicted terrible losses. The formerly proud peoples of the Powhatan Confederacy, the Chickahominy, Mattaponi, Pamunkey, Nansemond, and Paspahegh were reduced to a handful of families amounting to just 5 percent of their earlier population. A treaty signed in the aftermath of Bacon's Rebellion supposedly guaranteed them certain lands and rights similar to those enjoyed by the colonists. But, as in Massachusetts, their lands were slowly encroached upon by whites, confining them to a few small enclaves. The result was a fatal undermining of the American Indian's society and economy, since many young men were compelled to labor for their white neighbors, a far cry from their former role as warriors and hunters. Their self-esteem was further undermined by various acts of the Virginia legislature, which prohibited intermarriage in 1691 and banned American Indians from testifying in court in 1705. Living in an increasingly alien environment drove many to alcoholism. Soon the language of the Powhatan people itself was being lost, the final stage in the destruction of these once-proud people.

The same decline was evident in Maryland. The last nation of any note here was the Piscataway people, who successfully reconciled the changes wrought by the newcomers with

---

[3] The extent of the Indian decline, however, has been challenged. See Daniel R. Mandrell, *Behind the Frontier: Indians in Eighteenth-century Eastern Massachusetts* (Lincoln, 1996); and Jean M. O'Brien, *Dispossession by Degrees: Indian Land and Identity in Natick, Massachusetts, 1650–1790* (Cambridge, England, 1997). For the feminization of Indian poverty, see Ruth Wallis Herndon and Ella Wilcox Sekatau, "The Right to a Name: Narragansett People and Rhode Island Officials in the Revolutionary Era," in Colin G. Calloway, ed., *After King Philip's War: Presence and Persistence in Indian New England* (Hanover, 1997), 113–40.

their own way of life for sixty years, until the line of settlement began to encroach on their lands in the 1680s. By this time the Piscataways were less useful as guardians of the frontier, since the Marylanders now looked to the Iroquois for that purpose. In 1697 the remaining members moved to fresh lands in the Ohio Valley, leaving only a few pockets of Nanticoke, Patuxent, and Conoy peoples submerged among their white and African neighbors.

It was a similar story in the Carolinas, where the principal tidewater nations, the Tuscaroras and Yamasee, had been broken by war in 1711 and 1715. At the end of hostilities the Tuscaroras' numbers had been reduced from five thousand to perhaps twenty-five hundred. They were then offered sanctuary by the Five Nations, to whom they were linguistically related, on the upper reaches of the Susquehanna River, but several hundred opted to remain in North Carolina instead. Here they were grouped by the provincial authorities in a reservation on the north side of the Roanoke River under a single sachem, Tom Blount. Elevation of one individual in this manner was alien to American Indian culture and helped to complete the destruction of their clans. The Tuscaroras, who had previously been important participants in the fur trade, no longer had access to furs and trade with the western nations. Soon white settlements began to encroach on the reservation, and the North Carolinian authorities proved even less ready than the New Englanders to protect their native peoples from unscrupulous white traders and land speculators. In deepening poverty, the remnants frequently had to sell pieces of land. By 1760 their numbers had decreased to three hundred; most of these moved northward in the next few years to join their brethren in Iroquoia.

After their defeat in 1715 by South Carolina, the Yamasee similarly sought refuge with a friendly confederacy away from the white settlements. Since they spoke a Muskogean language, they all traveled south to join the Guale (Seminole) Indians in northern Florida. By 1770 Governor James Bull could only express astonishment "that in this province, settled in 1670 . . . then swarming with tribes of Indian, there now remain, except the few Catawba, nothing of them but their names, within three hundred miles of our sea coast." After almost three hundred years the European invaders still failed to appreciate the destructive effects of their diseases, trade, and warfare on the indigenous inhabitants. But even if they had understood, they would not have been troubled, since the decline of the Indians was seen as the necessary price of progress.[4]

Despite this downward spiral, historians and anthropologists are keen to emphasize the importance of the American Indian legacy for the European newcomers along the eastern seaboard. They not only helped Europeans to survive in the early days, but introduced them to many new plants, crops, and medicines. In addition, they enriched their language with such words as caucus, moccasin, powwow, and toboggan. They also taught European Americans much about the art of warfare in the New World and exposed them to new ideas about nature and the ecology. Though the process of acculturation was undoubtedly one sided, without "Indians" there would have been no "Americans."

---

[4] Only in the past few decades have Americans begun to view the European impact as one of conquest rather than peaceful settlement; of ecological degradation rather than environmental improvement; and of race and class rather than one of equality and democracy. For a discussion of these changing views, see Andrew R. L. Cayton and Fredrika J. Teute, eds, *Contact Points: American Frontiers from the Mohawk Valley to the Mississippi, 1750–1830* (Chapel Hill, 1998), 1–15.

2 THE NATIONS OF THE NORTHERN FRONTIER

The destruction or dispersal of the coastal nations brought the advancing whites into contact with a new series of peoples along the fall line of the Allegheny Mountains. For convenience these will be divided into two groups, northern and southern.

The most important peoples on the northern frontier were the Micmacs of Nova Scotia and New Brunswick; the Abenakis on the borders of Maine and New Hampshire; the Five Nations of the Iroquois in northern New York; and the Lenni Lenape, or Delaware, in northeastern Pennsylvania.

The Micmacs were an Algonquian-speaking people who relied on hunting and fishing for their subsistence. According to a seventeenth-century observer, they caught seals in January; hunted beaver, otter, moose, and caribou in February and March; devoted themselves during the spring and summer to catching the cod and shellfish that abounded along the coasts; and in the fall returned to hunting elk and beaver until the annual cycle began again.

Because of the predominance of hunting in the Micmac economy, their villages were less permanent than those of the nations in southern New England. They lived in conical tepees made of skins, which could be easily moved to a location convenient for whichever activity they were engaged in. The rest of their material culture was similarly determined by these economic considerations. Among their most important items before the arrival of the Europeans were the birchbark canoe, leather-thonged snowshoe, moccasin, and toboggan.

The need for constant movement also affected the Micmacs' social structure. The basic unit was the household, or nuclear family. This unit was usually part of a local group headed by a sagamore. The sagamores were simply household heads whose ability led other families to seek their protection. The exercise of authority was thus remarkably democratic, for the sagamores had few privileges other than the right to part of a young, unattached male hunter's catch.

During the spring and summer, when the Micmacs gathered along the coast and tidal rivers to catch fish, several groups joined together to form a band, the equivalent of a village community in less nomadic peoples. It was then that formal conferences were held. With the onset of winter they broke up into smaller units again, to make hunting easier.

As with most hunter-gatherers, families were patrilineal, the children taking the name of their father. Relations between the sexes were similar to those prevailing in European and African societies. The men did the physically dangerous work, leaving the household management and child rearing to the women. During pregnancy almost no concessions were made to alleviate a woman's daily routine. When her contractions began she would go into the woods accompanied by one or two females and deliver her baby in a crouching position. The newborn child would first be washed in the nearest stream, or snow in winter. The woman then returned to the task on which she had been engaged some hours beforehand.

The two sexes were separated socially early in life. Boys were instructed in the art of hunting and fishing; girls gathered firewood, fetched water, and helped their elders cook, make clothes, and process skins. Once a girl had shown proficiency in these tasks and had reached puberty, she was considered ready for betrothal. Although marriages were often arranged, the Micmacs placed few restrictions on the choice of a partner.

A common practice among the Micmacs and other northeastern Algonquian peoples was for the young man to do bride service for his future father-in-law for two years, during which period sexual relations between the couple were forbidden. At the end of this probation, the prospective husband would go out hunting to prepare a feast for the marriage ceremony. The celebration was attended by the village shaman, sagamore, parents, and other kin; speeches were made offering advice and encouragement to the young couple; and feasting and dancing then followed.

Religious powers were vested in the shaman, or witch doctor, who also dispensed medicines and other remedies for preserving life. The Micmacs believed in a supreme spirit whom they associated with the sun. They also worshiped Gluskap, a mighty warrior, whom they believed would help them in their hour of need. Like most American Indian peoples, they held nature in high reverence, believing that the spirits of animals, such as the beaver and bear, must be respected.

The Micmacs were one of the first North American native peoples to trade with Europeans, notably the French, whose fishermen frequented their area of settlement from the 1530s onwards. Most of this commerce involved the exchange of furs for hatchets, guns, textiles, and other useful items. This trade was regularized by Champlain after he had established Quebec, and the Micmacs thereafter remained staunch allies of the French.

Unfortunately the 1713 Treaty of Utrecht consigned the Micmac lands in Nova Scotia to Britain, which soon made attempts to settle the area. Although the French government was reluctant to become openly involved in time of peace, the Micmacs determined to fight for their homes. They were encouraged by a Jesuit priest, the Abbé Le Loutre, who had a mission at Bay Verte on the isthmus connecting Nova Scotia to the mainland. A series of raids was launched to confine the British to their principal settlement at Annapolis Royal, and until 1750 the Micmacs were indeed generally successful in their endeavors to defend their homes.

Their Abenaki neighbors to the south were less successful. The Abenaki, another Algonquian-speaking people, inhabited a large territory stretching from the coast of Maine to the St. Lawrence near Montreal. They included a number of nations, known collectively as the Eastern and Western Abenaki. Among the Eastern Abenaki peoples were the Maliseet, Kennebec, Pigwacket, and Penobscot. The Western Abenaki included the Sokoki and Penacook nations.

Like the Micmacs, the Abenaki were primarily hunters, fishermen, and gatherers. The eastern tribes especially had easy access to the sea and relied heavily on fish. Their economic cycle was accordingly similar to that of the Micmacs. The western bands, in contrast, had to rely more on hunting and the gathering of nuts and berries, though fish was plentiful in the region's many streams and lakes. Nevertheless, the Western Abenaki found it advantageous to engage in agriculture by growing corn and squashes, and as a result their settlements were more permanent. Indeed, by the eighteenth century their tepees were being replaced by log cabins surrounded by a fortified stockade.

Like most hunting societies, social structures were necessarily fluid and remarkably egalitarian. Though only certain families could supply a sagamore, heredity itself was never sufficient to justify chieftainship; personal leadership and character were considered essential. The Western Abenaki had both a civil and a war chief.

Families were patrilineal, and the basic unit was the household, which usually consisted of two or more nuclear families related through the male line. The household

DOCUMENT 25

The Micmacs ridicule the French, 1677, reprinted in Colin G. Calloway, *The World Turned Upside Down: Indian Voices from Early America* (Boston, 1994), 50–2.

[Though allies of the French, the Micmacs did not adopt European culture uncritically. Indeed, they remained disparaging about many French practices, as the following extract shows.]

Thou sayest of us also that we are the most miserable and most unhappy of all men, living without religion, without manners, without honour, without social order, and, in a word, without any rules, like the beasts in our woods and in our forests, lacking bread, wine, and a thousand other comforts which thou has in superfluity in Europe . . . I beg thee now to believe that, all miserable as we seem in thine eyes, we consider ourselves nevertheless much happier than thou in this, that we are very content with the little that we have; and believe also once for all, I pray, that thou deceivest thyself greatly if thou thinkest to persuade us that thy country is better than ours. For if France, as thou sayest, is a little terrestrial paradise, art thou sensible to leave it? And why abandon wives, children, relatives, and friends? Why risk thy life and thy property every year, and why venture thyself with such risk, in any season whatsoever, to storms and tempests of the sea in order to come to a strange and barbarous country which thou considerest the poorest and least fortunate of the world? Besides, since we are wholly convinced of the contrary, we scarcely take the trouble to go to France, because we fear, with good reason, lest we find little satisfaction there, seeing, in our own experience, that those who are natives thereof leave it every year in order to enrich themselves on our shores. We believe, further, that you are also incomparably poorer than we, and that you are only simple journeymen, valets, servants, and slaves, all masters and grand captains though you may appear, seeing that you glory in our old rags and in our miserable suits of beaver which can no longer be of use to us, and that you find among us, in the fishery for cod which you make in these parts, the wherewithal to comfort your misery and the poverty which oppresses you. As to us, we find all our riches and all our conveniences among ourselves, without trouble and without exposing our lives to the dangers in which you find yourselves constantly through your long voyages. And, whilst feeling compassion for you in the sweetness of our repose, we wonder at the anxieties and cares which you give yourselves night and day in order to load your ship. We see also that all your people live, as a rule, only upon cod . . . until things come to such a pass that if you wish some good morsels, it is at our expense; and you are obliged to have recourse to the Indians, who you despise so much, and to beg them to go a-hunting that you may be regaled. Now tell me this one little thing, if thou hast any sense: which of these two is the wisest and happiest – he who labours without ceasing and only obtains, and that with great trouble, enough to live on, or he who rests in comfort and finds all that he needs in the pleasure of hunting and fishing? . . . Learn now, my brother, once and for all, because I must open to thee my heart: there is no Indian who does not consider himself more happy and more powerful than the French.

normally took the name of an animal, such as turtle, beaver, otter, or bear, following the pattern of other native peoples.

The Abenaki were indulgent parents; children were admonished rather than physically punished. Both sexes began training for their allotted roles from the age of five or six. Boys went hunting, fishing, and fighting; girls gathered plants, prepared food, and dressed skins. Courtship was initiated by the man through an intermediary, who accompanied his request with a string of wampum. The woman could refuse by returning the gift.

Since the middle of the seventeenth century the Abenaki had desired an accommodation with the English. Following King Philip's War, they sought a treaty with Massachusetts recognizing their independence. Sadly, nothing came of the negotiations. As the English settlements in New Hampshire and southern Maine expanded, so the Abenaki were forced to continue hostilities, looking to the French for support.

A French alliance was advantageous because French settlements posed no threat to the Abenaki. The problem was that successive governors in Montreal offered only halfhearted support, being reluctant to ally with the Abenaki for fear of angering the English, especially in peacetime. The French also had close links with the Micmacs, who feared that the Abenaki might steal their trade, and therefore agreed to help only if the Abenaki would resettle along the St. Lawrence. This they refused to do except in an occasional emergency.

Nevertheless, the French Catholic church at least was ready to answer the call of this distressed people. Missionary work at this time was conducted principally by the Jesuits, who made conversion easy by requiring only outward conformity to the practices of Catholicism. Unlike the Puritans, they did not insist that the American Indians understand the theology underlying their religion. Indeed, the Jesuits allowed them to retain many of their old customs, especially if these could be equated with Christian beliefs. From 1694 the most active missionary was Sebastian Rale.

The Abenaki people most immediately affected by the tide of English settlement were the Norridgewock Indians of the Kennebec River, where Rale had his mission. The Norridgewocks repeatedly tried diplomacy to effect an amicable outcome, since they had no wish to become the clients of France and were keen to trade with the English. All attempts to negotiate, however, were frustrated by the unacceptable demands of the Massachusetts authorities, who insisted on hostages to secure conformity with their wishes. Almost all the Norridgewock attacks after 1688 were defensive, aimed at protecting their homes.

Nineteenth-century American historians like Francis Parkman cast Rale as an evil priest who connived in the sending of war parties against peaceful English settlements. In reality Rale constantly tried to mediate between the parties, seeking only to do what was best for his mission in a difficult situation. Certainly he was not the stooge of French imperial ambition as traditionally portrayed.[5]

The lack of effective French assistance forced the Norridgewock Indians to struggle alone. The Abenaki never had any political organization. Indeed, the other Abenaki peoples wanted to remain neutral since, like all the eastern nations, they depended on European trade for essential goods. They therefore sought good relations with both European nations, though eventually most chose to support the French.

---

[5] Francis Parkman, *France and England in North America*, 7 vols (Boston, 1865–92). The contrary viewpoint is argued by Morrison in *The Embattled North-East*. For an analysis of Parkman's writings, see Francis Jennings, "Francis Parkman: A Brahmin among Untouchables," *William and Mary Quarterly*, XLII, 1985, 305–28.

The brave attempt of the Norridgewock people to protect their way of life finally ended in 1724 when Governor Shute of Massachusetts sent an expedition in which Rale was killed and his mission destroyed. The remnants fled to the French settlement of St. Francis, near Sorel, to await an opportunity for revenge and a chance to return home. The other Abenaki peoples decided that diplomacy might once again be the more prudent course and in 1727 concluded a treaty with Massachusetts. It did them little good, since controversy quickly arose as to what had been agreed at Casco Bay. The British claimed that the Abenaki had recognized the authority of the Crown and had accepted responsibility for the recent hostilities. The Abenaki, in contrast, asserted that they had merely agreed to stop fighting so that the British could open a store on their coast. Despite all the Abenakis' efforts, the two sides were as far apart as ever, and the prospects for peace were not promising.

The frontier of New York, in contrast, was relatively peaceful in the period 1714–50 because New York was shielded by the powerful confederacy of the Iroquois Five Nations. Since the 1660s the Iroquois had been linked to New York by a chain of friendship which had continued ever since, albeit with varying enthusiasm. One reason for its endurance was the slow growth of New York's population, due to the manorial system. The Iroquois simply did not experience the same pressure on their lands as other nations living in proximity to the English.

More has been written about the Iroquois than about any other American Indian nation, to some extent just because they maintained their independence for so long. Another reason for their perceived importance was their strategic location guarding the principal pathways to the west by way of the Mohawk River. In addition their numerical strength, amounting perhaps to fifteen thousand people, gave them a reputation far beyond what was actually deserved.[6]

Until the mid-fifteenth century the Iroquois had been five separate nations. Then one of their chiefs, Hiawatha, had a vision from the Prophet Dekanawidah telling him to join hands with his neighbors to end their bloody conflicts. The vision implied that at some future date a great covenant of peace under the Iroquois would stretch from sea to sea. The covenant initially included only the five Iroquoian-speaking Mohawk, Oneida, Onondaga, Cayuga, and Seneca nations. Every year fifty sachems, representing the families who had originally sanctioned the league, met at the great long house of the Onondagas to exchange presents, usually belts of wampum, and to renew their vows of peace and friendship.

Oratory played a special role at these meetings, as for all Indian conferences. With no written records other than the symbols on wampum belts, such speeches were essential to ensure that the history of each nation was remembered. The orations were also a matter of diplomatic courtesy. The Iroquois in particular believed that proceedings could begin only after an exchange of condolences for recent losses. European observers failed to appreciate this custom when they criticized Indian speakers for being unacceptably loquacious.

This annual gathering of the Iroquois was generally misconstrued by Europeans as being something akin to a great confederacy for political and military cooperation, which

---

[6] For the historiography of the Iroquois, see Daniel K. Richter and James H. Merrell, eds, *Beyond the Covenant Chain: The Iroquois and their Neighbors in Indian North America, 1600–1800* (Syracuse, 1987); and Dean R. Snow, *The Iroquois* (Cambridge, Mass., 1994).

Plate 39 Portrait of Sa Ga Yeath Qua Pieth Tow (called Brant), a Mohawk chief
who visited London in 1710, by John Verelst, 1710. The cloak was a gift in
London, but the white cloth shirt also reflects European influence on the
Iroquois by this time. The National Archives of Canada, C-092418.

is more than it was. Undoubtedly views were exchanged at the annual council, but the
gathering in no way reduced the independence of the individual nations or clans since the
descendants of the original families that had sanctioned the league were not necessarily
influential now. Hence the most easterly members of the confederacy, the Mohawks, continued their policy of friendship with the English, while the most westerly, the Seneca,
generally looked to the French. The basic purpose of the confederacy was merely to ensure
that its members did not feud with each other.

The lack of cohesion was exacerbated because each nation was fragmented into clans,
which were a form of extended family and usually carried the name of some animal – bear,
wolf, deer, or turtle. An additional factor was that each clan was allocated to one of two

moieties to help in the conduct of war or peace, the burial of relatives, and other matters of emotive importance. But all clan members lived together in what was a village community, except that it was taboo for anyone to marry another person of the same clan. Each clan jealously guarded its independence.

Iroquoian culture placed great emphasis on war. All males were expected to be warriors to maintain the system of retributive justice. Although crimes within the Five Nations had to be compensated on an agreed scale, Iroquoian culture demanded simple revenge against outsiders, especially in the case of death. Known as mourning war, this culture required either a member of the offending nation to be slain or a suitable captive brought back to be adopted in replacement. The Iroquois believed that unless retribution was exacted the soul of the departed person could not rest in peace.

For most of the seventeenth century the Iroquois war parties went northward and westward to attack the Chippewas, Hurons, and Ottawas, as well as the Susquehannocks to the south. These clashes are usually called the Beaver Wars. Although competition for the beaver trade was certainly one cause of hostilities, other explanations were the desire to avenge warriors killed in battle and the need to replace kinfolk struck down by pathogens. Often all three reasons for fighting applied to one target, as in the war against the Huron, who were suspected of having caused Iroquois deaths by the use of malevolent spirits. For five decades the Iroquois carried out attacks on their enemies, culminating in 1684 with their humiliating defeat of the French. It proved a pyrrhic victory, since the French not only reinforced their colony but united the surrounding peoples in alliance against the Iroquois. The result was a series of bitter defeats (see chapter 9, section 4). After the 1701 treaty with the French, it proved necessary to make peace with these traditional foes. Thereafter the most popular war path was southward against the Siouan-speaking Catawba and even the Iroquoian-speaking Cherokee. These expeditions were not always successful, and each foray necessitated further war parties to exact vengeance for previous losses.

A key element in the Iroquoian economy was hunting, both for food and for furs to trade. After 1701 some readjustment was necessary, if only because of the decline in beaver, but the Iroquois continued to hunt game for meat and furs, often traveling hundreds of miles to do so. These expeditions led to accidental clashes with other nations, thus sparking off new blood feuds. An alternative – and safer – source of protein closer to home was fish, which was plentiful in the lakes and rivers. As in all American Indian societies, both hunting and fishing were very largely male occupations.

Whatever their image as warriors and hunters, agriculture always played a larger role in the economy of the Iroquois than in that of the Abenaki. The main crops were corn, squash, beans, and tobacco; and except for the initial clearing of land, all the cultivation was done by the women. Each clan normally grew just enough for its own survival, for like most native peoples, the Iroquois never considered growing surplus crops on a commercial basis, even though this might have eased some of the problems caused by the decline in game.

The Iroquois lived in semipermanent stockaded villages. Like most of the eastern nations, their houses were built of sapling stakes bent together and covered with bark. Their rectangular shape (much longer than wide) gave rise to the term "the long house." The grand council chamber at Onondaga was at one time almost three hundred feet in length, though most were much smaller, being between 80 and 150 feet, holding six to ten households. Each household had its own compartment but shared a hearth with the family on the opposite side of a central corridor. Platforms were built for sleeping on, with a series of holes in the middle of the roof to let out the smoke. Earlier, a whole matrilineage had lived in one of these structures, but by the eighteenth century the traditional extended family was apparently breaking down into more compact nuclear groups, thus stimulating the construction of small log cabins. This in turn encouraged the abandonment of compact fortified villages for more dispersed settlements.

The Iroquois were matrilineal in their family structure. A man married into his wife's family, and his children took the mother's clan name. It was to a woman's relatives that the family looked for support. Inheritance was accordingly through the female line, which helped prevent the concentration of power in the eldest son and the development of patriarchy. In addition, the senior matron was also responsible for choosing the sachem to represent the clan at the grand council. This led one seventeenth-century Frenchman to observe how "All real authority is vested in them [the Iroquois women]. The lands, the fields and their harvest all belong to them. They are the souls of the Councils and the arbiters of peace and war . . . The children are their domain, and it is through their blood that the order of succession is transmitted." However, being matrilineal did not make the Iroquois matriarchal. At clan gatherings the men did all the talking and made decisions about war and peace, land disposals, and other matters of common interest, though the influence of Indian women may have declined as contact with Europeans increased. The latter invariably insisted on dealing with men in matters of diplomacy and trade. The only occasion when a clan matron had decisive influence was if she requested the launch of a mourning war party to avenge a death in her family, which male relatives were bound to respect.

Normally only certain families provided sachems. To this extent the Iroquois introduced an element of heredity into their choice of leader, though the matrilineal principle meant that only the brother of a sachem or one of his sister's sons could succeed. In practice most sachems were chosen for their hunting prowess, warrior skills, and wisdom, which collectively had gained them the respect of their clan. In particular they were expected to have shown stoical qualities in the face of adversity, though every male was expected to possess fortitude.

Relations between the sexes, as with most native peoples, were remarkably egalitarian. Although men and women had different roles, this was never used to justify unequal status, as in European societies. The key to survival was reciprocity, not individual aggrandisement: gender was complementary, not competitive. Hence women could initiate both courtship and divorce, in the latter instance by placing her partner's possessions outside the door of her family's longhouse.

The Iroquois were indulgent parents, and their children were normally not weaned until the age of three or four. This system may have demonstrated affection, but it also reduced fertility by prolonging lactation. Like all native inhabitants the Iroquois had no concept of sin and allowed their children every freedom, short of conduct dangerous to the safety of the clan. In general the children were encouraged to play games imitative of adult life. Thus boys hunted in the woods while girls attended their mothers in the house or garden.

From early childhood, the Iroquois were reminded of the ever-present threat of death. Such conditioning was especially necessary for the males, who were expected to be brave not only in battle but also when put to death if captured by an enemy. Most nations tortured their captives unless they adopted them, doing so less for sadistic pleasure than for the performing of a ritual in which the victim could demonstrate his courage. The Iroquois warrior was expected to withstand a whole night's torture, beginning with the burning of his legs and other parts of his anatomy. These preliminaries might be interrupted by feasting, in which the victim would participate. The torture would then continue, often with the captive singing to show his defiance, until his vital organs were cut out. This final act usually took place at sunrise, after which the heart and other parts of the body were eaten by the families of those taking part. This practice has led some observers to suggest a link with the sacrifices of the Aztecs, but the real reason for eating the heart was the belief that it would transfer the bravery of the deceased warrior to his captors. Europeans commented on the barbarity of these rituals; in reality they were little worse than the public executions of criminals broken on the wheel or hung, drawn, and quartered.

The religion of the Iroquois, as of most tribes, centered on the worship of nature, which was held to contain both good and evil spirits following the creation of the earth by Sky woman.[7] These spirits were customarily portrayed by painted masks called the False Faces, which were worn at various times of the year to ward off misfortune. They paid particular attention to the seasons, for which thanks and expressions of hope were offered. Among the more important observances were the midwinter ceremony, when fires were stirred; the thunder ceremony to celebrate the arrival of spring; the planting ceremony when the first crops were sown; the strawberry ceremony to celebrate the start of summer; the green corn ceremony, when the first corn could be eaten; and the harvest ceremony, when the last crops were safely gathered in. At these gatherings, offerings of tobacco were usually made, dances performed, feasts held, and speeches of thanks delivered. In addition it was customary during the midwinter and green corn ceremonies to name newborn children and those entering adulthood. Also important in Iroquois culture were dreams, through which the Iroquois believed a person's soul communicated its desires. These wishes then had to be implemented, no matter what the cost, otherwise sickness or disaster would result.

Since the seventeenth century the French had made various efforts to convert the Iroquois. While the confederacy remained in forest strongholds, the missions made little progress, though some Mohawks, Onondagas, and Oneidas were enticed to the Jesuit communities near the St. Lawrence at Caughnawaga. In the 1700s a number of Mohawks also converted to Anglicanism as did others in the aftermath of the Great Awakening, but the majority held fast to their traditional beliefs.

Nevertheless, by the turn of the eighteenth century the Iroquois were beginning to succumb to the insidious effects of their contacts with the European. The triple assaults of disease, technology, and lack of game had seriously weakened them at a time when the Europeans were continuing to grow. Smallpox was the most deadly disease, its disfiguring effects driving many to suicide. But equally destructive was the growing technological dependence of the Iroquois. They now hunted with guns, built houses with axes, and used other imported implements in their daily lives. European cloth had replaced their traditional skins. This dependence proved dangerous because the American Indians were unable to master the technology to make their own items in the future. They could not even repair

---

[7] See chapter 2, section 3, for the Iroquois view of the creation.

their guns. At the same time many of their traditional skills, like pottery making, were being forgotten.[8]

Finally, the lack of game meant that the Iroquois soon had little to trade for European goods and were thus of increasingly little use except as a buffer between the two white empires. As long as the Iroquois could sustain the illusion of holding the balance of power, both European powers were ready to supply them with arms and other goods. When that illusion was destroyed, the confederacy was likely to be economically and diplomatically crippled.

The Iroquois were not insensitive to the dangers facing them. In 1701 they opted for a policy of neutrality in respect to the two white nations, to allow them to rebuild their strength while playing off one European power against the other.[9] Then in 1722 the Iroquois invited the Tuscaroras to join the confederacy, conferring on them around 1750 the status of sixth nation, with representation on the grand council at Onondaga. In 1744 the Iroquois also provided the Delawares with new lands on the upper Susquehanna, though in a manner which ultimately did them no good. And throughout the period they continued to adopt rather than kill individuals captured in war, so that some of the clans became so mixed as to have lost much of their racial distinctiveness. Heterogeneity proved both a strength and weakness. While adoption brought recruits, the lack of racial awareness, however admirable by present-day standards, turned out to be an Achilles' heel. In contrast, the French and British, now advancing from the north and east, never forgot such invidious distinctions.

Unfortunately, the Iroquois were too scattered and isolated to assess the full nature of the perils confronting them, though there were a number of warning signs. One was the settlement of German immigrants on Mohawk territory at the mouth of Schoharie Creek near a fortified post, Fort Hunter. Another was the Kayaderosseras patent of Lord Cornbury, which granted a huge area of Mohawk land to a group of New York speculators, allegedly without Mohawk consent. But equally alarming was the increasing presence of the European military on the Great Lakes. In 1720 the French established a post at Niagara, whereupon the British built one at Oswego in 1727. The Five Nations had to accept both these incursions, if only to make their balancing act more credible. Fortunately, the fighting between Britain and France during the 1740s did not affect the area of New York. But by 1750 both European nations were about to dispute control of the Ohio. With hostile Delaware and Shawnee also in the area the claims of the Five Nations to suzerainty over the territory were likely to be severely tested.

To the south of Iroquoia the principal nation in the backcountry of Pennsylvania was the Algonquian-speaking Delaware, or Lenni Lenape. Originally they had inhabited much of southern New York and New Jersey, but they had been pushed back by white settlement to the upper reaches of the Delaware River. They were never one nation, being divided into two linguistic groups: the Munsee, or northern Delaware, and the Unami, or lower Delaware.

---

[8]   Richard White, *The Roots of Dependency: Subsistence, Environment, and Social Change among the Choctaws, Pawnee, and Navajos* (Lincoln, 1983) argues that it was the introduction of market values which proved most destructive to Indian society.

[9]   This meant in practice that the Seneca, Cayuga, and Onondaga nations maintained their links with the French, while the Oneida and Mohawk peoples continued their traditional friendship with the British.

DOCUMENT 26

The Iroquois reject English missionaries, circa 1710, reprinted in Karen Ordahl Kupperman, ed., *Major Problems in American Colonial History: Documents and Essays* (Lexington, Mass., 1993), 489.

[The Iroquois were sufficiently confident of their culture to reject the offer of missionaries, who they believed would corrupt the Indian way of life. But they were aware too of their dependency on European technology, hence the desirability of having blacksmiths to instruct them in metal working.]

It appears by the answer of one of the Indian chiefs or Sachems to Governor Hunter, at a conference in this town [Albany], that the English do not pay so much attention to a work of so much consequence as the French do, and that they do not send such able men to instruct the Indians, as they ought to do. For after Governor Hunter had presented these Indians, by order of Queen Anne, with many clothes and other presents, of which they were fond, he intended to convince them still more of her Majesty's good-will and care for them, by adding *that their good mother, the Queen, had not only generously provided them with fine clothes for their bodies, but likewise intended to adorn their souls by the preaching of the gospel; and that to this purpose some ministers should be sent to them to instruct them.* The governor had scarce ended, when one of the oldest sachems got up and answered *that in the name of all the Indians, he thanked their gracious good queen and mother for the fine clothes she had sent them; but that in regard to the ministers, they had already had some among them . . . who instead of preaching the holy gospel to them had taught them to drink to excess, to cheat, and to quarrel among themselves because in order to get furs they had brought brandy along with which they filled the Indians and deceived them.* He then intreated the governor to take from them these preachers, and a number of other Europeans who resided amongst them, for, before they came among them the Indians had been an honest, sober, and innocent people, but now most of them had become rogues. He pointed out that they formerly had the fear of God, but that they hardly believed his existence at present; that if he (the governor) would do them any favor, he should send two or three blacksmiths amongst them, to teach them to forge iron, in which they were inexperienced.

The Delawares were largely agrarian in their means of subsistence, growing corn and legumes, though like all American Indians they relied on hunting for meat. Land was cleared by the traditional method of slashing and burning, which also helped keep down the forest undergrowth and thereby facilitated the catching of deer and other game.

The Delawares lived mainly in small, semipermanent villages, some of which were stockaded, though others were merely a series of dwellings scattered along a convenient stretch of river. Their houses were made of birch saplings covered with bark. Some structures were similar to the Iroquois long house, being up to one hundred feet long to accommodate several families.

Like most east coast nations the Delaware were matrilineal in their family structure. The men hunted and fished while the women tended the crops, managed the household, and brought up the children. Babies were born in a separate hut and then strapped to a cradle board for twelve months. Girls were secluded during their first menstruation, after which they could become betrothed; they advertised their eligibility by means of a special headdress. Proposals of marriage were made through intermediaries. Marriage usually followed within a year and was marked by a feast. Relations between the sexes were relaxed, though fidelity was expected. Divorce was by mutual consent.

The religion of the Delaware was similar to that of their Indian neighbors. Animal spirits had to be propitiated if a hunt was to be successful, while dreams were thought to give the individual an insight into the spirit world. However, like many native peoples, the Delawere were amenable to European ideas, though dissent inevitably occurred over how far they should adopt Christianity.

Initially relations with the English were generally harmonious, not least because William Penn made particular efforts to negotiate proper land purchases. The Delawares were content to sell some territory, seeing the advantage of trade and assistance against other, more aggressive neighbors. And they were not disappointed, since the Quakers, almost alone out of all the English settlers, showed respect for the indigenous inhabitants and their customs.

Then in the 1730s Penn's sons, Thomas and John, took over the proprietorship of Pennsylvania. More interested in developing their lands than in protecting the American Indians, they were abetted in their quest by Penn's former secretary, James Logan. All three had ceased attending Quaker meetings, signaling a weakening of any moral commitment to treat the native inhabitants as equals. The situation was the more volatile because numerous Germans and Scots-Irish were now entering Pennsylvania in search of land.

The result was increasing pressure on the Delawares, for the arrival of the new immigrants offered the Penns the prospect of huge profits from land sales if they could remove the native inhabitants. A means was found in the Walking Treaty of 1735, which emanated from Thomas Penn's claim to have discovered an ancient deed granting his father an area as far as a man could walk in one and a half days. Penn arranged for a relay of runners to mark out the boundary. The Delawares had no illusions about the fraudulent interpretation of the deed. Like all the native peoples, they had little knowledge of the white man's laws and no written records of their own. They had trustingly based their security for fifty years on their original treaties with William Penn. Although they totaled about four thousand people, their warriors were too few and their settlements too exposed for outright resistance.

Not that the Penn brothers had a completely free hand, since they still had to deal with the Quakers in the assembly. It was partly to circumvent this obstacle that Thomas and John Penn enlisted the aid of the Iroquois. The two sides had several interests in common. Apart from land, the Penns wanted to open trade with the western tribes, which they could do only with the agreement of the Iroquois. The latter believed that the subjection of the Delawares would increase their power and influence. Accordingly, in 1744 a treaty was concluded at Lancaster. The Iroquois claimed suzerainty over the Delawares, whom they claimed to have conquered and reduced to the status of women, and told them to move to the Susquehanna River. In return the proprietors received the lands thus vacated, along with the blessing of the Iroquois for a western trade route.

The combined pressure of the proprietors and the Iroquois confederacy was too strong for the Delawares to withstand unaided. Some like Chief Teedyuscung adopted Christianity in an abortive attempt to keep their lands. Others sought refuge with the Moravian missionaries at Gnadenhutten near Bethlehem. But many refused to accept such clearly fraudulent proceedings and migrated to the Ohio country to join the Shawnee, another Algonquian-speaking people who had lost their hunting lands to the Iroquois during the Beaver Wars and then suffered at the hands of the Cherokee and Catawba early in the eighteenth century. The two soon represented a formidable combination, not least because of their mutual resentments. They only awaited an opportunity for revenge.

It was about this time that the western Delawares began to develop a new philosophy which taught their people that only by abandoning the ways of the white man could they ever again enjoy their former, happy state. Unfortunately for the Delawares, the British were soon to follow them into the Ohio, leaving them no escape. The only consolation was that the French, too, were anxious to halt the British advance and offered potent support should any conflict develop.

3 THE NATIONS OF THE SOUTHERN FRONTIER

The principal nations of the southern frontier after 1715 were the Siouan-speaking Catawba, the Iroquoian-speaking Cherokee, and the Muskogean-speaking Creek.

The Catawba had originally come from the Siouan area of the plains sometime in the sixteenth century. In the process, they had changed from being nomadic hunters to farmers living in stockaded villages, growing corn, beans, and squash. They lived on the border between North and South Carolina, sandwiched between the Tuscaroras to the east and the Cherokee to the west.

Until 1715 the term Catawba was unknown, being a phrase of convenience first coined by the Europeans to describe the Esaw, Sugaree, and Shuteree tribes living on the Catawba River in the vicinity of Sugar Creek. When these three nations refrained from supporting the Yamasee, they were permitted to accommodate the other Siouan peoples displaced by the recent hostilities, among whom were the coastal Waccamaw and Santee and the more inland Congaree, Saponi, Ocaneechee, and Cheraw.

This consolidation revealed that the Siouan peoples could overcome old hostilities and cultures to build a new community. Not that their integration was complete, since each tribe lived in its own village. To help bridge these differences, a council of headmen was periodically held, though its authority was necessarily limited. Ties were also reinforced by communal hunting, war parties, and trade.

Despite these adoptions the numbers of the Catawba were never large, amounting to perhaps two thousand people concentrated in seven towns.

The presence of other powerful confederacies in the region meant that the Catawba had to be warriors. Like the Iroquois, they practiced the mourning war ritual, which suited both admirably. The first clash occurred about 1670, seemingly from an accidental meeting while hunting. Whatever the cause, from that time on Iroquois war parties traveled south to strike at the Catawba, who then hit back as they retreated. Unfortunately for the Catawba, after 1715 the Iroquois attacks were backed up by the assistance of the Tuscaroras. The fighting became so intense that the provincial authorities in Virginia, South Carolina, and New York made efforts in the 1740s to end the warfare in order to unite the native peoples against the French. The Catawba by this time were ready for peace, having been deserted by the Cherokee. A treaty was accordingly signed at Albany in 1751, but it proved of limited duration. Iroquois mourning war ritual remained a dominant requirement, and individual clans continued to fight the Catawba despite the agreement at Albany. Here again was proof of the limited power of the Iroquois grand council.

The Catawba's relations with the British were generally harmonious, as they were not sufficiently numerous to be a threat but had enough prowess to be useful guardians of the frontier. They were useful, too, in tracking down runaway slaves. In addition the two sides enjoyed a thriving trade, exchanging deerskins for guns, ammunition, cloth, pans, and other manufactured goods.

Nevertheless, by the 1750s the Catawba were increasingly under threat. Disease continued to diminish their numbers, and there were no more coastal Indians to adopt. Equally insidious was the advancing line of white settlement. Since 1729 the authorities in Charleston had encouraged development of the backcountry to protect the coastal plantations from another Indian war. Now a new tide of settlement was approaching from the north, along the great wagon road from Pennsylvania through Virginia and North Carolina. By 1755 the Catawba towns were virtually encircled.

The result was a repetition of what had happened to coastal peoples elsewhere. The settlers cut down the trees, drove away the game, cleared the land, erected fences, built roads, diverted streams, stocked the countryside with domestic livestock, and destroyed the Catawba economy in the process. Earlier the Catawba had been able to conduct a thriving trade in skins to meet their needs. Now they were increasingly dependent on the colonial government – even for food when a drought occurred in 1755. Only their reputation as warriors sustained them in the eyes of the whites.

The Catawba recognized their precarious situation, and as early as 1748 they debated the wisdom of joining the Chickasaw or Creek nations. Essentially they had three options: removal, resistance, or reservation status. Removal to unknown lands was both risky and unappealing. Resistance was no longer realistic, though the buildings and fences of some intruders were burnt. The majority wished to stay and decided the best way was through accommodation. The Catawba hoped that gratitude for past services and current usefulness would ensure them a future too. Hence at a meeting in 1754 they promised to respect the colonists' laws, explaining that the recent theft of livestock and other items had merely been the result of exuberance on the part of the younger warriors. They had put their lives at risk fighting the enemies of the British, only to be refused help when returning hungry from the battle. The Indians had also had property stolen and were constantly being plied with drink. Nevertheless, they were ready to fight with their British allies.

While the Spanish, French, Cherokee, Creek, and Chickasaw posed a threat, the Catawba were still welcome in Charleston. They were also able to play the South Carolinians off against the Virginians and North Carolinians who were anxious for their support. But should the military balance shift decisively in favor of the British, such bargaining power would be lost. As it was, the Catawba were now on the verge of being a dependent people, with a homeland little more than a reservation.[10]

---

[10] The descent into reservation status occurred quicker than anyone anticipated. In 1759 smallpox killed over half the tribe, reducing their number to five hundred. At the same time the defeat of the French and Cherokee meant that Catawba warrior skills were no longer marketable. The Catawba responded by requesting that their lands be surveyed to distinguish and protect them from white claims, effectively establishing a reservation.

Farther inland to the southwest were the Cherokee, who were linguistically an Iroquoian people. They resided in the mountains of southern Appalachia, where the borders of Georgia, the Carolinas, and Tennessee now meet, concentrated in three groups – the lower, middle, and upper towns – comprising some sixty settlements.

The Cherokee were one of the most numerous Indian peoples, having a population of around twelve thousand at the turn of the eighteenth century. Like the Iroquois, their towns were based on clans and were politically independent. The lower towns favored the British; the middle towns tried to be neutral; while the upper towns looked to the French at New Orleans, reflecting their different economic interests and location on the tributaries of the Tennessee River. But the Cherokee clans, like those of the Iroquois, never fought each other. Diversity in their foreign relationships was not incompatible with harmony at home.

Like most eastern nations, the seven Cherokee clans were matrilineal. They, too, had relaxed notions of sexual morality; a man might have more than one wife if he could support her. However, their religion had a greater spatial sense than that of the Iroquois, for they divided the universe into three parts: the upper world of the spirits, the middle world of human beings, and the underworld of the dead. Most of their gods were similar to those of other nations: the sun, moon, and corn deities. Justice was enacted through the clan system.

Hunting was an important part of the Cherokee economy, since the region abounded with deer, which provided food for the villages and skins to trade at Charleston. Like all the southeastern nations, they also engaged in agriculture, principally the growing of Indian corn. Their farming was among the most advanced of any native people, and had been further boosted by Cherokee readiness to cultivate European and African foods such as peaches, melons, apples, onions, and cabbages. Initially they rejected European livestock, for as one chief explained, "the buffalo are our cows, the deer our sheep . . . [and] bear our hogs." However, by the end of the colonial period they had begun keeping cattle, horses, and hogs to balance the decline in game. The same trend influenced other aspects of Cherokee culture. Traditionally, their houses were constructed of the customary saplings bent together, normally covered with thatch. However, by the 1750s the Cherokee, too, were beginning to construct log cabins, now that iron axes were available.

From an early stage the Cherokee were keen to trade with the European newcomers, if only to surpass their neighboring rivals, the Creeks and Chickasaw. Perhaps more than most they appreciated the initial advantage of copying white culture in its material and technological aspects. This desire for access to British goods led them to assist the South Carolinians in their war against the Yamasee. Once the latter had been destroyed, the Cherokee became South Carolina's main line of defense against more distant tribes like the Choctaw, who were falling under French influence in Louisiana. This was a role which the lower and middle towns were happy to play, since it gave them control of the trade with Charleston. Nevertheless, like all tribes, the Cherokee eventually found trade with Europeans to be a mixed blessing. As one tribesman noted in 1753, "The Cloaths we wear, we cannot make ourselves, they are made for us. We use their ammunition with which to kill deer. We cannot make our Guns, they are made for us. Every necessary Thing in Life we must have from the white People." It was a relationship of unequals.

Although the Cherokee were linguistically Iroquoian, this connection did not prevent hostilities between them and the northern confederacy. Fortunately the Iroquois found it

Plate 40 A draught of the Creek nation, 1757. The Public Record Office, London. Reproduced by kind permission of the controller of Her Majesty's Stationery Office. Crown copyright.

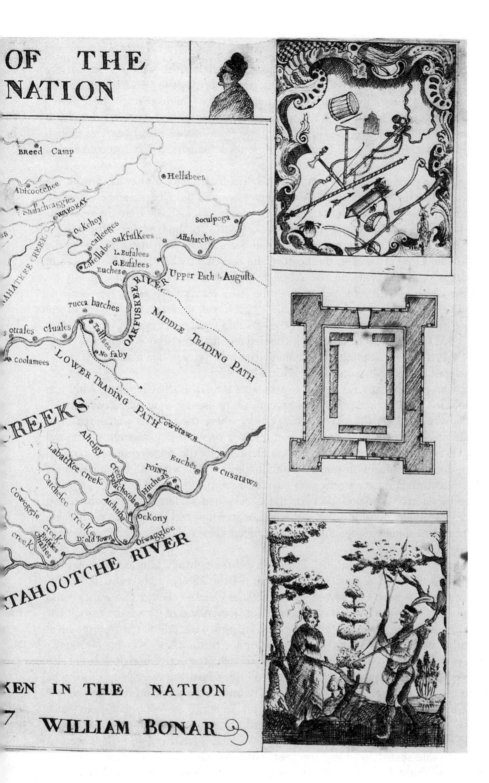

OF THE
NATION

Breed Camp

Hellabees

Abicootchee

Shahachaggies

WAKOKAY

ockchoy

calleeges

oakfulKees

Soculpoga

L.Eufalees

Altahatche

LaHellabe

G.Eufalees

Euches

Upper Path to Augusta

tucca hatches

MIDDLE TRADING PATH

otrafes

cluales

tallises

No faby

coolamees

LOWER TRADING PATH

coweta.ws

CREEKS

Ahetgy

Creek

Cowetaws

Labatikee creek

POINT

Euches

cusataws

Catchelee creek

Pucachooche

Hitchea.s

Atchuba

Coweogie creek

ockony

D: old Town

Otwaggloe

creek

TAHOOTCHE RIVER

KEN IN THE NATION
7 WILLIAM BONAR

difficult to reach them in their mountain retreats. Nevertheless this warring between the two principal allies of the British finally led to concerted efforts by the New York and South Carolina governments to arrange a peace, in the hope that the Cherokee might be deployed against the Spanish in St. Augustine. A treaty was concluded in 1742; however, the sachems of both nations could not prevent individual villages from further blood feuding, though hostilities did decline. Indeed, some Iroquois war parties actually stayed with the Cherokee before attacking other opponents.

The last major native people to confront the British settlements after 1715 were the Creeks. "Creek," like Catawba, was a term of convenience to describe a number of tribes, some of which did not even speak a Muskogean language. Among them were the remnants of the Guales of northern Florida and the Yamasee of South Carolina, while on the western fringes were the Natchez, another people who had been driven from their homes by the French in the late 1720s. However, the heart of the confederacy comprised two groups of Muskogean-speaking settlements on the Alabama and Chattahoochee rivers, usually referred to as the Upper and Lower Creek, though the latter were known as the Apalachicola by the Spanish. The principal settlements of the Upper Creek were Abeika, Okfuskee, and Okchai; those of the Lower Creek, Coweta, Cussita, and Oconee. Estimates of the Creek population varied from 15,000 to 25,000, distributed among some sixty settlements. What is not in doubt is that their readiness to accommodate other groups had made them one of the most powerful confederacies in eastern North America.

In their economy and sustenance the Creeks were similar to the Cherokee. Although they hunted for food, they relied principally on corn and pulses for their subsistence, which grew particularly well along the rich alluvial valleys where their towns were sited. The deerskin trade was similarly important, since it allowed them to buy firearms, cloth, and metal tools, all of which had become indispensable items by the mid-eighteenth century. Most of their commerce was with traders from Charleston, Augusta, and Savannah, who brought their goods to the Creek towns on packhorse trains.

Like most Eastern Woodland peoples, the Creeks had a clan structure which was organized into two main divisions: red and white, signifying war and peace. With these moieties were the customary designations of bear, deer, beaver, turkey, wildcat, and wolf. Lineage and kin were matrilineal.

Gender roles were fairly traditional. The men did the fighting, hunting, and clearing of the land, while the women reared the children, fed the family, and tended the crops. Indeed, the men and women often lived apart since the Creeks believed that purity could best be achieved by the separation of opposites. Thus women had to withdraw during their menstrual cycles and also at childbirth. The men in turn were prohibited from physical contact with the women when hunting or preparing for battle.

Marriages might be negotiated by clan leaders, though prospective husbands could also initiate proceedings by sending gifts to the intended bride's matrilineage. Spouses had to be from another clan. In the past, skill in warfare and hunting were the main requirements for a groom, but by the middle of the eighteenth century an ability to secure European goods was often the yardstick by which a man was judged, though personal attraction was still important. However, brides always had the right to refuse a husband, and single women enjoyed considerable sexual freedom, not least with visiting traders. Married women in contrast had to be faithful, though divorce was possible by mutual consent. Polygamy had once been common among the sachems, but seems to have declined as the cost of European goods rose relative to the value of deerskins. Keeping more than one wife had become prohibitive.

Creek towns were usually situated by a river where there was good land, access to freshwater fish, and ready communication with neighboring communities. Though the towns were fairly compact they were not protected by palisades: the inhabitants relied instead on their knowledge of the rivers and countryside for defence. Their houses were traditionally constructed of birch saplings, though by 1750s log cabins were becoming more popular. At the centre of each town was a small square, formed by the council chamber and private dwellings. Here ball games could be played.

Before 1760 European acculturation was limited to the import of tools, weapons, and cloth. After the Spanish had been expelled from Apalachicola in 1681, no missionaries had been allowed to establish their value systems or challenge the traditional Creek religious practices of the green corn dance or belief in a great creator and supreme being. Even in economic matters the Creeks still felt able to deal with the Europeans on an equal footing. However, as for the Catawba, this was shortly to change, especially when the white-tailed deer became scarce through overhunting. Prior to 1760 the Creek peoples had vigorously refused to keep domestic animals since they invariably took pasture from the deer and strayed on to the Indians' fields. They also undercut the price of venison. But as the deer became scarcer some chiefs began keeping cattle, a further sign that the traditional Creek economy was being undermined.

Contacts between the Creeks and the British had occurred following the establishment of South Carolina and these were further increased after the founding of Georgia in 1733. The Creeks, like all the native peoples, wanted European goods and technology so that they could confront their traditional enemies, notably the Cherokee and Choctaw. Earlier in the 1680s they had approached the Spanish at St. Augustine but were rebuffed because of Spain's ties with the Apalachee Indians. The Creeks hereafter looked to the English for allies and joined them in a number of military operations against east and west Florida at the turn of the eighteenth century which resulted in the destruction of the Spanish missions (see chapter 18, section 1).

Even so relations were not always harmonious. Profiteering by English traders was widespread, and in 1715 the Creeks supported the Yamasee in their war with South Carolina. Relations were patched up in 1716 and thereafter enjoyed something of a golden era, despite the presence of a French post among the Upper Creeks at the convergence of the Coosa and Tallapoosa rivers. The superior quantity if not quality of the British goods ensured that the garrison at Fort Toulouse were never able to compete commercially. Nevertheless, the French presence was useful since it allowed the Creeks, like the Iroquois, to play off the British against the French, thus ensuring better prices and gifts.[11]

The native Americans are often portrayed as having had no pleasures other than those associated with war and hunting. In reality all the native peoples played games, especially the young men as part of their training for war. Most popular were ball games, notably lacrosse. Another such game involved kicking a piece of leather against a post or posts in a kind of football. Often one clan or town challenged another to a contest (see Document 27). Throwing spears at a rolling object was also popular, the aim being to lodge the spear

---

[11]   For Creek relations with the French, see chapter 18, section 4.

DOCUMENT 27

The Indian ball game, quoted in Jerald T. Milanich, *The Timucua* (Oxford, 1996), 182–3.

[As Father Escobo, a Spanish observer, notes, the ball game was played not only for pleasure but to keep the warriors fit. The game itself appears to have been a combination of football and soccer.]

They arrange themselves twenty on a side and play the game in a brisk athletic manner. The ball carrier handles it smartly and he plays such an effective game with his sure shots that we can state that he scores on each shot. They erect goal posts made from pine trees about seven feet tall and on top of this goal they place a figure. Suddenly the forty players dash to the field, commence playing, and the game has begun with a rush. It is a rough game which many times proves to be costly to some unfortunate player who gets seriously injured. These seasonal games last for one month.

Even if the one carrying the ball returns to the game on the following day, he will try to move in a different direction. His adversary, however, will be just as fast, attempting to intercept him with his hands and feet and throw him to the ground. While the other thirty-eight struggle among themselves, these two carry on the fight between themselves. Each one attacks his opponent and tries to cast him to the ground. If some persons assist the one who is carrying the ball because he is their friend, they are disqualified and never again will be allowed to play. The two teams fight as if they were in a real battle and each one tries to get a good grip on his adversary. . . .

In Castile [Spain] the hands are used in playing ball, these Indians play ball with their feet. They propel the ball with their feet directly at the goal. I have seen fifteen; then fifty direct shots, until the player gave up because he was exhausted. That number was the maximum allowed by the rules of the game. . . .

Those assisting the one who propels the ball carry on such a quarrel that they do not respect brother, or even father or son. The opponent tries to break up the locking of arms. If one loses his grip, another will come to the rescue and clasp the arm. So it is a continuous war until time is called. The one holding the ball with his foot will kick the ball straight at the goal. If he makes his mark, his friends go wild because the reward is worth the struggle and it is considered an act of great skill to hit the mark.

closest to where the object stopped. Lastly, gambling was widespread, using peach stones or other objects as dice.

The position of the American Indian nations along the Appalachian and Allegheny frontier in 1750 was similar to that of the coastal nations at the beginning of the seventeenth century. They were still relatively strong, despite the ravages of disease, but all were threatened by the advancing line of British settlement. Unlike the native peoples in the seventeenth century, they had to contend with the conflicting ambitions of three imperial powers: Britain, France, and Spain. While the European forces were balanced, the native people could still play an important role. But should one of them win decisively, the position of the indigenous peoples would be profoundly and detrimentally affected.

The question remains why the American Indians were so slow to appreciate the dangers threatening them, compared to the Japanese, say, on the arrival of Commodore Perry. One reason was their isolation. For each nation the arrival of the Europeans was a recent phenomenon whose consequences were difficult for them to assess. What they did appreciate was the advantages of European goods. And although they were frequently ill-treated, they usually believed that their differences could be negotiated. In this respect the American Indians simply failed to understand the depth of white contempt for them and their culture, perhaps because of their own lack of racial prejudice and notions of cultural superiority.

The major obstacle to an effective native response was, however, linguistic. When the Europeans arrived there were between two hundred and three hundred languages spoken in North America. Even those speaking the same family of languages did not find communication easy. Hence American Indians' awareness was generally limited to a particular area, restricting even more their ability to confront the Europeans' superior resources and complex institutions.

16

The Institutions of Government

1691	The Virginian treasury comes under the control of the House of Burgesses.
	John Locke publishes *Two Treatises of Government*.
1708	Lord Cornbury is recalled as governor of New York for maladministration.
1718	Governor Spotswood is defeated in his appeal to the Virginia electorate.
1719	The Massachusetts House of Representatives claims sole right to name its speaker.
1720	An attempt is made to prevent the South Carolina assembly from adjourning without the Crown's permission.
	Gordon and Trenchard begin publication of *Cato's Letters*.
1725	The Maryland assembly claims sole legislative competence against the provincial council.
	A Massachusetts explanatory charter gives the governor a veto over the choice of a speaker.
1728	The Crown attempts to obtain a permanent salary for the governor of Massachusetts.
1732	William Cosby is appointed governor of New York.
1733	The Zenger trial takes place in New York.
1734	Gabriel Johnston is appointed governor of North Carolina; the Albemarle region secedes from the assembly.
1738	The South Carolina assembly attempts to prevent the council from amending money bills.
1740	The Privy Council requires all bills to contain a suspending clause.
1742	The proprietary party is defeated in an election in Pennsylvania.
1747	Governor Wentworth refuses to extend representation for the New Hampshire assembly.

1750   Jonathan Mayhew gives a sermon against "unlimited submission."

1752   The Privy Council instructs that all judicial appointments are to be at the king's pleasure.

Georgia becomes a royal colony and is granted an assembly.

1758   Virginia passes the Twopenny Act.

1 THE ROYAL FRAMEWORK

B Y THE END of the 1720s colonial government had acquired the pattern it would retain until the Revolution. Every province had a governor, council, and assembly elected by the freemen. However, there were significant differences between one province and another in the manner of selecting the governor and council. In the royal colonies of New Hampshire, Massachusetts, New York, New Jersey, Virginia, and the Carolinas, the king appointed the governor, who in turn chose the council. The only exception was Massachusetts, where the house of representatives selected the councilors in agreement with the governor.

Under the proprietary system in Maryland and Pennsylvania, the proprietor chose the governor and council subject to the consent of the monarch. In the corporate colonies of Rhode Island and Connecticut, on the other hand, the freemen elected not only the assembly and council but the governor, too, though the king could theoretically exercise a veto.

Before the Glorious Revolution the colonists' political relationship with England had been confined largely to the Crown; and this situation did not change after 1689. Until 1760 Parliament was little concerned with the administration of the colonies beyond ensuring that the mercantilist framework was in place. Their internal management was still the responsibility of the king and was jealously protected as part of the royal prerogative. Most of the routine administration was performed by the Board of Trade, which answered to the Privy Council, where most major decisions about the colonies were made.

The king's principal representative in each colony was the governor. In many respects he performed the same function as the monarch in England. He was head of the executive, approved all appointments on behalf of the king, and was responsible for the execution of the laws. He also summoned the local assemblies by the issue of writs, similarly proroguing or dismissing them in the manner of Parliament. He was in addition commander in chief of the local forces with responsibility for the defense of the province. On paper his powers were formidable.

To help administer the colony, the governor had a number of officials, including a secretary, attorney general, deputy auditor, and naval officer. He also had a council, which was a cross between the Privy Council and the House of Lords, having executive, judicial, and legislative functions. This body assisted the governor in all administrative matters and was also the highest provincial court of appeal. In addition, it had legislative responsibilities, constituting an upper house for the passage of bills. The only provincial exception to this rule was Pennsylvania, which had a unicameral legislature under the charter of 1701.

The third branch of English government was the judiciary, which was responsible for dealing with those who broke the law or were in some kind of civil dispute. In medieval times judges had been officers of the king and dismissible at his pleasure. However, since the 1701 Act of Settlement they could no longer be removed except by impeachment in the House of Commons. This granting of tenure during "good behaviour" had been instigated to ensure their independence and to check abuses by the executive branch of government.

The colonial judiciary had not yet attained this eminence. Indeed, in many respects it was still a branch of the executive. Colonial judges did not enjoy security of tenure but could be removed "at the pleasure" of the king. The reasons for this were various. Before 1689 justice had been the responsibility of part-time members of the council, who by definition had only limited knowledge of the law. Thereafter all the colonies created separate bodies to act as a superior court of judicature, probate, and admiralty. Nevertheless, the Crown still felt that colonial judges were not sufficiently trained to be given tenure for life. Perhaps most important was the belief that the colonial judiciary, like colonial assemblies, could not enjoy the same exalted status as its counterpart in England. Mercantilism dictated that all colonial institutions be subordinate to the mother country, and making judges independent was incompatible with that aim.

2 LOCAL GOVERNMENT: TOWN MEETING AND COUNTY COURT

Most colonists dealt only with the lowest strata of government. They were remote even from the provincial capital, and very few ever made the journey to the mother country.

The structure of local government varied considerably from province to province. In New England the town was its principal element. Originally, only church members could participate, but since the end of the seventeenth century a property qualification had been instituted instead. The voters elected a wide range of officials: constables, tax assessors, highway surveyors, and tithingmen. Most important were the selectmen, who had general responsibility for the town, determining taxes and dispensing justice for minor offenses. However, one responsibility not granted them was the distribution of town lands, which after 1692 lay with the proprietors or founding families, acting separately. Elections were annual.

The New England provinces also had a system of county courts, consisting of a panel of justices appointed by the governor. Their main business was to act as an intermediate judicial stage between the petty misdemeanors handled by the selectmen and the major crimes involving "life, limb, banishment, or divorce" dealt with by the provincial superior court.

The middle colonies had a more varied system of local government. New York City was governed by a mayor, aldermen, and councillors. Under Governor Dongan's charter of 1686, the aldermen and councillors were elected by the free male inhabitants. Since the posts of mayor, sheriff, recorder, and town clerk were still chosen by the governor, however, the citizens' real power was limited. Like the New England selectmen, the mayor and aldermen acted as justices of the peace.

Most of the rest of the province was divided into counties, with a sheriff and panel of justices appointed by the governor. Some counties, like Suffolk on Long Island, also had towns structured on the New England model, in which all freeholders had the vote. In addition, the Van Rensselaer patroonship remained, though with greatly restricted legal and administrative authority. The other manors merely gave their possessors ownership of the land. Local government was exercised either by the county courts or by town officers elected by the inhabitants.

Pennsylvania had a similarly complex structure of local government but was also in some respects the least representative of the northern colonies. Philadelphia was governed by a closed corporation on the English model with a mayor, aldermen, and councillors, who coopted someone as a vacancy arose. The rest of the province was divided into counties, with a sheriff and bench of justices appointed by the proprietor or his representatives.

However, in 1711 the assembly reduced the powers of the justices when it created county tax commissioners, positions which became elective in 1722. The post of sheriff was also partially democratized. The freemen elected two nominees, leaving the governor to make the final choice. There was a similar arrangement concerning the townships into which each county was divided. The inhabitants elected two nominees for constable and local tax assessor, giving the governor the final say. There were no town meetings.

The third middle colony, New Jersey, had a system similar to that of New England; towns elected their own officials and county justices were appointed by the governor. However, the representative element was strengthened by the requirement that the justices, when dealing with administrative rather than judicial matters, were assisted by a panel of supervisors, elected by the freemen of each township in the county.

The southern colonies, in contrast, had almost no representative element in their local government. They followed English practice, especially in the Chesapeake. At the lowest level was the parish, whose governing body was the vestry. This body was invariably self-coopting and chosen from the gentry. Its responsibilities included appointing Anglican ministers, the upkeep of the established church, the provision of welfare for the indigent sick and elderly, and the setting of a parish rate.

The next level of local government in the South was the county court, which consisted of a panel of justices, technically appointed by the governor, but in effect also self-coopting, since they filled vacancies by recommending names to the governor. The justices also selected the sheriff and other court officials. They dealt with most legal matters such as hearing civil actions and petty misdemeanors, the verifying of wills, and the sale of lands. The county courts also shared responsibility with the parishes for roads, bridges, and ferries. The only southern province to diverge from this county court pattern was South Carolina, where most judicial and administrative tasks continued to be handled by the vestries.

Local government was clearly not representative, especially in the South. Only the New England town was fully elective, and its system has been paid much attention in the belief that it provided the bedrock of America's subsequent democracy.

It is often supposed that representative institutions are by definition democratic, but as the study of New England itself shows, such an assumption is not valid. During the seventeenth century only church members or proprietors could participate in the affairs of most New England towns, and even then only the wealthier members were elected to positions of authority. Popular acquiescence in the authority of the elite was almost complete. Only in the last two decades of the century was their domination challenged in a growing number of disputes about taxes, the level of the minister's salary, election returns, and the distribution of town lands. One consequence was increased litigation. The saints were finding it more difficult to settle matters behind closed doors.

The consensus broke down for various reasons. In Massachusetts, one factor was the granting of a new charter in 1691, under which any male who possessed taxable property worth £20 could participate in town affairs. This qualification was a considerable reduction from the previous requirement of £80 under the 1670 franchise law, but it was still a far cry from the concept of one man, one vote. Nevertheless, more electors meant greater diversity of opinion. The need for voters to be in good standing in the church also seems to have been abandoned at this time. Although the colony still outwardly conformed to the values of its forebears, it no longer had the same commitment to them, perhaps being influenced by the spread of materialism as the towns became more susceptible to market forces.

A further cause of discord was the monopoly of the proprietary families over the distribution of unsettled lands. This was increasingly resented by the other inhabitants who had subsequently bought land, held office, and paid their taxes – only to remain excluded from entitlement to any dividend. Frequent attempts were made to widen access, but all were defeated by the general court because of its reluctance to interfere with the rights of private property. However, the proprietors of many communities eventually found it prudent to admit to their ranks the more prominent residents who were still excluded from their number.

Analysis of the specific disputes, however, shows that there was another factor responsible for the loss of the consensus on local government: the growth of many towns. Community and agreement were possible when a town comprised just a few families pioneering in the wilderness. Eighty years later the population of many towns had increased several times. In the case of Dedham, founded in 1636, the initial grant from the general court had been very extensive. By the 1700s the spread of the population had effectively created new centers of population at Bellingham, Walpole, and Needham. These communities found it inconvenient to have their affairs managed from Dedham and increasingly wanted their own minister, school, town meeting, and selectmen. The result was a bitter series of disputes which in 1728 compelled the general court to intervene; in the end Dedham had to be divided into three precincts.

Many other New England towns suffered similar disruption. Gloucester had originally been a small farming community. From the second decade of the eighteenth century a thriving port began to develop in the area known as Gloucester Harbor. When a new church was required in the mid-1730s the wealthy merchants there determined to have it rebuilt in their own part of town close to the harbor. The farmers and fishermen of the older Annisquam region of Gloucester resisted bitterly, since their control of the community was already being undermined in other respects. The controversy rumbled on until 1742, when the general court allowed the creation of two separate parishes.[1]

The primary force behind these disputes was not a demand for democracy but rather a geographically motivated desire for reallocation of local government responsibilities. The towns continued to be run by small enclaves of relatively privileged people, in a manner far removed from the spirit of a modern democracy. One indication of their restrictive nature was their unwillingness to admit strangers, especially if they appeared to have no visible means of support. The first six decades of the eighteenth century witnessed a huge increase in the number of people being "warned out."

Another reason for dissension after 1740 was religion. During the Great Awakening congregations in many towns became divided between the New and Old Lights over the selection of ministers, destroying the unanimity of the old order. Along the way the inhabitants became accustomed to electioneering, speech making, and all other aspects of politics.

---

[1] See Kenneth A. Lockridge, *A New England Town, the First Hundred Years: Dedham, Massachusetts, 1636–1736* (New York, 1970); and Edward M. Cook, Jr., *The Fathers of the Towns: Leadership and Community Structure in Eighteenth Century New England* (Baltimore, 1976). For Gloucester, see Christine Leigh Heyrman, *Commerce and Culture: The Maritime Communities of Colonial Massachusetts, 1690–1750* (New York, 1984). The argument that consensus was breaking down is disputed by Michael Zuckerman, *Peaceable Kingdoms: New England Towns in the Eighteenth Century* (New York, 1970).

This process in turn prepared the ground for the later growth of a more truly democratic spirit, though only after the colonial period had ended.

Elsewhere local government remained relatively static in the hands of the traditional authorities. In the middle colonies towns did not have large landholdings and no problems arose concerning the location of their churches or government. Any excess population simply emigrated to the next county and sought incorporation as required.

A similar picture pertained in the South, where the planter elites dominated government at both a local and provincial level. Many of those appointed to the county courts were also members of the council or house of representatives and were thus able to use their visits to St. Mary's, Williamsburg, New Bern, or Charleston to confirm themselves or their relatives as sheriffs and county justices.

Not until the last decades of the colonial period did the arrival of a new population in the backcountry pose a challenge to this cozy arrangement. Interestingly, the response varied from one province to another. Virginia acted quickly to establish vestries and county courts. The tidewater elite welcomed the new settlers both as a barrier against the Shawnee and other western nations and also as a means of increasing the value of their own lands. Accordingly, in 1738 Orange County was established on the eastern side of the Blue Ridge Mountains, followed in 1745 by Augusta County in the valley itself. Although these counties were not elective, they did reflect the newcomers' desire for some framework of government. In addition, the vestries were left almost entirely free of Episcopalian influence, to avoid offending the religious sensibilities of the newcomers.

In the Carolinas, by way of contrast, the authorities paid little attention to the new settlements in the piedmont. North Carolina created counties but staffed them with the tidewater elite, who used their position to further their own interests. In South Carolina the new settlements were simply administered as extensions of the existing coastal parishes. This lack of attention to the political needs of the backcountry population was to cause serious trouble after 1760 with the rise of the Regulator movement.

3   THE PROVINCIAL ASSEMBLY: CROWN VERSUS PEOPLE

After 1689 all twelve mainland colonies had an assembly, as did the main British West Indian islands. As already noted, these had been won only after protracted struggles during the seventeenth century and were looked on as grants of favor rather than of right. Officially that view had not altered, but the Glorious Revolution in England, with its emphasis on property rights, had strengthened the assemblies' position considerably.

Although the origins of the different assemblies had been diverse, by 1700 they had two main functions. The first was to make local laws for the convenience of colonial inhabitants – London was too far away to meet every legislative requirement. Second, the provincials believed that the assemblies, like Parliament, should act as watchdogs. The experience of the seventeenth century had demonstrated that the rights of the individual subject were constantly under threat from the executive branch of government.

The assemblies normally met in the spring or fall, when the roads were passable and the weather temperate. The sessions usually lasted about four weeks. Most representatives were not professional politicians and were anxious to return home to their occupations as farmers and merchants.

The main business was to vote taxes essential to cover the expenses of government, such as the salaries of the governor and the few other permanent officials. Members also addressed any other subjects which required government attention: poor crops, natural disasters, or lapses in law and order. Most sessions were not controversial, though an issue like paper currency might cause dispute.

The right to vote for members of the assembly varied from colony to colony but always required a property qualification. In most places it was equivalent to the English forty-shilling freehold, that is, ownership of a property with a rental value of forty shillings. In Virginia, for example, the law of 1736 required that a voter possess either twenty-five acres of improved land with a house of four hundred square feet or one hundred acres of unimproved land.

Historians have long been divided as to just how democratic the provincial franchise was. At one time it was popular to argue that because wages were high and property was cheap, almost any male could qualify for the vote. In the past twenty years writers have tended to emphasize the hidden costs of land ownership, the high incidence of tenant farming, and the presence of considerable poverty in both town and country, all of which suggest a lower proportion of enfranchised settlers, perhaps 50 percent of white males.[2]

Since all women, African-Americans, and American Indians were excluded from the political process, judged by modern standards the American colonies were not democratic.[3] Nor did they pretend to be, for although the representatives referred to themselves as the popular part of the system, they did so only in contrast to its monarchical and aristocratic components. Before 1760 no one believed that a crude head count could be the basis of political legitimacy. The popular view was that government should be a mixture of monarchy, aristocracy, and democracy, the three legitimate forms of government outlined by Aristotle. Democracy alone was thought likely to degenerate into mobocracy, the worst of all conditions, since property itself would be at risk. Here lies one of the crucial differences between eighteenth-century and present-day America. In colonial times the belief that owning property should be a requirement for participation in the political process was an unquestioned assumption on both sides of the Atlantic.

Nevertheless, although the colonists and the British agreed on the fundamentals of political behavior before 1760, there were two basic differences in interpretation which

---

[2] For a discussion of the provincial franchise, see Robert J. Dinkin, *Voting in Provincial America: A Study of Elections in the Thirteen Colonies, 1689–1776* (Westport, 1977). The view that land was cheap, wages high, and voting qualifications easily obtainable is argued by Robert E. Brown, *Middle Class Democracy and the Revolution in Massachusetts, 1691–1780* (Ithaca, 1955). For a recent analysis of electoral practices in Virginia, see John Gilman Kolp, *Gentlemen and Freeholders: Electoral Politics in Colonial Virginia* (Baltimore, 1998). He shows that there were wide variations in voter participation depending on the issues and local circumstances. In some counties only 25 percent of males voted; in others the figure was as high as 75 percent. See also chapter 11, section 3.

[3] Inevitably there were a few exceptions. In some places in Massachusetts, widows with property were occasionally allowed to vote, as were American Indians, in, for example, Stockbridge in western Massachusetts. For more information on the latter, see Brown, *Middle Class Democracy*, 40–4, 89. Some free African-Americans may also have voted in the South until the second decade of the eighteenth century, when both North and South Carolina passed laws to make the franchise exclusively white, as did Virginia in 1723. For more information, see Dinkin, *Voting in Provincial America*, 33. Five colonies also specifically excluded Catholics from the franchise: Virginia, New York, Maryland, Rhode Island, and South Carolina. Another four excluded Jews. See Chilton Williamson, *American Suffrage: From Property to Democracy, 1760–1860* (Princeton, 1960), 15–16.

caused periodic dispute. One concerned the rights of the provincial assemblies, the other concerned issues of legislative policy.

The main points of contention in regard to the rights of the assemblies centered on their ability to control their membership, choose a speaker, audit expenditure, and adjourn when they wanted. Since these were all rights enjoyed by the House of Commons, the lower houses generally believed that they should enjoy them too. The British, however, regarded such claims as unacceptable, believing that if granted, they would weaken royal government and undermine the whole purpose of the imperial relationship. In their view the colonies were constitutionally akin to borough corporations, which also held royal charters allowing them to make byelaws and raise local taxes. Such institutions could never be equated with the majesty of Parliament; what the colonists assumed to be rights were in British eyes merely privileges.

Hence when Francis Nicholson was appointed governor of South Carolina in 1720 he was warned how "the members of several assemblies in the plantations have of late assumed to themselves privileges no ways belonging to them." One such assumption was that "of being protected from suits at law during the term of the assemblies." Freedom from arrest was something that only members of Parliament ought to enjoy. Equally unacceptable was the practice of many assemblies to adjourn "themselves at pleasure without taking leave from his Majesty's governor first obtained." This habit suggested that it was the assemblies which were determining business, not the Crown.

The same reasoning induced the Crown to ensure that the speaker of the house was at least approved by the governor, so that some control could be exerted over that body's proceedings. This policy produced a fierce battle in Massachusetts during the 1720s. The clash began in 1719 when the house nominated Elisha Cooke, Jr., to be speaker. The recently arrived Governor Shute vetoed the nomination because Cooke had been critical of his predecessor. The assembly disputed Shute's right to do this and decided to adjourn, whereupon Shute dissolved the house and called new elections. The house remained adamant over its choice of speaker and in the end Shute appealed to the Privy Council, which issued an explanatory charter in 1725 affirming the right of the governor to veto the nominee of the lower house. Significantly, the assembly accepted this ruling, fearing that further obstruction might mean the loss of the 1691 charter.

The extension of representation was another area of dispute. The Crown took the view that representation was a privilege which only it could grant. The lower houses asserted that it was part of their inherent right to determine their own membership. The matter was potentially explosive, since the need for additional representation often arose in light of the continuing westward spread of the population. In practice the lower houses were not always quick to act, since the creation of new constituencies would weaken the influence of the existing tidewater areas. In most colonies the Crown did permit limited increases in representation. Nevertheless, from 1747 to 1752 the issue provoked a bitter dispute in New Hampshire between the assembly and Governor Wentworth, who asserted that membership had been fixed at the time of the original charter and could not be unilaterally increased by the house.

The most heated battles between the Crown and the provincial representatives were fought over the control of finance. Though the assemblies had gained the right of initiating taxation, the Crown continued to fight a rearguard action for a permanent source of revenue, especially to pay the governors' salaries. The British were terrified that their officials would be blackmailed into making concessions if their salaries had to be renewed annually.

In reality only one episode lived up to the authorities' apprehensions, after Governor Shute refused to accept the Massachusetts assembly's nomination for the speakership. The house first responded by reducing his stipend and then in 1720 refused to pay him at all. Matters finally came to a head in 1728, when Shute's successor, Governor Burnet, was instructed to demand a permanent revenue, hinting at possible parliamentary action in the event of a negative response. The house refused but did offer the governor an increased stipend on the old conditions. Burnet continued to resist, even proroguing the assembly to Salem, and the issue dragged on until his death in September 1729. In the end the next governor, Jonathan Belcher, accepted the increase and the subject quietly dropped. The royal representatives were ultimately reluctant to involve Parliament, for fear of reducing the royal prerogative. Equally, the assembly was not unaware that a further confrontation might lead to the loss or amendment of the charter.

Another financial matter which caused dispute was the issue and audit of money. The Crown took the view that taxes were "aids to the king" which gave it the right to dispose of the money as it wished. To this end the governors were strictly enjoined to ensure that all monies were issued through their own hands. But several assemblies argued that what the people had granted should be spent only as they designated.

Unfortunately for the Crown, it had already lost this battle in a number of colonies during the confusion of the late seventeenth century. In Virginia the issue of money since 1691 had been exercised by the treasurer, who was appointed by the house. A similar practice prevailed in South Carolina, where a weakened proprietary government had given way. In the aftermath of Governor Cornbury's corrupt stewardship, New York had adopted the same practice, arguing successfully that the assembly must protect the public from such notorious peculation. Once a precedent had been set it was almost impossible to reverse.

The control of expenditure was most controversial in wartime, when emergency levies were imposed. On these occasions the lower houses frequently specified that commissioners were to accompany the army to supervise military expenditures. Similar tactics were adopted in the financing of presents to the American Indians. The Crown feared that the assemblies would thereby gain control of these important areas of policy and thus undermine the royal prerogative. The Massachusetts house of representatives caused offence in this respect in 1720 when it tried to supervise the running of several military posts in Maine by the direct vetting of expenditures.

One other matter of constitutional dispute concerned the tenure of judges. In both North Carolina and New Jersey attempts were made to give colonial judges commissions on the English basis of good behavior rather than at the king's pleasure, in order to protect their appointments from executive interference. As already noted, the Crown did not believe that colonial judges were sufficiently competent or mindful of imperial requirements to be given tenure for life. Moreover, as most judges were only paid, like governors, on a yearly basis, they would be substituting dependence on the executive for one on the legislature, an even less desirable relationship. In 1752 the Privy Council issued a general directive that all judicial appointments were to be at the king's pleasure. The issue did not become really contentious until after 1760.

Finally, in several royal colonies attempts were made to restrict the powers of the council on the grounds that it was an arm of the executive, not the legislative, branch of government. The most sensitive area in this respect was the right of councils to amend money bills. In South Carolina the assembly refused the council this right from the late

1730s, claiming the same exclusive power over taxation as the House of Commons did in England. In some provinces the response of the councils was to differentiate between their executive and legislative functions by excluding the governor from the latter deliberations. In New Jersey Governor Lewis Morris voluntarily withdrew when bills from the lower house were under discussion. However, in South Carolina the appointment of expatriates from England led the assembly to demand the council's exclusion from all legislative matters, arguing that it was improper for placemen to be involved in the making of laws.

Intermingled with these constitutional issues were other policy matters which provoked conflict between the Crown and provincial assemblies. Here again, Massachusetts was in the forefront though for a time it seemed that the appointment of a native Bostonian, Jonathan Belcher, as governor in 1730 would help calm the situation after the acrimonious disputes about the speakership and payment of the governor's salary.[4] Belcher decided that the key to a successful administration was to build his own party in the assembly. During his first year he dismissed fifty-one justices of the peace and other local officials, replacing them with persons linked to potential sympathizers in the assembly. The evidence suggests that he offended more than he cajoled, which proved unfortunate when the Land Bank became a burning issue at the end of the 1730s. By then Belcher had too many enemies to control the situation.

The disallowance of the Land Bank, however, was to prove a turning point in the politics of Massachusetts. In 1741 Belcher was replaced by William Shirley, partly because of intrigues by his opponents and in part because of his poor handling of the bank issue. Though an Englishman, Shirley had first come to the colony in 1731 and had served Belcher as advocate general of the admiralty court. A man of considerable charm and ability, unlike Belcher he did not try to change the leadership of the assembly, preferring to work with those already there. Shirley's adept handling of the final stages of the Land Bank issue, his subsequent willingness to accept paper money, and his organization of the expedition against Louisburg in 1745 brought the old antagonistic relationship between the executive and the legislature almost to a close.

He was also helped by the growth of a Court party and a more pragmatic Country party leadership (see section 4 below). Massachusetts was exceptional among the colonies in the intensity and duration of its quarrels with the Crown, which were exacerbated partly by its long tradition of self-government during the seventeenth century. It took time for these commonwealth traditions to die.

New York had problems of a different kind. Riddled with faction for much of the seventeenth century, in 1702 it had the misfortune to receive Lord Cornbury as governor. Cornbury came with only one end in view, to make himself rich. He siphoned off money from the provincial treasury and made lavish land grants, playing one faction off against another to his own advantage. He also grossly offended all the inhabitants by dressing as a transvestite.[5] He was equally cavalier in his treatment of New Jersey, of which he was simultaneously governor. His final affront was to ignore the Toleration Act of 1689 by

---

4   See chapter 10, section 4, for details about the Land Bank.
5   This aspect of Cornbury's character has been challenged by Patricia U. Bonomi, "Lord Cornbury Redressed: The Governor and Problem Portrait," *William and Mary Quarterly*, LI, 1994, 106–18. See also Patricia U. Bonomi, *The Lord Cornbury Scandal* (Chapel Hill, 1998), in which she argues that the charges against Cornbury were largely inventions by his political opponents.

imprisoning the Presbyterian minister Francis Makemie in 1707 for preaching. Although Cornbury was related to Queen Anne, the Whig administration in London insisted on recalling him, thus illustrating the new commitment to honesty which permeated government after 1689.

The appointment of Robert Hunter as governor in 1708 initiated a period of relative harmony. Hunter was a cultivated man, whose good manners and fine sense of judgment enabled him to steer between the opposing Leislerian and Anglo-Dutch factions. No less important was his ability to sort out the province's finances, including the grant of a five-year revenue to the Crown, though he only achieved this by acknowledging the right of the assembly to appoint the provincial treasurer, a significant concession in the struggle to control finance. The good relations between the executive and legislature continued under his successor, Governor Burnet, until the latter's removal to Massachusetts in 1727.

Unfortunately New York was to suffer from another high-handed governor in the early 1730s. William Cosby, like Cornbury, was related to the English aristocracy, and he too wanted to revive his fortune. When he failed to secure some perquisites he created a special court of chancery to handle the case. This episode not only offended the chief justice, Lewis Morris, but also led John Peter Zenger to publish his *New York Weekly Journal*. Ultimately, Cosby upset too many people and in 1736 he was recalled.

After the departure of Cornbury, New Jersey in contrast witnessed little conflict between the Crown and assembly – at least until the governorship of Lewis Morris, when paper currency became an issue following the Privy Council's ban on further emissions. This led Morris to veto a bill for the issue of £40,000 in 1742, even though the assembly offered him an increased stipend and inserted a suspending clause as requested by the Privy Council. The assembly responded by withholding his salary. Morris then called new elections, but to no avail, even though he dissolved the assembly three more times and purged his council. The issue was resolved only by his death and the appointment of Jonathan Belcher, who was prepared to be more flexible, following his experience as governor in Massachusetts. His salary was paid, even though the Privy Council subsequently vetoed the currency bill. The assembly finally got its way in 1754 when financial necessity overruled the council's objections (see chapter 10, section 4).

Unlike New York and New Jersey, Virginia experienced a prolonged period of political harmony from 1720 to the early 1750s. In some respects this was surprising, given the earlier conflict between the imperial authorities and the members of the planter elite. Indeed, the 1700s had witnessed an attempt by Governor Spotswood to break the planters' power, culminating in his appeal to the Virginia electorate in 1718 "to choose men of Estates and Family's of moderation . . . dutiful to their superiors." The attempt failed, and Spotswood, unable to beat his opponents, joined them, buying large tracts of land and becoming a planter himself. He also humored the grandees by allowing them similar concessions and thus avoiding political controversy. Governor Gooch continued this policy, and the harmony was disrupted only following the appointment of Robert Dinwiddie in 1751. Two issues then clouded the scene: the pistole fee controversy of 1752–4 and the Twopenny Act of 1758.

The pistole was a Spanish coin equal to three and a half dollars, which Dinwiddie wanted to levy on every grant of land. Similar fees were permitted in most colonies, but in Virginia the House of Burgesses had been responsible for legislating all fees since the late seventeenth century, following the extortionate activities of governors like Lord Culpepper.

DOCUMENT 28

Lord Cornbury instructed to obtain a permanent salary, 1703, reprinted in W. Keith Kavenagh, *Foundations of Colonial America: A Documentary History* (New York, 1973), II, 1118–19.

[No issue in the period 1700–40 was more sensitive than that of a permanent salary for royal officials, the fear being that the assemblies would use its annual renewal as a means of exerting pressure on the Crown. In the case of New Jersey, the government was anxious to make a fresh start now that the colony was a royal province. The initiative failed partly because Cornbury, in accepting gifts, flagrantly ignored his instructions and had to be recalled.]

Whereas we have appointed you our Governor-in-Chief of our province of New Jersey in America, and there being no provision made, as we yet understand, for the support of yourself or of the governor or lieutenant governor of the said province for the time being, we do hereby signify to you our royal will and pleasure that, at the first meeting of the Assembly after the receipt thereof, you do acquaint them with our expectation that, in regard of our receiving our good subjects of that province under our immediate protection and government, they do forthwith settle a constant and fixed allowance on you our governor. . . .

In consideration whereof we are hereby pleased to direct that neither you our governor, nor any governor, lieutenant governor, commander-in-chief or president of the council of our said province for the time being, do give your or their consent to the passing of any law or act for any gift or present to be made to you or them by the assembly, and that neither you nor they do receive any gift or present from the Assembly or others, on any account or in any manner whatsoever, upon pain of our highest displeasure and of being recalled from that our government.

Dinwiddie's demand threatened the authority of the lower house by setting a precedent for similar impositions in the future. His bid for more income accordingly failed.

The Twopenny Act was a rather different issue, being a temporary measure to regulate Virginia's commodity money, tobacco. The poor harvest of 1758 meant that prices fixed in tobacco suddenly become much higher in real terms, causing considerable hardship, especially for debtors. The House of Burgesses accordingly intervened in September 1758 to regulate the price in the interests of equity. The Anglican clergy, whose salaries were paid in tobacco and who now stood to make a considerable profit, were understandably displeased. They appealed to the Privy Council and won their case on the grounds that the Twopenny Act did not have a clause suspending its operation until the consent of the Crown had been obtained. The clergy then sought redress in the courts for reimbursement of their stipend. This issue rumbled on after 1760, helping to sow doubts about the efficacy of the provincial assemblies to pass emergency legislation.

The suspending clause was not otherwise a serious issue before 1760. Perhaps only 5 percent of bills were disallowed for want of such a clause, or indeed for any other reason.

Plate 41   Portrait of Major General Robert Hunter, by Sir Godfrey Kneller, ca. 1720.
Collection of the New York Historical Society, New York City.

Connecticut had fewer than six measures challenged in over a hundred years: in South Carolina a mere twenty out of four hundred were challenged between 1719 and 1760. Many temporary bills were permitted in recognition that emergency action had been necessary. When measures were disallowed it was usually because they contravened the laws of trade. For instance, the 1723 Virginia tax on imported slaves was annulled at the prompting of British merchants who saw it as a threat to their commercial interests. At no time before 1760, however, did such disallowance threaten a serious constitutional disturbance. The colonies generally accepted the right of the Privy Council to exercise judicial review to ensure compatibility with the laws of Britain.

The proprietary colonies were likewise not free from political controversy between their legislative and executive branches of government. Pennsylvania probably had more disputes than any other colony, continuing the tradition set during the first twenty years when David Lloyd led his country supporters against Penn and his wealthy backers in Philadelphia. In 1716 a bitter dispute over the right of Quakers to affirm rather than take an oath on the Bible in legal and administrative proceedings was stirred up by Governor Charles Gookin, despite the English Toleration Act of 1689 which allowed Quakers to affirm.

There were periods of calm following the death of Penn in 1718. During the 1720s the main areas of contention occurred within the assembly itself when a former governor, William Keith, tried to wrest control from Lloyd in a battle for the speakership. The harmony between the executive and legislature continued even when Thomas Penn arrived in 1732 to restore the fortunes of his family.

The outbreak of war in 1739, however, was another matter, as it immediately raised the issue of defense. This issue had nearly cost William Penn his province fifty years before, and Thomas was determined not to repeat this experience. To meet the crucial need to form a militia, he set about building a party from the minority groups which could challenge the Quaker country party in the assembly. Despite his organization of gangs of seamen to intimidate the voters, however, he was signally rebuffed in the 1742 election, not least because the Quakers organized their own guard of shipwrights known as the White Oaks. This defeat led to talk of disfranchising the Quakers, while they in turn considered an appeal to the Crown for a royal charter. The antagonism became even more bitter with the steady distancing of the proprietary family from the Quaker religion. One sign of this was Penn's choice of Richard Peters, an Anglican clergyman, to be provincial secretary.

The dispute over defense dragged on until 1747, when Benjamin Franklin appeared as peacemaker. Though associated with the Quaker party, Franklin was more flexible than the acrimonious Lloyd. Hence a bill was finally passed in 1748 for the support of a volunteer militia. This allowed the non-Quaker population to defend itself without contravening the conscientious objections of the Friends. Fortunately, hostilities with Spain and France did not greatly affect Pennsylvania, involving no more than some privateering between the Capes of Delaware. The issue was to resurface, however, during the last French and Indian War, with rather more serious consequences.

Maryland, the other proprietary colony, also had its share of disputes. Although the Calvert family had been dispossessed of its governing rights in 1689, these had been restored in 1715 following Benedict Calvert's conversion to Anglicanism. Initially it was feared that the family had acted merely for political convenience, since several Catholics immediately claimed positions of authority in the provincial government. In the event the proprietor refused to support them, and Protestant fears were calmed by a further act in

1718, requiring all officeholders to take oaths of loyalty to the Hanoverian monarchs and abjure the temporal authority of the pope. After this anti-Catholic fears subsided.

Thereafter attention shifted to the relationship between the council and the assembly. In reality this was a continuation of the old battle against the proprietary authority, since the Calverts controlled the council's membership. In 1725 the assembly claimed to be "the people's representatives for whom all laws are made" and proceeded to whittle down the powers of the upper house, denying them in 1740 the right to amend money bills. Disputes also developed concerning fees and the right of the proprietor to a permanent revenue.

Only the corporate colonies of Connecticut and Rhode Island completely avoided overt tension between their legislative and executive branches of government. Since both were elected by the freemen, they enjoyed a close harmony of interests. Conflict arose mainly over the administrative details of royal government. Connecticut clashed with the customs authorities over which ports were to issue clearance papers, and in 1731 the colony was reprimanded for not sending all the amendments to its laws to London for approval. Its governor, however, received nothing more than a reprimand.

One ameliorating factor between the Crown and colonies was the system of agents to represent the provincial assemblies in London. Essentially the agents were lobbyists, whose task was to ensure favorable consideration of colonial interests by the authorities at the center of the empire. Among their targets were the Board of Trade and Privy Council, but ordinary members of parliament were also lobbied since they could influence legislation affecting the colonies. The principal merchants who traded with North America were another important target, since they could give valuable support both inside and outside Westminster. The system provided a safety valve whereby the views of the colonists and imperial authorities could be reconciled to the benefit of both.

Nevertheless, historians have tended to see the disputes between the central and local authorities as evidence of a drift toward independence. They argue that the imperial system was too inflexible, saddling the colonies with incompetent officials, offering insufficient reward to native-born white Americans, and containing fundamental constitutional inconsistencies.[6]

Certainly the Crown sent too many ineffective place seekers, who were doubly incompetent since almost all were total strangers to America. But colonial opposition to them did not constitute disloyalty to the Crown, only a protest against its representatives. Many of these disputes in any case were motivated by a desire for office. Once that objective had been attained, those who had vociferously condemned a particular measure or official often adopted what they had so recently denounced. The quality of governors also improved as the century progressed, one reason being the stricter guidelines drawn up by the Board of Trade. Though some infractions of these rules did take place, the worst excesses of Cornbury and his predecessors were not to be repeated. When governors fell foul of the population it was because of their lack of judgment, not peculation or extortion. In addition the Crown sent out many good governors, notably the veteran Nicholson and his successor, Spotswood,

---

[6] See especially Leonard W. Labaree, *Royal Government in America: A Study of the British Colonial System before 1783* (New Haven, 1930); and Jack P. Greene, *The Quest for Power: The Lower Houses of Assembly in the Southern Royal Colonies, 1689–1776* (Chapel Hill, 1963). The thesis is restated in Jack P. Greene, *Peripheries and Center: Constitutional Development in the Extended Politics of the British Empire and the United States, 1607–1785* (Athens, 1986).

in Virginia, and the able Robert Hunter of New York. Even the era of the Duke of Newcastle from 1725 to 1760 was not as wanting in ability as has usually been suggested. Where able men were appointed, comparative harmony was the result, as Shirley demonstrated in Massachusetts.[7]

Another popular explanation of the conflict between the Crown and the assemblies is that the Board of Trade and Privy Council saddled the governors with rigid instructions which prevented them from dealing with each situation as it arose. But most of the hundred-odd articles were designed to introduce the incumbent to the routine of provincial administration, while other provisions merely asserted the need for a godly atmosphere. The most controversial directives were those already outlined: to prevent the assemblies from accumulating too many privileges and to ensure that the mercantilist system was observed. In any case, under emergency conditions many governors ignored the strict letter of their instructions and took contrary actions which the Board of Trade and Privy Council retrospectively had to accept. No governor who had shown himself adept was removed for being flexible.

Ironically, it was often locally born governors like Lewis Morris who were most inflexible, not having the confidence of appointees from Britain as to how far they could ignore their instructions. For example, William Burnet accepted a paper money bill from the New Jersey assembly in 1723, even without a suspending clause, in return for a better salary. Morris felt he had no such latitude and suffered prolonged confrontation as his reward.

A further criticism of the colonial system of government is that it offered too little in the way of rewards for the local elites. No provincials were raised to the peerage, and only two were rewarded with baronetcies: William Phips, for his capture of Port Royal; and William Pepperell for the capture of Louisburg in 1745. Even the imperious Joseph Dudley failed to secure such an honor, while William Byrd II was snubbed on two counts. Not only did he not receive the governorship of Virginia, he also failed to secure a bride from the ranks of the British aristocracy which would have advanced his political influence and self-esteem. Such rebuffs may have fueled resentment against the imperial connection, since many visiting provincials often suffered an identity crisis in Britain, not least when disparaging comments were made about their country being a suitable receptacle for convicts and indigents.[8]

Many provincials, though, were appointed to the most senior administrative positions of governor or lieutenant governor. In Massachusetts, local men held the governorship for

---

[7] For a fuller analysis of Shirley, see John A. Shutz, *William Shirley: King's Governor of Massachusetts* (Chapel Hill, 1961). The view that the period was one of drift is argued by James A. Henretta, *"Salutary Neglect": Colonial Administration under the Duke of Newcastle* (Princeton, 1972); and Stanley N. Katz, *Newcastle's New York: Anglo-American Politics, 1732–1753* (Cambridge, Mass., 1968). Both Henretta and Katz were influenced by the British historian Sir Lewis Namier, who argued that patronage was the sole consideration in mid-eighteenth-century British politics. More favorable to Newcastle is Philip S. Haffenden, "Colonial Appointments and Patronage under the Duke of Newcastle, 1724–1739," *English Historical Review*, LVII, 1963, 417–35; and Richard Middleton, "The Duke of Newcastle and the Conduct of Patronage during the Seven Years' War, 1757–1762," *British Journal for Eighteenth Century Studies*, XII, 1989, 175–86. Behind the distribution of offices Newcastle had a serious political objective: the maintenance of the 1689 Revolution settlement.

[8] For a discussion of Byrd's wounded pride and the alienation of other members of the Virginia gentry, see Kenneth A. Lockridge, "Colonial Self Fashioning: Paradoxes and Pathologies in the Construction of Genteel Identity in Eighteenth Century America," in Ronald Hoffman, Mechal Sobel, and Fredrika Teute, eds, *Through a Glass Darkly: Reflections on Personal Identity in Early America* (Chapel Hill, 1997), 274–339.

thirty-five out of the fifty years following the Glorious Revolution, and almost all the men appointed in Rhode Island and Connecticut were colonials, though New England was perhaps the exception. Appointees in Virginia, New York, and South Carolina invariably came from the mother country.

Nevertheless, colonial elites everywhere could look to places on the council and positions in the judiciary. The superior courts were staffed by local men, even though most had no formal legal training. The same was true of the councils, where in addition to executive, legislative, and judicial responsibilities, membership allowed participation in the special perquisite of granting lands. A large number of positions were also available in the county courts, town meetings, and provincial militias, creating in the local inhabitants a strong sense of running their own affairs. The only areas of government not staffed exclusively by colonials were the customs, vice-admiralty judgeships, and a few positions (like colony secretary) for which British-born governors liked to bring over their own men. Until the 1760s thwarted ambition does not appear to have been a serious political problem.

The final reason for asserting that the imperial system was doomed is that the Crown and the assemblies had incompatible views about their constitutional relationship. Although the colonists paid homage to the king and acknowledged the concept of aristocracy, their emphasis on Locke's view that government was a trust for the benefit of the people was hardly compatible with the British view of the constitution.

Representative assemblies seemingly had an inexorable tendency to extend their control. The question remains: was this aggrandisement driven by incompatible ideological differences or was it merely a reflection of marginally divergent opinions? On balance the answer seems to lie with the latter, since the colonial intention was not to dismantle or deny the legitimacy of royal government. The assemblies believed that they were merely performing their proper role in watching over the executive. In any case, greater activity by the assemblies did not necessarily mean a decline in the powers of the Crown. Hence although governors occasionally voiced the need for parliamentary intervention, no one talked of radical restructuring or ultimate separation from Britain, even in Massachusetts. Such talk occurred only after 1760.

4 PARTIES AND FACTIONS IN THE AGE OF WALPOLE

One reason for not seeing the period 1715–60 solely in terms of a developing conflict between the Crown and the assemblies is that both intercolonial and intracolonial disputes were equally prevalent.

Most intercolonial conflict occurred over boundaries. Imprecise wording and lack of proper surveys prior to the drafting of the seventeenth-century charters meant that every colony had some dispute with its neighbors. Connecticut and Rhode Island remained in disagreement over their boundary until 1728. Massachusetts and New Hampshire were in contention during the 1730s. New Hampshire and New York had to negotiate in the 1740s, while from 1748 onwards there were disturbances on the Massachusetts border with New York when squatters invaded the Livingston manor. Pennsylvania and Maryland had a long-running dispute over their border, while Connecticut claimed the northeast corner of Pennsylvania by virtue of its 1664 charter.

Political strife in this period, however, was actually most prevalent between rival groups inside each colony. Disputes were carried on under various guises, for at that time political parties were not considered legitimate. In a just polity where magistrates did their duty, subjects were expected to be loyal. Factiousness was equated with self-interest. Accordingly, all those who were politically active argued that they were acting for the common good. This was the key to legitimacy in government or opposition.

The nature of the struggles varied from colony to colony. In some they revolved around commerce and agriculture, in others they were the result of religious and ethnic disagreements. Elsewhere the conflicts can be explained in terms of tidewater versus piedmont. Often it was a mixture of all three.

In Massachusetts the conflict was perhaps one of the clearest cases of commerce versus country. In Boston a nucleus of the wealthier classes, especially those involved in trade with Britain, like the Dudley and Hutchinson families, always affected to support the executive. At times they and their allies in the other seaports and market-oriented constituencies were sufficiently powerful to dominate the assembly, where Thomas Hutchinson was speaker for two years. Most of the country towns, jealous of such commercial wealth, opposed them.

The conduct of politics in Massachusetts was influenced by another ingredient. As Robert Zemsky has shown, a number of politicians in the country party began their careers by shaking the political tree as the prelude to climbing it. Among them were men like James Otis, Sr., Robert Hale, and John Choate. All were effectively professional politicians who used their skills to manage the untutored backcountry members in the House of Representatives. Their behavior did not result in constant battle with the Crown or commercial interests, since an accommodation was their ultimate objective. Even Elisha Cooke, Jr., the most vitriolic member of the country party, indicated a willingness to support Governor Belcher in the 1730s.[9]

In Connecticut political tensions tended to be sectional, with the older towns of the Connecticut River valley and New Haven arrayed against the more recent eastern settlements, like the burgeoning commercial centers of Norwich and New London. The older towns had been formed by religious covenants which still permeated their political culture. The newer towns, in contrast, had been founded as commercial ventures and reflected their more materialistic origins. They demanded cheap credit through the issue of paper currency, which was anathema to the older towns.

In New York the political lines were not always clear. Locals called the divisions court and country, later commentators preferred the terms Whig and Tory, but town and country would often be more appropriate, since New York City, with its strong commercial interests, often found itself ranged against the farming communities of the Hudson River and Long Island. Divisions sometimes also took on a religious complexion, especially between the Anglicans and Presbyterians, while ethnicity was a third factor with such a mixture of English, Dutch, Scottish, Huguenot, and German inhabitants.

New York City was generally dominated by the large Anglo-Dutch families, whose interests were increasingly commercial rather than landed and who also tended to be

---

[9]   See Robert Zemsky, *Merchants, Farmers and River Gods: An Essay on Eighteenth Century American Politics* (Boston, 1971). A similar interpretation is followed by Stephen E. Patterson, *Political Parties in Revolutionary Massachusetts* (Madison, 1973); and Richard L. Bushman, *King and People in Provincial Massachusetts* (Chapel Hill, 1985).

Anglican. Their leaders were Adolphe Philipse and later James DeLancey. The country party was led by Lewis Morris and Philip Livingston. The latter was a Presbyterian. Although large landowners themselves, Morris and Livingston cultivated the support of the "middling sort" of small farming communities of the Hudson, including the Dutch, together with the growing artisan class in New York City. The main arguments after 1710 centered on the question of taxation: should the provincial government be financed by quitrents or customs? Quitrents would bear more heavily on the small farms: customs burdens would fall chiefly on the commerce of New York. Defense was another intermittent issue. The tidewater area around the city believed that the frontier counties should look after themselves.

During Hunter's governorship, the Morris group dominated, since Hunter wanted to reduce the power of the elite. Governor Burnet initially continued this alliance when he arrived in 1720, but as support for the Philipse faction increased in the assembly, Burnet began to look to them. This was the situation which greeted Cosby on his arrival in 1731. Cosby's injudicious action over his salary perquisites and prosecution of John Peter Zenger quickly discredited his political allies. Accordingly, in the mid-1730s the Morris faction once more achieved ascendancy, only to find the situation reversed again in the 1750s when the DeLanceys came back into power. Although both sides claimed to be representing the people, and cultivated their votes at election time, none of this maneuvering involved much principle, for as Philip Livingston confessed during the Cosby episode, "We change Sides as Serves our Interest best not the Country's."

New Jersey was similarly riven by sectionalism, religious antagonism, and differing economic interests. Early in its history it also had a problem with absentee landowners, since many proprietors preferred to be domiciled in the relative comfort of New York or Philadelphia rather than in the wilds of east or west New Jersey.

However, with the governorship of Robert Hunter, most took up residence in the province to provide an effective governing elite, helping to alleviate the divisions between the east and the west. But most important was the development of tolerance between the Anglicans and Quakers, who dominated the upper and lower houses of the General Assembly even though they made up only one-quarter of the population. They were helped in their electoral dominance by the inability of the Presbyterians, Dutch Reformed, and Baptists to work together or to vote in sufficient numbers.[10]

Several other factors helped the development of a more cooperative spirit. One was the need for unity to combat the overweening power of New York and Philadelphia. Another was that New Jersey fortunately had no exposed frontier to defend. Finally, all the contending parties agreed to keep government to a minimum, thus avoiding contentious issues that bedeviled other provincial governments.

Nevertheless, this harmony broke down in the 1740s when doubts arose over the validity of various land titles. Since obtaining their original grant in 1664, the Elizabeth and Newark associates had continued issuing patents well beyond the original area, following additional acquisitions from the Indians, thus causing conflict with the proprietary titles

---

[10] For a revisionist view, see Thomas Purvis, *Proprietors, Patronage, and Paper Money: Legislative Politics in New Jersey, 1703–1776* (New Brunswick, 1986). See also Benjamin H. Newcomb, *Political Partisanship in the American Middle Colonies, 1700–1776* (Baton Rouge, 1995); and Brendan McConville, *Those Daring Disturbers of the Public Peace: The Struggle for Property and Power in Early New Jersey* (Ithaca, 1999). Newcomb plays down the importance of the subsequent land title disputes.

purchased from Berkeley and Carteret. In 1745 the East Jersey proprietors decided to challenge the activities of the Elizabeth and Newark associates in the courts, provoking numerous evictions and riots, during which the inmates of several jails were released. The struggle was then transferred to the council and the assembly. The council, representing the large landowners, demanded a draconian public order act to intimidate the rioters into accepting new proprietary patents requiring the payment of quitrents. The assembly, representing the smaller farmers and property owners, preferred conciliation, seeing the disturbances as essentially a conflict between two sets of landowners. Eventually the assembly got its way. An amnesty was granted; and tempers cooled when many of the small farmers, who had been unaware of the legal pitfalls of purchasing land in New Jersey, finally had their titles confirmed.

We have already seen that Pennsylvania's politics were dominated by the conflict between the proprietary family and the Quakers. Here too there was an element of town versus country. The wealthy commercial elements in Philadelphia were frequently in conflict with the small Quaker farming communities in Bucks and Chester counties. From the 1720s onwards the demographic balance of Pennsylvania began to change following the influx of large numbers of Germans and Scots-Irish. Until 1755 these newcomers were too remote or inexperienced to participate regularly in the political process. In general they supported the Quakers because of the latters' opposition to the attempts of the Penn family to raise the price of land, but eventually, after 1760, they were to undermine both the proprietary and Quaker factions.

In the South the factional fighting was generally less pronounced. A principal reason was that the presence of large numbers of slaves made the grandees readier both to cooperate with one another and to listen to those who owned small farms. The result was a tacit political consensus, which in Virginia led to a mere one-third of constituencies being contested after 1728. This *rapprochement* was briefly threatened in 1735 over the Tobacco Inspection Act, which many small farmers believed would exclude their produce from the market. Otherwise this harmony was marred only by the occasional dispute between the council and the assembly. The council was dominated by older members of the elite, who sought to protect their interests from attack by the younger generation in the house. Another cause of occasional discord was competing economic interests, such as those between the Ohio and Loyal Land companies in Virginia.[11]

The one exception to consensus politics was North Carolina, where the number of African-Americans was significantly smaller. The main conflict here was between the northern and southern parts of the province. The northern counties around Albemarle Sound were settled mainly by people from Virginia who, as in their former colony, produced tobacco. The southern area around Cape Fear had been populated largely by people from South Carolina, who cultivated rice and made pitch and tar for the navy. Until the 1730s the northern counties dominated the legislature. But as the Cape Fear region expanded, it began to demand more representation and the removal of the provincial capital from Edenton to New Bern. These demands were effectively realized in 1734 when Governor

---

[11] Marc Egnal, *A Mighty Empire: The Origins of the American Revolution* (Ithaca, 1988), suggests that the lines of political action were divided between optimists, who wanted to expand as quickly as possible, and pessimists, who were inclined to conserve what had already been won.

Gabriel Johnston, a planter from the Cape Fear region, took office. The northern counties responded by refusing to pay their taxes and seceding from the assembly. Eventually, in 1754 a new governor, Arthur Dobbs, secured a compromise involving a more equitable distribution of seats, though a permanent site for the capital still had to be decided. One factor bringing the two regions closer was the arrival of the Scots-Irish, Germans, and other groups in the piedmont area, who posed a challenge to both north and south.

Any system of government is bound to produce political discord; such conflict is part of the human condition. Perhaps more noteworthy than the occasional lack of harmony was the essential stability of colonial institutions between 1714 and 1760. Compared with the seventeenth century the period after 1715 saw few, if any, serious disturbances. No governors had to flee for their lives, nor were royal troops called upon to put down any insurrection. One reason for this relative calm was the greater stability of Britain itself. Another was the new maturity of the colonies. They were no longer isolated frontier settlements, ready to seize arms at the first alarm, and the change was reflected in their politics, which were now conducted within a clear constitutional framework. It was this very maturity that was to be so important after 1760.

5 TOWARD A REPUBLICAN IDEOLOGY

The American colonists were practical people. They concentrated on specific issues, like their entitlement to a representative assembly. They had no ideology in the modern sense.

Nevertheless, most historians believe that an embryonic republican ideology began to develop after 1689, making possible the rapid appearance of an alternative political creed after 1763 when Britain and the colonies came into open conflict.

The sources of this ideology have been variously identified. One was the tradition of Protestant dissent. New Englanders in particular held strong critical views of the Anglican church and, by implication, the English state. Their views were shared by other dissenting groups like the Presbyterians. None was overtly antimonarchical; their quarrel was with the unreformed church. There was much in their theology, however, which was incompatible with the kind of hierarchical authority then sought by kings. James I had asserted in 1603 that no bishops would mean no king. Subsequent events proved him right when Charles I was executed and a commonwealth form of government imposed.

The tradition of religious dissent was subsequently subsumed into the Whig party after the restoration of Charles II. Many Whigs, like the Earl of Shaftesbury, Algernon Sydney, and John Locke had served during the Cromwellian era. It was their distrust of monarchical power, allied to a hatred of Catholicism, which led to the Exclusion crisis of 1681 when an attempt was made to deprive James II of his right to the throne. The Whigs also played a key role in the Glorious Revolution of 1689.

Most English Whigs thereafter became supporters of the Crown, since the monarchy was now constrained by Parliament, where the Whigs had a majority following the revolutionary settlement. But a small band continued to remember their more radical traditions. Among them were the publicists Thomas Gordon and John Trenchard. After 1714 they and other "real" Whigs became increasingly alarmed at the apparent corruption of successive ministries under Sir Robert Walpole, fearing that his use of patronage to control the House of Commons would lead to the reimposition of tyranny. They expressed their opposition in various publications, notably the *Independent Whig* and *Cato's Letters*. These eighteenth-century "commonwealth"-style papers were sometimes read in America, where they reminded their transatlantic readers of the need for vigilance if virtuous government and a free people were to survive. This "commonwealth" mentality was well demonstrated by the Boston minister, Jonathan Mayhew. In a 1750 sermon entitled *Discourse Concerning Unlimited Submission*, he told his congregation on the anniversary of the execution of Charles I: "For a nation thus abused to arise unanimously and to resist their prince even to the dethroning him, is not criminal, but a reasonable way of vindicating their liberties and just rights." Or as Andrew Eliot wrote more succinctly in 1765, "when tyranny is abroad, submission is a crime."

The writings on natural law of Enlightenment philosophers like Pufendorf, Vattel, Grotius, Montesquieu, and Voltaire formed a third strand in the embryonic republican ideology. These philosophers provided a rationale for government based on reason, justice, and the laws of nature. The most influential member of this school was John Locke. Locke's intention on publishing his *Two Treatises of Government* in 1691 was to justify the Glorious Revolution. In practice, his arguments found little support even among English Whigs, for Locke stated that all authority must emanate from the people, to whom both monarch and Parliament were accountable. Government was a trust, and if rulers abused their authority the people could remove them, since their consent alone could confer legitimacy. This radical view offered a basis for government quite different from the existing European notions of divine right, prescriptive inheritance, or even parliamentary omnipotence. Significantly, it was this rationale which the Americans adopted when denying British authority in 1776.

A fourth strand in this incipient republicanism was provided by the classical historians of Greece and Rome, often interpreted and elucidated by Renaissance authors. These demonstrated how a society could conduct itself in an enlightened, constitutional, and virtuous fashion. Classical republicanism appealed to all those looking for a system of government not based on religion in which the good of the commonwealth came before the interests of the individual. But there were dangers too in such precedents, as history showed. The writings of Plutarch, Livy, Cicero, and Tacitus were full of dire warnings about the fate of the Roman republic, where a decline in virtue had allowed vicious tyrants like Nero and Caligula to take control. How happy in contrast were the Germans, Tacitus asserted, because they had retained their simple ways. These perils were seemingly confirmed by the experience of some eighteenth-century colonials. When John Dickinson studied law in London he was appalled at the apparent corruption of British politics. As he told his father, "It is grown a vice here to be virtuous." He could only reflect that "unbounded licentiousness . . . is the unfailing cause of the destruction of all empires." The colonists should take note.

Lastly, educated Americans were familiar with the writings of Aristotle, the great political scientist of the ancient world. His analysis of the three legitimate forms of government – monarchy, aristocracy, and democracy – taught colonials that, theoretically at least, constitutional monarchy was not the only legitimate system.

Of course such knowledge was limited to the few before 1760. Conventional wisdom suggested that the British constitution was the best, since it uniquely combined all three types of government defined by Aristotle. Natural rights were merely an interesting concept, not something the colonials needed to seek, since they already had their rights as Englishmen. When colonial legislators came into conflict with imperial authority they always resorted to English legal precedents like Magna Carta, the Petition of Right, Habeas Corpus, and the Bill of Rights.

Nevertheless the absence of the king three thousand miles away in London was subtly inducing a republican mentality among the colonists. Public mention of his name was necessarily a formality. Most colonists did not even have portraits to identify him, and there was no formal aristocracy or court. Consequently, by 1760 the veneer of monarchy was dangerously thin, though few yet realized this.[12]

---

[12] This subconscious drift towards a republican mentality is argued by Richard L. Bushman, *King and People in Provincial Massachusetts* (Chapel Hill, 1985). Other important writings on the topic include Bernard Bailyn, *The Ideological Origins of the American Revolution* (Cambridge, Mass., 1967); Gordon S. Wood, *The Creation of the American Republic, 1776–1787* (Chapel Hill, 1969); Caroline Robbins, *The Eighteenth Century Commonwealthman: Studies in the Transmission, Development, and Circumstance of English Liberal Thought from the Restoration of Charles II until the War with the Thirteen Colonies* (Cambridge, Mass., 1959); J. G. A. Pocock, *The Machiavellian Moment: Florentine Political Thought and the Atlantic Republican Tradition* (Princeton, 1975); and Edmund S. Morgan, *Inventing the People: The Rise of Popular Sovereignty in England and America* (New York, 1988).

17

Immigration and Expansion, 1714–50

1685	The revocation of the Edict of Nantes by Louis XIV increases the Huguenot exodus from France.
1704	The first sewer is built in Boston.
1707	The Act of Union between England and Scotland opens the door to Scottish emigration to America.
1709	Swiss Mennonites arrive at Pequea Creek, Pennsylvania.
1710	Palatine Germans settle on the Schoharie River, New York.
1717	The first Scots-Irish arrive in the Delaware and at Boston.
1720	Massachusetts passes an act to discourage Irish immigration. Lutheran and German Reformed immigration into Pennsylvania begins.
1730	The first settlements in the Shenandoah Valley are established.
1732	A charter is issued for the establishment of Georgia.
1735	The first Moravians arrive in Pennsylvania.
1740	Settlers arrive in the North Carolina piedmont.
1749	A lighting scheme is introduced into Philadelphia's streets.
1750	Settlement begins in the South Carolina backcountry.
1760	Philadelphia becomes the third largest city in the British Empire. Fire destroys four hundred houses in Boston.

1 THE GERMANS AND SCOTS-IRISH

T HE SEVENTEENTH CENTURY is usually portrayed as a period of settlement; the eighteenth century as one of consolidation. Before 1700 English men and women streamed forth to found a series of colonies driven by economic and religious necessity. Thereafter immigration dried up. But while this portrait may have held true for New England, it is not correct for the rest of the colonies. The South greatly increased its importation of African slaves, while all the colonies outside New England attracted new sources of white settlement.

What is true is that there was a relative decline in emigration from England after 1700. One reason was a lessening of persecution, another was an improvement in living standards there. A third was industrialization, which provided new opportunities at home. Even so, America continued to lure people from England, as the hope of a better existence still had considerable appeal, especially for those who had friends and relatives there. Others, perhaps 30,000, came as a result of the 1718 Transportation Act. It is likely that 75,000 persons of English extraction went to America in the period 1700–60.

A steady stream of Scots also crossed the Atlantic. The inhabitants of the northern kingdom had been excluded from England's overseas possessions during the seventeenth century. Some lowland Scots did settle in East New Jersey around Perth Amboy, after its purchase by Scottish Quakers. But after the 1707 Act of Union the door was open. Some Scots left as a result of the Jacobite uprisings of 1715 and 1745; many more departed for economic reasons. In time these Scottish immigrants were to be especially important in commerce, not least the tobacco trade. Perhaps 20,000 Scots came to America in this period.

A further group to appear before the turn of the eighteenth century were the Huguenots, or French Protestants. Most came following Louis XIV's revocation of the Edict of Nantes in 1685, which until then had assured them religious toleration. The Huguenots were generally welcomed, as their numbers were not large enough to constitute a threat and they brought many valuable skills as coopers, gunsmiths, clock makers, and textile workers. These skills, added to their thrift and diligence, soon enabled them to prosper. They improved their position still further by learning English and integrating with the rest of the community, even to the extent of joining the existing Anglican church. Perhaps five thousand Huguenots had arrived by 1750. They were especially numerous in New York, where they founded the town of New Rochelle, and in South Carolina.

A few hundred Jews also came to America from Britain during the latter part of the colonial period. Their commercial talents enabled them to prosper in the major seaports of Newport, New York, Philadelphia, and Charleston, where the first American synagogues were established. By the time of the French and Indian war, merchants like David and Moses Franks of Philadelphia were sufficiently established to secure contracts for supplying the British army with provisions.

The two most important sources of white immigration in the eighteenth century, however, were from Germany and Ireland. In both countries the population was initially driven from Europe rather than attracted to America, their uprooting being the familiar product of the search for economic opportunity and a desire for greater religious freedom.

The first Germans to come to America arrived with Francis Pastorius in 1683 at the invitation of William Penn. Their numbers were small. German emigration became

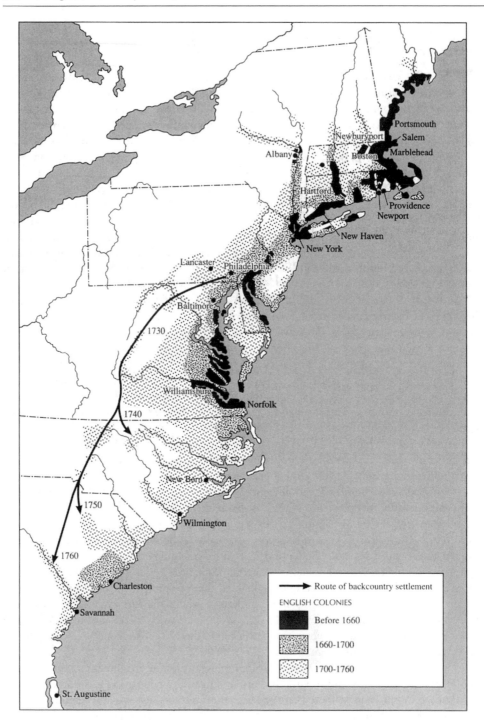

Map 11 Immigration and expansion, 1700–60.

substantial only after 1690, the year in which the Palatine prince decided to become a Catholic. Severe persecution ensued as he attempted to convert his subjects. In addition the devastation of the principalities of Baden, Württemberg, and the Palatine during the wars of 1689–1713 led many to consider emigration as the only possible escape. Most Germans looked for refuge elsewhere in central and eastern Europe: America was never the promised land for more than a small minority during the colonial period. German emigration proceeded in two main waves. First came the pietist sects, erroneously called Palatines, like the Mennonites and Dunkers. Later came a second, larger wave from among members of the established Lutheran and Reformed churches after European hostilities had ended in the 1720s.

Initially, departures were necessarily restricted by the fighting in Europe, though some emigrants did escape. In 1709 a group of Swiss Mennonites made its way to Pequea Creek in Lancaster County, Pennsylvania. The following year 2,500 Rhinelanders arrived in New York, assisted by financial aid from the British government. The Whig ministry believed that Dutch commercial success in the seventeenth century had resulted partly from the nation's tolerant religious policy. Hence the exodus of German and French Protestants might be put to good use, especially, it was hoped, in producing hemp for the navy.

In the event a change of ministry meant that no further aid was forthcoming, and it was some time before the refugees finally found shelter on the Schoharie Creek to the west of Albany. The lack of suitable land and the indifference of the New York authorities led most Germans to look instead to Pennsylvania, where the early Mennonites had received a welcome because their pietist beliefs were close to those of the Quakers. Soon other groups were arriving in the Delaware, notably the Amish people, an offshoot of the Mennonites, who settled in Lancaster County. Other newcomers were the Dunkers, or Baptists, who found homes there and in Berks County.

The end of the war in Europe brought a new exodus around 1720. These emigrants increasingly belonged to the main Lutheran and German Reformed churches, and their reasons for emigrating were more economic than religious. The Upper Rhineland in particular was experiencing a population explosion that meant ever smaller farms and less opportunity. In the mid-1730s, however, the Moravians, an evangelical branch of the Lutheran church, began to arrive, following their expulsion from Austria by the archbishop of Salzburg.

The total number of German-speaking immigrants during this period is difficult to assess, but it certainly approached one hundred thousand and caused one-third of Pennsylvania's population to be of German origin by 1760. The numbers were so high that fears were expressed for the survival of the English inhabitants. In 1727 a bill was passed requiring all immigrants to take an oath of loyalty, and in the early 1740s there was talk of barring from office anyone who did not speak English, the first demonstration of that later phenomenon known as nativism. As Franklin commented, "Why should the Palatine boors be suffered to swarm into our settlements, and by herding together, establish their language and manners, to the exclusion of ours."[1] He was referring not only to the continued use of the German language but to the fact that Germans lived in their own enclaves socialized

---

[1] Quoted in Stephanie Grauman Wolf, *Urban Village: Population, Community, and Family Structure in Germantown, Pennsylvania, 1683–1800* (Princeton, 1976), 138–9.

in their own taverns, drank coffee rather than tea, worshiped in their own churches, and seemingly failed to become politically involved. However, this freedom to live as they pleased, which they had so often been denied in Europe, was the reason Germans were so appreciative of "the famous English Liberty." As peasants in Germany, they had a variety of compulsory feudal obligations in the form of taxes, military service, and the provision of labor. In any case many became naturalized so they could vote, recognizing the need to protect their interests on such issues as religious freedom, the land policies of the proprietary family, the availability of paper money, and the defence of the frontier. The problem of assimilation, in fact, concerned mainly the first generation. Except for pietist groups like the Amish, most Germans were keen to assimilate, especially with regard to their children's upbringing, understanding of the law, and participation in the provincial economy. Many newcomers anglicized their names, from Holz to Wood and Zimmermann to Carpenter. Ironically, these settlers were shortly to become known as Pennsylvania Dutch, a corruption of *Deutsch*, meaning German.[2]

The Germans were to prove able colonists. Most of them were peasants who needed only settled conditions to prosper, being hardworking, Godfearing, and thrifty. Not all farmed immediately. Many came as redemptioners, hoping to pay off the costs of passage either by borrowing from relatives already there or by becoming servants for a time. This practice was bitterly criticized by the Reverend Gottlieb Mittelberger, who came to America in 1750 to investigate. He asserted: "It often happens that whole familes, husband, wife and children, are separated by being sold to different purchasers, especially when they have not paid any part of their passage-money." Mittelberger, however, was anxious to dissuade others from coming. He accordingly painted a picture of hardship on the voyage and disappointment on arrival.[3] In fact, since most redemptioners traveled in groups and possessed property, usually only one or two had to be sold into servitude, and they were generally redeemed by the rest of their family within a short time. Some German emigrants in any case saw servitude as an apprenticeship which it was useful to complete before buying a farm. Some took ten to fifteen years before purchasing a property of their own.

Unlike most English-speaking colonists, the Germans, or at least the Mennonites, cherished their farms and sought to improve the land rather than merely exploit it. This attitude often encouraged them to take over farms which the original owners had decided were no longer viable. And like the Puritans in New England, they rarely moved until the pressure of population forced the third generation to look elsewhere for land. The result was that they generally prospered, and their husbandry was one reason that Pennsylvania prospered in turn. Though one of the last provinces to be founded, by 1760 Pennsylvania contained over 300,000 people, making it the third most populous colony in America and the one with the highest per capita income.

The second major ethnic group to arrive in the period 1715–60 was the Scots-Irish from Northern Ireland, where religious persecution also played a part. Although the Presbyterian Scots-Irish had been brought to Ireland by the Protestant James I, they

---

[2]   However, the speed of assimilation is questioned by A. G. Roeber, *Palatines, Liberty and Property: German Lutherans in Colonial British America* (Baltimore, 1993); and Aaron S. Fogleman, *Hopeful Journeys: German Immigration, Settlement, and Political Culture in Colonial America, 1717–1775* (Philadelphia, 1996).

[3]   Gottlieb Mittelberger, *Journey to Pennsylvania* (1756), edited and translated by Oscar Handlin and John Clive (Cambridge, Mass., 1960). See Document 29.

suffered considerable persecution, not least the requirement to pay tithes to the established Episcopalian church. Then in 1665 the Anglican-dominated parliament in Dublin passed an Act of Uniformity requiring all ministers to conduct services according to the Book of Common Prayer. The effect was to bar Presbyterian ministers not only from holding church services, including marriage ceremonies and funerals, but also from operating schools. However, for the first thirty-five years the act was only intermittently enforced. Then at the turn of the eighteenth century a more militant Anglican church, as elsewhere, attempted to make its supremacy effective in practice as well as in theory. This culminated in the 1704 Test clause of the Popery Act which barred all dissenters from holding any public office in central or local government.

The Scots-Irish had economic grievances too. Although Ireland was a dominion of the British Crown, it had been excluded from the mercantilist system, like Scotland before 1707. The worst blow had been the 1699 Woollen Act prohibiting Irish wool exports to Britain. This ban particularly hurt the northern province of Ulster, where a textile industry was developing. Finally, most Scots-Irish were tenant farmers. Many of their leases were due to lapse in 1717, and the only prospect they faced was higher rents. The coming of peace in Europe induced many merchants to offer passage on their outward voyages, and for some Scots-Irish the chance proved irresistible.

Accordingly, in 1717 several shiploads of emigrants set off from Ireland to seek a better life. In a few cases whole congregations emigrated, though when the restrictions against the Presbyterian ministry were eased shortly thereafter, this phenomenon ended.[4] Once a precedent had been set, however, others were ready to follow, especially since the economic problems remained. Initially, many headed for New England, believing that they would be welcomed there. When the inhabitants discovered that the newcomers were Presbyterians, however, relations quickly deteriorated, culminating in the burning of the newcomers' church at Worcester. Hostility was so great that in 1720 the Massachusetts assembly passed a bill to discourage any further immigration from Ireland. A few groups did manage to establish themselves in New Hampshire and Maine, where the settling of the frontier was considered more important than the maintenance of religious orthodoxy. Among the new settlements were the towns of Londonderry and Belfast.

Initially the southern colonies were also unattractive to the emigrants from Ireland. The domination of Maryland, Virginia, and the Carolinas by the plantation system with its slave workforce restricted both the demand for white labor and the availability of land, though attempts were made to lure them to the South Carolina backcountry in the 1730s with bounties to increase the white population. Another apparent obstacle was the presence of the Anglican church, which made further persecution a possibility.

New York had little appeal because its manorial system left little freehold land available for settlement. After being tenants in Ireland the emigrants were determined not to

---

[4] In 1719 the Dublin Parliament, under pressure from the more liberal Whig ministry in England, passed a limited Toleration Act allowing Presbyterians to hold religious services. At the same time it passed a Partial Indemnity Act which suspended the Test clause, allowing Presbyterians to hold public office on a grace and favor basis. Some of the restrictions on Irish trade with the American colonies were also relaxed in 1731 by an act of Parliament, 4 George II, c. 15. Marriages between Presbyterians were eventually legalized in 1737, though not for mixed marriages, which still had to be performed by an Anglican minister. The formal ban on office-holding was only removed in 1780, while tithes remained payable until 1870.

DOCUMENT 29

Gottlieb Mittelberger on the perils of crossing the Atlantic, 1750, reprinted in Merrill Jensen, ed., *English Historical Documents*, Vol. IX: *American Colonial Documents to 1776* (New York, 1955), 464–9.

[Although conditions on Atlantic crossings had improved since the seventeenth century, they could still be extremely uncomfortable and perilous, as this extract reveals. Nor were the immigrants' problems necessarily over once land was sighted.]

When the ships have for the last time weighed their anchors near the city of Kaupp [Cowes] in Old England, the real misery begins with the long voyage. For from there the ships, unless they have good wind, must often sail 8, 9, 10 to 12 weeks before they reach Philadelphia. But even with the best wind the voyage lasts 7 weeks.

During the voyage there is on board these ships terrible misery, stench, fumes, horror, vomiting, many kinds of seasickness, fever, dysentery, headache, heat, constipation, boils, scurvy, cancer, mouth-rot, and the like, all of which come from old and sharply salted food and meat, also from very bad and foul water, so that many die miserably.

Add to this want of provisions, hunger, thirst, frost, heat, dampness, anxiety, want, afflictions and lamentations, together with other trouble, as the lice abound so frightfully, especially on sick people, that they can be scraped off the body. The misery reaches the climax when a gale rages for 2 or 3 nights and days, so that every one believes that the ship will go to the bottom with all human beings on board. In such a visitation the people cry and pray most piteously. . . .

That most of the people get sick is not surprising, because, in addition to all other trials and hardships, warm food is served only three times a week, the rations being very poor and very little. . . . The water which is served out on the ships is often very black, thick and full of worms, so that one cannot drink it without loathing, even with the greatest thirst. . . .

At length, when, after a long and tedious journey, the ships come in sight of land, so that the promontories can be seen, which the people were so eager and anxious to reach, all creep from below on deck to see the land from afar, and they weep for joy and pray and sing, thanking and praising God. . . . But alas!

When the ships have landed at Philadelphia after their long voyage, no one is permitted to leave them except those who pay for their passage or can give good security; the others, who cannot pay, must remain on board the ships till they are purchased. . . . The sick always fare the worst, for the healthy are naturally preferred first, and so the sick and wretched must often remain on board in front of the city for 2 or 3 weeks, and frequently die. . . .

have any more landlords. Nor was there any need to do so, for as the former governor of New York, Lord Bellomont observed, "What man will be such a fool as to become a base tenant . . . when for crossing the Hudson River that man can for a song purchase a good freehold."[5] Accordingly it was to New Jersey and Pennsylvania that the newcomers looked. Only there did the Quakers ensure the absence of religious persecution; and only Pennsylvania offered freehold land on easy terms, not least because the proprietary family was anxious to increase the value of its holdings.

Thus was the steady stream of Scots-Irish directed to Pennsylvania at the rate of over two thousand a year in the peak periods of 1717–19, 1727–9, 1740–3, and the early 1750s, when economic conditions were at their worst in Ireland. Perhaps a third of those emigrating went as families with sufficient resources to pay their passage and buy land on arrival. The rest, mainly single young men and women, took the traditional option of traveling as indentured servants. The men might hope in due course to buy land or become a craftsman. The women could look forward to a good marriage at the end of their service as the best means of securing a better life.

Initially, the newcomers, at least those who had the means, went to Lancaster County and the frontier areas of Cumberland and York, including the Susquehanna Valley and its tributary, the Juniata River. They were assisted by the readiness of the proprietary family to buy out the American Indians, though by the 1730s most of the best land in eastern Pennsylvania had been distributed. To the west lay only the uninviting Allegheny Mountains, but land was known to exist in the Shenandoah, or Great Valley of Virginia. The newcomers, accordingly, began trekking down through Maryland to the junction of the Shenandoah and Potomac rivers at Harper's Ferry. They were encouraged to make the journey because the northwestern part of Virginia was not suitable for plantation agriculture, while the Anglican church there was too weak to pose a threat. The Virginian authorities in any case welcomed the newcomers as a means of protecting their frontiers from attack by the French and Indians. The settlers might also prevent runaway slaves from setting up maroon communities. Lastly, the Virginian elite wanted to sell them lands which they had patented for this purpose. Accordingly, in 1738 Frederick and Augusta counties were organized where new arrivals could apply for a survey and obtain a patent. Prices ranged from £3 to £11 a hundred acres, depending on location and availability.

The Scots-Irish were not the only participants in this trek. They were joined by many Germans, Scots, and people of English descent. The coastal areas were experiencing a demographic explosion of their own. In the period 1720–60 Connecticut's population rose from 60,000 to 140,000; Maryland's from 60,000 to 160,000; and Virginia's similarly from 130,000 to 310,000. Land was now almost unobtainable in the tidewater except for the wealthy, resulting in an exodus by all groups. In Frederick County in the Shenandoah 38 percent of the population were English, 30 percent German, and only 28 percent Scots-Irish, though for the valley as a whole the figures were 25 percent English, 31 percent German, and 38 percent Scots-Irish.

The search for land accordingly continued. Since the mountains remained forbiddingly impenetrable, the settlers turned southeast from the Shenandoah, arriving in the backcountry

---

[5] Quoted in Michael Kammen, *Colonial New York: A History* (New York, 1975), 179. This view has been challenged by Sung Bok Kim, *Landlord and Tenant in Colonial New York: Manorial Society, 1664–1775* (Chapel Hill, 1978).

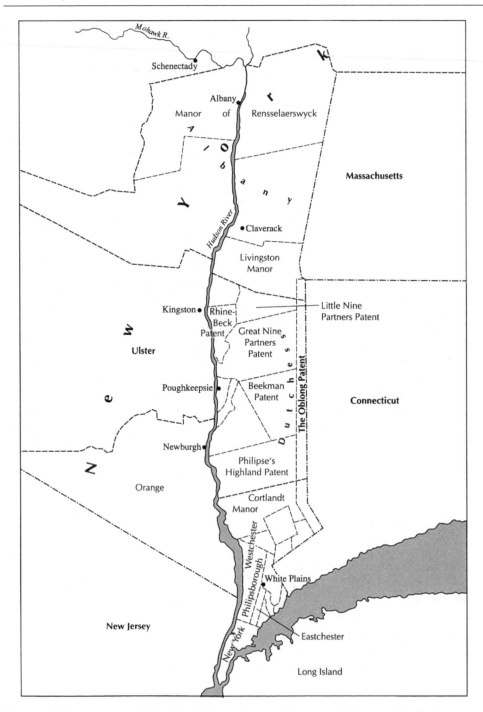

Map 12 The manors of New York. From Patricia Bonomi, A *Factious People* (New York, 1971).

of North Carolina from 1740 onwards. Here they found what had until now been a sparsely populated area. By 1750 an advanced guard of settlers had reached South Carolina, where they were welcomed as a protective screen against the still powerful Cherokee, Catawba, and Creek nations. South Carolina also saw them as a useful balance to the province's large number of slaves.

It is hard to calculate precisely the total number of Scots-Irish immigrants to America; the most scholarly assessment suggests that about 100,000 people left Ireland in the period 1717–60. Higher estimates have been given but seem suspect in light of the limited Scots-Irish population in Ireland. Of course emigration from Ireland could have included other groups, like the descendants of those who settled following Cromwell's conquest since passenger lists for the period 1717–20 reveal many departures from ports outside Ulster, notably Dublin, Cork, and Waterford. Many Catholics may also have taken ship, changing their religion and anglicizing their names so that they could make a frest start on the other side of the Atlantic. As early as 1692 Edward Randolph had noted that Somerset County in Maryland was "pestered with Scotch and Irish." The presence of Catholic immigrants could explain why the authorities in Massachusetts acted with such hostility.[6]

In any event, Scots-Irish settlers were sufficiently numerous to make up 10 percent of the population by the end of the colonial period. Their presence was especially noticeable in Pennsylvania, where they constituted over 30 percent of the population. In time this influence was to have a profound effect on the politics of that province. Until 1760, however, the newcomers were too isolated and underrepresented to have much impact in Philadelphia, let alone in the southern colonies, though the evidence from Opequon Creek in Frederick County, Virginia, suggests that they played their part in local government as justices of the peace and members of the militia, along with their German neighbors. Ethnic divisions in the backcountry seem to have been less severe than along the coast, suggesting that the frontier had a unifying effect for the white population at least.[7]

Compared with the Germans, the Scots-Irish, were not good farmers. They were more like earlier English settlers, concerned only with exploiting the land quickly. They preferred to cut the trees down, build a crude log cabin, and grow whatever was possible regardless of the long-term consequences for the land. This attitude explains why so many of them moved after a few years. The French visitor J. Hector St. John Crèvecoeur later commented that, on average, out of every twelve families emigrating to America, nine Germans succeeded, seven Scots, but only four Scots-Irish. However, when making his comparison, Crèvecoeur selected the Mennonites, who were exceptional even among the Germans, and more recent work suggests that, where the Scots-Irish secured good land, their farming practices differed little from those of other European settlers.[8]

The Scots-Irish have enjoyed a reputation as frontierspeople. Certainly a number of them did excel as traders and frontierspeople, though not all Irish frontierspeople were

---

[6]   For a discussion of Catholic emigration to America before 1776, see David N. Doyle, *Ireland, Irishmen and Revolutionary America, 1760–1820* (Cork, 1981), 59–61; and Kerby A. Miller, *Emigrants and Exiles: Ireland and the Irish Exodus to North America* (New York, 1985), 137–49.

[7]   See Warren R. Hofstra, "Land, Ethnicity, and Community in the Opequon Settlement, Virginia, 1730–1800," in H. Blethen Tyler and Curtis W. Wood, Jr., eds, *Ulster and North America: Transatlantic Perspectives on the Scotch Irish* (Tuscaloosa, 1997).

[8]   See Tyler and Curtis, eds, *Ulster and North America*.

of Scots-Irish descent. George Croghan, for example, came from Dublin of Anglican parents. But the vast majority of the Scots-Irish stayed on the eastern side of the Allegheny Mountains, since conditions in Tyrone and Fermanagh bore little resemblence to the terrain and climate of North America. As one settler from Belfast commented on arriving in South Carolina: "We were oppressed with fears, on divers account, especially of being massacred by the Indians, or bitten by snakes, or torn by wild beasts, or being lost and perishing in the woods." Settling one frontier in Ireland did not necessarily qualify them to do so again.[9]

In reality the Scots-Irish, like most groups, became frontier settlers only by necessity. The frontier was where the land was cheapest or could be squatted on without payment of rent. Once settled, the Scots-Irish, like all Europeans, did their best to destroy the frontier by cutting down the trees, plowing the land, and building roads, houses, and churches. They, too, wanted to send their surplus produce to market so that they could enjoy a better standard of living. Roaming the woods had little attraction in itself, except for the tiny minority who traded with the native peoples. For the Presbyterian Scots-Irish, as for the Puritans of New England, the wilderness was a dark, forbidding place, occupied only by savages and wild beasts. They only began leaving their communities in the Shenandoah Valley, for example, when the growth of population by 1783 required members of the third generation to find new lands in Kentucky and Tennessee.

Not surprisingly, one effect of the Scots-Irish settlement was a deterioration in relations with the American Indians. The Quakers, as already mentioned, did their best to deal fairly with the indigenous inhabitants. No such compunction swayed the Presbyterian Scots-Irish. For them the American Indian was a heathen outside the moral law. Like most European settlers, they believed the native peoples to be guilty of ignoring the parable of the talents. As one squatter told the proprietary land agent, "It was against the laws of God and nature that so much land should be idle while so many Christians wanted it to work on." James Logan noticed early on how the Scots-Irish were "very rough" with the Delawares. The result was a bitter harvest of trouble in the 1750s, when the battle to control the Ohio Valley began.

2   THE FOUNDING OF GEORGIA

The settling of the backcountry was not the only expansion taking place at this time. In the 1730s a more formal colony was begun on the southern flank of South Carolina and named Georgia in honor of the king. The prime mover behind this scheme was Colonel (later General) James Oglethorpe.

---

[9]   The view that the Scots-Irish were especially heroic frontier settlers owes much to Theodore Roosevelt, *The Winning of the West* (New York, 1910). Roosevelt was writing at a time when exploitation of the American West was equated with progress. His attitude also reflected his own concept of manhood, typified by his formation of the Rough Riders during the war with Spain in 1898, rather than a historian's view. A more realistic account is to be found in James G. Leyburn, *The Scots-Irish: A Social History* (Chapel Hill, 1962). See also Tyler and Wood, eds, *Ulster and North America*; and David Colin Crass et al., eds, *The Southern Colonial Backcountry: Interdisciplinary Perspectives on Frontier Communities* (Knoxville, 1998).

A number of considerations prompted his design. After a career in the army Oglethorpe devoted himself to helping the poor of London, notably those imprisoned for debt. He suggested settling them in America, just as the Elizabethans had sought to do with their beggars. But there were other considerations too. South Carolina, which had become an important colony, was isolated from the other provinces and had many potential enemies. A new settlement on its southern border would offer valuable protection. Several plans had been proposed since the Yamasee war but had failed for want of money. The need for action remained, however. The land south of the Savannah River had until the 1680s been controlled by Spain through its missions with the Guale or Yamasee peoples, and it was feared that the Spanish might revive their influence.

Since money was required, Oglethorpe took his scheme to Parliament. Funding was duly agreed to, though a charter still had to be obtained from the Crown. The charter was issued on June 9, 1732, to a group of twenty trustees, headed by John Viscount Percival. The trustees were granted the status of a corporation with power to elect their own council, grant lands, enact laws, and raise taxes. To avoid a conflict of interest with their charitable aims, however, no trustees could hold any paid office or receive land. In addition, their responsibilities were to terminate after twenty-one years in favor of the Crown. In the meantime they had to make regular reports to the Secretary of State and Board of Trade and cooperate with the Crown's revenue officers.

The device of appointing trustees indicated a shift in public attitudes; crude profiteering in the manner of the seventeenth century was no longer acceptable as a model for colonization, though the commercial motives behind the scheme had some similarities with past endeavors. In this case the climate of Georgia was thought to be suitable for growing the mulberry trees on which silkworms spin their cocoons, and every farm was to have fifty bushes. Similar hopes were entertained for potash and viticulture. Moral arguments also resurfaced; the settlement would provide the American Indians with a Christian example and give the colonists an opportunity to redeem themselves by hard work. However, the new venture would not have an established church. Liberty of conscience would be granted to all except papists.

Since the scheme was to benefit the poor, Oglethorpe and Percival placed a limit on the size of landholdings. They were determined that this settlement should not follow the example of the other southern colonies, with their large plantations and discrepancies of wealth. No grant of land was to exceed five hundred acres. In addition, the settlers in receipt of charity who had not purchased their lands could neither sell nor alienate their holdings, nor divide them into portions of less than fifty acres. This restriction was designed to avoid the creation of a class of either very rich or very poor people. Georgia was to remain a land of yeoman farmers.

The paternalistic nature of the settlement was reflected in one other respect. There was to be no assembly, even though such bodies were now established in all the other mainland colonies. The power of making laws was to remain with the trustees, though their enactments had to "be reasonable and not contrary or repugnant to the laws" of England. Finally, the scheme placed considerable emphasis on defense. The new colony was to be laid out in compact townships to which everyone would be confined, thus facilitating defense in general and the formation of a militia in particular.

Prospective settlers were to receive free passage and be given cattle, land, and subsistence until they established themselves. The period of support was not expected to be more than twelve months, for the situation was quite different from that which prevailed in the seventeenth century. As Oglethorpe argued, "Carolina abounds with provisions, the climate is known, and there are men to instruct in the seasons and nature of cultivating the soil." He concluded: "By such a colony many families who would otherwise starve will be provided for . . . the people of Great Britain to whom these necessitous families were a burden will be relieved; numbers of manufacturers will be here employed for supplying them with clothes, working tools and other necessaries; and the power of Britain . . . will be increased by the addition of so many religious and industrious inhabitants."[10]

The first batch of 114 settlers left England with Oglethorpe toward the end of 1732, arriving at the Savannah River early in 1733. Few of the new arrivals were released debtors, the trustees having vetted the settlers so carefully as to eliminate such people. The passage had been well organized and only two emigrants had died on the voyage, a great improvement over the experience of pioneers a century earlier. Also propitious was Oglethorpe's choice of an easily defensible bluff as the site for the first town, which he then proceeded to survey in a military fashion. The new settlement, Savannah, was laid out as a series of squares, which were in turn divided into house lots, with gardens and farms to the rear.

Oglethorpe also aided the settlement by sensibly negotiating with the local native peoples. Most of the Guale or Yamasee had withdrawn toward St. Augustine, but a clan of Creeks known as the Yamacraw remained, under their sachem, Tomochichi. After talking to Oglethorpe, Tomochichi helped negotiate a treaty with the main Creek nation recognizing the right of the emigrants to settle, though Oglethorpe was also assisted by Mary Musgrove, the wife of a South Carolina trader, whose mother claimed chiefly lineage among the lower Creek. The Creeks welcomed the British as a counterbalance to the Spanish in Florida and the French along the Gulf at Biloxi and Mobile.

Meanwhile the settlers, organized in gangs, began clearing the ground and building houses, spurred by the knowledge that within a year they would be laboring on their own behalf. Soon other groups arrived. Among them were some Moravians from Austria and a boatload of Sephardic Jews from London. Oglethorpe was not pleased about the appearance of the latter, since like most of his countrymen he held antisemitic views. Nevertheless, he accepted them, since they included several doctors and other useful people.

However promising the initial twelve months, America was soon to prove once more the graveyard of European experiments in social engineering. The trustees expected gratitude from the recipients of their charity. Instead the settlers grumbled, not least at the restrictions on where they could settle and what they could do with their land. They were particularly alienated by the decision in January 1735 to prohibit slavery. The trustees believed that this ban would encourage the settlement of "English and Christian inhabitants" who alone could be relied on in war. If the dream of a white yeoman society was to be effected, then slavery must be excluded, a point seemingly reinforced by the Stono Rebellion in 1739.[11]

---

[10] For a copy of the charter, see W. Keith Kavenagh, *Foundations of Colonial America: A Documentary History*, 3 vols (New York, 1973), III, 1822–32.

[11] The plan to ban slavery was strongly supported by William Byrd II, who commented from his experience of living in Virginia: "I am sensible of many bad consequences of multiplying these Ethiopians amongst us. They blow up the pride, and ruin the Industry of our White People, who seeing a Rank of poor Creatures below them, detest work for fear it should make them look like Slaves". Quoted in Karen Ordahl Kupperman, ed., *Major Problems in American Colonial History: Documents and Essays* (Lexington, Mass., 1993).

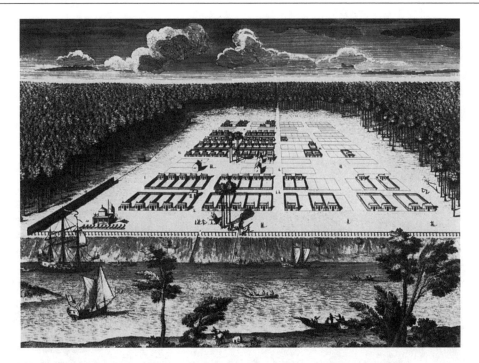

Plate 42   View of Savannah. University of Georgia Libraries.

The settlers took a very different view. Most of those arriving in Georgia after the first few years were South Carolinians who viewed being yeoman farmers as a recipe for poverty. They wanted to become large-scale planters and knew from experience that the use of slaves was the only means of rapid expansion.

The trustees' paternalism was also evident in their attempt to prevent the importation of rum and other spirits. The trustees claimed that the Creeks desired such a ban because of the "great disorders among them occasioned by the use of the said liquors." In reality the trustees feared the effect alcohol might have on their own settlers, some of whom had only recently been plucked from the streets of London, where gin cost a penny a gallon and disorder was equally prevalent.

For a time criticism was diverted by the war against Spain. But after the fighting died down in the early 1740s, the trustees slowly had to give way on various aspects of their model society. The attempt to settle people in compact towns had never been a success. Now the restrictions on both the size of farms and the right to sell had to be removed. From 1742 holdings of up to two thousand acres were allowed. That same July the ban on liquor was removed, if only to help Georgian merchants trading with the West Indies.

Finally, in August 1750 the trustees conceded the right to own slaves as "an encouragement to the inhabitants." For a time their antislavery views had been supported by the Scottish settlers at Darien and the German Moravians at Ebenezer. But the South Carolinians in Savannah kept up their demands. One last straw may have been the encouragement they received from George Whitefield on one of his revivalist tours. Not that the trustees gave

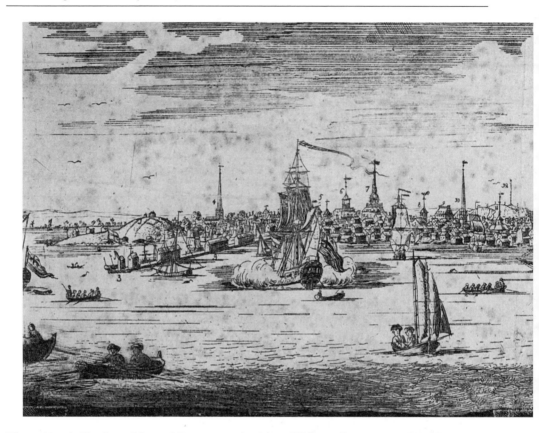

Plate 43   A *Northeast View of Boston*, attributed to William Burgis, ca. 1723. Courtesy of the Essex Institute, Salem, Massachusetts.

in completely, for under their new decree anyone keeping four slaves had to employ at least one able-bodied white male servant; also, no African-Americans were to be trained as apprentices, as in other colonies. In addition, the trustees tried to revive their plans for a silk industry by requiring slave owners to keep one female trained "in the art of winding or reeling of silk." Lastly an import duty was to be levied on all slaves entering the colony to support the government and pay for a Christian ministry.

These concessions in fact represented almost the last act of the trustees. Two years later they handed over their authority to the Crown and Georgia became a royal colony, with a governor, council, and provincial assembly.

The trustees' stewardship was not without result. By 1752, 4,500 whites and 1,500 Africans had been settled in Georgia. Parliament, however, had expended £137,000 in the process. The trustees' idealistic hopes had faded. Some silk was produced at Ebenezer for a few years, but little remained of the plan to resettle London's poor, develop compact towns, or create a new class of yeoman farmer. Georgia quickly adopted the pattern of South Carolina. Rice plantations, owned by a wealthy elite and worked by African slaves, dominated the tidewater, while small struggling farms were the norm elsewhere.

3   THE URBAN FRONTIER

While the backcountry and frontier areas were being developed, a rather different expansion was taking place in the east. The growth of the American town was under way.

Until the eighteenth century American towns were little more than villages, except for Boston, which by 1689 had a population of 7,000 inhabitants. No other settlement had more than 3,000 people, the figure usually set by demographers today as the minimum necessary for an urban environment.

After 1715 other towns began to grow, shedding off their village origins. By 1720 Boston had 12,000 people but Philadelphia, with some 10,000 inhabitants, was catching up fast. New York had a population of 7,000, while Newport and Charleston each contained close to 4,000 people.

The reason for this pattern of growth was the role these settlements played in the economies of their respective areas. Their first-class harbors provided an entrepôt for their respective hinterlands, both for the marketing of their produce and the distribution of imported goods. This commerce in turn supported a growing number of laborers, artisans,

Plate 44 *South East Prospect of the City of Philadelphia*, by Peter Cooper. The Library
Company of Philadelphia.

and other craftsmen, together with a professional class of, for example, lawyers and doctors.
Hence by 1760 Philadelphia had 23,000 inhabitants, New York 18,000, Boston 16,000,
Charleston 8,000, and Newport 7,500. Only Boston had failed to sustain a rapid rate of
growth, having already reached a population of 16,000 by 1740. Its restricted hinterland
and competition for its traditional trades had resulted in a prolonged period of stagnation.

Growth was not limited to these five towns; by 1760 two more Massachusetts seaports,
Salem and Marblehead, exceeded 3,000 inhabitants, while a number of other towns were
approaching this figure. In New England these included Portsmouth, New Hampshire;
Newburyport, Massachusetts; Providence, Rhode Island; and New Haven and Hartford,
Connecticut. In the middle colonies, Albany in New York and Lancaster in southeast
Pennsylvania were similar in size. In the South Baltimore, Norfolk, and Savannah were also
approaching 3,000 inhabitants. Historians have also detected signs of urban activity in the
piedmont of Virginia and North Carolina, where the growing wheat trade was creating
centers of commerce.[12]

All these places were ports on the coast or on large rivers leading to the sea. Only
Lancaster was a genuine inland center, the result of the rapid influx of German and Scots-
Irish settlers. Nevertheless, impressive as the growth of towns was, the number of people
living in them as a proportion of the total population had actually declined, from 9 percent
to 6 percent. As fast as the towns had expanded, the countryside had grown even faster.

---

[12] See especially Joseph A. Ernst and H. Roy Merrens, " 'Camden's Turrets Pierce the Skies': The Urban Process
in the Southern Colonies during the Eighteenth Century," *William and Mary Quarterly*, XXX, 1973, 549–74.
However, this thesis about southern backcountry towns has been challenged by H. Wellenreuther, "Urbanization
in the Colonial South," *William and Mary Quarterly*, XXXI, 1974, 653–71.

The five major towns posed special problems for their inhabitants, the most serious of which was fire. Boston suffered several bad fires in the seventeenth century, notably in 1676 and 1679, leading to the town's purchase of the first fire engine in America equipped with buckets and hand pumps. In 1691 the general court passed an ordinance that all buildings in the town were to be of brick. Still the fires raged, and in 1717 the town organized its first volunteer fire company to replace the militia units which had formerly been used. A bonus of £5 was paid to the first one arriving at the scene of a conflagration. Since the act of 1691 was frequently ignored, their services continued to be in demand. The year 1760 witnessed the worst fire of all, in which four hundred houses were destroyed.

Similar legislation was adopted by the other major towns, though Philadelphia and Charleston, with their spacious streets and house lots, were less at risk. But a serious fire in Charleston in 1740 emphasized the need for building regulations to be enforced.

Fire was not the only hazard in the cities. Disease and epidemics were a considerable danger too, not least because of the constant influx of newcomers, the close proximity in which people lived, and the lack of sanitation. The link between these elements was not always understood, though the desirability of keeping the streets clean was recognized. Once again Boston took the lead. Following the example of Christopher Wren in London, it began the construction of sewers beneath the main thoroughfares into which householders could pour their offal and other waste material. The first sewer, completed in 1704, was the work of a private individual, Francis Thresher, but the selectmen were quick to encourage others to follow his example by the promise of compensation. New York began to build its first sewer shortly afterward. These improvements were one reason the inhabitants of the emerging cities of America remained relatively healthy in comparison with their European counterparts.

Drinking water was secured mainly from underground wells, though many citizens wisely avoided using them in summer, preferring fermented beverages instead. Some

Plate 45 *This View of Charlestown . . .* , etching with engraving by William Henry Toms after Bishop Roberts, 1737–9. I. N. Phelps Stokes Collection, Miriam and Ira D. Wallach Division of Art, Prints and Photographs, the New York Public Library, Astor, Lenox and Tilden Foundations.

epidemics were inevitable. Boston suffered several smallpox outbreaks, and yellow fever appeared regularly in Charleston every summer, reaching as far north as New York in 1702 when five hundred people perished. By 1750 the adoption of inoculation for smallpox and of quarantine procedures for other diseases substantially reduced the incidence of these particular threats.

Linked to the need for sewers was the need to attend to the condition of the streets. As the population grew, the number of carts and coaches made these intolerable, especially in winter, when rain and snow turned them into a quagmire. From 1690 Boston once more set the tone by having its streets paved with cobblestones. This improvement was often carried out in conjunction with drainage improvements. By 1760 all the large towns had made considerable progress in this direction.

The reason for Boston's lead in municipal improvements, apart from its being the first town to experience such problems, was its system of government. The annual election of selectmen made it more responsive. Most other towns had nonelective corporations. Charleston was most disadvantaged in this respect, having to rely on commissioners appointed by the provincial legislature, who were frequently unsympathetic to its problems.

Private initiatives were therefore still essential to bring about urban improvements. One of the most notable of these was in public lighting. Before 1750 the only street lighting came from oil lamps provided by individuals on a random and voluntary basis. Then in 1749, a group of Philadelphia's citizens, led by the Quaker John Smith, agreed to provide lamps and pay someone to light them each evening. Their action prompted the assembly to pass an act the next year in support of this initiative. The measure was so well received that within ten years all the major towns had adopted similar schemes, using whale oil as lighting fuel. However, such improvements rarely extended beyond the wealthier parts of a town, leaving the poorer inhabitants to do without until the following century.

One reason for the popularity of street lighting was another urban problem, crime. Its emergence may have been the result of increased poverty in the 1730s when America's first workhouses were established in Boston, New York, and Philadelphia. Crime may also have been caused by declining religious zeal among a now cosmopolitan population. In addition, the concentration of so many people undoubtedly provided temptations and opportunities which were not available in the country. With robberies and burglaries on the increase, all the townsfolk wanted better protection, especially at night. Hence, in addition to their lighting, every town made provision for increased night patrols.

By 1760 life for the inhabitants of the five largest towns was quite different from that of the rest of the population. Most townspeople worked for a cash wage and had specialist occupations. As a result they purchased their food, clothing, and other requirements from retail shops or large markets. Everywhere the concept of the just price had been superseded by the mechanism of the marketplace. And although churchgoing remained popular, the ideal of the godly man had been replaced by that of the good citizen, someone who was concerned for the well-being of the community and its environment.

By 1760 the major cities were sufficiently advanced to impress visitors from Europe. The Swede Peter Kalm commented on the "grandeur and perfection of Philadelphia," while one British naval officer said of New York in 1756 that "the nobleness of the town surprised me more than the fertile appearance of the country . . . I had no idea of finding a place in America, consisting of near two thousand houses, elegantly built of brick. . . . Such is this city that very few in England can rival it."[13] Indeed, in their municipal developments the American towns were ahead of their British provincial counterparts. Civic pride and the desire for refinement were everywhere evident.

The cities represented the cutting edge of colonial society, where fashion and ideas were most advanced. Some have argued that this was also true of politics. Although only 6 percent of the population lived in them, the towns provided that leadership and organization which was lacking elsewhere.[14]

---

[13]　Quoted in Carl Bridenbaugh, *Cities in Revolt: Urban Life in America, 1743–1776* (New York, 1955), 41–2.

[14]　This theme is argued by Gary B. Nash, *The Urban Crucible: Social Change, Political Consciousness, and the Origins of the American Revolution* (Cambridge, Mass., 1979).

18

Imperial Neighbors: Spain and France in Florida, New Mexico, Texas, and Louisiana

1513	Juan Ponce de Leon explores the coast of Florida.
1539–42	Francisco Vázquez de Coronado explores New Mexico.
1565	St. Augustine founded by Pedro Menéndez de Avilés.
1573	The Spanish Crown publishes its *Royal Orders for New Discoveries*, banning slavery and the enforced conversion of the natives.
1595	The Franciscans arrive to convert the Florida Indians.
1598	Juan de Oñate conquers the Pueblo towns on the Rio Grande.
1630	The conversion of the Apalachee in Western Florida begins.
1670	The Founding of Charleston.
1673	The French discover the Mississippi.
1680	The revolt of the Pueblo People.
1681	The revolt of the Apalachicola or the Lower Creek.
1684–7	The failure of La Salle to establish a colony in the Gulf of Mexico.
1693	New Mexico reoccupied by Diego de Vargas.
1699	The French establish themselves at Biloxi.
1702–8	The final destruction of the Spanish missions in Florida, except at St. Augustine.
1716	Spanish missions established in East Texas.
1718	New Orleans founded by the French as the capital of Louisiana.
1729	The defeat of the Natchez Indians by the French.
1733	The founding of Georgia.
1742	The Spanish are defeated at the Battle of the Bloody Swamp in Georgia.

W hile Britain's colonies were expanding rapidly along the eastern seaboard, other European powers were also extending their control over areas that were later to become part of the United States. The efforts of Spain and France in Florida, New Mexico, Texas, and Louisiana are usually overlooked by historians of colonial America whose focus has been on the English-speaking colonies of the eastern seaboard.[1] It is to rectify this omission that this chapter is included.

1 FLORIDA

As mentioned in chapter 1, the first permanent European settlement in what is now continental United States was St. Augustine in Florida. Its establishment by Spain in 1565 was the result of the attempt by French Huguenots, under Jean Ribaut, to establish a colony near the mouth of the St. Johns River. From the Spanish perspective, the interlopers were not only foreigners but pirates and heretics too. However, the Spanish recognized that it was not enough to destroy Ribaut's colony. A permanent settlement was required if Spain was to sustain its claim to the area.

Another consideration was the need for a base to support Spain's Treasure Fleets as they made their way through the Straits of Florida, since this was a favorite place for French, Dutch, and English corsairs to lie in wait. The consequence of these piratical attacks had been a severe loss of revenue to the Spanish Crown.

Lastly, a permanent presence in Florida was deemed necessary because the Spanish, more than any other European nation, felt a moral imperative to convert the native peoples to Christianity. It had been one of the conditions of the papal bull of 1493 authorizing Spain to take possession of the New World. Of course, such a policy would serve other useful objectives too. Conversion meant Hispanicization, no small consideration in view of Spain's lack of population and the size of its empire. Although several hundred thousand Spaniards emigrated to the New World in the first flush of enthusiasm,[2] few wanted to go to the borderlands once it was realized that conditions there were harsh and the prospects unpromising. A loyal Indian population would therefore consolidate Spanish control, solve the endemic labor problem, and allow sustained development. Finally, priests were much cheaper than soldiers. Only a few were initially required while conversion offered the prospect of a loyal population rather than a sullen underclass waiting to revolt.

The task of destroying the French colony and asserting Spain's claims to the area was entrusted to Pedro Menéndez de Avilés, a prominent mariner and entrepreneur. To cut costs, Philip II effectively agreed to make the enterprise a joint venture. The king would provide naval and military assistance, while Menéndez supplied the rest. In return he was appointed *adelantado* or proprietor of the region, with the right to exploit all lands to the north of New Spain, as Mexico was then called.

Menéndez more than fulfilled his responsibilities. After founding St. Augustine and destroying the fledgling French colony, he proceeded to establish various forts around the

---

[1] For a discussion of the historical treatment of the non-English-speaking colonies in North America north of the Rio Grande, see David J. Weber, *The Spanish Frontier in North America* (Hartford, 1992), 1–7, 335–9.
[2] It is calculated that, by 1650, approximately 450,000 Spaniards had emigrated to the New World.

Plate 46 Portrait of Pedro Menéndez de Avilés, engraving, 1791. Courtesy St. Augustine Historical Society.

coast of Florida, including one at Tampa Bay, another at Charlotte Harbor, three on the St. Johns River and one, Santa Elena, on Port Royal Sound.[3] Not that success came easily, for in 1568 the French made a revenge counter-attack which resulted in the destruction of the three forts on the St. Johns River. Nevertheless, Menéndez, driven by personal pride, was determined to succeed and he pawned much of his estate to buy fresh supplies in Cuba. Just when things seemed at their bleakest, reinforcements arrived from Spain.

In the midst of this activity, Menéndez had not forgotten the third reason for settling Florida, the conversion of the Indians. Several Jesuits had accompanied Menéndez from Spain and they began establishing missions among the Timucuan people near St. Augustine and the Guale Indians further up the coast. An attempt was also made, as noted in chapter 2, to establish a mission in the Chesapeake at Ajacán. However, without military support, the latter enterprise quickly ended with the killing of the eight Jesuits. The limits of Spanish power had been reached, at least for the present.

Menéndez quit the province in 1572, which proved unfortunate for the Spanish cause in Florida, since his successors did not have the same energy or conviction. Most of the missions were abandoned, and when Sir Francis Drake visited St. Augustine on a privateering expedition in 1586, it proved an easy target, since its only defense was a log fort. Drake's visit

---

[3] The Point of Santa Elena had been the original choice of Philip II in 1557 for a military and naval base. Two attempts were made to establish the site in the years 1559–60; both failed.

might well have led to the abandonment of Florida entirely but for the continued need for a base at the northern end of the Florida Straits. In the event it was decided to concentrate resources at St. Augustine rather than Santa Elena, the current capital, which was too far to the north to be an effective naval base and was in consequence abandoned that same year. Almost the entire Hispanic population of five hundred was now concentrated in just one settlement, and half of this comprised the garrison. The prospects were not auspicious.

Nevertheless, the hope of extending Spain's presence in Florida by the conversion of the natives had not been abandoned, for within a decade a new attempt was made to effect this. The difference this time was that the emphasis was to be firmly on the spiritual rather than on the military way of doing things. The new policy began in 1595 with the arrival of twelve Franciscan friars, who were preferred to the Jesuits because they were seemingly less hostile to the civil power, being a religious order dedicated to individual poverty, chastity, and self-denial, not corporate aggrandizement. Missions were accordingly quickly reestablished among the Timucuan people around St. Augustine and among the Guale along the coast. The latter offered some resistance when attempts were made to alter their marriage and inheritance customs, and five Franciscans were killed within two years of their arrival. The friars nevertheless persisted. One way of limiting the danger was to establish the missions on offshore islands, from where they could win the trust of the local inhabitants.

The episode demonstrated what was to prove a perennial dilemma for the Franciscans. Unprotected missionaries were clearly vulnerable to Indian attack. However, the presence of soldiers usually threatened the mission's spiritual purpose, since the troops invariably set a poor example. Apart from cursing, drinking, and gambling, they often mistreated the native peoples, molesting their women and abusing their men. But, without soldiers, the missionaries faced the risk of martyrdom and failure. Hence a compromise was usually necessary with the Franciscans being accompanied by a small military detachment until such time as their presence was accepted and their security assured. The dilemma posed by the need for protection and the incompatibility of the military for a spiritual enterprise was still being debated when the Franciscans entered California in the late 1760s.

One difference from the early decades of Spain's presence in the New World was that soldiers were no longer used to perform forced conversions. By the end of the sixteenth century the Spanish had come to realize that conversion at the point of a sword was both bad theology and self-defeating, since it merely stimulated hostility and resistance. The desire for conversion must come from the native people themselves. The *Royal Orders for New Discoveries*, published in 1573, accordingly banned such practices, though, once the Indians had been baptized, the military might be used to prevent subsequent apostasy. Indeed, any Indian seeking to leave the church or questioning its doctrines was usually brutally punished.

In the initial stages the Franciscans had various stratagems for winning over the native peoples. One was by demonstrating their extraordinary bravery and endurance as they walked barefoot in hair shirts over long distances. Other ploys included the wearing of ornate vestments, the use of sacred images, the chanting of music, and reciting of the liturgy. Indian curiosity could also be reinforced by gifts. As elsewhere in North America, the peoples of Florida were often predisposed to welcome Europeans, believing that they could help them against traditional enemies. The friars in addition offered the possibility of access to European goods, while their seemingly superior knowledge and apparent magical powers might ensure protection against natural disasters, especially the diseases which did not apparently affect the newcomers. It was unnecessary, in any case, for a whole tribe to invite the friars to a village. Often the invitation came from a particular faction anxious to harness the magic of the Catholic church to enhance their own power. This underlined another difference from the methods of earlier conquistadors, who attempted to supplant the native leadership entirely. The friars recognized that while the host chiefs or caciques remained loyal they could be used to consolidate the mission, especially by exploiting their traditional position as the giver and receiver of gifts. The difference now was that the Spanish gave the gifts, usually of clothing and metal implements, while the caciques ensured that the *encomienda* system of tribute in food and labour was efficiently levied.

Once a foothold had been established, the process of conversion could begin. To aid this process a church was usually built and potential adherents invited to live nearby, for it was a maxim of the friars that converts must live within sound of the mission bell. Once a sympathetic climate had been created, pagan idols could be smashed and native rituals discountenanced. Church attendance could then be encouraged, simple catechisms taught, and attention paid to the formal observance of Christian sexual mores. The last stage was baptism, after which converts were expected to attend services regularly and go to confession.

Equally important to successful conversion was the process of secular acculturation, since it was assumed that pagans could not become true Christians until they lived like Christians. Hence every encouragement was given to get the converts to dress, cook, talk, and compose themselves like Spaniards. Particular attention was devoted to the education of the young, since they were more malleable and less resistant to new ideas and could become powerful allies in the battle to win the hearts and minds of a community. To aid this process the friars were expected to learn the native language, but this was one task that many failed to do.

The missions, of course, were never simply spiritual entities, for no friar could succeed unless he enjoyed material support from the host community. Indeed a principal reason for converting the native peoples was to turn them into productive subjects of the Crown. Hence the importance of work in the service of God was constantly emphasized. But the world of work was also important for the process of acculturation. By introducing the natives to new crops, livestock, and systems of agriculture, the friars hoped their attitudes could be radically changed. Hence horses, cattle, sheep, goats, pigs, and chickens were all introduced, as were European crops like wheat and barley and fruits like oranges, peaches, watermelons, and pomegranates. Similarly, useful skills like carpentry, joinery, and metal working were encouraged to keep the native men and women within constant reach of the friars and control of the Spanish.[4] By 1620 this pattern had allowed the Franciscans to establish missions along the coast as far as St. Catherine's Island, in present-day Georgia, where the mission of Santa Catalina was placed.

Nevertheless there was no room for complacency for by the 1620s the English had established themselves in the Chesapeake. The Spanish in consequence decided to expand

---

[4]   Turning the native peoples into European-style yeoman farmers was to have a long tradition among European Americans. Perhaps the most notorious attempt was the Dawes Severalty Act of 1887, which sought to end tribal attachments by giving each head of household 160 acres and the promise of citizenship if the land was kept for twenty-five years.

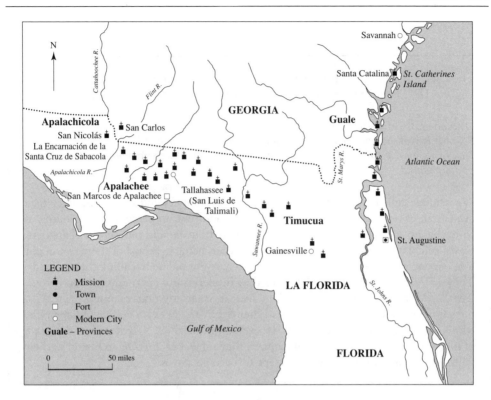

Map 13 Missions in Spanish Florida, ca. 1674–5. From David Weber, *The Spanish Frontier in North America* (Yale, 1992), 101 (map drawn specifically for Professor Weber's book by Don Bufkin).

their influence across northern Florida to the western Timucua and Apalachee peoples. Apart from excluding the English, they also hoped to open a road to New Spain round the Gulf of Mexico. There was in any case little to interest the Spanish south of St. Augustine. The Calusa Indians in the lower peninsular practiced little agriculture, being necessarily hunter gatherers in that swampy terrain. The western Timucua and Apalachee people, on the other hand, were primarily agriculturists. This made them a much more promising target, since, being relatively sedentary, they could more easily be isolated from their pagan neighbors and exploited for their labor.

The first contacts with the Apalachee may have been as early as 1610. However, they were a proud people, having successfully repulsed earlier Spanish incursions under Pánfilo de Narváez in 1528 and Hernando de Soto in 1539–40. Hence it was not until the 1630s that the first formal missions were established, when the Apalachee's loss of population and relative weakness finally induced them to look more favorably on the Spanish. The result was another extension of the mission system, producing a string of new posts across northern Florida to the Gulf of Mexico near Tallahassee and beyond (see map 13). This development was particularly advantageous to the Spanish, since agriculturally the Apalachee were among the most advanced peoples of the region. The understanding was that, in return for Spanish protection and religious instruction, the Apalachee would provide food

DOCUMENT 30

The Difficulties posed by the New Order for Native Americans, printed in Meynard Geiger, *The Franciscan Conquest of Florida, 1573–1618* (Washington, 1937).

[The contrast between the native people's previous existence and that imposed by the Spanish is well documented here by one of the Florida chiefs. Given the sacrifices and lack of reciprocity by the Franciscans, it is easy to see why the native peoples rebelled so frequently.]

We who are called Christians, experience only hindrances and vexations. They take away from us our women, allowing us but one, and that, in perpetuity, forbidding us to exchange them for others. They prohibit us from having our dances, banquets, feasts, celebrations, games and wars, in order that, being deprived of these, we might lose our ancient valor and skill . . . They persecute our old men, calling them wizards. They are not satisfied with our labor for they hinder us from performing it on certain days . . . All they do, is to reprimand us, treat us in an injurious manner, oppress us, preach to us and call us bad Christians. They deprive us of every vestige of happiness, which our ancestors obtained for us, in exchange for which they hold out the hope of joys of Heaven. In this deceitful manner, they subject us, holding us bound to their wills. What have we to hope for except to become slaves.

and labor not only for the missions but also for the maintenance of a road to St. Augustine, along which they sent considerable quantities of corn.

The period 1635–75 proved to be the high-water mark of the Spanish mission system. During these years the Franciscans operated between forty and seventy missions, catering for perhaps 26,000 Hispanicized natives, who were organized in four provinces: Timucua in central Florida; Guale along the Georgia coast; Apalachee on the northeastern edge of the gulf; and Apalachicola to the west. Not that it was a golden age for the native inhabitants. Disease continued to diminish their ranks, whether Christian or pagan. The population of Apalachee, for instance, was around 30,000 in 1617, but by 1676 was little more than 8,000.[5] And whatever the benefits of Spanish military protection or spiritual sustenance, many aspects of the Spanish system were not well received. Most offensive was the *repartimiento*. This was a modified version of the *encomienda* system whereby the Spanish levied tribute in money, goods, or services. In theory the *repartimiento* was limited to periodic labor on public works, for which the Indians were to be paid, the most important requirements being the maintenance of the Camino Real (or royal road), the carrying of supplies to St. Augustine, and the building of fortifications. In practice the system often operated little differently from the *encomienda* and was open to abuse, both by the friars and

---

[5]   For a discussion of the population of the southeastern nations during this period, see Marvin T. Smith, "Aboriginal Depopulation in the Post Contact Southeast," in Charles Hudson and Carmen Chaves Tesser, eds, *The Forgotten Centuries: Indians and Europeans in the American South, 1521–1704* (Athens, 1994), 257–75.

the Spanish ruling class, since the native peoples were frequently forced to work on the settlers' farms when they should have been attending their own crops. Nor was there any reduction in these demands, even though the native population was in decline. Another grievance was that stocks of native grain were on occasion sequestrated with minimal compensation. Lastly their women were frequently abused, while any protest was met with a severe whipping. The unhappiness of the native peoples was demonstrated by a series of revolts, notably by the Guale in 1645 and the early 1680s; the Apalachee in 1647; the Timucua in 1655; and Apalachicola in 1675 and 1681. However, the Indians failed to cooperate and the only successful revolt was that of the Apalachicola, or Lower Creek, in 1681. Elsewhere the revolts were suppressed and their leaders hanged. In such circumstances many Indians, including converts, ran away, further aggravating the decline in population.[6]

The result of these disturbances and the diminishing population was that the Spanish were not as strong as they might have been to face the challenge posed by the English. Admittedly, for the first six decades, the fears caused by the founding of Jamestown in 1607 had not been realized. Nevertheless the weakness of Spain in Florida was cruelly revealed in 1665 when an English buccaneer from Jamaica, Captain John Davis, attacked St. Augustine and ransacked the town. The garrison managed to hold on to Fort San Marcos, but the incident emphasized the need for stronger defences. Fortunately, this time the lesson was learnt, for during the next few years the old wooden fort was replaced by one made of stone. The mission Indians, of course, provided the labor.

The improvements to St. Augustine were none too soon for news arrived in 1670 that the English had established a colony in South Carolina. Spain and England were now technically at peace and on the point of signing a treaty respecting each other's possessions across the Atlantic. However, both sides recognized that the activities of the other were incompatible with their own pretensions regarding the area. The Spanish still wanted to possess as much of North America as possible, while the newcomers were equally determined to restrict, if not entirely destroy, the Spanish hold on Florida.

What followed was a graphic contrast in imperial methods. The Spanish continued to rely on the power of the Catholic church, backed by a limited military presence, to sustain their cause. They believed that converting and holding the allegiance of the native people was the key to the struggle for North America. The English objective, in contrast, was the development of a market, in which they were well equipped to engage, since they had plenty of goods to exchange for deerskins and slaves. In crude terms, the imperial struggle was now one of religion versus trade, with God on one side and mammon on the other.

As a result hostilities continued, despite the treaty of 1670. The Spanish made the first move in 1675 by advancing toward Charleston, though they got no further than St. Helena Island. The English responded by arming the Yamasee Indians to attack the Guale missions.

---

[6] The idea of a golden age in the Spanish mission system in Florida was first advanced by Herbert E. Bolton, *The Spanish Borderlands: A Chronicle of Old Florida and the Southwest* (New Haven, 1921). Bolton was endeavoring to counteract the "black legend" about the Spanish era as one of economic repression and religious intolerance, rather than one of reciprocity and self-sufficiency. The "golden age" was subsequently challenged by Robert Allen Matter, *Pre-Seminole Florida: Spanish Soldiers, Friars and Indian Missions, 1513–1763* (New York, 1990), who argued that the missions were far from successful, either spiritually or economically, since they merely hastened the extirpation of the Indian population. A similar view is taken by Amy Turner Bushnell, *Situado and Sabana: Spain's Support System for the Presidio and Mission Provinces of Florida* (Athens, 1994).

This was not difficult since the Yamasee were easily lured by the prospect of slaves, horses, and other booty. Indian captives at this point were as valuable to the Carolinians as deerskins, since they could be shipped to Barbados in exchange for African slaves. The first mission to fall was Santa Catalina in 1680, the most northern outpost. Unfortunately, the other missions were equally exposed, since the Spanish in St. Augustine preferred to concentrate their resources on protecting the more productive provinces of Apalachee and Timucua. As a result, within six years the Guale missions had been destroyed.

The Spanish were correct in thinking that the threat to Florida was not limited to eastern Florida, for in 1686 news arrived that Dr Henry Woodward, an English trader and envoy of the Carolina proprietors, had arrived among the Apalachicola or Lower Creek people with a large train of packhorses loaded with weaponry. This would clearly be a prelude to an attack on the Apalachee missions with their valuable grain supplies. The Spanish accordingly decided to launch a preemptive strike against both the Apalachicola and Charleston itself. Neither scheme was a success. The Charleston expedition got no further than Edisto Island, while the invasion of Apalachicola merely encouraged the Creeks to hit back, encouraged by the prospect of slaves and other booty.

Unfortunately for the Spanish, this was not the only threat to their North American hegemony, for in 1684 they learnt that the French, under René Robert Cavelier, Sieur de La Salle, were attempting to establish a colony in the Gulf of Mexico. This was still something that the Spanish refused to allow. Hence, despite their weakened situation, they determined to attempt what they had done in 1565 when dealing with Ribaut and the Huguenots. They would first destroy the French settlement and then establish a permanent base of their own. It proved a case of easier said than done. The Gulf above the Rio Grande, with its swamps, bayous, and shallow waters, was almost unknown to the Spanish and it took nearly three years to find the French settlement, by which time it had been abandoned. Establishing a Spanish fort in the area took even longer because of financial constraints and the difficulty of finding a suitable site. Not until 1698 was the decision made to build the new post at Pensacola and within months it was shown to serve no useful purpose. In the first place it was irrelevant to the defence of the Apalachee missions. Secondly, with the signing of a peace in Europe in 1697, the Spanish found it diplomatically impossible to uproot the French when they did finally establish themselves at Biloxi Bay in 1699, just a few miles from Pensacola itself.

However, the problems of Spain in this part of North America only really began in 1702 with Queen Anne's War – or the War of Spanish Succession as it is usually called in Europe. Though the French and Spanish royal families were now united by dynastic ties, the alliance brought few advantages to Spain. Indeed, her ability to defend her interests in America was even less than before because of political weakness at home. The initiative accordingly passed to the English in Charleston where, early in 1702, Governor James Moore secured approval for a scheme to drive the Spanish out of Florida entirely by a daring raid on St. Augustine. Moore failed in his principal objective because of the strength of the fortifications of San Marcos. However, he not only sacked the town but destroyed all the remaining missions along the east coast and on the St. Johns River. Nor was this the end to his destructive designs, for late in 1703 he invaded the province of Apalachee, in company with the Creeks and Yamasee. Here he destroyed some fourteen missions and executed several Spanish officials when they were unable to ransom themselves. The bitter animosity between the British and Spanish was demonstrated by Moore's treatment of one friar, Father Parga, who had his legs hacked off before being burnt at the stake. The result was the enforced evacuation of Apalachee by both the Spanish and the native peoples, who were dispersed in every direction. Finally, late in 1708, a third raid was launched under Colonel John Barnwell. This time the objective was western Timucua, which completed the ruin of the Spanish mission system in Florida. During this period some 10,000 Christian Indians were either killed, enslaved, or forced to run away. A pitiful remnant of about three hundred took refuge under the guns of the San Marcos castle, it being unsafe even to venture into the town.

Spanish Florida never recovered from this terrible ordeal, being in effect reduced to one principal settlement, the town of St. Augustine. After 1708 the only other posts were a few satellite missions between St. Augustine and the St. Johns River. A mission and fort were subsequently rebuilt in 1718 at St. Marks on the northeast shore of the Gulf for the remnants of the Apalachee people. The colony also received an influx of several hundred Yamasee, following their war with South Carolina. However, the prosperity of the colony could not recover while border warfare continued, even though the European powers were formally at peace following the signing of the Treaty of Utrecht in 1713. Spanish acceptance of the Yamasee refugees angered the Carolinians since they interpreted this as an indication of Spain's underlying hostility. Relations were also not improved by the giving of sanctuary at St. Augustine to runaway slaves (see chapter 14, section 5).

To prevent further incursions by the Yamasee, the South Carolinians in 1721 established a fort at the mouth of the Altamaha River. Then in 1727, following further Yamasee raids, a force under Colonel Palmer launched a reprisal expedition almost to the gates of St. Augustine itself. Although Spanish diplomatic pressure was successful in getting the fort on the Altamaha removed, the tranquility did not last. In 1733 George II granted the area between the Savannah and Altamaha rivers for the new colony of Georgia, which threatened to bring the line of English settlement even closer to the heartland of the Spanish colony.

Although Florida survived the subsequent conflict known as King George's War, suffering only one serious invasion in the period 1739–48, its position remained weak (see chapter 19, section 1). St. Augustine itself and the immediate region had a total population of under 3,000 by mid-century. Of these, some five hundred were soldiers, 1,500 ethnic Spanish, and the remainder Hispanicized Indians, African slaves, and free blacks living in the village of Mose.[7] The other two settlements, St. Marks and Pensacola, each had perhaps 150 soldiers and 500 other inhabitants. Everywhere the missions had all but collapsed. By 1759 there were only seventy-nine Indians in the two villages near St. Augustine and just twenty-five at St. Marks. Moreover, none of the settlements produced any thing of value. They were no longer able even to feed themselves, being essentially military garrisons, surviving only with constant help from the Spanish treasury. Florida was effectively in the same situation as it had been in 1565. It was a poor reward after almost two hundred years of effort.

2   NEW MEXICO

The colonizing of New Mexico began, like Florida, as a result of the twin impulses of missionary zeal and conquistador greed. The area was first extensively explored by Francisco

---

[7]   For further information on Mose, see chapter 14, section 5.

Plate 47 Taos Pueblo. From Calvin Roberts and Susan Roberts, *A History of New Mexico* (University of New Mexico, 1991), 39. Courtesy New Mexico Economic Department and Tourism Department.

Vázquez de Coronado in 1540–2, looking for the seven cities of Cíbola, a fabled Indian kingdom, which it was believed would produce wealth equal to that of the Aztec and Inca empires. However, after two years of desultory marching through present-day Arizona, New Mexico, Texas, Oklahoma, and Kansas, Coronado had to acknowledge that there were no great Indian civilizations to be found. Nevertheless, his expedition did reveal along the Rio Grande and adjacent areas a relatively advanced Indian population which used irrigation in its agriculture, built multi-storied brick houses, lived in compact villages (pueblos), and was also skilled in weaving, pottery, and basketry. In addition, the inhabitants had yet to experience Christianity.

Despite this, another fifty years passed before a serious attempt was made to settle the region, by which time other considerations had come to the fore. One was the need to protect the silver mines of Zacatecas in northern New Spain, since the Spanish were fearful that the English or French might find an overland route to attack this precious asset. Another incentive was the belief that somewhere to the north lay the long sought passage to China, which it was imperative to discover before it fell under foreign control. In addition, the presence of relatively advanced Indian civilizations offered the prospect of wealth through the exploitation of their labor in an *encomienda*-style plantation system. Finally, there was still the possibility that gold and silver might be found, either above or below ground.

Consequently, when Juan de Oñate approached King Philip II for a commission to colonize the area and convert the native people, it was readily granted. Oñate was a Mexican-born Spanish aristocrat who had extensive interests in the Zacatecas mines. He was also distantly related, through his wife, to Cortes and Moctezuma. The terms of his *adelantado* were that he must bear all the expenses, though he would have extensive rights over the land, with the power to award the status of *hidalgo*, a lesser nobleman, to his principal followers. No royal forces would accompany him, since Oñate was unlikely to meet European opponents.

The lack of royal support did not worry Oñate, being an extremely wealthy man, and he accordingly began assembling a force on the Rio Grande near the later site of El Paso. In the expedition were some five hundred persons, including 130 soldiers, ten Franciscans, and sundry colonists with their wives, children, servants, and slaves. The entourage also included a large number of cattle and other livestock.

Oñate initially met little resistance when he crossed the Rio Grande in April 1598. The Pueblo communities had experienced visits from the Spaniards over many years, and most had ended in considerable loss of Indian life. It made sense, therefore, to treat the newcomers with respect. However, it seems that some Pueblos actually welcomed the Spaniards as protectors against the nomadic Apache, whose raids had recently increased. Oñate accordingly continued northwards along the Rio Grande, finally siting his headquarters at a pueblo on the west side of the river, which he renamed San Gabriel. Here a church was built and the town reshaped to meet the needs of the newcomers. However, the site soon became overcrowded and proved unsuitable for defence. Within ten years Oñate had moved his capital twenty miles southwards to a place that he named Santa Fe.

Although Oñate's arrival had not been resisted this did not mean that he was greeted with enthusiasm, especially when the Pueblos discovered that they were to be menial laborers working their own lands for the benefit of the settlers and clergy. When the Pueblo of Acoma, which sat on top of a seemingly impregnable *mesa*, resisted the Spanish extortion by killing eleven of Oñate's men, including his nephew, the *adelantado* responded by offering the inhabitants a choice of slavery or death. The Acoma declined the offer, believing their town to be impregnable. In this they proved mistaken. During the subsequent fighting, some 500 men and 300 women and children were killed, out of a total population of 1,380. The survivors were then put on trial. All, except children under twelve, were condemned to twenty-five years' servitude. However, males over twenty-five were also to have one foot cut off, as a reminder to other Pueblos of the consequences of rebellion. Oñate justified his cruelty by arguing that, as the Acoma had taken an oath of obedience to the Spanish king, they had not only committed murder but treason too. Such treatment in any case was the only way of saving heathen souls. The Franciscans agreed.

After this brutal demonstration of Spanish power, many Pueblo settlements reluctantly accepted Spanish authority, both civil and military, which in some respects mirrored the Indian duality of religious and civil chiefs. The difference now was that the chiefs were at the bottom of the political, religious, and economic order while the friars and soldiers were on top. Once this switch had been effected a concerted attempt could be made to eradicate all traces of the Indians' religion and culture. Indian icons were destroyed and replaced with those of the cross and the Virgin Mary. Attempts were also made to change Indian sexual mores, which had permitted both polygamy and serial monogamy. Indeed to Spanish eyes the carnal behavior of the native women, not least with the newcomers, appeared the height of profanity. Of course the Spanish, like the English, had no appreciation of Indian attitudes to fertility, hospitality, and sex. To the Indians sex was something beautiful, to be enjoyed rather than hidden in shame behind a monogamous relationship.

Initially the friars were not without success, though chance often played a part in this. Their first arrival in 1598 coincided with the ending of a drought, which made Christianity seem more powerful than the native religion. The coincidence proved so potent that the friars thereafter always attempted, when on a new mission, to arrive just before the rainy season. In addition, some medical feats helped to give the newcomers an appearance of magic and invincibility. The friars also turned the Indian custom of gift giving to their advantage. In Pueblo society those unable to reciprocate gifts were deemed inferior. The friars, by offering tools, seeds, and livestock, were able in return to secure submission to the new order. Another ploy was to draw parallels between Pueblo beliefs and Christian liturgy. Thus the Indian Corn Mother became the Virgin Mary, while the cult of the rain spirits, or *katsinas*, was superseded by veneration of the saints. In addition, the traditional prayer sticks used to summon the rain spirits were replaced by the cross. Flagellation also had a useful parallel since it could be equated with the native practice of flogging their leaders to see if they could endure pain. Finally the friars' abstinence from sexual activity reinforced the native notion that these were men of extraordinary power. Pueblo men abstained from sex before hunting and war, believing this gave them greater power, both spiritual and physical. To abstain permanently seemed miraculous.

As a result many voluntary conversions were made, though in reality they were often the result of a starving population desperate for the necessities of life, while the understanding of such converts struggling with a strange language must have been limited.

Conversion went hand in hand with a restructuring of Indian civil society. The adoption of European-style farming, especially the keeping of domestic animals, considerably strengthened Spanish authority since it meant a downgrading of hunting, the prerogative of the former civil chiefs. Their role as warriors was also undermined, since warfare was now primarily the responsibility of the Spanish. Indeed in many respects Indian society was turned on its head, at least for the old governing elite. The priestly class had been discredited by their failure to conjure sufficient magic to defeat the Spanish, while the civil chiefs had nothing to sustain their authority now that they had no gifts to distribute. Even the institution of marriage was controlled by the priests.

Nevertheless, developing the colony proved difficult for both Oñate and his successors. Oñate himself was recalled in 1612 on charges of abusing his authority, not least over the Indians. He had also nearly bankrupted himself, thus leaving the Crown a potentially expensive legacy. The result was a debate about abandoning the enterprise. But, as with Florida, knowledge that the French and English were attempting to establish themselves in North America tipped the scales.[8] The Franciscans in any case were anxious to continue their missionary work, arguing that those already converted should not be abandoned. In the event a compromise was arranged: Florida and New Mexico would be retained, but no further attempt would be made to settle California. A few missions were subsequently built on the lower peninsula from 1697, but upper California remained outside Spanish control until toward the end of the colonial period.

The qualms of the Spanish Crown about New Mexico had at least one positive effect in that it made the Franciscans even more determined to take advantage of their reprieve. Indeed they were now fired by the vision of a colony of godly Indian communities, separated as much as possible from the corrupting influences of the Spanish inhabitants. As a result, by the late 1620s they had established almost fifty churches and residencies along a two-hundred-mile stretch of the Rio Grande. The arrival in 1629 of eight more friars allowed additional missions to be established further afield among the Acoma, Zuni, and Hopi peoples.[9] It seemed that Oñate's policy of "War by fire and blood" had been successful in inducing the Pueblo Indians to accept the newcomers and their religion. But apart from Spanish military superiority, other factors were at work in effecting the response of the native people. One was the desirability of Spanish protection against the Apache. Another was the apparent immunity of the Spanish from the diseases which afflicted the native peoples. Many Indians also recognized that if they embraced the friars, they would be spared the worst excesses of the Spanish soldiery. Nevertheless, it seemed to the Franciscans at this point that the whole of North America was within their grasp, if only they were given adequate support.

Unfortunately, the secular aspects of New Mexico presented a less heartening picture. One reason was a lack of people. The Hispanic population never exceeded 1,500 during the seventeenth century, though the number of Indians acknowledging Spanish authority may have been as high as 17,000. The slow growth was a consequence of the isolation of the province. San Gabriel and Santa Fe were almost eight hundred miles from the nearest Spanish settlements in northern Mexico. Even El Paso, founded in 1659, was nearly as remote. New Mexico in consequence could expect a supply convoy only once every three years, and frequently the period was longer. This meant that there were no real markets to stimulate the economy and attract settlers. Another reason was the lack of marketable

---

[8] The Spanish still had only the haziest notion of the geography of North America, believing that Jamestown and Quebec were much closer to New Mexico than they actually were.

[9] The extent to which the villages of the Zuni and Hopi actually accepted Christianity, but simply tolerated the friars to avoid military reprisals, is noted by Weber, *Spanish Frontier*, 97–8.

commodities. The settlers mainly supported themselves by ranching and raising crops. But even with cheap Indian labor, the rewards were scanty. Surplus horses, sheep, and cattle were periodically sent to New Spain, but the numbers were necessarily small and the quality poor after such a long trek. Hides and salt were also produced, but only in small quantities. The only other export commodity – an illegal one under the royal ordinance of 1573 – was the sale of slaves. Prisoners captured from the Apache could always be sold in New Spain as labor for the mines. The policy, however, was of dubious benefit since the officials who organized these slaving expeditions did so for personal profit, indifferent to the retaliation that the Apache were likely to inflict on the outlying Pueblo communities.

In these circumstances New Mexico was not an attractive place for Spanish settlement and investment. The climate was harsh, resulting in fierce heat in the summer and bitter cold in the winter, when the communion wine sometimes froze. The Hispanic population accordingly could only grow through its own fertility and that meant a mestizo population, given the lack of Spanish women.

Another constraint on growth was the need to rely on the *encomienda* system. Unlike Florida, New Mexico had no royal military establishment so that the settlers had to rely on their own prowess as soldiers. *Encomenderos* had originally been appointed to fight the Moors in Spain. In return for defending the frontier the Crown granted them the right to exact tribute from any subject peoples. However, when the system was adopted in the Americas, it was so grossly abused that in 1542 Charles V had attempted to stop it. Unfortunately, his good intentions were impossible to implement, since the *encomienda* was too advantageous, given the Crown's perennial lack of revenue and need to provide defence in remote places like New Mexico. Hence, the natives in Oñate's province had to endure its full rigors. Tribute was usually levied in both goods and services, which, when added to the friars' demands for labor to build, repair and, feed the missions, amounted to a harsh exploitative regime. What made the situation even more repressive was that the demands on each individual increased as the Indian population declined, and many Indians effectively fell into permanent servitude, which did nothing for the economic health of the colony.

Unfortunately economic exploitation was not the limit of Indian complaint. Other grievances included the sexual abuse of their women and misuse of their land, much of which was now appropriated for the use of the church and settlers. The sense of injustice was not diminished when officials like the governor and even some friars, who should have protected the Indians, were foremost in practicing such abuses. The result, even among Christian Indians, was a serious undermining of support for the Spanish cause. This was very damaging since by the last quarter of the seventeenth century the religion of the conquistadors had seemingly lost much of its magic. The ravages of disease continued, as did other natural calamities like droughts, which were severe in the 1660s and 1670s. Nor were the Spanish always successful in shielding the Pueblos from Apache raids, which simultaneously undermined respect for their temporal power.

In this situation many Pueblos began to return to their traditional gods, which even the most zealous neophytes had never entirely abandoned. The evidence suggests that many ceremonies continued to be observed in the *kivas*, or ceremonial chambers, whenever Spanish backs were turned. This renaissance was helped by moral lapses among the Spanish themselves. While the priests preached the need for monogamy among the laity and abstinence for themselves, their exhortations were more often breached than observed by the Spanish themselves. Finally, respect for authority was not increased by the frequent disputes between officials and friars over the spoils of Indian labor. In 1659 Governor Lopez de Mendizabal actually asked several Pueblos to list their complaints against the friars, including any sexual misdemeanors, as an excuse for taking control of the Indians' labor himself.

Throughout the seventeenth century sporadic revolts had occurred as a result of Spanish misrule, but until 1680 the Pueblo peoples seemingly lacked the ability to combine against their oppressors. The Spanish certainly believed so. However, the difficult climatic conditions of the 1660s and 1670s, combined with the ever-increasing demands of the Spanish for tribute and a renewed attempt to suppress Pueblo dancing and *kivas*, drove a majority of the native inhabitants secretly to agree on a concerted bid for freedom. Some two dozen communities took part in the uprising in August 1680, overcoming the difficulty of coordinating people who spoke six different languages. One factor making for success was the presence of a dynamic leader, Popé. Five years earlier he had participated in a Pueblo religious revival for which he had been savagely whipped. Popé, an inhabitant of San Juan, organized the plot from Taos, which had previously rebelled. The Spanish received warnings two days beforehand of the planned uprising, but failed to realize its magnitude. Many settlers in consequence were surprised in the fields, as at Jamestown in 1622. Santa Fe itself was soon besieged by two thousand Indians. Inside were about a thousand Spaniards and loyal Indians, though only a small number of these were capable of bearing arms. Accordingly, after six weeks, the governor decided to abandon the capital and retreat down the Rio Grande to El Paso, whither another fifteen hundred had already fled. The plan was a desperate one, but Popé's own forces had suffered heavy losses and for this reason allowed their opponents to escape. Nevertheless, the Pueblo people of New Mexico had done what Opechancanough had failed to do in Virginia: drive out the invader. In the process about four hundred Spanish had been killed, including twenty-one missionaries.

In the weeks that followed Popé encouraged his followers to destroy all traces of the Spanish occupation, both secular and religious, in an effort to cleanse and restore the native way of life. He was only partially successful. Most Pueblos found European tools, livestock, and crops too useful to dispense with entirely. Nevertheless the success of the uprising can be measured by the fact that thirteen years were to pass before the Spanish returned to New Mexico.

During this time the refugees at El Paso waited for an opportunity to recover their former way of life. That they finally succeeded owed much to the resolution of one man, Diego de Vargas, who, on being appointed governor of the province, determined to restore Spanish authority. He was in large part able to regain the initiative because the Pueblo communities were once more divided amongst themselves. Popé had alienated many of his supporters by acting in the manner of a Spanish governor. In this situation many Pueblos were ready to play the Spanish off against their rivals, as Vargas found during a preliminary foray in 1692, when twenty-three towns offered their loyalty and friendship. This encouraged Vargas to march back the following year for a permanent stay. Even so he had to fight his way into Santa Fe, where he hanged seventy rebels, and had to continue campaigning for another year. Moreover, the Franciscans found that, without a continuous military presence, they could no longer remain in their missions, as before. Indeed within three years another rebellion broke out. This time many Pueblos were abandoned, the inhabitants preferring to flee to their Hopi and Apache neighbors, who remained outside Spanish authority.

The revolt had several consequences. One was a further decline in population. This was despite the abandonment of the *encomienda* system. Although the Spanish refused to blame themselves for the disaster, they recognized that the systematic exploitation of the natives would have to be alleviated. The result was the adoption of the less extortionate *repartimiento* labor requirement, although abuses such as the forced sale of corn continued. Another concession was that each Pueblo was allowed more freedom in the nomination of their village officers, whose task was to liaise with the Spanish civil administration. Previously these officials had been appointed by the friars. Arms were also occasionally issued so that the Pueblos could assume responsibility for their own defence. Lastly, religious concessions were made as the Franciscans recognized the need to be more accommodating of native customs and beliefs. As a result, New Mexico experienced something of a modest revival. While many missions were not rebuilt, some new ones were established, notably at Albuquerque in 1706.

Even so New Mexico was not without its problems. Border raids continued, and indeed increased with the appearance of new foes like the Comanche. The defence of the frontier was more difficult now because the Plains peoples had access to European weapons from the French settlements in the Mississippi valley. They also had horses, thus cancelling out the previous advantage of the Spanish. Thus one expedition sent to drive out French traders from the Kansas area in 1720 met with disaster at the hands of the Pawnee, when thirty-five men, a third of the Santa Fe garrison, were killed. The resources simply did not exist to mount a mission in revenge. The balance of power had dramatically shifted.

Meanwhile, the institution of slavery continued, despite the official ban, being too valuable in a society that had little else to sustain it. Most male captives were still sent to the silver mines in Mexico, though some were retained as laborers and a few turned into skilled craftsmen such as blacksmiths, masons, weavers, and silversmiths. Most females were deployed as domestics in the predominantly Spanish towns of Santa Fe, Santa Cruz and Albuquerque. Historians have often credited the Spanish with operating a more benign form of slavery, permitting marriage, allowing access to the courts and limiting the period of service. In practice, these regulations, which were designed for African slavery, were rarely observed. Few marriages were recorded while even freed Indians were often kept tied to their owners by fictitious obligations in a form of debt peonage. Beatings were common and sexual harassment endemic.

By mid-century the Spanish population of New Mexico had perhaps reached 6,500 of whom some 2,500 live around El Paso. The number of Hispanicized Indians was approximately 10,000, but still declining because of the maltreatment of the native population. In many ways the province was little different from what it had been during the previous century, consisting of a string of Pueblo settlements along the Rio Grande. There were no schools or hospitals other than what were provided by the friars. Perhaps the greatest changes were in the economy. The reduced availability of Indian labor meant that New Mexico now had to rely more on trade with the surrounding Indian nations. This in turn required a relaxation of the ban on the selling of guns, which the Spanish had always enforced as a means of controlling the natives. Refusal now meant that the Indians would simply turn to the French in the Mississippi valley for supplies, with the consequent loss of custom. Mammon had finally triumphed over God in Spain's imperial priorities.

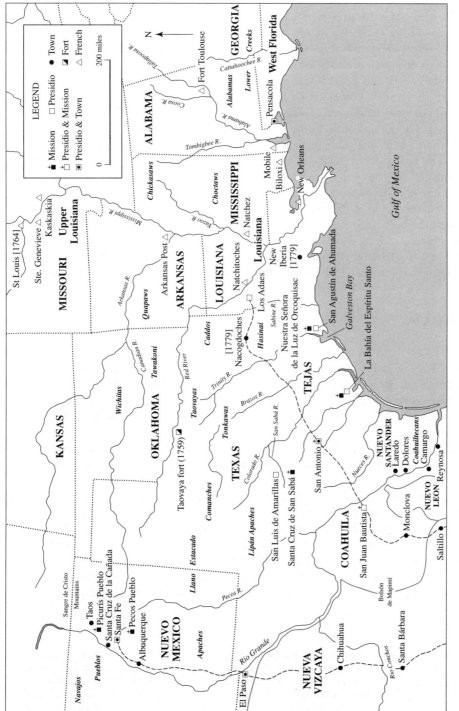

Map 14 Spanish, French, and Indian settlements in the Gulf of Mexico in the mid-eighteenth century. From David Weber, *The Spanish Frontier in North America* (Yale, 1992), 185 (map drawn specifically for Professor Weber's book by Don Bufkin).

Unfortunately, New Mexico lacked the goods to exploit the new opportunities effectively. The reasons for this were twofold. One was the weakness of Spanish manufacturing.[10] The second was the restrictive nature of the Spanish mercantilist system, which required all goods to travel in Spanish ships to a designated port like Vera Cruz. This placed Spain's colonies in an economic strait-jacket, throttling their ability to compete. The only beneficiaries were French and English smugglers.

Finally the colony continued to be impeded by racial and class distinctions. The Spanish, whether the landowning *hidalgos* or yeoman farmers, remained rigidly attached to their notions of honor and birth. Purity of blood was considered essential, for the protection of which women were kept subordinate to the wishes of their patriarchs, especially regarding marriage. The rest of the population, namely the Pueblo Indians, mestizos, and household slaves remained in degraded circumstances. Like the Moors in sixteenth-century Spain, their only function was to work for the benefit of the elite. The result was a society which inhibited enterprise and initiative.

Spanish New Mexico faced a dilemma. Although its regulation by imperial Spain provided a measure of security, it also prevented its effective development. On the other hand, to open the colony to market forces would bring in foreign elements and dilute Spain's political, cultural, and religious control. Neither option was particularly encouraging.

3 TEXAS

Spain had fought hard for two centuries to exclude other European powers from the Gulf of Mexico, but eventually had to accept a French presence at Biloxi Bay in 1699. That did not mean that the Spanish had resigned themselves to losing the area. Rather it stimulated them to take preventive action to limit the damage. The principal fear was that the French would pioneer an overland route from the Mississippi to New Mexico to siphon off its trade. The result was a new Spanish interest in the region, especially the area that came to be Texas, which until the end of the seventeenth century had been entirely neglected.

Even before the French established themselves at Biloxi, the Spanish hoped to gain control of the region through their traditional strategy of using Franciscan missions to win over the native inhabitants. Their main target this time was the Caddo peoples living between the Trinity, Sabine, and Red rivers. The Caddo were attractive because, like the Pueblo people, they were relatively sedentary and had a well-developed agriculture. The Caddo were organized into three confederacies: the Hasinai or Tejas (Texas), the Kadohadacho, and the Natchitoches. They comprised in total about twenty-five communities.

The first plan, drawn up in 1690, was for a mission near the Trinity River, 500 miles north of the Rio Grande. The danger as always was that the post would be too remote to

---

[10]   Historians have advanced many reasons for the economic decline of Spain: the expulsion of the Moors and Jews, the most dynamic elements in the population; the excessive dependence on bullion, which fueled inflation and undermined Spanish manufactures; a mercantilist system, which was totally designed for the benefit of metropolitan Spain; the Catholic church, which laid insufficient stress on the work ethic; and a culture that glorified war and adventure at the expense of more mundane economic activity; see J. H. Elliot, *Spain and its World, 1500–1700: Selected Essays* (New Haven, 1989).

defend or have any real effect. The likelihood of this was greatly increased when Father Mazanet, the mission leader, dismissed most of his escort, fearing that the soldiers would set the Caddo a bad example. In the event an outbreak of disease rather than the behavior of the military defeated the venture. The Caddo rightly blamed the Spanish for the arrival of smallpox and ordered the friars to leave, which they did, not having the same zest for martyrdom as their predecessors. No immediate attempt was made to return. The problems in New Mexico and the failure of La Salle meant that for the moment Spain had neither the resources nor the need for such a venture.

However, by the turn of the eighteenth century a French presence on the Mississippi had become a reality and the Spanish recognized that, unless they reoccupied East Texas, French influence among the native tribes would grow, with all its attendant dangers. Accordingly, in 1716 an expedition was dispatched under Captain Domingo Ramón to make contact once more with the Caddo. Ramón's force was small, just seventy-five persons, among whom were twenty soldiers and ten friars. By the time Ramón reached the Natchitoches tribe on the Red River he found a French post already there. Since France and Spain were now at peace, Ramón had to accept this *fait accompli* and establish instead two mission posts nearby, called San Miguel de los Adaes and Dolores de los Ais, from which he hoped to contain any further French incursion. But to prevent East Texas from being totally isolated, the viceroy of New Spain simultaneously ordered the building of a mission on the San Antonio River to act as a way-station between the two. The new town, begun in 1718, was to be called San Antonio.

Despite this peaceful progress the Spanish soon faced further challenges to their position in East Texas. In 1719 Spain went to war with England, France, and Austria over her territorial claims in Italy. This provided the French with an opportunity to attack the Spanish in the Gulf. First Pensacola and then the East Texas missions were overrun, leaving San Antonio as Spain's most advanced post. Not that the Spanish were prepared to accept such an outcome permanently. An army of five hundred men was assembled on the Rio Grande by the Marquis de San Miguel de Aguayo, but by the time he was ready to attack, peace had already been signed in Europe. Aguayo, therefore, merely had to escort the French trespassers back to their former post at Natchitoches.

Before returning to New Spain, Aguayo arranged to leave a more formidable garrison of two hundred and fifty men, a hundred of whom were quartered at Los Adaes. This now became the provincial capital, despite its closeness to the French at Natchitoches. Militarily Spain was not to be threatened again in East Texas during the colonial period, though this was largely the result of Franco-Spanish friendship in Europe rather than of Aguayo's military arrangements.

Unfortunately, there was just one weakness in the Spanish position. As in New Mexico and Florida, the missions lacked economic viability. At times they could not even feed themselves, having to buy what they needed from their French neighbors. This gravely weakened Spain's hold over the Indian peoples, since orthodox Christianity and the threat of force no longer had the same potency as in the past. In the new market era of the eighteenth century, guns and other manufactures were what the native peoples expected if the Spanish were to retain their respect. Gift giving had always been a yardstick of a person's importance in Indian culture and without generous distribution of presents the missions had little to offer the Indians, since they could always go to the French for arms and ammunition.

But the missions had lost their potency for other reasons too. The clergy no longer exuded the same zeal as in the days of the Counter-Reformation, when religion had dominated the thoughts of European peoples. As a result conversions declined. Indeed baptism was most frequent when Indians were on the point of death and hoping for a miracle cure. Others frequented the missions merely for the sake of a meal. Lastly the missions found it difficult to operate when so many were hostile to their aims. Three of the East Texas missions were accordingly abandoned in 1731 and their personnel withdrawn to Los Adaes or San Antonio. But even at the latter they were not safe as bands of Apache continued their raids for horses and other goods.

Such insecurity further stunted the colony's growth, since it deterred others from settling in the territory. The result was that by 1730 the province still had only five hundred Hispanic people, with perhaps another thousand Hispanicized natives. The following year fifty settlers arrived from Tenerife to start farms around San Antonio, but soon found that their efforts were ineffectual without additional labor and that was unobtainable. The Indians of Texas now worked solely for the missions on a voluntary basis, for compulsion was no longer and option, given the paucity of their numbers and the need to appease the few who remained. The economic prospects improved a little in 1749 when peace was agreed with the Apache, which allowed more extensive ranching. The market, though, was only a local one, being restricted to the supply of food and other services to the military. This was not a recipe for growth. Even by 1760 the three principal settlements of San Antonio, Los Adaes, and La Bahia (near the mouth of the San Antonio River) had barely 1,200 Hispanic inhabitants. The number of mission Indians was even smaller. The future of Texas was not seemingly bright.

4 LOUISIANA

As already noted, from 1682 the French had been trying to establish themselves in the Gulf of Mexico and Mississippi Valley. Their reasons were varied, but one was a desire to expand their empire. As noted in chapter 1, the French had been distracted from overseas ventures by domestic political and religious strife for much of the previous century. Now, under Louis XIV, France had become the most powerful country in Europe, the equivalent of a twentieth-century superpower, and it was fitting that she should take her place in the imperial order. Since 1608 the French had been settling the St. Lawrence Valley, but Canada had proved a financial liability. The sugar islands of Martinique and Guadeloupe in the West Indies had been highly successful, but were not sufficient to make France an imperial power like Spain or even England, whose colonial possessions were expanding significantly.

There were, of course, a number of differences between the French and Spanish imperial efforts in the Gulf of Mexico. By 1680 the French had no illusions about discovering cities of gold or instant riches, though hopes remained of finding mineral wealth and a passage to China. In general French intentions were more hard headed. The possession of Canada had at least given them control of the northern fur trade which was then at its peak. Now the French wanted to develop it further to the south and west to exclude their English rivals.

Compared to the Spanish, the French were also more practical in their attitudes toward the native peoples. While they sought to convert the Indians, they did not have the same obsession about absolute obedience and conformity. The priests, who were mainly Jesuits, were content to introduce the natives to Christianity in stages. They allowed them to keep many of their traditional customs, preferring to emphasize the similarities rather than the differences between their respective religions. There was also no attempt to extract forced labor. It was enough that the Indians brought their furs to exchange for French goods. This symbiotic relationship helped align most of the native peoples west of the Allegheny mountains with the French. Their one failure in eastern North America was with the Iroquois, and even the Five Nations eventually adopted a neutral stance after 1700.[11]

French involvement in Louisiana was initially a result of their Canadian fur-trade operations. By the 1660s French *coureurs de bois* (travelers of the woods) began exploring the region of the Great Lakes where they heard Indian tales that a mighty river flowed away from New France, indicating the possibility of a passage to the Pacific. This roused considerable curiosity, not least in the mind of Father Jacques Marquette, the Jesuit in charge of the mission at Michilimackinac, and Louis Joliet, a trader and explorer from Quebec. In May 1673 they set off to establish the truth of these rumors. The party traveled up Green Bay before ascending the Fox River. They next crossed over a desolate portage to the Wisconsin River which at length took them to the Mississippi on June 17, 1673. They then proceeded downstream, passing the junction with the Missouri, which opened a new possibility for a passage to the Pacific, since it was clear by this time that the Mississippi led directly to the Gulf of Mexico. On July 17, 1673, near the mouth of the Arkansas River, the explorers decided to return, aware of the reception they would receive if they ran into the Spanish. They chose a slightly different route back via the Illinois and Chicago rivers, arriving in Green Bay at the end of September.

Despite these discoveries it took another nine years for the entire course of the Mississippi river to be explored by René Robert Cavelier, Sieur de La Salle. La Salle's motives, like those of many earlier Spanish conquistadors, was to seek new lands and make his fortune, either by trade, mineral wealth, or the discovery of a route to the east. In hopes of the latter he called his estate near Montreal "La Chine" or China. His first attempt at that objective was by way of the Ohio River but the enterprise was not successful. This was in 1669 before Joliet and Marquette had found the Mississippi. La Salle was only ready to try again in 1678, this time with a formal commission from Louis XIV to explore the Mississippi and establish forts. He had his first view of the river in December 1680, but required another year to assemble sufficient men and supplies for his main expedition. He finally entered the Mississippi on February 6, 1682. As he proceeded downstream he noted much promising countryside, both for hunting and agriculture. The mouth of the river was reached on April 6, 1682 where three days later formal possession was proclaimed on behalf of Louis XIV. The party then retraced its passage up the Mississippi.

La Salle recognized that a mere proclamation was insufficient to establish French claims to the territory. Physical occupation was required. Accordingly, in February 1684 he proposed the establishment of a colony two hundred miles up the Mississippi to render it safe from Spanish attack. His request was granted and he set off in July 1684 with four ships, including a royal frigate, heading directly for the Gulf of Mexico with approximately two hundred soldiers and three hundred colonists. Hopes were high, but unbeknown disaster

---

[11] For the Iroquois's relations with the French., see chapter 8, section 3; and chapter 15, section 2.

awaited, just as it had for earlier Spanish explorers of the region. La Salle's main problem was finding the mouth of the river. Unwittingly he thought his first sighting of the mainland was the coast of Apalachee, when in reality he was 300 miles west of his objective. A temporary refuge, Fort St. Louis, was built in Matagorda Bay, near the mouth of the San Antonio River, while further attempts were made to find the Mississippi amid the islands, bayous, and channels that dotted the area. Further setbacks were not long in coming. One of La Salle's ships went aground, while the naval officer in charge of the frigate, having failed to find the mouth of the Mississippi further east, returned to France. This left La Salle with no shipping, since his other two vessels had remained at Santo Domingo. He then made three attempts, from 1685 to 1687, to set off on foot to find the Mississippi and get help from New France. On the third such attempt, in January 1687, he was murdered by his own mutinous soldiers, most of whom, together with the settlers, died of starvation, disease, or death at the hands of the Indians. By the spring of 1689, when the Spanish finally succeeded in finding Fort St. Louis, it was an abandoned ruin.

Nevertheless, the same concerns that had fueled support for La Salle resurfaced at the end of the century, being given added impetus in 1697 by the signing of the Treaty of Ryswick. This ceded to France the western portion of Hispaniola or the island of Santo Domingo (now Haiti), providing her with a convenient base from which to launch a new attempt at colonization. In addition, the French remained concerned that the English might try to establish themselves in the region. Accordingly, when a new proposal for a colony in the lower Mississippi valley was submitted to Louis XIV by Pierre Le Moyne, Sieur d'Iberville, and his younger brother, Jean-Baptiste Le Moyne, Sieur de Bienville, it was readily accepted and a force similar to that of La Salle's commissioned, though the brothers were more careful in their choice of subordinates. Iberville left France in October 1698 and, like La Salle, reached the Gulf coast via Santo Domingo toward the end of January 1699. But although he discovered the mouth of the Mississippi, he decided to make his initial settlement in Biloxi Bay, not having sufficient time to find a suitable location in the river itself before his vessels returned to France. It proved a serious mistake since the land around Biloxi was barren and the site had to be abandoned within three years in favour of a new position at Mobile, not far from the recently established Spanish post at Pensacola. Fortunately the two nations were now at peace. Equally fortunate was the friendliness of the native peoples who were ready to trade food for goods. Some soldiers were even sent to lodge with the Indians, who were glad to offer such hospitality in exchange for protection against the Creeks.

The period following the Treaty of Ryswick proved in retrospect not to have been a good time for colonizing Louisiana, since France quickly became involved in another major conflict in Europe, the War of Spanish Succession. The only benefit for the new colony from this was that France was now allied with Spain rather than against her. Nevertheless the effect was to put the survival of Louisiana in doubt. The lower Mississippi Valley was not suitable for European agriculture and, starved of resources, had nothing to stimulate its development. The only economically successful parts of the new colony were the mission posts in the upper Mississippi Valley at Kaskaskia, Cahokia, and Peoria, where more traditional styles of farming were possible. Accordingly, many of the province's four hundred settlers went northwards to take advantage of this more accommodating climate and environment. The Illinois settlements now became the chief source of provisions for the rest of the colony, especially wheat to which the average Frenchman felt a divine entitlement.

The settlements also made a significant contribution to the fur trade, being well placed to tap the hinterland of the western Great Lakes region.

Even this modest success was seemingly put in jeopardy in 1712 when the French king granted a monopoly on Louisiana's trade to a leading French merchant, Antoine Crozat, by way of repayment for helping finance the recent war in Europe. Fortunately Crozat was not an armchair investor. He quickly organized a survey which defined more precisely the limits of Louisiana, and set about establishing trading posts on all the important rivers, notably on the Red River at Nachitoches, as the Spanish shortly discovered. Even so he found it hard to make a profit.

Accordingly, in 1717 Crozat handed over his patent to a subsidiary of the Company of the Indies. This was just before the 1721 South Sea Bubble when speculative fever was rife in both Britain and France and there was plenty of money for investment schemes, especially in exotic far-away places. In many respects Louisiana now experienced a phase similar to that of Virginia during the period of Sir Edwin Sandys. Like Sandys, the new directors believed that population growth was the key to success. Accordingly during the next four years they sent some 7,000 white immigrants and 2,000 West African slaves, mainly Wolof and Bambara people from Senegal, to the colony. Moreover, as at Jamestown, lands were granted to certain privileged individuals or concessionaires for the development of plantations. Changes were also made to the judicial and administrative systems. A superior council for the whole colony was established which in turn divided Louisiana into nine districts: New Orleans, Biloxi, Mobile, the Alabamas, Natchez, Yazoo, Natchitoches, Arkansas, and Illinois. The council also arranged for the creation of two religious districts, one under the Capuchins, the other under the Jesuits. Lastly a well-sited levee along the Mississippi was chosen in 1718 for the capital, which was to be called New Orleans.

Louisiana thus experienced dramatic growth in the years 1717–26, although, as at Jamestown, many of the new arrivals died or went back home, for the census of 1726 indicated a total population of just under 4,000. Of the whites, 1,663 were *habitants* who were free to work for themselves and acquire land, another 245 were *engagés* or indentured servants who still had contractual obligations to complete, and 332 were military personnel. Slaves accounted for the rest, comprising 1,385 blacks and 159 Indians.[12] But the most dramatic change, compared to the pre-1718 colony, was the emergence of tobacco plantations, which accounted for most of the African slaves. Not that the fur trade had been entirely supplanted, for on average deerskins worth £50,000 were exported each year, though the figure exceeded £100,000 on occasion. Much depended on the native peoples.

Relations with the Indians had generally been good, at least until the mid-1720s. The coastal or "*petite*" nations were almost invariably friendly. Devastated by disease, they welcomed the French as traders and protectors. The coastal peoples had rarely had good relations with the Spanish because of their insistence on conversion and refusal to sell guns. However, as the French advanced into the interior, they came into contact with larger, more powerful nations. Among the more important were the Creeks who lived to the north and east of Mobile; the Natchez on the Mississippi River above New Orleans; the Choctaw

---

[12]   This information is from Daniel H. Usner, Jr., *Indians, Settlers and Slaves in a Frontier Exchange Economy: The Lower Mississippi Valley before 1783* (Chapel Hill, 1992).

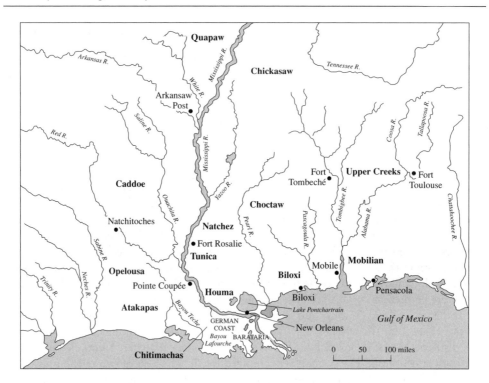

Map 15   The Lower Mississippi Valley in the 1730s. From Daniel H. Usner, Jr.,
*Indians, Settlers and Slaves in a Frontier Exchange Economy: The Lower
Mississippi Valley before 1783* (Chapel Hill, 1992), 51.

on the upper reaches of the Pearl River; and the Chickasaw further north between the
Yazoo and Tennessee Rivers (see map 15).

Contact was first made with the Creeks after the founding of Mobile in 1702 when an
attempt was made to wean them from the English. The same reasoning led to the building
in 1717 of Fort Toulouse at the junction of the Coosa and Tallapoosa rivers (see chapter 15,
section 3). Unfortunately the French, like the Spanish, did not always have sufficient goods
of the right quality and price. The French attempted to overcome this want by sending
various chiefs to France to impress them with the wealth and power of their nation. Greater
attempts were also made to understand Indian culture. Many, like Bienville, learnt Indian
languages, while young French boys were sent to live with the natives so that they could
become interpreters. Nevertheless, although the French made some headway with the Upper
Creeks, their success was limited, since the English traders were soon back with their wares.

The French were also constrained by a lack of trade goods in their dealings with the
nations along the Mississippi Valley. As a result they had to be selective in their choice of
allies, preferring the Natchez and Choctaw to the Chickasaw. Despite such favoritism,
relations with the Natchez in particular proved difficult. The Natchez were one of the more
advanced nations in the region, being almost the sole surviving example of a Mississippi
mound-building culture. They were a proud people and had earlier been deeply offended
when Governor Antoine de La Mothe Cadillac failed to pay his respects to the paramount
chief or sun king while traveling down the Mississippi in 1715. Fortunately, Bienville was

able to patch up relations after a show of force and the building of a military post and trading center called Fort Rosalie.

However relations broke down irretrievably, as in Virginia a hundred years earlier, when the Indies Company began to encourage tobacco planting near the natives' principal settlements, changing the landscape in the process. The Natchez were also now aware of the dangers of living too close to the white settlers and their diseases. From 1722 onwards they retaliated against the encroachments of the settlers by attacking their livestock and crops. The French in return took hostages and demanded compensation. The final straw came in 1729 when the French commander at Fort Rosalie ordered the Natchez to vacate one of their principal settlements so that he could establish a plantation for himself. This utter disregard for the Natchez made them determined to attempt what Opechancanough had tried to do at Jamestown: liquidate the entire white presence as the only way of preserving their culture and livelihood.

Despite rumors of the Indians' impending design, the French at Fort Rosalie were totally surprised when the plan was executed on November 28, 1729. Within hours some 235 French men, women, and children had been killed and nearly 300 African slaves taken, though some of the latter may have been involved in the uprising. However, the Natchez had not been able to attack New Orleans itself, nor were they supported by the neighboring peoples, many of whom now rallied to the French cause, most importantly the Choctaw. The French were also fortunate that their African slaves at New Orleans did not rebel, though there was widespread fear that they might do so. The French were accordingly able to mobilize sufficient forces to hunt down their foe, who were either killed or sold into slavery in Santo Domingo, though some managed to take refuge with the Chickasaw and Creeks.

Although the colony survived the Natchez war, the Indies Company's control did not. With the colony on the verge of starvation, the members decided that Louisiana was too unprofitable a prospect to be worth keeping. Accordingly, they surrendered their charter to the king in January 1731. The management of the colony was now placed in the hands of a royal council, which delegated the day-to-day running to a royal governor, the veteran Bienville. This was a similar outcome to that in Virginia after the massacre of 1622. However, unlike Virginia, there was to be no boom in the economy. Louisiana's tobacco growers simply could not compete in the European market with their counterparts in the Chesapeake and elsewhere. Indigo, another cash crop, was equally disappointing, while sugar was not thought to be feasible because of the length of the growing season. Many planters accordingly had to turn to the more mundane occupation of providing France's Caribbean islands with timber, naval stores, cereals, and cattle. The only other economic lifeline remained the fur trade.

With the defeat of the Natchez, the Choctaw now became the principal allies of the French. The Choctaw, a Muskogean-speaking people, had at least 20,000 inhabitants, but had long been disadvantaged by the difficulty of securing arms to fight their traditional enemies, the Creeks and Chickasaw. In many ways they now formed a partnership similar to the one between the Iroquois and New York, though relations were not always harmonious, especially when the French failed to give them a fair price for their peltry. The Choctaw also felt that they had been poorly rewarded for their assistance against the Natchez. In consequence a faction led by Chief Red Shoes attempted to open negotiations with the English at Savannah, after its founding in 1733. Ultimately the advantages of the French alliance were too great for most Choctaws while their old enemy the Chickasaw remained a threat.

We have already seen that the French had found it impractical to form alliances with all the nations in the region, most notably the Chickasaw, who in consequence looked elsewhere for their arms and other goods. This brought the danger that English merchants and soldiers might come into the Mississippi Valley. The Chickasaw also gave offence by giving refuge to some of the Natchez and were suspected of encouraging that tribe to continue their attacks against isolated French settlements. After a number of incidents Bienville determined to punish them by striking at the Chickasaw heartland between the Yazoo, Tennessee, and Tombigbee rivers. To make the attack more effective, Bienville mobilized additional forces from Illinois. The main advance began from Mobile on April 1, 1736 but failed to take the Chickasaw's principal fort, partly because of a lack of co-ordination and the inadvertent betrayal of Bienville's plans by the Illinois force commander. Over a hundred men were killed during the campaign. As a result Bienville did not advance against the Chickasaw again for another three years until he had assembled a much larger and better supplied force. This time the Chickasaw were ready to sue for peace, offering to surrender the English traders and Natchez refugees, together with several chiefs as hostages. But Bienville's victory proved a hollow one. Once the French had returned home in February 1740, the Chickasaw resumed their trading with the English. Nor had the war done much for relations with the Choctaw, since they received little reward for supporting the French. Even worse, in 1745 the distribution of presents was cut while the price of trade goods doubled. The result was a civil war among the Choctaw as various factions disputed which European nation to ally with. This led to many deaths among both the white and Indian communities.

Because of this turmoil, the European American population of lower Louisiana was still only 3,200 by 1750, though the African-American population had shown rather more robust growth at 4,500. Another 1,300 whites and some 300 blacks lived in the Illinois country. Compared to the English colonies, such increase was pedestrian. Not that the economy was totally stagnant. The fur trade continued to flourish and tobacco increased as the plantations acquired more slaves. Some landowners also diversified successfully into indigo and timber products, while a little rice was cultivated for domestic consumption, using the skills of the Wolof and Bambara peoples. One planter even experimented with sugar, though without success. The smallness of the population meant that both demand for and production of these commodities was necessarily limited, resulting in a lack of resources and revenue. Even by 1760 Louisiana still had difficulty feeding itself and remained a financial liability for the Crown.

The reasons why settlers refused to come to Louisiana were varied. In part it was a chicken and egg situation. Until a sufficient population had created a vibrant economy, Louisiana necessarily remained backward and unappealing, which in turn deterred others from coming. In addition, the relatively large number of slaves may have dissuaded some French from emigrating since their presence excluded whites from various kinds of employment. Another factor may have been the lack of representative institutions to check a frequently corrupt and incompetent administration; for every aspect of colonial life was determined by officials appointed by the Crown.[13]

---

[13] For a discussion of the reasons why the French were reluctant to emigrate, see Peter N. Moogk, "Reluctant Exiles: Emigrants from France in Canada before 1760," *William and Mary Quarterly*, XLVI, 1989, 463–505.

Conditions for most groups in Louisiana, accordingly, remained harsh and unattractive. Apart from places of worship, there were no public buildings and few facilities of any kind other than those provided by the clergy. The most notable of these was the Ursuline Convent, which was established in 1727 to provide a military hospital and school for the daughters of the elite. The Ursulines also helped care for the province's orphans. But for most of the population there was effectively no educational provision. Medical facilities were also rudimentary, comprising one small hospital for the poor, which was established at New Orleans in 1735, following a bequest from a local fisherman.

However, by mid-century the ratio of European men to women was relatively balanced, with 1,700 males to 1,500 women. This meant that family life was possible for most whites, though the common soldiers still had to rely on Indian and African women. The Code Noir of 1724 attempted to stop such relationships. Nevertheless, these practices continued. Indeed, some soldiers attempted to protect themselves and their Indian spouses by formally marrying them, though this was not an option for those with African partners.

For women, Louisiana offered the familiar opportunities and disadvantages of a frontier society. A favorable sex ratio meant that nearly all could marry if they wished. At the same time they had the disadvantages of living in a harsh environment where manual work of all kinds was constantly required, except by members of the elite. The harshness of their life probably explains why a group of New Orleans women decided in 1730 to ask the Ursuline Convent for permission to form a sorority, or female confraternity, to be called the Children of Mary. Most of the members were drawn from the elite, though a number were from the ranks of artisans and poorer sort. Their stated purpose was to honor the Blessed Virgin by holding regular prayer meetings and by doing good works. Most important was their readiness to help the Ursuline nuns visit the sick, relieve the poor, and instruct the children of the province, both free and slave. The confraternity undoubtedly helped the women of New Orleans to live more meaningful lives by allowing them to participate in these activities.

The one group for whom things did not generally improve was the African slaves. Unlike the whites, the 4,000 Africans did not enjoy equal sex ratios, there being as late as 1760 approximately three men to every two women. Familial relationships were in consequence denied to many. However, in the early decades their treatment had been fairly benign, as in other infant European settlements. Most had been allowed time to engage in market activities such as the growing of vegetables and sale of venison. Others had been employed as skilled craftsmen. A few had been sufficiently trusted to be armed during the war with the Natchez. The benign nature of French slavery was reflected in the Code Noir of 1724 which guaranteed African slaves a minimum amount of food and clothing as well as provision for their baptism and marriage. The importance of the family was underlined by the ban on the separate sale of husband, wife, and children under fourteen years of age.

But a gap remained between the law in theory and in practice, as the estate of Joseph Dubreuil, a large planter, shows. On his death in 1754, thirty-one couples were sold with their children (if any), but eight women were sold without their partners. Moreover, estate records show that all slaves faced the daily hazard of ill treatment. Runaways could be mutilated without restraint since no masters were ever punished for killing their slaves, despite instances of gross cruelty. One reason for the increasingly harsh conditions was the growth of a plantation economy, which confined most slaves to the production of cash crops. Some still went hunting and others had the relative freedom of being employed as boatmen, wagon drivers, or cowboys. A few slaves in New Orleans continued to be trained as blacksmiths, cartwrights, carpenters, cabinetmakers, masons, and coopers. But, for most, the development of a plantation economy, as in the English-speaking colonies, was in many respects a backward step.

Nevertheless, black slaves still managed to develop their own culture, comprising a mixture of European and African ingredients. Many, for example, adopted the religion of their masters while retaining voodoo. Similarly they developed a Creole language, consisting of French words but African grammar. Those who found conditions intolerable after 1740 could flee to the maroon communities that began to flourish in the Cypress swamps of the delta. Here they could cut wood, grow crops, and even take their surpluses to the New Orleans market. Africans never entirely lost their self-respect or capacity to adapt in a dignified manner.

A number of blacks also gained their freedom legally. In this respect the French were more generous than their English counterparts. Some were rewarded for their duties as militiamen, others for outstanding service to grateful owners. A number of black women were also liberated by their French partners on the birth of a child to protect the latter's status, despite an edict that all manumissions had to be vetted by the Superior Council of the province. Another theoretical constraint on mixed race unions was the ban on the transference of property to blacks to sustain the supremacy of the white patriarchal order. In practice some white men did protect their partners and offspring by surreptitiously transferring property to them. As a result free blacks accounted for 10 percent of the African population by 1760. The majority, especially free, single, black women, resided in the area of New Orleans where employment was generally available. Even so, life remained harsh and perilous for such persons on the margins of society.[14]

Except for the French in the St. Lawrence Valley, both Spain and France had only a tenuous presence on the North American continent north of the twenty-fifth parallel. The number of inhabitants in their respective territories amounted to a few thousand at most. The British colonies in contrast had a population of one million by 1750, and this was likely to double in less than a generation if the existing demographic trends continued. Traditionally, American historians have implied that this disparity was the result of white Anglo-Saxon Protestant virtue. More recently, the emphasis has been on material factors like climate and geography in the colonization process.[15] But if numbers were to be the deciding factor in the struggle for empire, the long-term survival of the Spanish and French colonies was not a cause for optimism.[16]

---

[14] In this context it should perhaps be noted that the Spanish attempted to end the practice of interracial liaisons between whites and blacks, whether slave or free, in its Code of 1777. The French practice of recognizing slave unions was also ended.

[15] For an example of the old triumphalist view of the struggle between Britain and France, see Francis Parkman, *Montcalm and Wolfe* (New York, 1884). For a discussion relating to the nineteenth century, see Reginald Horseman, *Race and Manifest Destiny: The Origins of American Racial Anglo-Saxonism* (Cambridge, Mass, 1981).

[16] Ironically it is Mexicans and other Hispanic peoples who are now winning the numbers game in the peopling of the American South and Southwest.

19

Britain, France, and Spain: The Imperial Contest, 1739–60

1713	The Treaty of Utrecht ends the War of the Spanish Succession.
1720	The French establish a fort at Niagara.
1727	The British build a fort at Oswego.
1739	The War of Jenkins' Ear with Spain breaks out.
1740	In the expedition to Cartagena the colonists are collectively called "Americans" for the first time.
	General Oglethorpe's attack on St. Augustine fails.
1745	The New Englanders capture Louisburg.
1747	The Ohio Company is founded.
1748	The Treaty of Aix-la-Chapelle ends the War of the Austrian Succession.
	The Treaty of Logstown opens the trail to Pickawillany in the West.
1750	Dr Thomas Walker passes through the Cumberland Gap.
1754	The French establish Fort Duquesne (Pittsburgh) at the forks of the Ohio.
	A plan of union is unveiled at the Albany Congress.
1755	General Braddock is defeated.
1756	Oswego falls.
1757	Fort William Henry falls.
1758	Louisburg, Fort Frontenac, and Fort Duquesne are taken.
1759	General Wolfe takes Quebec; Rogers's rangers massacre the St. Francis Indians.
1760	General Amherst takes Montreal and receives the surrender of New France.
1763	The Peace of Paris ends the French and Indian War.

1 THE WAR OF JENKINS' EAR

ALTHOUGH THE TREATY of Utrecht in 1713 seemingly settled the boundaries of Britain and France in North America, the British colonies were expanding so rapidly that another contest was almost inevitable.

The treaty was in any case unsatisfactory respecting the boundary of Nova Scotia, or Acadia, as the French called it, the ceding of which left five thousand French people under British control. This change of status was fiercely resented by the Acadians, who continued to receive support from their compatriots in Canada, backed by the Jesuit missionaries and their Micmac allies. Every attempt by the British at Annapolis Royal to administer an oath of loyalty was met with a rebuff. The position of the British was not eased when the French constructed a new fort at Louisburg on Cape Breton Island to protect the approaches to Canada and dominate the fishery.

To the west, another potential cause of trouble after 1713 was the establishment of rival trading posts at Niagara and Oswego. Britain and France each wanted to gain access to the western nations and to restrict the commerce of the other. This rivalry threatened a resumption of the struggles of the seventeenth century during which the French and the Iroquois had fought a long and bitter contest for control of the fur trade. These dangers prompted the Board of Trade in London in September 1721 to propose a tripartite policy of building forts, regulating the Indian trade, and settling the backcountry beyond the mountains. However, the necessary enthusiasm for such a scheme was lacking at Westminster and another thirty years were to pass before something similar was attempted.

As it turned out, the next war was with Spain, so that attention was initially focused on the Caribbean. The conflict arose over the treatment of British commerce in the aftermath of the Treaty of Utrecht. That agreement allowed the British South Sea Company to supply Spain's American empire with slaves and one annual shipload of goods, but it had been shamefully abused, for the company had constantly restocked its vessel with fresh goods. Smuggling was also rife elsewhere, much of it carried out by colonial vessels and abetted by the Spanish Creoles, who needed colonial imports to survive. Spanish officials, however, simultaneously enforced Spain's mercantilist system through the *guarda costa*, or coast guard, and in the process a number of detainees were ill-treated. Among them was a Captain Jenkins, whose ear was allegedly cut off. The opposition in Parliament used the episode to embarrass the government of Sir Robert Walpole. Walpole himself was inclined toward peace, but the furor over the treatment of Britain's commerce compelled him to declare war.

In the early months of 1739 a British expedition under Admiral Vernon managed to capture the Spanish base of Porto Bello. This success encouraged the British to mount a more ambitious attack in 1740 against Cartagena, the departure point for Spain's treasure fleets. Recalling previous colonial enthusiasm in 1711, Britain requested that the colonists raise some units themselves. The call met with a good response after appeals by Governor Gooch of Virginia. Eventually four battalions were raised from eleven colonies. Interestingly, this occasion was the first on which the provincials were called Americans. The expedition itself was a poorly executed failure and proved a disaster for the colonial volunteers, many of whom died of disease or malnutrition. The colonists also found regular discipline distasteful, since most had enlisted for adventure and profit. They got neither, and their dissatisfaction greatly increased when many were detained for service with the

Royal Navy. This insult was not forgotten; when the fleet called at Boston in 1747 for provisions and the recovery of deserters the result was a serious riot.

Equally unrewarding was General Oglethorpe's scheme to attack St. Augustine. Like Vernon, Oglethorpe sought local recruits and succeeded in raising over one thousand volunteers, many from neighboring South Carolina, similarly lured by the prospect of booty. Alas, here too the colonial hopes were blighted, for after besieging St. Augustine for a month, Oglethorpe decided that his forces were too weak to continue and retreated with little to show for his effort. Fortunately, he was more successful in his defense of Georgia. When the Spanish counterattacked there in 1742, they were decisively repulsed near the settlement of Frederica in the Battle of the Bloody Swamp.

Meanwhile, in Europe war had broken out once more between France and Britain. For the colonists the renewed conflict again focused attention on the northern colonial frontier. It has often been suggested that Britain's European wars were of no interest to the colonists, but this argument is not borne out by the evidence. In fact, the call to arms was especially popular in New England, since it continued the old struggle against Catholic New France. Other motives were also at work, however. The colonists increasingly recognized that only the defeat of France could bring peace to the back country and give New England control of the fishery. The dangers posed by Louisburg were emphasized in 1744 when its garrison destroyed the fishing village of Canso at the northern end of Nova Scotia and then besieged Annapolis Royal, which Massachusetts was helping to garrison.

Accordingly in 1745 Governor Shirley persuaded the general court to launch an attack on Louisburg itself. Massachusetts had a proud tradition of organizing its own campaigns, notably the attack on Quebec in 1690. Some three thousand men were quickly voted for the enterprise; contingents also came from Connecticut and New Hampshire. The operation was greatly assisted by a squadron of Royal Navy frigates under Sir Peter Warren, which ensured that the expedition not only reached its objective but was able to isolate the garrison inside. Morale in Louisburg was low, and the French surrendered on June 16.

The capture of Louisburg had a similar effect to that of Vernon's earlier exploits at Porto Bello; it stimulated the government in London to look for further success in America. Orders were sent to New England to have supplies ready for an attack up the St. Lawrence in 1746 and another force in New York prepared to invade Canada via Crown Point. Alas, the operation was to be a repeat of 1709. The British fleet and army never arrived, having been diverted to attack the French coast at the last moment.

This fiasco effectively concluded military operations for the colonists. William Johnson, New York's agent for Indian affairs, momentarily persuaded the Mohawks to attack some outlying French settlements near the St. Lawrence, but this action merely produced a retaliatory assault on Saratoga. Skirmishing continued on the New England frontier. The peace which was finally signed at Aix-la-Chapelle in 1748 proved a great disappointment to the New England provinces, for the British negotiators returned Louisburg to the French in exchange for territorial concessions elsewhere. It seemed that Britain's American interests were doomed to be subordinated to its European ones.

2   THE STRUGGLE FOR THE OHIO

As already mentioned, by the middle of the eighteenth century the expansion of the British colonies was already making land harder to find east of the Allegheny Mountains. Although the southern piedmont still offered opportunities, by the end of the 1740s more farsighted settlers were beginning to look beyond the mountains.

Such ambitions posed a number of problems. Little was known of this area except that the American Indian nations were likely to resent any incursion into their territory and could call on the French or Spanish for assistance. Though traders like George Croghan had penetrated the mountains, their incursions were recent, and prior to them the British had relied on intermediaries for trade with the interior.

What might be daunting to an individual could more easily be accomplished by a group. The first frontier in the seventeenth century had been developed largely by joint stock companies. Similar organizations were now being formed to tackle this second frontier. The first was the Ohio Company of Virginia, organized in 1747 by Thomas Lee, a member of the Virginia council. Its aims were the promotion of both trade and settlement. Lee initially sought a charter from the Virginia assembly but later decided to apply to the Privy Council instead, perhaps to attract London investors. The grant was for 500,000 acres, and the royal charter stated that the company was to build a fort and settle one hundred families within two years on the forks of the Ohio. A start was made with the dispatch of Christopher Gist to explore the area and set up a trading post.

The activities of the Ohio Company prompted the establishment of a rival group, the Loyal Land Company. The principal persons behind this were Colonel John Lewis and John Robinson, the speaker of the Virginia House of Burgesses. These men resented the Ohio Company's direct approach to the Privy Council, preferring that such matters be determined by the local authorities. The Loyal Land Company received a grant of 800,000 acres from the House of Burgesses on what was later to be the borders of Virgina, Kentucky, and Tennessee. It also employed a surveyor, Dr Thomas Walker, who set out on his exploratory mission in the same year as Gist. Walker passed through the Cumberland Gap but failed to find open country beyond and reported that there was little land worth settling. Walker's analysis underlined the continued ignorance about the countryside beyond the mountains.

The activities of these Virginian land companies prompted rival interest from Pennsylvania. The difference there was that since the Quakers had always insisted on fair dealings with the native peoples, no land company was likely to be incorporated by the provincial assembly. For the present, Pennsylvanian interest was limited to trade. The 1744 Treaty of Lancaster had already secured Iroquois permission for a route, and negotiations were completed at Logstown in 1748 for the opening of a trail through the Ohio country. The principal negotiators were Croghan and Conrad Wieser, a second-generation Palatine. Croghan himself spoke both Delaware and Shawnee; by 1750 his mule trains had successfully crossed the mountains and opened a series of trading posts, the most notable being the village of Pickawillany on the Miami River.

These activities did not go unnoticed by the French, who not only saw their own trade diminished as a result but also realized that the affiliations of the native peoples would be compromised unless something was done to stop the British. Their main fear was that the link between New France and Louisiana would be broken.

The French therefore initiated a series of moves to confine the British colonies to a narrow strip along the coast east of the Allegheny Mountains. First, an expedition was organized under Coleron de Bienville to inform the American Indians of France's title to their territory. Then in 1752 the French destroyed the village of Pickawillany, and eliminated the presence of the British traders. Next they extended the chain of forts between the

Great Lakes and the Mississippi, strengthening Niagara and building a new post on the shores of Lake Erie at Presquile, followed by two more at Venango and Fort Le Boeuf. By 1753 only the River Ohio required fortification to complete the chain.

The French attempt to exclude the British from westward expansion could no longer be tolerated by the government in London, because of a fundamental shift in Britain's trade. Since the middle of the seventeenth century the sugar islands of the West Indies had been Britain's most prized colonial possessions. By 1750, however, trade with the mainland colonies had begun to surpass that with the West Indies, not least because the export of manufactured goods was now as important as the importation of enumerated commodities. In the words of the Duke of Newcastle, King George II's leading minister, "The French claim almost all North America except a line to the sea, to which they would confine all our colonies, and from whence they may drive us whenever they please." And he vehemently affirmed. "That is what we must not, We will not suffer."[1] A watershed had been reached in British colonial policy. The Walpolean era of salutary neglect was at an end.

The British government accordingly instituted a number of measures. The Board of Trade, under the energetic Lord Halifax, began to expend large sums for the establishment of a new town and harbor in Nova Scotia, to be called Halifax, which had been started in 1749 to secure the vulnerable northeastern approaches. At the same time further pressure was put on the Acadians to take an oath of allegiance. Elsewhere the Board of Trade ordered the Ohio Company to abide by its charter and establish a fort on the banks of that river. Everywhere the colonial governments were instructed to meet force with force if they found the French trespassing on the king's territory. In addition the Board of Trade sent a circular letter to the northern colonies urging them to negotiate with the native peoples and, most important, to persuade the Iroquois to resume their traditional alliance. To achieve these and other objectives the colonies were to consider establishing a common war chest.

The result was the Albany Congress of June 1754, attended by delegates from New Hampshire, Massachusetts, Connecticut, Rhode Island, New York, Pennsylvania, and Maryland. It was a landmark in colonial cooperation. Never before had there been such wide participation. True, the New England provinces had long cooperated with one another, while the southern colonies had occasionally given cross-border assistance, as in the Tuscarora and Yamasee wars. Otherwise, previous efforts at cooperation had been confined to meetings of royal officials, like Bellomont's conference of governors in 1700.

At Albany a number of "presents" were first given to the representatives of the Five Nations, though with little result. The sachems affected to be tired of fighting Britain's wars without adequate support and wisely decided to see who was the likely winner before committing themselves. The conference then turned to the question of a common war fund. This issue provoked a wide-ranging discussion of a plan of colonial union drawn up by Franklin. His scheme was that there should be a president general appointed by the Crown and a grand council elected by the colonial assemblies. Representation would depend on each colony's respective population. The grand council, or congress, was to have legislative power, though the president would be able to veto any measure. The new body was to be responsible for defense, relations with native peoples, and lands "not now within the bounds of particular colonies." It would be financed by quitrents on all new grants.

---

[1] Newcastle to the Earl of Albemarle, September 5, 1754, Newcastle Papers, British Library.

DOCUMENT 31

The Albany plan of union, 1754, reprinted in W. Keith Kavenagh, *Foundations of Colonial America: A Documentary History* (New York, 1973), II, 1374–5

[This ambitious scheme proposed to link the colonies together in a defensive union. In some respects it was even more ambitious than the Articles of Confederation under which the American colonies conducted the War of Independence.]

The Plan of Union (as finally adopted). It is proposed that humble application be made for an act of Parliament of Great Britain by virtue of which one general government may be formed in America, including all the said colonies, within and under which government each colony may retain its present constitution, except in the particulars wherein a change may be directed by the said act as hereafter follows.

President-General and Grand Council. That the said general government be administered by a President-General, to be appointed and supported by the Crown, and a Grand Council, to be chosen by the representatives of the people of the several colonies met in their respective assemblies.

Election of Members. The [several] House of Representatives . . . shall choose members for the Grand Council in the following proportion, that is to say, Massachusetts Bay, 7; New Hampshire, 2; Connecticut 5; Rhode Island 2; New York 4; New Jersey 3; Pennsylvania 6; Maryland 4; Virginia 7; North Carolina 4; South Carolina 4. Total 48.

Place of First Meeting. The City of Philadelphia

New Election. There shall be a new election of the members of the Grand Council every three years. . . .

Meetings of the Grand Council. The Grand Council shall meet once in every year, and oftener if occasion require, at such time and place as they adjourn to at the last preceding meeting or as they shall be called to meet at by the President-General on any emergency. . . .

Assent of the President-General and his Duty. The assent of the President-General be requisite to all acts of the Grand Council and that it be his office and duty to cause them to be carried into execution.

Power of the President-General and Grand Council: Treaties of Peace and War. That the President-General, with the advice of the Grand Council, hold or direct all Indian treaties in which the general interest of the colonies may be concerned; and make peace or declare war with Indian nations.

Indian Trade. That they make such laws as they judge necessary for regulating all Indian trade.

Indian Purchases. That they make all purchases, from Indians for the Crown, of lands not now within the bounds of particular colonies or that shall not be within their bounds when some of them are reduced to more convenient dimensions.

New Settlements. That they make new settlements on such purchases by granting lands in the King's name, reserving a quitrent to the Crown.

Laws to Govern them. That they make laws for regulating and governing such new settlements till the Crown shall think fit to form them into particular governments.

Raise Soldiers and equip vessels. That they raise and pay soldiers and build forts for the defense of any of the colonies, and equip vessels of force to guard the coasts. . . .

Power to make laws, lay duties. That for these purposes they have power to make laws and lay and levy such general duties, imposts, or taxes as to them shall appear most equal and just.

Quorum. That a quorum of the Grand Council, empowered to act with the President-General, do consist of twenty-five members; among whom there shall be one or more from a majority of the colonies.

Laws to be Transmitted. That the laws made by them for the purposes aforesaid, shall not be repugnant, but as near as may be, agreeable to the laws of England, and shall be transmitted to the King in council for approbation.

Officers, how appointed. That all military commission officers, whether for land or sea service, to act under this general constitution, shall be nominated by the President-General, but the approbation of the Grand Council is to be obtained before they receive their commissions. And all civil officers are to be nominated by the Grand Council and to receive the President-General's approbation before they officiate.

Each Colony may defend itself on an Emergency. That the particular as well as civil establishments in each colony remain in their present state, the general constitution notwithstanding; and that on sudden emergencies any colony may defend itself and lay the accounts of expense thence arising before the President-General and General Council. . . .

The scheme proved too ambitious to be acceptable either to the Crown or to the provincial assemblies, both of which apprehended a loss of authority; in addition it reminded many New Englanders of the hated Dominion of New England. Nevertheless, it was a remarkable initiative, which was to surface again in 1775.

While the conference was in session, the first hostilities broke out. In 1753 the governor of Virginia, Robert Dinwiddie, had sent a young militia officer, George Washington, to warn the French to stop encroaching on the Ohio. Then, early in 1754, Dinwiddie sent a group to construct a fort on the forks of the Ohio. These men were subsequently surprised by a much larger French and American Indian force which proceeded to occupy the site themselves. Dinwiddie then sent Washington, now a militia colonel, back with a contingent to expel them. But although Washington routed a small vanguard of the French, he was subsequently surrounded at a makeshift encampment called Fort Necessity, where he was compelled to surrender and admit his guilt for starting hostilities.

This episode was intrinsically no more important than many previous skirmishes, the difference being that on this occasion both crowns felt their prestige was at stake. When

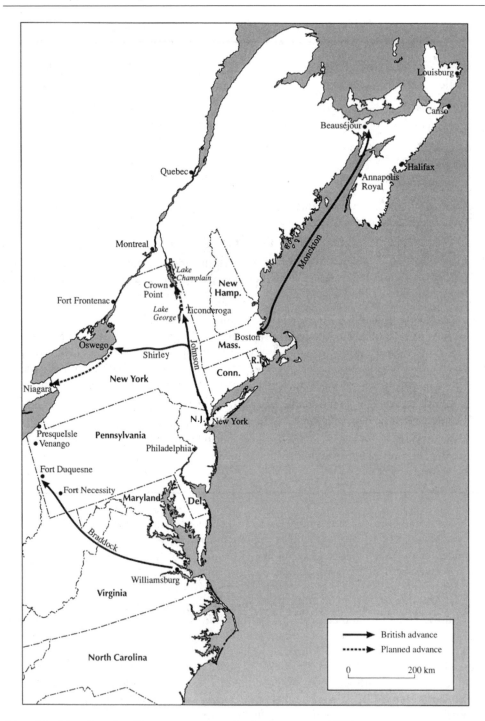

Map 16 The British offensive to secure the backcountry, 1755.

news of Washington's setback reached London, Newcastle's ministry determined to launch a four-pronged offensive to secure the frontier. First, a force of two regular regiments from Britain under the command of General Braddock was to do what Washington had failed to do on the Ohio. At the same time the middle and New England colonies were to be harnessed in a double offensive: one against Niagara by Governor Shirley and the New England troops; the other under William Johnson, who was to advance north with his Mohawks and New York volunteers against Ticonderoga and Crown Point, two French forts on New York's northern border. Finally, a mixed force of regulars and provincials was to attack the French post of Beauséjour. Located at the neck of the peninsula joining Nova Scotia to the mainland, this post was seen as the key to French influence in the area.

Braddock arrived in Virginia in February 1755 and conferred with the neighboring governors, but his appearance elicited few offers of assistance. Pennsylvania was especially tardy, its assembly resorting to the usual tactics of making every issue part of its struggle with the proprietary government. It voted £20,000 of paper currency but did not include a suspending clause as required in the proprietary instructions. This obtuseness partly stemmed from the province's traditional pacifist conviction that any war was wrong. Pennsylvanians may also have been reluctant to contribute to an expedition which was being launched from Virginia and likely to benefit that colony.

Maryland had no western territory and therefore no interest in the conflict. Finally, the Carolinas claimed that they were too poor and had too many other enemies to worry about the struggle for the Ohio. The net result was that Braddock had difficulty acquiring both supplies and transport and was saved only when Franklin, in his capacity as postmaster general, managed to hire some wagons and horses.

Farther north there were difficulties of a different kind. Although Shirley managed to raise a substantial force of New Englanders, fierce rivalry existed between him and Johnson, reflecting the conflicting interests of New England and New York. Therefore, although Johnson was supposed to recruit some of the Five Nations for Shirley's attack on Niagara, he made little attempt to do so. And since both men experienced difficulty supplying their forces, their campaigns were seriously delayed.

These setbacks set the scene for the disastrous events to follow. First came news that Braddock's mission had been an abysmal failure. True, he had succeeded in crossing the mountains, but his forces had then been ambushed a few miles from his objective by a mixed force of Canadians and American Indians. The British troops had little time to acclimatize to the demands of warfare in America, and after three hours they fled from the field. According to Adam Stephens, one of the attendant Virginians, the "Indians crept up hunting us as they would do a herd of Buffaloes. . . . The British troops were thunderstuck to feel the effects of a heavy fire and see no enemy." Stephens concluded that "you might as well send a cow in pursuit of a hare as an English soldier loaded in his way." The incident began a fierce debate over whether British troops should be used in America at all.[2]

---

[2] Adam Stephens to Sir John Hunter, July 18, 1755, Newcastle Papers, British Library. The debate over the suitability of deploying British regulars has generated a substantial literature. Most nineteenth-century writers like Francis Parkman argued that the regulars were unsuitable for warfare in America, unlike the colonists who had been brought up to wilderness fighting from birth; this view was also adopted by many more recent writers, notably Howard H. Peckham, *The Colonial Wars, 1689–1762* (Chicago, 1962); and Douglas E. Leach, *Arms for Empire:*

But at least Braddock had got to his objective. The provincials at Lake George and Oswego failed to advance at all. They found the logistics of moving whole armies through a wilderness beyond their means. Johnson's failure was fortuitously disguised by his repulse of a French force under Baron Dieskau, who ill-advisedly attacked his fortifications on Lake George after a long march and without cannon. For this Johnson received a baronetcy.

The only other success was achieved by Colonel Robert Monckton, who commanded an expedition which captured Fort Beauséjour and thus secured Nova Scotia against further attack by land. The Acadians were then given one last chance to take the oath of loyalty. When they refused they were rounded up and deported to the mainland, losing most of their property in the process, for their settlements were destroyed to prevent them being reoccupied. Few arrangements were made for their reception, and many perished on the journey or died of sickness. Some were successfully resettled, but others made heroic efforts to return to Canada to fight for their lands once more. The episode revealed the harshness of war for a civilian population caught between the ambitions of two competing powers.

One immediate result of Braddock's defeat was to set the frontier ablaze, for the Delaware and Shawnee tribes saw it as an opportunity to avenge themselves on the Pennsylvanians. They had been kept in check only by the hope that the Quakers might still obtain justice for them and by the need to secure arms and other supplies. Now the French victory convinced them that they had nothing more to fear or gain from the British. Naturally the price of French assistance was the promise of support on the frontier. Though the native war parties were generally careful to spare the Quakers, other settlements were attacked without mercy. In some areas the line of habitation was pushed back fifty miles.

Pennsylvania was not the only colony to be attacked. Virginia had to raise a regiment under Washington to repel similar assaults by the Shawnee and Delaware. New York did not escape either, even though the Iroquois were supposedly friendly, for their pretensions to control the area were now cruelly exposed. Nearly all the native peoples from Maine to Virginia took the opportunity proffered by the French victories to seek revenge. Only in the Carolinas, where the Cherokee supported the British, did the backcountry remain quiet.

The events of 1755 had revealed how woefully ill prepared the colonists were for the conflict now facing them. Most of their militias simply did not have the training or equipment for the present contest. An observer of the Virginia militia in 1739 had noted the "Diversity of Weapons and Dresses, the Unsizeableness of the Men, and the Want of the least Grain of Discipline in their Officers or them." The situation had not improved. In addition, it was almost impossible to deploy them outside the tidewater, where most of the inhabitants lived. Indeed, except in New England, those living along the coast usually saw

---

A *Military History of the British Colonies in North America, 1607–1763* (New York, 1973). The contrary view is argued by Stanley M. Pargellis, *Lord Loudoun in America* (New Haven, 1933); Lawrence Henry Gipson, *The British Empire before the American Revolution*, vol. VI, *The Years of Defeat, 1754–1757*, and vol. VII, *The Victorious Years, 1758–1760* (New York, 1946–9); Peter E. Russell, "Redcoats in the Wilderness: British Officers and Irregular Warfare in Europe and America, 1740–1760," *William and Mary Quarterly*, XXXV, 1978, 628–52; and most recently by Harold E. Selesky, *War and Society in Colonial Connecticut* (Yale, 1989). For a sympathetic account of Braddock, see Stanley M. Pargellis, "Braddock's Defeat," *American Historical Review*, XLI, 1936, 253–69; Lee S. McCardell, *Ill-Starred General: Braddock of the Coldstream Guards* (Pittsburgh, 1986); and Fred Anderson, *Crucible of War: The Seven Years' War and the Fate of Empire in British North America, 1754–1766* (New York, 2000), 105–7, who points out that Washington never criticized Braddock for the disaster.

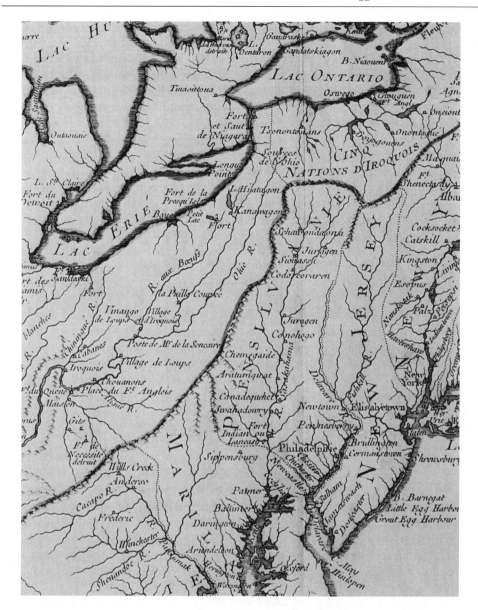

Plate 48 French map of North America, 1756, showing Fort Necessity "détruit" (destroyed), near lower left corner. Photographed by Stephen Davison.

little reason to help the frontier inhabitants. The conflict might be two or three hundred miles away, the causes not obviously important (other than protecting the interests of wealthy speculators), while those under attack were often of a different religion and ethnic origin who should learn to look after themselves.

The alternative to using the militia was to call for volunteers. However, the system of raising volunteer units had many defects, not least because such units were raised for only one campaign at a time. As the lieutenant governor of New York, Cadwallader Colden, subsequently commented, "Being only levied in the spring and disbanded in the fall they must often disappoint their general's expectations." Poor performance was to be expected "from men educated for the plough or trades in time of peace who never before saw an Enemy."[3] A century earlier the average settler had been accustomed to defending himself at a moment's notice. Now even the redoubtable Scots-Irish fled to the more populated regions when the Shawnee and Delaware struck.

The fact was that the scale of warfare had changed significantly. As Lord Loudoun, the next British commander in chief, shortly commented, the first settlers had been adventurers who were expected to support themselves. "Then their only enemies were Indians; but as the colonies began to flourish, our [French] neighbours . . . began to make encroachments and soon after to raise regular troops." Places like Ticonderoga and Niagara were no longer simple wooden structures; they were built of stone. It required skilled engineers and a siege train to batter them into submission.[4] The kind of raid launched by Phips in the seventeenth century could no longer obtain a decisive result. By early 1756 it was clear that further British aid was needed if the French were to be stopped.

3   THE CONQUEST OF CANADA

Despite the setbacks in 1755, the British government resolved to persevere with its objectives, even though France was threatening to invade Britain itself early in 1756. For once it was America which was engulfing Europe in war. First, a new commander, Lord Loudoun, was sent to replace Braddock, who had died in the engagement on the Ohio. Accompanying him were two more regiments of regulars. Plans were also made to raise four battalions from among the German inhabitants of Pennsylvania, to be officered by Swiss and other German-speaking professionals.

Unfortunately, the threat to invade Britain delayed Loudoun's departure, and he arrived too late to prevent the Marquis de Montcalm from seizing Oswego in August 1756. The fort had been garrisoned with the remnants of Shirley's force from the 1755 campaign, but its defenses were poorly constructed and the place was short of supplies. Oswego had been an important trading post and window to the west for New York since 1727; its loss was a grievous blow.

The provincials were no more successful elsewhere. A New England force had been gathered at Lake George under the command of John Winslow, who experienced all the supply difficulties that had dogged Shirley and Johnson the previous year. When Loudoun tried to amalgamate the provincial forces with his own, he met resistance. Previously the Duke of Cumberland, the captain general of the British army, had decreed that no colonial should rank ahead of any regular officer. A British lieutenant could thus give orders to a provincial colonel, creating much resentment in the process, although the colonial lack of military experience partly justified this rule.

---

[3]   Cadwallader Colden to Peter Collinson, August 23, 1758, Colden Papers, *New York Historical Society Collections*, V (New York, 1921), 253.
[4]   Lord Loudoun to Sir Charles Hardy, November 21, 1756, Loudoun Papers, Huntington Library.

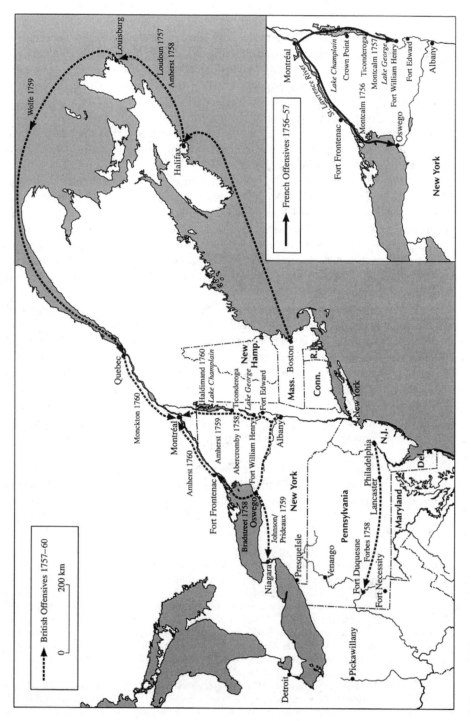

Map 17 The struggle for Canada, 1756–60.

The provincial rank and file were equally disenchanted with Loudoun's plans to create a joint force. They had witnessed the severity of regular discipline and had no wish to experience it themselves. Most of them were the sons of freeholders who expected to become farmers themselves in due course. Soldiering was merely an interlude to earn some money and experience a bit of adventure. Having signed up for one campaign, they were determined not to have their service prolonged, which they feared would be the result if they served alongside the regulars. To New Englanders especially, military service was a contract which both parties must observe. If the government broke its part of the bargain, then desertion was no crime. Their officers recognized this, realizing that they must appeal to their men's better nature rather than command through brute discipline. Such views were quite alien to the British officer corps.[5]

Colonial distrust of the military also gave Loudoun considerable difficulty in getting the supplies he needed from the provincial assemblies, though he did have one success in Pennsylvania when a number of Quakers agreed to retire to facilitate the conduct of the war. A great deal of antagonism had been generated against the Quakers because of their failure to protect the backcountry. Unfortunately, the new assembly remained just as opposed to the proprietary family as the previous one and inserted a clause taxing the proprietary estates into the bill appropriating money for the war, which the Penn family vetoed as a result. In reality little had changed.

For the 1757 campaign Loudoun and his staff concluded that the present scheme of attacking the French in the backcountry would not do. A more radical approach was needed, namely an assault on the center of French power in the St. Lawrence. To this end Loudoun requested an army of ten thousand regulars and a sizable fleet. His plans coincided with the creation of a new ministry in London headed by William Pitt and the Duke of Devonshire. They had come into office on a wave of public anger following the loss of the island of Minorca, which was imputed to the incompetence of the Newcastle ministry. The new government promised a more vigorous conduct of the war, authorizing eight additional regiments, or eight thousand men, plus a fleet of twelve ships of the line with orders to attack Louisburg and Quebec.[6]

Loudoun's plan was to transport most of the regulars by sea, leaving a holding force to prevent another incursion such as had happened at Oswego the previous year. Loudoun by now thoroughly distrusted the military capabilities of the provincials but, realizing that

---

[5]   For an analysis of the colonial soldier, see Fred W. Anderson, *A People's Army: Massachusetts Soldiers and Society in the Seven Years' War* (Chapel Hill, 1984). See also Fred W. Anderson, "Why Did Colonial New Englanders Make Bad Soldiers?: Contractual Principles and Military Conduct During the Seven Years' War," *William and Mary Quarterly*, XXXVIII, 1981, 395–417. In *War and Society*, Selesky challenges the view that colonial soldiers came from middle-ranking colonial families, arguing that most of the volunteers were from the lowest strata of society.

[6]   The admission of Pitt to the ministry has traditionally been seen as the beginning of a more dynamic conduct of the war. See Howard Peckham, *The Colonial Wars, 1689–1762* (Chicago, 1964); and Douglas Edward Leach, *Arms for Empire: A Military History of the British Colonies in North America, 1607–1763* (New York, 1973). In a more critical analysis, Stanley M. Pargellis, *Lord Loudoun in North America* (New Haven, 1933), suggests that Pitt interfered unnecessarily. For a recent evaluation of Pitt's war leadership, see Richard Middleton, *The Bells of Victory: The Pitt–Newcastle Ministry and the Conduct of the Seven Years' War, 1757–1762* (Cambridge, England, 1985). He argues that many of the policies ascribed to Pitt were already in operation before his admission to office and that his powers as a war minister were circumscribed by constitutional constraints.

he could not do without them, he visited the several provincial capitals between Boston and Philadelphia during the spring of 1757. Unfortunately, his brusque manner merely exacerbated the existing conflicts between the civilian and military authorities. One dispute concerned recruitment by the British regiments. Many indentured servants were enlisting with the army to escape the drudgery of their work. Their defection represented a serious loss to their masters, many of whom were men of influence, even magistrates; and they were quick to use their powers to obstruct the military.

Another point of tension concerned quartering. In Britain, the Mutiny Act allowed the army to quarter its men on local inns and taverns. The colonists argued that this legislation did not apply to America. Most American taverns in any case were gin shops, with no stabling or accommodation. Loudoun accordingly began billeting his men in private houses. The colonists quickly protested, appealing to the English Bill of Rights, which forbade this practice. Loudoun then pointed out that it was inconsistent to accept one act of Parliament but not another. He believed that the colonies were in the same constitutional position as Scotland, where quartering on the local population was allowed. When the magistrates refused to act, Loudoun ordered his officers to take the matter into their own hands, lodging the largest number of men on the offending magistrates themselves. Similar difficulties occurred over the army's demand for wagons and horses, which Loudoun also believed he could demand as of right.

The degree of hostility should not be exaggerated. Most colonials recognized that the army needed quarters, transport, and supplies. In 1755 New York passed an act allowing the impressment of ship's carpenters and boatmen for the Niagara and Lake George campaigns; and in 1756 it provided for the billeting of troops and passed another measure allowing the impressment of carriages. Even Pennsylvania passed an act in March 1756 approving the military use of farmers' wagons. Later the inhabitants of Cumberland County gratefully elected Colonel Stanwix to be one of their representatives in recognition of his services.

The southern colonies were the least cooperative in respect of the war effort. Maryland never contributed anything after 1757, seeing no advantage to itself from the war. As in Pennsylvania, the lower house remained at loggerheads with the proprietary government, so that even when the house granted supplies, it did so in a manner which the proprietors felt bound to reject. Virginia was not much better. Washington complained bitterly about the parsimonious attitude of "our chimney corner politicians," as he called the members of the House of Burgesses. He was equally critical of the magistrates, men "tenacious of liberty," who "condemn all proceedings technically illegal, without considering their necessity." In reality the Virginian authorities merely reflected the attitude of the ordinary inhabitants, most of whom had no interest in advancing the cause of the Ohio Company and its wealthy proprietors. South Carolina, though welcoming British troops, continued to plead its isolation and the dangers of a slave uprising as the reason for not providing assistance.[7]

Nevertheless, substantial contributions from New England and the middle colonies enabled Loudoun to sail for Halifax in June 1757 with a considerable armada to await the forces from Britain.

Alas, events again did not work out as planned. Although Loudoun arrived in good time, the forces from Britain did not appear before July, by which time the French had

---

[7] George Washington to the Earl of Loudoun, January 10, 1757, Loudoun Papers, Huntington Library.

gathered a powerful fleet at Louisburg. Without command of the sea, Loudoun dared not proceed in case his army became trapped on the barren wastes of Cape Breton Island. Even if the French fleet remained in port, Louisburg was almost impossible to attack, since French naval guns could bombard the besieging force.

While Loudoun pondered this checkmating of his plan, Montcalm struck again, this time against Fort William Henry at the foot of Lake George. The garrison there was over two thousand strong, backed up by further regular and colonial forces at Fort Edward on the Hudson. Montcalm had barely six thousand troops, including American Indians. Nevertheless, General Webb at Fort Edward decided he was not strong enough to march until reinforced by the provincial militias of New England, giving Montcalm all the opportunity he needed. The French general had already led his troops two hundred miles bearing cannon through a seemingly impassable wilderness, and he now obtained his reward. The French success was unfortunately marred by the brutal behavior of their native allies, many of whom had been promised revenge or plunder. They accordingly rushed in, first scalping the sick before attacking the rest. Although the garrison had been granted the honors of war, including the right to keep its arms, the troops had not been allowed any ammunition. Between one hundred and two hundred were killed and a similar number carried off captive.[8]

This defeat concluded what had been a most unhappy year for the British. From April to July the country had no ministry because Pitt and Newcastle were unable to work together. In New England there was even talk of reviving the seventeenth-century Confederation of the United Colonies so that the war could be prosecuted independently of the British. The scheme came to nothing because early in 1758 news arrived that the government, with Pitt firmly back in power, had made important concessions. First, the issue of rank was settled. In future colonial officers would rank with the regulars, albeit as the most junior in each category. Next, the abrasive Loudoun was to be replaced by a new commander in chief, General Abercromby. Third, the British treasury would feed and arm the colonial troops; the provincials would merely have to provide their pay, and even this expense would be reimbursed.

This about-face instantly transformed the provincial attitude. At Boston Loudoun had been seeking two thousand men from Massachusetts, only to be faced by weeks of procrastination. The news of Pitt's letter induced the assembly immediately to vote seven thousand men. A similar response came from Connecticut, while New York also agreed to meet its quota of twenty-four hundred. Of the northern colonies, only Pennsylvania proved difficult, though supplies and men were finally secured after the proprietary government had agreed to be more flexible. Even the Virginia House of Burgesses voted to raise two regiments of one thousand men, now that the major expense would be borne by the British, since this allowed the payment of a large bounty and eliminated the need for a compulsory draft from the militia. Otherwise the lives of the propertied classes might have been put at risk.

---

[8] The incident has traditionally been used to portray French and native savagery, the implication being that Anglo-Saxon methods were more civilized. This attitude has long typified British and American accounts of their various wars. See especially Francis Parkman, *Montcalm and Wolfe* (Boston, 1884), comparing his account of the massacre at Fort William Henry with the attack by Rogers's rangers on the St. Francis Indians in 1759. For a critical analysis of Parkman, see Francis Jennings, "Francis Parkman: A Brahmin among Untouchables," *William and Mary Quarterly*, XLII, 1985, 305–28. For a recent, more neutral account of the episode, see Ian K. Steele, *Betrayals: Fort William Henry and the "Massacre"* (New York, 1990).

For 1758 the ministry decided upon a three-pronged offensive. General Amherst, supported by the fleet, was to command an army of fourteen thousand regulars in another attempt against Louisburg and Quebec. Abercromby was to advance north from New York toward Montreal with eight thousand British and twenty thousand provincial troops. Finally, Brigadier John Forbes, commanding a mixed force of two thousand regulars and five thousand provincials, would advance westward in a new effort to capture Fort Duquesne at the forks of the Ohio.

The attack on Louisburg was successful, the fortress finally capitulating early in July 1758. After Amherst had secured it, however, it was too late to move on to Quebec. Forbes, too, was successful, though as a result of numerous troubles he reached his objective only in November. The Maryland assembly refused aid even for the three hundred troops it had previously supplied at Fort Frederick. Next, Forbes found his native allies difficult to control. The Cherokee alone observed Pitt's timetable for an offensive starting in May. When it seemed that the British would never advance the American Indians began to drift away, carrying their supplies with them. Fortunately Forbes received assistance from an unexpected quarter. The Pennsylvania Quakers, assisted by the Moravian missionary Frederick Post, finally succeeded in negotiating a peace with the western Delawares by giving them promises of a better-regulated trade and assurances about their hunting lands, which were formally ratified at Easton in October 1758 before the governors of Pennsylvania and New Jersey. By this time representatives of other western nations were indicating a similar desire to negotiate. As a result the French were abandoned at a critical time and there was no repetition of Braddock's defeat. The French commander eventually burned Fort Duquesne rather than surrender it.

These successes were marred only by a setback on the northern front, where the largest number of men were deployed. Although the provincial forces were slow to muster, Abercromby reached his first objective, the fortress of Ticonderoga, early in July. He then heard that Montcalm was expecting reinforcements of three thousand Canadians and American Indians. Although Ticonderoga was a stone fortification, Abercromby reasoned that if he stormed the outer entrenchments which held most of Montcalm's six thousand men, he would be able to take the fort at his leisure. It proved a fatal miscalculation. Montcalm had protected his army with a breastwork of trees lined with sharpened stakes. When the assault began, the British were unable to break through the enemy's lines, and over fifteen hundred regulars and three hundred colonials were killed or wounded as a result. The carnage was so severe that Abercromby decided to retreat back down Lake George to reorganize his shattered command.

The report of French reinforcements proved false, but Abercromby refused to advance again until he heard that Montcalm had withdrawn to face Amherst in the St. Lawrence. Offensive action was not given up altogether, however. Abercromby's ambitious quartermaster, Colonel John Bradstreet, had long advocated an attack on the French post of Frontenac on Lake Ontario. He argued that this post must now be denuded of troops, given the operations elsewhere, and that its destruction would strike a blow against the French chain linking Canada with Louisiana and help Forbes in his attempt on Fort Duquesne. Abercromby sensibly agreed, giving Bradstreet a force of twenty-five hundred men mainly from New York. Bradstreet began his advance in August and found the French defenses negligible. Frontenac was burned, along with several boats and numerous stores. But Bradstreet made no attempt to hold the post or reoccupy Oswego, judging the French ability to

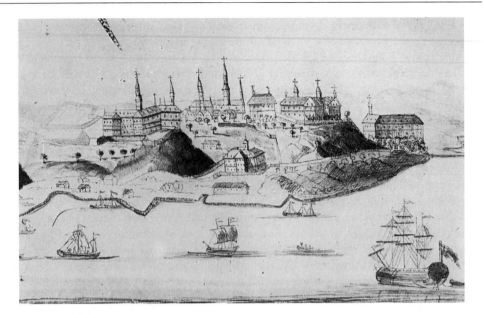

Plate 49 View of Quebec. The Mansell Collection, London.

retaliate too formidable. Nevertheless, a major blow to French power had been delivered, of which the Iroquois especially took note.

Despite the overall success of the 1758 campaign, the ministry felt that there could be no relaxation of military activity until the whole of Canada had been conquered. Thus for 1759 a similar three-pronged campaign was devised. This time the amphibious forces under General Wolfe were to sail directly for Quebec. Amherst himself would succeed Abercromby in an operation to take Ticonderoga and Crown Point before proceeding to Montreal. Finally, General Prideaux and Sir William Johnson would advance on Niagara (Forbes having died at the end of the last campaign). As in 1758, the colonists would be mainly involved in the overland operations.

Wolfe sailed from Halifax on June 4, 1759, arriving off Quebec at the beginning of July. For the next ten weeks he searched in vain for a way through the French defenses until he was able to scale the cliffs, known as the Heights of Abraham, above the city. In the ensuing battle he was killed, as was Montcalm, but he left Quebec in British hands.

Amherst's campaign was, by comparison, a pedestrian affair. Once more the provincials found it difficult to keep to Pitt's timetable. With Montcalm at Quebec, however, the British capture of Ticonderoga and Crown Point was now assured. Amherst then found it necessary to gain naval command of Lake Champlain, by which time it was too late to advance on Montreal. Nevertheless, his advance meant that the backcountry of New York and western Massachusetts was now secure.

In the west, Prideaux and Johnson were also victorious at Niagara. After surrounding the fort they successfully defeated a force sent to relieve it. Although Prideaux was killed, Johnson carried the operation to a successful conclusion on July 25, 1759.

It was during this campaign that Major Robert Rogers and his rangers made their famous raid on the St. Francis Indians near Sorel. The St. Francis Indians were Abenaki

Plate 50 *The Death of Wolfe*, by Benjamin West. The Mansell Collection, London.

people who had been driven from their homes on the Merrimac, Connecticut, and Kennebec rivers. The attack has traditionally been seen as a heroic feat of arms. Certainly the march itself tested the troops to the limit. Unfortunately, the attack on the village amounted to little more than a massacre of women and children, for there were few warriors present when the assault took place early on the morning of October 6. First, the houses were set alight; then the survivors were shot as they attempted to swim across the St. Francis River. Moreover, the retreat was anything but glorious. After splitting into small groups to evade pursuit, many of the attackers got lost and perished in the woods or were captured by the Indians. A dispirited Rogers only reached safety in early December when he reported to Amherst the extent of his misfortunes. Although the St. Francis inhabitants had perpetrated some outrages, the episode provided one more demonstration of British inhumanity toward the native people.

These British victories in 1759 convinced most of the American Indians that further support for France was inadvisable. The only hitch in this change of heart was the outbreak of hostilities with the Cherokee. In the aftermath of Forbes's campaign they had clashed with some of the backcountry settlers while returning home and looking for food. The South Carolinian government called for assistance to chastise them. Perhaps it was not coincidental that the first settlers were now beginning to encroach on Cherokee lands. Despite the mountainous nature of the terrain, a Scottish Highland regiment, together with some provincial forces, marched into the Cherokee heartland, first under Colonel Montgomery in 1760 and then under Colonel Grant in 1761. Both operations were conducted with some skill, avoiding several ambushes along the way. In the brutal fashion of contemporary Anglo-Saxon warfare, they destroyed first the lower and then the middle towns of the Cherokee, thus convincing the native peoples of the necessity for peace.

Although the British had now achieved their original war aims, they could not relax their campaign until the whole of Canada had been conquered. Hence orders were again issued by Pitt for a final campaign in 1760 to win Montreal. Although the same generous financial terms were offered, Pitt felt it necessary to warn against colonial complacency, since notions of peace were being expressed. In the event, Governor Thomas Pownall secured only four thousand men from Massachusetts.

The campaign plan for 1760 was similar to that of the previous year. Three armies were to converge on Montreal. General Murray was to advance from Quebec, General Haldimand was to resume the northward movement by way of Lake Champlain, while Amherst himself would advance with the main force via the River Mohawk and Lake Ontario to approach from the west. Significantly, this time the army was accompanied by a large body of Iroquois, though a contemptuous Amherst determined that such fickle allies should not benefit from the plunder they clearly anticipated. The campaign itself was nearly ruined when Murray was defeated by the French under the Chevalier Levis early in the spring before the ice in the river had melted. For a few weeks it was not certain whether Quebec itself might fall to the French again. Fortunately, British reinforcements arrived by river and the French were forced to retire. Thereafter, all three British armies advanced steadily, finally linking up near Montreal at the beginning of September. The position of the French was now hopeless, and they surrendered on September 7, 1760.

Though the surrender of Montreal effectively ended hostilities on mainland America, fighting between Britain and France continued elsewhere in Europe and the Caribbean. In 1761 the British decided to attack the French island of Martinique, for which colonial volunteers were sought to supplement the regular forces. The following year, when Spain came into the war as an ally of France, similar colonial support was sought for the expedition against Havana.

Success greeted both these and other ventures, so that by the end of 1762 Britain was able to negotiate a handsome peace. There was some debate in the press over whether to keep the French sugar islands of Guadeloupe and Martinique rather than Canada. The government, however, stuck to its original aim of securing the backcountry of the mainland colonies. Canada was therefore retained and the sugar islands handed back. Britain was now in possession of the whole of eastern North America from Hudson Bay to the Mississippi, for Spain ceded Florida to secure the return of Cuba. The only link France retained with the continent was two small islands near the Newfoundland fishery, Louisiana having been ceded also to Spain as compensation for supporting France in the war.

These terms caused despair among the Spanish in Florida and the French in Canada and Louisiana. The inhabitants of St. Augustine took ship for Cuba, while most of the French in Illinois crossed the Mississippi to found St. Louis, though they did so before learning that France had ceded the territory to Spain. The French Canadians, on the other hand, were too numerous to think of moving. They also had firmer treaty rights guaranteeing their religion, property, and legal customs. Nearly all of them stayed.

The signing of the Peace of Paris in February 1763 seemed to herald a glittering era for Britain as a world power with possessions in every corner of the globe. A new king, George III, had recently ascended the throne to begin what promised to be an Augustan age.

Equally promising were the American colonists' prospects. The doubling of their population every twenty-five years made it possible that within a century America might become the center of the British empire.

Least rosy was the situation of the American Indians. The Iroquois, among others, had made a fine art of playing one European power against another. Now they could no longer do so and were instead seriously threatened by the flood of settlers who followed the redcoats. In addition, most of the other principal nations on the frontier, including the Micmac, Abenaki, Delaware, Shawnee, and Cherokee peoples, had suffered serious military losses. True, the American Indians had signed formal treaties, but their experience of the white man's honoring of such commitments could induce no optimism. With the fur trade continuing to decline and the price of goods rising, the economic and environmental prospects of the native peoples were bleak indeed.

The Peace of Paris thus marked the end of one momentous chapter and the beginning of another for all three groups. The British now had to consider how to manage their new empire, the colonists how to exploit it, and the American Indians how to survive in it.

Part IV

The Path to Independence

20

The Rights of British America, 1760–66

1760 (Oct.) George III accedes to the throne.

1761 (Feb.) Writs of Assistance are challenged in Massachusetts.
(Dec.) A ban on colonial land grants is introduced.

1763 (April) George Grenville becomes first lord of the Treasury.
(May) Pontiac's War begins.
(Oct.) Proclamation concerning western lands is issued.
(Dec.) Conestoga Indians are killed by the Paxton Boys.

1764 (April) The Sugar Act is passed.
(April) The Currency Act is passed.

1765 (March) The Stamp Act is passed.
(May) The Quartering Act is passed.
(May) The Virginia Resolves are passed.
(August) Boston riots take place.
(Oct.) The Stamp Act Congress meets.
(Nov.) The Stamp Act is due to come into effect.

1766 (March) The Declaratory Act is passed and the Stamp Act is repealed.

Plate 51   Portrait of George III, by Allan Ramsey. James E. Roberts Fund, Indianapolis Museum of Art.

1   THE EMPIRE IN 1760

T HE FALL OF Montreal in 1760 was greeted with considerable joy. Colonists everywhere not only felt pride in the achievement but sensed a glorious destiny awaiting
the British. The notion that Britain's North American empire would collapse within
fifteen years would have been viewed with incredulity. True, a few Britons warned of the
dangers of colonial separation, but only as a distant eventuality. Concern was also voiced
that the removal of the French might make the colonists less dependent. As General
Murray commented after the conquest of Canada, a continued French presence there might
guarantee their good behavior.

The colonials themselves were much more optimistic about their status as British
subjects. When Benjamin Franklin and others speculated about the future, their favorite
scenario was that America would become the center of the British world. As the population
and resources of the colonies grew, the heirs of George III would see the wisdom of moving
across the Atlantic to be at the center of their dominions. The idea that the colonies would
shortly secede from the empire and become independent republics seemed ludicrous.

There are several reasons for the universal inability of contemporaries to foresee the
course of events. Most important was the fact that the colonists themselves had no clear
American identity. Outside New England the loyalties of the inhabitants were confined
primarily to their own colony and then to the mother country. Although economic ties
between the colonies were growing, there were still few bonds even among the 60 percent
of colonists who were of English descent. As Franklin commented in 1760, the continental
colonies were "not only under different governors, but have different forms of government,
different laws, different interests, and some of them different religious persuasions and
manners." The only common institutions were those derived from Britain, notably the
monarchy, Parliament, the common law, the English language, and British culture. The
word *American* was still infrequently used, especially by the colonists themselves.[1]

Another reason few people anticipated drastic change was that Britain's own constitutional polity seemed well calculated to protect colonial liberties. Those colonists who
thought about such matters were proud of their British heritage and links with the Crown.
Since 1689 most inhabitants (other than African-Americans) subscribed to the view that
Britain had the freest constitution in the world. Such pride was strengthened by the process
of anglicization and the recent triumph of British arms. Even in Massachusetts, as Thomas
Hutchinson noted, a general satisfaction existed with the state of affairs. This sentiment was
reflected in the warm reception given to Governor Francis Bernard on his arrival in 1760.

Yet within thirteen years of the Peace of Paris the colonists were proclaiming their
independence. One explanation for this dramatic change is that, despite the apparently
robust state of the empire, certain long-term factors came to a head which made the
relationship ultimately incompatible. One, as already noted in chapter 16, was the intellectual environment of the colonial elites, which was germinating the seeds of a republican
ideology. Another was the considerable economic and political success of the colonies by
1760. They had grown so fast and reached such maturity that a different, less restrictive

---

[1] For the development of an American identity, see Richard Merritt, *Symbols of American Community, 1735–
1775* (New Haven, 1966).

relationship with the mother country was required. Distance too was a problem, given that the centrifugal forces of colonial self-interest were always likely to conflict with the centripetal demands of imperial control.

The danger of conflict had also increased because both sides had sharply different perceptions of their relationship and the location of authority. Since 1689 the British had convinced themselves that sovereignty must lie with the center, as embodied in the monarch, lords, and commons. This view was reinforced by their mercantilist attitudes and belief in a unitary state, which prevented them from imagining any system which was not controlled by London. The colonists, on the other hand, were equally convinced, though they had yet to articulate the view, that power must be shared with the periphery. Otherwise their provincial assemblies would count for nothing.

Lastly, the growth of English nationalism after 1740 was an irritant to the Anglo-American relationship, since it often led to denigration of people living on the periphery of the Empire. The colonists' comfortable assumption that they were equal partners with metropolitan Englishmen was to be increasingly undermined after 1763. The consequence was a sense of rejection and search for a new identity that would more accurately reflect their view of themselves and the world.[2]

The potential for conflict was kept in check until 1763 by three things: British concern for property rights; the resistance of the Crown to Parliament's involvement in the colonies; and the fact that the empire was managed largely by the local elites. Except for governorships and a few other posts, the colonial elites constituted the governing class, benefiting from their power and status in numerous ways.

This mutually convenient equilibrium was to be upset as a consequence of the French and Indian War. In the first place, this conflict widened the colonists' provincial horizons. Although colonial units did not serve as a single force, many of them fought alongside units from other colonies. Assemblies also enjoyed additional responsibilities which made them increasingly impatient of imperial control, especially in regard to paper money and the need for suspending clauses. Suddenly the umbilical cord of maternal union was threatening to become a noose.

Second, the war affected British perceptions of the empire's effectiveness. Among the more serious flaws detected were colonial violations of the imperial laws of trade, especially the commerce with the French and Spanish West Indies, which had not stopped even on the outbreak of war. Although Rhode Island was the worst offender, it was clear that all the colonies were contravening the navigation system to some extent. Another flaw exposed by the conflict was the difficulty of obtaining colonial support. When the provincial assemblies did vote supplies, they were invariably in the form of paper money. This form, as already noted, was increasingly unacceptable to the imperial authorities, pressed as they were by British merchants.[3]

But the war had other consequences too which altered Britain's view of the imperial relationship. One was the need to defend the newly conquered territories. The peace left Britain responsible for 70,000 French Canadians, several hundred Spanish subjects in Florida, and perhaps 150,000 western Indians, none of whom was well disposed to living under the

---

[2] See T. H. Breen, "Ideology and Nationalism on the Eve of the American Revolution: Revisions Once More in Need of Revising," *Journal of American History*, LXXXIV 1997, 13–39.

[3] For the background to the issue of paper money, see chapter 10, section 4.

authority of George III. A standing army would be necessary to maintain order. This was quite a novel situation for the British in North America. So too was the expense. The war had doubled the national debt, much of the increase due to operations in America, leading to an added burden on the British taxpayer. Now the costs of empire were to be increased in peacetime too. During the war many army officers and government officials had been impressed by the wealth of the colonies: the well-kept plantations, productive farms, spacious houses, and presence of luxury goods. It seemed only fair that the colonials should at least pay a share of the new peacetime costs of empire, having reaped much of the benefit from the recent war.

All of these considerations led the government in London to conclude that reform was necessary. Sir Robert Walpole's old policy of "salutary neglect," leaving the empire to run itself, was clearly flawed. Better management was required through a strengthening of the executive by making the governors and other officials less dependent on the provincial assemblies for their salaries. This thinking was well expressed by Thomas Pownall, the former governor of Massachusetts, who early in 1764 published a pamphlet entitled *The Administration of the Colonies*, in which he argued for the creation of a single department to handle American affairs so that responsibility was no longer fragmented among several government ministries. Unless this was done, he believed, the colonies would slide into the economic and political orbit of France and Spain.

Other bureaucrats and politicians agreed, at least on the need to strengthen the imperial tie. Equally important, few now believed that the Crown had sufficient power to carry out such reform. Only the authority of Parliament would suffice.

The colonists naturally saw matters somewhat differently. They ascribed the recent military successes in large part to their own exertions, especially when they reflected on the performance of British commanders like General Braddock and Lord Loudoun. More important, for the colonists the expulsion of the French and Spanish meant that the danger was now over – and with it the need for a military presence. If troops were required, it was someone else's problem; the colonies had made their contribution in men and money.

The recent victory also had another effect on the colonists, namely a sense of liberation. Visionaries like Franklin could now dream of an empire stretching from the Atlantic to the Pacific. More prosaically, speculators and small farmers could see large profits or new livelihoods in these huge territories. As the Reverend Samuel Cooper lyrically commented, "What scenes of Happiness are we ready to figure to ourselves . . . our settlements extending themselves with Security on Every side, and changing a Wilderness into a fruitful Field."

The ending of the war also unleashed a desire for greater freedom in commercial matters. While most colonists accepted the mercantilist system, some necessarily felt aggrieved at its restrictiveness. One such irritant was the use of writs of assistance by the customs service. These permitted officers a right of general search for smuggled goods, specifying neither the names of the suspects nor the type of contraband in question. The system of writs had been widely abused, and in 1761 a group of Boston merchants determined to challenge their legality in the Massachusetts Superior Court. To present their case they engaged a rising young lawyer, James Otis, Jr., who argued that the writs were not justified by statute, were against natural equity, and were therefore illegal. Chief Justice Hutchinson, recognizing the controversial nature of the case, deferred judgment pending clarification from London. But Otis's action was so popular in Boston that he was shortly afterwards elected to the general court.

Plate 52   A London cockfight, by William Hogarth, ca. 1760, depicting the metropolitan corruption and depravity so feared by many colonials. The Mansell Collection, London.

Lastly, the imperial relationship was undermined in 1760 because the colonials harbored a number of suspicions about Britain. For one thing the war provoked widespread distrust of the regular army, whose recent quartering and recruiting practices had convinced many that it was a threat to liberty. These actions, exacerbated by the old fear of standing armies, lent substance to the belief that the existence of any peacetime force in America could be intended only for the subjugation of the colonists. As one Connecticut assemblyman commented on the news of Britain's decision to maintain an army in North America, "It seems determined to fix upon us a large Number of regular troops under pretence for our defence; but rather designed as a rod and a check over us."

A second cause for suspicion, especially in New England, was the activities of the Church of England. Rumors were rife that it was about to appoint a bishop for North America, for which American Anglicans had long campaigned to facilitate the ordination of ministers. It was believed that such an appointment would mean the creation of ecclesiastical courts and, eventually, an established church. The descendants of the Puritans could not but feel apprehensive, and their fears were not diminished by the appearance in 1761 of an Anglican mission in Cambridge, next to Harvard, the chief seminary of the Congregational Church. The result was a fierce pamphlet war in which the view was expressed that the recent defeat of the French had not resulted in the extirpation of popery.

Plate 53 Portrait of George Grenville, mezzotint by James Watson after W. Hoare. The Mansell Collection, London.

A third reason for distrust of Britain was the feeling of many educated colonists that corruption threatened their liberty. History showed that Greece and Rome had fallen, despite their military success, because of its corrosive effects on public morality. The opposition in Parliament was constantly denouncing the government as venal. Liberty was a tender plant, continually threatened by governmental power and its insidious agent, corruption. The colonies had better beware.

2 THE GRENVILLE MINISTRY AND IMPERIAL REFORM

The ending of the Seven Years' War in January 1763 gave the ministers a chance to address the problems posed by America. First, a bill was passed permitting the navy to assist the customs service in peacetime, clarifying previous legal uncertainties. At the same time the decision was made to station forty-four frigates and cutters off the coast of North America, a fivefold increase in the old prewar establishment.

A new broom was also sweeping clean at the Treasury. When George Grenville became first lord in April 1763, he discovered that the cost of collecting the navigation duties in America exceeded the yield. One reason was the readiness of the collectors to stay in London, leaving deputies to do their job across the Atlantic. Grenville quickly informed them that they should either return to America or relinquish their appointments. Most reluctantly obeyed. But for Grenville this step was only the beginning of his determined efforts to make the system more efficient.

Meanwhile other ministers were tackling the thorny problems of defense and the administration of the new territories. The general consensus was that an army of ten thousand men was needed in America. Any doubts about the advisability of establishing it were quickly suppressed when news arrived in the summer that the western Indians had commenced hostilities against the British.

The triumph of Britain in 1760 had been deeply disturbing for the Ottawa, Huron, Erie, Chippewa, Shawnee, Delaware, Wyandot, and Seneca nations who had traditionally allied with France. Before 1760 they had been able to safeguard their independence by playing one imperial power off against the other. Now they could no longer do this. Most had changed sides reluctantly in 1759, and then only on the understanding that a British victory would mean the evacuation of all military posts west of the Allegheny Mountains. Soon, however, the victorious British began making it clear that they no longer needed their former allies and thus no longer felt obliged to keep their promises. The forts remained. Even worse, settlers followed, in defiance of the treaties agreed at Easton and elsewhere.

The Indians were upset for other reasons too. One was the British insistence that all captives be returned. As mentioned in chapter 15, the Indians put much store in the successful adoption of captives. Many of these had accepted the Indian way of life and would now have to be returned against their will. Equally important was the fact that the customary supply of presents was being reduced.[4] These were especially necessary after 1760, since the recent conflict had so disrupted the Indians' hunting and planting cycles that they had little to trade or eat. Third, the Indians were unhappy with the prices and quality of the traders' goods. Finally, they were angry with the traders for using rum as a negotiating weapon to cheat them out of the few furs they did have. Unless the British government gave them help, the outlook for the western nations was bleak.

Unfortunately the Indian request for relief came just as the government in London was calling for economy. Amherst and the other commanders were in any case convinced that the Indians must learn to support themselves by growing their own food and exchanging their furs for other goods. The British military had no concept of the importance of gift culture to the Indian peoples. Amherst in particular was openly contemptuous of their way of life.

The accumulation of British indifference to the Indians' trade requirements, failure to intervene in the unscrupulous activities of the traders, demand for the return of prisoners, retention of the French military posts, and inability to control the flood of western settlers

---

[4]   The French, though more generous, were not beyond attempting economies themselves. See Catherine M. Desbarats, "The Cost of Early Canada's Native Alliances: Reality and Scarcity's Rhetoric," *William and Mary Quarterly*, LII, 1995, 609–30.

all threatened the tribes with disaster. Rumors abounded that the French would return to help. The final inducement to fight was the call by the Delaware prophet, Neolin, to drive out the "dogs clothed in red" so that the Indians could return to their ancient ways before the Europeans corrupted them. Among those listening to his message was Pontiac, an Ottawa chief. Soon warbelts were being exchanged throughout the Great Lakes and Ohio region, though the subsequent offensive was only loosely planned. Each nation took action as news of the hostilities arrived.

Through surprise attacks the Indians captured all the smaller posts at Michilimackinac, St. Joseph, Miami, Ouiatenon, LeBoeuf, Sandusky, PresqueIsle, and Venango, putting many of the garrisons' troops to death; at the same time they laid siege to the main forts at Pittsburgh, Niagara, and Detroit. Initially the situation was sufficiently desperate for Amherst to suggest planting blankets infected with smallpox to wipe out the native peoples' resistance, the first known scheme for biological warfare.[5] But the Indians lacked the equipment to capture these larger fortifications, nor did they have the resources to fight a prolonged war. As usual, their women and children were especially vulnerable. By the spring of 1764 Pontiac and the other leaders were seeking peace.

These events reinforced the imperial policy makers in their opinion that responsibility for the West could no longer be left to the colonists. Except for New York, no colony gave any significant help, leaving it primarily to the regulars under Gage, Bouquet, and Bradstreet to defeat the Indians. Second, there was a strong feeling in London that the conflict had occurred because the colonists had let unscrupulous traders cheat the Indians of their furs and lands through the sale of alcohol and worthless goods, as well as failing to prevent settlers from squatting on Indian territory.

Officials in London were thus prompted to devise a new policy for the West, promulgated as the Proclamation of 1763. In December 1761 the Crown had already forbidden the individual colonies from making any further land grants on their western boundaries, as they had done before the war. Now all settlement beyond a line running along the watershed of the Allegheny Mountains was strictly prohibited, that area being reserved solely for the Indians. In future, settlers seeking new lands were to be diverted either into Nova Scotia and the St. Lawrence Valley or southward into the Floridas.

The proclamation was designed to serve several complementary objectives. First, it would quieten the Indians and make it clear that the British intended to honor their recent treaties. Second, it would help channel new settlement where it was most needed, on the vulnerable flanks of the empire, overwhelming the French and Spanish populations with people loyal to the Crown. In addition it would prevent the development of new colonies beyond the mountains, which Whitehall now opposed because such remote settlements might develop their own manufacturing.

The reorganization of the West was completed in July 1764 with the appointment of two superintendents, John Stuart and Sir William Johnson, to supervise relations with the southern and northern Indians.[6] Diplomacy and trade had traditionally been the

---

[5]   Unknown to Amherst, the commander at Fort Pitt had already tried to do this, though with what effect remains uncertain. See Elizabeth A. Fenn, "Biological Warfare in Eighteenth Century North America: Beyond Jeffery Amherst," *Journal of American History*, LXXXVI, 2000, 1552–80.

[6]   These were not the first such officials to be appointed, two having been nominated at the start of the French and Indian War to elicit Indian support. However, the officers' powers were now expanded.

responsibility of the provincial authorities. Now all commerce with the Indians would have to take place at a designated post under the watchful eye of the imperial government.

The proclamation line and subsequent establishment of an Indian department seemed a neat solution to the new challenges facing Britain in North America. Unfortunately, like many paper solutions, it was to work out differently in practice.[7]

For the moment, however, the policy seemed statesmanlike. The only discernible problem was the cost, which reinforced the need to raise additional revenue, a task that fell to Grenville at the Treasury. Grenville was a lawyer by training with a lawyer's grasp of detail. Unfortunately he lacked vision, as did most British politicans at this time. All looked at America from the perspective of the immediate requirements of the mother country, placing these ahead of long-term considerations. The priority was to find money to pay the new costs of empire without increasing the burden on the home taxpayer. There appeared to be two ways of obtaining such revenue: either by new taxes or by administrative reform. Grenville determined to adopt both approaches in his Sugar or Revenue Act of 1764.

The first part of the act placed new duties on several items – among them coffee, indigo, pimento, and East Indian fabrics – though the most important article concerned molasses. The duty on this was to be reduced from the 1733 rate of sixpence a gallon to threepence. Unlike the old duties, however, the new rates were to be vigorously enforced. To ensure the effectiveness of his new measures, Grenville looked to ways of making the collecting service more efficient. Accordingly, all ships leaving colonial ports had to deposit a bond of up to £2,000 to ensure that their journey conformed with the laws of trade. There would be no more surreptitious trading with the French, Spanish, and Dutch.

The act also sought to strengthen the machinery for punishing offenders. The existing system of vice-admiralty courts had become ineffective because cases were generally referred to the common law courts, where juries invariably refused to convict smugglers. Worse, those acquitted often subsequently sued the customs officers for damages, undermining the morale and effectiveness of the service. To address this problem, Grenville now proposed that at the customs officer's discretion, all cases could be referred to one of the existing vice-admiralty courts or to a new superior court at Halifax. The advantage to the government was that since a vice-admiralty court contained no jury, the judge decided both the facts of the case and the guilt of the defendant. Convictions therefore were much more likely. Lastly, the act made it illegal to sue officers for wrongful prosecution where they had acted in good faith and with reasonable suspicion.

At the prompting of British merchants the Grenville ministry also allowed the House of Commons to pass a Currency Act, extending the 1751 New England ban on the emission of paper money to all the American colonies. During the war most assemblies had authorized large issues of paper currency, some of which had depreciated badly much to the chagrin of British merchants who were owed money. Henceforward no colonial currency

---

[7]   Historians disagree on the importance of the West as a cause of the Revolution. The Imperial school believed that the narrow selfishness of the colonists was one of the principal reasons why the empire disintegrated. See Lawrence Henry Gipson, *The British Empire before the American Revolution*, 15 vols (New York, 1936–70). Progressive writers argued that thwarted speculation was an important factor. See Thomas Abernathy, *Western Lands and the American Revolution* (Charlottesville, 1937). The tendency among scholars today is to downplay the West as an issue in the Revolution, though the argument about thwarted land speculation has been restated by Woody Holton, *Forced Founders: Indians, Debtors, Slaves and the Making of the American Revolution in Virginia* (Chapel Hill, 1999).

could have the force of legal tender. Assemblies could still issue bills, but British merchants or other creditors were not obliged to accept them. The threat of an uncontrolled colonial currency was to be eliminated.

While drafting the Sugar Bill, Grenville informed the colonial agents that a further measure was being contemplated, requiring the payment of a stamp duty on all legal documents, newspapers, books, pamphlets, and other paper products. He told them, however, that he would not proceed if they could propose an alternative way of raising £45,000 in revenue. The agents replied that they must first consult their assemblies. All they could suggest was a revival of the old wartime requisition system whereby each colony contributed according to its population. Since the failure of that system was well known, Grenville was convinced that only parliamentary action could rectify the shortfall. He accordingly introduced his measure in an almost empty House of Commons in February 1765. Infractions of the revenue laws in Britain were tried by a court of exchequer, but to simplify matters, Grenville determined that all breaches of the proposed Stamp Act would be handled by the vice-admiralty courts. Stamp duties had been raised in Britain since the end of the seventeenth century, and Grenville did not expect this measure to be either controversial or difficult to execute.

3 THE AMERICAN RESPONSE: THE RIGHTS OF BRITISH SUBJECTS

The initial American response to these measures was indeed muted. Speculators like George Washington saw the Proclamation of 1763 as a temporary measure to calm the Indian nations. Most pioneers in any case paid no attention, knowing that the government had too few personnel to enforce the proclamation. Provided squatters did not come too close to the military posts, they were safe, though some expulsions had taken place around Fort Pitt in 1761. The main deterrent to mass western emigration was still the hostility of the American Indians.

The Currency Act of 1764 also had only limited impact, at least in the short term. Attempts by the Crown to limit colonial paper money were not new. The act in any case did not outlaw existing emissions; and further issues could still be made, though without the force of legal tender. Other forms of money, like commodities, could also be used. In Virginia the use of paper money was still relatively new and the planters' anger was directed more at British merchants, who refused to extend them credit, than against the government. Those colonists most immediately affected were transatlantic merchants who, fearing an inability to pay their suppliers, began reducing their orders. The long-term consequences, which were perhaps more significant, developed as the notes still in circulation were withdrawn, causing varying difficulties for the community at large. Some historians thus see the Currency Act as one of the underlying causes of the Revolution.[8]

The Sugar Act, however, had a more immediate impact, not least because the colonies suffered an economic recession following the adjustment to a peacetime economy.

---

[8] The restrictiveness of the 1764 act was partially eased by another act in 1773 permitting the issue of legal tender paper currency for the payment of provincial taxes. See Joseph Albert Ernst, *Money and Politics in America, 1755–1775* (Chapel Hill, 1973).

Merchants and businesspeople everywhere were complaining about the lack of trade. Any measure which threatened to increase costs and close profitable loopholes was bound to be unpopular. This was especially true in New England and the middle colonies, where the threepenny duty on molasses threatened the prosperity of the rum industry. The measure also meant higher prices for so-called luxuries like coffee and silks, which many American consumers now considered essential items.

But unease was not confined to northern merchants and manufacturers. Assemblymen everywhere could see that the purpose of the new legislation was significantly different from previous navigation acts. Those laws had been aimed at the regulation of trade, even if by means of customs duties. The Sugar Act in contrast explicitly stated that its purpose was "improving the revenue."

This goal had profound implications for the provincial assemblies, which had long assumed that they had the sole right of raising taxes. Such exclusivity was essential if they were to act as watchdogs of the executive and protect the rights of the people, since the colonies had no representation in Parliament. If the Sugar Act was meekly accepted, other impositions might follow. Indeed the British might stop taxing themselves and let Americans pay for everything. Another provision that set alarm bells ringing was the extension of the vice-admiralty courts, which seemingly undermined one of the colonists' most precious rights, trial by jury. The fact that the king's subjects in Britain did not enjoy this right in revenue cases was overlooked.[9]

Following the legislation there were a number of protests by the provincial assemblies, though most of their petitions to Parliament concentrated on the economic hardships imposed by the Sugar Act. They went no further than to argue that the new measure violated the spirit, if not the letter, of the constitution: that no taxes should be levied in America without the consent of the people. Only New York and North Carolina overtly attacked the measure as unconstitutional. Massachusetts would have done so but was persuaded by Hutchinson that it would be prudent to emphasize instead the economic hardships of the measure. But as James Otis, Jr. commented, "One single Act of Parliament . . . has set people a thinking in six months, more than they had done in their whole lives."

These events prepared the ground for what was to follow. Initially, Grenville's notification of the impending Stamp Act caused little reaction, possibly because it was hoped that the traditional requisition system might be implemented. Then came the news early in May 1765 that Parliament had passed the Stamp Act two months previously. Most of the provincial assemblies were in recess. However, the Virginia House of Burgesses was still in session; and led by one of its younger members, Patrick Henry, it passed five resolutions condemning the measure. These asserted that it was a long-established convention of the British constitution that subjects should not be taxed without their consent or that of their representatives. In Virginia that right lay solely with the House of Burgesses, since it alone represented the people. Hence, the fifth resolution concluded, any attempt to divest the assembly of its rights had "a manifest tendency to destroy British as well as American freedom."

Next day the fifth resolution was overturned because the majority feared it was too inflammatory. However, newspapers throughout the colonies printed not only this but two

---

[9]   However, even Sir William Blackstone in his classic *Commentaries on the Laws of England* (Oxford, 1765–9); vol. 4, p. 281, was concerned by the extension of this practice and its potential for abuse.

additional resolutions: first, that the inhabitants were not obliged to obey the law; and, second, that anyone who attempted to obey it would be deemed "an enemy to this his Majesty's Colony." Equally inflammatory were the accounts of the debate. Henry was reported as saying, "In former times Tarquin and Julius had their Brutus, Charles had his Cromwell, and he did not doubt but some good American would stand up in favour of his Country."[10]

"No taxation without representation" now became the cry of all those opposed to the recent measures of the British administration. And the opposition was widespread, since the Stamp Act had succeeded in antagonizing all sections of the elite at once. The new duties would have to be paid by lawyers on all legal documents; by merchants posting bond on cargoes; by ministers of religion and other graduates receiving degrees; by farmers patenting land; by innkeepers seeking licenses; by masters agreeing articles of indenture; and by printers publishing newspapers, almanacs, and pamphlets. Nor was resentment confined to the elite. Equally damaging was the anxiety created among the rest of the population fearful for their continued employment if higher taxes were imposed.

In Massachusetts the mood of the community was already sullen when reports of the events in Virginia arrived. The economy remained depressed, while the merchants were still angry about the activities of the customs officers. Then on August 8, 1765, the newspapers published the names of those appointed to distribute the new stamps. Here were the declared enemies of the people! Boston was not without a tradition of violence. For decades boisterous mobs had gathered on November 5 to celebrate Pope's day when Guy Fawkes was burnt in effigy. What was new this time was that a group emerged, calling itself the Loyal Nine or Sons of Liberty, to orchestrate the popular discontent.[11]

Popular anger finally erupted on August 14 in Boston when a mob led by Ebenezer Mackintosh, a shoemaker, burnt an effigy of Andrew Oliver, the newly appointed stamp distributor, before attacking his wharf and house. Without protection and fearing for his life, Oliver quickly promised to resign his commission – even though he had yet to receive it. Similar pressure was placed on the distributors in other colonies, all of whom resigned. However, in Massachusetts worse was to follow. A second riot occurred on Monday, August 26, when the house of Lieutenant Governor Hutchinson was attacked and wrecked after rumors circulated that Hutchinson, a relative of Oliver's, was one of the authors of the Stamp Act. Discontent among Boston's unemployed was undoubtedly another factor accounting for the attack.[12]

Meanwhile moves were afoot to organize constitutional opposition. The previous year the Massachusetts assembly had attempted to correspond with the other colonies about the

---

[10] The authorship of the two additional resolutions and the responsibility for publishing them have never been resolved. See Edmund S. Morgan and Helen M. Morgan, *The Stamp Act Crisis: Prologue to Revolution* (New York, 1963).

[11] The phrase "Sons of Liberty" was coined by Isaac Barre during the passage of the Stamp Act. He was one of the few MPs to oppose the measure.

[12] For an account of street politics during the Stamp Act crisis, see Gary P. Nash, *The Urban Crucible: Social Change, Political Consciousness, and the Origins of the American Revolution* (Cambridge, Mass., 1979); Morgan and Morgan, *The Stamp Act Crisis*; Charles S. Olton, *Artisans for Independence: Philadelphia Mechanics and the American Revolution* (Syracuse, 1975); Jesse Lemisch, "Jack Tar in the Streets: Merchant Seamen in the Politics of Revolutionary America," *William and Mary Quarterly*, XXV, 1968, 371–407; and Paul A. Gilje, *The Road to Mobocracy: Popular Disorder in New York City, 1763–1834* (Chapel Hill, 1987).

DOCUMENT 32

Resolves of the Stamp Act Congress, October 1765, reprinted in Merrill Jensen, ed., *English Historical Documents*, vol. IX: *American Colonial Documents to 1776* (London, 1955), 672–3.

[The object of the resolves was not only to overturn the Stamp Act and the right of Parliament to tax (Articles 1–6) but to protest against the denial of the right to trial by jury (Articles 7–8) and the economic consequences of recent British policy (Articles 9–12). However, their failure to condemn the constitutionality of the Sugar Act concerning its revenue changes fostered the illusion in Britain that the colonists objected only to internal taxation, a misunderstanding which led to the 1767 Townshend duties.]

1) That His Majesty's subjects in these colonies, owe the same allegiance to the Crown of Great Britain, that is owing from his subjects born within the realm, and all due subordination to that august body, the Parliament of Britain.

2) That his Majesty's liege subjects in these colonies are entitled to all the inherent rights and liberties of his natural born subjects within the kingdom of Great Britain.

3) That it is inseparably essential to the freedom of a people, and the undoubted right of Englishmen, that no taxes should be imposed on them, but with their own consent, given personally, or by their representatives.

4) That the people of these colonies are not, and from their local circumstances, cannot be represented in the House of Commons in Great Britain.

5) That the only representatives of the people of these colonies, are persons chosen therein, by themselves; and that no taxes ever have been, or can be constitutionally imposed on them, but by their respective legislature.

6) That all supplies to the Crown, being free gifts of the people, it is unreasonable and inconsistent with the principles and spirit of the British constitution, for the people of Great Britain to grant to his Majesty the property of the colonists.

7) That trial by jury is the inherent and invaluable right of every British subject in these colonies.

8) That the late Act of Parliament, entitled an Act for granting and applying certain Stamp Duties . . . by imposing taxes on the inhabitants of these colonies, and the said Act and other Acts, by extending the jurisdiction of the courts of admiralty beyond its ancient limits, have a manifest tendency to subvert the rights and liberties of the colonists.

9) That the duties imposed by several late Acts of Parliament, from the peculiar circumstances of these colonies, will be extremely burthensome and grievous, and from the scarcity of specie, the payment of them absolutely impracticable.

10) That as the profits of the trade of these colonies ultimately centre in Great Britain, to pay for the manufactures which they are obliged to take from thence, they eventually contribute very largely to all supplies granted there to the Crown.

11) That the restrictions imposed by several late Acts of Parliament, on the trade of these colonies, will render them unable to purchase the manufactures of Great Britain.

> 12) That the increase, prosperity and happiness of these colonies, depend on the full and free enjoyment of their rights and liberties, and an intercourse with Great Britain, mutually affectionate and advantageous.
>
> 13) That it is the right of the British subjects in these colonies, to petition the king or either house of Parliament.

Sugar Act. Now there was wider recognition of the need for coordination, since the united voice of the colonies was likely to be more effective than thirteen disparate responses. Consequently, Massachusetts's call for a congress in New York that October met with considerable approval. In the event only nine provinces sent delegates, but those present still succeeded in drafting thirteen resolves protesting the British measures. The first eight concentrated on the constitutional issues of taxation, representation, and trial by jury. Four of the last five emphasized the economic inadvisability of the new laws, which would make it impossible for the colonies to buy British manufactured goods and thus result in economic distress on both sides of the Atlantic.

The Stamp Act resolves were couched in respectful language and were highly conservative. They made it clear that the colonists were not seeking to change the imperial relationship; they merely wanted a return to the system as it had operated before 1763. If there were revolutionaries, they were the British.

These points were discussed by numerous writers on both sides of the Atlantic, especially the issue of representation. British writers like Treasury Secretary Thomas Whately and Soame Jenyns, a member of the Board of Trade, advanced the view that the colonists were virtually represented, being in the same position as the inhabitants of cities like Manchester and Birmingham, who also did not have the vote. The point was that Parliament acted collectively, taking account of the interests of the whole nation.

This view was totally rejected by American writers like Daniel Dulany, a Maryland lawyer, in his pamphlet *Considerations on the Propriety of Imposing Taxes on the British Colonies*. He pointed out that the inhabitants of Leeds, Halifax, Manchester, or Birmingham could always make their views known to a neighboring member of Parliament. Americans, given their geographic distance, were unable to do this. The debate revealed a fundamental difference in attitudes to representation. Americans saw their elected representatives as delegates whose first duty was to the interests of their constituents. The British, in contrast, believed members of Parliament were there to represent the whole nation. But, whatever view was expressed, the crisis made newspapers and pamphlets a formidable vehicle for expressing political opinion. Even the government found it expedient to resort to print.

To make the colonial protest more effective, the merchants of New York and elsewhere attempted to organize a boycott of British goods. Since trade was depressed many agreed to do this because it provided them with the chance to sell surplus stock. Among the New Yorkers were several "she merchants" or women traders. Paradoxically, the boycott received considerable support from consumers, who believed that persuading the government to remove the offending tax was the best way of protecting their purchasing power.

Meanwhile the street protests continued. On October 31, the day before the Stamp Act was supposed to come into force, the Sons of Liberty in Boston compelled Oliver to reaffirm his intention to refuse the post of distributor; and in New York the lieutenant governor was burnt in effigy outside the gates of Fort George. The mob then attacked an officer's house and several brothels, which the rioters believed were patronized by British soldiers. Only the surrender of the stamps to the City Hall calmed the situation. In every colony the courts were closed, though attempts were made to open them. On the other hand many ships set sail, having persuaded the customs officers to let them leave with unstamped papers. All now waited to see what Britain would do.

Many historians have argued that the conflict with Britain unleashed a struggle between rich and poor, giving ordinary people an opportunity to demand political rights. As Carl Becker put it, "the American Revolution was not about home rule but who should rule at home."[13] Most active in this struggle were artisans and mechanics, common seamen, and other underprivileged groups like small farmers and the urban unemployed. Opposed to them were the wealthier propertied classes who wanted to control the Revolution to protect their private interests.

The thesis has declined in popularity in the past twenty-five years, though it still has its adherents.[14] One problem in discussing class conflict has been the lack of definition. The colonies were certainly afflicted by various conflicts at this time, as the next section shows, but it is not clear that these were linked to the imperial confrontation.

What can be said is that the disputes with Britain did permit participation by groups which had not previously been active. In part this was a result of the Patriot[15] leadership's readiness to use the language of liberty as a means of eliciting support. The constant rhetoric about the sovereignty of the people gave an unintended boost to popular politics. Thus in Charleston blacks also took up the cry of liberty, even though Henry Laurens described their chanting as thoughtless imitation. Similarly, in Massachusetts during the Boston riots, Mackintosh demonstrated the new awareness of the urban poor, though the elite quickly discarded him and his supporters when they threatened to get out of control. Clearly the common people – including some women and blacks – had been given a chance to influence events and were to do so again. This was especially true of New York, where an ethnically mixed population and a divided elite opened the door for others to become involved.[16]

---

[13] Carl Becker, *The History of Political Parties in the Province of New York, 1760–1776* (Madison, 1909). Becker was a member of the Progressive school, which argued that class conflict was the key to understanding the American Revolution. Other members of the school included Arthur Meier Schlesinger, Sr., *The Colonial Merchants and the American Revolution, 1763–1776* (New York, 1918); James Truslow Adams, *Revolutionary New England* (Boston, 1923); James Franklin Jameson, *The American Revolution Considered as a Social Movement* (Princeton, 1926); Elisha P. Douglas, *Rebels and Democrats: The Struggle for Equal Political Rights and Majority Rule during the American Revolution* (Chapel Hill, 1955); and Jackson Turner Main, *The Social Structure of Revolutionary America* (Princeton, 1965).

[14] See especially Alfred Young, ed., *The American Revolution: Explorations in the History of American Radicalism* (DeKalb, 1976); Nash, *The Urban Crucible*; Edward Countryman, *The American Revolution* (New York, 1985); and Mary Lou Lustig, *Privilege and Prerogative: New York's Provincial Elite, 1710–1776* (Madison, 1995).

[15] It was about this time that opponents of the ministry first began to be called Patriots.

[16] For the activities of women during this period, see Mary Beth Norton, *Liberty's Daughters: The Revolutionary Experience of American Women, 1750–1800* (Boston, 1980); and Linda Kerber, *Women of the Republic: Intellect and Ideology in Revolutionary America* (Chapel Hill, 1980). For African-Americans, see Ira Berlin and Ronald Hoffman, eds, *Slavery and Freedom in the Age of the American Revolution* (Charlottesville, 1983); Gary P. Nash, *Forging Freedom: The Formation of Philadelphia's Black Community, 1720–1840* (Cambridge Mass., 1988); and William D. Pierson, *Black Yankee: The Development of an Afro-American Subculture in Eighteenth Century New England* (Amherst, 1988).

The extent and violence of the American response caught the British by surprise. Fortunately for those who wanted a peaceful outcome, a change of government had occurred. Grenville had been replaced by Lord Rockingham, who had no particular commitment to the Stamp Act. The Rockingham Whigs also had close links with the British merchants who were beginning to suffer from the disruption to their trade. But even the Rockingham Whigs had to avoid the impression of giving way to mob violence. Hence Rockingham's ministry first passed the Declaratory Act, reaffirming the power of Parliament over the colonies in "all cases whatsoever." Then it repealed the Stamp Act. Another concession to the colonies was the lowering of the molasses duty to one penny a gallon.

If the government had not made these concessions and had attempted to enforce the Stamp Act instead, the separation from Britain might have begun eight years earlier than it did. The Americans now had some common principles which they were determined to assert. They also had a stronger sense of an identity that was different from the British. Equally significant was the nullification of the machinery of royal government during the crisis. Governors were isolated, royal officials intimidated, and Parliament's authority defied. A majority of the population, from farmers to militia members, had supported the Patriots; this majority included most of the elite, for whom opposition was but a short step to taking control.

4   INTERNAL CONFLICT

Though the disputes between Britain and the colonies dominate accounts of the period 1760–76, some attention must be paid to other, simultaneous conflicts, unrelated or only marginally connected to the imperial disputes. Historians have traditionally conveyed the impression that the colonists, with the exception of a few Tories and selfish grandees, were united during the era of the American Revolution. In reality there were "divisions throughout the whole."

The activities of the Paxton Boys in Pennsylvania form one such episode. As noted in chapter 17, Pennsylvania had been subject to a flood of Irish and German immigrants. While these groups had been welcomed on economic grounds, they had not been politically accommodated, since the Quakers were anxious to keep control of the assembly. Consequently, the five western counties (where most immigrants settled) had a total of just ten seats, whereas Bucks, Chester, and Philadelphia had twenty-six.[17]

For the first forty years this lack of representation had not troubled the westerners. Seats in the provincial assembly seemed a needless luxury while they were establishing themselves. Then came the French and Indian War. Suddenly the western counties found themselves without adequate protection and blamed the assembly, dominated as it was by men who apparently believed in peace at any price. In 1756 a number of strict Friends did temporarily step down so that the moderates led by Franklin could vote war supplies. However, the strict Quakers returned with the ending of hostilities in 1760. Then in May 1763 a new frontier war broke out with the Indian nations. Once more homesteads were burnt and men, women, and children killed. Again the Quaker-dominated assembly gave no adequate protection; worse, it seemed in league with the killers, offering them protection and support.

---

[17]   Ensuring equal representation was a problem for all colonies and, later, states with a constantly westward-moving population.

DOCUMENT 33

The Remonstrance of the Paxton Boys, February 13, 1764, reprinted in Merrill Jensen, ed., *English Historical Documents*, vol. IX: *American Colonial Documents to 1776* (London, 1955), 615.

[The anger of the western settlers in Pennsylvania and their inability to consider the view of the Indians, who had suffered similarly at the hands of the whites, is vividly expressed in this document. For the Paxton Boys, the only good Indian was a dead one or one who had been expelled.]

During the late and present Indian War, the frontiers of this province had been repeatedly attacked and ravaged by skulking parties of the Indians, who have with the most savage cruelty murdered men, women, and children, without distinction, and have reduced near a thousand families to the most extreme distress. It grieves us to the very heart to see such of our frontier inhabitants as have escaped savage fury with the loss of their parents, their children, their wives or relatives, left destitute by the public, and exposed to the most cruel poverty and wretchedness, while upwards of an hundred and twenty of these savages, who are with great reason suspected of being guilty of these horrid barbarities, under the mask of friendship, have procured themselves to be taken under the protection of the government, with a view to elude the fury of the brave relatives of the murdered, and are now maintained at the public expense. Some of these Indians now in the barracks of Philadelphia, are confessedly a part of the Wyalusing Indians, which tribe is now at war with us, and the others are the Moravian Indians, who, living with us under the cloak of friendship, carried on a correspondence with our known enemies on the Great Island. We cannot but observe, with sorrow and indignation, that some persons in this province are at pains to extenuate the barbarous cruelties practised by these savages on our murdered brethren and relatives, which are shocking to human nature; and must pierce every heart but that of the hardened perpetrators or their abettors; nor is it less distressing to hear others pleading that, although the Wyalusing Tribe is at war with us, yet that part of it which is under the protection of the government may be friendly to the English, and innocent.

   In what nation under the sun was it ever the custom that when a neighbouring nation took up arms, not an individual should be touched but only the persons who offered hostilities. Who ever proclaimed war with a part of a nation, and not with the whole? Had these Indians disapproved of the perfidy of their tribe, and been willing to cultivate and preserve friendship with us, why did they not give notice of the war before it happened, as it is known to be the result of long deliberations, and a preconcerted combination among them? Why did they not leave their tribe immediately and come among us before there was ground to suspect them, or war was actually waged with their tribe: No, they stayed amongst them, were privy to their murders and ravages, until we had destroyed their provisions, and when they could no longer subsist at home, they come, not as deserters, but as friends, to be maintained through the winter, that they may be able to scalp and butcher us in the spring.

In this emergency a number of westerners, mainly Scots-Irishmen from the township of Paxton, took the law into their own hands. They had long suspected the Christian Indians in the settled areas of collusion with their more warlike kinfolk to the west. A party of some sixty "Paxton Boys" therefore attacked the Indian settlement of Conestoga, murdering six of the inhabitants; the rest took refuge in the Lancaster jail. Despite a proclamation by the governor denouncing the atrocity, the group returned a few days later, broke into the jail, and butchered the remaining fourteen.

A much larger force of 250 men then set off from Paxton for Philadelphia to finish the job of killing the settlement Indians and deal with the Quakers too. In the event the Paxton Boys got no further than Germantown. Here they were met by Franklin and other assemblymen, who managed to reach an accord with the two leading Paxton spokesmen, Matthew Smith and James Gibson. It was agreed that additional representation would be given to the western counties and proper measures taken against enemy Indians, while an amnesty would be granted for those involved in the recent murders. Clearly in future the native people were to have no place in Pennsylvania, for as Franklin himself commented: "The spirit of killing all Indians, Friends and Foes, spread amazingly thro the whole Country. The Action was almost universally approved by the common People." It was a sad end to the ideals of the Quaker colony.

The agreement with the Paxton Boys was to have important consequences for Pennsylvania, since it began a process of political realignment. The Quakers believed that the proprietors had made common cause with the westerners during the crisis and decided to seek an end to proprietary government by asking the Crown for a royal charter. This move proved fateful, since it prevented the Quakers from taking the popular side in the ensuing Stamp Act controversy. The void was quickly filled by the Scots-Irish, Germans, and their urban allies who created a new Patriot party. Indicative of the Quaker discomfiture was the defection of the White Oaks Association of Philadelphia shipwrights. Although they initially stayed loyal to the Quakers during the Stamp Act crisis, by 1770 they had joined the Patriot opposition in demanding more representation and a lower property qualification for voting. The result was ultimately to make the Quakers a party of Tories and Loyalists, hastening their political demise.

Meanwhile a different sort of conflict was raging over land on the eastern borders of New York. New England's rapid population growth meant that farmers from Connecticut, Massachusetts, and New Hampshire were pushing north and west in search of fresh land. To the northwest families began settling the area that was to become Vermont with patents from New Hampshire, even though the land was claimed by New York. The problem was exacerbated by the Privy Council's failure to define New Hampshire's western boundary, which was finally declared to be the Connecticut River in 1764. New York then began issuing its own patents to the area, insisting that families already settled there must seek new titles. The New Hampshire patentees vigorously resisted this measure, since it meant a lengthy and costly journey to New York City. As previously noted, the questioning of land titles always caused trouble, and this occasion proved to be no exception. In 1769 the settlers around Bennington, led by Ethan Allen, organized themselves as the Green Mountain Boys with the aim of expelling the New York surveyors and anyone with a title from that province. The dispute was still not settled by the time of independence and caused considerable embarrassment to the Patriot cause.

New York was also embroiled in a similar dispute with Massachusetts. Here too the problem was caused by Yankee farmers looking for more land, this time on the adjacent manorial estates of the Livingston and Van Rensselaer families, and compounded by an imprecise boundary. The dispute was intensified because it involved two incompatible land systems. The New York landowners wanted only tenants on their land; the Massachusetts families were determined to be freeholders. The first clashes occurred in 1751 but subsided when the war with France intervened.

However, the end of the war brought renewed tension, not only in western Massachusetts but along the border with Connecticut, affecting the Philipse and Courtland manors. To increase the pressure, the trespassers from Connecticut craftily offered the tenants already on those estates freehold titles. The Stamp Act riots in New York encouraged them to continue their invasion. When they marched on the city to press their case, however, they were shunned by the Sons of Liberty and compelled to retire. The governor then asked for military assistance, and the squatters had to flee to Connecticut, ending the trouble on the lower Hudson.

Unfortunately these events sparked off renewed violence on the Livingston and Van Rensselaer manors to the north; four men, including a deputy, were killed when squatters resisted arrest by the Albany County sheriff. With order apparently having broken down, the governor asked once more for military assistance. The tenants were then subdued and the Massachusetts squatters driven back across the provincial boundary, but not for long. The issue caused so much anger in Massachusetts that there was talk of "a formal rupture," which encouraged many squatters to return. Heavily outnumbered, the Van Rensselaer family ultimately had to give up the eastern portion of the Claverak manor. The issue was finally settled in 1773, after negotiations between Hutchinson and Governor Tryon led to the drawing of a clearly marked boundary twenty miles from the Hudson River.

The New England land hunger also caused friction between Connecticut and Pennsylvania. Connecticut had no frontier of its own, only a border with New York. However, a group calling itself the Susquehanna Company, founded in 1753, was endeavoring to settle the valley of the Wyoming River, a tributary of the Susquehanna River, in northern Pennsylvania. The company claimed this area by virtue of Connecticut's 1664 charter, which theoretically extended the colony's boundaries from the Atlantic to the "South Sea." To strengthen its claim, the company had secretly purchased six million acres from the Iroquois during the 1754 Albany Congress.

Once again, differing land systems bedeviled the dispute, since the Pennsylvania authorities were determined to collect quitrents, which the New Englanders were equally determined to resist. But it was not until 1769, when the Susquehanna Company dispatched its first settlers, that the battle for possession really began. The Connecticut settlers, initially outnumbered, sought the assistance of the Paxton Boys in a seesaw struggle for control. Only the outbreak of fighting between Britain and the colonies halted the violence. This dispute also continued beyond the colonial period.[18]

The New England and middle colonies were not alone in experiencing backcountry disturbances during the American Revolution. The Carolinas were also afflicted though, as in Pennsylvania, the conflict there was between the eastern establishment and an expanding

---

[18]   One territorial dispute which was settled was the border between Pennsylvania and Maryland, which had been at issue since 1681. An agreed line was finally established by two British surveyors, Charles Mason and Jeremiah Dixon.

western population rather than an intercolonial struggle. Another similarity was that the problems were aggravated by religious differences. The Carolina low country was largely Anglican, the interior predominantly Presbyterian and Baptist.

The principal grievance in both colonies concerned local government, which the malcontents wanted better regulated – hence their name "the Regulators." In South Carolina, however, the complaint concerned the lack of any system at all. Instead of creating new parishes, the tidewater authorities in Charleston simply extended the existing parishes. This meant that many people in the piedmont not only had to travel two or three hundred miles to obtain a marriage license, have a will attested, or patent their land but also then had to pay an exorbitant fee for the privilege. At the same time there was little provision for law and order. The few deputies available were frequently in league with the bandits who infested the countryside. A further problem was that there were no local courts to dispense justice once the criminals were caught. The result was widespread rustling and other violent crime, much of it perpetrated by hunters, who opposed the spread of farming because it destroyed the game.

The response of the backcountry farming community, which now numbered some substantial slave owners among its ranks, was to take the law into its own hands by forming the first vigilante groups in American history. Posses were organized, the gangs tracked down, and their leaders summarily executed. Eventually, in 1769 the Charleston authorities took notice of the situation by passing a bill giving the backcountry people four new districts, a circuit court, proper jails, and sheriffs to deal with delinquents. They also agreed to fixed statutory fees for all public officials and three additional representatives in the assembly. But relations remained sufficiently strained for the tidewater Patriots early in 1775 to dispatch a special committee, including a Baptist and Presbyterian minister, to win support for the Continental Association. Even then the settlement of Ninety Six continued to be sufficiently resentful of its treatment by the tidewater that it opted to remain neutral rather than supportive of the Patriot cause on the outbreak of hostilities with Britain in 1775.

In North Carolina the complaint of the backcountry settlers was not so much the lack of local government but rather the corruption rife in the existing system. The tidewater government had created a system of county courts. However, most of the positions were filled by members of the eastern elite whose principal concern was to make money by the collection of fees. The activities of Edmund Fanning, the register of deeds for Orange County and colonel of the militia, were especially notorious. The westerners were also angry that the elite had preempted much of the best land without settling it, evicting as squatters anyone who attempted to do so.

Another complaint was the system of taxation, especially the use of poll taxes and collection of quitrents. These bore heavily on the westerners, who believed that payment ought to be proportional to a person's estate. The prohibition against payment in kind was also unfair to them, since the western counties had little specie and many westerners were being imprisoned for debt as a result. What made the Regulators angry was that much of the money was being squandered on a new capital at New Bern.

Despite the presentation of several petitions, the legislature did little to meet the complaints of the western counties. The petitioners themselves were seemingly powerless, since appointees to the county court had to be coopted and the western counties were underrepresented in the assembly. The result was a recourse to more violent methods. Late in September 1770 a group of mainly Scots-Irish farmers led by James Hunter, William Butler, and Herman Husband descended on the Orange County courthouse at Hillsborough. Here they beat several court officials in front of the judge before proceeding to wreck Fanning's house. The assembly responded by passing a Riot Act which made the Regulators' actions punishable by death, though it also passed legislation favoring some of the Regulators' demands; cheaper procedures for settling small debts; the regulation of fees; an end to the unfair sequestration of property for debt; and the creation of new counties to give better access to the courts.

Unfortunately the Regulators ignored these concessions, threatening instead to march on New Bern to overturn the alleged inequities of the Riot Act. This response compelled Governor Tryon to advance into the backcountry to settle the issue, accompanied by the more dependable units of the eastern militia. He finally caught up with two thousand Regulators at the River Alamance in May 1771. After a further attempt at negotiation failed, Tryon ordered his forces to fire. Some three hundred opponents were killed, while the rest scattered. Five of the ringleaders were summarily hanged; many others fled for safety across the mountains into eastern Tennessee. Once the belated reforms of the assembly began to work, peace was finally restored. But the situation was still sufficiently tense in 1774 for the eastern Patriots to send, as their colleagues in South Carolina were shortly to do, two visiting Presbyterian ministers from Pennsylvania into the backcountry to elicit support for the struggle against Britain.

Although the episodes concerning the Paxton Boys, New York manor riots, Green Mountain Boys, Wyoming Valley settlements and Carolina Regulators occurred at different times and in different places, they do share some common elements. All were indirectly the result of an expanding population caused by a high birthrate and continued immigration. Most contained an element of rich versus poor; several concerned the conflict between east and west.

The struggle between tidewater and piedmont is a constant theme in American history. It developed partly as a consequence of differing cultures. Easterners distrusted westerners as uncivilized backwoodsmen who lived in a state of barbarism and believed that they, as the more civilized element in society, had a legal and moral responsibility to ensure that the West was settled in an orderly fashion.[19] This meant respect for legally acquired property and the institutions of government, without which the development of the backcountry would be impossible.

Westerners bitterly resented such views. They believed that only the labor of those working the land gave title to it. They resented the claims of absentee proprietors who preempted the best tracts by signing a piece of paper. It was especially galling to westerners that those securing such patents did not need the land for their own families and had no intention of personally developing their claims. Westerners regarded such behavior as profiteering and exploitation of the worst kind.

Nevertheless these conflicts were not class war in the Marxist sense. The westerners had no desire to change the fundamental structure of society. Their aim was not the destruction of property but its acquisition. What they wanted was an opportunity to enjoy the fruits of their labor without being exploited by an overprivileged elite.

---

[19] Eastern distaste for the interior is well illustrated in Charles Woodmason's writings about the South Carolina backcountry. Woodmason, an Anglican minister, undoubtedly exaggerated his account, since most of the population were dissenters. See Richard Slotkin, *Regeneration Through Violence: The Mythology of the American Frontier, 1600–1860* (Middletown, 1973).

21

Revolution and Independence, 1767–76

1766 (Jan.) The New York assembly refuses to implement the Quartering Act.

1767 (June) The Revenue Act (Townshend duties) is passed.
(Oct.) Boston makes a first attempt at a nonimportation agreement.
(Nov.) Publication of *Letters from a Farmer* begins.

1768 (Feb.) Massachusetts sends circular letter to all colonial assemblies.
(March) Second nonimportation agreement is reached.
(June) The *Liberty* riot takes place.
(Sept.) A convention of Massachusetts towns is held.

1769 (Feb.) Parliament passes resolves calling for firmer action.

1770 (March) The Boston Massacre takes place.
(April) Townshend duties are removed (except on tea).

1772 (June) The *Gaspee* is burnt.
(Oct.) The Boston committee of correspondence is formed.

1773 (March) The Virginia Intercolonial committee of correspondence is established.
(Dec.) The Boston Tea Party takes place.

1774 (March) The Boston Port Act is passed.
(May) The Massachusetts Government Act is passed.
(Sept.–Oct.) The First Continental Congress is held.

1775 (March) An act restraining New England trade is passed.
(April) The Battle of Lexington and Concord is fought; Second Continental Congress is held.
(Aug.) A royal proclamation calls for suppression of the rebellion.

1776 (Jan.) *Common Sense* is published.
(April) American ports are opened to all nations.
(May) New state constitutions are authorized.
(July) The Declaration of Independence is signed.

1 THE STRUGGLE RENEWED: THE TOWNSHEND DUTIES

Although most colonists celebrated the repeal of the Stamp Act, they soon found that the old relationship was not to be resumed. Parliament had made only a tactical concession in repealing the Stamp Act. The belief remained that Parliament had the right to tax and that the Americans ought to make a greater contribution to the costs of empire. Many Britons were concerned that this wider competence of Parliament to legislate had been implicitly questioned. Hence it was only a matter of time before an attempt was made to assert the claims laid down in the Declaratory Act.

Trouble was already developing with New York over the quartering of troops. The right to quarters had been a source of dispute since the French and Indian War. In May 1765 the Grenville ministry, determined to clarify the situation, passed an act requiring each colony to provide barracks or accommodation in empty warehouses for all troops stationed within its borders and to supply them with firewood, candles, food, and drink.

Most colonies were only marginally affected by this measure, since the troops were stationed either in Canada, Florida, or beyond the Allegheny Mountains. New York was affected because it was the entry point for forces going to the West. Its assembly decided, in light of the Stamp Act debate, that the Quartering Act was tantamount to a tax and should be rejected. When news of this refusal reached London early in 1767, the ministry of Lord Chatham, which had succeeded the Rockingham government, passed an act suspending the New York assembly from all legislative activity until it complied with the terms of the Quartering Act. At a stroke Parliament had overturned the rights of a colony. Only the unpopularity of New York with the other colonies and its readiness to climb down before the new act was implemented prevented a major constitutional confrontation.

By this time the British government was once more on the verge of taxing the Americans, since the need for revenue was as pressing as ever. During the repeal of the Stamp Act Franklin had led Parliament to believe that Americans objected only to internal taxes. Chatham's chancellor of the exchequer, Charles Townshend, accordingly decided to test this view and turn the American flank, as Grenville had in 1764, by raising revenue in the guise of a navigation act for the regulation of trade. Townshend expected initially a modest £40,000 from taxes on the items selected: glass, paint, tea, and paper. However, the proceeds were to be used not only for defense but for "defraying the Charge of the Administration of Justice, and the Support of Civil Government." The old fear that recalcitrant assemblies might not pay royal officials their salaries had resurfaced. The act also affirmed the legality of writs of assistance in response to the appeal for clarification from the Massachusetts Superior Court.

Townshend, like Grenville, also believed that more revenue could be raised by reforming the administrative machinery, especially the customs service. Supervision from London was too distant to be effective. He therefore sponsored another bill establishing a separate Board of American Customs, to be located in Boston. Townshend died shortly after this, but the government continued his reforming policy by further strengthening the vice-admiralty courts. The court in Halifax had proved too remote for most prosecutions. A new act was accordingly passed authorizing additional courts, which the Privy Council decreed should be at Halifax, Boston, Philadelphia, and Charleston. The new courts were to have both appellate powers and original jurisdiction. But to calm colonial fears about rapacious officials, the act stipulated that judges were to be paid a fixed salary and were expressly forbidden "to take any fee or gratuity whatsoever."

The final step in the ministerial scheme was the appointment in January 1768 of a secretary of state for America to coordinate policy, as Pownall had recommended in 1764. However, the powers of the new office were to be limited to those formerly exercised by the southern secretary of state. The first incumbent was the Earl of Hillsborough, a large land-owner and member of the Anglo-Irish elite.

The American reaction to Townshend's program was initially muted, and for a short while it seemed that his ploy might work. But protests were not long in appearing. In October the residents of Boston attempted to organize a ban on the importation of all luxury goods. Then in November John Dickinson, a Philadelphia lawyer, initiated a series of articles called *Letters from a Farmer*. He began by warning of the dangerous implications for all the colonies of the recent suspension of the New York assembly. Then he affirmed that any tax, even for the regulation of trade, was unacceptable if it was intended to raise revenue. Next he turned to the equally pernicious plan to use the Townshend revenues to pay the salaries of royal officials, which would dangerously weaken the assemblies. With so many parasitical officials, the royal executive had to be kept accountable to the colonial legislature; otherwise the colonies would sink to the abject condition of Ireland, which had been sucked dry of its wealth by foreign placemen. But all protests should be peaceable. Dickinson did not want a repetition of the Stamp Act riots.

Dickinson's letters, which were reprinted throughout the mainland colonies, started a fresh and vigorous debate. Among those alerted to the dangerous actions of the imperial government was the Massachusetts House of Representatives, which early in 1768 sent a circular letter to all the colonial assemblies protesting the recent Townshend duties and arguing that such legislation constituted a breach of the colonists' fundamental rights as British subjects. The opposition in Massachusetts was now led by Samuel Adams, a former Boston tax collector and caucus politician. Adams argued that Parliament too was bound by the laws, and thus could not unilaterally overturn them, an early example of how the colonists were beginning to use natural rights to reinforce their position. This was a process that would continue until 1776 when the rights of Englishmen were entirely expunged from the Patriots' political language. It was also one more factor compelling the colonists to redefine their identity. If they could not enjoy equal rights with Englishmen across the Atlantic, then they would have to defend their lives and property as Americans.

The denigrating tone of the circular letter not surprisingly offended the British author-ities, who demanded that Massachusetts rescind it and that those assemblies to which it had been sent ignore it. Refusal to comply would mean instant dissolution. The Virginia House of Burgesses responded by drafting its own circular letter and was promptly dismissed. All the assemblies eventually suffered the same fate.

Meanwhile Patriots in the major seaports were once more considering an economic boycott as the best means of getting the British to desist from their current policies. Boston had already attempted limited action against luxury goods, but a town meeting in March 1768 adopted a much more stringent nonimportation agreement, exempting only essential items required by the New England fishing industry. Other towns soon followed, though with some reluctance, especially on the part of Philadelphia. This time the merchant community was divided. Nonimportation was unpopular with transatlantic merchants but generally supported by coastal operators and traders with the West Indies like John Hancock, who would be less affected by the ban and were most active in smuggling.[1]

Nonimportation was also popular in the wider community. Many artisans, like the White Oaks, believed that it would increase the demand for American manufactured goods and provide them with work. They were especially vociferous in New York, where they sought to gain control of the movement from the more cautious merchants. Women also seized the opportunity to be active by ensuring that their households did not drink tea; several hundred signed agreements in Boston during 1770 not to consume this item. Other women contributed by using their looms to produce linen and woolen cloth so that the colonies were less dependent on the mother country.

Lastly, nonimportation appealed to all those who believed that the colonists were becoming too materialistic. The consumers of imported luxuries should give up their sinful ways, since they were otherwise assisting the imperial design of enslaving America. Those who failed to do so justly had their names published in the newspapers. Overall, nonimportation provided considerable scope for popular activity because it touched the lives of ordinary people, offering them a means of relevant and effective action.

In this climate further friction was perhaps inevitable, especially after the arrival of the new Board of Commissioners in Boston, where Hancock was leading the resistance to the local collectors. When it was alleged that Hancock had locked a customs officer in a cabin while unloading a cargo of Madeira wine from his ship, the *Liberty*, the officers seized the vessel and secured it alongside the *Romney* warship. The result was a riot during which both the officers and the customs commissioners had to flee to Castle William for safety. The government responded by calling in the military, believing that Boston was now a city without law and order. Four regiments were dispatched, two from Nova Scotia and two from Ireland, to sustain the civil government. Calls were also made in Parliament for suspects to be sent to England for trial under an old statute from the time of Henry VIII.

Since the assembly was still dissolved because of its refusal to rescind the circular letter, Adams turned in this crisis to the Boston town meeting. Condemning the proposed use of a standing army as a reversion to Stuart tyranny, he appealed for a special convention of the Massachusetts towns to debate the matter. Governor Bernard warned that this constituted an attempt to call the assembly without royal consent and was tantamount to treason. The convention still met but, faced with the imminent arrival of the troops and conscious of its precarious legal position, dispersed on September 22 without reaching any resolution. It none the less set a precedent for future extralegal assemblies.

Equally important was the fact that Massachusetts was not alone in its defiance. When Parliament passed a series of resolutions in February 1769 condemning the province, the Virginia House of Burgesses in Williamsburg responded with a set of its own resolutions.

---

[1] The merchants of the Revolutionary era have generally incurred harsh criticism, especially from Progressive historians, who argued that they put economic self-interest before patriotic principle. See Arthur Schlesinger, Sr., *The Colonial Merchants and the American Revolution, 1763–1776* (New York, 1918). More sympathetic is Benjamin W. Labaree, *Patriots and Partisans: The Merchants of Newburyport, 1764–1815* (Cambridge, Mass., 1962). Labaree pointed out that the merchants were not a monolithic group and that their affiliations were determined by the trade in which they were engaged. For a more recent assessment, see Edward C. Papenfuse, *In Pursuit of Profit: The Annapolis Merchants in the Era of the American Revolution, 1763–1805* (Baltimore, 1975); and John W. Tyler, *Smugglers and Patriots: Boston Merchants and the Advent of the American Revolution* (Boston, 1986).

Plate 54   *The Boston Massacre,* engraving/cartoon by Paul Revere. The Mansell
Collection, London.

Plate 55   Portrait of Samuel Adams, by John Singleton Copley, ca. 1770. Deposited by the City of Boston. Courtesy of the Museum of Fine Arts, Boston.

These asserted the right of the assemblies to correspond with one another, condemned the proposal to send suspects to England as "highly derogatory of the rights of British subjects," and reaffirmed the sole right of the assemblies to levy taxes. When the governor sent a message dissolving the assembly, the members simply adjourned to the Raleigh Tavern to adopt a nonimportation agreement. Defiance had become second nature.

Meanwhile hopes that the military could quieten the situation were proving false. In New York the constant conflict between off-duty soldiers and local Patriots over the siting of the liberty pole near Fort George resulted in a serious riot in January 1770. Miraculously, no one was killed. The same did not prove the case in Boston, where after a few months relations began to deteriorate, as off-duty soldiers competed for additional jobs and stole the hearts of local girls. Brawls occurred despite the efforts of the officers to prevent them. Then on March 5, 1770, an angry mob confronted a military detachment under Captain Preston guarding the customs house. Church bells rang, perhaps as a prearranged signal of trouble. In the subsequent confusion the soldiers opened fire, killing five rioters, including Crispus Attucks, an African-American slave. Thousands of people rushed from the surrounding countryside ready to fight, and the angry populace were pacified only by the arrest of the guard and the prompt withdrawal of the remaining troops to Castle William. The British policy of using the army to support the civil authority had been an abject failure.

2 INTERLUDE, 1770–1773

The withdrawal of troops from Boston initiated a period of greater calm. The government was now headed by Lord North, a skillful parliamentarian who preferred conciliation to confrontation. In April 1770 North decided to remove all the Townshend duties except that on tea, which he maintained as a symbol of Parliament's right to tax. Though some Patriots determined to continue the struggle until this too was withdrawn, the removal of the other duties helped undermine the nonimportation movement, first in Philadelphia, then in New York, and finally in Boston.

Another factor which may have weakened the Patriots' opposition was the government's change of stance on the West. The Proclamation of 1763 had left various Indians and white settlers on the wrong side of the line. It had also taken no account of either the demographic pressures caused by renewed immigration or the fertility of the population, both of which were driving a constant stream of settlers westward in search of land.[2] Accordingly in 1768 the boundary with the northern nations was renegotiated by Johnson in the Treaty of Fort Stanwix and with the southern nations by Stuart in the Treaty of Hard Labor. As a result eastern Tennessee and Kentucky around the Watauga and Holston rivers were opened to settlement. At the same time the licensing of traders was handed back to the colonial authorities. Equally encouraging to western developers in 1772 was the removal of Hillsborough, who had opposed all western expansion, as American secretary of state. His successor, Lord Dartmouth, was more disposed to western colonies, especially after

---

[2] By 1770 some 12,000 people a year were coming to America from the British Isles, three times the number arriving before the French and Indian War. See Bernard Bailyn, *Voyagers to the West: Emigration from Britain to America on the Eve of the Revolution* (New York, 1986).

a judicious distribution of stock in London by James Wharton, a leading member of the Vandalia Company.

Unfortunately the appearance of calm was deceptive. In Massachusetts suspicions went too deep for meaningful reconciliation. Patriots like Samuel Adams were convinced that Lord North's ministry was engaged in a conspiracy to undermine American liberty. They were encouraged in these notions by the persecution of John Wilkes in England, which similarly seemed to threaten liberty. The Patriots accordingly arranged for the Boston Massacre to be commemorated each year in a speech reminding the inhabitants of the continued danger of enslavement.

Further evidence of sinister intent was not long in appearing. One of the original objections to the Townshend duties was that they were to be used to pay the salaries of royal officials, making them independent of the colonial legislatures. So far no attempt had been made to implement this policy. Then in June 1772 Hutchinson announced that he was to receive his salary directly from the British government. Even worse, it was announced in September that judges too would henceforth receive their salaries from the Crown. This meant that Britain would have control not only of the executive but also of the judiciary since the judges' independence was already compromised by the Crown's refusal to grant them tenure during good behavior.[3]

When Hutchinson refused to summon the assembly to discuss the matter, Adams and his colleagues turned once more to the Boston town meeting. The outcome was an agreement to establish a committee of correspondence "to state the Rights of the Colonists and of this Province in particular," which were to be circulated to all the Massachusetts towns. The tone was uncompromising, claiming the manifest desire of the imperial government to enslave the inhabitants. Reference was now made to the "assumed" power rather than the right of Parliament to legislate. Over half the towns responded, most of them favorably, the least responsive being the settlements in the Connecticut River valley, where the landed elite known as the "River Gods" exercised restraint.[4]

One practical way for the Massachusetts Patriots to thwart the plans of North's ministry was to persuade the judges not to accept a royal salary but to receive their stipend as usual from the assembly. Within twelve months all but one had agreed, induced in part by the offer of a large increase. Only the chief justice, Peter Oliver, refused. The assembly then began drawing up articles of impeachment, a procedure that even the British House of Commons rarely exercised. At the same time it demanded the dimissal of Hutchinson, following the disclosure of some letters in which he suggested that the liberties of the colonists might have to be curtailed.

There was turmoil elsewhere too. In Rhode Island the activities of one of the navy's cutters, the *Gaspee*, so angered the merchants that they boarded it one night after it had run aground, wounded its commander, and burnt the vessel. This outrage against officers and property of the Crown led to the establishment of a special commission of inquiry, with authority to send suspects to England for trial.

---

[3] For previous disputes on this issue, see chapter 16, section 3.

[4] For the politicization of the New England countryside, see Richard D. Brown, *Revolutionary Politics in Massachusetts: The Boston Committee of Correspondence and the Towns, 1772–1774* (Cambridge, Mass., 1970); Robert A. Gross, *The Minutemen and their World* (New York, 1976); and Gary Nobles, *Divisions Throughout the Whole: Politics and Society in Hampshire County, Massachusetts, 1740–1775* (New York, 1983).

To the government's chagrin, nothing came of the investigation, since the commission was met with silence. Nevertheless the talk of sending accused persons to England confirmed the colonists' fears that their liberty was threatened, since it was an ancient right of Englishmen to be tried at the scene of their alleged crime. The alarm spread even to Virginia where younger members of the planter elite, among them Thomas Jefferson, Richard Henry Lee, and Patrick Henry, were convinced that the commission could only be explained as part of a giant imperial conspiracy. They decided to set up an intercolonial committee of correspondence to monitor British actions throughout the continent. Within twelve months all the colonies except Pennsylvania, where the Quakers prevented such action, had done the same.

In this situation only a spark was needed to set the situation ablaze once more. Ironically it was provided by a seemingly innocuous piece of legislation intended to help the East India Company out of its financial difficulties. Previously the company had had to dispose of its tea on the London market, paying an import duty in the process. The North ministry now passed an act allowing the company to sell its tea directly to consignees in America. Though the 1767 Townshend duty would still be levied on arrival in America, the tea would be much cheaper, being subject to only one duty and thus ensuring wider sales and greater profits for the company. North may also have calculated that cheaper tea would tempt the Americans into paying the duty, thus acknowledging Parliament's right to tax.

If this was his aim, it proved a gross miscalculation. Since 1770 the Sons of Liberty had been conducting a desultory campaign to prevent the drinking of British tea. Now their cause was given a considerable boost – first, from the merchants who had previously shipped tea from Britain and now stood to lose business; second, from all those who had been smuggling Dutch tea and would similarly lose their market; and third, from Patriot activists who believed that the measure was a diabolical imperial design to trick Americans into acknowledging Parliament's right to tax. People gathered in all the major ports demanding that the tea be sent back. As usual it was in Boston that the people took decisive action. When Hutchinson refused the *Dartmouth* and two other vessels permission to leave because they had technically failed to clear customs, Adams and the town leaders arranged for a group of supporters, disguised as Indians, to board the vessels and throw the tea, worth £10,000, into the harbor. Although similar events elsewhere were less violent, they were no less ominous. Handbills warned captains and merchants not to handle the tea for fear of being tarred and feathered.

3 THE INTOLERABLE ACTS

The destruction of the tea proved the last straw for the British, who believed that they had done everything possible to accommodate the Americans. The only response had been violence, this time against the property of the East India Company, one of the country's most prestigious corporations, in which many members of Parliament held stock. Since conciliation had failed, firmness would now have to be tried – and quickly too, if the colonies were not to slide into insubordination. Clearly an example must be made of Massachusetts and the town of Boston, where dastardly attempts were being made to impeach the chief justice for his refusal to accede to popular pressure concerning his salary. Not that the ministers in London believed that the popular party had much

Plate 56 The practice of tarring and feathering, lithograph by Philip Dawe, 1774. The
Library of Congress, Washington, D.C.

support, being convinced that it consisted of little more than a small group of men who
were subverting the true affections of the people. Once these wicked persons had been
removed, the loyal majority would revert to their traditional respect for the Crown and
Parliament.

A series of measures was therefore devised to deliver that firm government and restore an errant province to obedience. First, Parliament passed the Boston Port Act, closing the harbor until the town paid compensation to the East India Company. Then North's ministry passed its key measure, the Massachusetts Government Act, replacing the 1691 charter with a new frame of government, the first time that Parliament had enacted such a measure. In future the council was to be appointed solely by the governor, as in other royal colonies, not from a list submitted by the House of Representatives. No longer would the governor have to work with a hostile group of men. Second, restrictions were to be placed on town meetings: in future these could meet only once a year to elect their officials. All other meetings would require the consent of the governor, thus preventing the Patriots from manipulating these gatherings for their nefarious ends. Third, the governor was authorized to appoint sheriffs without the consent of the council, and they in turn were to impanel juries. No longer would the judicial system work to the disadvantage of the Crown in cases of treason and sedition.

To strengthen government further and temporarily prevent the intimidation of officials, North's ministry passed a third measure, the Administration of Justice Act. For the next three years any royal official accused of a crime could be tried in Britain or another colony, to avoid the kind of situation that had threatened Preston and his men in the aftermath of the Boston Massacre. The British government also added another Quartering Act, reiterating the Crown's right to billet troops in "uninhabited houses, outhouses, barns or other buildings." Finally, to implement the new policy, the government appointed Thomas Gage, the commander in chief in North America, governor of Massachusetts in place of the now discredited Hutchinson.

Coincidentally a bill was also being passed for the better government of Quebec. For twelve years the province had been governed without any participation by the French Canadians. All this was to change in what today is acknowledged to have been an enlightened piece of legislation. Britain still felt it "inexpedient to call an assembly," given the inhabitants' lack of familiarity with such institutions, but a council drawn from the local population was to be appointed to promulgate laws for the better government of the country. Among those included in these new arrangements were the French-speaking western settlements. The hope was that a new enlarged province, controlling most of the fur trade, would increase revenues while keeping costs down. Accordingly a clause was included transferring all lands north of the Ohio River to the province of Quebec.

If the British ministers thought that these measures would restore order in Massachusetts and respect elsewhere, they could not have been more misguided. The colonies might have ignored the plight of New York in 1767 when its assembly was threatened with supension, but none could ignore the measures now being passed, which at a stroke overturned the rights of one of Britain's oldest colonies. The measures were indeed "intolerable," doubly so when Roman Catholics in Canada were being given special consideration.

The government had inadvertently made the Quebec Act into a fifth means of oppression. Congregational ministers in New England were especially vociferous in their opposition to the act as a device of the agents of anti-Christ to bring down the Puritan commonwealth. The measure was unpopular too with speculators and land companies, since the transfer of the northwestern territory to Quebec threatened to make their schemes more difficult. The legislatures of Virginia, Connecticut, and Massachusetts were especially upset, since their charter rights to the territory were being overturned.

In this crisis Adams called a meeting of Boston's inhabitants and its correspondence committee. A suggestion by some of the merchants to pay damages to the East India Company was contemptuously brushed aside in favor of economic sanctions. These were to be implemented by a Solemn League and Covenant, whereby the signatories would cease all trade with Britain after August 31 and boycott anyone refusing to subscribe to the agreement. It was clear, however, that support would have to be sought from the other colonies if the full weight of Britain's displeasure was to be resisted. Accordingly, the House of Representatives issued calls for a Congress to be held that September in Philadelphia. Agreement was quickly secured from all the mainland colonies except Georgia, where the threat of war with the Creeks was a restraining factor. Elsewhere the anger was so great that even when the colonial legislatures were recessed or dissolved – as in Virginia, Maryland, New Hampshire, New Jersey, Delaware, and North Carolina – informal assemblies or conventions were summoned for the election of representatives to attend the Congress.

It was not clear whether much could be achieved. When John Adams, a cousin of Samuel Adams and a rising Patriot leader in his own right, arrived as delegate for Massachusetts, he commented how the members constituted "a collection of strangers." But the participants were highly motivated to cooperate by the need, as Franklin was to put it on a later occasion to either "all hang together [i.e. cooperate], or, most assuredly . . . all hang separately." This feeling was eloquently expressed by Patrick Henry when he affirmed that he was attending "not as a Virginian but as an American." In this spirit Congress quickly agreed that each colony should have one vote – both to placate the smaller ones and to surmount the lack of statistics about each colony's relative wealth and population. Delegates also agreed on a two-part agenda to define America's rights and decide how to defend them.

Nevertheless divisions soon appeared among the delegates. Although these have usually been described in terms of radicals versus conservatives, it would be more appropriate to designate them hardliners versus moderates. The moderates, led by Joseph Galloway of Pennsylvania, were as keen as the hardliners to overturn the Intolerable Acts and limit the sovereignty of Parliament. But they wanted to resolve the crisis positively by renegotiating the imperial relationship. Galloway therefore presented the delegates with a plan whereby a colonial Congress or Grand Council, with a president chosen by the king, would raise revenue for imperial purposes in America. It would also have the right to veto all Westminster legislation affecting the colonies, while Parliament in turn could veto any legislation (other than taxation) passed by the Grand Council. Sovereignty over America would be shared.

The hardliners, however, were as suspicious of an American parliament as of a British one. In their view the British were solely responsible for the crisis. The only solution was a return to the pre-1763 situation, though with one important difference: Parliament must give up all claim to sovereignty over the colonies, since history showed that its authority was usurped. It could for convenience regulate trade in the interest of the whole empire. Otherwise, the constitutional connection with Britain must be limited to the Crown, as defined in the colonial charters.

The hardliners narrowly won. An early indication of the outcome was their success on September 17 in getting Congress to adopt the Suffolk County Resolves, which had just been drafted at a special convention by Joseph Warren, a leading Boston Patriot. These called for taxes in Massachusetts to be withheld; the militia to be put into a state of readiness; and all colonial officials to obey the authority of the general court, now reconstituted as a colonial congress, until the disputes with Britain had been resolved. Defiance was preferred to conciliation. Then the hardliners won the vote to shelve Galloway's plan of union by six colonies to five. In reality the plan was doomed from the start, being far too revolutionary for the British also, since it undermined their concept of a centralized, unitary state located in Britain.

The hardliners were now firmly in control. Congress drew up a Declaration of Rights, strongly defending the colonial position on the basis of "the immutable laws of nature, the principles of the English constitution and the several charters or compacts" of each colony. The message was clear: North's ministry must climb down. No concessions could be contemplated regarding the legislative rights of the Americans. Respect must also be given to other rights like trial by jury, the sending of petitions, and freedom from a standing army.

To ensure recognition of these rights, Congress proposed three measures: the sending of an address to the people of Great Britain; the dispatch of a message of loyalty to the king; and the adoption of the plan for an economic boycott. This last was to include both imports and exports, as well as the nonconsumption of articles already imported into America. Nonconsumption was to begin immediately and nonimportation to come into effect on December 1. In contrast, the prohibition on exports was to start only in September 1775, a concession to the South because of its dependency on overseas markets for its cash crops. The delay also amounted to recognition that nonimportation would have a more immediate effect than an export ban.

To enforce the boycott, each colony was to form an association, with local committees in every county, city, and town chosen "by those who are qualified to vote." They were to inspect warehouses, customs house books, and ships' holds. Any colonists not observing the boycott were to be shunned and have their names published in the newspapers. While not actively supporting violence, these steps sent a clear signal to "the enemies of American liberty" of what might happen. Previous nonimportation schemes had been weakened by the lack of consistent enforcement, which had created fears that some were profiting at the expense of others. The Continental Association, in contrast, was to operate in every colony at every level, in both town and country.

The association did not intend to be purely negative; it also planned to harness the moral sense of the American people by urging them to "encourage frugality, economy and industry" through the promotion of "agriculture, arts and the manufactures of this country." At the same time those taking the oath to the association were required to pledge that they would give up "every species of extravagence and dissipation, especially all horse racing, and all kinds of gaming, cock fighting, exhibition of shows, plays and other expensive diversions." The values of seventeenth-century dissent were still much in evidence.[5]

Among those zealously subscribing to the cause were fifty-one members of the Society of Patriotic Ladies at Edenton, North Carolina, who announced their determination to do everything possible to support "the public good." Never before had women organized so publicly for a political objective. Others were quick to do the same, helping to change women's consciousness about their role and place in society. As a Connecticut woman wrote, carding two pounds of wool had made her feel "Nationly."

---

[5] Such pledges proved especially hard for the Virginian gentry. See Rhys Isaac, *The Transformation of Virginia, 1740–1790* (Chapel Hill, 1995).

Meanwhile a revolution in political authority was taking place. In Massachusetts the assembly had used the Continental Congress's adoption of the Suffolk Resolves as authority to assume the powers of government. First, a committee of safety was formed with responsibity for the militia, one of its tasks being the organization of special companies of "minutemen" who were to be ready at a moment's notice in the event of an emergency. A treasurer was also appointed to supervise the collection of revenue for the purchase of weapons and other necessary items. Cannon were also seized, albeit peacefully, from Fort William and Mary at Portsmouth in neighboring New Hampshire. Other colonies took similar action. In Virginia, George Washington and the planters of Fairfax County began reorganizing the militia with money raised from a three-shilling tithe authorized by the colonial congress. Inspection committees everywhere were enforcing the association.

Conversely, the position of the royal government deteriorated rapidly. In Massachusetts the members of the new "mandamus" council were quickly intimidated either into resigning their appointments or fleeing to Boston to seek the protection of Gage's troops, an example followed by other royal officials who defied the authority of the colonial congress. Among those to succumb was Israel Williams, one of the Connecticut Valley "River Gods." His family and relatives had dominated Hampshire County since the time of John Pynchon. It was due to their influence that Hampshire County and neighboring Berkshire County played only a minor role during the Stamp Act and later kept the Boston committee of correspondence at bay. But times had changed, as Williams found when he tried to stay loyal to the royal administration. Many of the new towns beyond the river owed nothing to the old establishment. One day a mob of angry freeholders followed him to his home and locked him in a smokehouse for two days to consider his position, while a more radical and popular leadership took control under Joseph Hawley.[6]

However, most officials, for example justices of the peace and sheriffs, were happy to accept the new order. As members of the elite, it was in their interest to do so. Many served on the local committees to enforce the association. As the militias exercised, Gage found his authority restricted to Boston. Even here he felt obliged to start fortifying the approaches to the town. Occasional detachments went out to encourage the Loyalists, but with little effect. As Gage warned officials in London, he was no longer dealing with a rabble "but the freeholders and farmers of New England." His estimate by late fall was that twenty thousand troops were urgently needed to restore royal authority in the northern provinces. The only interim measure he could recommend was the suspension of the Intolerable Acts to calm the situation.

A physical clash was almost inevitable, given that North's ministry was still bent on coercion. Although he offered to suspend the taxing power of Parliament if each colony made a suitable contribution to the imperial exchequer, North simultaneously introduced an act restraining the trade of New England in response to the Continental Association.

---

[6]   Robert J. Taylor, *Western Massachusetts in the Revolution* (Providence, 1954), argues that radicalization of the region began only with the passage of the Intolerable Acts. Gregory H. Nobles, *Divisions Throughout the Whole: Politics and Society in Hampshire County, Massachusetts, 1740–1775* (New York, 1983), suggests that the erosion of the old elite's power began with the Great Awakening. But caution is required when considering the extent to which Hampshire County was radicalized, since Hawley was a cousin of Williams. A case of everything changing and nothing changing?

DOCUMENT 34

Massachusetts's account of Lexington and Concord, reprinted in Merrill Jensen, ed., *English Historical Documents*, vol. IX: *American Colonial Documents to 1776* (London, 1955), 828–9.

[The Massachusetts provincial congress recognized the importance of winning the propaganda battle by publishing its version of events. Most crucial was the need to establish that the British had fired first without provocation and had then committed further atrocities against a peaceful citizenry, thereby justifying colonial retaliation.]

By the clearest depositions relative to this transaction, it will appear that on the night preceding the 19 April instant, a body of the king's troops, under the command of Colonel Smith, were secretly landed at Cambridge with an apparent design to take or destroy the military and other stores provided for the defence of this colony, and deposited at Concord; that some inhabitants of the colony on the night aforesaid, whilst travelling peaceably on the road between Boston and Concord, were seized and greatly abused by armed men who appeared to be officers of General Gage's army; that the town of Lexington by these means was alarmed, and a company of the inhabitants mustered on the occasion; that the regular troops on their way to Concord marched into the said town of Lexington, and the said company, on their approach, began to disperse; that notwithstanding this, the regulars rushed on with great violence and first began hostilities by firing on said Lexington Company, whereby they killed eight and wounded several others, that the regulars continued to fire until those of said company who were neither killed nor wounded had made their escape; that Colonel Smith with the detachment then marched to Concord where a number of provincials were again fired on by the troops, and two of them killed, and several wounded, before the provincials fired on them; and that these hostile measures of the troops produced an engagement that lasted through the day in which many of the provincials, and more of the regular troops, were killed and wounded.

To give a particular account of the ravages of the troops as they retreated from Concord to Charlestown, would be very difficult, if not impracticable. Let it suffice to say that a great number of houses on the road were plundered and rendered unfit for use; several were burnt; women in childbed were driven by the soldiery naked into the streets, old men, peaceably in their houses were shot dead; and scenes exhibited as would disgrace the annals of the most uncivilized nation.

The ministers reasoned that if the New Englanders wanted to trade, they must do so solely with mainland Britain and Ireland, being excluded even from the Newfoundland fishery. The measure was shortly afterwards extended to all the other colonies, except New York and North Carolina, which were erroneously thought to have rejected the association's boycott. Plans were also made to send more troops. Finally, Gage was ordered in a letter dated January 27, 1775, to be more decisive in enforcing the Coercive Acts. The British

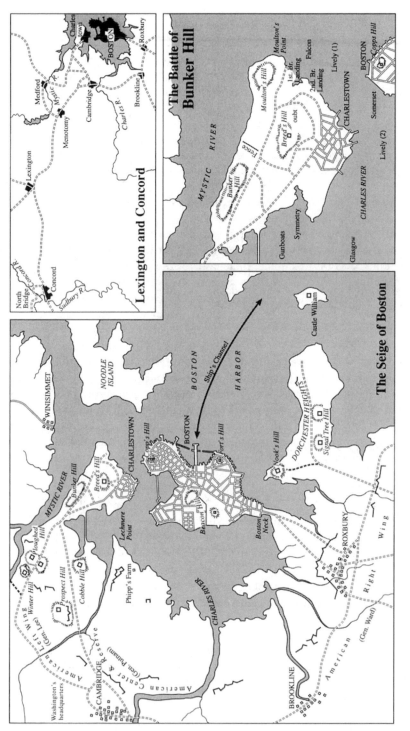

Lexington and Concord

The Battle of Bunker Hill

The Seige of Boston

Map 18 Military operations in the vicinity of Boston, April 1775–March 1776.

government was confident that a determined stand would soon bring the colonists to heel. As to their military capabilities, these were surely minimal.

Two principal options were open to Gage: either to seize the Patriot leaders or to capture some arms which they were known to be stockpiling at Concord and Worcester. Gage decided that the latter course was more realistic, and on the night of April 18 he ordered Colonel Francis Smith to march on Concord with a force of several hundred grenadiers and light infantry.

Despite all Gage's attempts at secrecy, news of the troops' departure was carried from Boston by Paul Revere, one of Boston's Sons of Liberty. In executing his mission, Revere was assisted by a network of Patriots who provided him with a boat to cross the harbor and a horse at Charleston so that he could raise the alarm on his way to Concord. Among those answering his warning were the militiamen of Lexington; and it was these men that Smith's forces encountered on their way early on the morning of April 19 at the edge of the town green. The advance guard under Major Pitcairn, not wishing to have a hostile force on its flank, ordered the colonials to disperse. When they hesitated in doing so, shooting broke out, and eight colonists were killed.[7] The British regulars then proceeded to Concord, where they found little except an increasing number of angry militia members. When some buildings were set ablaze, the Americans began firing from behind houses and other defensive positions. A running battle resulted as the British retreated back to Boston. Smith was saved only by the arrival of substantial reinforcements under Lord Percy, equipped with cannon. British casualties amounted to 273, the Americans suffered 92. The war had begun with an American success. Equally significant, Boston, the main center of British power, had been put under siege by the New England militias.

4   WAR AND INDEPENDENCE

The result of the events at Lexington and Concord was a general recognition on both sides that war was now inevitable. Congress had fortunately arranged to reconvene early in May 1775 to review the success of its previous measures. The new session opened on May 10, 1775, in a mood of grim determination.

The actions of the Massachusetts militia were immediately endorsed. However, the 15,000 men encamped around Boston needed to be organized into an effective army if the siege was to continue. It was accordingly agreed that a Continental Army should be formed consisting of 30,000 men, of whom 13,500 would be drawn from Massachusetts. The next question was that of command. The Massachusetts delegates, still eager to gain support from outside New England, suggested George Washington. Washington had a considerable reputation as a commander dating from his years of service during the French and Indian War. He had recently impressed Congress with his military knowledge, not least because of his attendance in full uniform. He had also offered to raise a regiment at his own expense. As a leading Virginian, his appointment would consolidate support from the southern provinces. The proposal met with approval.

---

[7]   There has been endless debate over which side fired the first shot and thus bears responsibility for the start of hostilities. The question is unimportant in the wider context, since both sides expected hostilities and were ready to fight. See Document 34.

Plate 57 George Washington in the uniform of a colonel in the Virginia Militia, by Charles Wilson Peale. Washington/Curtis/Lee Collection, Washington and Lee University, Lexington, Virginia.

A debate was then held on the question of whether the Indians and Canadians should be courted. The duplicity of appealing to the French inhabitants while demanding the rescission of the Quebec Act could not be entirely overlooked. On the other hand the advantage of depriving the British of an important base from which to launch an invasion also had to be considered. Congress therefore decided to overcome its prejudice against Catholics and appeal to the Canadians to join the American fight against despotism in "defence of our common liberty."

No such appeal was made to the American Indians. The assumption was that they could not be meaningful participants in the conflict. On the other hand they could cause great distress to the backcountry if recruited by the British. Congress decided therefore to encourage the Indians to be neutral. At a conference with the Six Nations in August 1775 the Iroquois were told that the struggle between Britain and the Americans was a "family affair" which did not concern them. As long as they stayed out of the conflict, the Americans would not invade Iroquoia and would also leave the roads open for trade. This suited the Iroquois admirably, since they could once more adopt their old policy of holding the balance between two competing forces. A similar conference was held at Pittsburgh in September with the Seneca, Wyandot, Shawnee, and Delaware peoples.

Meanwhile important events had been taking place in Boston. On June 17, two days after the appointment of Washington, Gage determined to test the Americans' resolve by attacking their positions on the Charlestown peninsula at Breed's Hill and nearby Bunker Hill. Again the Americans surprised the British with the stubbornness of their resistance. Two hundred and twenty-six redcoats were killed and a further 828 wounded before the colonials were driven back. The American losses were 140 killed and 271 wounded.

But fighting alone was not enough for victory. Winning the political argument was also essential. Congress accordingly published a defense of its actions entitled *A Declaration of the Causes and Necessity for Taking up Arms*. This document asserted that the Americans had had no choice but to defend their liberties. The alternative was enslavement by a despotic Parliament seeking absolute jurisdiction.

One consequence of the escalating conflict was that Congress now instructed Massachusetts to govern itself according to its 1691 charter. It was of course effectively doing this already, but congressional authorization constituted one more step toward independence. Ostensibly Congress was still seeking an accommodation whereby the colonies would retain their link with the Crown. But privately, many radical hardliners were beginning to see independence as the only outcome. Nevertheless, the moderate majority still feared a total separation from the mother country. To appease them, therefore, Congress agreed to petition George III once more, asking him to acknowledge the colonists' grievances. John Dickinson, now leader of the moderates, drafted the petition.[8]

Throughout the colonies the events of that spring led to the final collapse of royal government. Until Lexington and Concord, most governors and officials had continued in office, though increasingly sidelined by the local congresses, committees of correspondence, county courts, and town meetings. Now, like Governor Dunmore of Virginia, they fled to the nearest royal ship. They had little option once local Patriots generally followed the example of Mecklenburg County, North Carolina, declaring royal government to be "wholly

---

[8] Galloway had ruined himself politically by writing a pamphlet denouncing Congress and its membership.

suspended." Anyone there still holding a commission from the Crown was to be considered an enemy of the people.

The officials' flight did little to embolden the rest of the Loyalist population. Those refusing to subscribe to the Continental Association were usually confronted by a mob. Most quickly succumbed or found themselves in jail. The rest kept their heads down and waited for the Crown to deliver them.

Herein lay one of the Loyalists' principal weaknesses: their reluctance to take the initiative. As colonials, they felt it was not their place to lead. Another weakness was that the Loyalists tended to be drawn from minority ethnic groups like the Scots in North Carolina or religious minorities like the Anglicans and Quakers. In addition to being few in number they found cooperation, even among themselves, difficult. Another problem was the varying intensity of Loyalist feeling, which ranged from those who were prepared to die for their king to those whose convictions were no more than lukewarm. Thus although Loyalists numbered one-fifth of the population – and even constituted a majority in some parts of the middle colonies – they were almost universally ineffective. In the few areas where they did organize they were quickly crushed, as in the case of the Scottish Highlanders around Cape Fear, who were defeated in the Battle of Moore's Creek Bridge near Wilmington, North Carolina, in February 1776 before regular reinforcements could arrive.

The Loyalists' weakness and Patriots' conviction of the justice of their cause could have only one result, independence. Though there were still only a few who realized it, a number of factors were beginning to make a final break with Britain inevitable. One was the British response to events in America. Further bad news simply made the government in London more determined. In August 1775 it declared the colonies to be in a state of rebellion, which meant that the perpetrators of the conflict were all to be punished as traitors of the realm. Then in December 1775 the Prohibitory Act placed a total ban on colonial trade, making all ships and their cargoes liable to confiscation. The government also planned a large increase in both the army and navy, including the hiring of several thousand Hessian mercenaries.

The British ministers were encouraged in their course for several reasons: They believed that Britain was right; they had faith in its military and naval might; and they assumed that the vast majority of the colonists were naturally loyal. This was also the reaction of the British people at large, for as Franklin observed, most of them were petty tyrants on the issue of America.

The result of this British intransigence was to make the Patriots too more determined, driving them toward separation. Other factors conspired to the same conclusion. Near the end of 1775 the first informal contacts with the French revealed that no assistance would be forthcoming until the Americans declared themselves independent. And in November southern Patriots were shocked when Lord Dunmore offered freedom to Virginia's male slaves if they would join the royal forces. Northerners too feared that the British were recruiting the Mohawk Indians to attack the backcountry. Everyone was appalled by the decision to recruit German mercenaries to shed American blood. To the colonists it seemed that the British were prepared to go to any lengths to make the colonists submit.

The response of the Patriots was to widen hostilities. As early as May 1775 forces from Connecticut and Vermont had seized Fort Ticonderoga.[9] In the fall Congress ordered an

---

[9] The Vermont forces were as keen to secure weapons for possible use against New York as against the forces of the Crown.

attack on Canada, despite the lack of any positive response from the French Canadians. Though the assault on Quebec by Benedict Arnold and Richard Montgomery was ultimately unsuccessful it raised the stakes. Both sides accepted that it was now a war with no limits, as the bombardment and burning of Norfolk by British forces in January 1776 demonstrated. Not long afterwards Congress decided it too would "engage the Indians in the service of the United Colonies."

Of paramount importance was Washington's success in forcing the British out of Boston. The key to his victory lay in the earlier capture of Ticonderoga. Some of the cannon seized there had been dragged in winter through very difficult terrain to the Dorchester heights overlooking Boston. The Patriots' appearance there early in March 1776 made the British position untenable. Unwilling to risk another Bunker Hill, General Howe, the new commander in chief, determined to withdraw. Boston, the center of rebellion, was thus freed. It was a considerable boost to American confidence, not least on the issue of independence.

By now events off the battlefield had changed the climate of public opinion. Until the spring of 1776 the moderate majority remained apprehensive about severing relations with Britain. One reason was that there were no immediate precedents for such an act. The Dutch were the most recent example of a people who had defied an imperial power when they declared independence from Spain, but that revolt had occurred two centuries ago. The classical Roman Republic, which many Americans affected to admire, dated from even further back in history. The theory of natural rights, though a reassuring concept, provided no practical guidance on how to achieve independence. If anything, it threatened to plunge the American people into a state of chaos – without institutions, law, or property – the exact opposite of what the colonists were fighting for.

It was to dispel such fears that Thomas Paine, a former excise officer and son of an English Quaker, produced his pamphlet *Common Sense*. Unlike the learned contributions of John Adams, James Wilson, and other colonial commentators, it was written with great clarity and in plain language that all could understand. Paine pointed out that the British monarchy had originated not in a just compact but through conquest by the Normans. Kings always brought misery, not justice, to their peoples; and the "Royal Brute of Britain" was no exception. Moreover, the revered British constitution was a mockery, since one branch of government (the executive) had corrupted the other two. As to the dangers facing Americans once they separated from Britain, these were grossly exaggerated. The common people were far too sensible of their own interest to throw the country into disorder. Reconciliation in any case was impossible after the events of April 19, 1775. A declaration of independence on the other hand would bring foreign assistance. Americans had a glittering future in prospect and they should seize it. It was time to reject Europe, which represented the past, and embrace a New World based on simplicity, equity, and reason.

The pamphlet sold a remarkable one hundred thousand copies within three months of being published. Its popularity can be attributed partly to the fact that Paine successfully dispelled the most commonly held fears regarding republican government and, even more important, presented a convincing picture of republicanism as a desirable political system. Readers now realized that republicanism meant not simply a world without monarchs and other privileged orders like hereditary aristocracies and established churches but a society in which merit was recognized; disinterest guided leaders' action; and the people were devoted to simplicity, frugality, and civic virtue. For these reasons America could and *would* succeed where the republics of classical antiquity had failed.

The way was now clear for the irrevocable step to be taken. Early in April 1776 Congress announced the opening of America's ports to the shipping of all nations. This declaration did not simply defy the Prohibitory Act, it overturned the entire mercantilist navigation system so essential to the British view of empire. Six days later North Carolina made the first explicit call for independence.

Equally important in effecting a final rupture was the readiness of each colony to consider new republican forms of government, in which sovereignty lay with the people rather than the king. Congress accepted the necessity for this on May 15, 1776, when it instructed all the colonies to adopt governments "best conducive to the happiness and safety of their constituents in particular and America in general." The matter had already been considered by John Adams in his pamphlet, *Thoughts on Government*, which he wrote to counter some of Paine's more extreme ideas. Adams believed that there should be three branches of government as in Britain: an executive, legislature, and judiciary. However, these should be separate and equal to check and balance one another, preventing the abuses which had so disfigured the British constitution. All positions should be filled by annual popular election.

The first colony to metamorphose into a state was New Hampshire. Its constitution of January 1776 was very conservative, however, the main innovation being a provision for the election of a president by the legislature in place of an appointed royal governor. Otherwise its frame of government was similar to that of Massachusetts under the 1629 charter, making New Hampshire a self-governing commonwealth.

More significant was the redrafting of the Virginian constitution. The principal author of this was George Mason, a wealthy planter and slave owner. For Mason the most important consideration was Locke's concept of government as a trust exercised on behalf of the people. Consequently Virginia began its constitution making with a bill of rights, not a frame of government. But unlike the 1689 English bill, which was more concerned with the privileges of Parliament, Mason's document focused on the rights of the individual as derived from the immutable laws of nature. Hence together with their former rights as British subjects, Mason gave Virginians freedom of the press, access to office holding, the franchise (for those having sufficient "permanent common interest with and attachment to the community"), and "the free exercise of religion."

Only then did Mason and his colleagues define the three branches of government. However, they ignored Adams's advice about the separation of powers in the case of the executive and legislature, preferring to make the former dependent on the latter. To Mason and most Patriots at this time, it was the powers of the executive that seemed in most need of restraint.

The Virginia state constitution set an example which most other fledgling states followed during the next few months and years. Mason's intention was to conserve what the people of Virginia already enjoyed. The outcome was a mixture of radical and traditional concepts of government. The House of Burgesses became a House of Delegates; the council became a senate. However, the latter lost its executive and judicial functions to maintain the principle of the separation of powers. The franchise remained the same, as it did essentially in all the budding states. Citizens still had to own property or pay taxes to be able to vote, though the minimum was reduced in some cases. One main difference in the seven new constitutions drafted by July 1776 was that restrictions were placed on the executive branch. In Virginia the governor was now to be chosen by joint ballot of the legislature; and governors elsewhere were to be closely scrutinized by the people's representatives. In addition all public figures were to be answerable to the people by means of frequent election. Herein lay the most revolutionary feature of the new constitutions. Never before had sovereignty been placed so completely in the hands of the people. Never before had the powers of government been written down so that those in authority could be held to account.[10]

However, in assessing the extent to which the state constitutions broke with the past it must be remembered that they granted few, if any, rights to women, African-Americans, and American Indians. When Abigail Adams wrote to John Adams in March 1776 that Congress should draft a new code of laws remembering "the ladies," he laughed. "In Practice you know we are the subjects. We have only the Name of Masters" and to give up that "would completely subject us to the Despotism of the Peticoat." His jesting ignored the role that women would play in mobilizing their menfolk for military service, sustaining a war economy, and ensuring that farms and businesses were managed effectively. But however dismissive Adams tried to be, the subject had been raised, something inconceivable twenty years earlier.

There was a similar lack of rights accorded to African-Americans. The only offer of liberation was that made by Lord Dunmore. The risk for the several hundred who answered his call was high. They first had to find Dunmore, who after a defeat at Great Bridge in December 1775 was largely confined to a warship. Even then they had no guarantee that the British would honor their promise, while recapture was certain to mean severe punishment at the hands of former masters. Nevertheless, many were glad to make the attempt. Some two hundred gathered on Sullivan's Island at the mouth of Charleston harbor and a similar number on Tybee Island near Savannah to await the British. Unfortunately the local Patriots arrived first, resulting in the massacre of a number of those assembled. But even more took advantage of the confusion to search for a better life of their own. Ironically a few found service with the Continental army, despite Congress's ban on black recruitment in November 1775. Manpower was too scarce, as Washington pointed out.

The attitudes of European Americans on the issue of slavery were in fact starting to change. While drafting the Declaration of Independence, Jefferson wanted to include a denunciation of George III for allowing the slave trade, but he was overruled by the other southern delegates, who saw this as a condemnation of slavery itself. But Jefferson was not alone in his views; many others recognized that the Patriot rhetoric of liberty was incompatible with the enslavement of African-Americans. A ban on the importation of slaves had already been agreed as part of the Continental Association, while some representatives even began to talk about ending slavery itself through gradual manumission.[11]

---

[10] The radical nature of the Revolution has been much debated by historians. Nineteenth- and twentieth-century Whig nationalists like George Bancroft, Charles McIlwain, and Robert E. Brown emphasized the uniquely democratic nature of the Revolution. Progressives like Carl Becker, Charles Beard, and Arthur Schlesinger, Sr., argued that it was essentially a battle between reactionary elites and a democratic majority. More recently Gordon S. Wood has argued in *The Radicalism of the American Revolution* (New York, 1992) that the Revolution began conservatively but later had revolutionary consequences.

[11] Vermont claimed to be the first state to ban slavery, though it had yet to achieve statehood in 1777. Pennsylvania provided for gradual abolition in a 1780 statute declaring that all children born thereafter to slaves were free. Massachusetts achieved full abolition in 1783 when its courts ruled that the 1780 constitution declaring that "all men are born free and equal" had made slavery illegal. In the South some planters like George Washington arranged to manumit their slaves after their death as part of the arrangements for their estates.

DOCUMENT 35

Massachusetts slaves argue for freedom, reprinted in Richard D. Brown, ed., *Major Problems in the Era of the American Revolution, 1760–1791: Documents and Essays* (Lexington, Mass., 1992), 308–9.

[The constant talk about liberty and resisting oppression even affected the African-American community. In this petition four slaves ask for concessions so that they can buy their freedom and return to Africa.]

Sir, the efforts made by the legislature of this province in their last sessions to free themselves from [British] slavery, gave us, who are in that deplorable state, a high degree of satisfaction. We expect great things from men who have made such a noble stand against the designs of their *fellow-men* to enslave them. We cannot but wish and hope Sir, that you will have the same grand object, we mean civil and religious liberty, in view in your next session. The divine spirit of *freedom*, seems to fire every humane breast on this continent, except such as are bribed to assist in executing the execrable plan [of the ministry].

We are very sensible that it would be highly detrimental to our present masters, if we were allowed to demand all that of *right* belongs to us for past services; this we disclaim. Even the *Spaniards*, who have not those sublime ideas of freedom that English men have, are conscious that they have no right to all the services of their fellow-men, we mean the *Africans*, whom they have purchased with their money; therefore they allow them one day in a week to work for themselves, to enable them to earn money to purchase the residue of their time, which they have a right to demand in such portions as they are able to pay for (a due appraizement of their services being first made, which always stands at the purchase money). We do not pretend to dictate to you Sir, or to the Honorable Assembly, of which you are a member. We acknowledge our obligations to you for what you have already done, but as the people of this province seem to be actuated by the principles of equity and justice, we cannot but expect your house will again take our deplorable case into serious consideration, and give us that ample relief which, *as men*, we have a natural right to. . . .

We are willing to submit to such regulations and laws, as may be made relative to us, until we leave the province, which we determine to do as soon as we can, from our joint labors procure money to transport ourselves to some part of the Coast of *Africa*, where we propose a settlement.

In contrast, the Indian peoples received almost no consideration. No state accorded them citizenship. Pennsylvania typically referred to them as "savages," whom George III was using to reduce the province to an "abject submission." Similar sentiments were shortly to be expressed in the Declaration of Independence, which refers to the natives merely as "merciless Indian savages."

Plate 58   Portrait of Thomas Jefferson, engraving by Cornelius Tiebout after painting
by R. Peale, 1801. The Library of Congress, Washington, D.C.

Meanwhile Congress began its own metamorphosis into a more permanent and suitably republican institution. Two steps were required: the drafting of rules for its governance and an announcement to the world that America had ended its connection with Britain. Both steps were effectively agreed to on June 7 following a vote in favor of Richard Henry Lee's motion "That these United Colonies are, and of right ought to be, free and independent states."

Both tasks were delegated to committees. The committee to draft a "plan of confederation" was headed by John Dickinson and proved to have the more difficult task, since there were still deep divisons among the newly declared states. These were reinforced by fears about creating a new central government which might be as oppressive as the old. Nevertheless it was clear that some degree of unity must be effected if they were to defend their independence.

The committee on independence asked Thomas Jefferson to prepare a draft. He divided his document into two parts, beginning with a brief Lockean statement on the natural right of a people to independence when their inalienable rights were denied by an existing government. The second, more lengthy section listed the specific crimes George III had perpetrated, thereby nullifying his contractual right to govern the American people and making a republican frame of government necessary. Parliament was not mentioned, except indirectly as a "jurisdiction foreign to our Constitution." Of the twenty-seven charges enumerated, nine involved the subjection of the colonies to that foreign body; another six concerned recent punitive actions; eleven criticized restrictions on the colonial legislatures; three concerned abridgements of personal liberty; three declared the unconstitutionality of a standing army; three described interference with the judiciary; and one objected to the appointment of placemen. None mentioned the navigation laws or religious oppression; the draft emphasized that the Revolution was primarily about constitutional rights, not economic or sectarian interests.[12]

Congress voted for independence on July 2 and accepted the declaration itself on July 4, having it publicly proclaimed for the first time on July 8 in Philadelphia. It still had to be made good: no foreign nation was yet ready to brave the wrath of Britain by recognizing the American states; large numbers of Loyalists were actively opposed; and the British were about to invade New York to reassert royal authority. Nor could anyone tell where these events would lead. Several states still had to write their constitutions; rampant economic and political differences existed among the signatories; and everywhere civil strife was in the offing. The fragile bonds of society appeared close to breaking, promising a revolution of the worst kind.

Nevertheless, most Patriots were momentarily joyful. They sensed that Paine was right. Royal authority and the connection with Britain were like the pages of an old almanac, a thing of the past. A new book was ready to hand, titled the United States of America. It was something to celebrate and defend.

---

[12] For the view that mercantilism was a cause of the Revolution, see chapter 9, footnote 8. For a recent view that religion was a major factor, see J. C. D. Clark, *The Language of Liberty, 1660–1832: Political Discourse and Social Dynamics in the Anglo-American World* (Cambridge, England, 1993). See also Ronald Hoffman and Peter J. Albert, eds, *Religion in a Revolutionary Age* (Charlottesville, 1994).

Select Bibliography _____

BIBLIOGRAPHIES

David L. Ammerman and Philip D. Morgan, *Books about Early America: 2001 Titles* (Williamsburg, 1989).
Frank Freidel, ed., *Harvard Guide to American History* (Cambridge, Mass., 1974).

GENERAL TEXTS

Charles M. Andrews, *The Colonial Period of American History*, 4 vols (New Haven, 1934–8. Reprinted 1964).
Bernard Bailyn, *The Peopling of British North America: An Introduction* (New York, 1986).
Daniel Boorstin, *The Americans: The Colonial Experience* (New York, 1958).
Jon Butler, *Becoming America: The Revolution before 1776* (Cambridge, Mass., 2000).
Nicholas Canny, ed., *The Oxford History of the British Empire*, Vol. 1: *The Origins of Empire: British Overseas Enterprise to the Close of the Seventeenth Century* (Oxford and New York, 1998).
Edward Countryman, *Americans: A Collision of Histories* (New York, 1996).
Jack P. Greene, and J. R. Pole, eds, *Colonial British America: Essays in the New History of the Early Modern Era* (Baltimore, 1984).
David D. Hall, John M. Murrin, and Thad W. Tate, eds, *Saints and Revolutionaries: Essays on Early American History* (New York, 1984).
David Hawke, *The Colonial Experience* (Indianapolis, 1966).
David Freeman Hawke, *Everyday Life in Early America* (New York, 1988).
Jacob Judd, *Colonial America: A Basic History* (Krieger, 1998).
Michael Kammen, *People of Paradox: An Inquiry Concerning the Origins of American Civilization* (New York, 1972).
Stanley N. Katz, John M. Murrin, and Douglas Greenberg, eds, *Colonial America: Essays in Politics and Social Development*, 4th edn (New York, 1993).
Paul Robert Lucas, *American Odyssey, 1607–1789* (Englewood Cliffs, 1984).
Anthony McFarlane, *The British in the Americas, 1480–1815* (London, 1994).
Peter J. Marshall, ed., *The Oxford History of the British Empire*, Vol. 2: *The Eighteenth Century* (Oxford, 1998).
Donald William Meinig, *The Shaping of America: A Geographical Perspective on 500 Years of History*, Vol. 1: *Atlantic America, 1492–1800* (New Haven, 1986).
Gary B. Nash, *Red, White, and Black: The Peoples of Early America* (Englewood Cliffs, 1974).
R. C. Simmons, *The American Colonies from Settlement to Independence* (New York, 1976).

Ian K. Steele and Nancy L. Rhoden, *The Human Tradition in Colonial America* (Wilmington, 2000).
Esmond Wright, *The Search for Liberty: From Origins to Independence* (Oxford, 1994).

PRINTED DOCUMENTARY COLLECTIONS

James Axtell, *The Indian Peoples of Eastern America: A Documentary History of the Sexes* (New York, 1981).
Bernard Bailyn and Jane N. Garrett, eds, *Pamphlets of the American Revolution, 1750–1765* (Cambridge, Mass., 1965).
Warren M. Billings, ed., *The Old Dominion in the Seventeenth Century: A Documentary History of Virginia, 1606–1689* (Chapel Hill, 1975).
Paul Boyer and Stephen Nissenbaum, eds, *The Salem Witchcraft Papers: Verbatim Transcripts of the Legal Documents of the Salem Witchcraft Outbreak of 1692*, 3 vols (New York, 1977).
Richard D. Brown, *Major Problems in the Era of the American Revolution, 1760–1791: Documents and Essays* (Lexington, Mass., 1992).
Richard L. Bushman, ed., *The Great Awakening: Documents on the Revival of Religion, 1740–1745* (Chapel Hill, 1989).
Elizabeth Donnan, ed., *Documents Illustrative of the History of the Slave Trade to America*, 4 vols (Washington, 1930–5).
M. Farrand, ed., *Laws and Liberties of Massachusetts* (Cambridge, Mass., 1929).
Jack P. Greene, ed., *Settlements to Society, 1584–1763* (New York, 1966).
Alan Heimert and Andrew Delbanco, eds, *The Puritans in America: A Narrative Anthology* (Cambridge, Mass., 1985).
Merrill Jensen, ed., *English Historical Documents*, Vol. IX: *American Colonial Documents to 1776* (New York, 1955).
W. Keith Kavenagh, *Foundations of Colonial America: A Documentary History*, 3 vols (New York, 1973. Paperback edition, 6 vols, 1983).
Karen Ordahl Kupperman, ed., *Major Problems in American Colonial History: Documents and Essays* (Lexington, Mass., 1993).
Donald S. Lutz, ed., *Colonial Origins of the American Constitution: A Study in Legal, and Social History and Philosophy* (Indianapolis, 1998).
Perry Miller and T. H. Johnson, *The Puritans: A Source-Book of their Writings*, 2 vols (New York, 1938).
David B. Quinn, ed., *New American World: A Documentary History of North America to 1612*, 5 vols (New York, 1979).
Willie Lee Rose, ed., *A Documentary History of Slavery in North America* (New York, 1976).

DIARIES, JOURNALS, AND CONTEMPORARY HISTORIES

Carl Bridenbaugh, ed., *Gentleman's Progress: The Itinerarium of Dr Alexander Hamilton, 1744* (Chapel Hill, 1948).
Adolph B. Benson, ed., *Peter Kalm's Travels into North America: The English Version of 1770* (New York, 1937).
Robert Beverley, *The History and Present State of Virginia* [1705], edited by Louis B. Wright (Chapel Hill, 1947).
Colonel Benjamin Church, *Diary of King Philip's War, 1675–1676*, edited by Alan and Mary Simpson (Chester, 1975).
Everett Emerson, ed., *Letters from New England: The Massachusetts Bay Colony, 1629–1638* (Amherst, 1976).

Oscar Handlin and John Clive, eds, *Journey to Pennsylvania* [1756, Gottlieb Mittelberger] (Cambridge, Mass., 1960).

John Lawson, *A New Voyage to Carolina* [1709], edited by Hugh Talmage Lefler (Chapel Hill, 1967).

Michael McGiffert, ed., *God's Plot: The Paradoxes of Puritan Piety, Being the Autobiography and Journal of Thomas Shepard* [1640] (Amherst, 1972).

Alden T. Vaughan and Edward W. Clark, eds, *Puritans Among the Indians: Accounts of Captivity and Redemption, 1676–1724* (Cambridge, Mass., 1981).

REFERENCE WORKS

Jacob Ernest Cooke, *Encyclopedia of the North American Colonies*, 3 vols (New York, 1993).

Emory Elliott, ed., *Dictionary of Literary Biography*, Vol. XXIV: *American Colonial Writers, 1606–1734*; Vol. XXXI: *American Colonial Writers, 1735–1781* (Detroit, 1984–85).

John Mark Faragher, *The Encyclopedia of Colonial and Revolutionary America* (New York, 1990).

Alan Gallay, ed., *Colonial Wars of North America, 1512–1763: An Encyclopedia, Military History of the United States*, Vol. 5 (New York, 1996).

Daniel G. Reid et al., eds, *Dictionary of Christianity in America* (Downers Grove, 1990).

William C. Sturtevant, ed., *Handbook of North American Indians*, vols 1–15 (Washington, 1975–).

Alden T. Vaughan, ed., *Early American Indian Documents, Treaties and Laws, 1607–1789*, vols 1–20 (Frederick, 1983).

HISTORIOGRAPHICAL WORKS

James Axtell, "Columbian Encounters: 1992–1995," *William and Mary Quarterly*, LII, 1995, 650–96.

James Axtell, "Europeans, Indians and the Age of Discovery in American History Textbooks," *American Historical Review*, XCII, 1987, 621–32.

James Axtell, "The Ethnohistory of Early America: A Review Essay," *William and Mary Quarterly*, XXXV, 1978, 110–44.

Bernard Bailyn, "The Challenge of Modern Historiography," *American Historical Review*, LXXXVII, 1982, 1–24.

Richard R. Beeman, "The New Social History and the Search for Community in Colonial America," *American Quarterly*, XXIX, 1977, 422–43.

Wayne Bodle, "Themes and Directions in Middle Colonies Historiography, 1980–1994," *William and Mary Quarterly*, LI, 1994, 355–88.

Jon Butler, "The Future of American Religious History: Prospectus, Agenda, Transatlantic *Problématique*," *William and Mary Quarterly*, XLII, 1985, 167–83.

Nicholas Canny, "Writing Atlantic History; or, Reconfiguring the History of Colonial British America," *Journal of American History*, LXXXVI, 2000, 1093–14.

E. Wayne Carp, "Early American Military History: A Review of Recent Work," *Virginia Magazine of History and Biography*, XCIV, 1986, 259–84.

Charles L. Cohen, "The Post-Puritan Paradigm of Early American History," *William and Mary Quarterly*, LIV, 1997, 695–722.

Richard S. Dunn, "The Social History of Early New England," *American Quarterly*, XXIV, 1972, 661–79.

Douglas Greenberg, "The Middle Colonies in Recent American Historiography," *William and Mary Quarterly*, XXXVI, 1979, 396–427.

Philip F. Gura, "The Study of Colonial American Literature, 1966–1987: A Vade Mecum," *William and Mary Quarterly*, XLV, 1988, 305–41.

David D. Hall, "On Common Ground: The Coherence of American Puritan Studies," *William and Mary Quarterly*, XLIV, 1987, 193–229.

David D. Hall, "Witchcraft and the Limits of Interpretation," *New England Quarterly*, LVIII, 1985, 253–81.

Don Higginbotham, "The Early American Way of War: Reconnaissance and Appraisal," *William and Mary Quarterly*, XLIV, 1987, 230–73.

Richard R. Johnson, "Charles McClean Andrews and the Invention of American Colonial History," *William and Mary Quarterly*, XLIII, 1986, 519–41.

James H. Merrell, "Some Thoughts on Colonial Historians and American Indians," *William and Mary Quarterly*, XLVI, 1989, 94–119.

Richard Middleton, "British Historians and the American Revolution," *Journal of American Studies*, V, 1971, 43–58.

H. C. Porter, "Reflections on the Ethnohistory of Early Colonial North America," *Journal of American Studies*, XVI, 1982, 243–54.

Anita H. Rutman, "Still Planting the Seeds of Hope: The Recent Literature of the Early Chesapeake Region," *Virginia Magazine of History and Biography*, XCV, 1987, 3–24.

Thad W. Tate, "The Seventeenth Century Chesapeake and its Modern Historians," in Thad W. Tate and David L. Ammerman, eds, *The Chesapeake in the Seventeenth Century: Essays on Anglo-American Society* (Chapel Hill, 1979).

Peter H. Wood, "I Did the Best I Could for My Day: The Study of Early Black History during the Second Reconstruction, 1960 to 1976," *William and Mary Quarterly*, XXXV, 1978: 185–225.

CHAPTER 1 THE AGE OF EUROPEAN EXPLORATION

General

Jared Diamond, *Guns, Germs and Steel: A Short History of Everybody for the Last 13,000 Years* (London, 1997).

The Vikings, Spain, and Portugal

Emerson W. Baker et al., *American Beginnings: Exploration, Culture and Cartography in the Land of Norumbega* (Lincoln, 1994).

C. R. Boxer, *The Portuguese Seaborne Empire, 1415–1825* (London, 1968).

Paul E. Hoffman, *A New Andalucia and a Way to the Orient: The American Southeast during the Sixteenth Century* (Baton Rouge, 1990).

Gwyn Jones, *The Norse Atlantic Saga, Being the Norse Voyages of Discovery and Settlement to Iceland, Greenland and America* (New York, 1986).

Karen Ordahl Kupperman, ed., *America in European Consciousness, 1493–1750* (Chapel Hill, 1994).

L. N. McAlister, *Spain and Portugal in the New World, 1492–1700* (Oxford, 1984).

Samuel Eliot Morison, *The European Discovery of America*, 2 vols (New York, 1971).

Anthony Padgen, *Lords of all the World: Ideologies of Empire in Spain, Britain, and France, 1500–c.1800* (New Haven, 1995).

J. H. Parry, *The Discovery of South America* (New York, 1979).

J. H. Parry, *The Spanish Seaborne Empire* (Berkeley, 1990).

David Beers Quinn, *North America from Earliest Discovery to First Settlements: The Norse Voyages to 1612* (New York, 1975).

A. J. R. Russell-Wood, *A World on the Move: The Portuguese in Africa, Asia, and America, 1415–1808* (New York, 1993).

Erik Wahlgren, *The Vikings and America* (New York, 1986).

David J. Weber, *The Spanish Frontier in North America* (New Haven, 1992).

Robert S. Weddle, *The Gulf of Mexico in North American Discovery, 1500–1685* (College Station, 1985).

England

K. R. Andrews, N. P. Canny, and P. E. H. Hair, eds, *The Westward Enterprise: English Adventurers in Ireland, the Atlantic, and America 1480–1650* (Detroit, 1979).

Angus Calder, *Revolutionary Empire: The Rise of the English-speaking Empires from the Fifteenth Century to the 1780s* (New York, 1981).

Nicholas P. Canny, *The Elizabethan Conquest of Ireland: A Pattern Established, 1565–1576* (New York, 1976).

Nicholas P. Canny, ed., *Europeans on the Move: Studies on European Migration, 1500–1800* (Oxford, 1994).

Nicholas P. Canny, "The Ideology of English Colonization: From Ireland to America," *William and Mary Quarterly*, XXX, 1973, 575–98.

Nicholas P. Canny and Anthony Pagden, eds, *Colonial Identity in the Atlantic World, 1500–1800* (Princeton, 1987).

J. H. Elliott, *The Old World and the New, 1492–1650* (Cambridge, England, 1970).

R. Hakluyt, *The Principal Navigations, Voyages, Traffiques and Discoveries of the English Nation* (London, 1600. Reprinted 1927).

Karen Ordahl Kupperman, *Roanoke: The Abandoned Colony* (Totowa, 1984).

G. J. Marcus, *The Conquest of the North Atlantic* (New York, 1981).

David B. Quinn, *England and the Discovery of America, 1481–1620* (New York, 1974).

David B. Quinn, *The New American World: A Documentary History*, 5 vols (New York, 1979).

David B. Quinn, *Set Fair for Roanoke: Voyages and Colonies, 1584–1606* (Chapel Hill, 1985).

David B. Quinn and A. N. Ryan, *England's Sea Empire, 1550–1642* (London, 1983).

CHAPTER 2   THE PEOPLES OF EASTERN NORTH AMERICA

General

William W. Fitzhugh, ed., *Cultures in Contact: The Impact of European Contacts on Native American Institutions,* A.D. *1000–1800* (Washington, 1985).

Robert S. Grumet, *Historic Contact: Indian Peoples and Colonists in Today's Northeastern United States in the Sixteenth through Eighteenth Centuries* (Norman, 1995).

Bruce G. Trigger, ed., *Handbook of North American Indians*, Vol. 15: *Northeast* (Washington, 1978).

Bruce G. Trigger and Wilcomb E. Washburn, eds, *The Cambridge History of the Native Peoples of the Americas*. Vol. I: *North America* (New York, 1996).

Wilcomb E. Washburn, *The Indian in America* (New York, 1975).

The Precontact Background

Brian M. Fagan, *Ancient North America: The Archeology of a Continent* (London, 1990).

Jesse D. Jennings, ed., *Ancient North Americans* (San Francisco, 1978).

Alvin M. Josephy, ed., *America in 1492: The Worlds of the Indian Peoples before the Arrival of Columbus* (New York, 1992).

Timothy R. Pauketat and Thomas E. Emerson, eds, *Cahokia: Domination and Ideology in the Mississippian World* (Lincoln, 1997).

Lynda Norene Shaffer, *Native Americans before 1492: The Moundbuilding Centers of the Eastern Woodlands* (Armonk, NY, 1992).

Bruce D. Smith, ed., *Mississippian Emergence: The Evolution of Agricultural Societies in the Eastern Woodlands* (Washington, 1990).

The Columbian Impact

Alfred W. Crosby, *The Columbian Exchange: Biological and Cultural Consequences of 1492* (Westport, 1972).

Alfred W. Crosby, "Virgin Soil Epidemics as a Factor in the Aboriginal Depopulation in America," *William and Mary Quarterly*, XXXIII, 1976, 289–99.

John D. Daniels, "The Indian Population of North America in 1492," *William and Mary Quarterly*, XLIX, 1992, 298–320.

William M. Denevan, ed., *The Native Population of the Americas in 1492* (Madison, 1976).

Henry F. Dobyns, *Their Number Become Thinned: Native American Population Dynamics in Eastern North America* (Knoxville, 1983).

Wilbur R. Jacobs, "The Tip of an Iceberg: Pre-Columbian Indian Demography and Some Implications for Revisionism," *William and Mary Quarterly*, XXXI, 1974, 123–32.

Clark Spencer Larsen and George R. Milner, *In the Wake of Contact: Biological Responses to Conquest* (New York, 1994).

Neil Salisbury, "The Indians Old World: Native Americans and the Coming of Europeans," *William and Mary Quarterly*, LIII, 1996, 435–58.

Marvin T. Smith, "Aboriginal Depopulation in the Post Contact Southeast," in Charles Hudson and Carmen Chaves Tesser, eds, *The Forgotten Centuries: Indians and Europeans in the American South, 1521–1704* (Athens, 1994), 257–75.

David E. Stannard, *American Holocaust: Columbus and the Conquest of the New World* (New York, 1992).

Russell Thornton, *American Indian Holocaust and Survival: A Population History since 1492* (Norman, 1987).

John Verano and Douglas Ubelaker, *Disease and Demography in the Americas* (Washington, 1992).

Eastern North America, circa 1600

James Axtell, *After Columbus: Essays in the Ethnohistory of Colonial North America* (New York, 1988).

James Axtell, *Beyond 1492: Encounters in Colonial North America* (New York, 1992).

James Axtell, *The European and the Indian: Essays in the Ethnohistory of Colonial North America* (New York, 1981).

James Axtell, ed., *The Indian Peoples of Eastern America: A Documentary History of the Sexes* (New York, 1981).

James Axtell, *The Invasion Within: The Contest of Cultures in Colonial North America* (New York, 1985).

Kathleen J. Bragdon, *Native Peoples of Southern New England, 1500–1650* (Norman, 1996).

Colin G. Calloway, *New Worlds for All: Indians, Europeans, and the Remaking of Early America* (Baltimore, 1997).

William Cronon, *Changes in the Land: Indians, Colonists and the Ecology of New England* (New York, 1983).

Charlotte Gradie, "Spanish Jesuits in Virginia: The Mission that Failed," *Virginia Magazine of History and Biography*, XCVI, 1988, 131–56.

Charles Hudson and Carmen Chaves Tesser, eds, *The Forgotten Centuries: Indians and Europeans in the American South, 1521–1704* (Athens, 1994).

Paul Hulton, *America 1585: The Complete Drawings of John White* (Chapel Hill, 1984).

Shepard Krech III, ed., *Indians, Animals and the Fur Trade: A Critique of "Keepers of the Game"* (Athens, 1981).

Karen Ordahl Kupperman, *Indians and English: Facing off in Early America* (Cornell, 2000).

Karen Ordahl Kupperman, *Settling with the Indians: The Meetings of English and Indian Cultures in America, 1580–1640* (Totowa, 1980).

Calvin Martin, *Keepers of the Game: Indian–Animal Relationships and the Fur Trade* (Berkeley, 1978).

Jerald T. Milanich, *The Timucua* (Cambridge, Mass., 1996).

Michael Leroy Oberg, *Dominion and Civility: English Imperialism and Native America, 1585–1685* (Ithaca, 1999).

H. C. Porter, *The Inconstant Savage: England and the North American Indian, 1500–1660* (London, 1976).

Stephen R. Potter, *Commoners, Tribute and Chiefs: The Development of Algonquian Culture in the Potomac Valley* (Charlottesville, 1993).

Helen C. Rountree, ed., *Powhatan Foreign Relations, 1500–1722* (Charlottesville, 1993).

Helen C. Rountree, *The Powhatan Indians of Virginia: Their Traditional Culture* (Norman, 1989).

Helen C. Rountree and Thomas E. Davidson, *Eastern Shore Indians of Virginia and Maryland* (Charlottesville, 1997).

Howard S. Russell, *Indian New England before the Mayflower* (Hanover, 1980).

Neil Salisbury, *Manitou and Providence: Indians, Europeans and the Making of New England, 1500–1643* (New York, 1982).

Timothy Silver, *A New Face on the Countryside: Indians, Colonists and Slaves in South Atlantic Forests, 1500–1800* (New York, 1990).

Bruce C. Trigger, *Natives and Newcomers: Canada's "Heroic Age" Reconsidered* (Montreal, 1985).

Alden T. Vaughan, *New England Encounters: Indians and Euroamericans, ca. 1600–1850* (Boston, 2000).

Peter H. Wood, Gregory A. Waselkov, and M. Thomas Hatley, *Powhatan's Mantle: Indians in the Colonial Southeast* (Lincoln, 1989).

CHAPTER 3   THE ENGLISH ARRIVE: VIRGINIA, 1607–60

The Virginia Company

Charles M. Andrews, *The Colonial Period of American History: The Settlements*, 4 vols (Yale, 1964).

Philip L. Barbour, *Pocahontas and her World* (Boston, 1970).

Philip L. Barbour, *The Three Worlds of Captain John Smith* (Boston, 1964).

Warren M. Billings, *The Old Dominion in the Seventeenth Century: A Documentary History of Virginia, 1606–1689* (Chapel Hill, 1975).

Wesley F. Craven, *The Dissolution of the Virginia Company* (New York, 1932).

Carville V. Earle, "Environment, Disease, and Mortality in Early Virginia," in Thad W. Tate and David L. Ammerman, eds, *The Chesapeake in the Seventeenth Century: Essays on Anglo-American Society* (Chapel Hill, 1979).

Frederic W. Gleach, *Powhatan's World and Colonial Virginia: A Conflict of Cultures* (Lincoln, 1997).

Ivor Noel Hume, *The Virginia Adventure: Roanoke to James Towne: An Archaeological and Historical Odyssey* (New York, 1994).

Karen Ordahl Kupperman, "Apathy and Death in Early Jamestown," *Journal of American History*, LXVI, 1979, 24–40.

Karen Ordahl Kupperman, ed., *Captain John Smith: A Select Edition of his Writings* (Chapel Hill, 1988).

Karen Ordahl Kupperman, "Fear of Hot Climates in the Anglo-American Experience," *William and Mary Quarterly*, XLI, 1984, 213–40.

Edmund S. Morgan, "The First American Boom: Virginia 1618–1630," *William and Mary Quarterly*, XXVIII, 1971, 169–98.

Edmund S. Morgan, "The Labor Problem at Jamestown, 1607–1618," *American Historical Review*, LXXVI, 1971, 595–611.

Michael Leroy Oberg, *Dominion and Civility: English Imperialism and Native America, 1585–1685* (Ithaca, 1999).

Darrett B. Rutman and Anita H. Rutman, "Of Agues and Fevers: Malaria in the Early Chesapeake," *William and Mary Quarterly*, XXXIII, 1976, 31–60.

Thad W. Tate and David L. Ammerman, eds, *The Chesapeake in the Seventeenth Century: Essays on Anglo-American Society* (Chapel Hill, 1979).

Alden T. Vaughan, *American Genesis: Captain John Smith and the Founding of Virginia* (Boston, 1975).

Growth and Consolidation

Warren M. Billings, ed., *The Old Dominion in the Seventeenth Century: A Documentary History of Virginia, 1606–1689* (Chapel Hill, 1975).

Warren M. Billings, John E. Selby, and Thad W. Tate, *Colonial Virginia: A History* (New York, 1986).

T. H. Breen, ed., *Shaping Southern Society: The Colonial Experience* (New York, 1976).

T. H. Breen and Stephen Innes, *Myne Owne Ground: Race and Freedom on Virginia's Eastern Shore, 1640–1676* (New York, 1980).

Wesley Frank Craven, *White, Red, and Black: The Seventeenth-Century Virginian* (Charlottesville, 1971).

J. Douglas Deal, *Race and Class in Colonial Virginia: Indians, Englishmen, and Africans on the Eastern Shore during the Seventeenth Century* (New York, 1993).

Frederick Fausz, "Fighting 'Fire' with Firearms: The Anglo-Powhatan Arms Race in Early Virginia," *American Indian Culture and Research Journal*, III, 1979, 33–50.

Irene W. D. Hecht, "The Virginia Muster of 1624/5 as a Source of Demographic History," *William and Mary Quarterly*, XXX, 1973, 65–79.

Ivor Noel Hume, *Martin's One Hundred* (New York, 1981).

Jon Kukla, "Order and Chaos in Early America: Political and Social Stability in Pre-Restoration Virginia," *American Historical Review*, XC, 1985, 275–98.

Jon Kukla, *Political Institutions in Virginia, 1619–1660* (New York, 1989).

Edmund S. Morgan, *American Slavery, American Freedom: The Ordeal of Colonial Virginia* (New York, 1975).

James R. Perry, *The Formation of a Society on Virginia's Eastern Shore, 1615–1655* (Chapel Hill, 1990).

Martin H. Quitt, "Immigrant Origins of the Virginia Gentry: A Study of Cultural Transmission and Innovation," *William and Mary Quarterly*, XLV, 1988, 629–55.

Engel Sluiter, "New Light on the '20 Odd Negroes' Arriving in Virginia, August 1619," *William and Mary Quarterly*, LV, 1998, 421–34.

Alden T. Vaughan, "Blacks in Virginia: A Note on the First Decade," *William and Mary Quarterly*, XXIX, 1972, 469–78.

Alden T. Vaughan, " 'Expulsion of the Savages': English Policy and the Virginia Massacre of 1622," *William and Mary Quarterly*, XXXV, 1978, 57–84.

Alden T. Vaughan, *The Roots of American Racism: Essays on the Colonial Experience* (New York, 1995).

Betty Wood, *The Origins of American Slavery: Freedom and Bondage in the English Colonies* (New York, 1997).

CHAPTER 4   THE CONQUEST CONTINUES: NEW ENGLAND, 1620–60

The Pilgrim Fathers

William Bradford, *Of Plymouth Plantation, 1620–1647*, ed. Samuel Eliot Morison (New York, 1952).

William Cronon, *Changes in the Land: Indians, Colonists, and the Ecology of New England* (New York, 1983).

George D. Langdon, Jr., *Pilgrim Colony: A History of New Plymouth, 1620–1691* (New Haven, 1966).

Neil Salisbury, *Manitou and Providence: Indians, Europeans, and the Making of New England, 1500–1643* (New York, 1982).

Neil Salisbury, "Squanto: Last of the Patuxets," in David Sweet and Gary Nash, eds, *Struggle and Survival in Colonial America* (Berkeley, 1981), 228–44.

Massachusetts

David Grayson Allen, *In English Ways: The Movement of Societies and the Transferral of English Local Law and Custom to Massachusetts Bay in the Seventeenth Century* (Chapel Hill, 1981).

Virginia DeJohn Anderson, *New England's Generation: The Great Migration and the Formation of Society and Culture in the Seventeenth Century* (New York, 1991).

Ben Barker-Benfield, "Anne Hutchinson and the Puritan Attitude Toward Women," *Feminist Studies*, I, 1972, 65–96.

Emery Battis, *Saints and Sectaries: Anne Hutchinson and the Antinomian Controversy* (Chapel Hill, 1962).

Theodore Dwight Bozeman, *To Live Ancient Lives: The Primitivist Dimension in Puritanism* (Chapel Hill, 1988).

T. H. Breen, *The Character of a Good Ruler: Puritan Political Ideas, 1630–1730* (New Haven, 1970).

T. H. Breen, "Persistent Localism: English Social Change and the Shaping of New England Institutions," *William and Mary Quarterly*, XXXII, 1975, 3–28.

T. H. Breen, *Puritans and Adventurers: Change and Persistence in Early America* (New York, 1980).

T. H. Breen and Stephen Foster, "The Puritans' Greatest Achievement: A Study of Social Cohesion in Seventeenth Century Massachusetts," *Journal of American History*, LX, 1973/4, 5–22.

Francis J. Bremer, *Congregational Communion: Clerical Friendship in the Anglo-American Puritan Community, 1610–1692* (Boston, 1994).

Francis J. Bremer, *Puritan Crisis: New England and the English Civil Wars, 1630–1670* (New York, 1989).

Francis J. Bremer, *The Puritan Experiment: New England Society from Bradford to Edwards* (New York, 1976).

Alfred A. Cave, *The Pequot War* (Amherst, 1996).

Alfred A. Cave, "Who Killed John Stone? A Note on the Origins of the Pequot War," *William and Mary Quarterly*, XLIX, 1992, 509–21.

Cedric B. Cowing, *The Saving Remnant: Religion and the Settling of New England* (Urbana, 1995).

David Cressy, *Coming Over: Migration between England and New England in the Seventeenth Century* (New York, 1987).

A. L. Cummings, *The Framed Houses of Massachusetts Bay, 1625–1725* (Cambridge, Mass., 1979).

Bruce C. Daniels, *Puritans at Play, Leisure and Recreation in Colonial New England* (Basingstoke, 1995).

Andrew Delbanco, *The Puritan Ordeal* (Cambridge, Mass., 1989).

Richard S. Dunn, *Puritans and Yankees: The Winthrop Dynasty of New England, 1630–1717* (Princeton, 1962).

Stephen Foster, *The Long Argument: English Puritanism and the Shaping of New England Culture, 1570–1700* (Chapel Hill, 1991).

Stephen Foster, *Their Solitary Way: The Puritan Social Ethic in the First Century of Settlement in New England* (New Haven, 1971).

Alison Games, *Migration and the Origins of the English Atlantic World* (Cambridge, Mass., 1999).

Richard Godber, " 'The Cry of Sodom': Discourse, Intercourse, and Desire in Colonial New England," *William and Mary Quarterly*, LII, 1995, 259–86.

Philip F. Gura, *A Glimpse of Sion's Glory: Puritan Radicalism in New England, 1620–1660* (Middletown, 1984).

David D. Hall, ed., *The Antinomian Controversy, 1636–1638: A Documentary History* (Durham, 1990).

David D. Hall, "On Common Ground: The Coherence of American Puritan Studies," *William and Mary Quarterly*, XLIV, 1987, 193–229.

David D. Hall, *The Faithful Shepherd: A History of the New England Ministry in the Seventeenth Century* (Chapel Hill, 1972).

David D. Hall, *Worlds of Wonder, Days of Judgement: Popular Religious Belief in Early New England* (New York, 1989).

David D. Hall and David Grayson Allen, eds, *Seventeenth Century New England* (Boston, 1984).

E. Brooks Holifield, *Era of Persuasion: American Thought and Culture, 1521–1680* (Boston, 1989).

James Holstun, *A Rational Millennium: Puritan Utopias of Seventeenth-century England and America* (New York, 1987).

Stephen Innes, *Creating the Commonwealth: The Economic Culture of Puritan New England* (New York, 1995).

Francis Jennings, *The Invasion of America: Indians, Colonization and the Cant of Conquest* (Chapel Hill, 1975).

Ronald Dale Karr, " 'Why Should You Be So Furious?': The Violence of the Pequot War," *Journal of American History*, LXXXV, 1998, 876–909.

Lyle Koehler, "The Case of the American Jezebels: Anne Hutchinson and Female Agitation during the Years of Antinomian Turmoil, 1636–1640," *William and Mary Quarterly*, XXXI, 1974, 55–78.

Lyle Koehler, *A Search for Power: The "Weaker Sex" in Seventeenth Century New England* (Urbana, 1980).

David Thomas Konig, *Law and Society in Puritan Massachusetts: Essex County, 1629–1692* (Chapel Hill, 1979).

Benjamin W. Labaree, *Colonial Massachusetts: A History* (New York, 1979).

Douglas Edward Leach, *The Northern Colonial Frontier, 1607–1763* (New York, 1966).

Perry Miller, *Orthodoxy in Massachusetts, 1630–1650: A Genetic Study* (Cambridge, Mass., 1933).

Edmund S. Morgan, *The Puritan Dilemma: The Story of John Winthrop* (Boston, 1958).

Edmund S. Morgan, *Visible Saints: The History of a Puritan Idea* (New York, 1963).

Dane Morrison, *A Praying People: Massachusetts Acculturation and the Failure of the Puritan Mission, 1660–1690* (New York, 1995).

Carla Gardina Pestana, "The City upon a Hill under Siege: The Puritan Perception of the Quaker Threat to Massachusetts Bay, 1656–1661," *New England Quarterly*, LVI, 1983, 323–53.

Carla Gardina Pestana, "The Quaker Executions as Myth and History," *Journal of American History*, LXXX, 1993, 441–69.

Philip Ranlet, *Enemies of the Bay Colony* (New York, 1995).

James P. Rhonda, " 'We Are Well as We Are': An Indian Critique of Seventeenth Century Christian Missions," *William and Mary Quarterly*, XXXIV, 1977, 66–82.

Rosamond Rosenmeier, *Anne Bradstreet Revisited* (Boston, 1991).

Darrett B. Rutman, *American Puritanism: Faith and Practice* (Philadelphia, 1970).

Darett B. Rutman, *Winthrop's Boston: Portrait of a Puritan Town, 1630–1649* (Chapel Hill, 1965).

Neal Salisbury, "Red Puritans: 'The Praying Indians' of Massachusetts Bay and John Eliot," *William and Mary Quarterly*, XXXI, 1974, 27–54.

Ivy Schweitzer, *The Work of Self-representation: Lyric Poetry in Colonial New England* (Chapel Hill, 1991).

George Selement, *Keepers of the Vineyard: The Puritan Ministry and Collective Culture in Colonial New England* (Lanham, 1984).

Darren Staloff, *The Making of an American Thinking Class: Intellectuals and Intelligence in Puritan Massachusetts* (New York, 1998).

David E. Stannard, *The Puritan Way of Death: A Study in Religion, Culture, and Social Change* (New York, 1977).

William K. B. Stoever, *"A Faire and Easie Way to Heaven": Covenant Theology and Antinomianism in Early Massachusetts* (Middletown, 1978).

Frank Thistlethwaite, *Dorset Pilgrims: The Story of Westcountry Pilgrims who Went to New England in the Seventeenth Century* (London, 1989).

Roger Thompson, *Mobility and Migration: East Anglian Founders of New England, 1629–1640* (Amherst, 1994).

Alden T. Vaughan, *The New England Frontier: Puritans and Indians, 1620–1675* (Boston, 1965).

Peter White, ed., *Puritan Poets and Poetics: Seventeenth-century American Poetry in Theory and Practice* (University Park, 1985).

Selma R. Williams, *Divine Rebel: The Life of Anne Marbury Hutchinson* (New York, 1981).

Larzer Ziff, *Puritanism in America: New Culture in a New World* (New York, 1973).

Rhode Island, Connecticut, and New Hampshire

Sargent Bush, Jr., *The Writings of Thomas Hooker: Spiritual Adventure in Two Worlds* (Madison, 1980).

Jere R. Daniell, *Colonial New Hampshire: A History* (New York, 1981).

Bruce C. Daniels, *Dissent and Conformity on Narragansett Bay: The Colonial Rhode Island Town* (Middletown, 1983).

Timothy L. Hall, *Separating Church and State: Roger Williams and Religious Liberty* (Urbana, 1998).

Sydney V. James, *Colonial Rhode Island: A History* (New York, 1975).

Sydney V. James, *John Clarke and his Legacies: Religion and Law in Colonial Rhode Island, 1638–1750* (University Park, 1999).

Bruce H. Mann, *Neighbors and Strangers: Law and Community in Early Connecticut* (Chapel Hill, 1987).

Perry Miller, *Roger Williams: His Contribution to the American Tradition* (Indianapolis, 1953).

Edmund S. Morgan, *Roger Williams: The Church and the State* (New York, 1967).

Robert J. Taylor, *Colonial Connecticut: A History* (New York, 1979).

David E. Van Deventer, *The Emergence of Provincial New Hampshire, 1623–1741* (Baltimore, 1976).

CHAPTER 5   MARYLAND AND NEW YORK, 1624–60

Maryland

Lois Green Carr and Russell R. Menard, "Immigration and Opportunity: The Freedman in Early Colonial Maryland," in Thad W. Tate and David L. Ammerman, eds, *The Chesapeake in the Seventeenth Century: Essays on Anglo-American Society* (Chapel Hill, 1979), 206–42.

Lois Green Carr and Lorena S. Walsh, "The Planter's Wife: The Experience of White Women in Seventeenth Century Maryland," *William and Mary Quarterly*, XXXIV, 1977, 542–71.

Lois Green Carr, Russell R. Menard, and Lorena S. Walsh, *Robert Cole's World: Agriculture and Society in Early Maryland* (Chapel Hill, 1991).

Wesley Frank Craven, *The Southern Colonies in the Seventeenth Century* (Baton Rouge, 1949).

Carville V. Earle, *The Evolution of a Tidewater Settlement: All Hallows Parish, Maryland, 1650–1783* (Chicago, 1975).

David W. Jordan, *Foundations of Representative Government in Maryland, 1632–1715* (Cambridge, 1987).

Aubrey C. Land, *Colonial Maryland: A History* (New York, 1981).

Aubrey C. Land, *Law, Society and Politics in Early Maryland* (Baltimore, 1977).

Gloria L. Main, *Tobacco Colony: Life in Early Maryland, 1650–1720* (Princeton, 1982).

David B. Quinn, ed., *Early Maryland in a Wider World* (Detroit, 1982).

Russell R. Menard, *Economy and Society in Early Maryland* (New York, 1985).

Russell R. Menard, "From Servant to Freeholder: Status Mobility and Property Accumulation in Seventeenth Century Maryland," *William and Mary Quarterly*, XXX, 1973, 37–64.

Russell R. Menard, Lois Green Carr, and Lorena S. Walsh, "A Small Planter's Profits: The Cole Estate and the Growth of the Early Chesapeake Economy," *William and Mary Quarterly*, XL, 1983, 171–96.

Edward F. Terrar, *Social, Economic, and Religious Beliefs among Maryland Catholic Laboring People during the Period of the English Civil War, 1639–1660* (San Francisco, 1996).

Lorena S. Walsh, "Servitude and Opportunity in Charles County, Maryland, 1658–1705," in Aubrey C. Land, Lois Green Carr, and Edward C. Papenfuse, eds, *Law, Society, and Politics in Early Maryland* (Baltimore, 1977).

Lorena S. Walsh, " 'Till Death Us Do Part': Marriage and Family in Seventeenth Century Maryland," in Thad W. Tate and David L. Ammerman, eds, *The Chesapeake in the Seventeenth Century: Essays in Anglo-American Society* (Chapel Hill, 1979).

Lorena S. Walsh and Russell R. Menard, "Death in the Chesapeake: Two Life Tables for Men in Early Colonial Maryland," *Maryland Historical Magazine*, LXIX, 1974, 211–27.

New York

C. R. Boxer, *The Dutch Seaborne Empire, 1600–1800* (New York, 1965).

Thomas J. Condon, *New York Beginnings: The Commercial Origins of New Netherland* (New York, 1968).

Ada van Gastel, "Van der Donck's Description of the Indians: Additions and Corrections," *William and Mary Quarterly*, XLVII, 1990, 411–21.

Graham Russell Hodges, *Root and Branch: African Americans in New York and East Jersey, 1613–1863* (Chapel Hill, 1999).

Michael Kammen, *Colonial New York: A History* (New York, 1975).

Donna Merwick, *Possessing Albany, 1630–1710: The Dutch and English Experience* (Cambridge, England, 1990).

Oliver A. Rink, *Holland on the Hudson: An Economic and Social History of Dutch New York* (Ithaca, 1986).

George L. Smith, *Religion and Trade in New Netherland: Dutch Origins and American Development* (Ithaca, 1973).

William Smith, *The History of the Province of New York* (London, 1757. Reprinted New York, 1972).

Petrus Stuyvesant, *Correspondence, 1647–1653*, trans. Charles T. Gehring (Syracuse, 1998).

Allen W. Trelease, *Indian Affairs in Colonial New York: The Seventeenth Century* (Ithaca, 1960).

Bruce G. Trigger, "The Mohawk–Mahican War, 1624–1628: The Establishment of a Pattern," *Canadian Historical Review*, LII, 1971, 276–86.

Delaware

John A. Monroe, *Colonial Delaware: A History* (New York, 1978).

CHAPTER 6   THE RESTORATION ERA

The Return of Charles II

Robert M. Bliss, *Revolution and Empire: English Politics and the American Colonies in the Seventeenth Century* (New York, 1990).

Wesley Frank Craven, *The Colonies in Transition, 1660–1713* (New York, 1968).

J. R. Jones, *Charles II: Royal Politician* (London, 1987).

J. P. Kenyon, *Stuart England* (London, 1978).

J. M. Sosin, *English America and the Restoration Monarchy of Charles II: Transatlantic Politics, Commerce and Kinship* (Lincoln, 1981).

The Mercantilist System

Charles M. Andrews, *The Colonial Period of American History*, Vol. 4: *England's Commercial and Colonial Policy* (New Haven, 1938).

Joyce Oldham Appleby, *Economic Thought and Ideology in Seventeenth Century England* (Princeton, 1978).

K. G. Davies, *The North Atlantic World in the Seventeenth Century* (Minneapolis, 1974).

Ralph Davis, *The Rise of the Atlantic Economies* (Ithaca, 1973).

New York

Thomas J. Archdeacon, *New York City, 1661–1710: Conquest and Change* (Ithaca, 1976).

Randall H. Balmer, *A Perfect Babel of Confusion: Dutch Religion and English Culture in the Middle Colonies* (New York, 1989).

Thomas E. Burke, *Mohawk Frontier: The Dutch Community of Schenectady, New York, 1664–1710* (Ithaca, 1991).

David G. Hackett, *The Rude Hand of Innovation: Religion and Social Order in Albany, New York, 1652–1836* (New York, 1990).

Michael Kammen, *Colonial New York: A History* (New York, 1975).

Cathy Matson, " 'Damned Scoundrels' and 'Libertisme of Trade': Freedom and Regulation in Colonial New York's Fur and Grain Trades," *William and Mary Quarterly*, LI, 1994, 389–418.

Robert C. Ritchie, *The Duke's Province: A Study of New York Politics and Society, 1664–1691* (Chapel Hill, 1977).

Donald G. Shomette and Robert D. Haslach, *Raid on America: The Dutch Naval Campaigns of 1672–1674* (Columbia, 1988).

George L. Smith, *Religion and Trade in New Netherland: Dutch Origins and American Development* (Ithaca, 1973).

Dennis Sullivan, *The Punishment of Crime in Colonial New York: The Dutch Experience in Albany during the Seventeenth Century* (New York, 1997).

Allen W. Trelease, *Indian Affairs in Colonial New York: The Seventeenth Century* (Ithaca, 1960).

The Carolinas

Richard S. Dunn, *Sugar and Slaves: The Rise of the Planter Class in the English West Indies, 1624–1713* (Chapel Hill, 1972).

Walter Edgar, *South Carolina: A History* (Columbia, 1998).

Hugh T. Lefler and William S. Powell, *Colonial North Carolina: A History* (New York, 1973).

Richard B. Sheridan, *Sugar and Slavery: An Economic History of the British West Indies, 1623–1775* (Baltimore, 1973).

M. Eugene Sirmans, *Colonial South Carolina: A Political History, 1663–1763* (Chapel Hill, 1966).

Donna Spindel, *Crime and Society in North Carolina, 1663–1776* (Baton Rouge, 1989).

Rebecca Starr, *A School for Politics: Commercial Lobbying and Political Culture in Early South Carolina* (Baltimore, 1998).

Clarence L. Ver Steeg, *Origins of a Southern Mosaic: Studies of Early Carolina and Georgia* (Athens, 1975).

Richard Waterhouse, "England, the Caribbean, and the Settlement of Carolina," *Journal of American Studies*, IX, 1975, 259–81.

Richard Waterhouse, *A New World Gentry: The Making of a Merchant and Planter Class in South Carolina, 1670–1770* (New York, 1989).

Robert M. Weir, *Colonial South Carolina: A History* (New York, 1983).

CHAPTER 7 THE LATER YEARS OF CHARLES II

Virginia: Bacon's Rebellion

Charles M. Andrews, ed., *Narratives of the Insurrections, 1675–1690* (New York, 1915).

Warren M. Billings, ed., *The Old Dominion in the Seventeenth Century: A Documentary History of Virginia, 1606–1689* (Chapel Hill, 1975).

Warren M. Billings, John E. Selby, and Thad W. Tate, *Colonial Virginia: A History* (New York, 1986).

T. H. Breen, "A Changing Labor Force and Race Relations in Virginia," in T. H. Breen, *Puritans and Adventurers: Change and Persistence in Early America* (New York, 1980).

Mildred Campbell, "Social Origins of Some Early Americans," in James Morton Smith, ed., *Seventeenth-century America* (Chapel Hill, 1959), 63–89.

Wesley Frank Craven, *White, Red, and Black: The Seventeenth-century Virginian* (Charlottesville, 1971).

J. Douglas Deal, *Race and Class in Colonial Virginia: Indians, Englishmen and Africans on the Eastern Shore during the Seventeenth Century* (New York, 1993).

David W. Galenson, "The Social Origins of Some Early Americans: Rejoinder," with a reply by Mildred Campbell, *William and Mary Quarterly*, XXXVI, 1979, 264–86.

James Horn, *Adapting to a New World: English Society in the Seventeenth Century Chesapeake* (Chapel Hill, 1994).

James Horn, "Servant Emigration to the Chesapeake in the Seventeenth Century," in Thad W. Tate and David L. Ammerman, eds, *The Chesapeake in the Seventeenth Century: Essays on Anglo-American Society* (Chapel Hill, 1979).

Russell R. Menard, "From Servants to Slaves: The Transformation of the Chesapeake Labor System," *Southern Studies*, XVI, 1977, 355–90.

Edmund S. Morgan, *American Slavery, American Freedom: The Ordeal of Colonial Virginia* (New York, 1975).

Martin H. Quitt, *Virginia House of Burgesses, 1660–1706: The Social, Educational, and Economic Bases of Political Power* (New York, 1989).

John C. Rainbolt, *From Prescription to Persuasion: Manipulation of Seventeenth Century Virginia Economy* (Port Washington, 1974).

Darrett B. Rutman and Anita H. Rutman, " 'Now Wives and Sons-in-Law': Parental Death in a Seventeenth Century Virginia County," in Thad W. Tate and David L. Ammerman, eds, *The Chesapeake in the Seventeenth Century: Essays on Anglo-American Society* (Chapel Hill, 1979).

Darrett B. Rutman and Anita H. Rutman, *A Place in Time: Middlesex County, Virginia, 1650–1750* (New York, 1984).

Carole Shammas, "English-born and Creole Elites in Turn-of-the-century Virginia," in Thad W. Tate and David L. Ammerman, eds, *The Chesapeake in the Seventeenth Century: Essays on Anglo-American Society* (Chapel Hill, 1979).

William L. Shea, *The Virginia Militia in the Seventeenth Century* (Baton Rouge, 1983).

Wilcomb E. Washburn, *The Governor and the Rebel: A History of Bacon's Rebellion in Virginia* (Chapel Hill, 1957).

Stephen Saunders Webb, *1676: The End of American Independence* (New York, 1984).

Susan Westbury, "Women in Bacon's Rebellion," in Virginia Bernhard, Betty Brandon, Elizabeth Fox-Genovese and Theda Perdue, eds, *Southern Women: Histories and Identities* (Columbia, 1992).

Massachusetts and New England

Virginia DeJohn Anderson, "King Philip's Herds: Indians, Colonists, and the Problem of Livestock in Early New England," *William and Mary Quarterly*, LI, 1994, 601–24.

Sacvan Bercovitch, *The American Jeremiad* (Madison, 1978).

Colin G. Calloway, ed., *After King Philip's War: Presence and Persistence in Indian New England* (Hanover, 1997).

James F. Cooper, Jr., *Tenacious of their Liberties: The Congregationalist in Colonial Massachusetts* (New York, 1999).

James D. Drake, *King Philip's War: Civil War in New England, 1675–1676* (Amherst, 1999).

Richard S. Dunn, *Puritans and Yankees: The Winthrop Dynasty of New England, 1630–1717* (Princeton, 1962).

Richard P. Gildrie, *The Profane, the Civil, and the Godly: The Reformation of Manners in Orthodox New England, 1679–1749* (University Park, 1994).

Stephen Innes, *Creating the Commonwealth: The Economic Culture of Puritan New England* (New York, 1995).

Stephen Innes, "Land Tenancy and Social Order in Springfield, Massachusetts, 1652–1702," *William and Mary Quarterly*, XXXV, 1978, 33–56.

Francis Jennings, *The Invasion of America: Indians, Colonization and the Cant of Conquest* (Chapel Hill, 1975).

Benjamin W. Labaree, *Colonial Massachusetts: A History* (New York, 1979).

Patrick M. Malone, "Changing Military Technology among the Indians of Southern New England, 1600–1676," *American Quarterly*, XXV, 1973, 48–63.

John Frederick Martin, *Profits in the Wilderness: Entrepreneurship and the Founding of New England Towns in the Seventeenth Century* (Chapel Hill, 1991).

Perry Miller, *The New England Mind: The Seventeenth Century* (New York, 1939).

Gerald F. Moran and Maris Vinovskis, "The Puritan Family and Religion: A Critical Reappraisal," *William and Mary Quarterly*, XXXIX, 1982, 29–63.

Dane Morrison, *A Praying People: Massachusetts Acculturation and the Failure of the Puritan Mission, 1600–1690* (New York, 1995).

Mark A. Peterson, *The Price of Redemption: The Spiritual Economy of Puritan New England* (Stanford, 1997).

Robert G. Pope, *The Half-Way Covenant: Church Membership in Puritan New England* (Princeton, 1969).

Jenny Hale Pulsipher, "Massacre at Hurtleberry Hill: Christian Indians and English Authority in Metacom's War," *William and Mary Quarterly*, LIII, 1996, 458–86.

David M. Scobey, "Revising the Errand: New England's Ways and the Puritan Sense of the Past," *William and Mary Quarterly*, XLI, 1984, 3–31.

Richard C. Simmons, *Studies in the Massachusetts Franchise, 1631–1691* (New York, 1989).

Armstrong Starkey, *European and Native American Warfare, 1675–1815* (London, 1998).

Robert J. Taylor, *Colonial Connecticut: A History* (New York, 1979).

Mark Valeri, "Religious Discipline and the Market: Puritans and the Issue of Usury," *William and Mary Quarterly*, LIV, 1997, 747–68.

Alden T. Vaughan, *The New England Frontier, 1620–1675* (Boston, 1965).

New Jersey and Pennsylvania

Edwin B. Bronner, *William Penn's "Holy Experiment": The Founding of Pennsylvania, 1681–1701* (New York, 1962).

Jon Butler, " 'Gospel Order Improved: The Keithian Schism and the Exercise of Quaker Ministerial Authority in Pennsylvania," *William and Mary Quarterly*, XXXI, 1974, 431–52.

Wesley Frank Craven, *New Jersey and the English Colonization of North America* (Princeton, 1964).

Mary Maples Dunn, *William Penn, Politics and Commerce* (Princeton, 1967).

Richard S. Dunn and Mary Maples Dunn, eds, *The World of William Penn* (Philadelphia, 1986).

M. B. Endy, Jr., *William Penn and Early Quakerism* (Princeton, 1973).

Joseph E. Illick, *Colonial Pennsylvania: A History* (New York, 1976).

Barry Levy, *Quakers and the American Family: British Settlement in the Delaware Valley* (New York, 1988).

John A. Munroe, *Colonial Delaware: A History* (New York, 1978).

Gary B. Nash, *Quakers and Politics: Pennsylvania, 1681–1726* (Princeton, 1969).

William M. Offutt, Jr., *Of "Good Laws" and "Good Men": Law and Society in the Delaware Valley, 1680–1710* (Urbana, 1995).

John E. Pomfret, *Colonial New Jersey; A History* (New York, 1973).

John E. Pomfret, *The Province of East New Jersey, 1609–1702: A History of the Origins of an American Colony* (Princeton, 1956).

Jean R. Soderland et al., eds, *William Penn and the Founding of Pennsylvania, 1680–1684: A Documentary History* (Philadelphia, 1983).

CHAPTER 8   JAMES II AND THE GLORIOUS REVOLUTION

England and General Accounts

M. Ashley, *James II* (London, 1977).

J. Childs, *The Army, James II and the Glorious Revolution* (Manchester, 1980).

Michael G. Hall, *Edward Randolph and the American Colonies, 1676–1703* (Chapel Hill, 1960).

Michael G. Hall, Lawrence H. Leder, and Michael G. Kammen, eds, *The Glorious Revolution in America: Documents on the Colonial Crisis of 1689* (Chapel Hill, 1964).

Richard R. Johnson, "The Imperial Webb: The Thesis of Garrison Government in Early America Considered," *William and Mary Quarterly*, XLIII, 1986, 408–30.

J. R. Jones, *The Revolution of 1688 in England* (London, 1972).

David S. Lovejoy, *The Glorious Revolution in America* (New York, 1972).

J. M. Sosin, *English America and the Revolution of 1688* (Lincoln, 1982).

Ian Steele, "Governors or Generals?: A Note on Martial Law and the Revolution of 1689 in English America," *William and Mary Quarterly*, XLVI, 1989, 304–14.

Stephen Saunders Webb, "Army and Empire: English Garrison Government in Britain and America, 1569–1763," *William and Mary Quarterly*, XXXIV, 1977, 1–31.

Stephen Saunders Webb, "The Data and Theory of Restoration Empire," *William and Mary Quarterly*, XLIII, 1986, 431–59.

Stephen Saunders Webb, *The Governors-General: The English Army and the Definition of Empire, 1569–1681* (Chapel Hill, 1979).

Stephen Saunders Webb, *Lord Churchill's Coup: The Anglo-American Empire and the Glorious Revolution Reconsidered* (New York, 1995).

J. R. Western, *Monarchy and Revolution: The English State in the 1680s* (London, 1972).

Massachusetts

Bernard Bailyn, *The New England Merchants in the Seventeenth Century* (Cambridge, Mass., 1955).

Michael G. Hall, *The Last American Puritan: The Life of Increase Mather* (Middletown, 1987).

Richard R. Johnson, *Adjustment to Empire: The New England Colonies, 1675–1715* (New Brunswick, 1981).

Benjamin W. Labaree, *Colonial Massachusetts: A History* (New York, 1979).

David Levin, *Cotton Mather: The Young Life of the Lord's Remembrancer, 1663–1703* (Cambridge, Mass., 1978).

Robert Middlekauf, *The Mathers: Three Generations of Puritan Intellectuals, 1596–1728* (New York, 1971).

Michael J. Puglisi, *Puritans Besieged: The Legacies of King Philip's War in the Massachusetts Bay Colony* (Lanham, 1991).

New York

Joyce D. Goodfriend, *Before the Melting Pot: Society and Culture in Colonial New York City, 1664–1730* (Princeton, 1991).

Adrian Howe, "The Bayard Treason Trial: Dramatizing Anglo-Dutch Politics in Early Eighteenth-century New York City," *William and Mary Quarterly*, XLVII, 1990, 57–89.

Michael Kammen, *Colonial New York: A History* (New York, 1975).

Lawrence H. Leder, *Robert Livingston, 1654–1728, and the Politics of Colonial New York* (Chapel Hill, 1961).

Charles H. McCormick, *Leisler's Rebellion* (New York, 1989).

Donna Merwick, "Becoming English: Anglo-Dutch Conflict in the 1670s in Albany, New York," *New York History*, LXII, 1981, 389–414.

Donna Merwick, *Possessing Albany, 1630–1710: The Dutch and English Experience* (Cambridge, England, 1990).

John M. Murrin, "English Rights as Ethnic Aggression: The English Conquest, the Charter of Liberties of 1683, and Leisler's Rebellion in New York," in William Pencak and Conrad Edick Wright, eds, *Authority and Resistance in Early New York* (New York, 1988), 56–94.

Jerome R. Reich, *Leisler's Rebellion: A Study of Democracy in New York* (1953).

Robert C. Ritchie, *The Duke's Province: A Study of New York Politics and Society, 1664–1691* (Chapel Hill, 1977).

David William Voorhees, "The 'Fervent Zeale' of Jacob Leisler," *William and Mary Quarterly*, LI, 1994, 447–72.

Maryland

Lois Green Carr and David William Jordan, *Maryland's Revolution of Government, 1689–1692* (Ithaca, 1974).

David W. Jordan, *Foundations of Representative Government in Maryland, 1632–1715* (New York, 1988).

Aubrey C. Land, *Colonial Maryland: A History* (New York, 1981).

Aubrey C. Land, Lois Green Carr, and Edward C. Papenfuse, eds, *Law, Society, and Politics in Early Maryland* (Baltimore, 1977).

Russell R. Menard, *Economy and Society in Early Colonial Maryland* (New York, 1985).

Lorena S. Walsh, "Staying Put or Getting Out: Findings for Charles County, Maryland, 1650–1720," *William and Mary Quarterly*, XLIV, 1987, 89–103.

CHAPTER 9   THE ERA OF WILLIAM AND ANNE

British Imperial Policy

George H. Guttridge, *The Colonial Policy of William III in America and the West Indies* (Cambridge, England, 1922).

J. M. Sosin, *English America and Imperial Inconstancy: The Rise of Provincial Autonomy, 1696–1715* (Lincoln, 1985).

J. M. Sosin, *English America and the Revolution of 1688: Royal Administration and the Structure of Provincial Government* (Lincoln, 1982).

I. K. Steele, *Politics of Colonial Policy: The Board of Trade in Colonial Administration, 1696–1720* (New York, 1968).

The Salem Witchcraft Trials

Paul Boyer and Stephen Nissenbaum, *Salem Possessed: The Social Origins of Witchcraft* (Cambridge, Mass., 1974).

Paul Boyer and Stephen Nissenbaum, eds, *The Salem Witchcraft Papers: Verbatim Transcripts of the Legal Documents of the Salem Witchcraft Outbreak of 1692*, 3 vols (New York, 1977).

Elaine G. Breslaw, *Tituba, Reluctant Witch of Salem: Devilish Indians and Puritan Fantasies* (New York, 1996).

Laurie Winn Carlson, *A Fever in Salem* (Chicago, 2000).

John P. Demos, *Entertaining Satan: Witchcraft and the Culture of Early New England* (New York, 1982).

John P. Demos, "John Godfrey and his Neighbors: Witchcraft and the Social Web in Colonial Massachusetts," *William and Mary Quarterly*, XXXIII, 1976, 242–65.

John P. Demos, "Underlying Themes in the Witchcraft of Seventeenth Century New England," *American Historical Review*, LXXV, 1970, 1311–26.

Richard P. Gildrie, *Salem, Massachusetts, 1626–1683: A Covenant Community* (Charlottesville, 1975).

Richard Godbeer, *The Devil's Dominion: Magic and Religion in Early New England* (New York, 1992).

Larry Gragg, *The Salem Witch Crisis* (Westport, 1992).

David D. Hall, *Witch Hunting in Seventeenth Century New England: A Documentary History, 1638–1692* (Boston, 1990).

David D. Hall, "Witchcraft and the Limits of Interpretation," *New England Quarterly*, LVIII, 1985, 253–81.

Peter Charles Hoffer, *The Devil's Disciple: Makers of the Salem Witchcraft Trials* (Baltimore, 1996).

Peter Charles Hoffer, *The Salem Witchcraft Trials: A Legal History* (Lawrence, 1997).

Carol F. Karlsen, *The Devil in the Shape of a Woman: Witchcraft in Colonial New England* (New York, 1987).

Bryan F. Le Beau, *The Story of the Salem Witch Trials: "We Walked in Clouds and Could not See our Way"* (Upper Saddle River, NJ, 1998).

Elizabeth Reis, *Damned Women: Sinners and Witches in Puritan New England* (Ithaca, 1997).

Bernard Rosenthal, *Salem Story: Reading the Witch Trials of 1692* (Cambridge, England, 1993).

Keith Thomas, *Religion and the Decline of Magic* (New York, 1971).

Marion L. Starkey, *The Devil in Massachusetts: A Modern Enquiry into the Salem Witch Trials* (New York, 1950).

Richard Weisman, *Witchcraft, Magic and Religion in Seventeenth Century Massachusetts* (Amherst, 1984).

Pennsylvania

Richard S. Dunn and Mary Maples Dunn, *The World of William Penn* (Philadelphia, 1986).

J. William Fost, *A Perfect Freedom: Religious Liberty in Pennsylvania* (New York, 1990).

Gary B. Nash, *Quakers and Politics: Pennsylvania, 1681–1726* (Princeton, 1968).

Frederick B. Tolles, *Meeting House and Counting House: The Quaker Merchants of Colonial Philadelphia, 1682–1763* (Chapel Hill, 1948).

Frederick B. Tolles, *Quakers and the Atlantic Culture* (New York, 1960).

The Carolinas

Converse D. Clowse, *Economic Beginnings in Colonial South Carolina, 1670–1730* (Columbia, 1971).

Richard Haan, " 'The Trade Does Not Flourish as Formerly': The Ecological Origins of the Yamasee War of 1715," *Ethnohistory*, XXVIII, 1981, 341–58.

Hugh T. Lefler and William S. Powell, *Colonial North Carolina: A History* (New York, 1973).

Harry Roy Merrens, *Colonial North Carolina: A Study in Historical Geography* (Chapel Hill, 1964).

H. Roy Merrens, ed., *The Colonial South Carolina Scene: Contemporary Views, 1697–1774* (Columbia, 1977).

M. Eugene Sirmans, *Colonial South Carolina: A Political History, 1663–1763* (Chapel Hill, 1966).

Clarence L. Ver Steeg, *Origins of a Southern Mosaic: Studies of Early Carolina and Georgia* (Athens, 1975).

Peter H. Wood, *Black Majority: Negroes in Colonial South Carolina from 1670 through the Stono Rebellion* (New York, 1974).

The Wars of William and Anne

Emerson W. Baker and John G. Reid, *The New England Knight: Sir William Phips, 1651–1695* (Toronto, 1998).

John Demos, *The Unredeemed Captive: A Family Story from Early America* (New York, 1994).

Peter A. Dorsey, "Going to School with Savages: Authorship and Authority among the Jesuits of New France," *William and Mary Quarterly*, LV, 1998, 399–420.

Philip S. Haffenden, *New England in the English Nation, 1689–1713* (Oxford, 1973).

Eric Hinderaker, " 'The Four Indian Kings' and the Imaginative Construction of the First British Empire," *William and Mary Quarterly*, LIII, 1996, 487–526.

Richard R. Johnson, *Adjustment to Empire: The New England Colonies, 1675–1715* (New Brunswick, 1981).

Douglas Edward Leach, *Arms for Empire: A Military History of the British Colonies in North America, 1607–1763* (New York, 1973).

Douglas Edward Leach, *The Northern Colonial Frontier, 1607–1763* (New York, 1966).

Richard I. Melvoin, *New England Outpost: War and Society in Colonial Deerfield* (New York, 1989).

Howard H. Peckham, *The Colonial Wars, 1689–1762* (Chicago, 1964).

Marcus Rediker, *Between the Devil and the Deep Blue Sea: Marchant Seamen, Pirates and the Anglo-American Maritime World, 1700–1750* (New York, 1987).

Daniel K. Richter, "Cultural Brokers and Intercultural Politics: New York–Iroquois Relations, 1664–1701," *Journal of American History*, LXXV, 1988–9, 40–67.

Robert C. Ritchie, *Captain Kidd and the War against the Pirates* (Cambridge, Mass., 1986).

John D. Runcie, "The Problem of Anglo-American Politics in Bellomont's New York," *William and Mary Quarterly*, XXVI, 1969, 191–217.

CHAPTER 10   THE PROVINCIAL ECONOMY AND LABOR SYSTEM

General

Marc Egnal, *Divergent Paths: How Culture and Institutions have Shaped North American Growth* (New York, 1996).

Marc Egnal, "The Economic Development of the Thirteen Continental Colonies, 1720–1775," *William and Mary Quarterly*, XXXII, 1975, 191–218.

Marc Egnal, *New World Economies: The Growth of the Thirteen Colonies and Early Canada* (New York, 1998).

Stanley L. Engerman and Robert E. Gallman, eds, *The Cambridge Economic History of the United States*, Vol. 1: *The Colonial Era* (New York, 1996).

David W. Galenson, *White Servitude in Colonial America: An Economic Analysis* (New York, 1981).

Nancy F. Koehn, *The Power of Commerce: Economy and Governance in the First British Empire* (Ithaca, 1994).

John J. McCusker, *Essays in the Economic History of the Atlantic World* (New York, 1997).

John J. McCusker and Russell R. Menard, *The Economy of British North America, 1607–1789* (Chapel Hill, 1985).

Judith A. McGaw, ed., *Early American Technology: Making and Doing Things from the Colonial Era to 1850* (Chapel Hill, 1994).

Michael Merrill, "Putting 'Capitalism' in its Place: A Review of Recent Literature," *William and Mary Quarterly*, LII, 1995, 315–26.

Curtis P. Nettels, *The Roots of American Civilization: A History of American Colonial Life* (New York, 1963).

Edwin J. Perkins, *The Economy of Colonial America* (New York, 1988).

Ian K. Steele, *The English Atlantic, 1675–1740: An Exploration of Communication and Community* (New York, 1986).

Gary M. Walton and James F. Shepherd, *The Economic Rise of Early America* (New York, 1979).

James Walvin, *Fruits of Empire: Exotic Produce and British Trade, 1660–1800* (Macmillan, 1997).

The Southern Plantation System

Richard R. Beeman, *The Evolution of the Southern Backcountry: A Case Study of Lunenburg County, Virginia, 1746–1832* (Philadelphia, 1984).

T. H. Breen, *Tobacco Culture: The Mentality of the Great Tidewater Planters on the Eve of the Revolution* (Princeton, 1985).

Joyce Chaplin, *An Anxious Pursuit: Agricultural Innovation and Modernity in the Lower South, 1730–1815* (Chapel Hill, 1993).

Paul G. E. Clemens, *The Atlantic Economy and Colonial Maryland's Eastern Shore: From Tobacco to Grain* (Ithaca, 1980).

D. L. Coon, "Eliza Lucas Pinckney and the Reintroduction of Indigo Culture in South Carolina," *Journal of Southern History*, XLII, 1976, 61–76.

Christine Daniels, " 'WANTED: A Blacksmith who Understands Plantation Work': Artisans in Maryland, 1700–1810," *William and Mary Quarterly*, L, 1993, 743–67.

A. Roger Ekirch, "Bound for America: A Profile of British Convicts Transported to the Colonies, 1718–1775," *William and Mary Quarterly*, XLII, 1985, 184–200.

A. Roger Ekirch, *Bound for America: The Transportation of British Convicts to the Colonies, 1718–1775* (Oxford, 1987).

Charles Farmer, *In the Absence of Towns: Settlement and Country Trade in Southside Virginia, 1730–1800* (Lanham, 1993).

David W. Galenson, *Traders, Planters, and Slaves: Market Behavior in Early English America* (Cambridge, England, 1986).

David Klingaman, "The Significance of Grain in the Development of the Tobacco Colonies," *Journal of Economic History*, XXIX, 1969, 269–78.

Allan Kulikoff, "Households and Markets: Toward a New Synthesis of American Agrarian History," *William and Mary Quarterly*, L, 1993, 342–55.

Allan Kulikoff, *Tobacco and Slaves: The Development of Southern Cultures in the Chesapeake, 1680–1800* (Chapel Hill, 1986).

Johanna Miller Lewis, *Artisans in the North Carolina Backcountry* (Lexington, 1995).

Daniel C. Littlefield, *Rice and Slaves: Ethnicity and the Slave Trade in Colonial South Carolina* (Baton Rouge, 1981).

Russell R. Menard, "From Servants to Slaves: The Transformation of the Chesapeake Labor System," *Southern Studies*, XVI, 1977, 355–90.

Harry Roy Merrens, *Colonial North Carolina in the Eighteenth Century: A Study in Historical Geography* (Chapel Hill, 1964).

Kenneth Morgan, "The Organization of the Colonial American Rice Trade," *William and Mary Quarterly*, LII, 1995, 433–52.

Richard Pares, *Merchants and Planters* (Cambridge, England, 1960).

Jacob M. Price, *Capital and Credit in British Overseas Trade: The View from the Chesapeake, 1700–1776* (Cambridge, Mass., 1980).

Mary M. Schweitzer, "Economic Regulation and the Colonial Economy: The Maryland Tobacco Inspection Act of 1747," *Journal of Economic History*, XL, 1980, 551–69.

Abbot Emerson Smith, *Colonists in Bondage: White Servitude and Convict Labor in America, 1607–1776* (Chapel Hill, 1947).

Betty Wood, *Women's Work, Men's Work: The Informal Slave Economies of Lowcountry Georgia* (Athens, 1995).

Northern Farming and Commerce

Bernard Bailyn and Lotte Bailyn, *Massachusetts Shipping, 1697–1714* (Cambridge, Mass., 1959).

Richard Lyman Bushman, "Markets and Composite Farms in Early America," *William and Mary Quarterly*, LV, 1998, 351–74.

Charles F. Carroll, *The Timber Economy of Puritan New England* (Providence, 1973).

Jay Coughtry, *The Notorious Triangle: Rhode Island and the American Slave Trade, 1700–1807* (Philadelphia, 1981).

Bruce C. Daniels, "Economic Development in Colonial and Revolutionary Connecticut: An Overview," *William and Mary Quarterly*, XXXVII, 1980, 429–50.

Henry A. Gemery and Jan S. Hogendorn, eds, *The Uncommon Market: Essays in the Economic History of the Atlantic Slave Trade* (New York, 1979).

Joseph A. Goldenberg, *Shipbuilding in Colonial America* (Charlottesville, 1976).

James A. Henretta, "Families and Farms: *Mentalité* in Pre-industrial America," *William and Mary Quarterly*, XXXV, 1978, 3–32.

Adrienne D. Hood, "The Material World of Cloth: Production and Use in Eighteenth Century Rural Pennsylvania," *William and Mary Quarterly*, LIII, 1996, 43–66.

Stephen Innes, ed., *Work and Labor in Early America* (Chapel Hill, 1988).

Sung Bok Kim, *Landlord and Tenant in Colonial New York: Manorial Society, 1664–1775* (Chapel Hill, 1978).

Allan Kulikoff, "The Transition to Capitalism in Rural America," *William and Mary Quarterly*, XLVI, 1989, 120–44.

James T. Lemon, *The Best Poor Man's Country: A Geographical Study of Early Southeastern Pennsylvania* (Baltimore, 1972).

John J. McCusker, *Rum and the American Revolution: The Rum Trade and the Balance of Payments of the Thirteen Continental Colonies* (New York, 1989).

Cathy Matson, *Merchants and Empire: Trading in Colonial New York* (Baltimore, 1998).

Michael Merrill, "Cash is Good to Eat: Self-sufficiency and Exchange in the Rural Economy of the United States," *Radical History Review*, IV, 1977, 42–69.

Richard B. Morris, *Government and Labor in Early America* (New York, 1946).

John M. Murrin and Rowland Bertoff, "Feudalism, Communalism, and the Yeoman Freeholder: The American Revolution Considered as a Social Accident," in Stephen G. Kurtz and James H. Hutson, eds, *Essays on the American Revolution* (Chapel Hill, 1973).

Margaret Ellen Newell, *From Dependency to Independence: Economic Revolution in Colonial New England* (Ithaca, 1998).

Gilman M. Ostrander, "The Making of the Triangular Trade Myth," *William and Mary Quarterly*, XXX, 1973, 635–44.

Richard Pares, *Yankees and Creoles: The Trade between North America and the West Indies before the American Revolution* (Cambridge, England, 1956).

Bettye Hobbs Pruitt, "Self-sufficiency and the Agricultural Economy of Eighteenth Century Massachusetts," *William and Mary Quarterly*, XLI, 1984, 333–64.

Marcus Rediker, *Between the Devil and the Deep Blue Sea: Merchant Seamen, Pirates, and the Anglo-American Maritime World, 1700–1750* (New York, 1987).

Winifred B. Rothenberg, "The Emergence of a Capital Market in Rural Massachusetts, 1730–1838," *Journal of Economic History*, XLV, 1985, 796–99.

Winifred B. Rothenberg, *From Market-places to a Market Economy: The Transformation of Rural Massachusetts, 1750–1850* (Chicago, 1992).

Sharon V. Salinger, 'To Serve Well and Faithfully': Labor and Indentured Servants in Pennsylvania, 1682–1800 (New York, 1987).

Ronald Schultz, *The Republic of Labor: Philadelphia Artisans and the Politics of Class* (Oxford, 1993).

Max George Schumacher, *The Northern Farmer and his Markets during the Colonial Period* (New York, 1975).

Mary M. Schweitzer, *Custom and Contract: Household, Government and the Economy in Colonial Pennsylvania* (New York, 1987).

Daniel Vickers, *Farmers and Fishermen: Two Centuries of Work in Essex County, Massachusetts, 1630–1850* (Chapel Hill, 1994).

Peter O. Wacker and Paul G. E. Clements, *Land Use in Early New Jersey: A Historical Geography* (Newark, 1993).

The Mercantilist System

Thomas C. Barrow, *Trade and Empire: The British Customs Service in Colonial America, 1660–1776* (Cambridge, Mass., 1967).

Oliver M. Dickerson, *The Navigation Acts and the American Revolution* (Philadelphia, 1951).

Curtis P. Nettels, "British Mercantilism and the Economic Development of the Thirteen Colonies," *Journal of Economic History*, XII, 1952, 105–14.

Alison G. Olson, "The Board of Trade and London–American Interest Groups in the Eighteenth Century," *Journal of Imperial and Commonwealth History*, VIII, 1980, 33–50.

David R. Owen and Michael C. Tolley, *Courts of Admiralty in Colonial America: The Maryland Experience, 1634–1776* (Durham, NC, 1995).

James F. Shepherd and Gary M. Walton, *Shipping, Maritime Trade, and the Economic Development of Colonial North America* (Cambridge, England, 1972).

Ian K. Steele, *The English Atlantic, 1675–1740: An Exploration of Communication and Community* (New York, 1986).

Thomas M. Truxes, *Irish–American Trade, 1660–1783* (New York, 1989).

Money and Currency

Leslie V. Brock, *The Currency of the American Colonies, 1700–1764: A Study in Colonial Finance and Imperial Relations* (New York, 1975).

John J. McCusker, *Money and Exchange in Europe and America, 1600–1775: A Handbook* (Chapel Hill, 1978).

Curtis P. Nettels, *The Money Supply of the American Colonies before 1720* (Madison, 1934).

Robert Craig West, "Money in the Colonial American Economy," *Economic Inquiry*, XVI, 1978, 1–15.

Poverty and Prosperity

T. H. Breen, "Baubles of Britain: The American and Consumer Revolutions of the Eighteenth Century," *Past and Present*, CXIX, 1988, 73–104.

Cary Carson, Ronald Hoffman, and Peter J. Albert, eds, *Of Consuming Interests: The Style of Life in the Eighteenth Century* (Charlottesville, 1994).

Robert E. Cray, Jr., *Paupers and Poor Relief in New York City and its Rural Environs, 1700–1830* (Philadelphia, 1988).

David Harvey and Gregory Brown, *Common People and their Material World: Free Men and Women in the Chesapeake, 1700–1830* (Williamsburg, 1995).

Alice Hanson Jones, *Wealth of a Nation to Be: The America Colonies on the Eve of the Revolution* (New York, 1980).

Douglas Lamar Jones, "The Strolling Poor: Transiency in Eighteenth Century Massachusetts," *Journal of Social History*, VIII, 1975, 28–49.

James T. Lemon and Gary B. Nash, "The Distribution of Wealth in Eighteenth Century America: A Century of Change in Chester County, Pennsylvania, 1693–1802," *Journal of Social History*, II, 1968, 1–24.

Gloria L. Main, "Inequality in Early America: The Evidence from Probate Records of Massachusetts and Maryland," *Journal of Interdisciplinary History*, VII, 1977, 559–82.

Gary B. Nash, "Poverty and Poor Relief in Pre-revolutionary Philadelphia," *William and Mary Quarterly*, XXXIII, 1976, 3–30.

Gary B. Nash, *The Urban Crucible: Social Change, Political Consciousness, and the Origins of the American Revolution* (Cambridge, Mass., 1979).

Carla Gardina Pestana and Sharon V. Salinger, *Inequality in Early America* (Hanover, 1999).

Carole Shammas, *The Pre-industrial Consumer in England and America* (New York, 1990).

Lucy Simler, "Tenancy in Colonial Pennsylvania: The Case of Chester County," *William and Mary Quarterly*, XLIII, 1986, 543–69.

Billy G. Smith, *The "Lower Sort": Philadelphia's Laboring People, 1750–1800* (Ithaca, 1990).

Gregory A. Stiverson, *Poverty in a Land of Plenty: Tenancy in Eighteenth Century Maryland* (Baltimore, 1977).

Daniel Vickers, "Competency and Competition: Economic Culture in Early America," *William and Mary Quarterly*, XLVII, 1990, 3–29.

Lorena S. Walsh et al., "Toward a History of the Standard of Living in British North America," *William and Mary Quarterly*, XLV, 1988, 116–70.

CHAPTER 11   EUROPEAN-AMERICAN FAMILY AND SOCIETY

General

James A. Henretta et al., eds, *The Transformation of Early American History: Society, Authority, and Ideology* (New York, 1991).

Ronald Hoffman, Mechal Sobel, and Fredrika Teute, eds, *Through a Glass Darkly: Reflections on Personal Identity in Early America* (Chapel Hill, 1997).

The Family Structure

Linda Auwers Bissell, "From One Generation to Another: Mobility in Seventeenth Century Windsor, Connecticut," *William and Mary Quarterly*, XXXI, 1974, 79–110.

Kathleen Brown, *Good Wives, Nasty Wenches, and Anxious Patriarchs: Gender, Race and Power in Colonial Virginia* (Chapel Hill, 1996).

John Demos, *A Little Commonwealth: Family Life in Plymouth Colony* (New York, 1970).

John Demos, *Past, Present, and Personal: The Family and the Life Course in American History* (New York, 1986).

John Duffy, *Epidemics in Colonial America* (Baton Rouge, 1959).

Firth Haring Fabend, *A Dutch Family in the Middle Colonies, 1660–1800* (New Brunswick, 1989).

David Hackett Fischer, *Growing Old in America* (New York, 1977).

David H. Flaherty, *Privacy in Colonial New England* (Charlottesville, 1972).

Jay Fliegelman, *Prodigals and Pilgrims: The American Revolution against Patriarchal Authority, 1750–1800* (New York, 1982).

Vivian C. Fox and Martin H. Quitt, *Loving, Parenting, and Dying: The Family Cycle in England and America, Past and Present* (New York, 1980).

J. William Frost, *The Quaker Family in Colonial America: A Portrait of the Society of Friends* (New York, 1973).

Philip J. Greven, "Family Structure in Seventeenth Century Andover, Massachusetts," *William and Mary Quarterly*, XXIII, 1966, 234–56.

Philip J. Greven, *Four Generations: Population, Land, and Family in Colonial Andover, Massachusetts* (Ithaca, 1970).

Philip J. Greven, "Historical Demography and Colonial America," *William and Mary Quarterly*, XXIV, 1967, 438–54.

Winthrop D. Jordan and Sheila L. Skemp, eds, *Race and Family in the Colonial South* (Jackson, 1987).

Peter Laslett, ed., *Household and Family in Past Time: Comparative Studies in the Size and Structure of the Domestic Group* (Cambridge, England, 1972).

Gerda Lerner, *The Creation of Patriarchy* (Oxford, 1986).

Barry Levy, "The Birth of the 'Modern Family' in Early America: Quaker and Anglican Familes in the Delaware Valley, Pennsylvania, 1681–1750," in Michael Zuckerman, ed., *Friends and Neighbors: Group Life in America's First Plural Society* (Temple, 1982), 26–56.

Barry Levy, *Quakers and the American Family: British Settlement in the Delaware Valley* (New York, 1988).

Jan Lewis, "Domestic Tranquility and the Management of Emotion among the Gentry of Pre-revolutionary Virginia," *William and Mary Quarterly*, XXXIX, 1982, 135–49.

Jan Lewis, *The Pursuit of Happiness: Family and Values in Jefferson's Virginia* (New York, 1983).

Kenneth A. Lockridge, *On the Sources of Patriarchal Rage: The Commonplace Books of William Byrd and Thomas Jefferson and the Gendering of Power in the Eighteenth Century* (New York, 1992).

Gerald R. Moran and Maris A. Vinovskis, *Religion, Family, and the Life Course: Explorations in the Social History of Early America* (Ann Arbor, 1992).

Edmund S. Morgan, *The Puritan Family: Religion and Domestic Relations in Seventeenth Century New England* (New York, 1966).

Edmund S. Morgan, *Virginians at Home: Family Life in the Eighteenth Century* (Williamsburg, 1952).

David E. Narrett, *Inheritance and Family Life in Colonial New York City* (Ithaca, 1992).

David J. Russo, *Families and Communities: A New View of American History* (Nashville, 1974).

Carole Shammas, "Anglo-American Household Government in Comparative Perspective," *William and Mary Quarterly*, LII, 1995, 104–44.

Richard H. Shyrock, *Medicine and Society in America, 1660–1860* (New York, 1960).

Daniel Blake Smith, *Inside the Great House: Planter Family Life in Eighteenth Century Chesapeake Society* (Ithaca, 1980).

Daniel Blake Smith, "The Study of the Family in Early America: Trends, Problems and Prospects," *William and Mary Quarterly*, XXXIX, 1982, 3–28.

Daniel Scott Smith, "The Demographic History of Colonial New England," *Journal of Economic History*, XXXII, 1972, 165–83.

Daniel Scott Smith, "A Perspective on Demographic Methods and Effects in Social History," *William and Mary Quarterly*, XXXIX, 1982, 442–68.

Daniel Scott Smith, "Parental Power and Marriage Patterns: An Analysis of Historical Trends in Hingham, Massachusetts," *Journal of Marriage and the Family*, XXXV, 1973, 406–18.

Daniel Scott Smith, and M. S. Hindus, "Premarital Pregnancy in America, 1640–1971: An Overview and Interpretation," *Journal of Interdisciplinary History*, V, 1975, 537–70.

Lawrence Stone, *The Family, Sex, and Marriage in England, 1500–1800* (New York, 1977).

Roger Thompson, *Sex in Middlesex: Popular Mores in a Massachusetts County, 1649–1699* (Amherst, 1986).

Helena M. Wall, *Fierce Communion: Family and Community in Early America* (Cambridge, Mass., 1990).

John J. Waters, Jr., "Patrimony, Succession, and Social Stability: Guilford, Connecticut in the Eighteenth Century," *Perspectives in American History*, X, 1976, 131–60.

John J. Waters, Jr., "Family, Inheritance, and Migration in Colonial New England: The Evidence from Guilford, Connecticut," *William and Mary Quarterly*, XXXIX, 1982, 64–86.

Robert V. Wells, "Demographic Change and the Life Cycle of American Families," *Journal of Interdisciplinary History*, XI, 1971, 273–82.

Lisa Wilson, *Ye Heart of a Man: Domestic Life of Men in Colonial New England* (New Haven, 1999).

E. A. Wrigley and R. S. Schofield, *The Population History of England, 1541–1871: A Reconstruction* (London, 1981).

Children

Gillian Avery, *Behold the Child: American Children and their Books, 1621–1922* (Baltimore, 1992).

Ross W. Beales, Jr., "In Search of the Historical Child: Miniature Adulthood and Youth in Colonial New England," *American Quarterly*, XXVII, 1975.

Karin Calvert, *Children in the House: The Material Culture of Early Childhood, 1600–1800* (Boston, 1992).

John Demos, *Spare the Child: The Religious Roots of Punishment and the Psychological Impact of Physical Abuse* (New York, 1991).

Philip J. Greven, *The Protestant Temperament: Patterns of Child Rearing, Religious Experience, and the Self in Early America* (New York, 1977).

Peter Hoffer and N. E. H. Hull, *Murdering Mothers: Infanticide in England and New England, 1588–1803* (New York, 1981).

Susan E. Klepp, "Lost, Hidden, Obstructed, and Repressed: Contraceptive and Abortive Technology in the Early Delaware Valley," in Judith A. McGaw, ed., *Early American Technology: Making and Doing Things from the Colonial Era to 1850* (Chapel Hill, 1994).

Barry J. Levy, " 'Tender Plants': Quaker Farmers and Children in the Delaware Valley, 1681–1735," *Journal of Family History*, III, 1978, 116–35.

Catherine M. Scholten, *Childbearing in American Society: 1650–1850* (New York, 1985).

Peter Gregg Slater, *Children in the New England Mind in Death and in Life* (Hamden, 1977).

Glenn Wallach, *Obedient Sons: The Discourse of Youth and Generations in American Culture, 1630–1860* (Amherst, 1997).

Social Structure

Holly Brewer, "Entailing Aristocracy in Colonial Virginia: 'Ancient Feudal Restraints' and Revolutionary Reform," *William and Mary Quarterly*, LIV, 1997, 307–46.

Robert E. Brown, *Middle Class Democracy and the Revolution in Massachusetts, 1691–1780* (Ithaca, 1955).

Robert E. Brown and B. Katherine Brown, *Virginia, 1705–1786: Aristocracy or Democracy?* (East Lansing, 1964).

Lois Green Carr, Philip D. Morgan, and Jean B. Russo, eds, *Colonial Chesapeake Society* (Chapel Hill, 1989).

John Cary, "Statistical Method and the Brown Thesis on Colonial Democracy," *William and Mary Quarterly*, XX, 1963, 251–76.

Edward Countryman, "Stability and Class, Theory and History: The South in the Eighteenth Century," *Journal of American Studies*, XVII, 1983, 243–50.

Bruce C. Daniels, ed., *Power and Status: Office Holding in Colonial America* (Middletown, 1986).

Jack P. Greene, *The Intellectual Construction of America: Exceptionalism and Identity from 1492 to 1800* (Chapel Hill, 1993).

James A. Henretta, *The Evolution of American Society, 1700–1815: An Interdisciplinary Analysis* (Lexington, Mass., 1973).

James A. Henretta and Gregory H. Nobles, *Evolution and Revolution: American Society, 1600–1820* (Lexington, Mass., 1987).

Stephen Innes, *Labor in a New Land: Economy and Society in Seventeenth Century Springfield* (Princeton, 1983).

C. Ray Keim, "Primogeniture and Entail in Colonial Virginia," *William and Mary Quarterly*, XXV, 1968, 545–86.

Sung Bok Kim, "A New Look at the Great Landlords of Eighteenth Century New York," *William and Mary Quarterly*, XXVII, 1970, 581–614.

Kenneth A. Lockridge, *The Diary, and Life, of William Byrd II of Virginia, 1674–1744* (Chapel Hill, 1987).

Carla Gardina Pestana and Sharon V. Salinger, *Inequality in Early America* (Hanover, 1999).

Darrett B. Rutman and Anita H. Rutman, *A Place in Time: Middlesex County, Virginia, 1650–1750* (New York, 1984).

Robert Zemsky, *Merchants, Farmers and River Gods: An Essay on Eighteenth Century American Politics* (Boston, 1971).

Michael Zuckerman, "Tocqueville, Turner, and Turds: Four Stories of Manners in Early America," *Journal of American History*, LXXXV, 1998, 13–42.

CHAPTER 12   EUROPEAN-AMERICAN WOMEN

General

Mary Sumner Benson, *Women in Eighteenth Century America: A Study of Opinion and Social Usage* (New York, 1935; 2nd edn, Port Washington, 1966).

Carol Berkin, *First Generations: Women in Colonial America* (New York, 1996).

Virginia Bernhard, Betty Brandon, Elizabeth Fox-Genovese, and Theda Perdue, eds, *Southern Women: Histories and Identities* (Columbia, 1992).

Elaine Forman Crane, *Ebb Tide in New England: Women, Seaports, and Social Change, 1630–1800* (Boston, 1998).

Larry D. Eldridge, *Women and Freedom in Early America* (New York, 1997).

Sharon M. Harris, ed., *American Women Writers to 1800* (New York, 1996).

Ronald Hoffman and Peter J. Albert, eds, *Women in the Age of the American Revolution* (Charlottesville, 1989).

Esther Katz and Anita Rapone, *Women's Experience in America: An Historical Anthology* (New Brunswick, 1980).

Gerda Lerner, *The Majority Finds its Past: Placing Women in History* (New York, 1979).

Mary Beth Norton, "The Evolution of White Women's Experience in Early America," *American Historical Review*, LXXXIX, 1984, 593–619.

Mary Beth Norton, *Founding Mothers and Fathers: Gendered Power and the Forming of American Society* (New York, 1996).

Anne Firor Scott, *Unheard Voices: The First Historians of Southern Women* (Charlottesville, 1993).

Merril D. Smith, *Sex and Sexuality in Early America* (New York, 1998).

Roger Thompson, *Women in Stuart England and America: A Comparative Study* (Boston, 1974).

Paula A. Treckel, *To Comfort the Heart: Women in Seventeenth Century America* (New York, 1996).

Life Cycles

Linda Briggs Biemer, *Women and Property in Colonial New York: The Transition from Dutch to English Law, 1643–1727* (Ann Arbor, 1983).

Lois Green Carr and Lorena S. Walsh, "The Planter's Wife: The Experience of White Women in Seventeenth Century Maryland," *William and Mary Quarterly*, XXXIV, 1977, 542–71.

Nancy F. Cott, "Divorce and the Changing Status of Women in Eighteenth Century Massachusetts," *William and Mary Quarterly*, XXXIII, 1976, 586–614.

Cornelia Hughes Dayton, "Taking the Trade: Abortion and Gender Relations in an Eighteenth Century New England Village," *William and Mary Quarterly*, XLVIII, 1991, 19–49.

Mary Maples Dunn, "Saints and Sisters: Congregational and Quaker Women in the Early Colonial Period," *American Quarterly*, XXX, 1978, 582–601.

Thomas A. Foster, "Deficient Husbands: Manhood, Sexual Incapacity, and Male Marital Sexuality in Seventeenth-century New England," *William and Mary Quarterly*, LVI, 1999, 723–44.

Deborah Gough, "A Further Look at Widows in Early Southeastern Pennsylvania," *William and Mary Quarterly*, XLIV, 1987, 829–39.

Joan R. Gundersen and Gwen Victor Gampel, "Married Women's Legal Status in Eighteenth Century New York and Virginia," *William and Mary Quarterly*, XXXIX, 1982, 114–43.

Kevin J. Hayes, *A Colonial Woman's Bookshelf* (Knoxville, 1996).

N. E. H. Hull, *Female Felons: Women and Serious Crime in Colonial Massachusetts* (Urbana, 1987).

Alexander Kayssar, "Widowhood in Eighteenth Century Massachusetts: A Problem in the History of the Family," *Perspectives in American History*, VII, 1974, 83–118.

Linda K. Kerber, *Women of the Republic: Intellect and Ideology in Revolutionary America* (Chapel Hill, 1980).

Lyle Koehler, *A Search for Power: The Weaker Sex in Seventeenth Century New England* (Urbana, 1980).

Judith Walzer Leavitt, *Brought to Bed: Childbearing in America, 1750–1950* (New York, 1986).

J. A. Leo Lemay, ed., *Robert Bolling Woos Anne Miller: Love and Courtship in Colonial Virginia, 1760* (Charlottesville, 1990).

Mary Beth Norton, "Gender and Defamation in Seventeenth Century Maryland," *William and Mary Quarterly*, XLIV, 1987, 3–39.

Mary Beth Norton, *Liberty's Daughters: The Revolutionary Experience of American Women, 1750–1800* (Boston, 1980).

Marylynn Salmon, "Equality or Submersion?: Femme Couvert Status in Early Pennsylvania," in Carol Ruth Berkin and Mary Beth Norton, eds, *Women of America: A History* (Boston, 1979).

Marylynn Salmon, *Women and the Law of Property in Early America* (Chapel Hill, 1986).

Marylynn Salmon, "Women and Property in South Carolina: The Evidence from Marriage Settlements, 1730–1830," *William and Mary Quarterly*, XXXIX, 1982, 655–85.

Carole Shammas, Marylynn Salmon, and M. Dahlin, *Inheritance in America: From Colonial Times to the Present* (New Brunswick, 1987).

Merril D. Smith, *Breaking the Bonds: Marital Discord in Pennsylvania, 1730–1830* (New York, 1991).

Linda E. Speth and Alison Duncan Hirsch, *Women, Family, and Community in Colonial America: Two Perspectives* (New York, 1983).

Laurel Thatcher Ulrich, *Good Wives: Image and Reality in the Lives of Women in Northern New England, 1650–1750* (New York, 1982).

Alan D. Watson, "Women in Colonial North Carolina: Overlooked and Underestimated," *North Carolina Historical Review*, LVIII, 1981, 1–22.

Robert V. Wells, "Quaker Marriage Patterns in a Colonial Perspective," *William and Mary Quarterly*, XXIX, 1972, 415–42.

Lisa Wilson, *Life after Death: Widows in Pennsylvania, 1750–1850* (Philadelphia, 1992).

Employment

Rosalyn Baxandall, Linda Gordon, and Susan Reverby, eds, *America's Working Women: A Documentary History, 1600–Present* (New York, 1976).

Cornelia Hughes Dayton, *Women before the Bar: Gender, Law and Society in Connecticut, 1639–1789* (Chapel Hill, 1995).

Elizabeth A. Dexter, *Colonial Women of Affairs: Women in Business and the Professions in America before 1776* (Boston, 1931).

Joan M. Jensen, *Loosening the Bonds: Mid-Atlantic Farm Women, 1750–1850* (New Haven, 1986).

Jean P. Jordan, "Women Merchants in Colonial New York," *New York History*, LVIII, 1977, 416–36.

Cynthia A. Kierner, *Southern Women in Revolution, 1776–1800* (Columbia, 1998).

Cynthia A. Kierner, *Beyond the Household: Women's Place in the Early South, 1700–1835* (Ithaca, 1998).

Gloria L. Main, "Gender, Work, and Wages in Colonial New England," *William and Mary Quarterly*, LI, 1994, 39–66.

Deborah A. Rosen, *Courts and Commerce: Gender, Law, and the Market Economy in Colonial New York* (Columbus, 1997).

Jean Soderland, "Women's Authority in Pennsylvania and New Jersey Quaker Meetings, 1680–1760," *William and Mary Quarterly*, XLIV, 1987, 722–49.

Julia Cherry Spruill, *Women's Life and Work in the Southern Colonies* (Chapel Hill, 1938).

Laurel Thatcher Ulrich, "Wheels, Looms, and the Gender Division of Labor in the Eighteenth Century," *William and Mary Quarterly*, LV, 1998, 3–38.

Karin Wulf, *Not All Wives: Women of Colonial Philadelphia* (Ithaca, 2000).

CHAPTER 13   EUROPEAN-AMERICAN RELIGION, EDUCATION, AND CULTURE, 1689–1760

General

Jack P. Greene, *Pursuits of Happiness: The Social Development of Early Modern British Colonies and the Formation of American Culture* (Chapel Hill, 1988).

Ned C. Landsman, *From Colonials to Provincials: American Thought and Culture, 1680–1760* (New York, 1997).

Henry F. May, *The Enlightenment in America* (New York, 1976).

Esmond Wright, *Franklin of Philadelphia* (Cambridge, Mass., 1986).

Esmond Wright, ed., *Benjamin Franklin: His Life as He Wrote It* (Cambridge, Mass., 1990).

Religion

Sidney E. Ahlstrom, *A Religious History of the American People*, 2 vols (New Haven, 1972).

Randall H. Balmer, *A Perfect Babel of Confusion: Dutch Religion and English Culture in the Middle Colonies* (New York, 1989).

S. Charles Bolton, *Southern Anglicanism: The Church of England in Colonial South Carolina* (Westport, 1982).

Patricia U. Bonomi, *Under the Cope of Heaven: Religion, Society, and Politics in Colonial America* (New York, 1986).

Patricia U. Bonomi and Peter R. Eisenstadt, "Church Adherence in the Eighteenth Century British American Colonies," *William and Mary Quarterly*, XXXIX, 1982, 245–86.

Richard L. Bushman, ed., *The Great Awakening: Documents on the Revival of Religion, 1740–1745* (Chapel Hill, 1989).

Jon Butler, *Awash in a Sea of Faith: Christianizing the American People* (Cambridge, Mass., 1990).

Jon Butler, "Enthusiasm Described and Decried: The Great Awakening as Interpretive Fiction," *Journal of American History*, LXIX, 1982–3, 303–25.

Milton J. Coalter, *Gilbert Tennent, Son of Thunder* (Westport, 1986).

Ralph J. Coffman, *Solomon Stoddard* (Boston, 1978).

James F. Cooper, Jr., *Tenacious of their Liberties: The Congregationalist in Colonial Massachusetts* (New York, 1999).

John Tracy Ellis, *Catholics in Colonial America* (Baltimore, 1965).

Norman Fiering, *Jonathan Edwards's Moral Thought and its British Context* (Chapel Hill, 1981).

Edwin Scott Gaustad, *The Great Awakening in New England* (New York, 1957).

Christopher Grasso, *A Speaking Aristocracy: Transforming Public Discourse in Eighteenth Century Connecticut* (Chapel Hill, 2000).

Keith L. Griffin, *Revolution and Religion: American Revolutionary War and the Reformed Clergy* (New York, 1994).

Philip F. Gura, "Going Mr Stoddard's Way: William Williams on Church Privileges, 1693," *William and Mary Quarterly*, XLV, 1988, 489–98.

Timothy D. Hall, *Contested Boundaries: Itinerancy and the Reshaping of the Colonial American Religious World* (Durham, NC, 1994).

Nathan O. Hatch, *The Sacred Cause of Liberty: Republican Thought and the Millennium in Revolutionary New England* (New Haven, 1977).

Nathan O. Hatch and Harry S. Stout, *Jonathan Edwards and the American Experience* (New York, 1988).

Alan Heimert, *Religion and the American Mind from the Great Awakening to the Revolution* (Cambridge, Mass., 1966).

Rhys Isaac, "Evangelical Revolt: The Nature of the Baptists' Challenge to the Traditional Order in Virginia, 1765–1775," *William and Mary Quarterly*, XXXI, 1974, 345–66.

Rhys Isaac, "Religion and Authority: Problems of the Anglican Establishment in Virginia in the Era of the Great Awakening and the Parsons' Cause," *William and Mary Quarterly*, XXX, 1973, 3–36.

Alessa Johns, ed., *Dreadful Visitations: Confronting Natural Catastrophe in the Age of the Enlightenment* (New York, 1999).

James W. Jones, *The Shattered Synthesis: New England Puritanism before the Great Awakening* (New Haven, 1973).

Frank Lambert, *Inventing the "Great Awakening"* (Princeton, 1999).

Frank Lambert, *"Pedlar in Divinity": George Whitefield and the Transatlantic Revivals* (Princeton, 1994).

Brian F. Lee Beau, *Jonathan Dickinson and the Formative Years of American Presbyterianism* (Lexington, 1997).

Janet Moore Lindman, "Acting the Many Christian: White Evangelical Masculinity in Revolutionary Virginia," *William and Mary Quarterly*, LVII, 2000, 393–416.

Stephen L. Longenecker, *Piety and Tolerance: Pennsylvania German Religion, 1700–1850* (Metuchen, NJ, 1994).

David S. Lovejoy, *Religious Enthusiasm in the New World: Heresy to Revolution* (Cambridge, Mass., 1985).

Richard F. Lovelace, *The American Pietism of Cotton Mather: Origins of American Evangelicalism* (Grand Rapids, 1979).

Paul R. Lucas, " 'An Appeal to the Learned': The Mind of Solomon Stoddard," *William and Mary Quarterly*, XXX, 1973, 257–92.

Paul R. Lucas, *Valley of Discord: Church and Society along the Connecticut River, 1636–1725* (Hanover, 1976).

William G. McLoughlin, *Isaac Backus and the American Pietistic Tradition* (Boston, 1967).

William G. McLoughlin, *New England Dissent, 1630–1833: The Baptists and the Separation of Church and State* (Cambridge, Mass., 1971).

William G. McLoughlin, *Soul Liberty: The Baptists' Struggle in New England. 1630–1833* (Hanover, 1991).

Jack D. Marietta, *The Reformation of American Quakerism, 1748–1783* (Philadelphia, 1984).

Perry Miller, "Preparation for Salvation in Seventeenth Century New England," *Nature's Nation* (Cambridge, Mass., 1967).

Ian H. Murray, *Jonathan Edwards: A New Biography* (Edinburgh, 1987).

Peter S. Onuf, "New Lights in New London: A Group Portrait of the Separatists, 1740–1745," *William and Mary Quarterly*, XXXVII, 1980, 627–44.

Richard W. Pointer, *Protestant Pluralism and the New York Experience: A Study of Eighteenth Century Religious Diversity* (Bloomington, 1988).

Sally Schwartz, *A Mixed Multitude: The Struggle for Toleration in Colonial Pennsylvania* (New York, 1987).

Kenneth Silverman, *The Life and Times of Cotton Mather* (New York, 1984).

Bruce E. Steiner, "Anglican Officeholding in Pre-revolutionary Connecticut: The Parameters of New England Community," *William and Mary Quarterly*, XXXI, 1974, 369–406.

Harry S. Stout, *The New England Soul: Preaching and Religious Culture in Colonial New England* (New York, 1986).

Harry S. Stout, "Religion, Communications, and the Ideological Origins of the American Revolution," *William and Mary Quarterly*, XXXIV, 1977, 519–41.

William W. Sweet, *Religion in Colonial America* (New York, 1942).

Patricia J. Tracy, *Jonathan Edwards, Pastor: Religion and Society in Eighteenth-century Northampton* (New York, 1980).

Mark Valeri, *Law and Providence in Joseph Bellamy's New England: The Origins of the New Divinity in Revolutionary America* (Oxford, 1994).

Marilyn J. Westerkamp, *Triumph of the Laity: Scots-Irish Piety and the Great Awakening, 1625–1760* (New York, 1988).

Michael P. Winship, *Seers of God: Puritan Providentialism in the Restoration and Early Enlightenment* (Baltimore, 1996).

John Frederick Woolverton, *Colonial Anglicanism in North America* (Detroit, 1984).

Arthur J. Worrall, *Quakers in the Colonial Northeast* (Hanover, 1980).

J. William T. Youngs, Jr., *God's Messengers: Religious Leadership in Colonial New England, 1700–1750* (Baltimore, 1976).

Education

James Axtell, *The School upon a Hill: Education and Society in Colonial New England* (New Haven, 1974).

Bernard Bailyn, *Education in the Forming of American Society: Needs and Opportunities for Study* (Chapel Hill, 1960).

Whitfield J. Bell, Jr., *The Colonial Physician and Other Essays* (New York, 1975).

Stephen Botein, "The Legal Profession in Colonial North America," in Wilfred Prest, ed., *Lawyers in Early Modern Europe and America* (New York, 1981).

Richard D. Brown, *Knowledge is Power: The Diffusion of Information in Early America, 1700–1865* (New York, 1989).

Richard D. Brown, *The Strength of a People: The Idea of an Informed Citizenry in America, 1650–1870* (Chapel Hill, 1996).

Patricia Cline Cohen, *A Calculating People: The Spread of Numeracy in Early America* (Chicago, 1983).

Lawrence A. Cremin, *American Education: The Colonial Experience, 1607–1783* (New York, 1970).

Alan F. Day, *A Social Study of Lawyers in Maryland, 1660–1775* (New York, 1989).

Sandra M. Gustafson, *Eloquence is Power: Oratory and Performance in Early America* (Chapel Hill, 2000).

Peter Charles Hoffer, *Law and People in Colonial America* (Baltimore, 1992).

Lester S. King, *The Medical World of the Eighteenth Century* (Chicago, 1958).

Kenneth A. Lockridge, *Literacy in Colonial New England: An Enquiry into the Social Context of Literacy in the Early Modern West* (New York, 1974).

Robert Middlekauf, *Ancients and Axioms: Secondary Education in Eighteenth Century New England* (New Haven, 1963).

Richard B. Morris, *Studies in the History of American Law, with Special Reference to the Seventeenth and Eighteenth Centuries* (2nd edn, Philadelphia, 1959).

Howard Miller, *The Revolutionary College: American Presbyterian Higher Education, 1707–1837* (New York, 1976).

Samuel Eliot Morison, *The Founding of Harvard College* (Cambridge, Mass., 1935).

Lamar Riley Murphy, *Enter the Physician: The Transformation of Domestic Medicine, 1760–1860* (Tuscaloosa, 1991).

John M. Murrin, "The Legal Transformation: The Bench and Bar of Eighteenth Century Massachusetts," in Stanley N. Katz, ed., *Colonial America: Essays in Politics and Social Development* (Boston, 1971).

Richard Warch, *School of the Prophets: Yale College, 1701–1740* (New Haven, 1973).

Libraries, Literature, and the Press

Charles E. Clark, *The Public Print: The Newspaper in Anglo-American Culture, 1665–1740* (New York, 1994).

David A. Copeland, *Colonial American Newspapers: Character and Content* (Newark, 1997).

Richard Beale Davis, *A Colonial Southern Bookshelf: Reading in the Eighteenth Century* (Athens, 1979).

Thomas M. Davis, *A Reading of Edward Taylor* (Newark, 1992).

Norman Fiering, "The Transatlantic Republic of Letters: A Note on the Circulation of Learned Periodicals to Early Eighteenth Century America," *William and Mary Quarterly*, XXXIII, 1976, 642–60.

David D. Hall and John B. Hench, eds, *Needs and Opportunities in the History of the Book: America, 1639–1876* (Worcester, 1987).

William L. Joyce et al., eds, *Printing and Society in Early America* (Worcester, 1983).

Leonard W. Levy, *The Emergence of a Free Press* (New York, 1985).

William Pencak and Wythe W. Holt, Jr., *The Law in America, 1607–1861* (New York, 1989).

William David Sloan and Julie Hedgepeth Williams, *The Early American Press, 1690–1783* (Westport, 1994).

Jeffrey A. Smith, *Printers and Press Freedom: The Ideology of Early American Journalism* (New York, 1988).

John Tebbel, *A History of Book Publishing in the United States*, Vol. 1: *The Creation of an Industry, 1630–1865* (New York, 1972).

Julie Hedgepeth Williams, *The Significance of the Printed Word in Early America: Colonists' Thoughts on the Role of the Press* (Greenwood, 1999).

Edwin Wolf, *The Library of James Logan of Philadelphia, 1674–1751* (Philadelphia, 1974).

Science

Silvio A. Bedini, *Thinkers and Tinkers: Early American Men of Science* (New York, 1975).
Whitfield J. Bell, Jr., *The Colonial Physician and Other Essays* (New York, 1975).
I. Bernard Cohen, *Benjamin Franklin's Science* (Cambridge, Mass., 1990).
Colonial Society of Massachusetts Publications, *Medicine in Colonial Massachusetts, 1620–1820* (Boston, 1980).
Brooke Hindle, *The Pursuit of Science in Revolutionary America, 1735–1789* (Chapel Hill, 1956).
Brooke Hindle, ed., *America's Wooden Age: Aspects of its Early Technology* (Tarrytown, 1975).
Randolph Sidney Klein, ed., *Science and Society in Early America: Essays in Honor of Whitfield J. Bell, Jr.* (Philadelphia, 1986).
Ronald Numbers, ed., *Medicine in the New World: New Spain, New France, and New England* (Knoxville, 1987).
Raymond Phineas Stearns, *Science in the British Colonies of America* (Urbana, 1970).

The Arts

A. Owen Aldridge, *Early American Literature: A Comparatist Approach* (Princeton, 1982).
Waldron Phoenix Belknap, Jr., *American Colonial Painting: Materials for a History* (Cambridge, Mass., 1959).
Wendy Cooper, *In Praise of America: American Decorative Arts, 1650–1830* (New York, 1980).
Wayne Craven, *Colonial American Portraiture: The Economic, Religious, Social, Cultural, Philosophical, Scientific, and Aesthetic Foundations* (New York, 1986).
Richard Beale Davis, *Literature and Society in Early Virginia, 1608–1840* (Baton Rouge, 1973).
Emory Elliott, *Revolutionary Writers: Literature and Authority in the New Republic, 1725–1810* (New York, 1982).
Jonathan L. Fairbanks and Robert F. Trent, *New England Begins: The Seventeenth Century* (Boston, 1982).
Norman S. Grabo, *Edward Taylor* (Boston, rev. edn, 1988).
Philip F. Gura, "The Study of Colonial American Literature, 1966–1987, A Vade Mecum," *William and Mary Quarterly*, XLV, 1988, 305–41.
Sharon M. Harris, ed., *American Women Writers to 1800* (New York, 1996).
Graham Hood, *Charles Bridges and William Dering: Two Virginia Painters, 1735–1750* (Williamsburg, 1978).
J. A. Leo Lemay, ed., *Essays in Early Virginia Literature Honoring Richard Beale Davis* (New York, 1977).
Irving Lowens, *Music and Musicians in Early America* (New York, 1964).
Brooks McNamara, *The American Playhouse in the Eighteenth Century* (Cambridge, Mass., 1969).
Hugh F. Rankin, *The Theatre in Colonial America* (Chapel Hill, 1965).
Richard H. Saunders and Ellen G. Miles, *American Colonial Portraits, 1700–1776* (Washington, 1987).
David S. Shields, *Civil Tongues and Polite Letters in British America* (Chapel Hill, 1997).
David S. Shields, *Oracles of Empire: Poetry, Politics, and Commerce in British America, 1690–1750* (Chicago, 1990).
Kenneth Silverman, ed., *Colonial American Poetry* (New York, 1968).
Oscar G. Sonneck, *Early Concert-life in America, 1731–1800* (New York, 1949).
Louis B. Wright et al., *The Arts in America: The Colonial Period* (New York, 1966).

Popular Culture

Steven C. Bullock, *Revolutionary Brotherhood: Freemasonry and the Transformation of the American Social Order, 1730–1840* (Chapel Hill, 1996).

T. H. Breen, "Horses and Gentlemen: The Cultural Significance of Gambling among the Gentry of Virginia," *William and Mary Quarterly*, XXXIV, 1977, 239–57.

Jane Carson, *Colonial Virginians at Play* (Williamsburg, 1965).

David W. Conroy, *In Public Houses: Drink and the Revolution of Authority in Colonial Massachusetts* (Chapel Hill, 1995).

Bruce C. Daniels, *Puritans at Play: Leisure and Recreation in Colonial New England* (Basingstoke, 1995).

Jack P. Greene, *Landon Carter: An Inquiry into the Personal Values and Social Imperatives of the Eighteenth Century Virginia Gentry* (Charlottesville, 1965).

Daniel Walker Howe, *Making the American Self: Jonathan Edwards to Abraham Lincoln* (Cambridge, Mass., 1997).

Nancy L. Struna, *People of Prowess: Sport, Leisure, and Labor in Early Anglo-America* (Urbana, 1996).

Peter Thompson, *Rum Punch and Revolution: Tavern Going and Public Life in Eighteenth Century Philadelphia* (Philadelphia, 1999).

Architecture and Anglicization

Reinier Baarsen, Gervase Jackson-Stops, Philip M. Johnston, and Elaine Evans Dee, *Courts and Colonies: The William and Mary Style in Holland, England, and America* (New York, 1989).

T. H. Breen, "An Empire of Goods: The Anglicization of Colonial America, 1690–1776," *Journal of British Studies*, XXV, 1986, 467–99.

Richard L. Bushman, "American High Style and Vernacular Cultures," in Jack P. Greene and J. R. Pole, eds, *Colonial British America: Essays in the New History of the Early Modern Era* (Baltimore, 1984).

Richard L. Bushman, *The Refinement of America: Persons, Houses, Cities* (New York, 1992).

Jon Butler, *Becoming America: The Revolution before 1776* (Cambridge, Mass., 2000).

Cary Carson et al., "Impermanent Architecture in the Southern American Colonies," *Winterthur Portfolio: A Journal of Material Culture*, XVI, 1981, 135–96.

John Clive and Bernard Bailyn, "England's Cultural Provinces: Scotland and America," *William and Mary Quarterly*, XI, 1954, 200–13.

Abbott Lowell Cummings, *The Framed Houses of Massachusetts Bay, 1625–1725* (Cambridge, Mass., 1979).

James Deetz, *In Small Things Forgotten: The Archeology of Early American Life* (New York, 1977).

David Hackett Fischer, *Albion's Seed: Four British Folkways in America* (New York, 1989).

Jack P. Greene, *Imperatives, Behaviors, and Identities: Essays in Early American Cultural History* (Charlottesville, 1992).

John T. Kirk, *American Furniture and the British Tradition to 1830* (New York, 1982).

James D. Kornwolf, "So Good a Design." The Colonial Campus of the College of William and Mary: Its History, Background, and Legacy (Williamsburg, 1989).

William H. Pierson, Jr., *American Buildings and their Architects*, Vol. I: *The Colonial and Neoclassical Styles* (New York, 1970).

Daniel D. Reiff, *Small Georgian Houses in England and Virginia: Origins and Development through the 1750s* (Newark, 1986).

Michal J. Rozbicki, *The Complete Gentleman: Cultural Legitimacy in Plantation America* (Charlottesville, 1998).

Robert Blair St. George, *Conversing by Signs: Poetics of Implication in Colonial New England Culture* (Chapel Hill, 1998).

Robert Blair St. George, ed., *Material Life in America, 1600–1860* (Boston, 1988).

Barbara Wells Sarudy, *Gardens and Gardening in the Chesapeake, 1700–1805* (Baltimore, 1998).

Harold R. Shurtleff, *The Log Cabin Myth: A Study of the Early Dwellings of the English Colonists in North America* (Cambridge, Mass., 1939).

Dell Upton, *Holy Things and Profane: Anglican Parish Churches in Colonial Virginia* (Cambridge, Mass., 1987).

Thomas Tileston Waterman, *The Mansions of Virginia, 1706–1776* (Chapel Hill, 1946).

C. A. Weslager, *The Log Cabin in America: From Pioneer Days to the Present* (New Brunswick, 1969).

CHAPTER 14 AFRICAN-AMERICAN SOCIETY AND CULTURE, 1689–1760

General

Theodore W. Allen, *The Invention of the White Race*, Vol. 1: *Racial Oppression and Social Control* (New York, 1994); Vol. 2: *The Origins of Racial Oppression in Anglo-America* (New York, 1997).

Ira Berlin, "From Creole to African: Atlantic Creoles and the Origins of African-American Society in Mainland North America," *William and Mary Quarterly*, LIII, 1996, 251–88.

Ira Berlin, *Many Thousands Gone: The First Two Centuries of Slavery in North America* (Cambridge, Mass., 1998).

Robin Blackburn, *The Making of New World Slavery: From the Baroque to the Modern, 1492–1899* (New York, 1997).

Philip S. Foner, *History of Black Americans from Africa to the Emergence of the Cotton Kingdom* (Westport, 1975).

Stephan Palmié, *Slave Cultures and the Cultures of Slavery* (Knoxville, 1995).

John Thornton, *Africa and Africans in the Making of the Atlantic World, 1400–1680* (New York, 1992).

James Walvin, *Black Ivory: A History of British Slavery* (New York, 1992).

Betty Wood, *The Origins of American Slavery: Freedom and Bondage in the English Colonies* (New York, 1997).

Peter H. Wood, " 'I Did the Best I Could for My Day': The Study of Early Black History during the Second Reconstruction, 1960–1976," *William and Mary Quarterly*, XXXV, 1978, 185–225.

Donald R. Wright, *African-Americans in the Colonial Era: From African Origins through the American Revolution* (Arlington Heights, 1990).

The Slave Trade and African Background

Philip D. Curtin, *The Atlantic Slave Trade: A Census* (Madison, 1969).

K. G. Davies, *The Royal African Company* (London, 1957).

David Eltis and David Richardson, *Routes to Slavery: Direction, Ethnicity, and Mortality in the Transatlantic Slave Trade* (London, 1997).

J. C. Fage, "Slaves and Society in Western Africa, c. 1440–c. 1700," *Journal of African History*, XXI, 1981, 289–310.

Herbert S. Klein, *The Middle Passage: Comparative Studies in the Atlantic Slave Trade* (Princeton, 1978).

Herbert Klein, "Slaves and Shipping in Eighteenth Century Virginia", *Journal of Interdisciplinary History*, V, 1975, 383–412.

Daniel C. Littlefield, *Rice and Slaves: Ethnicity and the Slave Trade in Colonial South Carolina* (Baton Rouge, 1981).

Paul E. Lovejoy, *Transformations in Slavery: A History of Slavery in Africa* (Cambridge, England, 1983).

Paul E. Lovejoy, "The Volume of the Atlantic Slave Trade: A Synthesis," *Journal of African History*, XXIII, 1982, 483–7.

Patrick Manning, *Slavery and African Life: Occidental, Oriental, and African Slave Trades* (New York, 1990).

Daniel Pratt Mannix, *Black Cargoes: A History of the Atlantic Slave Trade, 1518–1865* (New York, 1962).

James Pope-Hennessy, *Sins of the Fathers: A Study of the Atlantic Slave Traders, 1441–1807* (New York, 1968).

James A. Rawley, *The Transatlantic Slave Trade: A History* (New York, 1981).

Mechal Sobel, *Trabelin' On: The Slave Journey to an Afro-Baptist Faith* (Princeton, 1979).

Barbara L. Solow, *Slavery and the Rise of the Atlantic System* (Cambridge, England, 1991).

Hugh Thomas, *The Slave Trade: The Story of the Atlantic Slave Trade, 1440–1870* (New York, 1997).

U. B. Thompson, *The Making of the African Diaspora in the Americas, 1441–1900* (London, 1988).

John Thornton, "The African Experience of the '20 and Odd Negroes' Arriving in Virginia in 1619," *William and Mary Quarterly*, LV, 1998, 421–34.

Susan Westbury, "Slaves of Colonial Virginia: Where They Came From," *William and Mary Quarterly*, XLII, 1985, 228–37.

The African-American Family, Work, and Culture

Ira Berlin, "Time, Space, and the Evolution of Afro-American Society on British Mainland North America," *American Historical Review*, LXXXV, 1980, 44–78.

Ira Berlin and Philip D. Morgan, eds, *Cultivation and Culture: Labor and the Shaping of Slave Life in the Americas* (Charlottesville, 1993).

Margaret Washington Creel, *"A Peculiar People": Slave Religion and Community-culture among the Gullahs* (New York, 1988).

Sylviane Diouf, *Servants of Allah: African Muslims Enslaved in the Americas* (New York, 1998).

Dena J. Epstein, *Sinful Tunes and Spirituals: Black Folk Music to the Civil War* (Urbana, 1977).

Leland Ferguson, *Uncommon Ground: Archaeology and Early Africa America, 1650–1800* (Washington, 1992).

Sylvia Frey and Betty Wood, *Come Shouting to Zion: African American Protestantism in the American South and British Caribbean to 1830* (Chapel Hill, 1998).

Michael A. Gomez, *Exchanging our Country Marks: The Transformation of African Identities in the Colonial and Antebellum South* (Chapel Hill, 1998).

Michael A. Gomez, "Muslims in Early America," *Journal of Southern History*, LX, 1994, 671–710.

Lorenzo J. Greene, *The Negro in Colonial New England, 1620–1776* (New York, 1942).

Joan Gunderson, "The Double Bonds of Race and Sex: Black and White Women in a Colonial Virginia Parish," *Journal of Southern History*, LII, 1986, 351–72.

Herbert G. Gutman, *The Black Family in Slavery and Freedom, 1750–1925* (New York, 1976).

Jacqueline Jones, "Race, Sex, and Self-evident Truths: The Status of Slave Women during the Era of the American Revolution," in Ronald Hoffman and Peter J. Albert, eds, *Women in the Age of the American Revolution* (Charlottesville, 1989).

Allan Kulikoff, "The Beginnings of the Afro-American Family in Maryland," in Aubrey C. Land, Lois Green Carr, and Edward C. Papenfuse, eds, *Law, Society, and Politics in Early Maryland* (Baltimore, 1977).

Allan Kulikoff, "The Origins of Afro-American Society in Tidewater Maryland and Virginia, 1700–1790," *William and Mary Quarterly*, XXXV, 1978, 226–50.

Allan Kulikoff, " 'A Prolifick People': Black Population Growth in the Chesapeake Colonies, 1700–1790," *Southern Studies*, XVI, 1977, 391–428.

Allan Kulikoff, *Tobacco and Slaves: The Development of Southern Cultures in the Chesapeake, 1680–1800* (Chapel Hill, 1986).

Jean Butenhoff Lee, "The Problem of Slave Community in the Eighteenth Century Chesapeake," *William and Mary Quarterly*, XLIII, 1986, 333–61.

Russell R. Menard, "The Maryland Slave Population, 1658 to 1730: A Demographic Profile of Blacks in Four Counties," *William and Mary Quarterly*, XXXII, 1975, 29–54.

Philip D. Morgan, *Slave Counterpoint: Black Culture in the Eighteenth-century Chesapeake and Lowcountry* (Chapel Hill, 1998).

Philip D. Morgan, "Slave Life in Piedmont Virginia, 1720–1800," in Lois Green Carr, Philip D. Morgan, and Jean Russo, eds, *Colonial Chesapeake Society* (Chapel Hill, 1989), 433–84.

Philip D. Morgan, "Work and Culture: The Task System and the World of Lowcountry Blacks, 1700–1800," *William and Mary Quarterly*, XXXIX, 1982, 563–99.

Philip D. Morgan and Michael L. Nicholls, "Slaves in Piedmont Virginia, 1720–1790," *William and Mary Quarterly*, XLVI, 1989, 211–51.

Patricia Morton, ed., *Discovering the Women in Slavery* (Athens, 1995).

Michael Mullin, *Africa in America: Slave Acculturation and Resistance in the American South and the British Caribbean, 1736–1831* (Urbana, 1992).

Patricia Samford, "The Archaeology of African American Slavery and Material Culture," *William and Mary Quarterly*, LIII, 1996, 87–114.

Erik R. Seeman, " 'Justice Must Take Plase': Three African Americans Speak of Religion in Eighteenth-century New England," *William and Mary Quarterly*, LVI, 1999, 393–414.

John F. Sensbach, *A Separate Canaan: The Making of an Afro-Moravian World in North Carolina, 1763–1840* (Chapel Hill, 1997).

Mechal Sobel, *The World They Made Together: Black and White Values in Eighteenth Century Virginia* (Princeton, 1987).

Thad W. Tate, *The Negro in Eighteenth Century Williamsburg* (Williamsburg, 1965).

John Thornton, "Central African Names and African-American Naming Patterns," *William and Mary Quarterly*, L, 1993, 727–42.

Lorena S. Walsh, *From Calabar to Carter's Grove: The History of a Virginia Slave Community* (Charlottesville, 1997).

Lorena S. Walsh, "Slave Life, Slave Society, and Tobacco Production in the Tidewater Chesapeake, 1620–1820", in Ira Berlin and Philip D. Morgan, eds, *Cultivation and Culture: Labor and the Shaping of Slave Life in the Americas* (Charlottesville, 1993).

Betty Wood, *Slavery in Colonial Georgia, 1730–1775* (Athens, 1984).

Peter H. Wood, *Black Majority: Negroes in Colonial South Carolina from 1670 through the Stono Rebellion* (New York, 1974).

Anne Elizabeth Yentsch, *A Chesapeake Family and their Slaves* (Cambridge, England, 1994).

White over Black: The Slave Codes

Warren S. Billings, "The Cases of Fernando and Elizabeth Key: A Note on the Status of Blacks in Seventeenth Century Virginia," *William and Mary Quarterly*, XXX, 1973, 467–74.

Thomas J. Davis, *A Rumour of Revolt: The "Great Negro Plot" in Colonial New York* (New York, 1985).

Sylvia Frey, *Like Water from the Rock: Black Resistance in a Revolutionary Age* (Princeton, 1991).

Graham Russell Hodges, *Slavery and Freedom in the Rural North: African Americans in Monmouth County, New Jersey, 1665–1865* (Madison, 1997).

Graham Russell Hodges, *Root and Branch: African Americans in New York and East New Jersey, 1613–1863* (Chapel Hill, 1999).

A. Leon Higginbotham, Jr., *In the Matter of Color: Race and the American Legal Process in the Colonial Period* (New York, 1978).

Winthrop D. Jordan, *White over Black: American Attitudes toward the Negro, 1550–1812* (Chapel Hill, 1968).

Marvin L. Michael Kay and Lorin Lee Cary, *Slavery in North Carolina, 1748–1775* (Chapel Hill, 1995).

Edward J. McManus, *Black Bondage in the North* (Syracuse, 1973).

Kenneth P. Minkema, "Jonathan Edwards on Slavery and the Slave Trade," *William and Mary Quarterly*, LIV, 1997, 823–34.

Edmund S. Morgan, *American Slavery, American Freedom: The Ordeal of Colonial Virginia* (New York, 1975).

Gerald W. Mullin, *Flight and Rebellion: Slave Resistance in Eighteenth Century Virginia* (New York, 1972).

Robert Olwell, *Masters, Slaves, and Subjects: The Culture of Power in the South Carolina Low Country, 1740–1790* (Ithaca, 1998).

Todd L. Savitt, *Medicine and Slavery: The Health Care and Diseases of Blacks in Antebellum Virginia* (Urbana, 1978).

Philip J. Schwartz, *Twice Condemned: Slaves and the Criminal Laws of Virginia, 1705–1865* (Baton Rouge, 1988).

Jean R. Soderland, *Quakers and Slavery: A Divided Spirit* (Princeton, 1985).

John Thornton, "The African Dimensions of the Stono Rebellion," *American Historical Review*, XCVI, 1991, 1101–13.

Larry E. Tise, *Proslavery: A History of the Defense of Slavery in America, 1701–1840* (Athens, 1987).

David Waldstreicher, "Reading the Runaways: Self-fashioning, Print Culture, and Confidence in Slavery in the Eighteenth-century Mid-Atlantic," *William and Mary Quarterly*, LVI, 1999, 243–72.

William M. Wiecek, "The Statutory Law of Slavery and Race in the Thirteen Mainland Colonies of British America," *William and Mary Quarterly*, XXXIV, 1977, 258–80.

Free African-Americans

Ira Berlin, *Slaves without Masters: The Free Negro in the Antebellum South* (New York, 1974).

Jane Landers, "Gracia Real de Santa Teresa de Mose: A Free Black Town in Spanish Colonial Florida," *American Historical Review*, XCV, 1990, 9–30.

William D. Piersen, *Black Yankees: The Development of an Afro-American Subculture in Eighteenth Century New England* (Amherst, 1988).

CHAPTER 15   AMERICAN INDIAN SOCIETY AND CULTURE, 1689–1760

General

James Axtell, *The European and the Indian: Essays in the Ethnohistory of Colonial North America* (New York, 1981).

James Axtell, "The White Indians of Colonial America," *William and Mary Quarterly*, XXXII, 1975, 55–88.

James Axtell and William C. Sturtevant, "The Unkindest Cut, or Who Invented Scalping," *William and Mary Quarterly*, XXXVII, 1980, 451–72.

Andrew R. L. Cayton and Fredrika J. Teute, *Contact Points: American Frontiers from the Mohawk Valley to the Mississippi, 1750–1830* (Chapel Hill, 1998).

Gregory Evans Dowd, *A Spirited Resistance: The North American Indian Struggle for Unity, 1745–1815* (Baltimore, 1992).

W. J. Eccles, "The Fur Trade and Eighteenth-century Imperialism," *William and Mary Quarterly*, XL, 1983, 341–62.

Robert S. Grumet, *Historic Contact: Indian Peoples and Colonists in Today's Northeastern United States in the Sixteenth through Eighteenth Centuries* (Norman, 1995).

Shepard Krech III, ed., *Indians, Animals, and the Fur Trade: A Critique of "Keepers of the Game"* (Athens, 1981).

Calvin Martin, ed., *The American Indian and the Problem of History* (New York, 1987).

Calvin Martin, *Keepers of the Game: Indian–Animal Relationships and the Fur Trade* (Berkeley, 1978).

James H. Merrell, "Some Thoughts on Colonial Historians and American Indians," *William and Mary Quarterly*, XLVI, 1989, 94–119.

Christopher L. Miller and George R. Hamell, "A New Perspective on Indian–White Contact: Cultural Symbols and Colonial Trade," *Journal of American History*, LXXIII, 1986–7, 311–28.

Armstrong Starkey, *European and Native American Warfare, 1675–1815* (Norman, 1998).

Helen Hornbeck Tanner and Adele Haste, *Atlas of Great Lakes Indian History* (Norman, 1987).

Bruce C. Trigger, ed., *Handbook of North American Indians*, Vol. XV: *The Northeast* (Washington, 1978).

A. T. Vaughan, "From White Man to Red Skin: Changing Anglo-American Perceptions of the American Indian," *American Historical Review*, LXXXVII, 1982, 917–53.

Wilcomb E. Washburn, *The Indian in America* (New York, 1975).

The Coastal Reservations

Colin G. Calloway, ed., *After King Philip's War: Presence and Persistence in Indian New England* (Hanover, 1997).

William Cronon, *Changes in the Land: Indians, Colonists, and the Ecology of New England* (New York, 1983).

Patrick Frazier, *The Mohicans of Stockbridge* (Lincoln, 1992).

Yasuhide Kawashima, *Puritan Justice and the Indian: White Man's Law in Massachusetts, 1630–1763* (Middletown, 1986).

Daniel R. Mandell, *Behind the Frontier: Indians in Eighteenth-century Eastern Massachusetts* (Lincoln, 1996).

Daniel R. Mandell, "Shifting Boundaries of Race and Ethnicity: Indian–Black Intermarriage in Southern New England, 1760–1880," *Journal of American History*, LXXXV, 1998, 466–501.

James H. Merrell, "Cultural Continuity among the Piscataway Indians of Colonial Maryland," *William and Mary Quarterly*, XXXVI, 1979, 548–71.

Jean M. O'Brien, *Dispossession by Degree: Indian Land and Identity in Natick, Massachusetts, 1650–1790* (Cambridge, England, 1997).

Ann Marie Plane, *Colonial Intimacies: Indian Marriages in Early New England* (Cornell, 2000).

James P. Ronda, "Generations of Faith: The Christian Indians of Martha's Vineyard," *William and Mary Quarterly*, XXXVIII, 1981, 369–94.

The Nations of the Northern Frontier

Richard Aquila, *The Iroquois Restoration: Iroquois Diplomacy on the Colonial Frontier, 1701–1754* (Detroit, 1983).

James W. Bradley, *Evolution of the Onondaga Iroquois: Accommodating Change, 1500–1655* (Syracuse, 1987).

Colin G. Calloway, *The Western Abenakis of Vermont, 1600–1800: War, Migration and the Survival of an Indian People* (Norman, 1990).

Jack Campisi and Laurence Hauptman, eds, *The Oneida Indian Experience. Two Perspectives* (Syracuse, 1988).

Mathew Dennis, *Cultivating a Landscape of Peace: Iroquois–European Encounters in Seventeenth Century America* (Ithaca, 1993).

William N. Fenton, *The False Faces of the Iroquois* (Norman, 1987).

William N. Fenton, *The Great Law and the Longhouse: A Political History of the Iroquois Confederacy* (Norman, 1998).

Michael K. Foster, Jack Campisi, and Marianne Mithun, eds, *Extending the Rafters: Interdisciplinary Approaches to Iroquoian Studies* (Albany, 1984).

Francis Jennings, *The Ambiguous Iroquois: The Covenant Chain Confederation of Indian Tribes with English Colonies from its Beginnings to the Lancaster Treaty of 1744* (New York, 1984).

Francis Jennings et al., eds, *The History and Culture of Iroquois Diplomacy: An Interdisciplinary Guide to the Treaties of the Six Nations and their League* (Syracuse, 1985).

Barry C. Kent, *Susquehanna's Indians* (Harrisburg, 1984).

Herbert C. Kraft, *The Lenape: Archeology, History and Ethnography* (Newark, Del., 1986).

Calvin Martin, "The European Impact on the Culture of a Northeastern Algonquian Tribe: An Ecological Interpretation," *William and Mary Quarterly*, XXXI, 1974, 3–26.

James H. Merrell, *Into the American Woods: Negotiators on the Pennsylvania Frontier* (New York, 1999).

Jane T. Merritt, "Dreaming of the Savior's Blood: Moravians and the Indian Great Awakening," *William and Mary Quarterly*, LIV, 1997, 723–46.

James T. Moore, *Indian and Jesuit: A Seventeenth Century Encounter* (Chicago, 1982).

Kenneth M. Morrison, *The Embattled North-East: The Elusive Ideal of Alliance in Abenaki–Euramerican Relations* (Berkeley, 1984).

Thomas Elliot Norton, *The Fur Trade in Colonial New York, 1686–1776* (Madison, 1974).

Daniel K. Richter, *The Ordeal of the Long House: The Peoples of the Iroquois League in the Era of European Colonization* (Chapel Hill, 1992).

Daniel K. Richter, "War and Culture: The Iroquois Experience," *William and Mary Quarterly*, XL, 1983, 528–59.

Daniel K. Richter and James H. Merrell, eds, *Beyond the Covenant Chain: The Iroquois and their Neighbors in Indian North America, 1600–1800* (Syracuse, 1987).

L. F. S. Upton, *Micmacs and Colonists: Indian–White Relations in the Maritimes, 1713–1867* (Vancouver, 1980).

Alden T. Vaughen, *New England Encounters: Indians and Euroamericans, ca.1600–1850* (Boston, 2000).

Anthony F. C. Wallace, *The Death and Rebirth of the Seneca* (New York, 1969).

Paul A. W. Wallace, *Indians in Pennsylvania* (Harrisburg, 1961).

C. A. Weslager, *The Delaware Indian Westward Migration* (Wallingford, 1978).

Richard White, *The Middle Ground: Indians, Empires and Republics of the Great Lakes Region, 1650–1815* (New York, 1991).

The Nations of the Southern Frontier

James Axtell, *The Indians' new South: Cultural Change in the Colonial Southeast* (Baton Rouge, 1997).

Kathryn E. Holland Braund, *Deerskins and Duffels: Creek Indian Trade with Anglo-America, 1685–1815* (Lincoln, 1993).

David H. Corkran, *The Cherokee Frontier: Conflict and Survival, 1740–1762* (Norman, 1966).

David H. Corkran, *The Creek Frontier, 1540–1783* (Norman, 1967).

Gary Goodwin, *Cherokees in Transition: A Study of Changing Culture and Environment prior to 1775* (Chicago, 1977).

Tom Hatley, *The Dividing Paths: Cherokees and South Carolinians through the Era of Revolution* (New York, 1993).

Sarah H. Hill, "Weaving History: Cherokee Baskets from the Springplace Mission," *William and Mary Quarterly*, LIII, 1996, 115–36.

Charles Hudson, *The Southeastern Indians* (Knoxville, 1976).

James H. Merrell, "The Indians' New World: The Catawba Experience," *William and Mary Quarterly*, XLI, 1984, 537–65.

James H. Merrell, *The Indians' New World: Catawbas and their Neighbours from European Contact through the Era of Removal* (Chapel Hill, 1989).

Michael P. Morris, *Trade and the Indians of the South east, 1700–1783* (Greenwood, 1999).

Theda Perdue, *Cherokee Women: Gender and Culture Change, 1700–1835* (Lincoln, 1998).

Theda Perdue, *Slavery and the Evolution of Cherokee Society, 1540–1866* (Knoxville, 1979).

John P. Reid, *A Better Kind of Hatchet: Law, Trade and Diplomacy in the Cherokee Nation during the Early Years of European Contact* (University Park, 1976).

John P. Reid, *A Law of Blood: The Primitive Law of the Cherokee Nation* (New York, 1970).

W. Stitt Robinson, *The Southern Colonial Froniter, 1607–1763* (Albuquerque, 1979).

Claudio Saunt, *A New Order of Things: Property, Power, and the Transformation of the Creek Indians, 1733–1816* (New York, 1999).

Richard White, *The Roots of Dependency: Subsistence, Environment, and Change among the Choctaws, Pawnees, and Navajos* (Lincoln, 1983).

Peter H. Wood, Gregory A. Waselkov, and M. Thomas Hatley, *Powhatan's Mantle: Indians in the Colonial Southeast* (Lincoln, 1989).

J. Leitch Wright, Jr., *Creeks and Seminoles: The Destruction and Regeneration of the Muscogulge People* (Lincoln, 1986).

J. Leitch Wright, Jr., *The Only Land They Knew: The Tragic Story of the American Indians in the Old South* (New York, 1981).

CHAPTER 16   THE INSTITUTIONS OF GOVERNMENT

Royal Government

H. V. Bowen, *Elites, Enterprise and the Making of the British Overseas Empire, 1688–1775* (Macmillan, 1996).

Jack P. Greene, *Negotiated Authorities: Essays on Colonial Political and Constitutional History* (Charlottesville, 1994).

Jack P. Greene, *Peripheries and Center: Constitutional Development in the Extended Politics of the British Empire and the United States, 1607–1788* (Athens, 1986).

Philip S. Haffenden, "Colonial Appointments and Patronage under the Duke of Newcastle, 1724–1739," *English Historical Review*, LXXVIII, 1963, 417–35.

James A. Henretta, *"Salutary Neglect": Colonial Administration under the Duke of Newcastle* (Princeton, 1972).

Michael G. Kammen, *Empire and Interest: The American Colonies and the Politics of Mercantilism* (Philadelphia, 1970).

Leonard W. Labaree, *Royal Government in America: A Study of the British Colonial System before 1783* (New Haven, 1930).

Richard Middleton, "The Duke of Newcastle and the Conduct of Patronage during the Seven Years' War, 1757–1762," *British Journal of Eighteenth Century Studies*, XII, 1989, 175–86.

Alison Gilbert Olson, *Making the Empire Work: London and American Interest Groups, 1690–1790* (Cambridge, Mass., 1992).

Local Government: Town and County

David Grayson Allen, "The Zuckerman Thesis and the Process of Legal Rationalization in Provincial Massachusetts," with a rebuttal by Michael Zuckerman, *William and Mary Quarterly*, XXIX, 1972, 443–68.

Richard R. Beeman, *The Evolution of the Southern Backcountry: A Case Study of Lunenburg County, Virginia, 1746–1832* (Philadelphia, 1984).

Richard R. Beeman, "Social Change and Cultural Conflict in Virginia: Lunenburg County, 1746–1774, *William and Mary Quarterly*, XXXV, 1978, 455–76.

Edward Byers, *The Nation of Nantucket: Society and Politics in an Early American Commercial Center, 1660–1820* (Boston, 1986).

Edward M. Cook, Jr., *The Fathers of the Towns: Leadership and Community Structure in Eighteenth Century New England* (Baltimore, 1976).

Edward M. Cook, Jr., "Social Behavior and Changing Values in Dedham, Massachusetts, 1700–1775," *William and Mary Quarterly*, XXVII, 1970, 546–80.

Bruce C. Daniels, *The Connecticut Town: Growth and Development, 1635–1790* (Middletown, 1979).

Bruce C. Daniels, *The Fragmentation of New England: Comparative Perspectives on Economic, Political, and Social Divisions in the Eighteenth Century* (Westport, 1988).

Bruce C. Daniels, *Town and County: Essays on the Structure of Local Government in the American Colonies* (Middletown, 1978).

Carville V. Earle, *The Evolution of a Tidewater Settlement System: All Hallow's Parish, Maryland, 1650–1783* (Chicago, 1975).

George W. Franz, *Paxton: A Study of Community Structure and Mobility in the Colonial Pennsylvania Backcountry* (New York, 1989).

Charles S. Grant, *Democracy in the Connecticut Frontier Town of Kent* (New York, 1961).

Christine L. Heyrman, *Commerce and Culture: The Maritime Communities of Colonial Massachusetts, 1690–1750* (New York, 1984).

Richard Holmes, *Communities in Transition: Bedford and Lincoln, Massachusetts, 1729–1850* (Ann Arbor, 1980).

Jessica Kross, *The Evolution of an American Town: Newtown, New York, 1624–1775* (Philadelphia, 1983).

Kenneth A. Lockridge, "Land, Population, and the Evolution of New England Society, 1630–1780," *Past and Present*, XXXIX, 1968, 62–80.

Kenneth A. Lockridge, *A New England Town, the First Hundred Years: Dedham, Massachusetts, 1636–1736* (New York, 1970).

Gwenda Morgan, *The Hegemony of the Law: Richmond County, Virginia, 1692–1776* (New York, 1989).

Gregory H. Nobles, *Divisions Throughout the Whole: Politics and Society in Hampshire County, Massachusetts, 1740–1775* (New York, 1983).

Sumner Chilton Powell, *Puritan Village: The Formation of a New England Town* (Middletown, 1963).

A. G. Roeber, "Authority, Law, and Custom: The Rituals of Court Day in Tidewater Virginia, 1720–1750," *William and Mary Quarterly*, XXXVII, 1980, 29–52.

Darrett B. Rutman, "Assessing the Little Communities of Early America," *William and Mary Quarterly*, XLIII, 1986, 163–78.

Darrett B. Rutman and Anita H. Rutman, *A Place in Time: Middlesex County, Virginia 1650–1750* (New York, 1984).

Stephanie G. Wolf, *Urban Village: Population, Community, and Family Structure in Germantown, Pennsylvania, 1683–1800* (Princeton, 1976).

Michael Zuckerman, *Peaceable Kingdoms: New England Towns in the Eighteenth Century* (New York, 1970).

The Provincial Assembly: Crown versus People

Michael Batinski, *Jonathan Belcher, Colonial Governor* (Lexington, 1996).

Richard L. Bushman, *King and People in Provincial Massachusetts* (Chapel Hill, 1985).

Jere R. Daniell, "Politics in New Hampshire under Governor Benning Wentworth, 1741–1767," *William and Mary Quarterly*, XXIII, 1966, 76–105.

Robert J. Dinkin, *Voting in Provincial America: A Study of Elections in the Thirteen Colonies, 1689–1776* (Westport, 1977).

Jack P. Greene, "Foundations of Political Power in the Virginia House of Burgesses, 1720–1776," *William and Mary Quarterly*, XVI, 1959, 485–506.

Jack P. Greene, "The Growth of Political Stability: An Interpretation of Political Development in the Anglo-American Colonies, 1660–1760," in John Parker and Carol Urness, eds, *The American Revolution: A Heritage of Change* (Minneapolis, 1975).

Jack P. Greene, "Legislative Turnover in British America, 1696–1775: A Quantitative Analysis," *William and Mary Quarterly*, XXXVIII, 1981, 442–63.

Jack P. Greene, "Political Mimesis: A Consideration of the Historical and Cultural Roots of Legislative Behavior in the British Colonies in the Eighteenth Century," with a reply by Bernard Bailyn, *American Historical Review*, LXXV, 1969–70, 337–67.

Jack P. Greene, *The Quest for Power: The Lower Houses of Assembly in the Southern Royal Colonies, 1689–1776* (Chapel Hill, 1963).

James H. Hutson, *Pennsylvania Politics, 1746–1770: The Movement for Royal Government and its Consequences* (Princeton, 1972).

Michael Kammen, *Deputyes and Libertyes: The Origins of Representative Government in Colonial America* (New York, 1969).

Michael Kammen, *A Rope of Sand: The Colonial Agents, British Politics, and the American Revolution* (Ithaca, 1968).

Stanley M. Katz, "Between Scylla and Charybdis: James DeLancey and Anglo-American Politics in Early Eighteenth Century New York," in Alison G. Olson and Richard M. Brown, eds, *Anglo-American Political Relations, 1675–1775* (New Brunswick, 1970).

Mary Lou Lustig, *Robert Hunter, 1666–1734: New York's Augustan Statesman* (Syracuse, 1983).

Edmund S. Morgan, *Inventing the People: The Rise of Popular Sovereignty in England and America* (New York, 1988).

J. R. Pole, *Political Representation in England and the Origins of the American Republic* (New York, 1966).

Thomas L. Purvis, " 'High Born, Long Recorded Families': Social Origins of New Jersey Assemblymen, 1703–1776," *William and Mary Quarterly*, XXXVII, 1980, 592–615.

Thomas L. Purvis, *Proprietors, Patronage, and Paper Money: Legislative Politics in New Jersey, 1703–1776* (New Brunswick, 1986).

John A. Schutz, *William Shirley, King's Governor of Massachusetts* (Chapel Hill, 1961).

Eugene R. Sheridan, *Lewis Morris, 1671–1746: A Study in Early American Politics* (Syracuse, 1981).

Bruce P. Stark, " 'A Factious Spirit': Constitutional Theory and Political Practice in Connecticut, 1740," *William and Mary Quarterly*, XLVII, 1990, 391–410.

Alan Tully, *William Penn's Legacy: Politics and Social Structure in Provincial Pennsylvania, 1726–1755* (Baltimore, 1977).

Parties and Factions in the Age of Walpole

Bernard Bailyn, *The Origins of American Politics* (New York, 1968).

Patricia U. Bonomi, *A Factious People: Politics and Society in Colonial New York* (New York, 1971).

Bruce C. Daniels, ed., *Power and Status. Office Holding in Colonial America* (Middletown, 1986).

Marc Egnal, *A Mighty Empire: The Origins of the American Revolution* (Ithaca, 1988).

A. Roger Ekirch, *"Poor Carolina": Politics and Society in Colonial North Carolina, 1729–1776* (Chapel Hill, 1981).

Joy B. Gilsdorf and Robert R. Gilsdorf, "Elites and Electorates: Some Plain Truths for Historians of Colonial America," in David D. Hall, John M. Murrin, and Thad W. Tate, eds, *Saints and Revolutionaries: Essays on Early American History* (New York, 1984).

Stanley Nider Katz, *Newcastle's New York: Anglo-American Politics, 1732–1753* (Cambridge, Mass., 1968).

John Gilman Kolp, "The Dynamics of Electoral Competition in Pre-Revolutionary Virginia," *William and Mary Quarterly*, XLIX, 1992, 652–74.

John Gilman Kolp, *Gentlemen and Freeholders: Electoral Politics in Colonial Virginia* (Baltimore, 1998).

Kenneth A. Lockridge, *Settlement and Unsettlement in Early America: Political Legitimacy before the Revolution* (Cambridge, England, 1981).

Brendan McConville, *These Daring Disturbers of the Public Peace: The Struggle for Property and Power in Early New Jersey* (Ithaca, 1999).

Benjamin Newcomb, *Political Partisanship in the American Middle Colonies, 1700–1776* (Baton Rouge, 1995).

Gregory Nobles, *Divisions Throughout the Whole: Politics and Society in Hampshire County, Massachusetts, 1740–1775* (New York, 1983).

Alison Gilbert Olson, *Anglo-American Politics, 1660–1775: The Relationship between Parties in England and Colonial America* (New York, 1973).

J. H. Plumb, *The Growth of Political Stability in England, 1675–1725* (London, 1967).

Thomas L. Purvis, " 'High Born, Long Recorded Families': Social Origins of New Jersey Assemblymen, 1703–1776," *William and Mary Quarterly*, XXXVII, 1980, 592–615.

Thomas L. Purvis, "Origins and Patterns of Agrarian Unrest in New Jersey, 1735–1754," *William and Mary Quarterly*, XXXIX, 1982, 600–27.

I. K. Steele, "The Empire and Provincial Elites: An Interpretation of Some Recent Writings on the English Atlantic, 1675–1740," *Journal of Imperial and Commonwealth History*, VIII, 1980, 2–32.

Charles S. Sydnor, *Gentlemen Freeholders: Political Practices in Washington's Virginia* (Chapel Hill, 1952).

Albert H. Tillson, Jr., *Gentry and Common Folk: Political Culture on a Virginia Frontier, 1740–1789* (Lexington, 1991).

Alan Tully, *Forming American Politics: Ideals, Interests, and Institutions in Colonial New York and Pennsylvania* (Baltimore, 1994).

Robert M. Weir, " 'The Harmony We Were Famous For': An Interpretation of Prerevolutionary South Carolina Politics," *William and Mary Quarterly*, XXVI, 1969, 473–501.

Robert M. Weir, *The Last American Freeman: Studies in the Political Culture of the Colonial and Revolutionary South* (Macon, 1986).

Robert Zemsky, *Merchants, Farmers, and River Gods: An Essay on Eighteenth Century American Politics* (Boston, 1971).

Political Ideology

Bernard Bailyn, *The Ideological Origins of the American Revolution* (Cambridge, Mass., 1967).

Richard Beeman, "Deference, Republicanism, and the Emergence of Popular Politics in Eighteenth-Century America," *William and Mary Quarterly*, XLIX, 1992, 401–30.

T. H. Breen, "Ideology and Nationalism on the Eve of the American Revolution: Revisions Once More in Need of Revising," *Journal of American History*, LXXXIV, 1997, 14–35.

J. M. Bumsted, " 'Things in the Womb of Time': Ideas of American Independence, 1633–1763," *William and Mary Quarterly*, XXXI, 1974, 533–64.

Richard L. Bushman, *King and People in Provincial Massachusetts* (Chapel Hill, 1985).

Robert M. Calhoon, *Dominion and Liberty: Ideology in the Anglo-American World, 1660–1801* (Arlington Heights, 1994).

H. Trevor Colbourn, *The Lamp of Experience: Whig History and the Intellectual Origins of the American Revolution* (Chapel Hill, 1965).

H. T. Dickinson, *Liberty and Property: Political Ideology in Eighteenth Century Britain* (New York, 1978).

Eliga H. Gould, *The Persistence of Empire: British Political Culture in the Age of the American Revolution* (Chapel Hill, 2000).

Lawrence H. Leder, *Liberty and Authority: Early American Political Ideology, 1689–1763* (Chicago, 1963).

Richard K. Mathews. *Virtue, Corruption, and Self-interest: Political Values in the Eighteenth Century* (Bethlehem, 1994).

Edmund S. Morgan, *Inventing the People: The Rise of Popular Sovereignty in England and America* (New York, 1988).

J. G. A. Pocock, *The Machiavellian Moment: Florentine Political Thought and the Atlantic Republican Tradition* (Princeton, 1975).

J. G. A. Pocock, *Virtue, Commerce, and History: Essays on Political Thought and History, Chiefly in the Eighteenth Century* (New York, 1985).

J. R. Pole, *The Gift of Government: Political Responsibility from the English Restoration to American Independence* (Athens, 1983).

Caroline Robbins, *The Eighteenth Century Commonwealthman: Studies in the Transmission, Development, and Circumstance of English Liberal Thought from the Restoration of Charles II until the War with the Thirteen Colonies* (Cambridge, Mass., 1959).

CHAPTER 17   IMMIGRATION AND EXPANSION, 1714–50

The Germans and Scots-Irish

Bernard Bailyn, *The Peopling of British North America: An Introduction* (New York, 1986).

Bernard Bailyn and Philip D. Morgan, *Strangers Within the Realm: Cultural Margins of the First British Empire* (Chapel Hill, 1991).

H. Tyler Blethen and Curtis W. Wood, Jr., *Ulster and North America: Transatlantic Perspectives on the Scotch-Irish* (Tuscaloosa, 1997).

Jon Butler, *The Huguenots in America: A Refugee People in New World Society* (Cambridge, Mass., 1983).

Nicholas Canny, ed., *Europeans on the Move: Studies on European Migration, 1500–1800* (Oxford, 1994).

David Colin Crass, ed., *The Southern Colonial Backcountry: Interdisciplinary Perspectives on Frontier Communities* (Knoxville, 1998).

R. J. Dickson, *Ulster Emigration to Colonial America, 1718–1775* (London, 1966).

David Dobson, *The Original Scots Colonists of Early America, 1612–1783* (Baltimore, 1989).

David Dobson, *Scottish Emigration to Colonial America, 1607–1785* (Athens, 1994).

A. Roger Ekirch, *Bound for America: The Transportation of British Convicts to the Colonies, 1718–1775* (Oxford, 1987).

Eli Faber, *A Time for Planting: The First Migration, 1654–1829, The Jewish People in America*, Vol. 1 (Baltimore, 1992).

Rory Fitzpatrick, *God's Frontiersmen: The Epic of the Scots-Irish* (London, 1989).

Aaron Spencer Fogleman, "From Slaves, Convicts, and Servants to free Passengers: The Transformation of Immigration in the Era of the American Revolution," *Journal of American History*, LXXXV, 1998/9, 43–76.

Aaron Spencer Fogleman, *Hopeful Journeys: German Immigration, Settlements, and Political Culture in Colonial America, 1717–1775* (Philadelphia, 1996).

Mark Haberlein, "German Migrants in Colonial Pennsylvania: Resources, Opportunities and Experience," *William and Mary Quarterly*, L, 1993, 555–74.

Arthur Hirsch, *The Huguenots of Colonial South Carolina* (Hamden, 1962).

Warren R. Hofstra, " 'The Extention of His Majesties Dominions': The Virginia Backcountry and the Reconfiguration of Imperial Frontiers," *Journal of American History*, LXXXIV, 1997/8, 1281–312.

George Lloyd Johnson Jr., *The Frontier in the Colonial South: South Carolina Backcountry, 1736–1800* (Greenwood, 1997).

Terry G. Jordan and Matti Kaups, *The American Backwoods Frontier: An Ethnic and Ecological Interpretation* (Baltimore, 1989).

Ned C. Landsman, *Scotland and its First American Colony, 1683–1765* (Princeton, 1985).

Hartmut Lehmann et al., *In Search of Peace and Prosperity: New Settlements in Eighteenth Century Europe and North America* (University Park, 2000).

W. C. Lehmann, *Scottish and Scotch-Irish Contributions to Early American Life and Culture* (Port Washington, 1978).

James G. Leyburn, *The Scotch-Irish: A Social History* (Chapel Hill, 1962).

Audrey Lockhart, *Some Aspects of Emigration from Ireland to the North American Colonies between 1660 and 1775* (New York, 1976).

Peter Mancall, *Valley of Opportunity: Economic Culture along the Upper Susquehanna* (Ithaca, 1991).

Jacob R. Marcus, *The Colonial American Jew, 1492–1776*, 3 vols (Detroit, 1970).

Duane Meyer, *The Highland Scots of North Carolina, 1732–1776* (Chapel Hill, 1953).

Robert D. Mitchell, *Commercialism and Frontier: Perspectives on the Early Shenandoah Valley* (Charlottesville, 1977).

Gregory H. Nobles, "Breaking into the Backcountry: New Approaches to the Early American Frontier, 1750–1880," *William and Mary Quarterly*, XLVI. 1989, 641–70.

Michael J. Puglisi, ed., *Diversity and Accommodation: Essays on the Cultural Composition of the Virginia Frontier* (Knoxville, 1997).

Robert W. Ramsey, *Carolina Cradle: Settlement of the Northwest Carolina Frontier, 1747–1762* (Chapel Hill, 1964).

James C. Riley, "Mortality on Long-distance Voyages in the Eighteenth Century," *Journal of Economic History*, XLI, 1981, 651–6.

A. G. Roeber, "In German Ways? Problems and Potentials of Eighteenth Century German Social and Emigration History," *William and Mary Quarterly*, XLIV, 1987, 750–74.

A. G. Roeber, *Palatines, Liberty, and Property: German Lutherans in Colonial British America* (Baltimore, 1993).

Richard Slotkin, *Regeneration through Violence: The Mythology of the American Frontier, 1600–1860* (Middletown, 1973).

Daniel B. Thorp, *The Moravian Community in Colonial North Carolina: Pluralism on the Southern Frontier* (Knoxville, 1989).

Lorena S. Walsh, "Staying Put or Getting Out: Findings for Charles County, 1650–1720," *William and Mary Quarterly*, XLIV, 1987, 89–103.

Robert V. Wells, *The Population of the British Colonies in America Before 1776: A Survey of Census Data* (Princeton, 1975).

Marianne Wokeck, "The Dynamics of German Speaking Emigration to British North America, 1683–1783," in Ida Altman and James Horn, eds, *"To Make America": European Emigration in the Early Modern Period* (Berkeley, 1991).

Stephanie Grauman Wolf, *Urban Village: Population, Community, and Family Structure in Germantown, Pennsylvania, 1683–1800* (Princeton, 1976).

Georgia

W. W. Abbot, *The Royal Governors of Georgia, 1754–1775* (Chapel Hill, 1959).

Kenneth Coleman, *Colonial Georgia: A History* (New York, 1976).

Kenneth Coleman, ed., *A History of Georgia* (Athens, 1977).

Harold E. Davis, *The Fledgling Province: Social and Cultural Life in Colonial Georgia, 1733–1776* (Chapel Hill, 1976).

Alan Gallay, *The Formation of a Planter Elite: Jonathan Bryan and the Southern Colonial Frontier* (Athens, 1989).

Alan Gallay, "Jonathan Bryan's Plantation Empire: Land, Politics, and the Formation of a Ruling Class in Colonial Georgia," *William and Mary Quarterly*, XLV, 1988, 253–79.

Harvey H. Jackson and Phinizy Spalding, eds, *Forty Years of Diversity: Essays on Colonial Georgia* (Athens, 1984).

Anthony W. Parker, *Scottish Highlanders in Colonial Georgia: The Recruitment, Emigration and Settlement at Darien, 1735–1748* (Athens, 1997).

Phinizy Spalding, *Oglethorpe in America* (Chicago, 1977).

Phinizy Spalding and Harvey H. Jackson, *Oglethorpe in Perspective: Georgia's Founder after Two Hundred Years* (Tuscaloosa, 1989).

Paul S. Taylor, *Georgia Plan: 1732–1752* (Berkeley, 1972).

Clarence L. Ver Steeg, *Origins of a Southern Mosaic: Studies of Early Carolina and Georgia* (Athens, 1975).

Betty Wood, *Slavery in Colonial Georgia, 1730–1755* (Athens, 1984).

Betty Wood, *Women's Work, Men's Work: The Informal Slave Economies of Lowcountry Georgia* (Athens, 1995).

The Colonial Town

J. B. Blake, *Public Health in the Town of Boston, 1630–1822* (Cambridge, Mass., 1959).

Carl Bridenbaugh, *Cities in Revolt: Urban Life in America, 1743–1776* (New York, 1955).

Carl Bridenbaugh, *Cities in the Wilderness: The First Century of Urban Life in America, 1625–1742* (New York, 1938).

Bruce C. Daniels, *Town and County: Essays on the Structure of Local Government in the American Colonies* (Middletown, 1978).

John Duffy, *Epidemics in Colonial America* (Baton Rouge, 1953).

Carville V. Earle and Ronald Hoffman, "Urban Development in the Eighteenth Century South," *Perspectives in American History*, X, 1976, 7–78.

Joseph A. Ernst and H. Roy Merrens, " 'Camden's Turrets Pierce the Skies!': The Urban Process in the Southern Colonies during the Eighteenth Century," *William and Mary Quarterly*, XXX, 1973, 549–74.

Douglas Greenberg, *Crime and Law Enforcement in the Colony of New York, 1691–1776* (Ithaca, 1976).

Douglas Lamar Jones, *Village and Seaport: Migration and Society in Eighteenth Century Massachusetts* (Hanover, 1981).

Susan E. Klepp, *Philadelphia in Transition: A Demographic History of the City and Its Occupational Groups, 1720–1830* (New York, 1989).

Gary B. Nash, *The Urban Crucible: Social Change, Political Consciousness, and the Origins of the American Revolution* (Cambridge, Mass., 1979).

G. B. Warden, *Boston, 1689–1776* (Boston, 1970).

Hermann Wellenreuther, "Urbanization in the Colonial South: A Critique," *William and Mary Quarterly*, XXXI, 1974, 653–68.

Lynne Withey, *Urban Growth in Colonial Rhode Island: Newport and Providence in the Eighteenth Century* (Albany, 1984).

Jerome H. Wood, Jr., *Conestoga Crossroads: Lancaster, Pennsylvania, 1730–1790* (Harrisburg, 1979).

CHAPTER 18   IMPERIAL NEIGHBORS: SPAIN AND FRANCE IN FLORIDA,
                     NEW MEXICO, TEXAS, AND LOUISIANA

General

Leslie Bethell, ed., *Colonial Latin America: The Cambridge History of Latin America*, 2 vols (Cambridge, 1984).

Stanley J. Palmer and Dennis Reinhartz, eds, *Essays on the History of North American Discovery and Exploration* (College Station, 1988).

Carl O. Sauer, *Seventeenth Century North America: The Land and the People as Seen by Europeans* (Berkeley, 1971).

Florida

John Francis Bannon, *The Spanish Borderlands Frontier, 1513–1821* (New York, 1970).

Herbert E. Bolton, *The Spanish Borderlands: A Chronicle of Old Florida and the Southwest* (New Haven, 1921).

Mark F. Boyd et al., *Here They Once Stood: The Tragic End of the Apalachee Missions* (1951, repr. Gainesville, 1999).

Amy Turner Bushnell, *Situado and Sabana: Spain's Support System for the Presidio and Mission Provinces of Florida* (Athens, 1994).

Kathleen A. Deagan, ed., *Spanish St. Augustine: The Archeology of a Colonial Creole Community* (New York, 1983).

Ernest F. Dibble and Earle W. Newton, *Spain and her Rivals on the Gulf Coast* (Pensacola, 1971).

John H. Hann, *Apalachee: The Land between the Rivers* (Gainesville, 1998).

John H. Hann, *A History of the Timucua Indians and Missions* (Gainesville, 1996).

John H. Hann and Bonnie G. McEwan, *The Apalachee Indians and Mission St. Luis* (Gainesville, 1998).

Paul E. Hoffman, *A New Andalucia and a Way to the Orient: The American Southeast during the Sixteenth Century* (Baton Rouge, 1990).

Charles Hudson and Carmen Chaves Tesser, *The Forgotten Centuries: Indians and Europeans in the American South, 1521–1704* (Athens, 1994).

Jane Landers, "Spanish Sanctuary: Fugitives in Florida, 1687–1790," *Florida Historical Quarterly*, LXII, 1984, 296–313.

Eugene Lyon, *The Enterprise of Florida: Pedro Menéndez de Avilés and the Spanish Conquest of 1565–1568* (Gainesville, 1976).

Bonnie G. McEwan, ed., *The Spanish Missions of "La Florida"* (Gainesville, 1993).

Robert Allen Matter, "Missions in the Defense of Spanish Florida, 1566–1710," *Florida Historical Quarterly*, LIV, 1975, 18–38.

Robert Allen Matter, *Pre-Seminole Florida: Spanish Soldiers, Friars, and Indian Missions, 1513–1763* (New York, 1990).

Jerald T. Milanich, *The Timucua* (Oxford, 1996).

John Jay TePaske, *The Governorship of Spanish Florida, 1700–1763* (Durham, 1964).

Jean Parker Waterbury, ed., *The Oldest City: St. Augustine, Saga of Survival* (St. Augustine, 1983).

David J. Weber, *The Spanish Frontier in North America* (Yale, 1992).

David J. Weber, "Turner, the Boltonians, and the Borderlands," *American Historical Review*, XCI, 1986, 66–81.

Randolph J. Widmer, *The Evolution of the Calusa: A Nonagricultural Chiefdom on the Southwest Florida Coast* (Tuscaloosa, 1988).

J. Leitch Wright, Jr., *Anglo-Spanish Rivalry in North America* (Athens, 1971).

New Mexico

Ramón A. Gutiérrez, *When Jesus Came, the Corn Mothers Went Away: Marriage, Sexuality, and Power in New Mexico, 1500–1846* (Stanford, 1991).

Elizabeth A. H. John, *Storms Brewed in Other Men's Worlds: The Confrontation of Indians, Spanish, and French in the Southwest, 1540–1795* (College Station, 1975).

Oakah L. Jones, *Nueva Vizcaya: Heartland of the Spanish Frontier* (Albuquerque, 1988).

Oakah L. Jones, *Los Paisanos: Spanish Settlers on the Northern Frontier of New Spain* (Norman, 1979).

Oakah L. Jones, *Pueblo Warriors and Spanish Conquest* (Norman, 1966).

Caroll L. Riley, *Rio del Norte: People of the Upper Rio Grande from Earliest Times to the Pueblo Revolt* (Salt Lake City, 1995).

Marc Simmons, *Albuquerque: A Narrative History* (Albuquerque, 1982).

Edward H. Spicer, *Cycles of Conquest: The Impact of Spain, Mexico, and the United States on the Indians of the Southwest, 1533–1960* (Tucson, 1962).

David Hurst Thomas, ed., *Columbian Consequences*, Vol. I: *Archaeological and Historical Perspectives on the Spanish Borderlands West* (Washington DC, 1989).

W. H. Timmons, *El Paso: A Borderlands History* (El Paso, 1990).

David J. Weber, ed., *Foreigners in their Native Land: Historical Roots of the Mexican Americans* (Albuquerque, 1973).

David J. Weber, *Myth and the History of the Hispanic Southwest: Essays by David J. Weber* (Albuquerque, 1988).

David J. Weber, ed., *New Spain's Far Northern Frontier: Essays on Spain in the American West* (Albuquerque, 1979).

Texas

Lawrence E. Aten, *Indians of the Upper Texas Coast* (New York, 1983).

Herbert E. Bolton, *Texas in the Middle Eighteenth Century: Studies in Spanish Colonial History and Administration* (1915; Austin, 1970).

William C. Foster, *Spanish Expeditions in Texas, 1689–1768* (Austin, 1995).

Jack Jackson, *Los Mestenos: Spanish Ranching in Texas, 1721–1821* (College Station, 1986).

David W. Meinig, *Imperial Texas: An Interpretive Essay in Cultural Geography* (Austin, 1969).

Gerald E. Poyo and Gilbert M. Hinojosa, "Spanish Texas and Borderlands Historiography in Transition: Implications for United States History," *Journal of American History*, LXXV, 1988–9, 393–416.

Louisiana

Ira Berlin, *Many Thousands Gone: The First Two Centuries of Slavery in North America* (Cambridge, Mass., 1998).

James Taylor Carson, *Searching for the Bright Path: The Mississippi Choctaws from Prehistory to Removal* (Lincoln, 1999).

John Anthony Caruso, *The Mississippi Valley Frontier: The Age of French Exploration and Settlement* (Indianapolis, 1966).

Emily Clark, "By All the Conduct of their Lives': A Laywomen's Confraternity in New Orleans, 1730–1744," *William and Mary Quarterly*, LIV, 1997, 769–94.

John G. Clark, *New Orleans, 1718–1812: An Economic History* (Baton Rouge, 1970).

Carl J. Ekberg, *French Roots in the Illinois Country: The Mississippi Frontier in Colonial Times* (Urbana, 1998).

Patricia K. Galloway, "Choctaw Factionalism and Civil War, 1746–1750," *Journal of Mississippi History*, XLIV, 1982, 289–327.

Patricia K. Galloway, ed., *La Salle and his Legacy: Frenchmen and Indians in the Lower Mississippi Valley* (Jackson, 1982).

Gwendolyn Midlo Hall, *Africans in Colonial Louisiana: The Development of Afro-Creole Culture in the Eighteenth Century* (Baton Rouge, 1992).

John Brice Harris, *From Old Mobile to Fort Assumption: A Story of the French Attempts to Colonize Louisiana and Destroy the Chickasaw Indians* (Nashville, 1959).

Thomas N. Ingersoll, *Mammon and Manon in Early New Orleans: The First Slave Society in the Deep South, 1718–1819* (Knoxville, 1999).

Joe Gray Taylor, *Louisiana: A Bicentennial History* (New York, 1976).

Tanis C. Thorne, *The Many Hands of my Relations: French and Indians on the Lower Missouri* (Columbia, 1996).

Daniel H. Usner, Jr., "American Indians in Colonial New Orleans," in Wood et al. eds, *Powhatan's Mantle*, 104–27.

Daniel H. Usner, Jr., *American Indians in the Lower Mississippi Valley: Social and Economic Histories* (Lincoln, 1998).

Daniel H. Usner, Jr., "From African Captivity to American Slavery; The Introduction of Black Laborers to Colonial Louisiana," *Louisiana History*, XX, 1979, 25–48.

Daniel H. Usner, Jr., "The Frontier Exchange Economy in the Lower Mississippi Valley in the Eighteenth Century," *William and Mary Quarterly*, XLIV, 1987, 165–92.

Daniel H. Usner, Jr., *Indians, Settlers and Slaves in a Frontier Exchange Economy: The Lower Mississippi Valley Before 1783* (Chapel Hill, 1992).

John A. Walthall and Thomas E. Emerson, *Calumet and Fleur-de-Lys: Archaeology of Indian and French Contact in the Midcontinent* (Washington, 1992).

Robert S. Weddle, *The French Thorn: Rival Explorers in the Spanish Sea, 1682–1762* (College Station, 1991).

Richard White, *The Roots of Dependency: Subsistence, Environment, and Social Change among the Choctaws, Pawnees, and Navajos* (Lincoln, 1983).

Patricia D. Woods, *French Indian Relations on the Southern Frontier, 1699–1762* (Ann Arbor, 1980).

Patricia D. Woods, "The French and the Natchez Indians in Louisiana: 1700–1731," *Louisiana History*, XIX, 1978, 413–35.

CHAPTER 19   BRITAIN, FRANCE, AND SPAIN: THE IMPERIAL CONTEST, 1739–60

General and the War of Jenkins' Ear

Lawrence Delbert Cress, *Citizens in Arms: The Army and the Militia in American Society to the War of 1812* (Chapel Hill, 1982).

W. J. Eccles, *The Canadian Frontier, 1534–1760* (New York, 1969).

W. J. Eccles, *Essays on New France* (Toronto, 1987).

W. J. Eccles, "The Fur Trade and Eighteenth Century Imperialism," *William and Mary Quarterly*, XL, 1983, 341–62.

John Ferling, *Struggle for a Continent: The Wars of Early America* (Arlington Heights, 1993).

John E. Ferling, *A Wilderness of Miseries: War and Warriors in Early America* (Westport, 1980).

Sylvia R. Frey, *The British Soldier in America: A Social History of Military Life in the Colonial Period* (Austin, 1981).

Lawrence Henry Gipson, *The British Empire before the American Revolution*, 15 vols (New York, 1936–70).

Don Higginbotham, "The Early American Way of War: Reconnaissance and Appraisal," *William and Mary Quarterly*, XLIV, 1987, 230–73.

Cornelius J. Jaenen, *The French Relationship with the Native Peoples of New France and Acadia* (Ottawa, 1984).

Douglas Edward Leach, *Arms for Empire: A Military History of the British Colonies in North America, 1607–1763* (New York, 1973).

Douglas Edward Leach, *Roots of Conflict: British Armed Forces and Colonial Americans, 1677–1763* (Chapel Hill, 1986).

Howard H. Peckham, *The Colonial Wars, 1689–1762* (Chicago, 1962).

John A. Schutz, *William Shirley, King's Governor of Massachusetts* (Chapel Hill, 1961).

George F. G. Stanley, *New France: The Last Phase, 1744–1760* (Toronto, 1968).

The Struggle for the Ohio

John R. Alden, *George Washington: A Biography* (Baton Rouge, 1984).

John R. Alden, *John Stuart and the Southern Colonial Frontier, 1754–1775* (Ann Arbor, 1944).

Daniel J. Beattie, "The Adaptation of the British Army to Wilderness Warfare, 1755–1763," in Maarten Ultee, ed., *Adapting to Conditions: War and Society in the Eighteenth Century* (University, Alabama, 1986).

Andrew R. L. Cayton and Fredrika J. Teute, *Contact Points: The American Frontier from the Mohawk Valley to the Mississippi, 1750–1830* (Chapel Hill, 1998).

Lawrence Henry Gipson, *The British Empire before the American Revolution*, Vols IV and V: *Zones of International Friction, 1748–1754* (New York, 1944–5).

Milton W. Hamilton, *Sir William Johnson: Colonial American, 1715–1763* (Port Washington, 1976).

Eric Hinderaker, *Elusive Empires: Constructing Colonialism in the Ohio Valley, 1673–1800* (New York, 1997).

Wilbur R. Jacobs, *Wilderness Politics and Indian Gifts: Anglo-French Rivalry along the Ohio and Northwest Frontier, 1748–1763* (Stanford, 1950).

Alfred P. James, *The Ohio Company: Its Inner History* (Pittsburgh, 1959).

Francis Jennings, *Empire of Fortune: Crowns, Colonies, and Tribes in the Seven Years' War in America* (New York, 1988).

P. E. Kopperman, *Braddock at the Monongahela* (Pittsburgh, 1977).

Lee McCardell, *Ill-starred General: Braddock of the Coldstream Guards* (Pittsburgh, 1986).

Michael N. McConnell, *A Country Between: The Upper Ohio Valley and its Peoples, 1724–1774* (Lincoln, 1992).

Peter R. Russell, "Redcoats in the Wilderness: British Officers and Irregular Warfare in Europe and America, 1740–1760," *William and Mary Quarterly*, XXXV, 1978, 629–52.

Timothy J. Shannon, *Indians and Colonists at the Crossroads of Empire: The Albany Congress of 1754* (Ithaca, 2000).

James Titus, *The Old Dominion at War: Society, Politics, and Warfare in Late Colonial Virginia* (Columbia, 1991).

Nicholas B. Wainwright, *George Croghan, Wilderness Diplomat* (Chapel Hill, 1959).

Anthony F. C. Wallace, *King of the Delawares: Teedyuscung, 1700–1763* (Syracuse, 1990).

The Conquest of Canada

Fred Anderson, *Crucible of War: The Seven Years' War and the Fate of Empire in British North America, 1754–1766* (New York, 2000).

Fred Anderson, *A People's Army: Massachusetts Soldiers and Society in the Seven Years' War* (Chapel Hill, 1984).

Fred Anderson, "A People's Army: Provincial Military Service in Massachusetts during the Seven Years' War," *William and Mary Quarterly*, XL, 1983, 499–527.

F. W. Anderson, "Why Did Colonial New Englanders Make Bad Soldiers? Contractual Principles and Military Conduct during the Seven Years' War," *William and Mary Quarterly*, XXXVIII, 1981, 395–417.

James T. Flexner, *Mohawk Baronet: A Biography of Sir William Johnson* (Syracuse, 1990).

J. Fortier, *Fortress of Louisburg* (Toronto, 1979).

Guy Fregault, *Canada: The War of the Conquest* (Toronto, 1969).

Sylvia R. Frey, *The British Soldier in America: A Social History of Military Life in the Colonial Period* (Austin, 1981).

Richard Middleton, *The Bells of Victory: The Pitt–Newcastle Ministry and the Conduct of the Seven Years' War, 1757–1762* (Cambridge, England, 1985).

Stanley M. Pargellis, *Lord Loudoun in North America* (New Haven, 1933).

Alan Rogers, *Empire and Liberty: American Resistance to British Authority, 1755–1763* (Berkeley, 1974).

Harold E. Selesky, *War and Society in Colonial Connecticut* (Yale, 1989).

Ian K. Steele, *Betrayals: Fort William Henry and the 'Massacre'* (New York, 1990).

CHAPTER 20   THE RIGHTS OF BRITISH AMERICA, 1760–66

General

Bernard Bailyn, *The Ideological Origins of the American Revolution* (Cambridge, Mass., 1967).

Colin Bonwick, *The American Revolution* (London, 1991).

Richard D. Brown, ed., *Major Problems in the Era of the American Revolution, 1760–1791: Documents and Essays* (Lexington, Mass., 1992).

Edward Countryman, *The American Revolution* (New York, 1985).

Marc Egnal, *A Mighty Empire: The Origins of the American Revolution* (Ithaca, 1988).

Lawrence Henry Gipson, *The Coming of the Revolution, 1763–1775* (New York, 1954).

Jack P. Greene, *Peripheries and Center: Constitutional Development in the Extended Polities of the British Empire and the United States, 1607–1788* (Athens, 1986).

Ronald Hoffman, John J. McCusker, and Russell Menard, eds, *The Economy of Early America: The Revolutionary Period, 1763–1790* (Charlottesville, 1988).

Robert Middlekauf, *The Glorious Cause: The American Revolution, 1763–1789* (New York, 1982).

Edmund S. Morgan, "The Puritan Ethic and the American Revolution," *William and Mary Quarterly*, XXIV, 1967, 3–43.

Ian K. Steele and Nancy L. Rhoden, *The Human Tradition in the American Revolution* (Wilmington, 2000).

The Empire in 1760

T. H. Breen, "Ideology and Nationalism on the Eve of the American Revolution: Revisions once more in Need of Revising," *Journal of American History*, LXXXIV, 1997, 14–35.

T. H. Breen, "Narrative of Commercial Life: Consumption, Ideology, and Community on the Eve of the American Revolution", *William and Mary Quarterly*, L, 1993, 471–501.

J. M. Bumsted, " 'Things in the Womb of Time': Ideas of American Independence, 1633–1763," *William and Mary Quarterly*, XXXI, 1974, 533–64.

Jack P. Greene, "The Seven Years' War and the American Revolution: The Causal Relationship Reconsidered," *Journal of Imperial and Commonwealth History*, VIII, 1980, 85–105.

James H. Kettner, *The Development of American Citizenship, 1608–1870* (Chapel Hill, 1978).

Richard L. Merritt, "The Colonists Discover America: Attention Patterns in the Colonial Press, 1735–1775," *William and Mary Quarterly*, XXI, 1964, 270–87.

Richard L. Merritt, *Symbols of American Community, 1735–1775* (New Haven, 1966).

British Policies, 1760–66

John Bullion, *A Great and Necessary Measure: George Grenville and the Genesis of the Stamp Act, 1763–1765* (Columbia, Missouri, 1982).

Walter S. Dunn, Jr., *Frontier Profit and Loss: The British Army and the Fur Traders, 1760–1764* (Westport, 1998).

Joseph A. Ernst, *Money and Politics in America, 1755–1775* (Chapel Hill, 1973).

Nancy Koehn, *The Power of Commerce: Economy and Governance in the First British Empire* (Ithaca, 1994).

P. Langford, *The First Rockingham Administration, 1765–1766* (Oxford, 1973).

Philip Lawson, *George Grenville: A Political Life* (Oxford, 1984).

John Shy, *Towards Lexington; The Role of the British Army in the Coming of the Revolution* (Princeton, 1965).

Jack M. Sosin, *Whitehall and the Wilderness: The Middle West in British Colonial Policy, 1760–1775* (Lincoln, 1961).

S. Taylor, "Whigs, Bishops and America: The Politics of Church Reform in Mid-Eighteenth Century England," *Historical Journal*, XXXVI, 1993, 331–56.

P. G. D. Thomas, *British Politics and the Stamp Act Crisis: The First Phase of the American Revolution, 1763–1767* (Oxford, 1975).

American Resistance

Thomas Perkins Abernethy, *Western Lands and the American Revolution* (New York, 1959).

Edward Countryman, *A People in Revolution: The American Revolution and Political Society in New York, 1760–1790* (Baltimore, 1981).

Paul A. Gilje, *The Road to Mobocracy: Popular Disorder in New York City, 1763–1834* (Chapel Hill, 1987).

Dirk Hoerder, *Crowd Action in Revolutionary Massachusetts, 1765–1780* (New York, 1977).

Bernard Knollenberg, *Origin of the American Revolution, 1759–1766* (New York, 1960).

Isaac Kramnick, *Republicanism and Bourgeois Radicalism* (Ithaca, 1992).

Jesse Lemisch, *Jack Tar vs. John Bull: The Role of New York's Seamen in Precipitating the Revolution* (New York, 1997).

Jesse Lemisch, "Jack Tar in the Streets: Merchant Seamen in the Politics of Revolutionary America," *William and Mary Quarterly*, XXV, 1968, 371–407.

Pauline Maier, *From Resistance to Revolution: Colonial Radicals and the Development of American Opposition to Britain, 1765–1776* (New York, 1972).

Edmund S. Morgan and Helen M. Morgan, *The Stamp Act Crisis: Prologue to Revolution* (New York, 1963).

Gary Nash, *The Urban Crucible: Social Change, Political Consciousness and the Origins of the American Revolution* (Cambridge, Mass., 1979).

Steven Rosswurm, *Arms, Country and Class: The Philadelphia Militia and the "Lower Sort" during the American Revolution* (New Brunswick, 1987).

Richard A. Ryerson, "Political Mobilization and the American Revolution: The Resistance Movement in Philadelphia, 1765 to 1776," *William and Mary Quarterly*, XXXI, 1974, 565–88.

Richard A. Ryerson, *The Revolution is Now Begun: The Radical Committees of Philadelphia, 1765–1776* (Philadelphia, 1978).

Ronald Schultz, *The Republic of Labor: Philadelphia Artisans and the Politics of Class, 1720–1830* (New York, 1993).

Thomas P. Slaughter, "The Tax Man Cometh: Ideological Opposition to Internal Taxes," *William and Mary Quarterly*, XLI, 1984, 566–91.

Thad W. Tate, "The Coming of the Revolution in Virginia: Britain's Challenge to Virginia's Ruling Class, 1763–1776," *William and Mary Quarterly*, XIX, 1962, 323–43.

Joseph S. Tiedemann, *Reluctant Revolutionaries: New York City and the Road to Independence, 1763–1776* (Ithaca, 1997).

Carl Ubbelode, *The Vice-Admiralty Courts and the American Revolution* (Chapel Hill, 1960).

John J. Waters Jr., *The Otis Family in Provincial and Revolutionary Massachusetts* (Chapel Hill, 1968).

Robert M. Weir, *"A Most Important Epoch": The Coming of the Revolution in South Carolina* (Columbia, 1970).

Internal Conflict

Michael A. Belleisles, *Revolutionary Outlaw: Ethan Allen and the Struggle for Independence on the Early American Frontier* (Charlottesville, 1993).

Richard Maxwell Brown, *The South Carolina Regulators* (Cambridge, Mass., 1963).

James H. Hutson, "An Investigation of the Inarticulate: Philadelphia's White Oaks," *William and Mary Quarterly*, XXVIII, 1971, 3–26.

James H. Hutson, *Pennsylvania Politics, 1746–1770: The Movement for Royal Government and its Consequences* (Princeton, 1972).

Marvin L. Kay, "The North Carolina Regulation, 1766–1776: A Class Conflict," in Alfred F. Young, ed., *The American Revolution: Explorations in the History of American Radicalism* (DeKalb, 1976).

Sung Bok Kim, *Landlord and Tenant in Colonial New York: Manorial Society, 1664–1775* (Chapel Hill, 1978).

Rachel N. Klein, "Ordering the Backcountry: The South Carolina Regulation," *William and Mary Quarterly*, XXXVIII, 1981, 661–80.

Rachel N. Klein, *The Unification of a Slave State; The Rise of the Planter Class in the South Carolina Backcountry, 1760–1808* (Chapel Hill, 1990).

Paul David Nelson, *William Tryon and the Course of Empire: A Life in British Imperial Service* (Chapel Hill, 1990).

Alan Taylor, *Liberty Men and Great Proprietors: The Revolutionary Settlement on the Maine Frontier, 1760–1820* (Chapel Hill, 1990).

Alfred F. Young, ed., *The American Revolution: Explorations in the History of American Radicalism* (Dekalb, 1976).

CHAPTER 21   REVOLUTION AND INDEPENDENCE, 1767–76

The Townshend Duties and British Policy

John Alden, *General Gage in America* (Baton Rouge, 1948).

John Brooke, *King George III* (London, 1972).

Bernard Donoughue, *British Politics and the American Revolution, 1773–1775* (London, 1964).

Ira D. Gruber "The American Revolution as a Conspiracy," *William and Mary Quarterly*, XXVI, 1969, 360–72.

Philip Lawson, *George Grenville: A Political Life* (Oxford, 1984).

Philip Lawson, *The Imperial Challenge: Quebec and Britain in the Age of the American Revolution* (Montreal, 1989).

Sir Lewis Namier and John Brooke, *Charles Townshend* (New York, 1964).

P. G. D. Thomas, *Lord North* (London, 1976).

P. G. D. Thomas, *Tea Party to Independence: The Third Phase of the American Revolution, 1773–1776* (Oxford, 1991).

P. G. D. Thomas, *The Townshend Duties Crisis: The Second Phase of the American Revolution, 1767–1773* (Oxford, 1987).

American Resistance

John Alden, *George Washington: A Biography* (Baton Rouge, 1984).

David Ammerman, *In the Common Cause: American Response to the Coercive Acts of 1774* (Charlottesville, 1974).

Richard Beeman, *Patrick Henry: A Biography* (New York, 1975).

Richard D. Brown, *Revolutionary Politics in Massachusetts: The Boston Committee of Correspondence and the Towns, 1772–1774* (Cambridge, Mass., 1970).

Noble E. Cunningham, Jr., *In Pursuit of Reason: The Life of Thomas Jefferson* (Baton Rouge, 1987).

John Ferling, *John Adams: A Life* (Knoxville, 1993).

David Hackett Fischer, *Paul Revere's Ride* (New York, 1994).

James Thomas Flexner, *Washington: The Indispensable Man* (Boston, 1974).

Milton E. Flower, *John Dickinson, Conservative Revolutionary* (Charlottesville, 1983).

William M. Fowler, *The Baron of Beacon Hill: A Biography of John Hancock* (Boston, 1979).

Robert A. Gross, *The Minutemen and their World* (New York, 1976).

Wood Holton, *Forced Founders: Indians, Debtors, Slaves, and the Making of the American Revolution in Virginia* (Chapel Hill, 1999).

Rhys Isaac, "Dramatizing the Ideology of the Revolution: Popular Mobilization in Virginia, 1774–1776," *William and Mary Quarterly*, XXXIII, 1976, 357–85.

Benjamin W. Labaree, *The Boston Tea Party* (New York, 1974).

Michael McDonnell, "Popular Mobilization and Political Culture in Revolutionary Virginia: The Failure of the Minutemen and the Revolution from Below," *Journal of American History*, LXXXV, 1998, 946–81.

Pauline Maier, *The Old Revolutionaries: Political Lives in the Age of Samuel Adams* (New York, 1980).

Jerrilyn Greene Marston, *King and Congress: The Transfer of Political Legitimacy, 1774–1776* (Princeton, 1987).

Charles Mayer, *Son of Thunder: Patrick Henry and the American Revolution* (New York, 1986).

John C. Miller, *Sam Adams: Pioneer in Propaganda* (Boston, 1936).

Gregory H. Nobles, *Divisions Throughout the Whole: Politics and Society in Hampshire County, Massachusetts, 1740–1775* (New York, 1983).

Merrill D. Peterson, *Thomas Jefferson and the New Nation: A Biography* (New York, 1970).

Bruce A. Ragsdale, *A Planters' Republic: The Search for Economic Independence in Revolutionary Virginia* (Madison, 1996).

Jack N. Rakove, *The Beginnings of National Politics: An Interpretative History of the Continental Congress* (New York, 1979).

Charles Royster, *A Revolutionary People at War: The Continental Army and American Character* (Chapel Hill, 1979).

Peter Shaw, *American Patriots and the Rituals of Revolution* (Cambridge, 1981).

Jayne E. Triber, *A True Republican: The Life of Paul Revere* (Amherst, 1998).

John W. Tyler, *Smugglers and Patriots: Boston Merchants and the Advent of the American Revolution* (Boston, 1986).

Esmond Wright, *Franklin of Philadelphia* (Cambridge, Mass., 1986).

Hiller B. Zobel, *The Boston Massacre* (New York, 1970).

Independence: The Ideological Origins

A. O. Aldridge, *Thomas Paine's American Ideology* (Newark, 1984).

Joyce Appleby, *Liberalism and Republicanism in the Historical Imagination* (Cambridge, Mass., 1992).

Bernard Bailyn, *The Ideological Origins of the American Revolution* (Cambridge, Mass., 1967).

J. C. D. Clark, *The Language of Liberty, 1660–1832: Political Discourse and Social Dynamics in the Anglo-American World* (Cambridge, England, 1993).

Francis D. Cogliano, *No King, No Popery: Anti-Catholicism in Revolutionary New England* (Westport, 1995).

Trevor Colbourn, *The Lamp of Experience: Whig History and the Intellectual Origins of the American Revolution* (Chapel Hill, 1965).

Eric Foner, *Tom Paine and Revolutionary America* (New York, 1976).

Jack Fruchtman, Jr., *Thomas Paine: Apostle of Freedom* (New York, 1994).

Jack P. Greene, *Pursuits of Happiness: The Social Development of Early Modern British Colonies and the Formation of American Culture* (Chapel Hill, 1988).

Jack P. Greene, *Negotiated Authorities: Essays on Colonial Political and Constitutional History* (Charlottesville, 1994).

Nathan O. Hatch, *The Sacred Cause of Liberty: Republican Thought and the Millennium in Revolutionary New England* (New Haven, 1977).

David Freeman Hawke, *Paine* (New York, 1974).

Merrill Jensen, *The Articles of Confederation: An Interpretation of the Social-constitutional History of the American Revolution, 1774–1781* (Madison, 1940).

Donald S. Lutz, *The Origins of American Constitutionalism* (Baton Rouge, 1988).

Pauline Maier, *American Scripture: Making the Declaration of Independence* (New York, 1997).

Jackson Turner Main, *The Upper House in Revolutionary America, 1763–1788* (Madison, 1967).

Edmund S. Morgan, *Inventing the People: The Rise of Popular Sovereignty in England and America* (New York, 1988).

Edmund S. Morgan, "The Puritan Ethic and the American Revolution," *William and Mary Quarterly*, XXIV, 1967, 3–43.

J. R. Pole, *The Pursuit of Equality in American History* (Berkeley, 1978).

J. R. Pole, *The Gift of Government: Political Responsibility from the English Restoration to American Independence* (Athens, 1983).

Paul A. Rahe, *Republics Ancient and Modern: Classical Republicanism and the American Revolution* (Chapel Hill, 1992).

John Philip Reid, *The Concept of Liberty in the Age of the American Revolution* (Chicago, 1988).

Robert A. Rutland, *The Birth of the Bill of Rights, 1776–1791* (Boston, 1983).

Barry Alan Shain, *The Myth of American Individualism: The Protestant Origins of American Political Thought* (Princeton, 1994).

Morton G. White, *The Philosophy of the American Revolution* (New York, 1978).

Garry Wills, *Inventing America: Jefferson's Declaration of Independence* (New York, 1978).

Gordon S. Wood, *The Creation of the American Republic, 1776–1787* (Chapel Hill, 1979).

Gordon S. Wood, *The Radicalism of the American Revolution* (New York, 1992).

Minorities

(1) Women

Joy Day Buel and Richard Buel, *In the Way of Duty: A Woman and her Family in Revolutionary America* (New York, 1984).

Elaine Forman Crane, *Ebb Tide in New England: Women, Seaports, and Social Change, 1630–1800* (Boston, 1998).

Edith B. Gelles, *Portia: The World of Abigail Adams* (Bloomington, 1992).

Joan R. Gundersen, *To be Useful to the World: Women in Revolutionary America, 1740–1790* (New York, 1996).

Susan J. Juster, *Disorderly Women: Sexual Politics and Evangelicalism in Revolutionary New England* (Ithaca, 1994).

Linda K. Kerber, *Women of the Republic: Intellect and Ideology in Revolutionary America* (Chapel Hill, 1980).

Mary Beth Norton, *Liberty's Daughters: The Revolutionary Experience of American Women, 1750–1800* (Boston, 1980).

Joan Hoff Wilson, "The Illusion of Change: Women and the American Revolution," in Alfred F. Young, ed., *The American Revolution: Explorations in the History of American Radicalism* (Dekalb, 1976).

Lynne Withey, *Dearest Friend: A Life of Abigail Adams* (New York, 1981).

(2) Tories and Loyalists

Bernard Bailyn, *The Ordeal of Thomas Hutchinson* (Cambridge, Mass., 1974).
Wallace Brown, *The Good Americans: The Loyalists in the American Revolution* (New York, 1969).
Robert M. Calhoon, *The Loyalists in Revolutionary America, 1760–1781* (New York, 1973).
Robert M. Calhoon, *The Loyalist Perception and other Essays* (Columbia, South Carolina, 1989).
John E. Ferling, *The Loyalist Mind: Joseph Galloway and the American Revolution* (University Park, 1977).
N. E. H. Hull, Peter Hoffer, and Steven L. Allen, "Choosing Sides: A Quantitative Study of the Personality Determinants of Loyalist and Revolutionary Political Affiliation in New York," *Journal of American History*, LXV, 1978, 344–66.
William H. Nelson, *The American Tory* (Oxford, 1961).
Mary Beth Norton, *The British Americans: the Loyalist Exiles in England, 1774–1789* (Boston, 1972).
William Pencak, *America's Burke: The Mind of Thomas Hutchinson* (Washington, 1982).
Janice Potter, *The Liberty We Seek: Loyalist Ideology in Colonial New York and Massachusetts* (Cambridge, Mass., 1983).
Philip Ranlet, *The New York Loyalists* (Knoxville, 1986).

(3) African-Americans

Ira Berlin and Ronald Hoffman, eds, *Slavery and Freedom in the Age of the American Revolution* (Charlottesville, 1983).
Patricia Bradley, *Slavery, Propaganda and the American Revolution* (Jackson, 1998).
Roger Bruns, ed., *Am I Not a Man and a Brother: The Antislavery Crusade of Revolutionary America, 1688–1788* (New York, 1977).
Sylvia Frey, *Water from the Rock: Black Resistance in a Revolutionary Age* (Princeton, 1991).
Ellen Gibson Wilson, *The Loyal Blacks* (New York, 1976).
Duncan McLeod, *Slavery, Race and the American Revolution* (Cambridge, 1974).
Gary Nash, *Forging Freedom: The Formation of Philadelphia's Black Community, 1720–1840* (Cambridge, Mass., 1988).
Benjamin Quarles, *The Negro in the American Revolution* (Chapel Hill, 1961).

(4) American Indians

Colin G. Calloway, *The American Revolution in Indian Country: Crisis and Diversity in Native American Communities* (Cambridge, England, 1995).
Robert M. Calhoon, Timothy M. Barnes, and George A. Rawlyk, *Loyalists and Community in North America* (Westport, 1994).
Louis De Vorsey, Jr., *The Indian Boundary in the Southern Colonies, 1763–1775* (Chapel Hill, 1966).
Barbara Graymont, *The Iroquois in the American Revolution* (Syracuse, 1972).
James H. Merrell, "Declarations of Independence: Indian-White Relations in the New Nation," in Jack P. Greene ed., *The American Revolution: Its Character and Limits* (New York, 1987).
James H. O'Donnell III, *Southern Indians in the American Revolution* (Knoxville, 1973).
Bernard Sheehan, *Seeds of Extinction: Jeffersonian Philosophy and the American Indian* (Chapel Hill, 1973).

Index ─────────────────────────────────

Page references for illustrations and maps are in italics; those for footnotes are followed by n.